1986

THE EMPIRICISTS

ANCHOR PRESS · DOUBLEDAY

THE EMPIRICISTS

JOHN LOCKE

AN ESSAY CONCERNING HUMAN UNDERSTANDING

Abridged by

PROFESSOR RICHARD TAYLOR

Department of Philosophy, Brown University

GEORGE BERKELEY

A TREATISE CONCERNING THE
PRINCIPLES OF HUMAN KNOWLEDGE

THREE DIALOGUES
BETWEEN HYLAS AND PHILONOUS,
IN OPPOSITION TO SCEPTICS AND ATHEISTS

DAVID HUME

AN ENQUIRY CONCERNING HUMAN UNDERSTANDING

DIALOGUES CONCERNING NATURAL RELIGION

Anchor Books
Anchor Press/Doubleday
Garden City, New York

Anchor Books Edition: 1974

ISBN: 0-385-09622-4

Printed in the United States of America

CONTENTS

John Locke

AN ESSAY CONCERNING HUMAN UNDERSTANDING

Abridged by

PROFESSOR RICHARD TAYLOR
Department of Philosophy, Brown University

INTRODUCTION

1. *An Inquiry into the Understanding pleasant and useful.*——Since it is the *understanding* that sets man above the rest of sensible beings, and gives him all the advantage and dominion which he has over them; it is certainly a subject, even for its nobleness, worth our labour to inquire into. The understanding, like the eye, whilst it makes us see and perceive all other things, takes no notice of itself; and it requires art and pains to set it at a distance and make it its own object. But whatever be the difficulties that lie in the way of this inquiry; whatever it be that keeps us so much in the dark to ourselves; sure I am that all the light we can let in upon our minds, all the acquaintance we can make with our own understandings, will not only be very pleasant, but bring us great advantage, in directing our thoughts in the search of other things.

2. *Design.*——This, therefore, being my purpose—to inquire into the original, certainty, and extent of *human knowledge*, together with the grounds and degrees of *belief*, *opinion*, and *assent*;—I shall not at present meddle with the physical consideration of the mind; or trouble myself to examine wherein its essence consists; or by what motions of our spirits or alterations of our bodies we come to have any *sensation*

by our organs, or any *ideas* in our understandings; and whether those ideas do in their formation, any or all of them, depend on matter or not. These are speculations which, however curious and entertaining, I shall decline, as lying out of my way in the design I am now upon. It shall suffice to my present purpose, to consider the discerning faculties of a man, as they are employed about the objects which they have to do with. And I shall imagine I have not wholly misemployed myself in the thoughts I shall have on this occasion, if, in this historical, plain method, I can give any account of the ways whereby our understandings come to attain those notions of things we have; and can set down any measures of the certainty of our knowledge; or the grounds of those persuasions which are to be found amongst men, so various, different, and wholly contradictory; and yet asserted somewhere or other with such assurance and confidence, that he that shall take a view of the opinions of mankind, observe their opposition, and at the same time consider the fondness and devotion wherewith they are embraced, the resolution and eagerness wherewith they are maintained, may perhaps have reason to suspect, that either there is no such thing as truth at all, or that mankind hath no sufficient means to attain a certain knowledge of it.

3. *Method.*——It is therefore worth while to search out the bounds between opinion and knowledge; and examine by what measures, in things whereof we have no certain knowledge, we ought to regulate our assent and moderate our persuasion. In order whereunto I shall pursue this following method:—

First, I shall inquire into the original of those *ideas*, notions, or whatever else you please to call them, which a man observes, and is conscious to himself he has in his mind; and the ways whereby the understanding comes to be furnished with them.

Secondly, I shall endeavour to show what *knowledge* the understanding hath by those ideas; and the certainty, evidence, and extent of it.

Thirdly, I shall make some inquiry into the nature and grounds of *faith* or *opinion*: whereby I mean that assent which we give to any proposition as true, of whose truth yet we have no certain knowledge. And here we shall have occasion to examine the reasons and degrees of *assent*.

4. *What Idea stands for.*——Before I proceed on to what I have thought on this subject, I must here in the entrance beg pardon of my reader for the frequent use of the word *idea*, which he will find in the following treatise. It being that term which, I think, serves best to stand for whatsoever is the *object* of the understanding when a man thinks, I have used it to express whatever is meant by *phantasm, notion, species*, or *whatever it is which the mind can be employed about in thinking*; and I could not avoid frequently using it.

I presume it will be easily granted me, that there are such *ideas* in men's minds: every one is conscious of them in himself; and men's words and actions will satisfy him that they are in others.

BOOK II.

CHAPTER I.

OF IDEAS IN GENERAL, AND THEIR ORIGINAL.

1. *Idea is the Object of Thinking.*——Every man being conscious to himself that he thinks; and that which his mind is applied about whilst thinking being the *ideas* that are there, it is past doubt that men have in their minds several ideas,—such as are those expressed by the words *whiteness, hardness, sweetness, thinking, motion, man, elephant, army, drunkenness*, and others: it is in the first place then to be inquired, *How he comes by them?*

I know it is a received doctrine, that men have native ideas, and original characters, stamped upon their minds in their very first being. This opinion I have at large examined already; and, I suppose what I have said in the foregoing Book will be much more easily admitted, when I have shown whence the understanding may get all the ideas it has; and by what ways and degrees they may come into the mind;—for which I shall appeal to every one's own observation and experience.

2. *All Ideas come from Sensation or Reflection.*——Let us

then suppose the mind to be, as we say, white paper, void of all characters, without any ideas:—How comes it to be furnished? Whence comes it by that vast store which the busy and boundless fancy of man has painted on it with an almost endless variety? Whence has it all the *materials* of reason and knowledge? To this I answer, in one word, from EXPERIENCE. In that all our knowledge is founded; and from that it ultimately derives itself. Our observation employed either, about external sensible objects, or about the internal operations of our minds perceived and reflected on by ourselves, is that which supplies our understandings with all the *materials* of thinking. These two are the fountains of knowledge, from whence all the ideas we have, or can naturally have, do spring.

3. *The Objects of Sensation.*——First, our Senses, conversant about particular sensible objects, do convey into the mind several distinct perceptions of things, according to those various ways wherein those objects do affect them. And thus we come by those *ideas* we have of *yellow, white, heat, cold, soft, hard, bitter, sweet,* and all those which we call sensible qualities; which when I say the senses convey into the mind, I mean, they from external objects convey into the mind what produces there those perceptions. This great source of most of the ideas we have, depending wholly upon our senses, and derived by them to the understanding, I call SENSATION.

4. *The Operations of our Minds, the other Source of them.*——Secondly, the other fountain from which experience furnisheth the understanding with ideas is,—the perception of the operations of our own mind within us, as it is employed about the ideas it has got;—which operations, when the soul comes to reflect on and consider, do furnish the understanding with another set of ideas, which could not be had from things without. And such are *perception, thinking, doubting, believing, reasoning, knowing, willing,* and all the different actings of our own minds;—which we being conscious of, and observing in ourselves, do from these receive into our understandings as distinct ideas as we do from bodies affecting our senses. This source of ideas every man has wholly in himself; and though it be not sense, as having nothing to do with external objects, yet it is very like it, and might properly enough be called *internal sense.* But as I call the other Sensation, so I call this REFLECTION, the ideas it affords being such only as the mind gets by reflecting on its own operations within itself. By reflection then, in the following part of this discourse, I

would be understood to mean, that notice which the mind takes of its own operations, and the manner of them, by reason whereof there come to be ideas of these operations in the understanding. These two, I say, viz. external material things, as the objects of SENSATION, and the operations of our own minds within, as the objects of REFLECTION, are to me the only originals from whence all our ideas take their beginnings. The term *operations* here I use in a large sense, as comprehending not barely the actions of the mind about its ideas, but some sort of passions arising sometimes from them, such as is the satisfaction or uneasiness arising from any thought.

5. *All our Ideas are of the one or the other of these.*—— The understanding seems to me not to have the least glimmering of any ideas which it doth not receive from one of these two. *External objects* furnish the mind with the ideas of sensible qualities, which are all those different perceptions they produce in us; and *the mind* furnishes the understanding with ideas of its own operations.

These, when we have taken a full survey of them, and their several modes, combinations, and relations, we shall find to contain all our whole stock of ideas; and that we have nothing in our minds which did not come in one of these two ways. Let any one examine his own thoughts, and thoroughly search into his understanding; and then let him tell me, whether all the original ideas he has there, are any other than of the objects of his senses, or of the operations of his mind, considered as objects of his reflection. And how great a mass of knowledge soever he imagines to be lodged there, he will, upon taking a strict view, see that he has not any idea in his mind but what one of these two have imprinted;—though perhaps, with infinite variety compounded and enlarged by the understanding, as we shall see hereafter.

6. *Observable in Children.*——He that attentively considers the state of a child, at his first coming into the world, will have little reason to think him stored with plenty of ideas, that are to be the matter of his future knowledge. It is *by degrees* he comes to be furnished with them. And though the ideas of obvious and familiar qualities imprint themselves before the memory begins to keep a register of time or order, yet it is often so late before some unusual qualities come in the way, that there are few men that cannot recollect the beginning of their acquaintance with them. And if it were

worth while, no doubt a child might be so ordered as to have but a very few, even of the ordinary ideas, till he were grown up to a man. But all that are born into the world, being surrounded with bodies that perpetually and diversely affect them, variety of ideas, whether care be taken of it or not, are imprinted on the minds of children. Light and colours are busy at hand everywhere, when the eye is but open; sounds and some tangible qualities fail not to solicit their proper senses, and force an entrance to the mind;—but yet, I think, it will be granted easily, that if a child were kept in a place where he never saw any other but black and white till he were a man, he would have no more ideas of scarlet or green, than he that from his childhood never tasted an oyster, or a pineapple, has of those particular relishes.

7. *Men are differently furnished with these, according to the different Objects they converse with.*——Men then come to be furnished with fewer or more simple ideas from without, according as the objects they converse with afford greater or less variety; and from the operations of their minds within, according as they more or less reflect on them. For, though he that contemplates the operations of his mind, cannot but have plain and clear ideas of them; yet, unless he turn his thoughts that way, and considers them *attentively*, he will no more have clear and distinct ideas of all the operations of his mind, and all that may be observed therein, than he will have all the particular ideas of any landscape, or of the parts and motions of a clock, who will not turn his eyes to it, and with attention heed all the parts of it. The picture, or clock may be so placed, that they may come in his way every day; but yet he will have but a confused idea of all the parts they are made up of, till he applies himself with attention, to consider them each in particular.

8. *Ideas of Reflection later, because they need Attention.*——And hence we see the reason why it is pretty late before most children get ideas of the operations of their own minds; and some have not any very clear or perfect ideas of the greatest part of them all their lives. Because, though they pass there continually, yet, like floating visions, they make not deep impressions enough to leave in their mind clear, distinct, lasting ideas, till the understanding turns inward upon itself, reflects on its own operations, and makes them the objects of its own contemplation. Children when they come first into it, are surrounded with a world of new things, which, by a

constant solicitation of their senses, draw the mind constantly to them; forward to take notice of new, and apt to be delighted with the variety of changing objects. Thus the first years are usually employed and diverted in looking abroad. Men's business in them is to acquaint themselves with what is to be found without; and so growing up in a constant attention to outward sensations, seldom make any considerable reflection on what passes within them, till they come to be of riper years; and some scarce ever at all.

9. *The Soul begins to have Ideas when it begins to perceive.*——To ask, at what *time* a man has first any ideas, is to ask, when he begins to perceive;—*having ideas*, and *perception*, being the same thing. I know it is an opinion, that the soul always thinks, and that it has the actual perception of ideas in itself constantly, as long as it exists; and that actual thinking is as inseparable from the soul as actual extension is from the body; which if true, to inquire after the beginning of a man's ideas is the same as to inquire after the beginning of his soul. For, by this account, soul and its ideas, as body and its extension, will begin to exist both at the same time.

10. *The Soul thinks not always; for this wants Proofs.*—— But whether the soul be supposed to exist antecedent to, or coeval with, or some time after the first rudiments of organization, or the beginnings of life in the body, I leave to be disputed by those who have better thought of that matter. I confess myself to have one of those dull souls, that doth not perceive itself always to contemplate ideas; nor can conceive it any more necessary for the soul always to think, than for the body always to move: the perception of ideas being (as I conceive) to the soul, what motion is to the body; not its essence, but one of its operations. And therefore, though thinking be supposed never so much the proper action of the soul, yet it is not necessary to suppose that it should be always thinking, always in action. That, perhaps, is the privilege of the infinite Author and Preserver of all things, who 'never slumbers nor sleeps'; but is not competent to any finite being, at least not to the soul of man. We know certainly, by experience, that we *sometimes* think; and thence draw this infallible consequence,—that there is something in us that has a power to think. But whether that substance *perpetually* thinks or no, we can be no further assured than experience informs us. For, to say that actual thinking is essential to the soul, and inseparable from it, is to beg what is in question, and not to

prove it by reason;—which is necessary to be done, if it be not a self-evident proposition. But whether this, 'That the soul always thinks,' be a self-evident proposition, that everybody assents to at first hearing, I appeal to mankind. It is doubted whether I thought at all last night or no. The question being about a matter of fact, it is begging it to bring, as a proof for it, an hypothesis, which is the very thing in dispute: by which way one may prove anything, and it is but supposing that all watches, whilst the balance beats, think, and it is sufficiently proved, and past doubt, that my watch thought all last night. But he that would not deceive himself, ought to build his hypothesis on matter of fact, and make it out by sensible experience, and not presume on matter of fact, because of his hypothesis, that is, because he supposes it to be so; which way of proving amounts to this, that I must necessarily think all last night, because another supposes I always think, though I myself cannot perceive that I always do so.

But men in love with their opinions may not only suppose what is in question, but allege wrong matter of fact. How else could any one make it an inference of mine, that a thing is not, because we are not sensible of it in our sleep? I do not say there is no *soul* in a man, because he is not sensible of it in his sleep; but I do say, he cannot *think* at any time, waking or sleeping, without being sensible of it. Our being sensible of it is not necessary to anything but to our thoughts; and to them it is; and to them it always will be necessary, till we can think without being conscious of it.

23. *A man begins to have ideas when he first has sensation. What sensation is.*——If it shall be demanded then, *when* a man *begins* to have any ideas, I think the true answer is,—*when he first has any sensation.* For, since there appear not to be any ideas in the mind before the senses have conveyed any in, I conceive that ideas in the understanding are coeval with *sensation; which is such an impression or motion made in some part of the body, as produces some perception in the understanding*. It is about these impressions made on our senses by outward objects that the mind seems *first* to employ itself, in such operations as we call perception, remembering, consideration, reasoning, &c.

24. *The Original of all our Knowledge.*——In time the mind comes to reflect on its own operations about the ideas got by sensation, and thereby stores itself with a new set of ideas, which I call ideas of reflection. These are the impres-

sions that are made on our senses by outward objects that are extrinsical to the mind; and its own operations, proceeding from powers intrinsical and proper to itself, which, when reflected on by itself, become also objects of its contemplation—are, as I have said, the original of all knowledge. Thus the first capacity of human intellect is,—that the mind is fitted to receive the impressions made on it; either through the senses by outward objects, or by its own operations when it reflects on them. This is the first step a man makes towards the discovery of anything, and the groundwork whereon to build all those notions which ever he shall have naturally in this world. All those sublime thoughts which tower above the clouds, and reach as high as heaven itself, take their rise and footing here: in all that great extent wherein the mind wanders, in those remote speculations it may seem to be elevated with, it stirs not one jot beyond those ideas which *sense* or *reflection* have offered for its contemplation.

CHAPTER II.

OF SIMPLE IDEAS.

1. *Uncompounded Appearances.*——The better to understand the nature, manner, and extent of our knowledge, one thing is carefully to be observed concerning the ideas we have; and that is, that some of them are *simple* and some *complex*.

Though the qualities that affect our senses are, in the things themselves, so united and blended, that there is no separation, no distance between them; yet it is plain, the ideas they produce in the mind enter by the senses simple and unmixed. For, though the sight and touch often take in from the same object, at the same time, different ideas;—as a man sees at once motion and colour; the hand feels softness and warmth in the same piece of wax: yet the simple ideas thus united in the same subject, are as perfectly distinct as those that come in by different senses. The coldness and hardness which a man feels in a piece of ice being as distinct ideas in the mind as the smell and whiteness of a lily; or as the taste of sugar, and smell of a rose. And there is nothing can be plainer to a man than the clear and distinct perception he has of those simple ideas; which, being each in itself uncompounded, contains in it nothing but *one uniform appearance, or conception in the mind,* and is not distinguishable into different ideas.

2. *The Mind can neither make nor destroy them.*——These simple ideas, the materials of all our knowledge, are suggested and furnished to the mind only by those two ways above mentioned, viz. sensation and reflection. When the understanding is once stored with these simple ideas, it has the power to repeat, compare, and unite them, even to an almost infinite variety, and so can make at pleasure new complex ideas. But it is not in the power of the most exalted wit, or enlarged understanding, by any quickness or variety of thought, to *invent* or *frame* one new simple idea in the mind, not taken in by the ways before mentioned: nor can any force of the understanding *destroy* those that are there. The dominion of man, in this little world of his own understanding being muchwhat the same as it is in the great world of visible things; wherein his power, however managed by art and skill, reaches no farther than to compound and divide the materials that are made to his hand; but can do nothing towards the making the least particle of new matter, or destroying one atom of what is already in being. The same inability will every one find in himself, who shall go about to fashion in his understanding one simple idea, not received in by his senses from external objects, or by reflection from the operations of his own mind about them. I would have any one try to fancy any taste which had never affected his palate; or frame the idea of a scent he had never smelt: and when he can do this, I will also conclude that a blind man hath ideas of colours, and a deaf man true distinct notions of sounds.

3. *Only the qualities that affect the senses are imaginable.*——This is the reason why—though we cannot believe it impossible to God to make a creature with other organs, and more ways to convey into the understanding the notice of corporeal things than those five, as they are usually counted, which he has given to man—yet I think it is not possible for any *man* to imagine any other qualities in bodies, howsoever constituted, whereby they can be taken notice of, besides sounds, tastes, smells, visible and tangible qualities. And had mankind been made but with four senses, the qualities then which are the objects of the fifth sense had been as far from our notice, imagination, and conception, as now any belong-

ing to a sixth, seventh, or eighth sense can possibly be;—which, whether yet some other creatures, in some other parts of this vast and stupendous universe, may not have, will be a great presumption to deny. He that will not set himself proudly at the top of all things, but will consider the immensity of this fabric, and the great variety that is to be found in this little and inconsiderable part of it which he has to do with, may be apt to think that, in other mansions of it, there may be other and different intelligent beings, of whose faculties he has as little knowledge or apprehension as a worm shut up in one drawer of a cabinet hath of the senses or understanding of a man; such variety and excellency being suitable to the wisdom and power of the Maker. I have here followed the common opinion of man's having but five senses; though, perhaps, there may be justly counted more;—but either supposition serves equally to my present purpose.

CHAPTER III.

OF SIMPLE IDEAS OF SENSE.

1. *Division of simple Ideas.*——The better to conceive the ideas we receive from sensation, it may not be amiss for us to consider them, in reference to the different ways whereby they make their approaches to our minds, and make themselves perceivable by us.

First, then, There are some which come into our minds *by one sense only.*

Secondly, There are others that convey themselves into the mind *by more senses than one.*

Thirdly, Others that are had from *reflection only.*

Fourthly, There are some that make themselves way, and are suggested to the mind *by all the ways of sensation and reflection.*

We shall consider them apart under these several heads.

Ideas of one Sense.——There are some ideas which have admittance only through one sense, which is peculiarly adapted to receive them. Thus light and colours, as white, red, yellow, blue; with their several degrees or shades and mixtures, as green, scarlet, purple, sea-green, and the rest, come in only by the eyes. All kinds of noises, sounds, and tones, only by the ears. The several tastes and smells, by the nose and palate. And if these organs, or the nerves which are the conduits to convey them from without to their audience in the brain,—the mind's presence-room (as I may so call it)—are any of them so disordered as not to perform their functions, they have no postern to be admitted by; no other way to bring themselves into view, and be perceived by the understanding.

The most considerable of those belonging to the touch, are heat and cold, and solidity: all the rest, consisting almost wholly in the sensible configuration, as smooth and rough; or else, more or less firm adhesion of the parts, as hard and soft, tough and brittle, are obvious enough.

2. *Few simple Ideas have Names.*——I think it will be needless to enumerate all the particular simple ideas belonging to each sense. Nor indeed is it possible if we would; there being a great many more of them belonging to most of the senses than we have names for. The variety of smells, which are as many almost, if not more, than species of bodies in the world, do most of them want names. Sweet and stinking commonly serve our turn for these ideas, which in effect is little more than to call them pleasing or displeasing; though the smell of a rose and violet, both sweet, are certainly very distinct ideas. Nor are the different tastes, that by our palates we receive ideas of, much better provided with names. Sweet, bitter, sour, harsh, and salt are almost all the epithets we have to denominate that numberless variety of relishes, which are to be found distinct, not only in almost every sort of creatures, but in the different parts of the same plant, fruit, or animal. The same may be said of colours and sounds. I shall, therefore, in the account of simple ideas I am here giving, content myself to set down only such as are most material to our present purpose, or are in themselves less apt to be taken notice of though they are very frequently the ingredients of our complex ideas; amongst which, I think, I may well account solidity, which therefore I shall treat of in the next chapter.

CHAPTER IV.

IDEA OF SOLIDITY.

1. *We receive this Idea from Touch.*——The idea of *solidity* we receive by our touch: and it arises from the resistance which we find in body to the entrance of any other body into the place it possesses, till it has left it. There is no idea which we receive more constantly from sensation than solidity. Whether we move or rest, in what posture soever we are, we always feel something under us that supports us, and hinders our further sinking downwards; and the bodies which we daily handle make us perceive that, whilst they remain between them, they do, by an insurmountable force, hinder the approach of the parts of our hands that press them. *That which thus hinders the approach of two bodies, when they are moved one towards another, I call solidity.* I will not dispute whether this acceptation of the word solid be nearer to its original signification than that which mathematicians use it in. It suffices that I think the common notion of solidity will allow, if not justify, this use of it; but if any one think it better to call it *impenetrability,* he has my consent. Only I have thought the term solidity the more proper to express this idea, not only because of its vulgar use in that sense, but also because it carries something more of positive in it than impenetrability; which is negative, and is perhaps more a consequence of solidity, than solidity itself. This, of all other, seems the idea most intimately connected with, and essential to body; so as nowhere else to be found or imagined, but only in matter. And though our senses take no notice of it, but in masses of matter, of a bulk sufficient to cause a sensation in us: yet the mind, having once got this idea from such grosser sensible bodies, traces it further, and considers it, as well as figure, in the minutest particle of matter that can exist; and finds it inseparably inherent in body, wherever or however modified.

2. *Solidity fills Space.*——This is the idea which belongs to body, whereby we conceive it to fill space. The idea of which filling of space is,—that where we imagine any space taken up by a solid substance, we conceive it so to possess it,

that it excludes all other solid substances; and will for ever hinder any other two bodies, that move towards one another in a straight line, from coming to touch one another, unless it removes from between them in a line not parallel to that which they move in. This idea of it, the bodies which we ordinarily handle sufficiently furnish us with.

6. *What Solidity is.*——If any one asks me, *What this solidity is,* I send him to his senses to inform him. Let him put a flint or a football between his hands, and then endeavour to join them, and he will know. If he thinks this not a sufficient explication of solidity, what it is, and wherein it consists; I promise to tell him what it is, and wherein it consists, when he tells me what thinking is, or wherein it consists; or explains to me what extension or motion is, which perhaps seems much easier. The simple ideas we have, are such as experience teaches them us; but if, beyond that, we endeavour by words to make them clearer in the mind, we shall succeed no better than if we went about to clear up the darkness of a blind man's mind by talking; and to discourse into him the ideas of light and colours. The reason of this I shall show in another place.

CHAPTER V.

OF SIMPLE IDEAS OF DIVERS SENSES.

Ideas received both by seeing and touching.——The ideas we get by more than one sense are, of *space* or *extension, figure, rest,* and *motion.* For these make perceivable impressions, both on the eyes and touch; and we can receive and convey into our minds the ideas of the extension, figure, motion, and rest of bodies, both by seeing and feeling. But having occasion to speak more at large of these in another place, I here only enumerate them.

CHAPTER VI.

OF SIMPLE IDEAS OF REFLECTION.

1. *Simple Ideas are the Operations of Mind about its other Ideas.*——The mind receiving the ideas mentioned in the foregoing chapters from without, when it turns its view inward upon itself, and observes its own actions about those ideas it has, takes from thence other ideas, which are as capable to be the objects of its contemplation as any of those it received from foreign things.

2. *The Idea of Perception, and Idea of Willing, we have from Reflection.*——The two great and principal actions of the mind, which are most frequently considered, and which are so frequent that every one that pleases may take notice of them in himself, are these two:—

Perception, or *Thinking*; and
Volition, or *Willing*.

The power of thinking is called the *Understanding*, and the power of volition is called the *Will*; and these two powers or abilities in the mind are denominated faculties.

Of some of the *modes* of these simple ideas of reflection, such as are *remembrance, discerning, reasoning, judging, knowledge, faith*, &c., I shall have occasion to speak hereafter.

CHAPTER VII.

OF SIMPLE IDEAS OF BOTH SENSATION AND REFLECTION.

1. *Ideas of Pleasure and Pain.*——There be other simple ideas which convey themselves into the mind by all the ways of sensation and reflection, viz. *pleasure* or *delight*, and its opposite, *pain*, or *uneasiness*; *power*; *existence*; *unity*.

2. *Mix with almost all our other Ideas.*——Delight or uneasiness, one or other of them, join themselves to almost all

our ideas both of sensation and reflection: and there is scarce any affection of our senses from without, any retired thought of our mind within, which is not able to produce in us pleasure or pain. By pleasure and pain, I would be understood to signify, whatsoever delights or molests us; whether it arises from the thoughts of our minds, or anything operating on our bodies. For, whether we call it satisfaction, delight, pleasure, happiness, &c., on the one side, or uneasiness, trouble, pain, torment, anguish, misery, &c., on the other, they are still but different degrees of the same thing, and belong to the ideas of pleasure and pain, delight or uneasiness; which are the names I shall most commonly use for those two sorts of ideas.

3. *As motives of our actions.*——The infinite wise Author of our being, having given us the power over several parts of our bodies, to move or keep them at rest as we think fit; and also, by the motion of them, to move ourselves and other contiguous bodies, in which consist all the actions of our body: having also given a power to our minds, in several instances, to choose, amongst its ideas, which it will think on, and to pursue the inquiry of this or that subject with consideration and attention, to excite us to these actions of thinking and motion that we are capable of,—has been pleased to join to several thoughts, and several sensations a perception of delight. If this were wholly separated from all our outward sensations, and inward thoughts, we should have no reason to prefer one thought or action to another; negligence to attention, or motion to rest. And so we should neither stir our bodies, nor employ our minds, but let our thoughts (if I may so call it) run adrift, without any direction or design, and suffer the ideas of our minds, like unregarded shadows, to make their appearances there, as it happened, without attending to them. In which state man, however furnished with the faculties of understanding and will, would be a very idle, inactive creature, and pass his time only in a lazy, lethargic dream. It has therefore pleased our wise Creator to annex to several objects, and the ideas which we receive from them, as also to several of our thoughts, a concomitant pleasure, and that in several objects, to several degrees, that those faculties which he had endowed us with might not remain wholly idle and unemployed by us.

7. *Ideas of Existence and Unity.*——*Existence* and *Unity* are two other ideas that are suggested to the understanding by every object without, and every idea within. When ideas are

in our minds, we consider them as being actually there, as well as we consider things to be actually without us;—which is, that they exist, or have existence. And whatever we can consider as one thing, whether a real being or idea, suggests to the understanding the idea of unity.

8. *Idea of Power.*——*Power* also is another of those simple ideas which we receive from sensation and reflection. For, observing in ourselves that we do and can think, and that we can at pleasure move several parts of our bodies which were at rest; the effects, also, that natural bodies are able to produce in one another, occurring every moment to our senses,—we both these ways get the idea of power.

9. *Idea of Succession.*——Besides these there is another idea, which, though suggested by our senses, yet is more constantly offered to us by what passes in our minds; and that is the idea of *succession.* For if we look immediately into ourselves, and reflect on what is observable there, we shall find our ideas always, whilst we are awake, or have any thought, passing in train, one going and another coming, without intermission.

10. *Simple Ideas the materials of all our Knowledge.*—— These, if they are not all, are at least (as I think) the most considerable of those simple ideas which the mind has, and out of which is made all its other knowledge; all which it receives only by the two forementioned ways of sensation and reflection.

Nor let any one think these too narrow bounds for the capacious mind of man to expatiate in, which takes its flight further than the stars, and cannot be confined by the limits of the world; that extends its thoughts often even beyond the utmost expansion of Matter, and makes excursions into that incomprehensible Inane. I grant all this, but desire any one to assign any *simple idea* which is not received from one of those inlets before mentioned, or any *complex idea* not made out of those simple ones. Nor will it be so strange to think these few simple ideas sufficient to employ the quickest thought, or largest capacity; and to furnish the materials of all that various knowledge, and more various fancies and opinions of all mankind, if we consider how many words may be made out of the various composition of twenty-four letters; or if, going one step further, we will but reflect on the variety of combinations that may be made with barely one of the above-mentioned ideas, viz. number, whose stock is inexhaustible and truly infinite: and what a large and immense field doth extension alone afford the mathematicians?

CHAPTER VIII.

SOME FURTHER CONSIDERATIONS CONCERNING OUR SIMPLE IDEAS OF SENSATION.

7. *Ideas in the Mind, Qualities in Bodies.*——To discover the nature of our *ideas* the better, and to discourse of them intelligibly, it will be convenient to distinguish them *as they are ideas or perceptions in our minds;* and *as they are modifications of matter in the bodies that cause such perceptions in us:* that so we may not think (as perhaps usually is done) that they are exactly the images and resemblances of something inherent in the subject; most of those of sensation being in the mind no more the likeness of something existing without us, than the names that stand for them are the likeness of our ideas, which yet upon hearing they are apt to excite in us.

8. *Our Ideas and the Qualities of Bodies.*——Whatsoever the mind perceives *in itself,* or is the immediate object of perception, thought, or understanding, that I call *idea;* and the power to produce any idea in our mind, I call *quality* of the subject wherein that power is. Thus a snowball having the power to produce in us the ideas of white, cold, and round,—the power to produce those ideas in us, as they are in the snowball, I call qualities; and as they are sensations or perceptions in our understandings, I call them ideas; which *ideas,* if I speak of sometimes as in the things themselves, I would be understood to mean those qualities in the objects which produce them in us.

9. *Primary Qualities of Bodies.*——Qualities thus considered in bodies are,

First, such as are utterly inseparable from the body, in what state soever it be; and such as in all the alterations and changes it suffers, all the force can be used upon it, it constantly keeps; and such as sense constantly finds in every particle of matter which has bulk enough to be perceived; and the mind finds inseparable from every particle of matter, though less than to make itself singly be perceived by our senses: v.g. Take a grain of wheat, divide it into two parts; each part has still solidity, extension, figure, and mobility: divide it again, and it retains still the same qualities; and so divide it on, till the parts become insensible; they must retain still each of them all those qualities. For division (which is all that a mill, or pestle, or any other body, does upon another, in reducing it to insensible parts) can never take away either solidity, extension, figure, or mobility from any body, but only makes two or more distinct separate masses of matter, of that which was but one before; all which distinct masses, reckoned as so many distinct bodies, after division, make a certain number. These I call *original* or *primary qualities* of body, which I think we may observe to produce simple ideas in us, viz. solidity, extension, figure, motion or rest, and number.

10. *Secondary Qualities of Bodies.*——*Secondly*, such qualities which in truth are nothing in the objects themselves but powers to produce various sensations in us by their primary qualities, i.e. by the bulk, figure, texture, and motion of their insensible parts, as colours, sounds, tastes, &c. These I call *secondary qualities*. To these might be added a *third* sort, which are allowed to be barely powers; though they are as much real qualities in the subject as those which I, to comply with the common way of speaking, call qualities, but for distinction, secondary qualities. For the power in fire to produce a new colour, or consistency, in *wax* or *clay*,—by its primary qualities, is as much a quality in fire, as the power it has to produce in *me* a new idea or sensation of warmth or burning, which I felt not before,—by the same primary qualities, viz. the bulk, texture, and motion of its insensible parts.

11. *How Bodies produce Ideas in us.*——The next thing to be considered is, how bodies produce ideas in us; and that is manifestly by impulse, the only way which we can conceive bodies to operate in.

12. *By motions, external, and in our organism.*——If then external objects be not united to our minds when they produce ideas therein; and yet we perceive these *original* qualities in such of them as singly fall under our senses, it is evident that some motion must be thence continued by our nerves, or animal spirits, by some parts of our bodies, to the brains or the seat of sensation, there to produce in our minds the particular ideas we have of them. And since the extension, figure, number, and motion of bodies of an observable bigness, may be perceived at a distance by the sight, it is evident some

singly imperceptible bodies must come from them to the eyes, and thereby convey to the brain some motion; which produces these ideas which we have of them in us.

13. *How secondary Qualities produce their ideas.*——After the same manner that the ideas of these original qualities are produced in us, we may conceive that the ideas of *secondary* qualities are also produced, viz. by the operation of insensible particles on our senses. For, it being manifest that there are bodies and good store of bodies, each whereof are so small, that we cannot by any of our senses discover either their bulk, figure, or motion,—as is evident in the particles of the air and water, and others extremely smaller than those; perhaps as much smaller than the particles of air and water, as the particles of air and water are smaller than peas or hail-stones;—let us suppose at present that the different motions and figures, bulk and number, of such particles, affecting the several organs of our senses, produce in us those different sensations which we have from the colours and smells of bodies; v.g. that a violet, by the impulse of such insensible particles of matter, of peculiar figures and bulks, and in different degrees and modifications of their motions, causes the ideas of the blue colour, and sweet scent of that flower to be produced in our minds. It being no more impossible to conceive that God should annex such ideas to such motions, with which they have no similitude, than that he should annex the idea of pain to the motion of a piece of steel dividing our flesh, with which that idea hath no resemblance.

14. *They depend on the primary Qualities.*——What I have said concerning colours and smells may be understood also of tastes and sounds, and other the like sensible qualities; which, whatever reality we by mistake attribute to them, are in truth nothing in the objects themselves, but powers to produce various sensations in us; and depend on those primary qualities, viz. bulk, figure, texture, and motion of parts as I have said.

15. *Ideas of primary Qualities are Resemblances; of secondary, not.*——From whence I think it easy to draw this observation,—that the ideas of primary qualities of bodies are resemblances of them, and their patterns do really exist in the bodies themselves, but the ideas produced in us by these secondary qualities have no resemblance of them at all. There is nothing like our ideas, existing in the bodies themselves. They are, in the bodies we denominate from them, only a power to

produce those sensations in us: and what is sweet, blue, or warm in idea, is but the certain bulk, figure, and motion of the insensible parts, in the bodies themselves, which we call so.

16. *Examples.*——Flame is denominated hot and light; snow, white and cold; and manna, white and sweet, from the ideas they produce in us. Which qualities are commonly thought to be the same in those bodies that those ideas are in us, the one the perfect resemblance of the other, as they are in a mirror, and it would by most men be judged very extravagant if one should say otherwise. And yet he that will consider that the same fire that, at one distance produces in us the sensation of warmth, does, at a nearer approach, produce in us the far different sensation of pain, ought to bethink himself what reason he has to say—that this idea of warmth, which was produced in him by the fire, is *actually in the fire*; and his idea of pain, which the same fire produced in him the same way, is *not* in the fire. Why are whiteness and coldness in snow, and pain not, when it produces the one and the other idea in us; and can do neither, but by the bulk, figure, number, and motion of its solid parts?

17. *The ideas of the Primary alone really exist.*——The particular bulk, number, figure, and motion of the parts of fire or snow are really in them,—whether any one's senses perceive them or no: and therefore they may be called *real* qualities, because they really exist in those bodies. But light, heat, whiteness, or coldness, are no more really in them than sickness or pain is in manna. Take away the sensation of them; let not the eyes see light or colours, nor the ears hear sounds; let the palate not taste, nor the nose smell, and all colours, tastes, odours, and sounds, *as they are such particular ideas,* vanish and cease, and are reduced to their causes, i.e. bulk, figure, and motion of parts.

18. *The secondary exist in things only as modes of the primary.*——A piece of manna of a sensible bulk is able to produce in us the idea of a round or square figure; and by being removed from one place to another, the idea of motion. This idea of motion represents it as it really is in manna moving: a circle or square are the same, whether in idea or existence, in the mind or in the manna. And this, both motion and figure, are really in the manna, whether we take notice of them or no: this everybody is ready to agree to. Besides, manna, by the bulk, figure, texture, and motion of its parts, has a power to produce the sensations of sickness, and some-

times of acute pains or gripings in us. That these ideas of sickness and pain are *not* in the manna, but effects of its operations on us, and are nowhere when we feel them not; this also every one readily agrees to. And yet men are hardly to be brought to think that sweetness and whiteness are not really in manna; which are but the effects of the operations of manna, by the motion, size, and figure of its particles, on the eyes and palate: as the pain and sickness caused by manna are confessedly nothing but the effects of its operations on the stomach and guts, by the size, motion, and figure of its insensible parts, (for by nothing else can a body operate, as has been proved): as if it could not operate on the eyes and palate, and thereby produce in the mind particular distinct ideas, which in itself it has not, as well as we allow it can operate on the guts and stomach, and thereby produce distinct ideas, which in itself it has not. These ideas, being all effects of the operations of manna on several parts of our bodies, by the size, figure, number, and motion of its parts;—why those produced by the eyes and palate should rather be thought to be really in the manna, than those produced by the stomach and guts; or why the pain and sickness, ideas that are the effect of manna, should be thought to be nowhere when they are not felt; and yet the sweetness and whiteness, effects of the same manna on other parts of the body, by ways equally as unknown, should be thought to exist in the manna, when they are not seen or tasted, would need some reason to explain.

19. *Examples.*——Let us consider the red and white colours in porphyry. Hinder light from striking on it, and its colours vanish; it no longer produces any such ideas in us: upon the return of light it produces these appearances on us again. Can any one think any real alterations are made in the porphyry by the presence or absence of light; and that those ideas of whiteness and redness are really in porphyry in the light, when it is plain *it has no colour in the dark?* It has, indeed, such a configuration of particles, both night and day, as are apt, by the rays of light rebounding from some parts of that hard stone, to produce in us the idea of redness, and from others the idea of whiteness; but whiteness or redness are not in it at any time, but such a texture that hath the power to produce such a sensation in us.

20. Pound an almond, and the clear white colour will be altered into a dirty one, and the sweet taste into an oily one.

What real alteration can the beating of the pestle make in any body, but an alteration of the texture of it?

21. *Explains how water felt as cold by one hand may be warm to the other.*——Ideas being thus distinguished and understood, we may be able to give an account how the same water, at the same time, may produce the idea of cold by one hand and of heat by the other: whereas it is impossible that the same water, if those ideas were really in it, should at the same time be both hot and cold. For, if we imagine *warmth*, as it is in our hands, to be nothing but a certain sort and degree of motion in the minute particles of our nerves or animal spirits, we may understand how it is possible that the same water may, at the same time, produce the sensations of heat in one hand and cold in the other; which yet *figure* never does, that never producing the idea of a square by one hand which has produced the idea of a globe by another. But if the sensation of heat and cold be nothing but the increase or diminution of the motion of the minute parts of our bodies, caused by the corpuscles of any other body, it is easy to be understood, that if that motion be greater in one hand than in the other; if a body be applied to the two hands, which has in its minute particles a greater motion than in those of one of the hands, and a less than in those of the other, it will increase the motion of the one hand and lessen it in the other; and so cause the different sensations of heat and cold that depend thereon.

23. *Three Sorts of Qualities in Bodies.*——The qualities, then, that are in bodies, rightly considered, are of three sorts:—

First, The bulk, figure, number, situation, and motion or rest of their solid parts. Those are in them, whether we perceive them or not; and when they are of that size that we can discover them, we have by these an idea of the thing as it is in itself; as is plain in artificial things. These I call *primary qualities*.

Secondly, The power that is in any body, by reason of its insensible primary qualities, to operate after a peculiar manner on any of our senses, and thereby produce in *us* the different ideas of several colours, sounds, smells, tastes, &c. These are usually called *sensible qualities*.

Thirdly, The power that is in any body, by reason of the particular constitution of its primary qualities, to make such a change in the bulk, figure, texture, and motion of *another body*, as to make it operate on our senses differently from what it did before. Thus the sun has a power to make wax white, and fire to make lead fluid. These are usually called *powers*.

The first of these, as has been said, I think may be properly called real, original, or primary qualities; because they are in the things themselves, whether they are perceived or not: and upon their different modifications it is that the secondary qualities depend.

The other two are only powers to act differently upon other things: which powers result from the different modifications of those primary qualities.

24. *The first are Resemblances; the second thought to be Resemblances, but are not; the third neither are, nor are thought so.*——But, though the two latter sorts of qualities are powers barely, and nothing but powers, relating to several other bodies, and resulting from the different modifications of the original qualities, yet they are generally otherwise thought of. For the *second* sort, viz. the powers to produce several ideas in us, by our senses, are looked upon as real qualities in the things thus affecting us: but the *third* sort are called and esteemed barely powers. v.g. The idea of heat or light, which we receive by our eyes, or touch, from the sun, are commonly thought real qualities existing in the sun, and something more than mere powers in it. But when we consider the sun in reference to wax, which it melts or blanches, we look on the whiteness and softness produced in the wax, not as qualities in the sun, but effects produced by powers in it. Whereas, if rightly considered, these qualities of light and warmth, which are perceptions in me when I am warmed or enlightened by the sun, are no otherwise in the sun, than the changes made in the wax, when it is blanched or melted, are in the sun. They are all of them equally *powers in the sun, depending on its primary qualities*; whereby it is able, in the one case, so to alter the bulk, figure, texture, or motion of some of the insensible parts of my eyes or hands, as thereby to produce in me the idea of light or heat; and in the other, it is able so to alter the bulk, figure, texture, or motion of the insensible parts of the wax, as to make them fit to produce in me the distinct ideas of white and fluid.

CHAPTER IX.

OF PERCEPTION.

1. *Perception the first simple Idea of Reflection.*——PERCEPTION, as it is the first faculty of the mind exercised about our ideas; so it is the first and simplest idea we have from reflection, and is by some called thinking in general. Though thinking, in the propriety of the English tongue, signifies that sort of operation in the mind about its ideas, wherein the mind is active; where it, with some degree of voluntary attention, considers anything. For in bare naked perception, the mind is, for the most part, only passive; and what it perceives, it cannot avoid perceiving.

2. *Reflection alone can give us the idea of what perception is.*——What perception is, every one will know better by reflecting on what he does himself, when he sees, hears, feels, &c., or thinks, than by any discourse of mine. Whoever reflects on what passes in his own mind cannot miss it. And if he does not reflect, all the words in the world cannot make him have any notion of it.

3. *Arises in sensation only when the mind notices the organic impression.*——This is certain, that whatever alterations are made in the body, if they reach not the mind; whatever impressions are made on the outward parts, if they are not taken notice of within, there is no perception. Fire may burn our bodies with no other effect than it does a billet, unless the motion be continued to the brain, and there the sense of heat, or idea of pain, be produced in the mind; wherein consists actual perception.

4. *Impulse on the organ insufficient.*——How often may a man observe in himself, that whilst his mind is intently employed in the contemplation of some objects, and curiously surveying some ideas that are there, it takes no notice of impressions of sounding bodies made upon the organ of hearing, with the same alteration that uses to be for the producing the idea of sound? A sufficient impulse there may be on the organ; but it not reaching the observation of the mind, there follows no perception: and though the motion that uses to

produce the idea of sound be made in the ear, yet no sound is heard. Want of sensation, in this case, is not through any defect in the organ, or that the man's ears are less affected than at other times when he does hear: but that which uses to produce the idea, though conveyed in by the usual organ, not being taken notice of in the understanding, and so imprinting no idea in the mind, there follows no sensation. So that wherever there is sense or perception, there some idea is actually produced, and present in the understanding.

8. *Sensations often changed by the Judgment.*——We are further to consider concerning perception, that the ideas we receive by sensation are often, in grown people, altered by the judgment, without our taking notice of it. When we set before our eyes a round globe of any uniform colour, v.g. gold, alabaster, or jet, it is certain that the idea thereby imprinted on our mind is of a flat circle, variously shadowed, with several degrees of light and brightness coming to our eyes. But we having, by use, been accustomed to perceive what kind of appearance convex bodies are wont to make in us; what alterations are made in the reflections of light by the difference of the sensible figures of bodies;—the judgment presently, by an habitual custom, alters the appearances into their causes. So that from that which is truly variety of shadow or colour, collecting the figure, it makes it pass for a mark of figure, and frames to itself the perception of a convex figure and an uniform colour; when the idea we receive from thence is only a plane variously coloured, as is evident in painting. To which purpose I shall here insert a problem of that very ingenious and studious promoter of real knowledge, the learned and worthy Mr. Molineux, which he was pleased to send me in a letter some months since; and it is this:—'Suppose a man *born* blind, and now adult, and taught by his *touch* to distinguish between a cube and a sphere of the same metal, and nighly of the same bigness, so as to tell, when he felt one and the other, which is the cube, which the sphere. Suppose then the cube and sphere placed on a table, and the blind man be made to see: *quære*, whether *by his sight*, *before he touched them*, he could now distinguish and tell which is the globe, which the cube?' To which the acute and judicious proposer answers, 'Not. For, though he has obtained the experience of how a globe, how a cube affects his touch, yet he has not yet obtained the experience, that what affects his touch so or so, must affect his sight so or so; or that a protuberant angle in

the cube, that pressed his hand unequally, shall appear to his eye as it does in the cube.'—I agree with this thinking gentleman, whom I am proud to call my friend, in his answer to this problem; and am of opinion that the blind man, at first sight, would not be able with certainty to say which was the globe, which the cube, whilst he only saw them; though he could unerringly name them by his touch, and certainly distinguish them by the difference of their figures felt. This I have set down, and leave with my reader, as an occasion for him to consider how much he may be beholden to experience, improvement, and acquired notions, where he thinks he had not the least use of, or help from them. And the rather, because this observing gentleman further adds, that 'having, upon the occasion of my book, proposed this to divers very ingenious men, he hardly ever met with one that at first gave the answer to it which he thinks true, till by hearing his reasons they were convinced.'

15. *Perception the Inlet of all materials of Knowledge.*——Perception then being the *first* step and degree towards knowledge, and the inlet of all the materials of it; the fewer senses any man, as well as any other creature, hath; and the fewer and duller the impressions are that are made by them; and the duller the faculties are that are employed about them, —the more remote are they from that knowledge which is to be found in some men. But this being in great variety of degrees (as may be perceived amongst men) cannot certainly be discovered in the several species of animals, much less in their particular individuals. It suffices me only to have remarked here,—that perception is the first operation of all our intellectual faculties, and the inlet of all knowledge in our minds. And I am apt too to imagine, that it is perception, in the lowest degree of it, which puts the boundaries between animals and the inferior ranks of creatures. But this I mention only as my conjecture by the by; it being indifferent to the matter in hand which way the learned shall determine of it.

CHAPTER X.

OF RETENTION.

1. *Contemplation.*——The next faculty of the mind, whereby it makes a further progress towards knowledge, is that which I call *retention*; or the keeping of those simple ideas which from sensation or reflection it hath received. This is done two ways.

First, by keeping the idea which is brought into it, for some time actually in view, which is called *contemplation*.

2. *Memory.*——The other way of retention is, the power to revive again in our minds those ideas which, after imprinting, have disappeared, or have been as it were laid aside out of sight. And thus we do, when we conceive heat or light, yellow or sweet,—the object being removed. This is *memory*, which is as it were the storehouse of our ideas. For, the narrow mind of man not being capable of having many ideas under view and consideration at once, it was necessary to have a repository, to lay up those ideas which, at another time, it might have use of. But, our *ideas* being nothing but actual perceptions in the mind, which cease to be anything when there is no perception of them; this laying up of our ideas in the repository of the memory signifies no more but this,—that the mind has a power in many cases to revive perceptions which it has once had, with this additional perception annexed to them, that *it has had them before*. And in this sense it is that our ideas are said to be in our memories, when indeed they are actually nowhere;—but only there is an ability in the mind when it will to revive them again, and as it were paint them anew on itself, though some with more, some with less difficulty; some more lively, and others more obscurely. And thus it is, by the assistance of this faculty, that we are said to have all those ideas in our understandings which, though we do not actually contemplate, yet we *can* bring in sight, and make appear again, and be the objects of our thoughts, without the help of those sensible qualities which first imprinted them there.

CHAPTER XI.

OF DISCERNING, AND OTHER OPERATIONS OF THE MIND.

1. *No Knowledge without Discernment.*——Another faculty we may take notice of in our minds is that of *discerning* and *distinguishing* between the several ideas it has. It is not enough to have a confused perception of something in general. Unless the mind had a distinct perception of different objects and their qualities, it would be capable of very little knowledge, though the bodies that affect us were as busy about us as they are now, and the mind were continually employed in thinking. On this faculty of distinguishing one thing from another depends the evidence and certainty of several, even very general, propositions, which have passed for innate truths;—because men, overlooking the true cause why those propositions find universal assent, impute it wholly to native uniform impressions; whereas it in truth depends upon this clear discerning faculty of the mind, whereby it *perceives* two ideas to be the same, or different. But of this more hereafter.

4. *Comparing.*——The COMPARING them one with another, in respect of extent, degrees, time, place, or any other circumstances, is another operation of the mind about its ideas, and is that upon which depends all that large tribe of ideas comprehended under *relation*; which, of how vast an extent it is, I shall have occasion to consider hereafter.

6. *Compounding.*——The next operation we may observe in the mind about its ideas is COMPOSITION; whereby it puts together several of those simple ones it has received from sensation and reflection, and combines them into complex ones. Under this of composition may be reckoned also that of *enlarging*, wherein, though the composition does not so much appear as in more complex ones, yet it is nevertheless a putting several ideas together, though of the same kind. Thus, by adding several units together, we make the idea of a dozen; and putting together the repeated ideas of several perches, we frame that of a furlong.

8. *Naming.*——When children have, by repeated sensations, got ideas fixed in their memories, they begin by degrees to learn the use of signs. And when they have got the skill to apply the organs of speech to the framing of articulate sounds, they begin to make use of words, to signify their ideas to others. These verbal signs they sometimes borrow from others, and sometimes make themselves, as one may observe among the new and unusual names children often give to things in the first use of language.

9. *Abstraction.*——The use of words then being to stand as outward marks of our internal ideas, and those ideas being taken from particular things, if every particular idea that we take in should have a distinct name, names must be endless. To prevent this, the mind makes the particular ideas received from particular objects to become general; which is done by considering them as they are in the mind such appearances,—separate from all other existences, and the circumstances of real existence, as time, place, or any other concomitant ideas. This is called ABSTRACTION, whereby ideas taken from particular beings become general representatives of all of the same kind; and their names general names, applicable to whatever exists conformable to such abstract ideas. Such precise, naked appearances in the mind, without considering how, whence, or with what others they came there, the understanding lays up (with names commonly annexed to them) as the standards to rank real existences into sorts, as they agree with these patterns, and to denominate them accordingly. Thus the same colour being observed to-day in chalk or snow, which the mind yesterday received from milk, it considers that appearance alone, makes it a representative of all of that kind; and having given it the name *whiteness*, it by that sound signifies the same quality wheresoever to be imagined or met with; and thus universals, whether ideas or terms, are made.

15. *The true Beginning of Human Knowledge.*——And thus I have given a short, and, I think, true *history of the first beginnings of human knowledge;*—whence the mind has its first objects; and by what steps it makes its progress to the laying in and storing up those ideas, out of which is to be framed all the knowledge it is capable of: wherein I must appeal to experience and observation whether I am in the right: the best way to come to truth being to examine things as really they are, and not to conclude they are, as we fancy of ourselves, or have been taught by others to imagine.

17. *Dark Room.*——I pretend not to teach, but to inquire; and therefore cannot but confess here again,—that external and internal sensation are the only passages I can find of knowledge to the understanding. These alone, as far as I can discover, are the windows by which light is let into this *dark room*. For, methinks, the understanding is not much unlike a closet wholly shut from light, with only some little openings left, to let in external visible resemblances, or ideas of things without: would the pictures coming into such a dark room but stay there, and lie so orderly as to be found upon occasion, it would very much resemble the understanding of a man, in reference to all objects of sight, and the ideas of them.

These are my guesses concerning the means whereby the understanding comes to have and retain simple ideas, and the modes of them, with some other operations about them.

I proceed now to examine some of these simple ideas and their modes a little more particularly.

CHAPTER XII.

OF COMPLEX IDEAS.

1. *Made by the Mind out of simple Ones.*——We have hitherto considered those ideas, in the reception whereof the mind is only passive, which are those simple ones received from sensation and reflection before mentioned, whereof the mind cannot make one to itself, nor have any idea which does not wholly consist of them. But as the mind is wholly passive in the reception of all its simple ideas, so it exerts several acts of its own, whereby out of its simple ideas, as the materials and foundations of the rest, the others are framed. The acts of the mind, wherein it exerts its power over its simple ideas, are chiefly these three: (1) Combining several simple ideas into one compound one; and thus all *complex ideas* are made. (2) The second is bringing two ideas, whether simple or complex, together, and setting them by one another, so as to take a view of them at once, without uniting them into one; by which way it gets all its *ideas of relations*. (3) The third is separating them from all other ideas that accompany them in their real existence: this is called abstraction: and thus all

its *general ideas* are made. This shows man's power, and its ways of operation, to be much the same in the material and intellectual world. For the materials in both being such as he has no power over, either to make or destroy, all that man can do is either to unite them together, or to set them by one another, or wholly separate them. I shall here begin with the first of these in the consideration of complex ideas, and come to the other two in their due places. As simple ideas are observed to exist in several combinations united together, so the mind has a power to consider several of them united together as one idea; and that not only as they are united in external objects, but as itself has joined them together. Ideas thus made up of several simple ones put together, I call *complex*;—such as are beauty, gratitude, a man, an army, the universe; which, though complicated of various simple ideas, or complex ideas made up of simple ones, yet are, when the mind pleases, considered each by itself, as one entire thing, and signified by one name.

2. *Made voluntarily.*——In this faculty of repeating and joining together its ideas, the mind has great power in varying and multiplying the objects of its thoughts, infinitely beyond what sensation or reflection furnished it with: but all this still confined to those simple ideas which it received from those two sources, and which are the ultimate materials of all its compositions. For simple ideas are all from things themselves, and of these the mind *can* have no more, nor other than what are suggested to it. It can have no other ideas of sensible qualities than what come from without by the senses; nor any ideas of other kind of operations of a thinking substance, than what it finds in itself. But when it has once got these simple ideas, it is not confined barely to observation, and what offers itself from without; it can, by its own power, put together those ideas it has, and make new complex ones, which it never received so united.

3. *Complex ideas are either of Modes, Substances, or Relations.*——*Complex ideas*, however compounded and decompounded, though their number be infinite, and the variety endless, wherewith they fill and entertain the thoughts of men; yet I think they may be all reduced under these three heads:—

1. *Modes.*
2. *Substances.*
3. *Relations.*

4. *Ideas of Modes.*——First, *Modes* I call such complex ideas which, however compounded, contain not in them the supposition of subsisting by themselves, but are considered as dependences on, or affections of substances;—such as are the ideas signified by the words triangle, gratitude, murder, &c. And if in this I use the word mode in somewhat a different sense from its ordinary signification, I beg pardon; it being unavoidable in discourses, differing from the ordinary received notions, either to make new words, or to use old words in somewhat a new signification; the later whereof, in our present case, is perhaps the more tolerable of the two.

5. *Simple and mixed Modes of simple ideas.*——Of these *modes*, there are two sorts which deserve distinct consideration:—

First, there are some which are only variations, or different combinations of the same simple idea, without the mixture of any other;—as a dozen, or score; which are nothing but the ideas of so many distinct units added together, and these I call *simple modes* as being contained within the bounds of one simple idea.

Secondly, there are others compounded of simple ideas of several kinds, put together to make one complex one;—v.g. beauty, consisting of a certain composition of colour and figure, causing delight to the beholder; theft, which being the concealed change of the possession of anything, without the consent of the proprietor, contains, as is visible, a combination of several ideas of several kinds: and these I call *mixed modes*.

6. *Ideas of Substances, single or collective.*——Secondly, the ideas of *substances* are such combinations of simple ideas as are taken to represent distinct *particular* things subsisting by themselves; in which the supposed or confused idea of substance, such as it is, is always the first and chief. Thus if to substance be joined the simple idea of a certain dull whitish colour, with certain degrees of weight, hardness, ductility, and fusibility, we have the idea of lead; and a combination of the ideas of a certain sort of figure, with the powers of motion, thought and reasoning, joined to substance, make the ordinary idea of a man. Now of substances also, there are two sorts of ideas:—one of *single* substances, as they exist separately, as of a man or a sheep; the other of several of those put together, as an army of men, or flock of sheep—which *collective* ideas

of several substances thus put together are as much each of them one single idea as that of a man or an unit.

7. *Ideas of Relation.*——Thirdly, the last sort of complex ideas is that we call *relation*, which consists in the consideration and comparing one idea with another.

Of these several kinds we shall treat in their order.

CHAPTER XIII.

COMPLEX IDEAS OF SIMPLE MODES.

1. *Simple modes of simple ideas.*——Though in the foregoing part I have often mentioned simple ideas, which are truly the materials of all our knowledge; yet having treated of them there, rather in the way that they come into the mind, than as distinguished from others more compounded, it will not be perhaps amiss to take a view of some of them again under this consideration, and examine those different modifications of the *same* idea; which the mind either finds in things existing, or is able to make within itself without the help of any extrinsical object, or any foreign suggestion.

Those modifications of any *one* simple idea (which, as has been said, I call *simple modes*) are as perfectly different and distinct ideas in the mind as those of the greatest distance or contrariety. For the idea of two is as distinct from that of one, as blueness from heat, or either of them from any number: and yet it is made up only of that simple idea of an unit repeated; and repetitions of this kind joined together make those distinct simple modes, of a dozen, a gross, a million.

CHAPTER XXI.

OF POWER.

1. *This Idea, how got.*——The mind being every day informed, by the senses, of the alteration of those simple ideas it observes in things without; and taking notice how one

comes to an end, and ceases to be, and another begins to exist which was not before; reflecting also on what passes within itself, and observing a constant change of its ideas, sometimes by the impression of outward objects on the senses, and sometimes by the determination of its own choice; and concluding from what it has so constantly observed to have been, that the like changes will for the future be made in the same things, by like agents, and by the like ways,—considers in one thing the possibility of having any of its simple ideas changed, and in another the possibility of making that change; and so comes by that idea which we call *power*. Thus we say, Fire has a power to melt gold, i.e. to destroy the consistency of its insensible parts, and consequently its hardness, and make it fluid; and gold has a power to be melted; that the sun has a power to blanch wax, and wax a power to be blanched by the sun, whereby the yellowness is destroyed, and whiteness made to exist in its room. In which, and the like cases, the power we consider is in reference to the change of perceivable ideas. For we cannot observe any alteration to be made in, or operation upon anything, but by the observable change of its sensible ideas; nor conceive any alteration to be made, but by conceiving a change of some of its ideas.

2. *Power, active and passive.*——Power thus considered is two-fold, viz. as able to make, or able to receive any change. The one may be called *active*, and the other *passive* power. Whether matter be not wholly destitute of active power, as its author, God, is truly above all passive power; and whether the intermediate state of created spirits be not that alone which is capable of both active and passive power, may be worth consideration. I shall not now enter into that inquiry, my present business being not to search into the original of power, but how we come by the *idea* of it. But since active powers make so great a part of our complex ideas of natural substances, (as we shall see hereafter,) and I mention them as such, according to common apprehension; yet they being not, perhaps, so truly *active* powers as our hasty thoughts are apt to represent them, I judge it not amiss, by this intimation, to direct our minds to the consideration of God and spirits, for the clearest idea of *active* power.

4. *The clearest Idea of active Power had from Spirit.*—— We are abundantly furnished with the idea of *passive* power by almost all sorts of sensible things. In most of them we cannot avoid observing their sensible qualities, nay, their very

substances, to be in a continual flux. And therefore with reason we look on them as liable still to the same change. Nor have we of *active* power (which is the more proper signification of the word power) fewer instances. Since whatever change is observed, the mind must collect a power somewhere able to make that change, as well as a possibility in the thing itself to receive it. But yet, if we will consider it attentively, bodies, by our senses, do not afford us so clear and distinct an idea of active power, as we have from reflection on the operations of our minds. For all power relating to action, and there being but two sorts of action whereof we have an idea, viz. thinking and motion, let us consider whence we have the clearest ideas of the powers which produce these actions. (1) Of thinking, body affords us no idea at all; it is only from reflection that we have that. (2) Neither have we from body any idea of the beginning of motion. A body at rest affords us no idea of any active power to move; and when it is set in motion itself, that motion is rather a passion than an action in it. For, when the ball obeys the motion of a billiard-stick, it is not any action of the ball, but bare passion. Also when by impulse it sets another ball in motion that lay in its way, it only communicates the motion it had received from another, and loses in itself so much as the other received: which gives us but a very obscure idea of an *active* power of moving in body, whilst we observe it only to *transfer*, but not *produce* any motion. For it is but a very obscure idea of power which reaches not the production of the action, but the continuation of the passion. For so is motion in a body impelled by another; the continuation of the alteration made in it from rest to motion being little more an action, than the continuation of the alteration of its figure by the same blow is an action. The idea of the *beginning* of motion we have only from reflection on what passes in ourselves; where we find by experience, that, barely by willing it, barely by a thought of the mind, we can move the parts of our bodies, which were before at rest. So that it seems to me, we have, from the observation of the operation of bodies by our senses, but a very imperfect obscure idea of *active* power; since they afford us not any idea in themselves of the power to begin any action, either motion or thought.

5. *Will and Understanding two Powers in Mind or Spirit.*——This, at least, I think evident,—That we find in ourselves a power to begin or forbear, continue or end several actions

of our minds, and motions of our bodies, barely by a thought or preference of the mind ordering, or as it were commanding, the doing or not doing such or such a particular action. This power which the mind has thus to order the consideration of any idea, or the forbearing to consider it; or to prefer the motion of any part of the body to its rest, and *vice versâ*, in any particular instance, is that which we call the *Will*. The actual exercise of that power, by directing any particular action, or its forbearance, is that which we call *volition* or *willing*. The forbearance of that action, consequent to such order or command of the mind, is called *voluntary*. And whatsoever action is performed without such a thought of the mind, is called *involuntary*. The power of perception is that which we call the *Understanding*. Perception, which we make the act of the understanding, is of three sorts:—1. The perception of ideas in our minds. 2. The perception of the signification of signs. 3. The perception of the connexion or repugnancy, agreement or disagreement, that there is between any of our ideas. All these are attributed to the understanding, or perceptive power, though it be the two latter only that use allows us to say we understand.

7. *Whence the idea of liberty and necessity.*——Everyone, I think, finds in himself a power to begin or forbear, continue or put an end to several actions in himself. From the consideration of the extent of this power of the mind over the actions of the man, which everyone finds in himself, arise the ideas of liberty and necessity.

8. *Liberty, what.*——All the actions that we have any idea of reducing themselves, as has been said, to these two, viz. thinking and motion; so far as a man has power to think or not to think, to move or not to move, according to the preference or direction of his own mind, so far is a man *free*. Wherever any performance or forbearance are not equally in a man's power; wherever doing or not doing will not equally *follow* upon the preference of his mind directing it, there he is not free, though perhaps the action may be voluntary. So that the idea of *liberty* is, the idea of a power in any agent to do or forbear any particular action, according to the determination or thought of the mind, whereby either of them is preferred to the other: where either of them is not in the power of the agent to be produced by him according to his volition, there he is not at liberty; that agent is under *necessity*. So that liberty cannot be where there is no thought, no

volition, no will; but there may be thought, there may be will, there may be volition, where there is no liberty. A little consideration of an obvious instance or two may make this clear.

9. *Supposes Understanding and Will.*——A tennis-ball, whether in motion by the stroke of a racket, or lying still at rest, is not by any one taken to be a free agent. If we inquire into the reason, we shall find it is because we conceive not a tennis-ball to think, and consequently not to have any volition, or *preference* of motion to rest, or *vice versâ*; and therefore has not liberty, is not a free agent; but all its both motion and rest come under our idea of necessary, and are so called. Likewise a man falling into the water, (a bridge breaking under him,) has not herein liberty, is not a free agent. For though he has volition, though he prefers his not falling to falling; yet the forbearance of that motion not being in his power, the stop or cessation of that motion follows not upon his volition; and therefore therein he is not free. So a man striking himself, or his friend, by a convulsive motion of his arm, which it is not in his power, by volition or the direction of his mind, to stop or forbear, nobody thinks he has in this liberty; every one pities him, as acting by necessity and constraint.

10. *Belongs not to Volition.*——Again: suppose a man be carried, whilst fast asleep, into a room where is a person he longs to see and speak with; and be there locked fast in, beyond his power to get out: he awakes, and is glad to find himself in so desirable company, which he stays willingly in, i.e. prefers his stay to going away. I ask, is not this stay voluntary? I think nobody will doubt it: and yet, being locked fast in, it is evident he is not at liberty not to stay, he has not freedom to be gone. So that liberty is not an idea belonging to volition, or preferring; but to the person having the power of doing, or forbearing to do, according as the mind shall choose or direct. Our idea of liberty reaches as far as that power, and no farther. For wherever restraint comes to check that power, or compulsion takes away that indifferency of ability to act, or to forbear acting, there liberty, and our notion of it, presently ceases.

11. *Voluntary opposed to involuntary, not to necessary.* ——We have instances enough, and often more than enough, in our own bodies. A man's heart beats, and the blood circulates, which it is not in his power by any thought or volition

to stop; and therefore in respect of these motions, where rest depends not on his choice, nor would follow the determination of his mind, if it should prefer it, he is not a free agent. Convulsive motions agitate his legs, so that though he wills it ever so much, he cannot by any power of his mind stop their motion, (as in that odd disease called *chorea sancti viti*), but he is perpetually dancing; he is not at liberty in this action, but under as much necessity of moving, as a stone that falls, or a tennis-ball struck with a racket. On the other side, a palsy or the stocks hinder his legs from obeying the determination of his mind, if it would thereby transfer his body to another place. In all these there is want of freedom; though the sitting still, even of a paralytic, whilst he prefers it to a removal, is truly voluntary. Voluntary, then, is not opposed to necessary, but to involuntary. For a man may prefer what he can do, to what he cannot do; the state he is in, to its absence or change; though necessity has made it in itself unalterable.

12. *Liberty, what.*——As it is in the motions of the body, so it is in the thoughts of our minds: where any one is such, that we have power to take it up, or lay it by, according to the preference of the mind, there we are at liberty. A waking man, being under the necessity of having some ideas constantly in his mind, is not at liberty to think or not to think; no more than he is at liberty, whether his body shall touch any other or no: but whether he will remove his contemplation from one idea to another is many times in his choice; and then he is, in respect of his ideas, as much at liberty as he is in respect of bodies he rests on; he can at pleasure remove himself from one to another. But yet some ideas to the mind, like some motions to the body, are such as in certain circumstances it cannot avoid, nor obtain their absence by the utmost effort it can use. A man on the rack is not at liberty to lay by the idea of pain, and divert himself with other contemplations: and sometimes a boisterous passion hurries our thoughts, as a hurricane does our bodies, without leaving us the liberty of thinking on other things, which we would rather choose. But as soon as the mind regains the power to stop or continue, begin or forbear, any of these motions of the body without, or thoughts within, according as it thinks fit to prefer either to the other, we then consider the man as a *free agent* again.

13. *Necessity, what.*——Wherever thought is wholly wanting, or the power to act or forbear according to the direction of thought, there necessity takes place. This, in an agent

capable of volition, when the beginning or continuation of any action is contrary to that preference of his mind, is called compulsion; when the hindering or stopping any action is contrary to his volition, it is called restraint. Agents that have no thought, no volition at all, are in everything *necessary agents.*

14. *Liberty belongs not to the Will.*——If this be so, (as I imagine it is,) I leave it to be considered, whether it may not help to put an end to that long agitated, and, I think, unreasonable, because unintelligible question, viz. *Whether man's will be free or no?* For if I mistake not, it follows from what I have said, that the question itself is altogether improper; and it is as insignificant to ask whether man's *will* be free, as to ask whether his sleep be swift, or his virtue square: liberty being as little applicable to the will, as swiftness of motion is to sleep, or squareness to virtue. Every one would laugh at the absurdity of such a question as either of these: because it is obvious that the modifications of motion belong not to sleep, nor the difference of figure to virtue; and when any one well considers it, I think he will as plainly perceive that liberty, which is but a power, belongs only to *agents,* and cannot be an attribute or modification of the will, which is also but a power.

15. *Volition.*——Such is the difficulty of explaining and giving clear notions of internal actions by sounds, that I must here warn my reader, that *ordering, directing, choosing, preferring,* &c., which I have made use of, will not distinctly enough express volition, unless he will reflect on what he himself does when he wills. For example, preferring, which seems perhaps best to express the act of volition, does it not precisely. For though a man would prefer flying to walking, yet who can say he ever wills it? Volition, it is plain, is an act of the mind knowingly exerting that dominion it takes itself to have over any part of the man, by employing it in, or withholding it from, any particular action. And what is the will, but the faculty to do this? And is that faculty anything more in effect than a power; the power of the mind to determine its thought, to the producing, continuing, or stopping any action, as far as it depends on us? For can it be denied that whatever agent has a power to think on its own actions, and to prefer their doing or omission either to other, has that faculty called will? *Will,* then, is nothing but such a power. *Liberty,* on the other side, is the power a *man* has to do or

forbear doing any particular action according as its doing or forbearance has the actual preference in the mind; which is the same thing as to say, according as he himself wills it.

16. *Powers belonging to Agents.*——It is plain then that the will is nothing but one power or ability, and *freedom* another power or ability so that, to ask, whether the will has freedom, is to ask whether one power has another power, one ability another ability; a question at first sight too grossly absurd to make a dispute, or need an answer. For, who is it that sees not that powers belong only to agents, and are attributes only of substances, and not of powers themselves? So that this way of putting the question (viz. whether the will be free) is in effect to ask, whether the will be a substance, an agent, or at least to suppose it, since freedom can properly be attributed to nothing else. If freedom can with any propriety of speech be applied to power, it may be attributed to the power that is in a man to produce, or forbear producing, motion in parts of his body, by choice or preference; which is that which denominates him free, and is freedom itself. But if any one should ask, whether freedom were free, he would be suspected not to understand well what he said; and he would be thought to deserve Midas's ears, who, knowing that rich was a denomination for the possession of riches, should demand whether riches themselves were rich.

19. *Powers are relations, not agents.*——I grant, that this or that actual thought may be the occasion of volition, or exercising the power a man has to choose; or the actual choice of the mind, the cause of actual thinking on this or that thing: as the actual singing of such a tune may be the cause of dancing such a dance, and the actual dancing of such a dance the occasion of singing such a tune. But in all these it is not one *power* that operates on another: but it is the mind that operates, and exerts these powers; it is the man that does the action; it is the agent that has power, or is able to do. For powers are relations, not agents: and that which has the power or not the power to operate, is that alone which is or is not free, and not the power itself. For freedom, or not freedom, can belong to nothing but what has or has not a power to act.

25. *The Will determined by something without it.*——Since then it is plain that, in most cases, a man is not at liberty, whether he will or no, (for, when an action in his power is proposed to his thoughts, he *cannot* forbear volition; he *must* determine one way or the other;) the next thing de-

manded is,—*Whether a man be at liberty to will which of the two he pleases, motion or rest?* This question carries the absurdity of it so manifestly in itself, that one might thereby sufficiently be convinced that liberty concerns not the will. For, to ask whether a man be at liberty to will either motion or rest, speaking or silence, which he pleases, is to ask whether a man can will what he wills, or be pleased with what he is pleased with? A question which, I think, needs no answer: and they who can make a question of it must suppose one will to determine the acts of another, and another to determine that, and so on *in infinitum.*

29. *What determines the Will.*——The will being nothing but a power in the mind to direct the operative faculties of a man to motion or rest, as far as they depend on such direction; to the question, What is it determines the will? the true and proper answer is, The mind. For that which determines the general power of directing, to this or that particular direction, is nothing but the agent itself exercising the power it has that particular way. If this answer satisfies not, it is plain the meaning of the question, What determines the will? is this,—What moves the mind, in every particular instance, to determine its general power of directing, to this or that particular motion or rest? And to this I answer,—The motive for continuing in the same state or action, is only the present satisfaction in it; the motive to change is always some uneasiness: nothing setting us upon the change of state, or upon any new action, but some uneasiness. This is the great motive that works on the mind to put it upon action, which for shortness' sake we will call determining of the will, which I shall more at large explain.

48. *The Power to suspend the Prosecution of any Desire makes way for Consideration.*——There being in us a great many uneasinesses, always soliciting and ready to determine the will, it is natural, as I have said, that the greatest and most pressing should determine the will to the next action; and so it does for the most part, but not always. For, the mind having in most cases, as is evident in experience, a power to *suspend* the execution and satisfaction of any of its desires; and so all, one after another; is at liberty to consider the objects of them, examine them on all sides, and weigh them with others. In this lies the liberty man has; and from the not using of it right comes all that variety of mistakes, errors, and faults which we run into in the conduct of our lives, and our endeavours after

happiness; whilst we precipitate the determination of our wills, and engage too soon, before due examination. To prevent this, we have a power to suspend the prosecution of this or that desire; as every one daily may experiment in himself. This seems to me the source of all liberty; in this seems to consist that which is (as I think improperly) called *free-will*. For, during this suspension of any desire, before the will be determined to action, and the action (which follows that determination) done, we have opportunity to examine, view, and judge of the good or evil of what we are going to do; and when, upon due examination, we have judged, we have done our duty, all that we can, or ought to do, in pursuit of our happiness; and it is not a fault, but a perfection of our nature, to desire, will, and act according to the last result of a fair examination.

73. *Recapitulation—Liberty of indifferency.*——To conclude this inquiry into *human liberty*, which, as it stood before, I myself from the beginning fearing, and a very judicious friend of mine, since the publication, suspecting to have some mistake in it, though he could not particularly show it me, I was put upon a stricter review of this chapter. Wherein lighting upon a very easy and scarce observable slip I had made, in putting one seemingly indifferent word for another that discovery opened to me this present view, which here, in this second edition, I submit to the learned world, and which, in short, is this: *Liberty* is a power to act or not to act, according as the mind directs. A power to direct the operative faculties to motion or rest in particular instances is that which we call the *will*. That which in the train of our voluntary actions determines the will to any change of operation is *some present uneasiness*, which is, or at least is always accompanied with that of *desire*. Desire is always moved by evil, to fly it: because a total freedom from pain always makes a necessary part of our happiness: but every good, nay, every greater good, does not constantly move desire, because it may not make, or may not be taken to make, any necessary part of our happiness. For all that we desire, is only to be happy. But, though this general desire of happiness operates constantly and invariably, yet the satisfaction of any particular desire *can be suspended* from determining the will to any subservient action, till we have maturely examined whether the particular apparent good which we then desire makes a part of our real happiness, or be consistent or inconsistent with it. The result of our judgment

upon that examination is what ultimately determines the man; who could not be *free* if his will were determined by anything but his own desire, guided by his own judgment. I know that liberty, by some, is placed in an indifferency of the man; antecedent to the determination of his will. I wish they who lay so much stress on such an antecedent indifferency, as they call it, had told us plainly, whether this supposed indifferency be antecedent to the thought and judgment of the understanding, as well as to the decree of the will. For it is pretty hard to state it between them, i.e. immediately *after* the judgment of the understanding, and *before* the determination of the will: because the determination of the will immediately follows the judgment of the understanding: and to place liberty in an indifferency, antecedent to the thought and judgment of the understanding, seems to me to place liberty in a state of darkness, wherein we can neither see nor say anything of it; at least it places it in a subject incapable of it, no agent being allowed capable of liberty, but in consequence of thought and judgment. I am not nice about phrases, and therefore consent to say with those that love to speak so, that liberty is placed in indifferency; but it is an indifferency which remains after the judgment of the understanding, yea, even after the determination of the will: and that is an indifferency not of the *man*, (for after he has once judged which is best, viz. to do or forbear, he is no longer indifferent,) but an indifferency of *the operative powers of the man*, which remaining equally able to operate or to forbear operating after as before the decree of the will, are in a state, which, if one pleases, may be called indifferency; and as far as this indifferency reaches, a man is free, and no further: v.g. I have the ability to move my hand, or to let it rest; that operative power is indifferent to move or not to move my hand. I am then, in that respect perfectly free; my will determines that operative power to rest: I am yet free, because the indifferency of that my operative power to act, or not to act, still remains; the power of moving my hand is not at all impaired by the determination of my will, which at present orders rest; the indifferency of that power to act, or not to act, is just as it was before, as will appear, if the will puts it to the trial, by ordering the contrary. But if, during the rest of my hand, it be seized with a sudden palsy, the indifferency of that operative power is gone, and with it my liberty; I have no longer freedom in that respect, but am under a necessity of letting my hand rest. On the other side, if my hand be put into motion by a convulsion, the indifferency of that operative faculty is taken away by that motion; and my liberty in that case is lost, for I am under a necessity of having my hand move. I have added this, to show in what sort of indifferency liberty seems to me to consist, and not in any other, real or imaginary.

Before I close this chapter, it may perhaps be to our purpose, and help to give us clearer conceptions about *power*, if we make our thoughts take a little more exact survey of *action*. I have said above, that we have ideas but of two sorts of action, viz. motion and thinking. These, in truth, though called and counted actions, yet, if nearly considered, will not be found to be always perfectly so. For, if I mistake not, there are instances of both kinds, which, upon due consideration, will be found rather passions than actions; and consequently so far the effects barely of *passive powers* in those subjects, which yet on their accounts are thought agents. For, in these instances, the substance that hath motion or thought receives the impression, whereby it is put into that action, purely from without, and so acts merely by the capacity it has to receive such an impression from some external agent; and such a power is not properly an active power, but a mere passive capacity in the subject. Sometimes the substance or agent puts itself into action by its own power, and this is properly *active power*. Whatsoever modification a substance has, whereby it produces any effect, that is called action: v.g. a solid substance, by motion, operates on or alters the sensible ideas of another substance, and therefore this modification of motion we call action. But yet this motion in that solid substance is, when rightly considered, but a passion, if it received it only from some external agent. So that the active power of motion is in no substance which cannot begin motion in itself or in another substance when at rest. So likewise in thinking, a power to receive ideas or thoughts from the operation of any external substance is called a power of thinking: but this is but a passive power, or capacity. But to be able to bring into view ideas out of sight at one's own choice, and to compare which of them one thinks fit, this is an active power. This reflection may be of some use to preserve us from mistakes about powers and actions, which grammar, and the common frame of languages, may be apt to lead us into. Since what is signified by verbs that grammarians call active, does not always signify action: v.g. this proposition: I *see* the moon, or a star, or I *feel* the heat of the sun, though expressed by a verb active, does not signify any action in me, whereby I operate on those substances, but only the reception of the ideas of light, roundness, and heat; wherein I am not active, but barely passive, and cannot, in that position of my eyes or body, avoid receiving them. But when I turn my eyes another way, or remove my body out of the sunbeams, I am properly active; because of my own choice, by a power within myself, I put myself into that motion. Such an action is the product of active power.

CHAPTER XXII.

OF MIXED MODES.

1. *Mixed Modes, what.*——Having treated of *simple modes* in the foregoing chapters, and given several instances of some of the most considerable of them, to show what they are, and how we come by them; we are now in the next place to consider those we call *mixed modes*; such are the complex ideas we mark by the names *obligation, drunkenness,* a *lie,* &c.; which consisting of several combinations of simple ideas of *different* kinds, I have called mixed modes, to distinguish them from the more simple modes, which consist only of simple ideas of the *same* kind. These mixed modes, being also such combinations of simple ideas as are not looked upon to be characteristical marks of any real beings that have a steady existence, but scattered and independent ideas put together by the mind, are thereby distinguished from the complex ideas of substances.

CHAPTER XXIII.

OF OUR COMPLEX IDEAS OF SUBSTANCES.

1. *Ideas of particular Substances, how made.*——The mind being, as I have declared, furnished with a great number of the simple ideas, conveyed in by the senses as they are found

in exterior things, or by reflection on its own operations, takes notice also that a certain number of these simple ideas go constantly together; which being presumed to belong to one thing, and words being suited to common apprehensions, and made use of for quick dispatch, are called, so united in one subject, by one name; which, by inadvertency, we are apt afterward to talk of and consider as one simple idea, which indeed is a complication of many ideas together: because, as I have said, not imagining how these simple ideas *can* subsist by themselves, we accustom ourselves to suppose some *substratum* wherein they do subsist, and from which they do result, which therefore we call *substance.*

2. *Our obscure Idea of Substance in general.*——So that if any one will examine himself concerning his notion of pure substance in general, he will find he has no other idea of it at all, but only a supposition of he knows not what *support* of such qualities which are capable of producing simple ideas in us; which qualities are commonly called accidents. If any one should be asked, what is the subject wherein colour or weight inheres, he would have nothing to say, but the solid extended parts; and if he were demanded, what is it that solidity and extension adhere in, he would not be in a much better case than the Indian before mentioned who, saying that the world was supported by a great elephant, was asked what the elephant rested on; to which his answer was—a great tortoise: but being again pressed to know what gave support to the broad-backed tortoise, replied—*something, he knew not what.* And thus here, as in all other cases where we use words without having clear and distinct ideas, we talk like children: who, being questioned what such a thing is, which they know not, readily give this satisfactory answer, that it is *something*: which in truth signifies no more, when so used, either by children or men, but that they know not what; and that the thing they pretend to know, and talk of, is what they have no distinct idea of at all, and so are perfectly ignorant of it, and in the dark. The idea then we have, to which we give the *general* name substance, being nothing but the supposed, but unknown, support of those qualities we find existing, which we imagine cannot subsist *sine re substante,* without something to support them, we call that support *substantia*; which, according to the true import of the word, is, in plain English, standing under or upholding.

3. *Of the Sorts of Substances.*——An obscure and relative idea of *substance in general* being thus made we come to have the ideas of *particular sorts of substances*, by collecting *such* combinations of simple ideas as are, by experience and observation of men's senses, taken notice of to exist together; and are therefore supposed to flow from the particular internal constitution, or unknown essence of that substance. Thus we come to have the ideas of a man, horse, gold, water, &c.; of which substances, whether any one has any other *clear* idea, further than of certain simple ideas co-existent together, I appeal to every one's own experience. It is the ordinary qualities observable in iron, or a diamond, put together, that make the true complex idea of those substances, which a smith or a jeweller commonly knows better than a philosopher; who, whatever *substantial forms* he may talk of, has no other idea of those substances, than what is framed by a collection of those simple ideas which are to be found in them: only we must take notice, that our complex ideas of substances, besides all those simple ideas they are made up of, have always the confused idea of something to which they belong, and in which they subsist: and therefore when we speak of any sort of substance, we say it is a thing having such or such qualities; as body is a thing that is extended, figured, and capable of motion; spirit, a thing capable of thinking; and so hardness, friability, and power to draw iron, we say, are qualities to be found in a loadstone. These, and the like fashions of speaking, intimate that the substance is supposed always *something besides* the extension, figure, solidity, motion, thinking, or other observable ideas, though we know not what it is.

4. *No clear or distinct idea of Substance in general.*——Hence, when we talk or think of any particular sort of corporeal substances, as horse, stone, &c., though the idea we have of either of them be but the complication or collection of those several simple ideas of sensible qualities, which we used to find united in the thing called horse or stone; yet, *because we cannot conceive how they should subsist alone, nor one in another,* we suppose them existing in and supported by some common subject; which support we denote by the name substance, though it be certain we have no clear or distinct idea of that thing we suppose a support.

5. *As clear an Idea of spiritual substance as of corporeal substance.*——The same thing happens concerning the operations of the mind, viz. thinking, reasoning, fearing, &c., which

we concluding not to subsist of themselves, nor apprehending how they can belong to body, or be produced by it, we are apt to think these the actions of some other *substance*, which we call *spirit*; whereby yet it is evident that, having no other idea or notion of matter, but something wherein those many sensible qualities which affect our senses do subsist; by supposing a substance wherein thinking, knowing, doubting, and a power of moving, &c., do subsist, we have as clear a notion of the substance of spirit, as we have of body; the one being supposed to be (without knowing what it is) the *substratum* to those simple ideas we have from without; and the other supposed (with a like ignorance of what it is) to be the *substratum* to those operations we experiment in ourselves within. It is plain then, that the idea of *corporeal substance* in matter is as remote from our conceptions and apprehensions, as that of *spiritual substance*, or spirit: and therefore, from our not having any notion of the substance of spirit, we can no more conclude its non-existence, than we can, for the same reason, deny the existence of body; it being as rational to affirm there is no body, because we have no clear and distinct idea of the substance of matter, as to say there is no spirit, because we have no clear and distinct idea of the substance of a spirit.

6. *Our ideas of particular Sorts of Substances.*——Whatever therefore be the secret abstract nature of substance in general, all the ideas we have of particular distinct sorts of substances are nothing but several combinations of simple ideas, co-existing in such, though unknown, cause of their union, as makes the whole subsist of itself. It is by such combinations of simple ideas, and nothing else, that we represent particular sorts of substances to ourselves; such are the ideas we have of their several species in our minds; and such only do we, by their specific names, signify to others, v.g. man, horse, sun, water, iron: upon hearing which words, every one who understands the language, frames in his mind a combination of those several simple ideas which he has usually observed, or fancied to exist together under that denomination; all which he supposes to rest in and be, as it were, adherent to that unknown common subject, which inheres not in anything else. Though, in the meantime, it be manifest, and every one, upon inquiry into his own thoughts, will find, that he has no other idea of any substance, v.g. let it be gold, horse, iron, man, vitriol, bread, but what he has barely of those sensible qualities, which he supposes to inhere; with a supposition of

such a *substratum* as gives, as it were, a support to those qualities or simple ideas, which he has observed to exist united together. Thus, the idea of the sun,—what is it but an aggregate of those several simple ideas, bright, hot, roundish, having a constant regular motion, at a certain distance from us, and perhaps some other: as he who thinks and discourses of the sun has been more or less accurate in observing those sensible qualities, ideas, or properties, which are in that thing which he calls the sun.

7. *Their active and passive Powers a great part of our complex Ideas of Substances.*——For he has the perfectest idea of any of the particular sorts of substances, who has gathered, and put together, most of those simple ideas which do exist in it; among which are to be reckoned its active powers, and passive capacities, which, though not simple ideas, yet in this respect, for brevity's sake, may conveniently enough be reckoned amongst them. Thus, the power of drawing iron is one of the ideas of the complex one of that substance we call a loadstone; and a power to be so drawn is a part of the complex one we call iron: which powers pass for inherent qualities in those subjects. Because every substance, being as apt, by the powers we observe in it, to change some sensible qualities in other subjects, as it is to produce in us those simple ideas which we receive immediately from it, does, by those new sensible qualities introduced into other subjects, discover to us those powers which do thereby mediately affect our senses, as regularly as its sensible qualities do it immediately: v.g. we immediately by our senses perceive in fire its heat and colour; which are, if rightly considered, nothing but powers in it to produce those ideas in *us*: we also by our senses perceive the colour and brittleness of charcoal, whereby we come by the knowledge of another power in fire, which it has to change the colour and consistency of *wood*. By the former, fire immediately, by the latter, it mediately discovers to us these several powers; which therefore we look upon to be a part of the qualities of fire, and so make them a part of the complex idea of it. For all those powers that we take cognizance of, terminating only in the alteration of some sensible qualities in those subjects on which they operate, and so making them exhibit to us new sensible ideas, therefore it is that I have reckoned these powers amongst the simple ideas which make the complex ones of the sorts of substances; though these powers considered in themselves, are truly complex ideas. And

in this looser sense I crave leave to be understood, when I name any of these *potentialities* among the simple ideas which we recollect in our minds when we think of *particular substances*. For the powers that are severally in them are necessary to be considered, if we will have true distinct notions of the several sorts of substances.

8. *And why.*——Nor are we to wonder that powers make a great part of our complex ideas of substances; since their secondary qualities are those which in most of them serve principally to distinguish substances one from another, and commonly make a considerable part of the complex idea of the several sorts of them. For, our senses failing us in the discovery of the bulk, texture, and figure of the minute parts of bodies, on which their real constitutions and differences depend, we are fain to make use of their secondary qualities as the characteristical notes and marks whereby to frame ideas of them in our minds, and distinguish them one from another: all which secondary qualities, as has been shown, are nothing but bare powers. For the colour and taste of opium are, as well as its soporific or anodyne virtues, mere powers, depending on its primary qualities, whereby it is fitted to produce different operations on different parts of our bodies.

9. *Three sorts of Ideas make our complex ones of Corporeal Substances.*——The ideas that make our complex ones of corporeal substances, are of these three sorts. First, the ideas of the primary qualities of things, which are discovered by our senses, and are in them even when we perceive them not; such are the bulk, figure, number, situation, and motion of the parts of bodies; which are really in them, whether we take notice of them or not. Secondly, the sensible secondary qualities, which, depending on these, are nothing but the powers those substances have to produce several ideas in us by our senses; which ideas are not in the things themselves, otherwise than as anything is in its cause. Thirdly, the aptness we consider in any substance, to give or receive such alterations of primary qualities, as that the substance so altered should produce in us different ideas from what it did before; these are called active and passive powers: all which powers, as far as we have any notice or notion of them, terminate only in sensible simple ideas. For whatever alteration a loadstone has the power to make in the minute particles of iron, we should have no notion of any power it had at all to operate on iron, did not its sensible motion discover it: and I doubt not, but there are

a thousand changes, that bodies we daily handle have a power to cause in one another, which we never suspect, because they never appear in sensible effects.

10. *Powers thus make a great Part of our complex Ideas of particular Substances.*——*Powers* therefore justly make a great part of our complex ideas of substances. He that will examine his complex idea of gold, will find several of its ideas that make it up to be only powers; as the power of being melted, but of not spending itself in the fire; of being dissolved in *aqua regia,* are ideas as necessary to make up our complex idea of gold, as its colour and weight: which, if duly considered, are also nothing but different powers. For, to speak truly, yellowness is not actually in gold, but is a power in gold to produce that idea in us by our eyes, when placed in a due light: and the heat, which we cannot leave out of our ideas of the sun, is no more really in the sun, than the white colour it introduces into wax. These are both equally powers in the sun, operating, by the motion and figure of its sensible parts, so on a man, as to make him have the idea of heat; and so on wax, as to make it capable to produce in a man the idea of white.

11. *The now secondary Qualities of Bodies would disappear, if we could discover the primary ones of their minute Parts.*——Had we senses acute enough to discern the minute particles of bodies, and the real constitution on which their sensible qualities depend, I doubt not but they would produce quite different ideas in us: and that which is now the yellow colour of gold, would then disappear, and instead of it we should see an admirable texture of parts, of a certain size and figure. This microscopes plainly discover to us; for what to our naked eyes produces a certain colour, is, by thus augmenting the acuteness of our senses, discovered to be quite a different thing; and the thus altering, as it were, the proportion of the bulk of the minute parts of a coloured object to our usual sight, produces different ideas from what it did before. Thus, sand or pounded glass, which is opaque, and white to the naked eye, is pellucid in a microscope; and a hair seen in this way, loses its former colour, and is, in a great measure, pellucid, with a mixture of some bright sparkling colours, such as appear from the refraction of diamonds, and other pellucid bodies. Blood, to the naked eye, appears all red; but by a good microscope, wherein its lesser parts appear, shows only some few globules of red, swimming in a pellucid liquor, and how

these red globules would appear, if glasses could be found that could yet magnify them a thousand or ten thousand times more, is uncertain.

15. *Our Ideas of spiritual Substances, as clear as of bodily Substances.*——Besides the complex ideas we have of material sensible substances, of which I have last spoken,—by the simple ideas we have taken from those operations of our own minds, which we experiment daily in ourselves, as thinking, understanding, willing, knowing, and power of beginning motion, &c., co-existing in some substance, we are able to frame the *complex idea of an immaterial spirit.* And thus, by putting together the ideas of thinking, perceiving, liberty, and power of moving themselves and other things, we have as clear a perception and notion of immaterial substances as we have of material. For putting together the ideas of thinking and willing, or the power of moving or quieting corporeal motion, joined to substance, of which we have no distinct idea, we have the idea of an immaterial spirit; and by putting together the ideas of coherent solid parts, and a power of being moved, joined with substance, of which likewise we have no positive idea, we have the idea of matter. The one is as clear and distinct an idea as the other: the idea of thinking, and moving a body, being as clear and distinct ideas as the ideas of extension, solidity, and being moved. For our idea of substance is equally obscure, or none at all, in both: it is but a supposed I know not what, to support those ideas we call accidents. It is for want of reflection that we are apt to think that our senses show us nothing but material things. Every act of sensation, when duly considered, gives us an equal view of both parts of nature, the corporeal and spiritual. For whilst I know, by seeing or hearing, &c., that there is some corporeal being without me, the object of that sensation, I do more certainly know, that there is some spiritual being within me that sees and hears. This, I must be convinced, cannot be the action of bare insensible matter; nor ever could be, without an immaterial thinking being.

16. *No Idea of abstract Substance either in Body or Spirit.*——By the complex idea of extended, figured, coloured, and all other sensible qualities, which is all that we know of it, we are as far from the idea of the substance of body, as if we knew nothing at all: nor after all the acquaintance and familiarity which we imagine we have with matter, and the many qualities men assure themselves they perceive and know in

bodies, will it perhaps upon examination be found, that they have any more or clearer primary ideas belonging to body, than they have belonging to immaterial spirit.

17. *Cohesion of solid parts and Impulse, the primary ideas peculiar to Body.*——The primary ideas we have *peculiar to body*, as contradistinguished to spirit, are the *cohesion of solid, and consequently separable, parts*, and a *power of communicating motion by impulse*. These, I think, are the original ideas proper and peculiar to body; for figure is but the consequence of finite extension.

18. *Thinking and Motivity.*——The ideas we have belonging and *peculiar to spirit*, are *thinking*, and *will*, or *a power of putting body into motion by thought, and, which is consequent to it, liberty*. For, as body cannot but communicate its motion by impulse to another body, which it meets with at rest, so the mind can put bodies into motion, or forbear to do so, as it pleases. The ideas of *existence, duration*, and *mobility*, are common to them both.

22. *Our complex idea of an immaterial Spirit and our complex idea of Body compared.*——Let us compare, then, our complex idea of an immaterial spirit with our complex idea of body, and see whether there be any more obscurity in one than in the other, and in which most. Our idea of *body*, as I think, is *an extended solid substance, capable of communicating motion by impulse*: and our idea of *soul, as an immaterial spirit*, is of *a substance that thinks, and has a power of exciting motion in body, by willing, or thought*. These, I think, are our complex ideas of soul and body, as contradistinguished; and now let us examine which has most obscurity in it, and difficulty to be apprehended. I know that people whose thoughts are immersed in matter, and have so subjected their minds to their senses that they seldom reflect on anything beyond them, are apt to say, they cannot comprehend a *thinking* thing, which perhaps is true: but I affirm, when they consider it well, they can no more comprehend an *extended* thing.

28. *Communication of Motion by Impulse, or by Thought, equally unintelligible.*——Another idea we have of body is, *the power of communication of motion by impulse*; and of our souls, *the power of exciting motion by thought*. These ideas, the one of body, the other of our minds, every day's experience clearly furnishes us with: but if here again we inquire how this is done, we are equally in the dark. For, in the communication of motion by impulse, wherein as much mo-

tion is lost to one body as is got to the other, which is the ordinariest case, we can have no other conception, but of the passing of motion out of one body into another; which, I think, is as obscure and inconceivable as how our minds move or stop our bodies by thought, which we every moment find they do. The increase of motion by impulse, which is observed or believed sometimes to happen, is yet harder to be understood. We have by daily experience clear evidence of motion produced both by impulse and by thought; but the manner how, hardly comes within our comprehension: we are equally at a loss in both. So that, however we consider motion, and its communication, either from body or spirit, the idea which belongs to spirit is at least as clear as that which belongs to body. And if we consider the active power of moving, or, as I may call it, motivity, it is much clearer in spirit than body; since two bodies, placed by one another at rest, will never afford us the idea of a power in the one to move the other, but by a borrowed motion: whereas the mind every day affords us ideas of an active power of moving of bodies; and therefore it is worth our consideration, whether active power be not the proper attribute of spirits, and passive power of matter. Hence may be conjectured that created spirits are not totally separate from matter, because they are both active and passive. Pure spirit, viz. God, is only active; pure matter is only passive; those beings that are both active and passive, we may judge to partake of both. But be that as it will, I think, we have as many and as clear ideas belonging to spirit as we have belonging to body, the substance of each being equally unknown to us; and the idea of thinking in spirit, as clear as of extension in body; and the communication of motion by thought, which we attribute to spirit, is as evident as that by impulse, which we ascribe to body. Constant experience makes us sensible of both these, though our narrow understandings can comprehend neither. For, when the mind would look beyond those original ideas we have from sensation or reflection, and penetrate into their causes, and manner of production, we find still it discovers nothing but its own short-sightedness.

37. *Recapitulation.*——And thus we have seen what kind of ideas we have of *substances of all kinds*, wherein they consist, and how we came by them. From whence, I think, it is very evident,

First, That all our ideas of the several *sorts* of substances are nothing but collections of simple ideas: with a supposition of *something* to which they belong, and in which they subsist: though of this supposed something we have no clear distinct idea at all.

Secondly, That all the simple ideas, that thus united in one common *substratum*, make up our complex ideas of several *sorts* of substances, are no other but such as we have received from sensation or reflection. So that even in those which we think we are most intimately acquainted with, and that come nearest the comprehension of our most enlarged conceptions, we cannot go beyond those simple ideas. And even in those which seem most remote from all we have to do with, and do infinitely surpass anything we can perceive in ourselves by reflection; or discover by sensation in other things, we can attain to nothing but those simple ideas, which we originally received from sensation or reflection; as is evident in the complex ideas we have of angels, and particularly of God himself.

Thirdly, That most of the simple ideas that make up our complex ideas of substances, when truly considered, are only *powers*, however we are apt to take them for positive qualities; v.g. the greatest part of the ideas that make our complex idea of *gold* are yellowness, great weight, ductility, fusibility, and solubility in *aqua regia*, &c., all united together in an unknown *substratum*: all which ideas are nothing else but so many relations to other substances; and are not really in the gold, considered barely in itself, though they depend on those real and primary qualities of its internal constitution, whereby it has a fitness differently to operate, and be operated on by several other substances.

CHAPTER XXVII.

OF IDENTITY AND DIVERSITY.

1. *Wherein Identity consists.*——Another occasion the mind often takes of comparing, is the very being of things, when, considering *anything as existing at any determined time and place*, we compare it with *itself existing at another time*, and thereon form the ideas of *identity* and *diversity*. When we see anything to be in any place in any instant of time, we are sure (be it what it will) that it is that very thing, and not

another which at that same time exists in another place, how like and undistinguishable soever it may be in all other respects: and in this consists *identity*, when the ideas it is attributed to vary not at all from what they were that moment wherein we consider their former existence, and to which we compare the present. For we never finding, nor conceiving it possible, that two things of the same kind should exist in the same place at the same time, we rightly conclude, that, whatever exists anywhere at any time, excludes all of the same kind, and is there itself alone. When therefore we demand whether anything be the *same* or no, it refers always to something that existed such a time in such a place, which it was certain, at that instant, was the same with itself, and no other. From whence it follows, that one thing cannot have two beginnings of existence, nor two things one beginning; it being impossible for two things of the same kind to be or exist in the same instant, in the very same place; or one and the same thing in different places. That, therefore, that had one beginning, is the same thing; and that which had a different beginning in time and place from that, is not the same, but diverse. That which has made the difficulty about this relation has been the little care and attention used in having precise notions of the things to which it is attributed.

2. *Identity of Substances.*——We have the ideas but of three sorts of substances: 1. *God.* 2. *Finite intelligences.* 3. *Bodies.*

First, *God* is without beginning, eternal, unalterable, and everywhere, and therefore concerning his identity there can be no doubt.

Secondly, *Finite spirits* having had each its determinate time and place of beginning to exist, the relation to that time and place will always determine to each of them its identity, as long as it exists.

Thirdly, The same will hold of every *particle of matter*, to which no addition or substraction of matter being made, it is the same. For, though these three sorts of substances, as we term them, do not exclude one another out of the same place, yet we cannot conceive but that they must necessarily each of them exclude any of the same kind out of the same place: or else the notions and names of identity and diversity would be in vain, and there could be no such distinctions of substances, or anything else one from another. For example: could two bodies be in the same place at the same time; then those two parcels of matter must be one and the same, take them great or little; nay, all bodies must be one and the same. For, by the same reason that two particles of matter may be in one place, all bodies may be in one place: which, when it can be supposed, takes away the distinction of identity and diversity of one and more, and renders it ridiculous. But it being a contradiction that two or more should be one, identity and diversity are relations and ways of comparing well founded, and of use to the understanding.

3. *Identity of modes and relations.*——All other things being but modes or relations ultimately terminated in substances, the identity and diversity of each particular existence of them too will be by the same way determined: only as to things whose existence is in succession, such as are the actions of finite beings, v.g. *motion* and *thought*, both which consist in a continued train of succession, concerning *their* diversity there can be no question: because each perishing the moment it begins, they cannot exist in different times, or in different places, as permanent beings can at different times exist in distant places; and therefore no motion or thought, considered as at different times, can be the same, each part thereof having a different beginning of existence.

4. *Principium Individuationis.*——From what has been said, it is easy to discover what is so much inquired after, the *principium individuationis*; and that, it is plain, is existence itself; which determines a being of any sort to a particular time and place, incommunicable to two beings of the same kind. This, though it seems easier to conceive in simple substances or modes; yet, when reflected on, is not more difficult in compound ones, if care be taken to what it is applied: v.g. let us suppose an atom, i.e. a continued body under one immutable superficies, existing in a determined time and place; it is evident, that, considered in any instant of its existence, it is in that instant the same with itself. For, being at that instant what it is, and nothing else, it is the same, and so must continue as long as its existence is continued; for so long it will be the same, and no other. In like manner, if two or more atoms be joined together into the same mass, every one of those atoms will be the same, by the foregoing rule: and whilst they exist united together, the mass, consisting of the same atoms, must be the same mass, or the same body, let the parts be ever so differently jumbled. But if one of these atoms be taken away, or one new one added, it is no longer

the same mass or the same body. In the state of living creatures, their identity depends not on a mass of the same particles, but on something else. For in them the variation of great parcels of matter alters not the identity: an oak growing from a plant to a great tree, and then lopped, is still the same oak; and a colt grown up to a horse, sometimes fat, sometimes lean, is all the while the same horse: though, in both these cases, there may be a manifest change of the parts; so that truly they are not either of them the same masses of matter, though they be truly one of them the same oak, and the other the same horse. The reason whereof is, that, in these two cases—a *mass of matter* and a *living body*—identity is not applied to the same thing.

5. *Identity of Vegetables.*——We must therefore consider wherein an oak differs from a mass of matter, and that seems to me to be in this, that the one is only the cohesion of particles of matter any how united, the other such a disposition of them as constitutes the parts of an oak; and such an organization of those parts as is fit to receive and distribute nourishment, so as to continue and frame the wood, bark, and leaves, &c., of an oak, in which consists the vegetable life. That being then one plant which has such an organization of parts in one coherent body, partaking of one common life, it continues to be the same plant as long as it partakes of the same life, though that life be communicated to new particles of matter vitally united to the living plant, in a like continued organization conformable to that sort of plants. For this organization, being at any one instant in any one collection of matter, is in that particular concrete distinguished from all other, and *is* that individual life, which existing constantly from that moment both forwards and backwards, in the same continuity of insensibly succeeding parts united to the living body of the plant, it has that identity which makes the same plant, and all the parts of it, parts of the same plant, during all the time that they exist united in that continued organization, which is fit to convey that common life to all the parts so united.

6. *Identity of Animals.*——The case is not so much different in *brutes* but that any one may hence see what makes an animal and continues it the same. Something we have like this in machines, and may serve to illustrate it. For example, what is a watch? It is plain it is nothing but a fit organization or construction of parts to a certain end, which, when a suffi-

cient force is added to it, it is capable to attain. If we would suppose this machine one continued body, all whose organized parts were repaired, increased, or diminished by a constant addition or separation of insensible parts, with one common life, we should have something very much like the body of an animal; with this difference, That, in an animal the fitness of the organization, and the motion wherein life consists, begin together, the motion coming from within; but in machines the force coming sensibly from without, is often away when the organ is in order, and well fitted to receive it.

7. *The Identity of Man.*——This also shows wherein the identity of the same *man* consists; viz. in nothing but a participation of the same continued life, by constantly fleeting particles of matter, in succession vitally united to the same organized body. He that shall place the identity of man in anything else, but, like that of other animals, in one fitly organized body, taken in any one instant, and from thence continued, under one organization of life, in several successively fleeting particles of matter united to it, will find it hard to make an embryo, one of years, mad and sober, the *same* man, by any supposition, that will not make it possible for Seth, Ismael, Socrates, Pilate, St. Austin, and Cæsar Borgia, to be the same man. For if the identity of *soul alone* makes the same *man*; and there be nothing in the nature of matter why the same individual spirit may not be united to different bodies, it will be possible that those men, living in distant ages, and of different tempers, may have been the same man: which way of speaking must be from a very strange use of the word man, applied to an idea out of which body and shape are excluded. And that way of speaking would agree yet worse with the notions of those philosophers who allow of transmigration, and are of opinion that the souls of men may, for their miscarriages, be detruded into the bodies of beasts, as fit habitations, with organs suited to the satisfaction of their brutal inclinations. But yet I think nobody, could he be sure that the *soul* of Heliogabalus were in one of his hogs, would yet say that hog were a *man* or *Heliogabalus*.

8. *Idea of Identity suited to the Idea it is applied to.*——It is not therefore unity of substance that comprehends all sorts of identity, or will determine it in every case; but to conceive and judge of it aright, we must consider what idea the word it is applied to stands for: it being one thing to be the same *substance*, another the same *man*, and a third the same *person*,

if *person, man,* and *substance,* are three names standing for three different ideas;—for such as is the idea belonging to that name, such must be the identity; which, if it had been a little more carefully attended to, would possibly have prevented a great deal of that confusion which often occurs about this matter, with no small seeming difficulties, especially concerning *personal* identity, which therefore we shall in the next place a little consider.

9. *Same man.*——An animal is a living organized body; and consequently the same animal, as we have observed, is the same continued *life* communicated to different particles of matter, as they happen successively to be united to that organized living body. And whatever is talked of other definitions, ingenious observation puts it past doubt, that the idea in our minds, of which the sound man in our mouths is the sign, is nothing else but of an animal of such a certain form. Since I think I may be confident, that, whoever should see a creature of his own shape or make, though it had no more reason all its life than a cat or a parrot, would call him still a *man;* or whoever should hear a cat or a parrot discourse, reason, and philosophize, would call or think it nothing but a *cat* or a *parrot;* and say, the one was a dull irrational man, and the other a very intelligent rational parrot.

11. *Personal Identity.*——This being premised, to find wherein personal identity consists, we must consider what *person* stands for;—which, I think, is a thinking intelligent being, that has reason and reflection, and can consider itself as itself, the same thinking thing, in different times and places; which it does only by that consciousness which is inseparable from thinking, and, as it seems to me, essential to it: it being impossible for any one to perceive without *perceiving* that he does perceive. When we see, hear, smell, taste, feel, meditate, or will anything, we know that we do so. Thus it is always as to our present sensations and perceptions: and by this every one is to himself that which he calls *self:*—it not being considered, in this case, whether the same self be continued in the same or divers substances. For, since consciousness always accompanies thinking, and it is that which makes every one to be what he calls self, and thereby distinguishes himself from all other thinking things, in this alone consists personal identity, i.e. the sameness of a rational being: and as far as this consciousness can be extended backwards to any past action or thought, so far reaches the identity of that

person; it is the same self now it was then; and it is by the same self with this present one that now reflects on it, that that action was done.

10. *Consciousness makes personal Identity.*——But it is further inquired, whether it be the same identical substance. This few would think they had reason to doubt of, if these perceptions, with their consciousness, always remained present in the mind, whereby the same thinking thing would be always consciously present, and, as would be thought, evidently the same to itself. But that which seems to make the difficulty is this, that this consciousness being interrupted always by forgetfulness, there being no moment of our lives wherein we have the whole train of all our past actions before our eyes in one view, but even the best memories losing the sight of one part whilst they are viewing another; and we sometimes, and that the greatest part of our lives, not reflecting on our past selves, being intent on our present thoughts, and in sound sleep having no thoughts at all, or at least none with that consciousness which remarks our waking thoughts,—I say, in all these cases, our consciousness being interrupted, and we losing the sight of our past selves, doubts are raised whether we are the same thinking thing, i.e. the same *substance* or no. Which, however reasonable or unreasonable, concerns not *personal* identity at all. The question being what makes the same person; and not whether it be the same identical substance, which always thinks in the same person, which, in this case, matters not at all: different substances, by the same consciousness (where they do partake in it) being united into one person, as well as different bodies by the same life are united into one animal, whose identity is preserved in that change of substances by the unity of one continued life. For, it being the same consciousness that makes a man be himself to himself, personal identity depends on that only, whether it be annexed solely to one individual substance, or can be continued in a succession of several substances. For as far as any intelligent being *can* repeat the idea of any past action with the same consciousness it had of it at first, and with the same consciousness it has of any present action; so far it is the same personal self. For it is by the consciousness it has of its present thoughts and actions, that it is *self to itself* now, and so will be the same self, as far as the same consciousness can extend to actions past or to come; and would be by distance of time, or change of substance, no more two persons, than a

man be two men by wearing other clothes to-day than he did yesterday, with a long or a short sleep between: the same consciousness uniting those distant actions into the same person, whatever substances contributed to their production.

11. *Personal Identity in Change of Substance.*——That this is so, we have some kind of evidence in our very bodies, all whose particles, whilst vitally united to this same thinking conscious self, so that *we feel* when they are touched, and are affected by, and conscious of good or harm that happens to them, are a part of ourselves; i.e. of our thinking conscious self. Thus, the limbs of his body are to every one a part of himself; he sympathizes and is concerned for them. Cut off a hand, and thereby separate it from that consciousness he had of its heat, cold, and other affections, and it is then no longer a part of that which is himself, any more than the remotest part of matter. Thus, we see the *substance* whereof personal self consisted at one time may be varied at another, without the change of personal identity; there being no question about the same person, though the limbs which but now were a part of it, be cut off.

12. *Personality in Change of Substance.*——But the question is, Whether if the same substance which thinks be changed, it can be the same person; or, remaining the same, it can be different persons?

And to this I answer: First, This can be no question at all to those who place thought in a purely material animal constitution, void of an immaterial substance. For, whether their supposition be true or no, it is plain they conceive personal identity preserved in something else than identity of substance; as animal identity is preserved in identity of life, and not of substance. And therefore those who place thinking in an immaterial substance only, before they can come to deal with these men, must show why personal identity cannot be preserved in the change of immaterial substances, or variety of particular immaterial substances, as well as animal identity is preserved in the change of material substances, or variety of particular bodies: unless they will say, it is one immaterial spirit that makes the same life in brutes, as it is one immaterial spirit that makes the same person in men; which the Cartesians at least will not admit, for fear of making brutes thinking things too.

13. *Whether in Change of thinking Substances there can be one Person.*——But next, as to the first part of the ques-

tion, Whether, if the same thinking substance (supposing immaterial substances only to think) be changed, it can be the same person? I answer, that cannot be resolved but by those who know what kind of substances they are that do think; and whether the consciousness of past actions can be transferred from one thinking substance to another. I grant were the same consciousness the same individual action it could not: but it being a present representation of a past action, why it may not be possible, that that may be represented to the mind to have been which really never was, will remain to be shown. And therefore how far the consciousness of past actions is annexed to any individual agent, so that another cannot possibly have it, will be hard for us to determine, till we know what kind of action it is that cannot be done without a reflex act of perception accompanying it, and how performed by thinking substances, who cannot think without being conscious of it. But that which we call the same consciousness, not being the same individual act, why one intellectual substance may not have represented to it, as done by itself, what *it* never did, and was perhaps done by some other agent—why, I say, such a representation may not possibly be without reality of matter of fact, as well as several representations in dreams are, which yet whilst dreaming we take for true—will be difficult to conclude from the nature of things. And that it never is so, will by us, till we have clearer views of the nature of thinking substances, be best resolved into the goodness of God; who, as far as the happiness or misery of any of his sensible creatures is concerned in it, will not, by a fatal error of theirs, transfer from one to another that consciousness which draws reward or punishment with it. How far this may be an argument against those who would place thinking in a system of fleeting animal spirits, I leave to be considered. But yet, to return to the question before us, it must be allowed, that, if the same consciousness (which, as has been shown, is quite a different thing from the same numerical figure or motion in body) can be transferred from one thinking substance to another, it will be possible that two thinking substances may make but one person. For the same consciousness being preserved, whether in the same or different substances, the personal identity is preserved.

14. *Whether, the same immaterial Substance remaining, there can be two Persons.*——As to the second part of the question, Whether the same immaterial substance remaining,

there may be two distinct persons; which question seems to me to be built on this,—Whether the same immaterial being, being conscious of the action of its past duration, may be wholly stripped of all the consciousness of its past existence, and lose it beyond the power of ever retrieving it again: and so as it were beginning a new account from a new period, have a consciousness that *cannot* reach beyond this new state. All those who hold pre-existence are evidently of this mind; since they allow the soul to have no remaining consciousness of what it did in that pre-existent state, either wholly separate from body, or informing any other body; and if they should not, it is plain experience would be against them. So that personal identity, reaching no further than consciousness reaches, a pre-existent spirit not having continued so many ages in a state of silence, must needs make different persons. Suppose a Christian Platonist or a Pythagorean should, upon God's having ended all his works of creation the seventh day, think his soul hath existed ever since; and should imagine it has revolved in several human bodies; as I once met with one, who was persuaded his had been the *soul* of Socrates (how reasonably I will not dispute; this I know, that in the post he filled, which was no inconsiderable one, he passed for a very rational man, and the press has shown that he wanted not parts or learning;)—would any one say, that he, being not conscious of any of Socrates's actions or thoughts, could be the same *person* with Socrates? Let any one reflect upon himself, and conclude that he has in himself an immaterial spirit, which is that which thinks in him, and, in the constant change of his body keeps him the same: and is that which he calls *himself*: let him also suppose it to be the same soul that was in Nestor or Thersites, at the siege of Troy, (for souls being, as far as we know anything of them, in their nature indifferent to any parcel of matter, the supposition has no apparent absurdity in it,) which it may have been, as well as it is now the soul of any other man: but he now having no consciousness of any of the actions either of Nestor or Thersites, does or can he conceive himself the same person with either of them? Can he be concerned in either of their actions? attribute them to himself, or think them his own, more than the actions of any other men that ever existed? So that this consciousness, not reaching to any of the actions of either of those men, he is no more one *self* with either of them than if the soul or immaterial spirit that now informs him had been created, and began to exist, when it began to inform his present body; though it were never so true, that the same *spirit* that informed Nestor's or Thersites' body were numerically the same that now informs his. For this would no more make him the same person with Nestor, than if some of the particles of matter that were once a part of Nestor were now a part of this man; the same immaterial substance, without the same consciousness, no more making the same person, by being united to any body, than the same particle of matter, without consciousness, united to any body, makes the same person. But let him once find himself conscious of any of the actions of Nestor, he then finds himself the same person with Nestor.

15. *The body, as well as the soul, goes to the making of a Man.*——And thus may we be able, without any difficulty, to conceive the same person at the resurrection, though in a body not exactly in make or parts the same which he had here,—the same consciousness going along with the soul that inhabits it. But yet the soul alone, in the change of bodies, would scarce to any one but to him that makes the soul the man, be enough to make the same man. For should the soul of a prince, carrying with it the consciousness of the prince's past life, enter and inform the body of a cobbler, as soon as deserted by his own soul, every one sees he would be the same *person* with the prince, accountable only for the prince's actions: but who would say it was the same *man*? The body too goes to the making the man, and would, I guess, to everybody determine the man in this case, wherein the soul, with all its princely thoughts about it, would not make another man: but he would be the same cobbler to every one besides himself. I know that, in the ordinary way of speaking, the same person, and the same man, stand for one and the same thing. And indeed every one will always have a liberty to speak as he pleases, and to apply what articulate sounds to what ideas he thinks fit, and change them as often as he pleases. But yet, when we will inquire what makes the same *spirit*, *man*, or *person*, we must fix the ideas of spirit, man, or person in our minds; and having resolved with ourselves what we mean by them, it will not be hard to determine, in either of them, or the like, when it is the same, and when not.

16. *Consciousness alone unites actions into the same Person.*——But though the same immaterial substance or soul does not alone, wherever it be, and in whatsoever state, make

the same *man*; yet it is plain, consciousness, as far as ever it can be extended—should it be to ages past—unites existences and actions very remote in time into the same *person*, as well as it does the existences and actions of the immediately preceding moment: so that whatever has the consciousness of present and past actions, is the same person to whom they both belong. Had I the same consciousness that I saw the ark and Noah's flood, as that I saw an overflowing of the Thames last winter, or as that I write now, I could no more doubt that I who write this now, that saw the Thames overflowed last winter, and that viewed the flood at the general deluge, was the same *self*,—place that self in what *substance* you please—than that I who write this am the same *myself* now whilst I write (whether I consist of all the same substance, material or immaterial, or no) that I was yesterday. For as to this point of being the same self, it matters not whether this present self be made up of the same or other substances—I being as much concerned, and as justly accountable for any action that was done a thousand years since, appropriated to me now by this self-consciousness, as I am for what I did the last moment.

17. *Self depends on Consciousness, not on Substance.*——*Self* is that conscious thinking thing,—whatever substance made up of, (whether spiritual or material, simple or compounded, it matters not)—which is sensible or conscious of pleasure and pain, capable of happiness or misery, and so is concerned for itself, as far as that consciousness extends. Thus every one finds that, whilst comprehended under that consciousness, the little finger is as much a part of himself as what is most so. Upon separation of this little finger, should this consciousness go along with the little finger, and leave the rest of the body, it is evident the little finger would be the person, the same person; and self then would have nothing to do with the rest of the body. As in this case it is the consciousness that goes along with the substance, when one part is separate from another, which makes the same person, and constitutes this inseparable self: so it is in reference to substances remote in time. That with which the consciousness of this present thinking thing *can* join itself, makes the same person, and is one self with it, and with nothing else; and so attributes to itself, and owns all the actions of that thing, as its own, as far as that consciousness reaches, and no further; as every one who reflects will perceive.

18. *Persons, not Substances, the Objects of Reward and Punishment.*——In this personal identity is founded all the right and justice of reward and punishment; happiness and misery being that for which every one is concerned for *himself*, and not mattering what becomes of any *substance*, not joined to, or affected with that consciousness. For, as it is evident in the instance I gave but now, if the consciousness went along with the little finger when it was cut off, that would be the same self which was concerned for the whole body yesterday, as making part of itself, whose actions then it cannot but admit as its own now. Though, if the same body should still live, and immediately from the separation of the little finger have its own peculiar consciousness, whereof the little finger knew nothing, it would not at all be concerned for it, as a part of itself, or could own any of its actions, or have any of them imputed to him.

19. *Which shows wherein Personal identity consists.*—— This may show us wherein personal identity consists: not in the identity of substance, but, as I have said, in the identity of consciousness, wherein if Socrates and the present mayor of Queinborough agree, they are the same person: if the same Socrates waking and sleeping do not partake of the same consciousness, Socrates waking and sleeping is not the same person. And to punish Socrates waking for what sleeping Socrates thought, and waking Socrates was never conscious of, would be no more of right, than to punish one twin for what his brother-twin did, whereof he knew nothing, because their outsides were so like, that they could not be distinguished; for such twins have been seen.

20. *Absolute oblivion separates what is thus forgotten from the person, but not from the man.*——But yet possibly it will still be objected,—Suppose I wholly lose the memory of some parts of my life, beyond a possibility of retrieving them, so that perhaps I shall never be conscious of them again; yet am I not the same person that did those actions, had those thoughts that I once was conscious of, though I have now forgot them? To which I answer, that we must here take notice what the word *I* is applied to; which, in this case, is the *man* only. And the same man being presumed to be the same person, I is easily here supposed to stand also for the same person. But if it be possible for the same man to have distinct incommunicable consciousness at different times, it is past doubt the same man would at different times make different

persons; which, we see, is the sense of mankind in the solemnest declaration of their opinions, human laws not punishing the mad man for the sober man's actions, nor the sober man for what the mad man did,—thereby making them two persons: which is somewhat explained by our way of speaking in English when we say such an one is 'not himself,' or is 'beside himself'; in which phrases it is insinuated, as if those who now, or at least first used them, thought that self was changed; the self-same person was no longer in that man.

BOOK IV.

CHAPTER I.

OF KNOWLEDGE IN GENERAL.

1. *Our Knowledge conversant about our Ideas only.*——Since the mind, in all its thoughts and reasonings, hath no other immediate object but its own ideas, which it alone does or can contemplate, it is evident that our knowledge is only conversant about them.

2. *Knowledge is the Perception of the Agreement or Disagreement of two Ideas.*——*Knowledge* then seems to me to be nothing but *the perception of the connexion of and agreement, or disagreement and repugnancy of any of our ideas.* In this alone it consists. Where this perception is, there is knowledge, and where it is not, there, though we may fancy, guess, or believe, yet we always come short of knowledge. For when we know that white is not black, what do we else but perceive, that these two ideas do not agree? When we possess ourselves with the utmost security of the demonstration, that the three angles of a triangle are equal to two right ones, what do we more but perceive, that equality to two right ones does necessarily agree to, and is inseparable from, the three angles of a triangle?

3. *This Agreement or Disagreement may be any of four sorts.*——But to understand a little more distinctly wherein

this agreement or disagreement consists, I think we may reduce it all to these four sorts:

I. *Identity*, or *diversity*.
II. *Relation*.
III. *Co-existence*, or *necessary connexion*.
IV. *Real existence*.

4. *First, Of Identity, or Diversity in ideas.*——As to the first sort of agreement or disagreement, viz. *identity* or *diversity*. It is the first act of the mind, when it has any sentiments or ideas at all, to perceive its ideas; and so far as it perceives them, to know each what it is, and thereby also to perceive their difference, and that one is not another. This is so absolutely necessary, that without it there could be no knowledge, no reasoning, no imagination, no distinct thoughts at all. By this the mind clearly and infallibly perceives each idea to agree with itself, and to be what it is; and all distinct ideas to disagree, i.e. the one not to be the other: and this it does without pains, labour, or deduction; but at first view, by its natural power of perception and distinction. And though men of art have reduced this into those general rules, *What is, is*, and *It is impossible for the same thing to be and not to be*, for ready application in all cases, wherein there may be occasion to reflect on it: yet it is certain that the first exercise of this faculty is about particular ideas. A man infallibly knows, as soon as ever he has them in his mind, that the ideas he calls *white* and *round* are the very ideas they are; and that they are not other ideas which he calls *red* or *square*. Nor can any maxim or proposition in the world make him know it clearer or surer than he did before, and without any such general rule. This then is the first agreement or disagreement which the mind perceives in its ideas; which it always perceives at first sight: and if there ever happen any doubt about it, it will always be found to be about the names, and not the ideas themselves, whose identity and diversity will always be perceived, as soon and clearly as the ideas themselves are; nor can it possibly be otherwise.

5. *Secondly, Of abstract Relations between ideas.*——The next sort of agreement or disagreement the mind perceives in any of its ideas may, I think, be called *relative*, and is nothing but the perception of the *relation* between any two ideas, of what kind soever, whether substances, modes, or any other. For, since all distinct ideas must eternally be known not to

be the same, and so be universally and constantly denied one of another, there could be no room for any positive knowledge at all, if we could not perceive any relation between our ideas, and find out the agreement or disagreement they have one with another, in several ways the mind takes of comparing them.

6. *Thirdly, Of their necessary Co-existence in Substances.*——The third sort of agreement or disagreement to be found in our ideas, which the perception of the mind is employed about, is *co-existence* or *non-co-existence* in the *same subject*; and this belongs particularly to substances. Thus when we pronounce concerning gold, that it is fixed, our knowledge of this truth amounts to no more but this, that fixedness, or a power to remain in the fire unconsumed, is an idea that always accompanies and is joined with that particular sort of yellowness, weight, fusibility, malleableness, and solubility in *aqua regia*, which make our complex idea signified by the word gold.

7. *Fourthly, Of real Existence agreeing to any idea.*——The fourth and last sort is that of *actual real existence* agreeing to any idea.

Within these four sorts of agreement or disagreement is, I suppose, contained all the knowledge we have, or are capable of. For all the inquiries we can make concerning any of our ideas, all that we know or can affirm concerning any of them, is, That it is, or is not, the same with some other; that it does or does not always co-exist with some other idea in the same subject; that it has this or that relation with some other idea; or that it has a real existence without the mind. Thus, 'blue is not yellow,' is of identity. 'Two triangles upon equal bases between two parallels are equal,' is of relation. 'Iron is susceptible of magnetical impressions,' is of co-existence. 'God is,' is of real existence. Though identity and co-existence are truly nothing but relations, yet they are such peculiar ways of agreement or disagreement of our ideas, that they deserve well to be considered as distinct heads, and not under relation in general; since they are so different grounds of affirmation and negation, as will easily appear to any one, who will but reflect on what is said in several places of this *Essay*.

CHAPTER II.

OF THE DEGREES OF OUR KNOWLEDGE.

1. *Of the degrees, or differences in clearness, of our Knowledge: I. Intuitive.*——All our knowledge consisting, as I have said, in the view the mind has of its own ideas, which is the utmost light and greatest certainty we, with our faculties, and in our way of knowledge, are capable of, it may not be amiss to consider a little the degrees of its evidence. The different clearness of our knowledge seems to me to lie in the different way of perception the mind has of the agreement or disagreement of any of its ideas. For if we will reflect on our own ways of thinking, we will find, that sometimes the mind perceives the agreement or disagreement of two ideas *immediately by themselves,* without the intervention of any other: and this I think we may call *intuitive knowledge.* For in this the mind is at no pains of proving or examining, but perceives the truth as the eye doth light, only by being directed towards it. Thus the mind perceives that *white* is not *black,* that a *circle* is not a *triangle,* that *three* are more than *two* and equal to *one and two.* Such kinds of truths the mind perceives at the first sight of the ideas together, by bare intuition; without the intervention of any other idea: and this kind of knowledge is the clearest and most certain that human frailty is capable of. This part of knowledge is irresistible, and, like bright sunshine, forces itself immediately to be perceived, as soon as ever the mind turns its view that way; and leaves no room for hesitation, doubt, or examination, but the mind is presently filled with the clear light of it. *It is on this intuition that depends all the certainty and evidence of all our knowledge*; which certainty every one finds to be so great, that he cannot imagine, and therefore not require a greater: for a man cannot conceive himself capable of a greater certainty than to know that any idea in his mind is such as he perceives it to be; and that two ideas, wherein he perceives a difference, are different and not precisely the same. He that demands a greater certainty than this, demands he knows not what, and shows only that he has a mind to be a sceptic, without being able to be

so. Certainty depends so wholly on this intuition, that, in the next degree of knowledge which I call demonstrative, this intuition is necessary in all the connexions of the intermediate ideas, without which we cannot attain knowledge and certainty.

2. *II. Demonstrative.*——The next degree of knowledge is, where the mind perceives the agreement or disagreement of any ideas, but not immediately. Though wherever the mind perceives the agreement or disagreement of any of its ideas, there be certain knowledge; yet it does not always happen, that the mind sees that agreement or disagreement, which there is between them, even where it is discoverable; and in that case remains in ignorance, and at most gets no further than a probable conjecture. The reason why the mind cannot always perceive presently the agreement or disagreement of two ideas, is, because those ideas, concerning whose agreement or disagreement the inquiry is made, cannot by the mind be so put together as to show it. In this case then, when the mind cannot so bring its ideas together as by their immediate comparison, and as it were juxta-position or application one to another, to perceive their agreement or disagreement, it is fain, *by the intervention of other ideas* (one or more, as it happens) to discover the agreement or disagreement which it searches; and this is that which we call *reasoning*. Thus, the mind being willing to know the agreement or disagreement in bigness between the three angles of a triangle and two right ones, cannot by an immediate view and comparing them do it: because the three angles of a triangle cannot be brought at once, and be compared with any other one, or two, angles; and so of this the mind has no immediate, no intuitive knowledge. In this case the mind is fain to find out some other angles, to which the three angles of a triangle have an equality; and, finding those equal to two right ones, comes to know their equality to two right ones.

3. *Demonstration depends on clearly perceived Proofs.*—— Those intervening ideas, which serve to show the agreement of any two others, are called *proofs*; and where the agreement and disagreement is by this means plainly and clearly perceived, it is called *demonstration*; it being *shown* to the understanding, and the mind made to see that it is so. A quickness in the mind to find out these intermediate ideas, (that shall discover the agreement or disagreement of any other,) and to apply them right, is, I suppose, that which is called *sagacity*.

4. *As certain, but not so easy and ready as Intuitive Knowledge.*——This knowledge, by intervening proofs, though it be certain, yet the evidence of it is not altogether so clear and bright, nor the assent so ready, as in intuitive knowledge. For, though in demonstration the mind does at last perceive the agreement or disagreement of the ideas it considers; yet it is not without pains and attention: there must be more than one transient view to find it. A steady application and pursuit are required to this discovery: and there must be a progression by steps and degrees, before the mind can in this way arrive at certainty, and come to perceive the argeement or repugnancy between two ideas that need proofs and the use of reason to show it.

5. *The demonstrated conclusion not without Doubt, precedent to the demonstration.*——Another difference between intuitive and demonstrative knowledge is, that, though in the latter all doubt be removed when, by the intervention of the intermediate ideas, the agreement or disagreement is perceived, yet before the demonstration there was a doubt; which in intuitive knowledge cannot happen to the mind that has its faculty of perception left to a degree capable of distinct ideas; no more than it can be a doubt to the eye (that can distinctly see white and black), Whether this ink and this paper be all of a colour. If there be sight in the eyes, it will, at first glimpse, without hesitation, perceive the words printed on this paper different from the colour of the paper: and so if the mind have the faculty of distinct perception, it will perceive the agreement or disagreement of those ideas that produce intuitive knowledge. If the eyes have lost the faculty of seeing, or the mind of perceiving, we in vain inquire after the quickness of sight in one, or clearness of perception in the other.

6. *Not so clear as Intuitive Knowledge.*——It is true, the perception produced by demonstration is also very clear; yet it is often with a great abatement of that evident lustre and full assurance that always accompany that which I call intuitive: like a face reflected by several mirrors one to another, where, as long as it retains the similitude and agreement with the object, it produces a knowledge; but it is still, in every successive reflection, with a lessening of that perfect clearness and distinctness which is in the first; till at last, after many removes, it has a great mixture of dimness, and is not at first

sight so knowable, especially to weak eyes. Thus it is with knowledge made out by a long train of proof.

7. *Each Step in Demonstrated knowledge must have Intuitive Evidence.*——Now, in every step reason makes in demonstrative knowledge, there is an intuitive knowledge of that agreement or disagreement it seeks with the next intermediate idea which it uses as a proof: for if it were not so, that yet would need a proof; since without the perception of such agreement or disagreement, there is no knowledge produced: if it be perceived by itself, it is intuitive knowledge: if it cannot be perceived by itself, there is need of some intervening idea, as a common measure, to show their agreement or disagreement. By which it is plain, that every step in reasoning that produces knowledge, has intuitive certainty; which when the mind perceives, there is no more required but to remember it, to make the agreement or disagreement of the ideas concerning which we inquire visible and certain. So that to make anything a demonstration, it is necessary to perceive the immediate agreement of the intervening ideas, whereby the agreement or disagreement of the two ideas under examination (whereof the one is always the first, and the other the last in the account) is found. This intuitive perception of the agreement or disagreement of the intermediate ideas, in each step and progression of the demonstration, must also be carried exactly in the mind, and a man must be sure that no part is left out: which, because in long deductions, and the use of many proofs, the memory does not always so readily and exactly retain; therefore it comes to pass, that this is more imperfect than intuitive knowledge, and men embrace often falsehood for demonstrations.

14. *III. Sensitive Knowledge of the particular Existence of finite beings without us.*——These two, viz. intuition and demonstration, are the degrees of our *knowledge*; whatever comes short of one of these, with what assurance soever embraced, is but *faith* or *opinion*, but not knowledge, at least in all general truths. There is, indeed, another perception of the mind, employed about *the particular existence of finite beings without us*, which, going beyond bare probability, and yet not reaching perfectly to either of the foregoing degrees of certainty, passes under the name of *knowledge*. There can be nothing more certain than that the idea we receive from an external object is in our minds: this is intuitive knowledge. But whether there be anything more than barely that idea in our

minds; whether we can thence certainly infer the existence of anything without us, which corresponds to that idea, is that whereof some men think there may be a question made; because men may have such ideas in their minds, when no such thing exists, no such object affects their senses. But yet here I think we are provided with an evidence that puts us past doubting. For I ask any one, Whether he be not invincibly conscious to himself of a different perception, when he looks on the sun by day, and thinks on it by night; when he actually tastes wormwood, or smells a rose, or only thinks on that savour or odour? We as plainly find the difference there is between any idea revived in our minds by our own memory, and actually coming into our minds by our senses, as we do between any two distinct ideas. If any one say, a dream may do the same thing, and all these ideas may be produced in us without any external objects; he may please to dream that I make him this answer:—1. That it is no great matter, whether I remove his scruple or no: where all is but dream, reasoning and arguments are of no use, truth and knowledge nothing. 2. That I believe he will allow a very manifest difference between dreaming of being in the fire, and being actually in it. But yet if he be resolved to appear so sceptical as to maintain, that what I call being actually in the fire is nothing but a dream; and that we cannot thereby certainly know, that any such thing as fire actually exists without us: I answer, That we certainly finding that pleasure or pain follows upon the application of certain objects to us, whose existence we perceive, or dream that we perceive, by our senses; this certainty is as great as our happiness or misery, beyond which we have no concernment to know or to be. So that, I think, we may add to the two former sorts of knowledge this also, of the existence of particular external objects, by that perception and consciousness we have of the actual entrance of ideas from them, and allow these three degrees of knowledge, viz. *intuitive, demonstrative,* and *sensitive*: in each of which there are different degrees and ways of evidence and certainty.

CHAPTER III.

OF THE EXTENT OF HUMAN KNOWLEDGE.

1. *First, it extends no further than we have Ideas.*——Knowledge, as has been said, lying in the perception of the agreement or disagreement of any of our ideas, it follows from hence, That,

First, we can have knowledge no further than we have *ideas.*

2. *It extends no further than we can perceive their Agreement or Disagreement.*——Secondly, That we can have no knowledge further than we can have *perception* of that agreement or disagreement. Which perception being: 1. Either by *intuition,* or the immediate comparing any two ideas; or, 2. By *reason,* examining the agreement or disagreement of two ideas, by the intervention of some others; or, 3. By *sensation,* perceiving the existence of particular things: hence it also follows:

3. *Intuitive Knowledge extends itself not to all the relations of all our Ideas.*——Thirdly, That we cannot have an *intuitive knowledge* that shall extend itself to all our ideas, and all that we would know about them; because we cannot examine and perceive all the relations they have one to another, by juxta-position, or an immediate comparison one with another. Thus, having the ideas of an obtuse and an acute angled triangle, both drawn from equal bases, and between parallels, I can, by intuitive knowledge, perceive the one not to be the other, but cannot that way know whether they be equal or no; because their agreement or disagreement in equality can never be perceived by an immediate comparing them: the difference of figure makes their parts incapable of an exact immediate application; and therefore there is need of some intervening qualities to measure them by, which is demonstration, or rational knowledge.

4. *Nor does Demonstrative Knowledge.*——Fourthly, It follows, also, from what is above observed, that our *rational knowledge* cannot reach to the whole extent of our ideas: because between two different ideas we would examine, we

cannot always find such mediums as we can connect one to another with an intuitive knowledge in all the parts of the deduction; and wherever that fails, we come short of knowledge and demonstration.

5. *Sensitive Knowledge narrower than either.*——Fifthly, *Sensitive knowledge* reaching no further than the existence of things actually present to our senses, is yet much narrower than either of the former.

6. *Our Knowledge, therefore, narrower than our Ideas.*——Sixthly, From all which it is evident, that the *extent of our knowledge* comes not only short of the reality of things, but even of the extent of our own ideas. Though our knowledge be limited to our ideas, and cannot exceed them either in extent or perfection; and though these be very narrow bounds, in respect of the extent of All-being, and far short of what we may justly imagine to be in some even created understandings, not tied down to the dull and narrow information that is to be received from some few, and not very acute, ways of perception, such as are our senses; yet it would be well with us if our knowledge were but as large as our ideas, and there were not many doubts and inquiries *concerning the ideas we have*, whereof we are not, nor I believe ever shall be in this world resolved. Nevertheless, I do not question but that human knowledge, under the present circumstances of our beings and constitutions, may be carried much further than it has hitherto been, if men would sincerely, and with freedom of mind, employ all that industry and labour of thought, in improving the means of discovering truth, which they do for the colouring or support of falsehood, to maintain a system, interest, or party they are once engaged in. But yet after all, I think I may, without injury to human perfection, be confident, that our knowledge would never reach to all we might desire to know concerning those ideas we have; nor be able to surmount all the difficulties, and resolve all the questions that might arise concerning any of them. We have the ideas of a *square*, a *circle*, and *equality*; and yet, perhaps, shall never be able to find a circle equal to a square, and certainly know that it is so. We have the ideas of *matter* and *thinking*, but possibly shall never be able to know whether any mere material being thinks or no; it being impossible for us, by the contemplation of our own ideas, without revelation, to discover whether Omnipotency has not given to some systems of matter, fitly disposed, a power to perceive and think, or else

joined and fixed to matter, so disposed, a thinking immaterial substance: it being, in respect of our notions, not much more remote from our comprehension to conceive that God can, if he pleases, superadd to matter a *faculty of thinking*, than that he should superadd to it *another substance with a faculty of thinking*; since we know not wherein thinking consists, nor to what sort of substances the Almighty has been pleased to give that power, which cannot be in any created being, but merely by the good pleasure and bounty of the Creator. For I see no contradiction in it, that the first Eternal thinking Being, or Omnipotent Spirit, should, if he pleased, give to certain systems of created senseless matter, put together as he thinks fit, some degrees of sense, perception, and thought: though, as I think I have proved, lib. iv. ch. 10, § 14, &c., it is no less than a contradiction to suppose matter (which is evidently in its own nature void of sense and thought) should be that Eternal first-thinking Being. What certainty of knowledge can any one have, that some perceptions, such as, v.g., pleasure and pain, should not be in some bodies themselves, after a certain manner modified and moved, as well as that they should be in an immaterial substance, upon the motion of the parts of body: Body, as far as we can conceive, being able only to strike and affect body, and motion, according to the utmost reach of our ideas, being able to produce nothing but motion; so that when we allow it to produce pleasure or pain, or the idea of a colour or sound, we are fain to quit our reason, go beyond our ideas, and attribute it wholly to the good pleasure of our Maker. For, since we must allow He has annexed effects to motion which we can no way conceive motion able to produce, what reason have we to conclude that He could not order them as well to be produced in a subject we cannot conceive capable of them, as well as in a subject we cannot conceive the motion of matter can any way operate upon?

But to return to the argument in hand: our knowledge, I say, is not only limited to the paucity and imperfections of the ideas we have, and which we employ it about, but even comes short of that too: but how far it reaches, let us now inquire.

7. *How far our Knowledge reaches.*——The affirmations or negations we make concerning the ideas we have, may, as I have before intimated in general, be reduced to these four sorts, viz. identity, co-existence, relation, and real existence.

I shall examine how far our knowledge extends in each of these:

8. *Firstly, Our Knowledge of Identity and Diversity in ideas extends as far as our Ideas themselves.*——First, as to *identity* and *diversity*. In this way of agreement or disagreement of our ideas, our intuitive knowledge is as far extended as our ideas themselves: and there can be no idea in the mind, which it does not, presently, by an intuitive knowledge, perceive to be what it is, and to be different from any other.

9. *Secondly, Of their Co-existence, extends only a very little way.*——As to the second sort, which is the agreement or disagreement of our ideas in *co-existence*, in this our knowledge is very short; though in this consists the greatest and most material part of our knowledge concerning substances. For our ideas of the species of substances being, as I have showed, nothing but certain collections of simple ideas united in one subject, and so co-existing together; v.g. our idea of flame is a body hot, luminous, and moving upward; of gold, a body heavy to a certain degree, yellow, malleable, and fusible: for these, or some such complex ideas as these, in men's minds, do these two names of the different substances, flame and gold, stand for. When we would know anything further concerning these, or any other sort of substances, what do we inquire, but what *other* qualities or powers these substances have or have not? Which is nothing else but to know what *other* simple ideas do, or do not co-exist with those that make up that complex idea?

10. *Because the Connexion between simple Ideas in substances is for the most part unknown.*——This, how weighty and considerable a part soever of human science, is yet very narrow, and scarce any at all. The reason whereof is, that the simple ideas whereof our complex ideas of substances are made up are, for the most part, such as carry with them, in their own nature, no *visible necessary* connexion or inconsistency with any other simple ideas, whose co-existence with them we would inform ourselves about.

11. *Especially of the secondary Qualities of Bodies.*——The ideas that our complex ones of substances are made up of, and about which our knowledge concerning substances is most employed, are those of their secondary qualities; which depending all (as has been shown) upon the primary qualities of their minute and insensible parts; or, if not upon them, upon something yet more remote from our comprehension;

it is impossible we should know which have a *necessary* union or inconsistency one with another. For, not knowing the root they spring from, not knowing what size, figure, and texture of parts they are, on which depend, and from which result those qualities which make our complex idea of gold, it is impossible we should know what *other* qualities result from, or are incompatible with, the same constitution of the insensible parts of gold; and so consequently must always co-exist with that complex idea we have of it, or else are inconsistent with it.

12. *Because necessary Connexion between any secondary and the primary Qualities is undiscoverable by us.*——Besides this ignorance of the primary qualities of the insensible parts of bodies, on which depend all their secondary qualities, there is yet another and more incurable part of ignorance, which sets us more remote from a certain knowledge of the co-existence or *inco-existence* (if I may so say) of different ideas in the same subject; and that is, that there is no discoverable connexion between any secondary quality and those primary qualities which it depends on.

13. *We have no perfect knowledge of their Primary Qualities.*——That the size, figure, and motion of one body should cause a change in the size, figure, and motion of another body, is not beyond our conception; the separation of the parts of one body upon the intrusion of another; and the change from rest to motion upon impulse; these and the like seem to have *some connexion* one with another. And if we knew these primary qualities of bodies, we might have reason to hope we might be able to know a great deal more of these operations of them one upon another: but our minds not being able to discover any connexion betwixt these primary qualities of bodies and the sensations that are produced in us by them, we can never be able to establish certain and undoubted rules of the *consequence* or *co-existence* of any secondary qualities, though we could discover the size, figure, or motion of those invisible parts which immediately produce them. We are so far from knowing *what* figure, size, or motion of parts produce a yellow colour, a sweet taste, or a sharp sound, that we can by no means conceive how *any* size, figure, or motion of any particles, can possibly produce in us the idea of any colour, taste, or sound whatsoever: there is no conceivable connexion between the one and the other.

14. *And seek in vain for certain and universal knowledge of unperceived qualities in substances.*——In vain, therefore,

shall we endeavour to discover by our ideas (the only true way of certain and universal knowledge) what other ideas are to be found constantly joined with that of *our* complex idea of any substance: since we neither know the real constitution of the minute parts on which their qualities do depend; nor, did we know them, could we discover any necessary connexion between them and any of the secondary qualities: which is necessary to be done before we can certainly know their necessary co-existence. So, that, let our complex idea of any species of substances be what it will, we can hardly, from the simple ideas contained in it, certainly determine the necessary co-existence of any other quality whatsoever. Our knowledge in all these inquiries reaches very little further than our experience. Indeed some few of the primary qualities have a necessary dependence and visible connexion one with another, as figure necessarily supposes extension; receiving or communicating motion by impulse, supposes solidity. But though these, and perhaps some others of our ideas have: yet there are so few of them that have a visible connexion one with another, that we can by intuition or demonstration discover the co-existence of very few of the qualities that are to be found united in substances: and we are left only to the assistance of our senses to make known to us what qualities they contain. For of all the qualities that are co-existent in any subject, without this dependence and evident connexion of their ideas one with another, we cannot know certainly any two to co-exist, any further than experience, by our senses, informs us. Thus, though we see the yellow colour, and, upon trial, find the weight, malleableness, fusibility, and fixedness that are united in a piece of gold; yet, because no one of these ideas has any evident dependence or necessary connexion with the other, we cannot certainly know that where any four of these are, the fifth will be there also, how highly probable soever it may be; because the highest probability amounts not to certainty, without which there can be no true knowledge. For this co-existence can be no further known than it is perceived; and it cannot be perceived but either in particular subjects, by the observation of our senses, or, in general, by the necessary connexion of the ideas themselves.

15. *Of Repugnancy to co-exist, our knowledge is larger.*—— As to the incompatibility or repugnancy to co-existence, we may know that any subject may have of each sort of primary qualities but one particular at once: v.g. each particular ex-

tension, figure, number of parts, motion, excludes all other of each kind. The like also is certain of all sensible ideas peculiar to each sense; for whatever of each kind is present in any subject, excludes all other of that sort: v.g. no one subject can have two smells or two colours at the same time. To this, perhaps will be said, Has not an opal, or the infusion of *lignum nephriticum*, two colours at the same time? To which I answer, that these bodies, to eyes differently placed, may at the same time afford different colours: but I take liberty also to say, that, to eyes differently placed, it is different parts of the object that reflect the particles of light: and therefore it is not the same part of the object, and so not the very same subject, which at the same time appears both yellow and azure. For, it is as impossible that the very same particle of any body should at the same time differently modify or reflect the rays of light, as that it should have two different figures and textures at the same time.

16. *Our Knowledge of the Co-existence of Powers in Bodies extends but a very little Way.*——But as to the powers of substances to change the sensible qualities of other bodies, which make a great part of our inquiries about them, and is no inconsiderable branch of our knowledge; I doubt as to these, whether our knowledge reaches much further than our experience; or whether we can come to the discovery of most of these powers, and be certain that they are in any subject, by the connexion with any of those ideas which to us make its essence. Because the active and passive powers of bodies, and their ways of operating, consisting in a texture and motion of parts which we cannot by any means come to discover; it is but in very few cases we can be able to perceive their dependence on, or repugnance to, any of those ideas which make our complex one of that sort of things. I have here instanced in the corpuscularian hypothesis, as that which is thought to go furthest in an intelligible explication of those qualities of bodies; and I fear the weakness of human understanding is scarce able to substitute another, which will afford us a fuller and clearer discovery of the necessary connexion and co-existence of the powers which are to be observed united in several sorts of them. This at least is certain, that, whichever hypothesis be clearest and truest, (for of that it is not my business to determine,) our knowledge concerning corporeal substances will be very little advanced by any of them, till we are made to see what qualities and powers of bodies have a

necessary connexion or repugnancy one with another; which in the present state of philosophy I think we know but to a very small degree: and I doubt whether, with those faculties we have, we shall ever be able to carry our general knowledge (I say not particular experience) in this part much further. Experience is that which in this part we must depend on. And it were to be wished that it were more improved. We find the advantages some men's generous pains have this way brought to the stock of natural knowledge. And if others, especially the philosophers by fire, who pretend to it, had been so wary in their observations, and sincere in their reports as those who call themselves philosophers ought to have been, our acquaintance with the bodies here about us, and our insight into their powers and operations had been yet much greater.

17. *Of the Powers that co-exist in Spirits yet narrower.*——If we are at a loss in respect of the powers and operations of bodies, I think it is easy to conclude we are much more in the dark in reference to spirits; whereof we naturally have no ideas but what we draw from that of our own, by reflecting on the operations of our own souls within us, as far as they can come within our observation. But how inconsiderable a rank the spirits that inhabit our bodies hold amongst those various and possibly innumerable kinds of nobler beings; and how far short they come of the endowments and perfections of cherubim and seraphim, and infinite sorts of spirits above us, is what by a transient hint in another place I have offered to my reader's consideration.

18. *Thirdly, Of Relations between abstracted ideas it is not easy to say how far our knowledge extends.*——As to the third sort of our knowledge, viz. the agreement or disagreement of any of our ideas in any other relation: this, as it is the largest field of our knowledge, so it is hard to determine how far it may extend: because the advances that are made in this part of knowledge, depending on our sagacity in finding intermediate ideas, that may show the relations and habitudes of ideas whose co-existence is not considered, it is a hard matter to tell when we are at an end of such discoveries; and when reason has all the helps it is capable of, for the finding of proofs, or examining the agreement or disagreement of remote ideas. They that are ignorant of Algebra cannot imagine the wonders in this kind are to be done by it: and what further improvements and helps advantageous to other parts of knowledge the sagacious mind of man may yet find

out, it is not easy to determine. This at least I believe, that the *ideas of quantity* are not those alone that are capable of demonstration and knowledge; and that other, and perhaps more useful, parts of contemplation, would afford us certainty, if vices, passions, and domineering interest did not oppose or menace such endeavours.

21. *Fourthly, Of the three real Existences of which we have certain knowledge.*——As to the fourth sort of our knowledge, viz. of the *real actual existence of things,* we have an intuitive knowledge of *our own existence,* and a demonstrative knowledge of the existence of a *God*: of the existence of *anything else,* we have no other but a sensitive knowledge; which extends not beyond the objects present to our senses.

CHAPTER IV.

OF THE REALITY OF KNOWLEDGE.

1. *Objection. 'Knowledge placed in our Ideas may be all unreal or chimerical.'*——I doubt not but my reader, by this time, may be apt to think that I have been all this while only building a castle in the air; and be ready to say to me:—

'To what purpose all this stir? Knowledge, say you, is only the perception of the agreement or disagreement of our own ideas: but who knows what those ideas may be? Is there anything so extravagant as the imaginations of men's brains? Where is the head that has no chimeras in it? Or if there be a sober and a wise man, what difference will there be, by your rules, between his knowledge and that of the most extravagant fancy in the world? They both have their ideas, and perceive their agreement and disagreement one with another. If there be any difference between them, the advantage will be on the warm-headed man's side, as having the more ideas, and the more lively. And so, by your rules, he will be the more knowing. If it be true, that all knowledge lies only in the perception of the agreement or disagreement of our own ideas, the visions of an enthusiast and the reasonings of a sober man will be equally certain. It is no matter how things are: so a man observe but the agreement of his own imaginations, and talk conformably, it is all truth, all certainty. Such castles in the air will be as strongholds of truth, as the demonstrations of Euclid. That an harpy is not a centaur is by this way as certain knowledge, and as much a truth, as that a square is not a circle.

'But of what use is all this fine knowledge of *men's own imaginations*, to a man that inquires after the reality of things? It matters not what men's fancies are, it is the knowledge of things that is only to be prized: it is this alone gives a value to our reasonings, and preference to one man's knowledge over another's, that it is of things as they really are, and not of dreams and fancies.'

2. *Answer. Not so, where Ideas agree with Things.*——To which I answer, That if our knowledge of our ideas terminate in them, and reach no further, where there is something further intended, our most serious thoughts will be of little more use than the reveries of a crazy brain; and the truths built thereon of no more weight than the discourses of a man who sees things clearly in a dream, and with great assurance utters them. But I hope, before I have done, to make it evident, that this way of certainty, by the knowledge of our own ideas, goes a little further than bare imagination: and I believe it will appear that all the certainty of general truths a man has lies in nothing else.

3. *But what shall be the criterion of this agreement?*——It is evident the mind knows not things immediately, but only by the intervention of the ideas it has of them. Our knowledge, therefore, is real only so far as there is a *conformity* between our ideas and the reality of things. But what shall be here the criterion? How shall the mind, when it perceives nothing but its own ideas, know that they agree with things themselves? This, though it seems not to want difficulty, yet, I think, there be two sorts of ideas that we may be assured agree with things.

4. *As, First, All Simple Ideas are really conformed to Things.*——The first are simple ideas, which since the mind, as has been showed, can by no means make to itself, must necessarily be the product of things operating on the mind, in a natural way, and producing therein those perceptions which by the Wisdom and Will of our Maker they are ordained and adapted to. From whence it follows, that simple ideas are not fictions of our fancies, but the natural and regular productions of things without us, really operating upon us; and so carry with them all the conformity which is intended;

or which our state requires: for they represent to us things under those appearances which they are fitted to produce in us: whereby we are enabled to distinguish the sorts of particular substances, to discern the states they are in, and so to take them for our necessities, and apply them to our uses. Thus the idea of whiteness, or bitterness, as it is in the mind, exactly answering that power which is in any body to produce it there, has all the real conformity it can or ought to have, with things without us. And this conformity between our simple ideas and the existence of things, is sufficient for real knowledge.

5. *Secondly, All Complex Ideas, except ideas of Substances, are their own archetypes.*——*Secondly,* All our complex ideas, *except those of substances,* being archetypes of the mind's own making, not intended to be the copies of anything, nor referred to the existence of anything, as to their originals, cannot want any conformity necessary to real knowledge. For that which is not designed to represent anything but itself, can never be capable of a wrong representation, nor mislead us from the true apprehension of anything, by its dislikeness to it: and such, excepting those of substances, are all our complex ideas. Which, as I have showed in another place, are combinations of ideas, which the mind, by its free choice, puts together, without considering any connexion they have in nature. And hence it is, that in all these sorts the ideas themselves are considered as the archetypes, and things no otherwise regarded, but as they are conformable to them. So that we cannot but be infallibly certain, that all the knowledge we attain concerning these ideas is real, and reaches things themselves. Because in all our thoughts, reasonings, and discourses of this kind, we intend things no further than as they are conformable to our ideas. So that in these we cannot miss of a certain and undoubted reality.

6. *Hence the reality of Mathematical Knowledge.*——I doubt not but it will be easily granted, that the knowledge we have of mathematical truths is not only certain, but real knowledge; and not the bare empty vision of vain, insignificant chimeras of the brain: and yet, if we will consider, we shall find that it is only of our own ideas. The mathematician considers the truth and properties belonging to a rectangle or circle only as they are in idea in his own mind. For it is possible he never found either of them existing mathematically, i.e. precisely true, in his life. But yet the knowledge he has of

any truths or properties belonging to a circle, or any other mathematical figure, are nevertheless true and certain, even of real things existing: because real things are no further concerned, nor intended to be meant by any such propositions, than as things really agree to those archetypes in his mind. Is it true of the *idea* of a triangle, that its three angles are equal to two right ones? It is true also of a triangle, wherever it *really exists.* Whatever other figure exists, that it is not exactly answerable to that idea of a triangle in his mind, is not at all concerned in that proposition. And therefore he is certain all his knowledge concerning such ideas is real knowledge: because, intending things no further than they agree with those his ideas, he is sure what he knows concerning those figures, when they have *barely an ideal existence* in his mind, will hold true of them also when they have *a real existence* in matter: his consideration being barely of those figures, which are the same wherever or however they exist.

7. *And of Moral.*——And hence it follows that moral knowledge is as capable of real certainty as mathematics. For certainty being but the perception of the agreement or disagreement of our ideas, and demonstration nothing but the perception of such agreement, by the intervention of other ideas or mediums; our moral ideas, as well as mathematical, being archetypes themselves, and so adequate and complete ideas; all the agreement or disagreement which we shall find in them will produce real knowledge, as well as in mathematical figures.

8. *Existence not required to make Abstract Knowledge real.*——For the attaining of knowledge and certainty, it is requisite that we have determined ideas: and, to make our knowledge real, it is requisite that the ideas answer their archetypes. Nor let it be wondered, that I place the certainty of our knowledge in the consideration of our ideas, with so little care and regard (as it may seem) to the real existence of things: since most of those discourses which take up the thoughts and engage the disputes of those who pretend to make it their business to inquire after truth and certainty, will, I presume, upon examination, be found to be general propositions, and notions in which existence is not at all concerned. All the discourses of the mathematicians about the squaring of a circle, conic sections, or any other part of mathematics, concern not the existence of any of those figures: but their demonstrations, which depend on their ideas, are the same, whether

there be any square or circle existing in the world or no. In the same manner, the truth and certainty of moral discourses abstracts from the lives of men, and the existence of those virtues in the world whereof they treat: nor are Tully's Offices less true, because there is nobody in the world that exactly practises his rules, and lives up to that pattern of a virtuous man which he has given us, and which existed nowhere when he writ but in idea. If it be true in speculation, i.e. in idea, that murder deserves death, it will also be true in reality of any action that exists conformable to that idea of murder. As for other actions, the truth of that proposition concerns them not. And thus it is of all other species of things, which have no other essences but those ideas which are in the minds of men.

9. *Nor will it be less true or certain, because Moral Ideas are of our own making and naming.*——But it will here be said, that if moral knowledge be placed in the contemplation of our own moral ideas, and those, as other modes, be of our own making, What strange notions will there be of justice and temperance? What confusion of virtues and vices, if every one may make what ideas of them he pleases? No confusion or disorder in the things themselves, nor the reasonings about them; no more than (in mathematics) there would be a disturbance in the demonstration, or a change in the properties of figures, and their relations one to another, if a man should make a triangle with four corners, or a trapezium with four right angles: that is, in plain English, change the names of the figures, and call that by one name, which mathematicians call ordinarily by another. For, let a man make to himself the idea of a figure with three angles, whereof one is a right one, and call it, if he please, *equilaterum* or *trapezium*, or anything else; the properties of, and demonstrations about that idea will be the same as if he called it a rectangular triangle. I confess the change of the name, by the impropriety of speech, will at first disturb him who knows not what idea it stands for: but as soon as the figure is drawn, the consequences and demonstrations are plain and clear. Just the same is it in moral knowledge: let a man have the idea of taking from others, without their consent, what their honest industry has possessed them of, and call this *justice* if he please. He that takes the name here without the idea put to it will be mistaken, by joining another idea of his own to that name: but strip the idea of that name, or take it such as it is in the

speaker's mind, and the same things will agree to it, as if you called it *injustice.* Indeed, wrong names in moral discourses breed usually more disorder, because they are not so easily rectified as in mathematics, where the figure, once drawn and seen, makes the name useless and of no force. For what need of a sign, when the thing signified is present and in view? But in moral names, that cannot be so easily and shortly done, because of the many decompositions that go to the making up the complex ideas of those modes. But yet for all this, the miscalling of any of those ideas, contrary to the usual signification of the words of that language, hinders not but that we may have certain and demonstrative knowledge of their several agreements and disagreements, if we will carefully, as in mathematics, keep to the same precise ideas, and trace *them* in their several relations one to another, without being led away by their names. If we but separate the idea under consideration from the sign that stands for it, our knowledge goes equally on in the discovery of real truth and certainty, whatever sounds we make use of.

10. *Misnaming disturbs not the Certainty of the Knowledge.*——One thing more we are to take notice of, That where God or any other law-maker, hath defined any moral names, there they have made the essence of that species to which that name belongs; and there it is not safe to apply or use them otherwise: but in other cases it is bare impropriety of speech to apply them contrary to the common usage of the country. But yet even this too disturbs not the certainty of that knowledge, which is still to be had by a due contemplation and comparing of those even nick-named ideas.

11. *Thirdly, Our complex Ideas of Substances have their Archetypes without us; and here knowledge comes short.*——*Thirdly,* There is another sort of complex ideas, which, being referred to archetypes without us, may differ from them, and so our knowledge about them may come short of being real. Such are our ideas of substances, which, consisting of a collection of simple ideas, supposed taken from the works of nature, may yet vary from them; by having more or different ideas united in them than are to be found united in the things themselves. From whence it comes to pass, that they may, and often do, fail of being exactly conformable to things themselves.

12. *So far as our complex ideas agree with those Archetypes without us, so far our Knowledge concerning Substances is*

real.——I say, then, that to have ideas of *substances* which, by being conformable to things, may afford us real knowledge, it is not enough, as in *modes*, to put together such ideas as have no inconsistence, though they did never before so exist: v.g. the ideas of sacrilege or perjury, &c., were as real and true ideas before, as after the existence of any such fact. But our ideas of substances, being supposed copies, and referred to archetypes without us, must still be taken from something that does or has existed: they must not consist of ideas put together at the pleasure of our thoughts, without any real pattern they were taken from, though we can perceive no inconsistence in such a combination. The reason whereof is, because we, knowing not what real constitution it is of substances whereon our simple ideas depend, and which really is the cause of the strict union of some of them one with another, and the exclusion of others; there are very few of them that we can be sure are or are not inconsistent in nature, any further than experience and sensible observation reach. Herein, therefore, is founded the reality of our knowledge concerning substances—That all our complex ideas of them must be such, and such only, as are màde up of such simple ones as have been discovered to co-exist in nature. And our ideas being thus true, though not perhaps very exact copies, are yet the subjects of real (as far as we have any) knowledge of them. Which (as has been already shown) will not be found to reach very far: but so far as it does, it will still be real knowledge. Whatever ideas we have, the agreement we find they have with others will still be knowledge. If those ideas be abstract, it will be general knowledge. But to make it real concerning substances, the ideas must be taken from the real existence of things. Whatever simple ideas have been found to co-exist in any substance, these we may with confidence join together again, and so make abstract ideas of substances. For whatever have once had an union in nature, may be united again.

18. *Recapitulation.*——Wherever we perceive the agreement or disagreement of any of our ideas, there is certain knowledge: and wherever we are sure those ideas agree with the reality of things, there is certain real knowledge. Of which agreement of our ideas with the reality of things, having here given the marks, I think, I have shown *wherein it is that certainty, real certainty, consists.* Which, whatever it was to others, was, I confess, to me heretofore, one of those desiderata which I found great want of.

CHAPTER IX.

OF OUR THREEFOLD KNOWLEDGE OF EXISTENCE.

1. *General Propositions that are certain concern not Existence.*——Hitherto we have only considered the essences of things; which being only abstract ideas, and thereby removed in our thoughts from particular existence, (that being the proper operation of the mind, in abstraction, to consider an idea under no other existence but what it has in the understanding,) gives us no knowledge of real existence at all. Where, by the way, we may take notice, that universal propositions of whose truth or falsehood we can have certain knowledge concern not existence: and further, that all particular affirmations or negations that would not be certain if they were made general, are only concerning existence; they declaring only the accidental union or separation of ideas in things existing, which, in their abstract natures, have no known necessary union or repugnancy.

2. *A threefold Knowledge of Existence.*——But, leaving the nature of propositions, and different ways of predication to be considered more at large in another place, let us proceed now to inquire concerning our knowledge of the *existence of things*, and how we come by it. I say, then, that we have the knowledge of *our own* existence by intuition; of the existence of *God* by demonstration; and of *other things* by sensation.

3. *Our Knowledge of our own Existence is Intuitive.*——As for *our own existence*, we perceive it so plainly and so certainly, that it neither needs nor is capable of any proof. For nothing can be more evident to us than our own existence. I think, I reason, I feel pleasure and pain: can any of these be more evident to me than my own existence? If I doubt of all other things, that very doubt makes me perceive my own existence, and will not suffer me to doubt of that. For if I know I feel pain, it is evident I have as certain perception of my own existence, as of the existence of the pain I feel: or if I know I doubt, I have as certain perception of the existence of the thing doubting, as of that thought which I *call doubt*. Experience then convinces us, that we have an *intui-*

tive knowledge of our own existence, and an internal infallible perception that we are. In every act of sensation, reasoning, or thinking, we are conscious to ourselves of our own being; and, in this matter, come not short of the highest degree of certainty.

CHAPTER X.

OF OUR KNOWLEDGE OF THE EXISTENCE OF A GOD.

1. *We are capable of knowing certainly that there is a God.*——Though God has given us no innate ideas of himself; though he has stamped no original characters on our minds, wherein we may read his being; yet having furnished us with those faculties our minds are endowed with, he hath not left himself without witness: since we have sense, perception, and reason, and cannot want a clear proof of him, as long as we carry *ourselves* about us. Nor can we justly complain of our ignorance in this great point; since he has so plentifully provided us with the means to discover and know him; so far as is necessary to the end of our being, and the great concernment of our happiness. But, though this be the most obvious truth that reason discovers, and though its evidence be (if I mistake not) equal to mathematical certainty: yet it requires thought and attention; and the mind must apply itself to a regular deduction of it from some part of our intuitive knowledge, or else we shall be as uncertain and ignorant of this as of other propositions, which are in themselves capable of clear demonstration. To show, therefore, that we are capable of *knowing,* i.e. *being certain* that there is a God, and *how we may come by* this certainty, I think we need go no further than *ourselves,* and that undoubted knowledge we have of our own existence.

2. *For Man knows that he himself exists.*——I think it is beyond question, that man has a clear idea of his own being; he knows certainly he exists, and that he is something. He that can doubt whether he be anything or no, I speak not to; no more than I would argue with pure nothing, or endeavour to convince nonentity that it were something. If any one pretends to be so sceptical as to deny his own existence, (for

really to doubt of it is manifestly impossible,) let him for me enjoy his beloved happiness of being nothing, until hunger or some other pain convince him of the contrary. This, then, I think I may take for a truth, which every one's certain knowledge assures him of, beyond the liberty of doubting, viz. that he is *something that actually exists.*

3. *He knows also that Nothing cannot produce a Being; therefore Something must have existed from Eternity.*——In the next place, man knows, by an intuitive certainty, that bare *nothing can no more produce any real being, than it can be equal to two right angles.* If a man knows not that nonentity, or the absence of all being, cannot be equal to two right angles, it is impossible he should know any demonstration in Euclid. If, therefore, we know there is some real being, and that nonentity cannot produce any real being, it is an evident demonstration, that *from eternity there has been something*; since what was not from eternity had a beginning; and what had a beginning must be produced by something else.

4. *And that eternal Being must be most powerful.*——Next, it is evident, that what had its being and beginning from another, must also have all that which is in and belongs to its being from another too. All the powers it has must be owing to and received from the same source. This eternal source, then, of all being must also be the source and original of all power; and so *this eternal Being must be also the most powerful.*

5. *And most knowing.*——Again, a man finds in *himself* perception and knowledge. We have then got one step further; and we are certain now that there is not only some being, but some knowing, intelligent being in the world. There was a time, then, when there was no knowing being, and when knowledge began to be; or else there has been also *a knowing being from eternity.* If it be said, there was a time when no being had any knowledge, when that eternal being was void of all understanding; I reply, that then it was impossible there should ever have been any knowledge: it being as impossible that things wholly void of knowledge, and operating blindly, and without any perception, should produce a knowing being, as it is impossible that a triangle should make itself three angles bigger than two right ones. For it is as repugnant to the idea of senseless matter, that it should put into itself sense, perception, and knowledge, as it is repugnant to the

idea of a triangle, that it should put into itself greater angles than two right ones.

6. *And therefore God.*——Thus, from the consideration of ourselves, and what we infallibly find in our own constitutions, our reason leads us to the knowledge of this certain and evident truth,—*That there is an eternal, most powerful, and most knowing Being*; which whether any one will please to call God, it matters not. The thing is evident; and from this idea duly considered, will easily be deduced all those other attributes, which we ought to ascribe to this eternal Being. If, nevertheless, any one should be found so senselessly arrogant, as to suppose man alone knowing and wise, but yet the product of mere ignorance and chance; and that all the rest of the universe acted only by that blind haphazard; I shall leave with him that very rational and emphatical rebuke of Tully (l. ii. De Leg.), to be considered at his leisure: 'What can be more sillily arrogant and misbecoming, than for a man to think that he has a mind and understanding in him, but yet in all the universe beside there is no such thing? Or that those things, which with the utmost stretch of his reason he can scarce comprehend, should be moved and managed without any reason at all?' *Quid est enim verius, quam neminem esse oportere tam stulte arrogantem, ut in se mentem et rationem putet inesse, in cælo mundoque non putet? Aut ea quæ vix summa ingenii ratione comprehendat, nulla ratione moveri putet?*

From what has been said, it is plain to me we have a more certain knowledge of the existence of a God, than of anything our senses have not immediately discovered to us. Nay, I presume I may say, that we more certainly know that there is a God, than that there is anything else without us. When I say we *know*, I mean there is such a knowledge within our reach which we cannot miss, if we will but apply our minds to that, as we do to several other inquiries.

7. *Our idea of a most perfect Being, not the sole Proof of a God.*——How far the *idea* of a most perfect being, which a man may frame in his mind, does or does not prove the *existence* of a God, I will not here examine. For in the different make of men's tempers and application of their thoughts, some arguments prevail more on one, and some on another, for the confirmation of the same truth. But yet, I think, this I may say, that it is an ill way of establishing this truth, and silencing atheists, to lay the whole stress of so important a

point as this upon that sole foundation: and take some men's having that idea of God in their minds, (for it is evident some men have none, and some worse than none, and the most very different,) for the only proof of a Deity; and out of an over fondness of that darling invention, cashier, or at least endeavour to invalidate all other arguments; and forbid us to hearken to those proofs, as being weak or fallacious, which our own existence, and the sensible parts of the universe offer so clearly and cogently to our thoughts, that I deem it impossible for a considering man to withstand them. For I judge it as certain and clear a truth as can anywhere be delivered, that 'the invisible things of God are clearly seen from the creation of the world, being understood by the things that are made, even his eternal power and Godhead.' Though our own being furnishes us, as I have shown, with an evident and incontestible proof of a Deity; and I believe nobody can avoid the cogency of it, who will but as carefully attend to it, as to any other demonstration of so many parts: yet this being so fundamental a truth, and of that consequence, that all religion and genuine morality depend thereon, I doubt not but I shall be forgiven by my reader if I go over some parts of this argument again, and enlarge a little more upon them.

8. *Recapitulation. Something from Eternity.*——There is no truth more evident than that *something* must be *from eternity.* I never yet heard of any one so unreasonable, or that could suppose so manifest a contradiction, as a time wherein there was perfectly nothing. This being of all absurdities the greatest, to imagine that pure nothing, the perfect negation and absence of all beings, should ever produce any real existence.

It being, then, unavoidable for all rational creatures to conclude, that *something* has existed from eternity; let us next see *what kind of thing* that must be.

9. *Two Sorts of Beings, cogitative and incogitative.*——There are but two sorts of beings in the world that man knows or conceives.

First, such as are purely material, without sense, perception, or thought, as the clippings of our beards, and parings of our nails.

Secondly, sensible, thinking, perceiving beings, such as we find ourselves to be. Which, if you please, we will hereafter call *cogitative* and *incogitative* beings; which to our present purpose, if for nothing else, are perhaps better terms than material and immaterial.

10. *Incogitative Being cannot produce a Cogitative Being.*——If, then, there must be something eternal, let us see what sort of being it must be. And to that it is very obvious to reason, that it must necessarily be a cogitative being. For it is as impossible to conceive that ever bare incogitative matter should produce a thinking intelligent being, as that nothing should of itself produce matter. Let us suppose any parcel of matter eternal, great or small, we shall find it, in itself, able to produce nothing. For example: let us suppose the matter of the next pebble we meet with eternal, closely united, and the parts firmly at rest together; if there were no other being in the world, must it not eternally remain so, a dead inactive lump? Is it possible to conceive it can add motion to itself, being purely matter, or produce anything? Matter, then, by its own strength, cannot produce in itself so much as motion: the motion it has must also be from eternity, or else be produced, and added to matter by some other being more powerful than matter; matter, as is evident, having not power to produce motion in itself. But let us suppose motion eternal too: yet matter, *incogitative* matter and motion, whatever changes it might produce of figure and bulk, could never produce thought: knowledge will still be as far beyond the power of motion and matter to produce, as matter is beyond the power of nothing or nonentity to produce. And I appeal to every one's own thoughts, whether he cannot as easily conceive matter produced by *nothing*, as thought to be produced by pure matter, when, before, there was no such thing as thought or an intelligent being existing? Divide matter into as many parts as you will, (which we are apt to imagine a sort of spiritualizing, or making a thinking thing of it,) vary the figure and motion of it as much as you please—a globe, cube, cone, prism, cylinder, &c., whose diameters are but 100,000th part of a *gry*, will operate no otherwise upon other bodies of proportionable bulk, than those of an inch or foot diameter; and you may as rationally expect to produce sense, thought, and knowledge, by putting together, in a certain figure and motion, gross particles of matter, as by those that are the very minutest that do anywhere exist. They knock, impel, and resist one another, just as the greater do; and that is all they can do. So that, if we will suppose *nothing* first or eternal, matter can never begin to be: if we suppose bare matter

without motion, eternal, motion can never begin to be: if we suppose only matter and motion first, or eternal, thought can never begin to be. For it is impossible to conceive that matter, either with or without motion, could have, originally, in and from itself, sense, perception, and knowledge; as is evident from hence, that then sense, perception, and knowledge, must be a property eternally inseparable from matter and every particle of it. Not to add, that, though our general or specific conception of matter makes us speak of it as one thing, yet really all matter is not one individual thing, neither is there any such thing existing as *one* material being, or *one* single body that we know or can conceive. And therefore, if matter were the eternal first cogitative being, there would not be one eternal, infinite, cogitative being, but an infinite number of eternal, finite, cogitative beings, independent one of another, of limited force, and distinct thoughts, which could never produce that order, harmony, and beauty which are to be found in nature. Since, therefore, whatsoever is the first eternal being must necessarily be cogitative; and whatsoever is first of all things must necessarily contain in it, and actually have, at least, all the perfections that can ever after exist; nor can it ever give to another any perfection that it hath not either actually in itself, or, at least, in a higher degree; it necessarily follows, that the first eternal being cannot be matter.

11. *Therefore, there has been an Eternal Cogitative Being.*——If, therefore, it be evident, that something necessarily must exist from eternity, it is also as evident, that that something must necessarily be a cogitative being: for it is as impossible that incogitative matter should produce a cogitative being, as that nothing, or the negation of all being, should produce a positive being or matter.

CHAPTER XI.

OF OUR KNOWLEDGE OF THE EXISTENCE OF OTHER THINGS.

1. *Knowledge of the existence of other Finite Beings is to be had only by actual Sensation.*——The knowledge of our own being we have by intuition. The existence of a God, reason clearly makes known to us, as has been shown.

The knowledge of the existence of *any other thing* we can have only by *sensation*: for there being no necessary connexion of real existence with any *idea* a man hath in his memory; nor of any other existence but that of God with the existence of any particular man: no particular man can know the existence of any other being, but only when, by actual operating upon him, it makes itself perceived by him. For, the having the idea of anything in our mind, no more proves the existence of that thing, than the picture of a man evidences his being in the world, or the visions of a dream make thereby a true history.

2. *Instance: Whiteness of this Paper.*——It is therefore the *actual receiving* of ideas from without that gives us notice of the existence of other things, and makes us know, that something doth exist at that time without us, which causes that idea in us; though perhaps we neither know nor consider how it does it. For it takes not from the certainty of our senses, and the ideas we receive by them, that we know not the manner wherein they are produced: v.g. whilst I write this, I have, by the paper affecting my eyes, that idea produced in my mind, which, whatever object causes, I call *white*; by which I know that that quality or accident (i.e. whose appearance before my eyes always causes that idea) doth really exist, and hath a being without me. And of this, the greatest assurance I can possibly have, and to which my faculties can attain, is the testimony of my eyes, which are the proper and sole judges of this thing; whose testimony I have reason to rely on as so certain, that I can no more doubt, whilst I write this, that I see white and black, and that something really exists that causes that sensation in me, than that I write or move my hand; which is a certainty as great as human nature is capable of, concerning the existence of anything, but a man's self alone, and of God.

3. *This notice by our Senses, though not so certain as Demonstration, yet may be called Knowledge, and proves the Existence of Things without us.*——The notice we have by our senses of the existing of things without us, though it be not altogether so certain as our intuitive knowledge, or the deductions of our reason employed about the clear abstract ideas of our own minds; yet it is an assurance that deserves the name of *knowledge*. If we persuade ourselves that our faculties act and inform us right concerning the existence of those objects that affect them, it cannot pass for an ill-grounded confidence: for I think nobody can, in earnest, be so sceptical

as to be uncertain of the existence of those things which he sees and feels. At least, he that can doubt so far, (whatever he may have with his own thoughts,) will never have any controversy with me; since he can never be sure I say anything contrary to his own opinion. As to myself, I think God has given me assurance enough of the existence of things without me: since, by their different application, I can produce in myself both pleasure and pain, which is one great concernment of my present state. This is certain: the confidence that our faculties do not herein deceive us, is the greatest assurance we are capable of concerning the existence of material beings. For we cannot act anything but by our faculties; nor talk of knowledge itself, but by the help of those faculties which are fitted to apprehend even what knowledge is.

But besides the assurance we have from our senses themselves, that they do not err in the information they give us of the existence of things without us, when they are affected by them, we are further confirmed in this assurance by other concurrent reasons:—

4. *Confirmed by concurrent reasons:—First, Because we cannot have ideas of Sensation but by the Inlet of the Senses.* ——I. It is plain those perceptions are produced in us by exterior causes affecting our senses: because those that want the *organs* of any sense, never can have the ideas belonging to that sense produced in their minds. This is too evident to be doubted: and therefore we cannot but be assured that they come in by the organs of that sense, and no other way. The organs themselves, it is plain, do not produce them: for then the eyes of a man in the dark would produce colours, and his nose smell roses in the winter: but we see nobody gets the relish of a pineapple, till he goes to the Indies, where it is, and tastes it.

5. *Secondly, Because we find that an Idea from actual Sensation, and another from Memory, are very distinct Perceptions.*——II. Because sometimes I find that *I cannot avoid the having those ideas produced in my mind.* For though, when my eyes are shut, or windows fast, I can at pleasure recal to my mind the ideas of light, or the sun, which former sensations had lodged in my memory; so I can at pleasure lay by *that* idea, and take into my view that of the smell of a rose, or taste of sugar. But, if I turn my eyes at noon towards the sun, I cannot avoid the ideas which the light or sun then produces in me. So that there is a manifest difference between

the ideas laid up in my memory, (over which, if they were there only, I should have constantly the same power to dispose of them, and lay them by at pleasure,) and those which force themselves upon me, and I cannot avoid having. And therefore it must needs be some exterior cause, and the brisk acting of some objects without me, whose efficacy I cannot resist, that produces those ideas in my mind, whether I will or no. Besides, there is nobody who doth not perceive the difference in himself between contemplating the sun, as he hath the idea of it in his memory, and actually looking upon it: of which two, his perception is so distinct, that few of his ideas are more distinguishable one from another. And therefore he hath certain knowledge that they are not *both* memory, or the actions of his mind, and fancies only within him; but that actual seeing hath a cause without.

6. *Thirdly, Because Pleasure or Pain, which accompanies actual Sensation, accompanies not the returning of those Ideas without the external Objects.*——III. Add to this, that many of those ideas are *produced in us with pain*, which afterwards we remember without the least offence. Thus, the pain of heat or cold, when the idea of it is revived in our minds, gives us no disturbance; which, when felt, was very troublesome; and is again, when actually repeated: which is occasioned by the disorder the external object causes in our bodies when applied to them: and we remember the pains of hunger, thirst, or the headache, without any pain at all; which would either never disturb us, or else constantly do it, as often as we thought of it, were there nothing more but ideas floating in our minds, and appearances entertaining our fancies, without the real existence of things affecting us from abroad. The same may be said of *pleasure*, accompanying several actual sensations. And though mathematical demonstration depends not upon sense, yet the examining them by diagrams gives great credit to the evidence of our sight, and seems to give it a certainty approaching to that of demonstration itself. For, it would be very strange, that a man should allow it for an undeniable truth, that two angles of a figure, which he measures by lines and angles of a diagram, should be bigger one than the other, and yet doubt of the existence of those lines and angles, which by looking on he makes use of to measure that by.

7. *Fourthly, Because our Senses assist one another's Testimony of the Existence of outward Things, and enable us to*

predict.——IV. Our *senses* in many cases *bear witness to the truth of each other's report,* concerning the existence of sensible things without us. He that *sees* a fire, may, if he doubt whether it be anything more than a bare fancy, *feel* it too; and be convinced, by putting his hand in it. Which certainly could never be put into such exquisite pain by a bare idea or phantom, unless that the pain be a fancy too: which yet he cannot, when the burn is well, by raising the idea of it, bring upon himself again.

Thus I see, whilst I write this, I can change the appearance of the paper; and by designing the letters, tell *beforehand* what new idea it shall exhibit the very next moment, by barely drawing my pen over it: which will neither appear (let me fancy as much as I will) if my hands stand still; or though I move my pen, if my eyes be shut: nor, when those characters are once made on the paper, can I choose afterwards but see them as they are; that is, have the ideas of such letters as I have made. Whence it is manifest, that they are not barely the sport and play of my own imagination, when I find that the characters that were made at the pleasure of my own thoughts, do not obey them; nor yet cease to be, whenever I shall fancy it, but continue to affect my senses constantly and regularly, according to the figures I made them. To which if we will add, that the sight of those shall, from another man, draw such sounds as I beforehand design they shall stand for, there will be little reason left to doubt that those words I write do really exist without me, when they cause a long series of regular sounds to affect my ears, which could not be the effect of my imagination, nor could my memory retain them in that order.

8. *This Certainty is as great as our Condition needs.*—— But yet, if after all this any one will be so sceptical as to distrust his senses, and to affirm that all we see and hear, feel and taste, think and do, during our whole being, is but the series and deluding appearances of a long dream, whereof there is no reality; and therefore will question the existence of all things, or our knowledge of anything: I must desire him to consider, that, if all be a dream, then he doth but dream that he makes the question, and so it is not much matter that a waking man should answer him. But yet, it he pleases, he may dream that I make him this answer, That the certainty of things existing in *rerum natura* when we have the testimony of our senses for it is not only as great as our frame can attain to,

but as our condition needs. For, our faculties being suited not to the full extent of being, nor to a perfect, clear, comprehensive knowledge of things free from all doubt and scruple; but to the preservation of us, in whom they are; and accommodated to the use of life: they serve to our purpose well enough, if they will but give us certain notice of those things, which are convenient or inconvenient to us. For he that sees a candle burning, and hath experimented the force of its flame by putting his finger in it, will little doubt that this is something existing without him, which does him harm, and puts him to great pain: which is assurance enough, when no man requires greater certainty to govern his actions by than what is as certain as his actions themselves. And if our dreamer pleases to try whether the glowing heat of a glass furnace be barely a wandering imagination in a drowsy man's fancy, by putting his hand into it, he may perhaps be wakened into a certainty greater than he could wish, that it is something more than bare imagination. So that this evidence is as great as we can desire, being as certain to us as our pleasure or pain, i.e. happiness or misery; beyond which we have no concernment, either of knowing or being. Such an assurance of the existence of things without us is sufficient to direct us in the attaining the good and avoiding the evil which is caused by them, which is the important concernment we have of being made acquainted with them.

9. *But reaches no further than actual Sensation.*——In fine, then, when our senses do actually convey into our understandings any idea, we cannot but be satisfied that there doth something *at that time* really exist without us, which doth affect our senses, and by them give notice of itself to our apprehensive faculties, and actually produce that idea which we then perceive: and we cannot so far distrust their testimony, as to doubt that such *collections* of simple ideas as we have observed by our senses to be united together, do really exist together. But this knowledge extends as far as the present testimony of our senses, employed about particular objects that do then affect them, and no further. For if I saw such a collection of simple ideas as is wont to be called *man*, existing together one minute since, and am now alone, I cannot be certain that the same man exists now, since there is no *necessary connexion* of his existence a minute since with his existence now: by a thousand ways he may cease to be, since I had the testimony of my senses for his existence. And if I

cannot be certain that the man I saw last to-day is now in being, I can less be certain that he is so who hath been longer removed from my senses, and I have not seen since yesterday, or since the last year: and much less can I be certain of the existence of men that I never saw. And, therefore, though it be highly probable that millions of men do now exist, yet, whilst I am alone, writing this, I have not that certainty of it which we strictly call knowledge; though the great likelihood of it puts me past doubt, and it be reasonable for me to do several things upon the confidence that there are men (and men also of my acquaintance, with whom I have to do) now in the world: but this is but probability, not knowledge.

10. *Folly to expect Demonstration in everything.*——Whereby yet we may observe how foolish and vain a thing it is for a man of a narrow knowledge, who having reason given him to judge of the different evidence and probability of things, and to be swayed accordingly; how vain, I say, it is to expect demonstration and certainty in things not capable of it; and refuse assent to very rational propositions, and act contrary to very plain and clear truths, because they cannot be made out so evident, as to surmount every the least (I will not say reason, but) pretence of doubting. He that, in the ordinary affairs of life, would admit of nothing but direct plain demonstration, would be sure of nothing in this world, but of perishing quickly. The wholesomeness of his meat or drink would not give him reason to venture on it: and I would fain know what it is he could do upon such grounds as are capable of no doubt, no objection.

11. *Past Existence of other things is known by Memory.*——As *when our senses are actually employed about any object,* we do know that it does exist; so *by our memory* we may be assured, that heretofore things that affected our senses have existed. And thus we have knowledge of the past existence of several things, whereof our senses having informed us, our memories still retain the ideas; and of this we are past all doubt, so long as we remember well. But this knowledge also reaches no further than our senses have formerly assured us. Thus, seeing water at this instant, it is an unquestionable truth to me that water doth exist: and remembering that I saw it yesterday, it will also be always true, and as long as my memory retains it always an undoubted proposition to me, that water did exist the 10th of July, 1688; as it will also be equally true that a certain number of very fine colours did

exist, which at the same time I saw upon a bubble of that water: but, being now quite out of sight both of the water and bubbles too, it is no more certainly known to me that the water doth now exist, than that the bubbles or colours therein do so: it being no more necessary that water should exist to-day, because it existed yesterday, than that the colours or bubbles exist to-day, because they existed yesterday, though it be exceedingly much more probable; because water hath been observed to continue long in existence, but bubbles, and the colours on them, quickly cease to be.

12. *The Existence of other finite Spirits not knowable, and rests on Faith.*——What ideas we have of spirits, and how we come by them, I have already shown. But though we have those ideas in our minds, and know we have them there, the having the ideas of spirits does not make us know that any such things do exist without us, or that there are any finite spirits, or any other spiritual beings, but the Eternal God. We have ground from revelation, and several other reasons, to believe with assurance that there are such creatures: but our senses not being able to discover them, we want the means of knowing their particular existences. For we can no more know that there are finite spirits really existing, by the idea we have of such beings in our minds, than by the ideas any one has of fairies or centaurs, he can come to know that things answering those ideas do really exist.

And therefore concerning the existence of finite spirits, as well as several other things, we must content ourselves with the evidence of faith; but universal, certain propositions concerning this matter are beyond our reach. For however true it may be, v.g., that all the intelligent spirits that God ever created do still exist, yet it can never make a part of our certain knowledge. These and the like propositions we may assent to, as highly probable, but are not, I fear, in this state capable of knowing. We are not, then, to put others upon demonstrating, nor ourselves upon search of universal certainty in all those matters; wherein we are not capable of any other knowledge, but what our senses give us in this or that particular.

13. *Only particular Propositions concerning concrete Existences are knowable.*——By which it appears that there are two sorts of propositions:—(1) There is one sort of propositions concerning the *existence* of anything answerable to such an idea: as having the idea of an elephant, phoenix, motion, or

an angel, in my mind, the first and natural inquiry is, Whether such a thing does anywhere exist? And this knowledge is only of particulars. No existence of anything without us, but only of God, can certainly be known further than our senses inform us. (2) There is another sort of propositions, wherein is expressed the agreement or disagreement of *our abstract ideas*, and their dependence on one another. Such propositions may be universal and certain. So, having the idea of God and myself, of fear and obedience, I cannot but be sure that God is to be feared and obeyed by me: and this proposition will be certain, concerning man in general, if I have made an abstract idea of such a species, whereof I am one particular. But yet this proposition, how certain soever, that 'men ought to fear and obey God' proves not to me the *existence* of *men* in the world; but will be true of all such creatures, whenever they do exist: which certainty of such general propositions depends on the agreement or disagreement to be discovered in those abstract ideas.

14. *And all general Propositions that are known to be true concern abstract Ideas.*——In the former case, our knowledge is the consequence of the existence of things, producing ideas in our minds by our senses: in the latter, knowledge is the consequence of the ideas (be they what they will) that are in our minds, producing there general certain propositions. Many of these are called *aeternae veritates*, and all of them indeed are so; not from being written, all or any of them, in the minds of all men; or that they were any of them propositions in any one's mind, till he, having got the abstract ideas, joined or separated them by affirmation or negation. But wheresoever we can suppose such a creature as man is, endowed with such faculties, and thereby furnished with such ideas as we have, we must conclude, he must needs, when he applies his thoughts to the consideration of his ideas, know the truth of certain propositions that will arise from the agreement or disagreement which he will perceive in his own ideas. Such propositions are therefore called *eternal truths*, not because they are eternal propositions actually formed, and antecedent to the understanding that at any time makes them; nor because they are imprinted on the mind from any patterns that are anywhere out of the mind, and existed before: but because, being once made about abstract ideas, so as to be true, they will, whenever they can be supposed to be made again at any time, past or to come, by a mind having those

ideas, always actually be true. For names being supposed to stand perpetually for the same ideas, and the same ideas having immutably the same habitudes one to another, propositions concerning any abstract ideas that are once true must needs be *eternal verities*.

CHAPTER XVII.

OF REASON.

1. *Various Significations of the word Reason.*——The word *reason* in the English language has different significations: sometimes it is taken for true and clear principles: sometimes for clear and fair deductions from those principles: and sometimes for the cause, and particularly the final cause. But the consideration I shall have of it here is in a signification different from all these; and that is, as it stands for a faculty in man, that faculty whereby man is supposed to be distinguished from beasts, and wherein it is evident he much surpasses them.

2. *Wherein Reasoning consists.*——If general knowledge, as has been shown, consists in a perception of the agreement or disagreement of our own ideas, and the knowledge of the existence of all things without us (except only of a God, whose existence every man may certainly know and demonstrate to himself from his own existence), be had only by our senses, what room is there for the exercise of any other faculty, but *outward sense* and *inward perception*? What need is there of *reason*? Very much: both for the enlargement of our knowledge, and regulating our assent. For it hath to do both in knowledge and opinion, and is necessary and assisting to all our other intellectual faculties, and indeed contains two of them, viz. *sagacity* and *illation*. By the one, it finds out; and by the other, it so orders the intermediate ideas as to discover what connexion there is in each link of the chain, whereby the extremes are held together; and thereby, as it were, to draw into view the truth sought for, which is that which we call *illation* or *inference*, and consists in nothing but the perception of the connexion there is between the ideas, in each step of the deduction; whereby the mind comes to see, either the certain

agreement or disagreement of any two ideas, as in demonstration, in which it arrives at *knowledge*; or their probable connexion, on which it gives or withholds its assent, as in *opinion*. Sense and intuition reach but a very little way. The greatest part of our knowledge depends upon deductions and intermediate ideas: and in those cases where we are fain to substitute assent instead of knowledge, and take propositions for true, without being certain they are so, we have need to find out, examine, and compare the grounds of their probability. In both these cases, the faculty which finds out the means, and rightly applies them, to discover certainty in the one, and probability in the other, is that which we call *reason*. For, as reason perceives the necessary and indubitable connexion of all the ideas or proofs one to another, in each step of any demonstration that produces knowledge; so it likewise perceives the probable connexion of all the ideas or proofs one to another, in every step of a discourse, to which it will think assent due. This is the lowest degree of that which can be truly called reason. For where the mind does not perceive this probable connexion, where it does not discern whether there be any such connexion or no; there men's opinions are not the product of judgment, or the consequence of reason, but the effects of chance and hazard, of a mind floating at all adventures, without choice and without direction.

3. *Reason in its four degrees.*——So that we may in *reason* consider these *four degrees*: the first and highest is the discovering and finding out of truths; the second, the regular and methodical disposition of them, and laying them in a clear and fit order, to make their connexion and force be plainly and easily perceived; the third is the perceiving their connexion; and the fourth, a making a right conclusion. These several degrees may be observed in any mathematical demonstration; it being one thing to perceive the connexion of each part, as the demonstration is made by another; another to perceive the dependence of the conclusion on all the parts; a third, to make out a demonstration clearly and neatly one's self; and something different from all these, to have first found out these intermediate ideas or proofs by which it is made.

14. *Our highest Degree of Knowledge is intuitive, without Reasoning.*——Some of the ideas that are in the mind, are so there, that they can be by themselves immediately compared one with another: and in these the mind is able to perceive that they agree or disagree as clearly as that it has them. Thus

the mind perceives, that an arch of a circle is less than the whole circle, as clearly as it does the idea of a circle: and this, therefore, as has been said, I call *intuitive knowledge*; which is certain, beyond all doubt, and needs no probation, nor can have any; this being the highest of all human certainty. In this consists the evidence of all those *maxims* which nobody has any doubt about, but every man (does not, as is said, only assent to, but) *knows* to be true, as soon as ever they are proposed to his understanding. In the discovery of and assent to these truths, there is no use of the discursive faculty, *no need of reasoning*, but they are known by a superior and higher degree of evidence. And such, if I may guess at things unknown, I am apt to think that angels have now, and the spirits of just men made perfect shall have, in a future state, of thousands of things which now either wholly escape our apprehensions, or which our short-sighted reason having got some faint glimpse of, we, in the dark, grope after.

15. *The next is got by Reasoning.*——But though we have, here and there, a little of this clear light, some sparks of bright knowledge, yet the greatest part of our ideas are such, that we cannot discern their agreement or disagreement by an immediate comparing them. And in all these we have *need of reasoning*, and must, by discourse and inference, make our discoveries. Now of these there are two sorts, which I shall take the liberty to mention here again:—

First, through Reasonings that are Demonstrative.——First, Those whose agreement or disagreement, though it cannot be seen by an immediate putting them together, yet may be examined by the intervention of other ideas which can be compared with them. In this case, when the agreement or disagreement of the intermediate idea, on both sides, with those which we would compare, is *plainly discerned*: there it amounts to *demonstration* whereby knowledge is produced, which, though it be certain, yet it is not so easy, nor altogether so clear as intuitive knowledge. Because in that there is barely one simple intuition, wherein there is no room for any the least mistake or doubt: the truth is seen all perfectly at once. In demonstration, it is true, there is intuition too, but not altogether at once; for there must be a remembrance of the intuition of the agreement of the medium, or intermediate idea, with that we compared it with before, when we compare it with the other: and where there be many mediums, there the danger of the mistake is the greater. For each agreement or disagreement of the ideas must be observed and seen in each step of the whole train, and retained in the memory, just as it is; and the mind must be sure that no part of what is necessary to make up the demonstration is omitted or overlooked. This makes some demonstrations long and perplexed, and too hard for those who have not strength of parts distinctly to perceive, and exactly carry so many particulars orderly in their heads. And even those who are able to master such intricate speculations, are fain sometimes to go over them again, and there is need of more than one review before they can arrive at certainty. But yet where the mind clearly retains the intuition it had of the agreement of any idea with another, and that with a third, and that with a fourth, &c., there the agreement of the first and the fourth is a demonstration, and produces certain knowledge; which may be called *rational knowledge*, as the other is intuitive.

16. *Secondly, to supply the narrowness of Demonstrative and Intuitive Knowledge we have nothing but Judgment upon probable reasoning.*——Secondly, There are other ideas, whose agreement or disagreement can no otherwise be judged of but by the intervention of others which have not a certain agreement with the extremes, but an *usual* or *likely* one: and in these it is that the *judgment* is properly exercised; which is the acquiescing of the mind, that any ideas do agree, by comparing them with such probable mediums. This, though it never amounts to knowledge, no, not to that which is the lowest degree of it; yet sometimes the intermediate ideas tie the extremes so firmly together, and the probability is so clear and strong, that *assent* as necessarily follows it, as *knowledge* does demonstration. The great excellency and use of the judgment is to observe right, and take a true estimate of the force and weight of each probability; and then casting them up all right together, choose that side which has the overbalance.

23. *Above, contrary, and according to Reason.*——By what has been before said of reason, we may be able to make some guess at the distinction of things, into those that are according to, above, and contrary to reason. 1. *According to reason* are such propositions whose truth we can discover by examining and tracing those ideas we have from sensation and reflection; and by natural deduction find to be true or probable. 2. *Above reason* are such propositions whose truth or probability we cannot by reason derive from those principles. 3. *Contrary to reason* are such propositions as are inconsistent

with or irreconcilable to our clear and distinct ideas. Thus the existence of one God is according to reason; the existence of more than one God, contrary to reason; the resurrection of the dead, above reason. *Above reason* also may be taken in a double sense, viz. either as signifying above probability, or above certainty: and in that large sense also, *contrary to reason*, is, I suppose, sometimes taken.

24. *Reason and Faith not opposite, for Faith must be regulated by Reason.*——There is another use of the word *reason*, wherein it is *opposed to faith*: which, though it be in itself a very improper way of speaking, yet common use has so authorized it, that it would be folly either to oppose or hope to remedy it. Only I think it may not be amiss to take notice, that, however faith be opposed to reason, faith is nothing but a firm assent of the mind: which, if it be regulated, as is our duty, cannot be afforded to anything but upon good reason; and so cannot be opposite to it. He that believes without having any reason for believing, may be in love with his own fancies; but neither seeks truth as he ought, nor pays the obedience due to his Maker, who would have him use those discerning faculties he has given him, to keep him out of mistake and error. He that does not this to the best of his power, however he sometimes lights on truth, is in the right but by chance; and I know not whether the luckiness of the accident will excuse the irregularity of his proceeding. This at least is certain, that he must be accountable for whatever mistakes he runs into: whereas he that makes use of the light and faculties God has given him, and seeks sincerely to discover truth by those helps and abilities he has, may have this satisfaction in doing his duty as a rational creature, that, though he should miss truth, he will not miss the reward of it. For he governs his assent right, and places it as he should, who, in any case or matter whatsoever, believes or disbelieves according as reason directs him. He that doth otherwise, transgresses against his own light, and misuses those faculties which were given him to no other end, but to search and follow the clearer evidence and greater probability. But since reason and faith are by some men opposed, we will so consider them in the following chapter.

CHAPTER XVIII.

OF FAITH AND REASON, AND THEIR DISTINCT PROVINCES.

1. *Necessary to know their boundaries.*——It has been above shown, 1. That we are of necessity ignorant, and want knowledge of all sorts, where we want ideas. 2. That we are ignorant, and want rational knowledge, where we want proofs. 3. That we want certain knowledge and certainty, as far as we want clear and determined specific ideas. 4. That we want probability to direct our assent in matters where we have neither knowledge of our own nor testimony of other men to bottom our reason upon.

From these things thus premised, I think we may come to lay down *the measures and boundaries between faith and reason*: the want whereof may possibly have been the cause, if not of great disorders, yet at least of great disputes, and perhaps mistakes in the world. For till it be resolved how far we are to be guided by reason, and how far by faith, we shall in vain dispute, and endeavour to convince one another in matters of religion.

2. *Faith and Reason, what, as contradistinguished.*——I find every sect, as far as reason will help them, make use of it gladly: and where it fails them, they cry out, It is matter of faith, and above reason. And I do not see how they can argue with any one, or ever convince a gainsayer who makes use of the same plea, without setting down strict boundaries between faith and reason; which ought to be the first point established in all questions where faith has anything to do.

Reason, therefore, here, as contradistinguished to *faith*, I take to be the discovery of the certainty or probability of such propositions or truths, which the mind arrives at by deduction made from such ideas, which it has got by the use of its natural faculties; viz. by sensation or reflection.

Faith, on the other side, is the assent to any proposition, not thus made out by the deductions of reason, but upon the credit of the proposer, as coming from God, in some extraordinary way of communication. This way of discovering truths to men, we call *revelation*.

3. *First, No new simple Idea can be conveyed by traditional Revelation.*——*First,* Then I say, that *no man inspired by God can by any revelation communicate to others any new simple ideas which they had not before from sensation or reflection.* For, whatsoever impressions he himself may have from the immediate hand of God, this revelation, if it be of new simple ideas, cannot be conveyed to another, either by words or any other signs. Because words, by their immediate operation on us, cause no other ideas but of their natural sounds: and it is by the custom of using them for signs, that they excite and revive in our minds latent ideas; but yet only such ideas as were there before. For words, seen or heard, recal to our thoughts those ideas only which to us they have been wont to be signs of, but cannot introduce any perfectly new, and formerly unknown simple ideas. The same holds in all other signs; which cannot signify to us things of which we have before never had any idea at all.

Thus whatever things were discovered to St. Paul, when he was rapt up into the third heaven; whatever new ideas his mind there received, all the description he can make to others of that place, is only this, That there are such things, 'as eye hath not seen, nor ear heard, nor hath it entered into the heart of man to conceive.' And supposing God should discover to any one, supernaturally, a species of creatures inhabiting, for example, Jupiter or Saturn, (for that it is possible there may be such, nobody can deny,) which had six senses; and imprint on his mind the ideas conveyed to theirs by that sixth sense: he could no more, by words, produce in the minds of other men those ideas imprinted by that sixth sense, than one of us could convey the idea of any colour, by the sound of words, into a man who, having the other four senses perfect, had always totally wanted the fifth, of seeing. For our simple ideas, then, which are the foundation, and sole matter of all our notions and knowledge, we must depend wholly on our reason, I mean our natural faculties; and can by no means receive them, or any of them, from traditional revelation. I say, *traditional revelation,* in distinction to *original revelation.* By the one, I mean that first impression which is made immediately by God on the mind of any man, to which we cannot set any bounds; and by the other, those impressions delivered over to others in words, and the ordinary ways of conveying our conceptions one to another.

4. *Secondly, Traditional Revelation may make us know Propositions knowable also by Reason, but not with the same Certainty that Reason doth.*——*Secondly,* I say that *the same truths may be discovered, and conveyed down from revelation, which are discoverable to us by reason, and by those ideas we naturally may have.* So God might, by revelation, discover the truth of any proposition in Euclid; as well as men, by the natural use of their faculties, come to make the discovery themselves. In all things of this kind there is little need or use of revelation, God having furnished us with natural and surer means to arrive at the knowledge of them. For whatsoever truth we come to the clear discovery of, from the knowledge and contemplation of our own ideas, will always be certainer to us than those which are conveyed to us by *traditional revelation.* For the knowledge we have that this revelation came at first from God, can never be so sure as the knowledge we have from the clear and distinct perception of the agreement or disagreement of our own ideas: v.g. if it were revealed some ages since, that the three angles of a triangle were equal to two right ones, I might assent to the truth of that proposition, upon the credit of the tradition, that it was revealed: but that would never amount to so great a certainty as the knowledge of it, upon the comparing and measuring my own ideas of two right angles, and the three angles of a triangle. The like holds in matter of fact knowable by our senses; v.g. the history of the deluge is conveyed to us by writings which had their original from revelation: and yet nobody, I think, will say he has as certain and clear a knowledge of the flood as Noah, that saw it; or that he himself would have had, had he then been alive and seen it. For he has no greater an assurance than that of his senses, that it is writ in the book supposed writ by Moses inspired: but he has not so great an assurance that Moses wrote that book as if he had seen Moses write it. So that the assurance of its being a revelation is less still than the assurance of his senses.

5. *Even Original Revelation cannot be admitted against the clear Evidence of Reason.*——In propositions, then, whose certainty is built upon the clear perception of the agreement or disagreement of our ideas, attained either by immediate intuition, as in self-evident propositions, or by evident deductions of reason in demonstrations we need not the assistance of revelation, as necessary to gain our assent, and introduce them into our minds. Because the natural ways of knowledge

could settle them there, or had done it already; which is the greatest assurance we can possibly have of anything, unless where God immediately reveals it to us: and there too our assurance can be no greater than our knowledge is, that it *is* a revelation from God. But yet nothing, I think, can, under that title, shake or overrule plain knowledge; or rationally prevail with any man to admit it for true, in a direct contradiction to the clear evidence of his own understanding. For, since no evidence of our faculties, by which we receive such revelations, can exceed, if equal, the certainty of our intuitive knowledge, we can never receive for a truth anything that is directly contrary to our clear and distinct knowledge; v.g. the ideas of one body and one place do so clearly agree, and the mind has so evident a perception of their agreement, that we can never assent to a proposition that affirms the same body to be in two distant places at once, however it should pretend to the authority of a divine revelation: since the evidence, first, that we deceive not ourselves, in ascribing it to God; secondly, that we understand it right; can never be so great as the evidence of our own intuitive knowledge, whereby we discern it impossible for the same body to be in two places at once. And therefore *no proposition can be received for divine revelation, or obtain the assent due to all such, if it be contradictory to our clear intuitive knowledge*. Because this would be to subvert the principles and foundations of all knowledge, evidence, and assent whatsoever: and there would be left no difference between truth and falsehood, no measures of credible and incredible in the world, if doubtful propositions shall take place before self-evident; and what we certainly know give way to what we may possibly be mistaken in. In propositions therefore contrary to the clear perception of the agreement or disagreement of any of our ideas, it will be in vain to urge them as matters of faith. They cannot move our assent under that or any other title whatsoever. For faith can never convince us of anything that contradicts our knowledge. Because, though faith be founded on the testimony of God (who cannot lie) revealing any proposition to us: yet we cannot have an assurance of the truth of its being a divine revelation greater than our own knowledge. Since the whole strength of the certainty depends upon our knowledge that God revealed it; which, in this case, where the proposition supposed revealed contradicts our knowledge or reason, will always have this objection hanging to it, viz. that we cannot tell how to conceive that to come from God, the bountiful Author of our being, which, if received for true, must overturn all the principles and foundations of knowledge he has given us; render all our faculties useless; wholly destroy the most excellent part of his workmanship, our understandings; and put a man in a condition wherein he will have less light, less conduct than the beast that perisheth. For if the mind of man can never have a clearer (and perhaps not so clear) evidence of anything to be a divine revelation, as it has of the principles of its own reason, it can never have a ground to quit the clear evidence of its reason, to give a place to a proposition, whose revelation has not a greater evidence than those principles have.

6. *Traditional Revelation much less.*——Thus far a man has use of reason, and ought to hearken to it, even in immediate and original revelation, where it is supposed to be made to himself. But to all those who pretend not to immediate revelation, but are required to pay obedience, and to receive the truths revealed to others, which, by the tradition of writings, or word of mouth, are conveyed down to them, reason has a great deal more to do, and is that only which can induce us to receive them. For matter of faith being only divine revelation, and nothing else, faith, as we use the word, (called commonly *divine faith*), has to do with no propositions, but those which are supposed to be divinely revealed. So that I do not see how those who make revelation alone the sole object of faith can say, That it is a matter of faith, and not of reason, to believe that such or such a proposition, to be found in such or such a book, is of divine inspiration; unless it be revealed that that proposition, or all in that book, was communicated by divine inspiration. Without such a revelation, the believing, or not believing, that proposition, or book, to be of divine authority, can never be matter of faith, but matter of reason; and such as I must come to an assent to only by the use of my reason, which can never require or enable me to believe that which is contrary to itself: it being impossible for reason ever to procure any assent to that which to itself appears unreasonable.

In all things, therefore, where we have clear evidence from our ideas, and those principles of knowledge I have above mentioned, reason is the proper judge; and revelation, though it may, in consenting with it, confirm its dictates, yet cannot in such cases invalidate its decrees: nor can we be obliged, where we have the clear and evident sentence of reason, to quit it for the contrary opinion, under a pretence that it is matter of faith: which can have no authority against the plain and clear dictates of reason.

7. *Thirdly, Things above Reason are, when revealed, the proper matter of faith.*——But, *Thirdly,* There being many things wherein we have very imperfect notions, or none at all; and other things, of whose past, present, or future existence, by the natural use of our faculties, we can have no knowledge at all; these, as being beyond the discovery of our natural faculties, and *above reason,* are, when revealed, *the proper matter of faith.* Thus, that part of the angels rebelled against God, and thereby lost their first happy state: and that the dead shall rise, and live again: these and the like, being beyond the discovery of reason, are purely matters of faith, with which reason has directly nothing to do.

8. *Or not contrary to Reason, if revealed, are Matter of Faith; and must carry it against probable conjectures of Reason.*——But since God, in giving us the light of reason, has not thereby tied up his own hands from affording us, when he thinks fit, the light of revelation in any of those matters wherein our natural faculties are able to give a probable determination; *revelation,* where God has been pleased to give it, *must carry it against the probable conjectures of reason.* Because the mind not being certain of the truth of that it does not evidently know, but only yielding to the probability that appears in it, is bound to give up its assent to such a testimony which, it is satisfied, comes from one who cannot err, and will not deceive. But yet, it still belongs to reason to judge of the truth of its being a revelation, and of the signification of the words wherein it is delivered. Indeed, if anything shall be thought revelation which is contrary to the plain principles of reason, and the evident knowledge the mind has of its own clear and distinct ideas; there reason must be hearkened to, as to a matter within its province. Since a man can never have so certain a knowledge, that a proposition which contradicts the clear principles and evidence of his own knowledge was divinely revealed, or that he understands the words rightly wherein it is delivered, as he has that the contrary is true, and so is bound to consider and judge of it as a matter of reason, and not swallow it, without examination, as a matter of faith.

9. *Revelation in Matters where Reason cannot judge, or but probably, ought to be hearkened to.*——First, Whatever proposition is revealed, of whose truth our mind, by its natural faculties and notions, cannot judge, that is purely matter of faith, and above reason.

Secondly, All propositions whereof the mind, by the use of its natural faculties, can come to determine and judge, from naturally acquired ideas, are matter of reason; with this difference still, that, in those concerning which it has but an uncertain evidence, and so is persuaded of their truth only upon probable grounds, which still admit a possibility of the contrary to be true, without doing violence to the certain evidence of its own knowledge, and overturning the principles of all reason; in such probable propositions, I say, an evident revelation ought to determine our assent, even against probability. For where the principles of reason have not evidenced a proposition to be certainly true or false, there clear revelation, as another principle of truth and ground of assent, may determine; and so it may be matter of faith, and be also above reason. Because reason, in that particular matter, being able to reach no higher than probability, faith gave the determination where reason came short; and revelation discovered on which side the truth lay.

10. *In Matters where Reason can afford certain Knowledge, that is to be hearkened to.*——Thus far the dominion of faith reaches, and that without any violence or hindrance to reason; which is not injured or disturbed, but assisted and improved by new discoveries of truth, coming from the eternal fountain of all knowledge. Whatever God hath revealed is certainly true: no doubt can be made of it. This is the proper object of faith: but whether it be a *divine* revelation or no, reason must judge; which can never permit the mind to reject a greater evidence to embrace what is less evident, nor allow it to entertain probability in opposition to knowledge and certainty. There can be no evidence that any traditional revelation is of divine original, in the words we receive it, and in the sense we understand it, so clear and so certain as that of the principles of reason: and therefore *Nothing that is contrary to, and inconsistent with, the clear and self-evident dictates of reason, has a right to be urged or assented to as a matter of faith, wherein reason hath nothing to do.* Whatsoever is divine revelation, ought to overrule all our opinions, prejudices, and interest, and hath a right to be received with full assent. Such

a submission as this, of our reason to faith, takes not away the landmarks of knowledge: this shakes not the foundations of reason, but leaves us that use of our faculties for which they were given us.

11. *If the Boundaries be not set between Faith and Reason, no Enthusiasm or Extravagancy in Religion can be contradicted.*——If the provinces of faith and reason are not kept distinct by these boundaries, there will, in matters of religion, be no room for reason at all; and those extravagant opinions and ceremonies that are to be found in the several religions of the world will not deserve to be blamed. For, to this crying up of faith in *opposition* to reason, we may, I think, in good measure ascribe those absurdities that fill almost all the religions which possess and divide mankind. For men having been principled with an opinion, that they must not consult reason in the things of religion, however apparently contradictory to common sense and the very principles of all their knowledge, have let loose their fancies and natural superstition; and have been by them led into so strange opinions, and extravagant practices in religion, that a considerate man cannot but stand amazed at their follies, and judge them so far from being acceptable to the great and wise God, that he cannot avoid thinking them ridiculous and offensive to a sober good man. So that, in effect, religion, which should most distinguish us from beasts, and ought most peculiarly to elevate us, as rational creatures, above brutes, is that wherein men often appear most irrational, and more senseless than beasts themselves. *Credo, quia impossibile est*: I believe, because it is impossible, might, in a good man, pass for a sally of zeal; but would prove a very ill rule for men to choose their opinions or religion by.

CHAPTER XIX.

OF ENTHUSIASM.

1. *Love of Truth necessary.*——He that would seriously set upon the search of truth, ought in the first place to prepare his mind with a love of it. For he that loves it not, will not take much pains to get it; nor be much concerned when he

misses it. There is nobody in the commonwealth of learning who does not profess himself a lover of truth: and there is not a rational creature that would not take it amiss to be thought otherwise of. And yet, for all this, one may truly say, that there are very few lovers of truth, for truth's sake, even amongst those who persuade themselves that they are so. How a man may know whether he be so in earnest, is worth inquiry: and I think there is one unerring mark of it, viz. The not entertaining any proposition with greater assurance than the proofs it is built upon will warrant. Whoever goes beyond this measure of assent, it is plain receives not the truth in the love of it; loves not truth for truth's sake, but for some other bye-end. For the evidence that any proposition is true (except such as are self-evident) lying only in the proofs a man has of it, whatsoever degrees of assent he affords it beyond the degrees of that evidence, it is plain that all the surplusage of assurance is owing to some other affection, and not to the love of truth: it being as impossible that the love of truth should carry my assent above the evidence there is to me, that it is true, as that the love of truth should make me assent to any proposition for the sake of that evidence which it has not, that it is true: which is in effect to love it as a truth, because it is possible or probable that it may not be true. In any truth that gets not possession of our minds by the irresistible light of self-evidence, or by the force of demonstration, the arguments that gain it assent are the vouchers and gage of its probability to us; and we can receive it for no other than such as they deliver it to our understandings. Whatsoever credit or authority we give to any proposition more than it receives from the principles and proofs it supports itself upon, is owing to our inclinations that way, and is so far a derogation from the love of truth as such: which, as it can receive no evidence from our passions or interests, so it should receive no tincture from them.

2. *A Forwardness to dictate another's beliefs, from whence.* ——The assuming an authority of dictating to others, and a forwardness to prescribe to their opinions, is a constant concomitant of this bias and corruption of our judgments. For how almost can it be otherwise, but that he should be ready to impose on another's belief, who has already imposed on his own? Who can reasonably expect arguments and conviction from him in dealing with others, whose understanding is not accustomed to them in his dealing with himself? Who does

violence to his own faculties, tyrannizes over his own mind, and usurps the prerogative that belongs to truth alone, which is to command assent by only its own authority, i.e. by and in proportion to that evidence which it carries with it.

3. *Force of Enthusiasm, in which reason is taken away.*——Upon this occasion I shall take the liberty to consider *a third ground of assent*, which with some men has the same authority, and is as confidently relied on as either faith or reason; I mean *enthusiasm*: which, laying by reason, would set up revelation without it. Whereby in effect it takes away both reason and revelation, and substitutes in the room of them the ungrounded fancies of a man's own brain, and assumes them for a foundation both of opinion and conduct.

4. *Reason and Revelation.*——*Reason* is *natural revelation*, whereby the eternal Father of light and fountain of all knowledge, communicates to mankind that portion of truth which he has laid within the reach of their natural faculties: *revelation* is *natural reason enlarged* by a new set of discoveries communicated by God immediately; which reason vouches the truth of, by the testimony and proofs it gives that they come from God. So that he that takes away reason to make way for revelation, puts out the light of both, and does muchwhat the same as if he would persuade a man to put out his eyes, the better to receive the remote light of an invisible star by a telescope.

5. *Rise of Enthusiasm.*——Immediate revelation being a much easier way for men to establish their opinions and regulate their conduct, than the tedious and not always successful labour of strict reasoning, it is no wonder that some have been very apt to pretend to revelation, and to persuade themselves that they are under the peculiar guidance of heaven in their actions and opinions, especially in those of them which they cannot account for by the ordinary methods of knowledge and principles of reason. Hence we see, that, in all ages, men in whom melancholy has mixed with devotion, or whose conceit of themselves has raised them into an opinion of a greater familiarity with God, and a nearer admittance to his favour than is afforded to others, have often flattered themselves with a persuasion of an immediate intercourse with the Deity, and frequent communications from the Divine Spirit. God, I own, cannot be denied to be able to enlighten the understanding by a ray darted into the mind immediately from the fountain of light: this they understand he has promised to do,

and who then has so good a title to expect it as those who are his peculiar people, chosen by him, and depending on him?

6. *Enthusiastic impulse.*——Their minds being thus prepared, whatever groundless opinion comes to settle itself strongly upon their fancies, is an illumination from the Spirit of God, end presently of divine authority: and whatsoever odd action they find in themselves a strong inclination to do, that impulse is concluded to be a call or direction from heaven, and must be obeyed: it is a commission from above, and they cannot err in executing it.

7. *What is meant by Enthusiasm.*——This I take to be properly *enthusiasm*, which, though founded neither on reason nor divine revelation, but rising from the conceits of a warmed or overweening brain, works yet, where it once gets footing, more powerfully on the persuasions and actions of men than either of those two, or both together: men being most forwardly obedient to the impulses they receive from themselves; and the whole man is sure to act more vigorously where the whole man is carried by a natural motion. For strong conceit, like a new principle, carries all easily with it, when got above common sense, and freed from all restraint of reason and check of reflection, it is heightened into a divine authority, in concurrence with our own temper and inclination.

8. *Enthusiasm accepts its supposed illumination without search and proof.*——Though the odd opinions and extravagant actions enthusiasm has run men into were enough to warn them against this wrong principle, so apt to misguide them both in their belief and conduct: yet the love of something extraordinary, the ease and glory it is to be inspired, and be above the common and natural ways of knowledge, so flatters many men's laziness, ignorance, and vanity, that, when once they are got into this way of immediate revelation, of illumination without search, and of certainty without proof and without examination, it is a hard matter to get them out of it. Reason is lost upon them, they are above it: they see the light infused into their understandings, and cannot be mistaken; it is clear and visible there, like the light of bright sunshine; shows itself, and needs no other proof but its own evidence: they feel the hand of God moving them within, and the impulses of the Spirit, and cannot be mistaken in what they feel. Thus they support themselves, and are sure

reasoning hath nothing to do with what they see and feel in themselves: what they have a sensible experience of admits no doubt, needs no probation. Would he not be ridiculous, who should require to have it proved to him that the light shines, and that he sees it? It is its own proof, and can have no other. When the Spirit brings light into our minds, it dispels darkness. We see it as we do that of the sun at noon, and need not the twilight of reason to show it us. This light from heaven is strong, clear, and pure; carries its own demonstration with it: and we may as naturally take a glow-worm to assist us to discover the sun, as to examine the celestial ray by our dim candle, reason.

9. *Enthusiasm how to be discovered.*——This is the way of talking of these men: they are sure, because they are sure: and their persuasions are right, because they are strong in them. For, when what they say is stripped of the metaphor of seeing and feeling, this is all it amounts to: and yet these similes so impose on them, that they serve them for certainty in themselves, and demonstration to others.

10. *The supposed internal Light examined.*——But to examine a little soberly this internal light, and this feeling on which they build so much. These men have, they say, clear light, and they see; they have awakened sense, and they feel: this cannot, they are sure, be disputed them. For when a man says he sees or feels, nobody can deny him that he does so. But here let me ask: This seeing, is it the perception of the truth of the proposition, or of this, that it is a revelation from God? This feeling, is it a perception of an inclination or fancy to do something, or of the Spirit of God moving that inclination? These are two very different perceptions, and must be carefully distinguished, if we would not impose upon ourselves. I may perceive the truth of a proposition, and yet not perceive that it is an immediate revelation from God. I may perceive the truth of a proposition in Euclid, without its being, or my perceiving it to be, a revelation: nay, I may perceive I came not by this knowledge in a natural way, and so may conclude it revealed, without perceiving that it is a revelation of God. Because there be spirits which, without being divinely commissioned, may excite those ideas in me, and lay them in such order before my mind, that I may perceive their connexion. So that the knowledge of any proposition coming into my mind, I know not how, is not a perception that it is from God. Much less is a strong persuasion that it

is true, a perception that it is from God, or so much as true. But however it be called light and seeing, I suppose it is at most but belief and assurance: and the proposition taken for a revelation, is not such as they *know* to be true, but *take* to be true. For where a proposition is known to be true, revelation is needless: and it is hard to conceive how there can be a revelation to any one of what he knows already. If therefore it be a proposition which they are persuaded, but do not know, to be true, whatever they may call it, it is not seeing, but believing. For these are two ways whereby truth comes into the mind, wholly distinct, so that one is not the other. What I see, I know to be so, by the evidence of the thing itself: what I believe, I take to be so upon the testimony of another. But this testimony I must know to be given, or else what ground have I of believing? I must see that it is God that reveals this to me, or else I see nothing. The question then here is: How do I know that God is the revealer of this to me; that this impression is made upon my mind by his Holy Spirit; and that therefore I ought to obey it? If I know not this, how great soever the assurance is that I am possessed with, it is groundless; whatever light I pretend to, it is but *enthusiasm*. For, whether the proposition supposed to be revealed be in itself evidently true, or visibly probable, or, by the natural ways of knowledge, uncertain, the proposition that must be well grounded and manifested to be true, is this, That God is the revealer of it, and that what I take to be a revelation is certainly put into my mind by Him, and is not an illusion dropped in by some other spirit, or raised by my own fancy. For, if I mistake not, these men receive it for true, because they presume God revealed it. Does it not, then, stand them upon to examine upon what grounds they presume it to be a revelation from God? or else all their confidence is mere presumption: and this light they are so dazzled with is nothing but an *ignis fatuus*, that leads them constantly round in this circle; *It is a revelation, because they firmly believe it*; and *they believe it, because it is a revelation.*

11. *Enthusiasm fails of Evidence, that the Proposition is from God.*——In all that is of divine revelation, there is need of no other proof but that it is an inspiration from God: for he can neither deceive nor be deceived. But how shall it be known that any proposition in our minds is a truth infused by God; a truth that is revealed to us by him, which he declares to us, and therefore we ought to believe? Here it is

that enthusiasm fails of the evidence it pretends to. For men thus possessed, boast of a light whereby they say they are enlightened, and brought into the knowledge of this or that truth. But if they know it to be a truth, they must know it to be so, either by its own self-evidence to natural reason, or by the rational proofs that make it out to be so. If they see and know it to be a truth, either of these two ways they in vain suppose it to be a revelation. For they know it to be true the same way that any other man naturally may know that it is so, without the help of revelation. For thus, all the truths, of what kind soever, that men uninspired are enlightened with, came into their minds, and are established there. If they say they know it to be true, because it is a revelation from God, the reason is good: but then it will be demanded how they know it to be a revelation from God. If they say, by the light it brings with it, which shines bright in their minds, and they cannot resist: I beseech them to consider whether this be any more than what we have taken notice of already, viz. that it is a revelation, because they strongly believe it to be true. For all the light they speak of is but a strong, though ungrounded persuasion of their own minds, that it is a truth. For rational grounds from proofs that it is a truth, they must acknowledge to have none; for then it is not received as a revelation, but upon the ordinary grounds that other truths are received: and if they believe it to be true because it is a revelation, and have no other reason for its being a revelation, but because they are fully persuaded, without any other reason, that it is true, then they believe it to be a revelation only because they strongly believe it to be a revelation; which is a very unsafe ground to proceed on, either in our tenets or actions. And what readier way can there be to run ourselves into the most extravagant errors and miscarriages, than thus to set up fancy for our supreme and sole guide, and to believe any proposition to be true, any action to be right, only because we believe it to be so? The strength of our persuasions is no evidence at all of their own rectitude: crooked things may be as stiff and inflexible as straight: and men may be as positive and peremptory in error as in truth. How come else the untractable zealots in different and opposite parties? For if the light, which every one thinks he has in his mind, which in this case is nothing but the strength of his own persuasion, be an evidence that it is from God, contrary opinions have the same title to be inspirations; and God will be not only the Father of lights, but of opposite and contradictory lights, leading men contrary ways; and contradictory propositions will be divine truths, if an ungrounded strength of assurance be an evidence that any proposition is a Divine Revelation.

12. *Firmness of Persuasion no Proof that any Proposition is from God.*——This cannot be otherwise, whilst firmness of persuasion is made the cause of believing, and confidence of being in the right is made an argument of truth. St. Paul himself believed he did well, and that he had a call to it, when he persecuted the Christians, whom he confidently thought in the wrong: but yet it was he, and not they, who were mistaken. Good men are men still liable to mistakes, and are sometimes warmly engaged in errors, which they take for divine truths, shining in their minds with the clearest light.

13. *Light in the Mind, what.*——Light, true light, in the mind is, or can be, nothing else but the evidence of the truth of any proposition; and if it be not a self-evident proposition, all the light it has, or can have, is from the clearness and validity of those proofs upon which it is received. To talk of any other light in the understanding is to put ourselves in the dark, or in the power of the Prince of Darkness, and, by our own consent, to give ourselves up to delusion to believe a lie. For, if strength of persuasion be the light which must guide us; I ask how shall any one distinguish between the delusions of Satan, and the inspirations of the Holy Ghost? He can transform himself into an angel of light. And they who are led by this Son of the Morning are as fully satisfied of the illumination, i.e. are as strongly persuaded that they are enlightened by the Spirit of God as any one who is so: they acquiesce and rejoice in it, are actuated by it: and nobody can be more sure, nor more in the right (if their own strong belief may be judge) than they.

14. *Revelation must be judged of by Reason.*——He, therefore, that will not give himself up to all the extravagances of delusion and error must bring this guide of his *light within* to the trial. God when he makes the prophet does not unmake the man. He leaves all his faculties in the natural state, to enable him to judge of his inspirations, whether they be of *divine* original or no. When he illuminates the mind with supernatural light, he does not extinguish that which is natural. If he would have us assent to the truth of any proposi-

tion, he either evidences that truth by the usual methods of natural reason, or else makes it known to be a truth which he would have us assent to by his authority, and convinces us that it is from him, by some marks which reason cannot be mistaken in. *Reason must be our last judge and guide in everything.* I do not mean that we must consult reason, and examine whether a proposition revealed from God can be made out by natural principles, and if it cannot, that then we may reject it: but consult it we must, and by it examine whether it be a revelation from God or no: and if reason finds it to be revealed from God, reason then declares for it as much as for any other truth, and makes it one of her dictates. Every conceit that thoroughly warms our fancies must pass for an inspiration, if there be nothing but the strength of our persuasions, whereby to judge of our persuasions: if reason must not examine their truth by something extrinsical to the persuasions themselves, inspirations and delusions, truth and falsehood, will have the same measure, and will not be possible to be distinguished.

George Berkeley

A TREATISE CONCERNING THE PRINCIPLES OF HUMAN KNOWLEDGE

PREFACE

What I here make public has, after a long and scrupulous inquiry, seemed to me evidently true, and not unuseful to be known, particularly to those who are tainted with scepticism, or want a demonstration of the existence and immateriality of God, or the natural immortality of the soul. Whether it be so or no, I am content the reader should impartially examine; since I do not think myself any further concerned for the success of what I written than as it is agreeable to truth. But to the end this may not suffer, I make it my request that the reader suspend his judgment till he has once, at least, read the whole through with that degree of attention and thought which the subject matter shall seem to deserve. For as there are some passages that, taken by themselves, are very liable (nor could it be remedied) to gross misinterpretation, and to be charged with most absurd consequences, which, nevertheless, upon an entire perusal will appear not to follow from them: so likewise, though the whole should be read over, yet if this be done transiently, it is very probable my sense may be mistaken; but to a thinking reader, I flatter myself, it will be throughout clear and obvious. As for the characters of novelty and singularity, which some of the following notions may seem to bear, it is, I hope, needless to make any apology on that account. He must surely be either very weak, or very little acquainted with the sciences, who shall reject a truth that is capable of demonstration, for no other reason but because it is newly known and contrary to the prejudices of mankind. Thus much I thought fit to premise, in order to prevent, if possible, the hasty censures of a sort of men, who are too apt to condemn an opinion before they rightly comprehend it.

INTRODUCTION

Philosophy being nothing else but the study of wisdom and truth, it may with reason be expected that those who have spent most time and pains in it should enjoy a greater calm and serenity of mind, a greater clearness and evidence of knowledge, and be less disturbed with doubts and difficulties than other men. Yet so it is, we see the illiterate bulk of mankind that walk the highroad of plain common sense, and are governed by the dictates of nature, for the most part easy and undisturbed. To them nothing that is familiar appears unaccountable or difficult to comprehend. They complain not of any want of evidence in their senses, and are out of all danger of becoming sceptics. But no sooner do we depart from sense and instinct to follow the light of a superior principle, to reason, meditate, and reflect on the nature of things, but a thousand scruples spring up in our minds concerning those things which before we seemed fully to comprehend. Prejudices and errors of sense do from all parts discover themselves to our view; and, endeavoring to correct these by reason, we are insensibly drawn into uncouth paradoxes, difficulties, and inconsistencies, which multiply and grow upon us as we advance in speculation, till at length, having wandered through many intricate mazes, we find ourselves just where we were, or, which is worse, sit down in a forlorn scepticism.

2. The cause of this is thought to be the obscurity of things, or the natural weakness and imperfection of our understandings. It is said the faculties we have are few, and those designed by nature for the support and comfort of life, and not to penetrate into the inward essence and constitution of things. Besides, the mind of man being finite, when it treats of things which partake of infinity it is not to be wondered at if it run into absurdities and contradictions, out of which it is impossible it should ever extricate itself, it being of the nature of infinite not to be comprehended by that which is finite.

3. But perhaps we may be too partial to ourselves in placing the fault originally in our faculties, and not rather in the wrong use we make of them. It is a hard thing to suppose

that right deductions from true principles should ever end in consequences which cannot be maintained or made consistent. We should believe that God has dealt more bountifully with the sons of men than to give them a strong desire for that knowledge which he had placed quite out of their reach. This were not agreeable to the wonted indulgent methods of Providence, which whatever appetites it may have implanted in the creatures, doth usually furnish them with such means as, if rightly made use of, will not fail to satisfy them. Upon the whole, I am inclined to think that the far greater part, if not all, of those difficulties which have hitherto amused philosophers, and blocked up the way to knowledge, are entirely owing to ourselves—that we have first raised a dust and then complain we cannot see.

4. My purpose therefore is, to try if I can discover what those principles are which have introduced all that doubtfulness and uncertainty, those absurdities and contradictions, into the several sects of philosophy; insomuch that the wisest men have thought our ignorance incurable, conceiving it to arise from the natural dullness and limitation of our faculties. And surely it is a work well deserving our pains to make a strict inquiry concerning the first principles of human knowledge, to sift and examine them on all sides, especially since there may be some grounds to suspect that those lets and difficulties, which stay and embarrass the mind in its search after truth, do not spring from any darkness and intricacy in the objects, or natural defect in the understanding, so much as from false principles which have been insisted on, and might have been avoided.

5. How difficult and discouraging soever this attempt may seem, when I consider how many great and extraordinary men have gone before me in the like designs, yet I am not without some hopes, upon the consideration that the largest views are not always the clearest, and that he who is short-sighted will be obliged to draw the object nearer, and may, perhaps, by a close and narrow survey, discern that which had escaped far better eyes.

6. In order to prepare the mind of the reader for the easier conceiving what follows, it is proper to premise somewhat, by way of introduction, concerning the nature and abuse of language. But the unraveling this matter leads me in some measure to anticipate my design, by taking notice of what seems to have had a chief part in rendering speculation intricate

and perplexed, and to have occasioned innumerable errors and difficulties in almost all parts of knowledge. And that is the opinion that the mind hath a power of framing *abstract ideas* or notions of things. He who is not a perfect stranger to the writings and disputes of philosophers must needs acknowledge that no small part of them are spent about abstract ideas. These are in a more especial manner thought to be the object of those sciences which go by the name of *logic* and *metaphysics*, and of all that which passes under the notion of the most abstracted and sublime learning, in all which one shall scarce find any question handled in such a manner as does not suppose their existence in the mind, and that it is well acquainted with them.

7. It is agreed on all hands that the qualities or modes of things do never really exist each of them apart by itself, and separated from all others, but are mixed, as it were, and blended together, several in the same object. But, we are told, the mind being able to consider each quality singly, or abstracted from those other qualities with which it is united, does by that means frame to itself abstract ideas. For example, there is perceived by sight an object extended, colored, and moved: this mixed or compound idea the mind resolving into its simple, constituent parts, and viewing each by itself, exclusive of the rest, does frame the abstract ideas of extension, color, and motion. Not that it is possible for color or motion to exist without extension; but only that the mind can frame to itself by *abstraction* the idea of color exclusive of extension, and of motion exclusive of both color and extension.

8. Again, the mind having observed that in the particular extensions perceived by sense there is something common and alike in all, and some other things peculiar, as this or that figure or magnitude, which distinguish them one from another; it considers apart or singles out by itself that which is common, making thereof a most abstract idea of extension, which is neither line, surface, nor solid, nor has any figure or magnitude, but is an idea entirely prescinded from all these. So likewise the mind, by leaving out of the particular colors perceived by sense that which distinguishes them one from another, and retaining that only which is common to all, makes an idea of color in abstract which is neither red, nor blue, nor white, nor any other determinate color. And, in like manner, by considering motion abstractedly not only from

the body moved, but likewise from the figure it describes, and all particular directions and velocities, the abstract idea of motion is framed; which equally corresponds to all particular motions whatsoever that may be perceived by sense.

9. And as the mind frames to itself abstract ideas of qualities or modes, so does it, by the same precision or mental separation, attain abstract ideas of the more compounded beings which include several coexistent qualities. For example, the mind having observed that Peter, James, and John resemble each other in certain common agreements of shape and other qualities, leaves out of the complex or compounded idea it has of Peter, James, and any other particular man, that which is peculiar to each, retaining only what is common to all, and so makes an abstract idea wherein all the particulars equally partake; abstracting entirely from and cutting off all those circumstances and differences which might determine it to any particular existence. And after this manner it is said we come by the abstract idea of man, or, if you please, humanity, or human nature; wherein it is true there is included color, because there is no man but has some color, but then it can be neither white, nor black, nor any particular color, because there is no one particular color wherein all men partake. So likewise there is included stature, but then it is neither tall stature, nor low stature, nor yet middle stature, but something abstracted from all these. And so of the rest. Moreover, there being a great variety of other creatures that partake in some parts, but not all, of the complex idea of man, the mind, leaving out those parts which are peculiar to men, and retaining those only which are common to all the living creatures, frames the idea of *animal*, which abstracts not only from all particular men, but also all birds, beasts, fishes, and insects. The constituent parts of the abstract idea of animal are body, life, sense, and spontaneous motion. By *body* is meant body without any particular shape or figure, there being no one shape or figure common to all animals, without covering, either of hair, or feathers, or scales, etc., nor yet naked: hair, feathers, scales, and nakedness being the distinguishing properties of particular animals, and for that reason left out of the *abstract idea*. Upon the same account the spontaneous motion must be neither walking, nor flying, nor creeping; it is nevertheless a motion, but what that motion is it is not easy to conceive.

10. Whether others have this wonderful faculty of abstract-

ing their ideas, they best can tell; for myself, I find indeed I have a faculty of imagining, or representing to myself, the ideas of those particular things I have perceived, and of variously compounding and dividing them. I can imagine a man with two heads, or the upper parts of a man joined to the body of a horse. I can consider the hand, the eye, the nose, each by itself abstracted or separated from the rest of the body. But then whatever hand or eye I imagine, it must have some particular shape and color. Likewise the idea of man that I frame to myself must be either of a white, or a black, or a tawny, a straight, or a crooked, a tall, or a low, or a middle-sized man. I cannot by any effort of thought conceive the abstract idea above described. And it is equally impossible for me to form the abstract idea of motion distinct from the body moving, and which is neither swift nor slow, curvilinear nor rectilinear; and the like may be said of all other abstract general ideas whatsoever. To be plain, I own myself able to abstract in one sense, as when I consider some particular parts or qualities separated from others, with which, though they are united in some object, yet it is possible they may really exist without them. But I deny that I can abstract from one another, or conceive separately, those qualities which it is impossible should exist so separated; or that I can frame a general notion, by abstracting from particulars in the manner aforesaid—which last are the two proper acceptations of 'abstraction.' And there are grounds to think most men will acknowledge themselves to be in my case. The generality of men which are simple and illiterate never pretend to abstract notions. It is said they are difficult and not to be attained without pains and study; we may therefore reasonably conclude that, if such there be, they are confined only to the learned.

11. I proceed to examine what can be alleged in defense of the doctrine of abstraction, and try if I can discover what it is that inclines the men of speculation to embrace an opinion so remote from common sense as that seems to be. There has been a late deservedly esteemed philosopher who, no doubt, has given it very much countenance, by seeming to think the having abstract general ideas is what puts the widest difference in point of understanding betwixt man and beast.

> The having of general ideas (saith he) is that which puts a perfect distinction betwixt man and brutes,

> and is an excellency which the faculties of brutes do by no means attain unto. For, it is evident we observe no footsteps in them of making use of general signs for universal ideas; from which we have reason to imagine that they have not the faculty of abstracting, or making general ideas, since they have no use of words or any other general signs.

And a little after:

> Therefore, I think, we may suppose that it is in this that the species of brutes are discriminated from men, and it is that proper difference wherein they are wholly separated, and which at last widens to so wide a distance. For, if they have any ideas at all, and are not bare machines (as some would have them), we cannot deny them to have some reason. It seems as evident to me that they do, some of them, in certain instances reason as that they have sense; but it is only in particular ideas, just as they receive them from their senses. They are the best of them tied up within those narrow bounds, and have not (as I think) the faculty to enlarge them by any kind of abstraction.

I readily agree with this learned author, that the faculties of brutes can by no means attain to abstraction. But then if this be made the distinguishing property of that sort of animals, I fear a great many of those that pass for men must be reckoned into their number. The reason that is here assigned why we have no grounds to think brutes have abstract general ideas is, that we observe in them no use of words or any other general signs; which is built on this supposition—that the making use of words implies the having general ideas. From which it follows that men who use language are able to abstract or generalize their ideas. That this is the sense and arguing of the author will further appear by his answering the question he in another place puts: "Since all things that exist are only particulars, how come we by general terms?" His answer is: "Words become general by being made the signs of general ideas." But it seems that a word becomes general by being made the sign, not of an abstract general idea, but of several particular ideas, any one of which it indifferently suggests to the mind. For example, when it is said "the change of motion is proportional to the impressed force," or that "whatever has extension is divisible," these propositions are to be understood of motion and extension in general; and nevertheless it will not follow that they suggest to my thoughts an idea of motion without a body moved, or any determinate direction and velocity, or that I must conceive an abstract general idea of extension, which is neither line, surface, nor solid, neither great nor small, black, white, nor red, nor of any other determinate color. It is only implied that whatever particular motion I consider, whether it be swift or slow, perpendicular, horizontal, or oblique, or in whatever object, the axiom concerning it holds equally true. As does the other of every particular extension, it matters not whether line, surface, or solid, whether of this or that magnitude or figure.

12. By observing how ideas become general we may the better judge how words are made so. And here it is to be noted that I do not deny absolutely there are general ideas, but only that there are any *abstract* general ideas; for in the passages we have quoted wherein there is mention of general ideas, it is always supposed that they are formed by abstraction, after the manner set forth in Sections 8 and 9. Now, if we will annex a meaning to our words, and speak only of what we can conceive, I believe we shall acknowledge that an idea which considered in itself is particular, becomes general by being made to represent or stand for all other particular ideas of the same sort. To make this plain by an example, suppose a geometrician is demonstrating the method of cutting a line in two equal parts. He draws, for instance, a black line of an inch in length: this, which in itself is a particular line, is nevertheless with regard to its signification general, since, as it is there used, it represents all particular lines whatsoever; so that what is demonstrated of it is demonstrated of all lines, or, in other words, of a line in general. And, as that particular line becomes general by being made a sign, so the *name* 'line,' which taken absolutely is particular, by being a sign is made general. And as the former owes its generality not to its being the sign of an abstract or general line, but of all particular right lines that may possibly exist, so the latter must be thought to derive its generality from the same cause, namely, the various particular lines which it indifferently denotes.

13. To give the reader a yet clearer view of the nature of abstract ideas and the uses they are thought necessary to, I

shall add one more passage out of the *Essay on Human Understanding*, which is as follows:

> *Abstract ideas* are not so obvious or easy to children or the yet unexercised mind as particular ones. If they seem so to grown men it is only because by constant and familiar use they are made so. For when we nicely reflect upon them, we shall find that general ideas are fictions and contrivances of the mind, that carry difficulty with them, and do not so easily offer themselves as we are apt to imagine. For example, does it not require some pains and skill to form the general idea of a triangle (which is yet none of the most abstract, comprehensive, and difficult); for it must be neither oblique nor rectangle, neither equilateral, equicrural, nor scalenon, but *all and none* of these at once? In effect, it is something imperfect that cannot exist, an idea wherein some parts of several different and *inconsistent* ideas are put together. It is true the mind in this imperfect state has need of such ideas, and makes all the haste to them it can, for the *conveniency of communication and enlargement of knowledge*, to both which it is naturally very much inclined. But yet one has reason to suspect such ideas are marks of our imperfection. At least this is enough to show that the most abstract and general ideas are not those that the mind is first and most easily acquainted with, nor such as its earliest knowledge is conversant about.

If any man has the faculty of framing in his mind such an idea of a triangle as is here described, it is in vain to pretend to dispute him out of it, nor would I go about it. All I desire is that the reader would fully and certainly inform himself whether he has such an idea or no. And this, methinks, can be no hard task for anyone to perform. What more easy than for anyone to look a little into his own thoughts, and there try whether he has, or can attain to have, an idea that shall correspond with the description that is here given of the general idea of a triangle, which is "neither oblique nor rectangle, equilateral, equicrural nor scalenon, but all and none of these at once"?

14. Much is here said of the difficulty that abstract ideas carry with them, and the pains and skill requisite to the form-

ing them. And it is on all hands agreed that there is need of great toil and labor of the mind, to emancipate our thoughts from particular objects, and raise them to those sublime speculations that are conversant about abstract ideas. From all which the natural consequence should seem to be, that so difficult a thing as the forming abstract ideas was not necessary for *communication*, which is so easy and familiar to all sorts of men. But, we are told, if they seem obvious and easy to grown men, it is only because by constant and familiar use they are made so. Now, I would fain know at what time it is men are employed in surmounting that difficulty, and furnishing themselves with those necessary helps for discourse. It cannot be when they are grown up, for then it seems they are not conscious of any such painstaking; it remains therefore to be the business of their childhood. And surely the great and multiplied labor of framing abstract notions will be found a hard task for that tender age. Is it not a hard thing to imagine that a couple of children cannot prate together of their sugar-plums and rattles and the rest of their little trinkets, till they have first tacked together numberless inconsistencies, and so framed in their minds abstract general ideas, and annexed them to every common name they make use of?

15. Nor do I think them a whit more needful for the enlargement of knowledge than for communication. It is, I know, a point much insisted on, that all knowledge and demonstration are about universal notions, to which I fully agree; but then it doth not appear to me that those notions are formed by abstraction in the manner premised: *universality*, so far as I can comprehend, not consisting in the absolute, *positive* nature or conception of anything, but in the *relation* it bears to the particulars signified or represented by it; by virtue whereof it is that things, names, or notions, being in their own nature *particular*, are rendered *universal*. Thus when I demonstrate any proposition concerning triangles, it is to be supposed that I have in view the universal idea of a triangle; which ought not to be understood as if I could frame an idea of a triangle which was neither equilateral, nor scalenon, nor equicrural; but only that the particular triangle I consider, whether of this or that sort it matters not, doth equally stand for and represent all rectilinear triangles whatsoever, and is in that sense *universal*. All which seems very plain and not to include any difficulty in it.

16. But here it will be demanded how we can know any

proposition to be true of all particular triangles, except we have first seen it demonstrated of the abstract idea of a triangle which equally agrees to all? For because a property may be demonstrated to agree to some one particular triangle, it will not thence follow that it equally belongs to any other triangle which in all respects is not the same with it. For example, having demonstrated that the three angles of an isosceles rectangular triangle are equal to two right ones, I cannot therefore conclude this affection agrees to all other triangles which have neither a right angle nor two equal sides. It seems therefore that, to be certain this proposition is universally true, we must either make a particular demonstration for every particular triangle, which is impossible, or once for all demonstrate it of the abstract idea of a triangle, in which all the particulars do indifferently partake and by which they are all equally represented. To which I answer, that, though the idea I have in view whilst I make the demonstration be, for instance, that of an isosceles rectangular triangle whose sides are of a determinate length, I may nevertheless be certain it extends to all other rectilinear triangles, of what sort or bigness soever. And that because neither the right angle nor the equality nor determinate length of the sides are at all concerned in the demonstration. It is true the diagram I have in view includes all these particulars, but then there is not the least mention made of them in the proof of the proposition. It is not said the three angles are equal to two right ones, because one of them is a right angle, or because the sides comprehending it are of the same length. Which sufficiently shows that the right angle might have been oblique and the sides unequal, and for all that the demonstration have held good. And for this reason it is that I conclude that to be true of any obliquangular or scalenon which I had demonstrated of a particular right-angled equicrural triangle, and not because I demonstrated the proposition of the abstract idea of a triangle. And here it must be acknowledged that a man may consider a figure merely as triangular, without attending to the particular qualities of the angles, or relations of the sides. So far he may abstract; but this will never prove that he can frame an abstract, general, inconsistent idea of a triangle. In like manner we may consider Peter so far forth as man, or so far forth as animal, without framing the forementioned abstract idea, either of man or of animal, inasmuch as all that is perceived is not considered.

17. It were an endless as well as an useless thing to trace the schoolmen, those great masters of abstraction, through all the manifold inextricable labyrinths of error and dispute which their doctrine of abstract natures and notions seems to have led them into. What bickerings and controversies, and what a learned dust have been raised about those matters, and what mighty advantage has been from thence derived to mankind, are things at this day too clearly known to need being insisted on. And it had been well if the ill effects of that doctrine were confined to those only who make the most avowed profession of it. When men consider the great pains, industry, and parts that have for so many ages been laid out on the cultivation and advancement of the sciences, and that notwithstanding all this the far greater part of them remains full of darkness and uncertainty, and disputes that are like never to have an end, and even those that are thought to be supported by the most clear and cogent demonstrations contain in them paradoxes which are perfectly irreconcilable to the understandings of men, and that, taking all together, a very small portion of them does supply any real benefit to mankind, otherwise than by being an innocent diversion and amusement—I say the consideration of all this is apt to throw them into a despondency and perfect contempt of all study. But this may perhaps cease upon a view of the false principles that have obtained in the world, amongst all which there is none, methinks, hath a more wide and extended sway over the thoughts of speculative men than this of *abstract* general ideas.

18. I come now to consider the *source* of this prevailing notion, and that seems to me to be *language*. And surely nothing of less extent than reason itself could have been the source of an opinion so universally received. The truth of this appears as from other reasons so also from the plain confession of the ablest patrons of abstract ideas, who acknowledge that they are made in order to naming; from which it is a clear consequence that if there had been no such thing as speech or universal signs there never had been any thought of abstraction. Let us examine the manner wherein words have contributed to the origin of that mistake. First, then, it is thought that every name has, or ought to have, one only precise and settled signification, which inclines men to think there are certain abstract, determinate ideas that constitute the true and only immediate signification of each general

name; and that it is by the mediation of these abstract ideas that a general name comes to signify any particular thing. Whereas, in truth, there is no such thing as one precise and definite signification annexed to any general name, they all signifying indifferently a great number of particular ideas. All which doth evidently follow from what has been already said, and will clearly appear to anyone by a little reflection. To this it will be objected that every name that has a definition is thereby restrained to one certain signification. For example, a triangle is defined to be 'a plane surface comprehended by three right lines,' by which that name is limited to denote one certain idea and no other. To which I answer that in the definition it is not said whether the surface be great or small, black or white, nor whether the sides are long or short, equal or unequal, nor with what angles they are inclined to each other; in all which there may be great variety, and consequently there is no one settled idea which limits the signification of the word triangle. It is one thing for to keep a name constantly to the same definition, and another to make it stand everywhere for the same idea; the one is necessary, the other useless and impracticable.

19. But to give a farther account how words came to produce the doctrine of abstract ideas, it must be observed that it is a received opinion that language has no other end but the communicating our ideas, and that every significant name stands for an idea. This being so and it being withal certain that names which yet are not thought altogether insignificant do not always mark out particular conceivable ideas, it is straightway concluded that they stand for abstract notions. That there are many names in use amongst speculative men which do not always suggest to others determinate, particular ideas, or in truth anything at all, is what nobody will deny. And a little attention will discover that it is not necessary (even in the strictest reasonings) significant names which stand for ideas should, every time they are used, excite in the understanding the ideas they are made to stand for: in reading and discoursing, names being for the most part used as letters are in algebra, in which, though a particular quantity be marked by each letter, yet to proceed right it is not requisite that in every step each letter suggest to your thoughts that particular quantity it was appointed to stand for.

20. Besides, the communicating of ideas marked by words is not the chief and only end of language, as is commonly sup-

posed. There are other ends, as the raising of some passion, the exciting to or deterring from an action, the putting the mind in some particular disposition; to which the former is in many cases barely subservient, and sometimes entirely omitted, when these can be obtained without it, as I think does not unfrequently happen in the familiar use of language. I entreat the reader to reflect with himself, and see if it doth not often happen, either in hearing or reading a discourse, that the passions of fear, love, hatred, admiration, disdain, and the like, arise immediately in his mind upon the perception of certain words, without any ideas coming between. At first, indeed, the words might have occasioned ideas that were fitting to produce those emotions; but, if I mistake not, it will be found that when language is once grown familiar, the hearing of the sounds or sight of the characters is oft immediately attended with those passions which at first were wont to be produced by the intervention of ideas that are now quite omitted. May we not, for example, be affected with the promise of a *good thing*, though we have not an idea of what it is? Or is not the being threatened with danger sufficient to excite a dread, though we think not of any particular evil likely to befall us, nor yet frame to ourselves an idea of danger in abstract? If anyone shall join ever so little reflection of his own to what has been said, I believe that it will evidently appear to him that general names are often used in the propriety of language without the speaker's designing them for marks of ideas in his own, which he would have them raise in the mind of the hearer. Even proper names themselves do not seem always spoken with a design to bring into our view the ideas of those individuals that are supposed to be marked by them. For example, when a schoolman tells me "Aristotle hath said it," all I conceive he means by it is to dispose me to embrace his opinion with the deference and submission which custom has annexed to that name. And this effect is often so instantly produced in the minds of those who are accustomed to resign their judgment to authority of that philosopher, as it is impossible any idea either of his person, writings, or reputation should go before. Innumerable examples of this kind may be given, but why should I insist on those things which everyone's experience will, I doubt not, plentifully suggest unto him?

21. We have, I think, shewn the impossibility of abstract ideas. We have considered what has been said of them by

their ablest patrons, and endeavored to show they are of no use for those ends to which they are thought necessary. And lastly, we have traced them to the source from whence they flow, which appears evidently to be language. It cannot be denied that words are of excellent use, in that by their means all that stock of knowledge which has been purchased by the joint labors of inquisitive men in all ages and nations may be drawn into the view and made the possession of one single person. But at the same time it must be owned that most parts of knowledge have been strangely perplexed and darkened by the abuse of words, and general ways of speech wherein they are delivered. Since therefore words are so apt to impose on the understanding, whatever ideas I consider, I shall endeavor to take them bare and naked into my view, keeping out of my thoughts so far as I am able those names which long and constant use hath so strictly united with them; from which I may expect to derive the following advantages:—

22. *First,* I shall be sure to get clear of all controversies *purely verbal*; the springing up of which weeds in almost all the sciences has been a main hindrance to the growth of true and sound knowledge. *Secondly,* this seems to be a sure way to extricate myself out of that fine and subtle net of *abstract ideas* which has so miserably perplexed and entangled the minds of men; and that with this peculiar circumstance, that by now much the finer and more curious was the wit of any man, by so much the deeper was he likely to be ensnared and faster held therein. *Thirdly,* so long as I confine my thoughts to my own ideas divested of words, I do not see how I can easily be mistaken. The objects I consider, I clearly and adequately know. I cannot be deceived in thinking I have an idea which I have not. It is not possible for me to imagine that any of my own ideas are alike or unlike that are not truly so. To discern the agreements or disagreements there are between my ideas, to see what ideas are included in any compound idea and what not, there is nothing more requisite than an attentive perception of what passes in my own understanding.

23. But the attainment of all these advantages doth *presuppose an entire deliverance from the deception of words,* which I dare hardly promise myself; so difficult a thing it is to dissolve an union so early begun, and confirmed by so long a habit as that betwixt words and ideas. Which difficulty seems

to have been very much increased by the doctrine of *abstraction*. For, so long as men thought abstract ideas were annexed to their words, it doth not seem strange that they should use words for ideas; it being found an impracticable thing to lay aside the word, and retain the abstract idea in the mind, which in itself was perfectly inconceivable. This seems to me the principal cause why those men who have so emphatically recommended to others the laying aside all use of words in their meditations, and contemplating their bare ideas, have yet failed to perform it themselves. Of late many have been very sensible of the absurd opinions and insignificant disputes which grow out of the abuse of words. And, in order to remedy these evils, they advise well that we attend to the ideas signified, and draw off our attention from the words which signify them. But how good soever this advice may be they have given others, it is plain they could not have a due regard to it themselves, so long as they thought the only immediate use of words was to signify ideas, and that the immediate signification of every general name was a determinate abstract idea.

24. But these being known to be mistakes, a man may with greater ease prevent his being imposed on by words. He that knows he has no other than particular ideas, will not puzzle himself in vain to find out and conceive the abstract idea annexed to any name. And he that knows names do not always stand for ideas will spare himself the labor of looking for ideas where there are none to be had. It were therefore to be wished that everyone would use his utmost endeavors to obtain a clear view of the ideas he would consider, separating from them all that dress and encumbrance of words which so much contribute to blind the judgment and divide the attention. In vain do we extend our view into the heavens and pry into the entrails of the earth, in vain do we consult the writings of learned men and trace the dark footsteps of antiquity; we need only draw the curtain of words, to hold the fairest tree of knowledge, whose fruit is excellent and within the reach of our hand.

25. Unless we take care to clear the first principles of knowledge from the embarrassment and delusion of words, we may make infinite reasonings upon them to no purpose: we may draw consequences from consequences, and be never the wiser. The farther we go, we shall only lose ourselves the more irrecoverably, and be the deeper entangled in difficulties

and mistakes. Whoever therefore designs to read the following sheets, I entreat him to make my words the occasion of his own thinking, and endeavor to attain the same train of thoughts in reading that I had in writing them. By this means it will be easy for him to discover the truth or falsity of what I say. He will be out of all danger of being deceived by my words, and I do not see how he can be led into an error by considering his own naked, undisguised ideas.

OF THE PRINCIPLES OF HUMAN KNOWLEDGE

It is evident to anyone who takes a survey of the objects of human knowledge, that they are either ideas (1) actually imprinted on the senses, or else such as are (2) perceived by attending to the passions and operations of the mind, or lastly (3) ideas formed by help of memory and imagination, either compounding, dividing, or barely representing those originally perceived in the aforesaid ways. By sight I have the ideas of lights and colors, with their several degrees and variations. By touch I perceive hard and soft, heat and cold, motion and resistance, and of all these more and less either as to quantity or degree. Smelling furnishes me with odors, the palate with tastes, and hearing conveys sounds to the mind in all their variety of tone and composition. And as several of these are observed to accompany each other, they come to be marked by one name, and so to be reputed as one thing. Thus, for example, a certain color, taste, smell, figure, and consistence, having been observed to go together, are accounted one distinct thing, signified by the name 'apple.' Other collections of ideas constitute a stone, a tree, a book, and the like sensible things; which, as they are pleasing or disagreeable, excite the passions of love, hatred, joy, grief, and so forth.

2. But besides all that endless variety of ideas or objects of knowledge, there is likewise something which knows or perceives them, and exercises divers operations, as willing, imagining, remembering, about them. This perceiving, active being is what I call *mind*, *spirit*, *soul*, or *myself*. By which words I do not denote any one of my ideas, but a thing entirely distinct from them wherein they exist, or, which is the

same thing, whereby they are perceived; for the existence of an idea consists in being perceived.

3. That neither our thoughts, nor passions, nor ideas formed by the imagination, exist without the mind, is what everybody will allow. And it seems no less evident that the various sensations or ideas imprinted on the sense, however blended or combined together (that is, whatever objects they compose), cannot exist otherwise than in a mind perceiving them. I think an intuitive knowledge may be obtained of this by anyone that shall attend to what is meant by the term 'exist' when applied to sensible things. The table I write on I say exists—that is, I see and feel it; and if I were out of my study I should say it existed—meaning thereby that if I was in my study I might perceive it, or that some other spirit actually does perceive it. There was an odor, that is, it was smelt; there was a sound, that is, it was heard; a color or figure, and it was perceived by sight or touch. This is all that I can understand by these and the like expressions. For as to what is said of the absolute existence of unthinking things without any relation to their being perceived, that seems perfectly unintelligible. Their *esse* is *percipi*, nor is it possible they should have any existence out of the minds or thinking things which perceive them.

4. It is indeed an opinion strangely prevailing amongst men, that houses, mountains, rivers, and in a word all sensible objects, have an existence, natural or real, distinct from their being perceived by the understanding. But with how great an assurance and acquiescence soever this principle may be entertained in the world, yet whoever shall find in his heart to call it in question may, if I mistake not, perceive it to involve a manifest contradiction. For what are the forementioned objects but the things we perceive by sense? and what do we perceive *besides our own ideas or sensations?* and is it not plainly repugnant that any one of these, or any combination of them, should exist unperceived?

5. If we thoroughly examine this tenet it will perhaps be found at bottom to depend on the doctrine of *abstract ideas.* For can there be a nicer strain of abstraction than to distinguish the existence of sensible objects from their being perceived, so as to conceive them existing unperceived? Light and colors, heat and cold, extension and figures—in a word the things we see and feel—what are they but so many sensations, notions, ideas, or impressions on the sense? And is it

possible to separate, even in thought, any of these from perception? For my part, I might as easily divide a thing from itself. I may, indeed, divide in my thoughts, or conceive apart from each other, those things which perhaps I never perceived by sense so divided. Thus I imagine the trunk of a human body without the limbs, or conceive the smell of a rose without thinking on the rose itself. So far, I will not deny, I can abstract, if that may properly be called abstraction which extends only to the conceiving separately such objects as it is possible may really exist or be actually perceived asunder. But my conceiving or imagining power does not extend beyond the possibility of real existence or perception. Hence, as it is impossible for me to see or feel anything without an actual sensation of that thing, so it is impossible for me to conceive in my thoughts any sensible thing or object distinct from the sensation or perception of it.

6. Some truths there are so near and obvious to the mind that a man need only open his eyes to see them. Such I take this important one to be, to wit, that all the choir of heaven and furniture of the earth, in a word all those bodies which compose the mighty frame of the world, have not any subsistence without a mind, that their *being* is to be perceived or known; that consequently so long as they are not actually perceived by me, or do not exist in my mind or that of any other created spirit, they must either have no existence at all, or else subsist in the mind of some Eternal Spirit; it being perfectly unintelligible, and involving all the absurdity of abstraction, to attribute to any single part of them an existence independent of a spirit. To be convinced of which, the reader need only reflect and try to separate in his own thoughts the *being* of a sensible thing from its *being perceived*.

7. From what has been said it follows there is not any other substance than *spirit* or that which perceives. But for the fuller proof of this point, let it be considered the sensible qualities are color, figure, motion, smell, taste, etc.—that is, the ideas perceived by sense. Now, for an idea to exist in an unperceiving thing is a manifest contradiction, for to have an idea is all one as to perceive; that therefore wherein color, figure, and the like qualities exist must perceive them; hence it is clear there can be no unthinking substance or *substratum* of those ideas.

8. But, say you, though the ideas themselves do not exist without the mind, yet there may be things *like* them, whereof

they are copies or resemblances, which things exist without the mind in an unthinking substance. I answer, an idea can be like nothing but an idea; a color or figure can be like nothing but another color or figure. If we look but never so little into our thoughts, we shall find it impossible for us to conceive a likeness except only between our ideas. Again, I ask whether those supposed originals or external things, of which our ideas are the pictures or representations, be themselves perceivable or no? If they are, then they are ideas and we have gained our point; but if you say they are not, I appeal to anyone whether it be sense to assert a color is like something which is invisible; hard or soft, like something which is intangible; and so of the rest. ANNOYING MAN

Locke

9. Some there are who make a distinction betwixt *primary* and *secondary* qualities. By the former they mean extension, figure, motion, rest, solidity or impenetrability, and number; by the latter they denote all other sensible qualities, as colors, sounds, tastes, and so forth. The ideas we have of these they acknowledge not to be the resemblances of anything existing without the mind, or unperceived, but they will have our ideas of the primary qualities to be patterns or images of things which exist without the mind, in an unthinking substance which they call *matter*. By *matter*, therefore, we are to understand an inert, senseless substance, in which extension, figure, and motion do actually subsist. But it is evident from what we have already shown, that extension, figure, and motion are only ideas existing in the mind, and that an idea can be like nothing but another idea, and that consequently neither they nor their archetypes can exist in an unperceiving substance. Hence, it is plain that the very notion of what is called *matter*, or *corporeal substance*, involves a contradiction in it.

10. They who assert that figure, motion, and the rest of the primary or original qualities do exist without the mind in unthinking substances, do at the same time acknowledge that color, sounds, heat, cold, and suchlike secondary qualities, do not; which they tell us are sensations existing in the mind alone, that depend on and are occasioned by the different size, texture, and motion of the minute particles of matter. This they take for an undoubted truth, which they can demonstrate beyond all exception. Now, if it be certain that those original qualities are inseparably united with the other sensible qualities, and not, even in thought, capable of being abstracted from them, it plainly follows that they exist only in

the mind. But I desire anyone to reflect and try whether he can, by any abstraction of thought, conceive the extension and motion of a body without all other sensible qualities. For my own part, I see evidently that it is not in my power to frame an idea of a body extended and moving, but I must withal give it some color or other sensible quality which is acknowledged to exist only in the mind. In short, extension, figure, and motion, abstracted from all other qualities, are inconceivable. Where therefore the other sensible qualities are, there must these be also, to wit, in the mind and nowhere else.

11. Again, *great* and *small*, *swift* and *slow*, are allowed to exist nowhere without the mind, being entirely relative, and changing as the frame or position of the organs of sense varies. The extension therefore which exists without the mind is neither great nor small, the motion neither swift nor slow, that is, they are nothing at all. But, say you, they are extension in general, and motion in general: thus we see how much the tenet of extended movable substances existing without the mind depends on the strange doctrine of *abstract ideas*. And here I cannot but remark how nearly the vague and indeterminate description of matter or corporeal substance, which the modern philosophers are run into by their own principles, resembles that antiquated and so much ridiculed notion of *materia prima*, to be met with in Aristotle and his followers. Without extension solidity cannot be conceived; since therefore it has been shewn that extension exists not in an unthinking substance, the same must also be true of solidity.

12. That *number* is entirely the creature of the mind, even though the other qualities be allowed to exist without, will be evident to whoever considers that the same thing bears a different denomination of number as the mind views it with different respects. Thus, the same extension is one, or three, or thirty-six, according as the mind considers it with reference to a yard, a foot, or an inch. Number is so visibly relative, and dependent on men's understanding, that it is strange to think how anyone should give it an absolute existence without the mind. We say one book, one page, one line; all these are equally units, though some contain several of the others. And in each instance, it is plain, the unit relates to some particular combination of ideas arbitrarily put together by the mind.

13. *Unity*, I know, some will have to be a simple or uncompounded idea, accompanying all other ideas into the mind.

That I have any such idea answering the word 'unity' I do not find; and if I had, methinks I could not miss finding it: on the contrary, it should be the most familiar to my understanding, since it is said to accompany all other ideas, and to be perceived by all the ways of sensation and reflection. To say no more, it is an *abstract idea.*

14. I shall farther add that, after the same manner as modern philosophers prove certain sensible qualities to have no existence in matter, or without the mind, the same thing may be likewise proved of all other sensible qualities whatsoever. Thus, for instance, it is said that heat and cold are affections only of the mind, and not at all patterns of real beings, existing in the corporeal substances which excite them, for that the same body which appears cold to one hand seems warm to another. Now, why may we not as well argue that figure and extension are not patterns or resemblances of qualities existing in matter, because to the same eye at different stations, or eyes of a different texture at the same station, they appear various, and cannot therefore be the images of anything settled and determinate without the mind? Again, it is proved that sweetness is not really in the sapid thing, because the thing remaining unaltered the sweetness is changed into bitter, as in case of a fever or otherwise vitiated palate. Is it not as reasonable to say that motion is not without the mind, since if the succession of ideas in the mind become swifter, the motion, it is acknowledged, shall appear slower without any alteration in any external object?

15. In short, let anyone consider those arguments which are thought manifestly to prove that colors and tastes exist only in the mind, and he shall find they may with equal force be brought to prove the same thing of extension, figure, and motion—though it must be confessed this method of arguing does not so much prove that there is no extension or color in an outward object, as that we do not know by sense which is the true extension or color of the object. But the arguments foregoing plainly show it to be impossible that any color or extension at all, or other sensible quality whatsoever, should exist in an unthinking subject without the mind, or in truth, that there should be any such thing as an outward object.

16. But let us examine a little the received opinion. It is said extension is a mode or accident of matter, and that matter is the *substratum* that supports it. Now I desire that you would explain to me what is meant by matter's *support-*

ing extension. Say you, I have no idea of matter and therefore cannot explain it. I answer, though you have no positive, yet, if you have any meaning at all, you must at least have a relative idea of matter; though you know not what it is, yet you must be supposed to know what relation it bears to accidents, and what is meant by its supporting them. It is evident 'support' cannot here be taken in its usual or literal sense—as when we say that pillars support a building; in what sense therefore must it be taken?

17. If we inquire into what the most accurate philosophers declare themselves to mean by *material substance*, we shall find them acknowledge they have no other meaning annexed to those sounds but the idea of *Being in general*, together with the relative notion of its supporting accidents. The general idea of Being appeareth to me the most abstract and incomprehensible of all other; and as for its supporting accidents, this, as we have just now observed, cannot be understood in the common sense of those words; it must therefore be taken in some other sense, but what that is they do not explain. So that when I consider the two parts or branches which make the signification of the words *material substance*, I am convinced there is no distinct meaning annexed to them. But why should we trouble ourselves any farther, in discussing this material *substratum* or support of figure and motion, and other sensible qualities? Does it not suppose they have an existence without the mind? And is not this a direct repugnancy, and altogether inconceivable?

18. But though it were possible that solid, figured, movable substances may exist without the mind, corresponding to the ideas we have of bodies, yet how is it possible for us to know this? Either we must know it by sense or by reason. As for our senses, by them we have the knowledge only of our sensations, ideas, or those things that are immediately perceived by sense, call them what you will; but they do not inform us that things exist without the mind, or unperceived, like to those which are perceived. This the materialists themselves acknowledge. It remains therefore that if we have any knowledge at all of external things, it must be by reason, inferring their existence from what is immediately perceived by sense. But what reason can induce us to believe the existence of bodies without the mind, from what we perceive, since the very patrons of matter themselves do not pretend there is any necessary connection betwixt them and our ideas? I say it is

granted on all hands (and what happens in dreams, frenzies, and the like, puts it beyond dispute) that *it is possible we might be affected with all the ideas we have now, though there were no bodies existing without, resembling them.* Hence, it is evident the supposition of external bodies is not necessary for the producing our ideas; since it is granted they are produced sometimes, and might possibly be produced always in the same order we see them in at present, without their concurrence.

19. But, though we might possibly have all our sensations without them, yet perhaps it may be thought easier to conceive and explain the manner of their production by supposing external bodies in their likeness rather than otherwise; and so it might be at least probable there are such things as bodies that excite their ideas in our minds. But neither can this be said; for though we give the materialists their external bodies, they by their own confession are never the nearer knowing how our ideas are produced, since they own themselves unable to comprehend in what manner body can act upon spirit, or how it is possible it should imprint any idea in the mind. Hence it is evident the production of ideas or sensations in our minds can be no reason why we should suppose matter or corporeal substances, since that is acknowledged to remain equally inexplicable with or without this supposition. If therefore it were possible for bodies to exist without the mind, yet to hold they do so, must needs be a very precarious opinion; since it is to suppose, without any reason at all, that God has created innumerable beings that are entirely useless, and serve to no manner of purpose.

20. In short, if there were external bodies, it is impossible we should ever come to know it; and if there were not, we might have the very same reasons to think there were that we have now. Suppose (what no one can deny possible) an intelligence without the help of external bodies, to be affected with the same train of sensations or ideas that you are, imprinted in the same order and with like vividness in his mind. I ask whether that intelligence hath not all the reason to believe the existence of corporeal substances, represented by his ideas, and exciting them in his mind, that you can possibly have for believing the same thing? Of this there can be no question; which one consideration were enough to make any reasonable person suspect the strength of whatever arguments

he may think himself to have for the existence of bodies without the mind.

21. Were it necessary to add any farther proof against the existence of matter after what has been said, I could instance several of those errors and difficulties (not to mention impieties) which have sprung from that tenet. It has occasioned numberless controversies and disputes in philosophy, and not a few of far greater moment in religion. But I shall not enter into the detail of them in this place, as well because I think arguments *a posteriori* are unnecessary for confirming what has been, if I mistake not, sufficiently demonstrated *a priori*, as because I shall hereafter find occasion to speak somewhat of them.

22. I am afraid I have given cause to think I am needlessly prolix in handling this subject. For, to what purpose is it to dilate on that which may be demonstrated with the utmost evidence in a line or two, to anyone that is capable of the least reflection? It is but looking into your own thoughts, and so trying whether you can conceive it possible for a sound, or figure, or motion, or color to exist without the mind or unperceived. This easy trial may perhaps make you see that what you contend for is a downright contradiction. Insomuch that I am content to put the whole upon this issue: if you can but conceive it possible for one extended movable substance, or, in general, for any one idea, or anything like an idea, to exist otherwise than in a mind perceiving it, I shall readily give up the cause; and, as for all that compages of external bodies you contend for, I shall grant you its existence, though you cannot either give me any reason why you believe it exists, or assign any use to it when it is supposed to exist. I say, the bare possibility of your opinion's being true shall pass for an argument that it is so.

23. But, say you, surely there is nothing easier than for me to imagine trees, for instance, in a park, or books existing in a closet, and nobody by to perceive them. I answer, you may so, there is no difficulty in it; but what is all this, I beseech you, more than framing in your mind certain ideas which you call books and trees, and the same time omitting to frame the idea of anyone that may perceive them? But do not you yourself perceive or think of them all the while? This therefore is nothing to the purpose; it only shews you have the power of imagining or forming ideas in your mind: but it doth not shew that you can conceive it possible the objects of

your thought may exist without the mind. To make out this, it is necessary that you conceive them existing unconceived or unthought of, which is a manifest repugnancy. When we do our utmost to conceive the existence of external bodies, we are all the while only contemplating our own ideas. But the mind taking no notice of itself, is deluded to think it can and doth conceive bodies existing unthought of or without the mind, though at the same time they are apprehended by or exist in itself. A little attention will discover to anyone the truth and evidence of what is here said, and make it unnecessary to insist on any other proofs against the existence of *material substance.*

24. It is very obvious, upon the least inquiry into our thoughts, to know whether it is possible for us to understand what is meant by the *absolute existence of sensible objects in themselves, or without the mind.* To me it is evident those words mark out either a direct contradiction, or else nothing at all. And to convince others of this, I know no readier or fairer way than to entreat they would calmly attend to their own thoughts; and if by this attention the emptiness or repugnancy of those expressions doth appear, surely nothing more is requisite for the conviction. It is on this therefore that I insist, to wit, that the absolute existence of unthinking things are words without a meaning, or which include a contradiction. This is what I repeat and inculcate, and earnestly recommend to the attentive thoughts of the reader.

25. All our ideas, sensations, notions, or the things which we perceive, by whatsoever names they may be distinguished, are visibly inactive: there is nothing of power or agency included in them. So that one idea or object of thought cannot produce or make any alteration in another. To be satisfied of the truth of this, there is nothing else requisite but a bare observation of our ideas. For, since they and every part of them exist only in the mind, it follows that there is nothing in them but what is perceived: but whoever shall attend to his ideas, whether of sense or reflection, will not perceive in them any power or activity; there is, therefore, no such thing contained in them. A little attention will discover to us that the very being of an idea implies passiveness and inertness in it, insomuch that it is impossible for an idea to do anything, or, strictly speaking, to be the cause of anything: neither can it be the resemblance or pattern of any active being, as is evident from Sec. 8. Whence it plainly follows that extension,

figure, and motion cannot be the cause of our sensations. To say, therefore, that these are the effects of powers resulting from the configuration, number, motion, and size of corpuscles, must certainly be false.

26. We perceive a continual succession of ideas, some are anew excited, others are changed or totally disappear. There is therefore some cause of these ideas, whereon they depend, and which produces and changes them. That this cause cannot be any quality or idea or combination of ideas, is clear from the preceding section. It must therefore be a substance; but it has been shewn that there is no corporeal or material substance: it remains therefore that the cause of ideas is an incorporeal active substance or Spirit.

27. A spirit is one simple, undivided, active being: as it perceives ideas it is called the *understanding*, and as it produces or otherwise operates about them it is called the *will*. Hence there can be no *idea* formed of a soul or spirit; for all ideas whatever, being passive and inert (*vide* Sec. 25), they cannot represent unto us, by way of image or likeness, that which acts. A little attention will make it plain to anyone, that to have an idea which shall be like that active principle of motion and change of ideas is absolutely impossible. Such is the nature of *spirit*, or that which acts, that it cannot be of itself perceived, but only by the effects which it produceth. If any man shall doubt of the truth of what is here delivered, let him but reflect and try if he can frame the idea of any power or active being, and whether he hath ideas of two principal powers, marked by the names *will* and *understanding*, distinct from each other as well as from a third idea of substance or being in general, with a relative notion of its supporting or being the subject of the aforesaid powers—which is signified by the name *soul* or *spirit*. This is what some hold; but, so far as I can see, the words *will, soul, spirit,* do not stand for different ideas, or, in truth, for any idea at all, but for something which is very different from ideas, and which, being an agent, cannot be like unto, or represented by, any idea whatsoever. Though it must be owned at the same time that we have some *notion* of soul, spirit, and the operations of the mind such as willing, loving, hating; inasmuch as we know or understand the meaning of these words.

28. I find I can excite ideas in my mind at pleasure, and vary and shift the scene as oft as I think fit. It is no more than willing, and straightway this or that idea arises in my

fancy; and by the same power it is obliterated and makes way for another. This making and unmaking of ideas doth very properly denominate the mind active. Thus much is certain and grounded on experience; but when we think of unthinking agents or of exciting ideas exclusive of volition, we only amuse ourselves with words.

29. But, whatever power I may have over my own thoughts, I find the ideas actually perceived by sense have not a like dependence on my will. When in broad daylight I open my eyes, it is not in my power to choose whether I shall see or no, or to determine what particular objects shall present themselves to my view; and so likewise as to the hearing and other senses, the ideas imprinted on them are not creatures of my will. There is therefore some other will or spirit that produces them.

30. The ideas of sense are more strong, lively, and distinct than those of the imagination; they have likewise a steadiness, order, and coherence, and are not excited at random, as those which are the effects of human wills often are, but in a regular train or series, the admirable connection whereof sufficiently testifies the wisdom and benevolence of its Author. Now the set rules or established methods wherein the mind we depend on excites in us the ideas of sense, are called the *laws of nature*; and these we learn by experience, which teaches us that such and such ideas are attended with such and such other ideas, in the ordinary course of things.

31. This gives us a sort of foresight which enables us to regulate our actions for the benefit of life. And without this we should be eternally at a loss: we could not know how to act anything that might procure us the least pleasure, or remove the least pain of sense. That food nourishes, sleep refreshes, and fire warms us; that to sow in the seed-time is the way to reap in the harvest; and, in general, that to obtain such or such ends, such or such means are conducive—all this we know, not by discovering any necessary connection between our ideas, but only by the observation of the settled laws of nature, without which we should be all in uncertainty and confusion, and a grown man no more know how to manage himself in the affairs of life than an infant just born.

32. And yet this insistent uniform working, which so evidently displays the goodness and wisdom of that governing Spirit whose will constitutes the laws of nature, is so far from leading our thoughts to Him, that it rather sends them wan-

dering after second causes. For, when we perceive certain ideas of sense constantly followed by other ideas and we know this is not of our own doing, we forthwith attribute power and agency to the ideas themselves, and make one the cause of another, than which nothing can be more absurd and unintelligible. Thus, for example, having observed that when we perceive by sight a certain round luminous figure we at the same time perceive by touch the idea or sensation called heat, we do from thence conclude the sun to be the cause of heat. And in like manner perceiving the motion and collision of bodies to be attended with sound, we are inclined to think the latter the effect of the former.

33. The ideas imprinted on the senses by the Author of nature are called *real things*; and those excited in the imagination, being less regular, vivid, and constant, are more properly termed *ideas*, or *images* of *things*, which they copy and represent. But then our sensations, be they never so vivid and distinct, are nevertheless ideas, that is, they exist in the mind, or are perceived by it, as truly as the ideas of its own framing. The ideas of sense are allowed to have more reality in them, that is, to be more strong, orderly, and coherent than the creatures of the mind; but this is no argument that they exist without the mind. They are also less dependent on the spirit, or thinking substance which perceives them, in that they are excited by the will of another and more powerful spirit; yet still they are *ideas*, and certainly no idea, whether faint or strong, can exist otherwise than in a mind perceiving it.

34. Before we proceed any farther it is necessary we spend some time in answering objections which may probably be made against the principles we have hitherto laid down. In doing of which, if I seem too prolix to those of quick apprehensions, I hope it may be pardoned, since all men do not equally apprehend things of this nature, and I am willing to be understood by everyone.

First, then, it will be objected that by the foregoing principles all that is real and substantial in nature is banished out of the world, and instead thereof a chimerical scheme of *ideas* takes place. All things that exist, exist only in the mind, that is, they are purely notional. What therefore becomes of the sun, moon, and stars? What must we think of houses, rivers, mountains, trees, stones; nay, even of our own bodies? Are all these but so many chimeras and illusions on the fancy? To all which, and whatever else of the same sort may be objected,

I answer that by the principles premised we are not deprived of any one thing in nature. Whatever we see, feel, hear, or anywise conceive or understand remains as secure as ever, and is as real as ever. There is a *rerum natura*, and the distinction between realities and chimeras retains its full force. This is evident from Sec. 29, 30, and 33, where we have shewn what is meant by *real things* in opposition to *chimeras* or ideas of our own framing; but then they both equally exist in the mind, and in that sense they are alike *ideas*.

35. I do not argue against the existence of any one thing that we can apprehend either by sense or reflection. That the things I see with my eyes and touch with my hands do exist, really exist, I make not the least question. The only thing whose existence we deny is that which *philosophers* call matter or corporeal substance. And in doing of this there is no damage done to the rest of mankind, who, I dare say, will never miss it. The atheist indeed will want the color of an empty name to support his impiety; and the philosophers may possibly find they have lost a great handle for trifling and disputation.

36. If any man thinks this detracts from the existence or reality of things, he is very far from understanding what hath been premised in the plainest terms I could think of. Take here an abstract of what has been said. There are spiritual substances, minds, or human souls, which will or excite ideas in themselves at pleasure; but these are faint, weak, and unsteady in respect of others they perceive by sense—which, being impressed upon them according to certain rules or laws of nature, speak themselves the effects of a mind more powerful and wise than human spirits. These latter are said to have more *reality* in them than the former; by which is meant that they are more affecting, orderly, and distinct, and that they are not fictions of the mind perceiving them. And in this sense the sun that I see by day is the real sun, and that which I imagine by night is the idea of the former. In the sense here given of 'reality' it is evident that every vegetable, star, mineral, and in general each part of the mundane system, is as much as a real being by our principles as by any other. Whether others mean anything by the term 'reality' different from what I do, I entreat them to look into their own thoughts and see.

37. It will be urged that thus much at least is true, to wit, that we take away all corporeal substances. To this my answer

is that if the word 'substance' be taken in the vulgar sense—for a combination of sensible qualities, such as extension, solidity, weight, and the like—this we cannot be accused of taking away. But if it be taken in a philosophic sense—for the support of accidents or qualities without the mind—then indeed I acknowledge that we take it away, if one may be said to take away that which never had any existence, not even in the imagination.

38. But after all, say you, it sounds very harsh to say we eat and drink ideas, and are clothed with ideas. I acknowledge it does so; the word 'idea' not being used in common discourse to signify the several combinations of sensible qualities which are called 'things'; and it is certain that any expression which varies from the familiar use of language will seem harsh and ridiculous. But this doth not concern the truth of the proposition, which in other words is no more than to say, we are fed and clothed with those things which we perceive immediately by our senses. The hardness or softness, the color, taste, warmth, figure, or suchlike qualities, which combined together constitute the several sorts of victuals and apparel, have been shewn to exist only in the mind that perceives them; and this is all that is meant by calling them 'ideas'; which word if it was as ordinarily used as 'things,' would sound no harsher nor more ridiculous than it. I am not for disputing about the propriety, but the truth of the expression. If therefore you agree with me that we eat and drink and are clad with the immediate objects of sense, which cannot exist unperceived or without the mind, I shall readily grant it is more proper or conformable to custom that they should be called things rather than ideas.

39. If it be demanded why I make use of the word 'idea,' and do not rather in compliance with custom call them 'thing'; I answer, I do it for two reasons:—first, because the term 'thing' in contradistinction to 'idea,' is generally supposed to denote somewhat existing without the mind; secondly, because 'thing' hath a more comprehensive signification than 'idea,' including spirit or thinking things as well as ideas. Since therefore the objects of sense exist only in the mind, and are withal thoughtless and inactive, I chose to mark them by the word 'idea,' which implies those properties.

40. But, say what we can, someone perhaps may be apt to reply, he will still believe his senses, and never suffer any arguments, how plausible soever, to prevail over the certainty of

them. Be it so; assert the evidence of sense as high as you please, we are willing to do the same. That what I see, hear, and feel doth exist, that is to say, is perceived by me, I no more doubt than I do of my own being. But I do not see how the testimony of sense can be alleged as a proof for the existence of anything which is not perceived by sense. We are not for having any man turn sceptic and disbelieve his senses; on the contrary, we give them all the stress and assurance imaginable; nor are there any principles more opposite to scepticism than those we have laid down, as shall be hereafter clearly shewn.

41. *Secondly*, it will be objected that there is a great difference betwixt real fire for instance, and the idea of fire, betwixt dreaming or imagining oneself burnt, and actually being so: if you suspect it to be only the idea of fire which you see, do but put your hand into it and you will be convinced with a witness. This and the like may be urged in opposition to our tenets. To all which the answer is evident from what hath been already said; and I shall only add in this place, that if real fire be very different from the idea of fire, so also is the real pain that it occasions very different from the idea of the same pain, and yet nobody will pretend that real pain either is, or can possibly be, in an unperceiving thing, or without the mind, any more than its idea.

42. *Thirdly*, it will be objected that we see things actually without or at distance from us, and which consequently do not exist in the mind; it being absurd that those things which are seen at the distance of several miles should be as near to us as our own thoughts. In answer to this, I desire it may be considered that in a dream we do oft perceive things as existing at a great distance off, and yet for all that, those things are acknowledged to have their existence only in the mind.

43. But, for the fuller clearing of this point, it may be worth while to consider how it is that we perceive distance and things placed at a distance by sight. For, that we should in truth see external space, and bodies actually existing in it, some nearer, others farther off, seems to carry with it some opposition to what hath been said of their existing nowhere without the mind. The consideration of this difficulty it was that gave birth to my *Essay towards a New Theory of Vision*, which was published not long since, wherein it is shewn that distance or outness is neither immediately of itself perceived by sight, nor yet apprehended or judged of by lines and angles,

or anything that hath a necessary connection with it; but that it is only suggested to our thoughts by certain visible ideas and sensations attending vision, which in their own nature have no manner of similitude or relation either with distance or things placed at a distance; but, by a connection taught us by experience, they come to signify and suggest them to us, after the same manner that words of any language suggest the ideas they are made to stand for; insomuch that a man born blind and afterwards made to see, would not, at first sight, think the things he saw to be without his mind, or at any distance from him. (See Sec. 41 of the forementioned treatise.)

44. The ideas of sight and touch make two species entirely distinct and heterogeneous. *The former are marks and prognostics of the latter.* That the proper objects of sight neither exist without mind, nor are the images of external things, was shewn even in that treatise; though throughout the same the contrary be supposed true of tangible objects—not that to suppose that vulgar error was necessary for establishing the notion therein laid down, but because it was beside my purpose to examine and refute it in a discourse concerning *vision*. So that in strict truth the ideas of sight, when we apprehend by them distance and things placed at a distance, do not suggest or mark out to us things actually existing at a distance, but only admonish us what ideas of touch will be imprinted in our minds at such and such distances of time, and in consequence of such or such actions. It is, I say, evident from what has been said in the foregoing parts of this treatise, and in Sec. 147 and elsewhere of the essay concerning vision, that visible ideas are the language whereby the governing Spirit on whom we depend informs us what tangible ideas he is about to imprint upon us, in case we excite this or that motion in our own bodies. But for a fuller information in this point I refer to the essay itself.

45. *Fourthly*, it will be objected that from the foregoing principles it follows things are every moment annihilated and created anew. The objects of sense exist only when they are perceived; the trees therefore are in the garden, or the chairs in the parlor, no longer than while there is somebody by to perceive them. Upon shutting my eyes all the furniture in the room is reduced to nothing, and barely upon opening them it is again created. In answer to all which, I refer the reader to what has been said in Sec. 3, 4, etc., and desire he will consider whether he means anything by the actual exist-

ence of an idea distinct from its being perceived. For my part, after the nicest inquiry I could make, I am not able to discover that anything else is meant by those words; and I once more entreat the reader to sound his own thoughts, and not suffer himself to be imposed on by words. If he can conceive it possible either for his ideas or their archetypes to exist without being perceived, then I give up the cause; but if he cannot, he will acknowledge it is unreasonable for him to stand up in defense of he knows not what, and pretend to charge on me as an absurdity the not assenting to those propositions which at bottom have no meaning in them.

46. It will not be amiss to observe how far the received principles of philosophy are themselves chargeable with those pretended absurdities. It is thought strangely absurd that upon closing my eyelids all the visible objects around me should be reduced to nothing; and yet is not this what philosophers commonly acknowledge, when they agree on all hands that light and colors, which alone are the proper and immediate objects of sight, are mere sensations that exist no longer than they are perceived? Again, it may to some perhaps seem very incredible that things should be every moment creating, yet this very notion is commonly taught in the schools. For the schoolmen, though they acknowledge the existence of matter, and that the whole mundane fabric is framed out of it, are nevertheless of opinion that it cannot subsist without the divine conservation, which by them is expounded to be a continual creation.

47. Farther, a little thought will discover to us that though we allow the existence of matter or corporeal substance, yet it will unavoidably follow, from the principles which are now generally admitted, that the particular bodies, of what kind soever, do none of them exist whilst they are not perceived. For, it is evident from Sec. 11 and the following sections, that the matter philosophers contend for is an incomprehensible somewhat, which hath none of those particular qualities whereby the bodies falling under our senses are distinguished one from another. But, to make this more plain, it must be remarked that the infinite divisibility of matter is now universally allowed, at least by the most approved and considerable philosophers, who on the received principles demonstrate it beyond all exception. Hence, it follows there is an infinite number of parts in each particle of matter which are not perceived by sense. The reason therefore that any particular

body seems to be of a finite magnitude, or exhibits only a finite number of parts to sense, is, not because it contains no more, since in itself it contains an infinite number of parts, but because the sense is not acute enough to discern them. In proportion therefore as the sense is rendered more acute, it perceives a greater number of parts in the object, that is, the object appears greater, and its figure varies, those parts in its extremities which were before unperceivable appearing now to bound it in very different lines and angles from those perceived by an obtuser sense. And at length, after various changes of size and shape, when the sense becomes infinitely acute the body shall seem infinite. During all which there is no alteration in the body, but only in the sense. Each body therefore, considered in itself, is infinitely extended, and consequently void of all shape or figure. From which it follows that, though we should grant the existence of matter to be never so certain, yet it is withal as certain, the materialists themselves are by their own principles forced to acknowledge, that neither the particular bodies perceived by sense, nor anything like them, exists without the mind. Matter, I say, and each particle thereof, is according to them infinite and shapeless, and it is the mind that frames all that variety of bodies which compose the visible world, anyone whereof does not exist longer than it is perceived.

48. If we consider it, the objection proposed in Sec. 45 will not be found reasonably charged on the principles we have premised, so as in truth to make any objection at all against our notions. For, though we hold indeed the objects of sense to be nothing else but ideas which cannot exist unperceived; yet we may not hence conclude they have no existence except only while they are perceived by us, since there may be some other spirit that perceives them though we do not. Wherever bodies are said to have no existence without the mind, I would not be understood to mean this or that particular mind, but all minds whatsoever. It does not therefore follow from the foregoing principles that bodies are annihilated and created every moment, or exist not at all during the intervals between our perception of them.

49. *Fifthly*, it may perhaps be objected that if extension and figure exist only in the mind, it follows that the mind is extended and figured; since extension is a mode or attribute which (to speak with the schools) is predicated of the subject in which it exists. I answer, those qualities are in the mind

only as they are perceived by it—that is, not by way of *mode* or *attribute*, but only by way of *idea*; and it no more follows the soul or mind is extended, because extension exists in it alone, than it does that it is red or blue, because those colors are on all hands acknowledged to exist in it, and nowhere else. As to what philosophers say of subject and mode, that seems very groundless and unintelligible. For instance, in this proposition, "a die is hard, extended, and square," they will have it that the word 'die' denotes a subject or substance, distinct from the hardness, extension, and figure which are predicated of it, and in which they exist. This I cannot comprehend: to me a die seems to be nothing distinct from those things which are termed its modes or accidents. And, to say a die is hard, extended, and square is not to attribute those qualities to a subject distinct from and supporting them, but only an explication of the meaning of the word 'die.'

50. *Sixthly*, you will say there have been a great many things explained by matter and motion; take away these and you destroy the whole corpuscular philosophy, and undermine those mechanical principles which have been applied with so much success to account for the phenomena. In short, whatever advances have been made, either by accident or modern philosophers, in the study of nature do all proceed on the supposition that corporeal substance or matter doth really exist. To this I answer that there is not any one phenomenon explained on that supposition which may not as well be explained without it, as might easily be made appear by an induction of particulars. To explain the phenomena, is all one as to shew why, upon such and such occasions, we are affected with such and such ideas. But how matter should operate on a spirit, or produce any idea in it, is what no philosopher will pretend to explain; it is therefore evident there can be no use of matter in natural philosophy. Besides, they who attempt to account for things do it not by corporeal substance, but by figure, motion, and other qualities, which are in truth no more than mere ideas, and, therefore, cannot be the cause of anything, as hath been already shewn. (See Sec. 25).

51. *Seventhly*, it will upon this be demanded whether it does not seem absurd to take away natural causes, and ascribe everything to the immediate operation of spirits? We must no longer say upon these principles that fire heats, or water cools, but that a spirit heats, and so forth. Would not a man

be deservedly laughed at, who should talk after this manner? I answer, he would so; in such things we ought to 'think with the learned, and speak with the vulgar.' They who to demonstration are convinced of the truth of the Copernican system do nevertheless say, "The sun rises," "The sun sets," or "comes to the meridian"; and if they affected a contrary style in common talk it would without doubt appear very ridiculous. A little reflection on what is here said will make it manifest that the common use of language would receive no manner of alteration or disturbance from the admission of our tenets.

52. In the ordinary affairs of life, any phrases may be retained, so long as they excite in us proper sentiments, or dispositions to act in such a manner as is necessary for our well-being, how false soever they may be if taken in a strict and speculative sense. Nay, this is unavoidable, since, propriety being regulated by custom, language is suited to the received opinions, which are not always the truest. Hence it is impossible, even in the most rigid, philosophic reasonings, so far to alter the bent and genius of the tongue we speak, as never to give a handle for cavilers to pretend difficulties and inconsistencies. But, a fair and ingenuous reader will collect the sense from the scope and tenor and connection of a discourse, making allowances for those inaccurate modes of speech which use has made inevitable.

53. As to the opinion that there are no corporeal causes, this has been heretofore maintained by some of the schoolmen, as it is of late by others among the modern philosophers, who though they allow matter to exist, yet will have God alone to be the immediate efficient cause of all things. These men saw that amongst all the objects of sense there was none which had any power or activity included in it; and that by consequence this was likewise true of whatever bodies they supposed to exist without the mind, like unto the immediate objects of sense. But then, that they should suppose an innumerable multitude of created beings, which they acknowledge are not capable of producing any one effect in nature, and which therefore are made to no manner of purpose, since God might have done everything as well without them: this I say, though we should allow it possible, must yet be a very unaccountable and extravagant supposition.

54. In the *eighth* place, the universal concurrent assent of mankind may be thought by some an invincible argument in

behalf of matter, or the existence of external things. Must we suppose the whole world to be mistaken? And if so, what cause can be assigned of so widespread and predominant an error? I answer, first, that, upon a narrow inquiry, it will not perhaps be found so many as is imagined do really believe the existence of matter or things without the mind. Strictly speaking, to believe that which involves a contradiction, or has no meaning in it, is impossible; and whether the foregoing expressions are not of that sort, I refer it to the impartial examination of the reader. In one sense, indeed, men may be said to believe that matter exists, that is, they *act* as if the immediate cause of their sensations, which affects them every moment, and is so nearly present to them, were some senseless unthinking being. But, that they should clearly apprehend any meaning marked by those words, and form thereof a settled speculative opinion, is what I am not able to conceive. This is not the only instance wherein men impose upon themselves, by imagining they believe those propositions which they have often heard, though at bottom they have no meaning in them.

55. But secondly, though we should grant a notion to be never so universally and steadfastly adhered to, yet this is weak argument of its truth to whoever considers what a vast number of prejudices and false opinions are everywhere embraced with the utmost tenaciousness, by the unreflecting (which are the far greater) part of mankind. There was a time when the antipodes and motion of the earth were looked upon as monstrous absurdities even by men of learning: and if it be considered what a small proportion they bear to the rest of mankind, we shall find that at this day those notions have gained but a very inconsiderable footing in the world.

56. But it is demanded that we assign a cause of this prejudice, and account for its obtaining in the world. To this I answer, that men knowing they perceived several ideas, whereof they themselves were not the authors (as not being excited from within nor depending on the operation of their wills) this made them maintain those ideas, or objects of perception had an existence independent of and without the mind, without ever dreaming that a contradiction was involved in those words. But philosophers having plainly seen that the immediate objects of perception do not exist without the mind, they in some degree corrected the mistake of the vulgar; but at the same time run into another which seems no less absurd,

to wit, that there are certain objects really existing without the mind, or having a subsistence distinct from being perceived, of which our ideas are only images or resemblances, imprinted by those objects on the mind. And this notion of the philosophers owes its origin to the same cause with the former, namely, their being conscious that they were not the authors of their own sensations, which they evidently knew were imprinted from without, and which therefore must have some cause distinct from the minds on which they are imprinted.

57. But why they should suppose the ideas of sense to be excited in us by things in their likeness, and not rather have recourse to *spirit*, which alone can act, may be accounted for, first, because they were not aware of the repugnancy there is, as well in supposing things like unto our ideas existing without, as in attributing to them power or activity. Secondly, because the Supreme Spirit, which excites those ideas in our minds, is not marked out and limited to our view by any particular finite collection of sensible ideas, as human agents are by their size, complexion, limbs, and motions. And thirdly, because His operations are regular and uniform. Whenever the course of nature is interrupted by a miracle, men are ready to own the presence of a superior agent. But, when we see things go on in the ordinary course they do not excite in us any reflection; their order and concatenation, though it be an argument of the greatest wisdom, power, and goodness in their creator, is yet so constant and familiar to us that we do not think them the immediate effects of a free spirit; especially since inconsistency and mutability in acting, though it be an imperfection, is looked on as a mark of freedom.

58. *Tenthly*, it will be objected that the notions we advance are inconsistent with several sound truths in philosophy and mathematics. For example, the motion of the earth is now universally admitted by astronomers as a truth grounded on the clearest and most convincing reasons. But, on the foregoing principles, there can be no such thing. For, motion being only an idea, it follows that if it be not perceived it exists not; but the motion of the earth is not perceived by sense. I answer, that tenet, if rightly understood, will be found to agree with the principles we have premised; for, the question whether the earth moves or no amounts in reality to no more than this, to wit, whether we have reason to conclude, from what has been observed by astronomers, that if we were

placed in such and such circumstances, and such or such a position and distance both from the earth and sun, we should perceive the former to move among the choir of the planets, and appearing in all respects like one of them; and this, by the established rules of nature which we have no reason to mistrust, is reasonably collected from the phenomena.

59. We may, from the experience we have had of the train and succession of ideas in our minds, often make, I will not say uncertain conjectures, but sure and well-grounded predictions concerning the ideas we shall be affected with pursuant to a great train of actions, and be enabled to pass a right judgment of what would have appeared to us, in case we were placed in circumstances very different from those we are in at present. Herein consists the knowledge of nature, which may preserve its use and certainty very consistently with what hath been said. It will be easy to apply this to whatever objections of the like sort may be drawn from the magnitude of the stars, or any other discoveries in astronomy or nature.

60. In the *eleventh* place, it will be demanded to what purpose serves that curious organization of plants, and the animal mechanism in the parts of animals: might not vegetables grow, and shoot forth leaves of blossoms, and animals perform all their motions as well without as with all that variety of internal parts so elegantly contrived and put together, which, being ideas, have nothing powerful or operative in them, nor have any necessary connection with the effects ascribed to them? If it be a Spirit that immediately produces every effect by a *fiat* or act of His will, we must think all that is fine and artificial in the works, whether of man or nature, to be made in vain. By this doctrine, though an artist hath made the spring and wheels, and every movement of a watch, and adjusted them in such a manner as he knew would produce the motions he designed, yet he must think all this done to no purpose, and that it is an Intelligence which directs the index, and points to the hour of the day. If so, why may not the Intelligence do it, without his being at the pains of making the movements and putting them together? Why does not an empty case serve as well as another? And how comes it to pass that whenever there is any fault in the going of a watch, there is some corresponding disorder to be found in the movements, which being mended by a skillful hand all is right again? The like may be said of all the clockwork of nature, great part whereof is so wonderfully fine and subtle as scarce to be discerned by

the best microscope. In short, it will be asked, how, upon our principles, any tolerable account can be given, or any final cause assigned of an innumerable multitude of bodies and machines, framed with the most exquisite art, which in the common philosophy have very apposite uses assigned them, and serve to explain abundance of phenomena?

61. To all which I answer, *first*, that though there were some difficulties relating to the administration of Providence, and the uses by it assigned to the several parts of nature, which I could not solve by the foregoing principles, yet this objection could be of small weight against the truth and certainty of those things which may be proved *a priori*, with the utmost evidence and rigor of demonstration. *Secondly*, but neither are the received principles free from the like difficulties; for, it may still be demanded to what end God should take those roundabout methods of effecting things by instruments and machines, which no one can deny might have been effected by the mere command of His will without all that apparatus; nay, if we narrowly consider it, we shall find the objection may be retorted with greater force on those who hold the existence of those machines without of mind; for it has been made evident that solidity, bulk, figure, motion, and the like have no *activity* or *efficacy* in them, so as to be capable of producing any one effect in nature. (See Sec. 25). Whoever therefore supposes them to exist (allowing the supposition possible) when they are not perceived does it manifestly to no purpose; since the only use that is assigned to them, as they exist unperceived, is that they produce those perceivable effects which in truth cannot be ascribed to anything but Spirit.

62. But, to come nigher the difficulty, it must be observed that though the fabrication of all those parts and organs be not absolutely necessary to the producing any effect, yet it is necessary to the producing of things in a constant regular way according to the laws of nature. There are certain general laws that run through the whole chain of natural effects; these are learned by the observation and study of nature, and are by men applied as well to the framing artificial things for the use and ornament of life as to the explaining various phenomena—which explication consists only in shewing the conformity any particular phenomenon hath to the general laws of nature, or, which is the same thing, in discovering the *uniformity* there is in the production of natural effects; as will

be evident to whoever shall attend to the several instances wherein philosophers pretend to account for appearances. That there is a great and conspicuous use in these regular constant methods of working observed by the Supreme Agent hath been shewn in Sec. 31. And it is no less visible that a particular size, figure, motion, and disposition of parts are necessary, though not absolutely to the producing any effect, yet to the producing it according to the standing mechanical laws of nature. Thus, for instance, it cannot be denied that God, or the Intelligence that sustains and rules the ordinary course of things, might if He were minded to produce a miracle, cause all the motions on the dial-plate of a watch, though nobody had ever made the movements and put them in it: but yet, if He will act agreeably to the rules of the mechanism, by Him for wise ends established and maintained in the creation, it is necessary that those actions of the watchmaker, whereby he makes the movements and rightly adjusts them, precede the production of the aforesaid motions; as also that any disorder in them be attended with the perception of some corresponding disorder in the movements, which being once corrected all is right again.

63. It may indeed on some occasions be necessary that the Author of nature display His overruling power in producing some appearance out of the ordinary series of things. Such exceptions from the general rules of nature are proper to surprise and awe men into an acknowledgment of the Divine Being; but then they are to be used but seldom, otherwise there is a plain reason why they should fail of that effect. Besides, God seems to choose the convincing our reason of His attributes by the works of nature, which discover so much harmony and contrivance in their make, and are such plain indications of wisdom and beneficence in their Author, rather than to astonish us into a belief of His Being by anomalous and surprising events.

64. To set this matter in a yet clearer light, I shall observe that what has been objected in Sec. 60 amounts in reality to no more than this:—ideas are not anyhow and at random produced, there being a certain order and connection between them, like to that of cause and effect; there are also several combinations of them made in a very regular and artificial manner, which seem like so many instruments in the hand of nature that, being hid as it were behind the scenes, have a secret operation in producing those appearances which are

seen on the theater of the world, being themselves discernible only to the curious eye of the philosopher. But, since one idea cannot be the cause of another, to what purpose is that connection? And, since those instruments, being barely *inefficacious perceptions* in the mind, are not subservient to the production of natural effects, it is demanded why they are made; or, in other words, what reason can be assigned why God should make us, upon a close inspection into His works, behold so great variety of ideas so artfully laid together, and so much according to rule; it not being credible that He would be at the expense (if one may so speak) of all that art and regularity to no purpose.

65. To all which my answer is, first, that the connection of ideas does not imply the relation of *cause and effect*, but only of a mark or *sign* with the thing *signified*. The fire which I see is not the cause of the pain I suffer upon my approaching it, but the mark that forewarns me of it. In like manner the noise that I hear is not the effect of this or that motion or collision of the ambient bodies, but the sign thereof. Secondly, the reason why ideas are formed into machines, that is, artificial and regular combinations, is the same with that for combining letters into words. That a few original ideas may be made to signify a great number of effects and actions, it is necessary they be variously combined together. And, to the end their use be permanent and universal, these combinations must be made by *rule*, and with *wise contrivance*. By this means abundance of information is conveyed unto us, concerning what we are to expect from such and such actions, and what methods are proper to be taken for the exciting such and such ideas; which in effect is all that I conceive to be distinctly meant when it is said that, by discerning a figure, texture, and mechanism of the inward parts of bodies, whether natural or artificial, we may attain to know the several uses and properties depending thereon, or the nature of the thing.

66. Hence, it is evident that those things which, under the notion of a cause co-operating or concurring to the production of effects, are altogether inexplicable, and run us into great absurdities, may be very naturally explained, and have a proper and obvious use assigned to them, when they are considered only as marks or signs for our information. And it is the searching after and endeavoring to understand those signs instituted by the Author of Nature, that ought to be the employment of the natural philosopher; and not the pretending to

explain things by corporeal causes, which doctrine seems to have too much estranged the minds of men from that active principle, that supreme and wise Spirit "in whom we live, move, and have our being."

67. In the *twelfth* place, it may perhaps be objected that—though it be clear from what has been said that there can be no such thing as an inert, senseless, extended, solid, figured, movable substance existing without the mind, such as philosophers describe matter—yet, if any man shall leave out of his idea of matter the positive ideas of extension, figure, solidity and motion, and say that he means only by that word an inert, senseless substance, that exists without the mind or unperceived, which is the *occasion of our ideas*, or at the presence whereof God is pleased to excite ideas in us: it doth not appear but that matter taken in this sense may possibly exist. In answer to which I say, first, that it seems no less absurd to suppose a substance without accidents, than it is to suppose accidents without a substance. But secondly, though we should grant this unknown substance may possibly exist, yet where can it be supposed to be? That it exists not in the mind is agreed; and that it exists not in place is no less certain—since all place or extension exists only in the mind, as hath been already proved. It remains therefore that it exists nowhere at all.

68. Let us examine a little the description that is here given us of *matter*. It neither acts, nor perceives, nor is perceived; for this is all that is meant by saying it is an inert, senseless, unknown substance: which is a definition entirely made up of negatives, excepting only the relative notion of its standing under or supporting. But then it must be observed that it supports nothing at all, and how nearly this comes to the description of a *nonentity* I desire may be considered. But, say you, it is the *unknown occasion*, at the presence of which ideas are excited in us by the will of God. Now, I would fain know how anything can be present to us, which is neither perceivable by sense nor reflection, nor capable of producing any idea in our minds, nor is at all extended, nor hath any form, nor exists in any place. The words 'to be present,' when thus applied, must needs be taken in some abstract and strange meaning, and which I am not able to comprehend.

69. Again, let us examine what is meant by *occasion*. So far as I can gather from the common use of language, that word signifies either the agent which produces any effect, or

else something that is observed to accompany or go before it in the ordinary course of things. But when it is applied to matter as above described, it can be taken in neither of those senses; for matter is said to be passive and inert, and so cannot be an agent or efficient cause. It is also unperceivable, as being devoid of all sensible qualities, and so cannot be the occasion of our perceptions in the latter sense: as when the burning my finger is said to be the occasion of the pain that attends it. What therefore can be meant by calling matter an *occasion*? The term is either used in no sense at all, or else in some very distant from its received signification.

70. You will perhaps say that matter, though it be not perceived by us, is nevertheless perceived by God, to whom it is the occasion of exciting ideas in our minds. For, say you, since we observe our sensations to be imprinted in an orderly and constant manner, it is but reasonable to suppose there are certain constant and regular occasions of their being produced. That is to say, that there are certain permanent and distinct parcels of matter, corresponding to our ideas, which, though they do not excite them in our minds, or anywise immediately affect us, as being altogether passive and unperceivable to us, they are nevertheless to God, by whom they are perceived, as it were so many occasions to remind Him when and what ideas to imprint on our minds; that so things may go on in a constant uniform manner.

71. In answer to this, I observe that, as the notion of matter is here stated, the question is no longer concerning the existence of a thing distinct from *spirit* and *idea*, from perceiving and being perceived; but whether there are not certain ideas of I know not what sort, in the mind of God which are so many marks or notes that direct Him how to produce sensations in our minds in a constant and regular method—much after the same manner as a musician is directed by the notes of music to produce that harmonious train and composition of sound which is called a tune, though they who hear the music do not perceive the notes, and may be entirely ignorant of them. But, this notion of matter seems too extravagant to deserve a confutation. Besides, it is in effect no objection against what we have advanced, to wit, that there is no senseless unperceived substance.

72. If we follow the light of reason, we shall, from the constant uniform method of our sensations, collect the goodness and wisdom of the Spirit who excites them in our minds;

but this is all that I can see reasonably concluded from thence. To me, I say, it is evident that the being of a spirit infinitely wise, good, and powerful is abundantly sufficient to explain all the appearances of nature. But as for *inert, senseless matter*, nothing that I perceive has any the least connection with it, or leads to the thoughts of it. And I would fain see anyone explain any the meanest phenomenon in nature by it, or shew any manner of reason, though in the lowest rank of probability, that he can have for its existence, or even make any tolerable sense or meaning of that supposition. For, as to its being an occasion, we have, I think, evidently shewn that with regard to us it is no occasion. It remains therefore that it must be, if at all, the occasion to God of exciting ideas in us; and what this amounts to we have just now seen.

73. It is worth while to reflect a little on the motives which inducted men to suppose the existence of *material substance*; that so having observed the gradual ceasing and expiration of those motives or reasons, we may proportionably withdraw the assent that was grounded on them. First, therefore, it was thought that color, figure, motion, and the rest of the sensible qualities or accidents, did really exist without the mind; and for this reason it seemed needful to suppose some unthinking *substratum* or substance wherein they did exist, since they could not be conceived to exist by themselves. Afterwards, in process of time, men being convinced that colors, sounds, and the rest of the sensible, secondary qualities had no existence without the mind, they stripped this *substratum* or material substance of those qualities, leaving only the primary ones, figure, motion, and suchlike, which they still conceived to exist without the mind, and consequently to stand in need of a material support. But, it having been shewn that none even of these can possibly exist otherwise than in a spirit or mind which perceives them, it follows that we have no longer any reason to suppose the being of matter; nay, that it is utterly impossible there should be any such thing, so long as that word is taken to denote an *unthinking substratum* of qualities or accidents wherein they exist without the mind.

74. But though it be allowed by the materialists themselves that matter was thought of only for the sake of supporting accidents, and, the reason entirely ceasing, one might expect the mind should naturally, and without any reluctance at all, quit the belief of what was solely grounded thereon; yet the prejudice is riveted so deeply in our thoughts, that we can

scarce tell how to part with it, and are therefore inclined, since the *thing* itself is indefensible, at least to retain the *name*, which we apply to I know not what abstracted and indefinite notions of being, or occasion, though without any show of reason, at least so far as I can see. For, what is there on our part, or what do we perceive, amongst all the ideas, sensations, notions which are imprinted on our minds, either by sense or reflection, from whence may be inferred the existence of an inert, thoughtless, unperceived occasion? And, on the other hand, on the part of an all-sufficient Spirit, what can there be that should make us believe or even suspect He is directed by an inert occasion to excite ideas in our minds?

75. It is a very extraordinary instance of the force of prejudice, and much to be lamented, that the mind of man retains so great a fondness, against all the evidence of reason, for a stupid thoughtless *somewhat*, by the interposition whereof it would as it were screen itself from the providence of God, and remove it farther off from the affairs of the world. But, though we do the utmost we can to secure the belief of *matter*, though, when reason forsakes us, we endeavor to support our opinion on the bare possibility of the thing, and though we indulge ourselves in the full scope of an imagination not regulated by reason to make out that poor possibility, yet the upshot of all is, that there are certain *unknown ideas* in the mind of God; for this, if anything, is all that I conceive to be meant by *occasion* with regard to God. And this at the bottom is no longer contending for the thing, but for the name.

76. Whether therefore there are such ideas in the mind of God, and whether they may be called by the name 'matter,' I shall not dispute. But, if you stick to the notion of an unthinking substance or support of extension, motion, and other sensible qualities, then to me it is most evidently impossible there should be any such thing; since it is a plain repugnancy that those qualities should exist in or be supported by an unperceiving substance.

77. But, say you, though it be granted that there is no thoughtless support of extension and the other qualities or accidents which we perceive, yet there may perhaps be some inert, unperceiving substance or *substratum* of some other qualities, as incomprehensible to us as colors are to a man born blind, because we have not a sense adapted to them. But, if we had a new sense, we should possibly no more doubt of their existence than a blind man made to see does of the

existence of light and colors. I answer, first, if what you mean by the word 'matter' be only the unknown support of unknown qualities, it is no matter whether there is such a thing or no, since it no way concerns us; and I do not see the advantage there is in disputing about what we know not *what*, and we know not *why*.

78. But, secondly, if we had a new sense it could only furnish us with new ideas or sensations; and then we should have the same reason against their existing in an unperceiving substance that has been already offered with relation to figure, motion, color, and the like. Qualities, as hath been shewn, are nothing else but *sensations* or *ideas*, which exist only in a *mind* perceiving them; and this is true not only of the ideas we are acquainted with at present, but likewise of all possible ideas whatsoever.

79. But, you will insist, what if I have no reason to believe the existence of matter? what if I cannot assign any use to it or explain anything by it, or even conceive what is meant by that word? yet still it is no contradiction to say that matter exists, and that this matter is in general a *substance*, or *occasion of ideas*; though indeed to go about to unfold the meaning or adhere to any particular explication of those words may be attended with great difficulties. I answer, when words are used without a meaning, you may put them together as you please without danger of running into a contradiction. You may say, for example, that twice two is equal to seven, so long as you declare you do not take the words of that proposition in their usual acceptation but for marks of you know not what. And, by the same reason, you may say there is an inert thoughtless substance without accidents which is the occasion of our ideas. And we shall understand just as much by one proposition as the other.

80. In the *last* place, you will say, what if we give up the cause of material substance, and stand to it that matter is an unknown *somewhat*—neither substance nor accident, spirit nor idea, inert, thoughtless, indivisible, immovable, unextended, existing in no place. For, say you, whatever may be urged against *substance* or *occasion*, or any other positive or relative notion of matter, hath no place at all, so long as this *negative* definition of matter is adhered to. I answer, you may, if so it shall seem good, use the word 'matter' in the same sense as other men use 'nothing,' and so make those terms convertible in your style. For, after all, this is what appears

to me to be the result of that definition, the parts whereof when I consider with attention, either collectively or separate from each other, I do not find that there is any kind of effect or impression made on my mind different from what is excited by the term 'nothing.'

81. You will reply, perhaps, that in the foresaid definition is included what doth sufficiently distinguish it from nothing: the positive abstract idea of *quiddity*, *entity*, or *existence*. I own, indeed, that those who pretend to the faculty of framing abstract general ideas do talk as if they had such an idea, which is, say they, the most abstract and general notion of all; that is, to me, the most incomprehensible of all others. That there are a great variety of spirits of different orders and capacities, whose faculties both in number and extent are far exceeding those the Author of my being has bestowed on me, I see no reason to deny. And for me to pretend to determine by my own few, stinted narrow inlets of perception, what ideas the inexhaustible power of the Supreme Spirit may imprint upon them were certainly the utmost folly and presumption—since there may be, for aught that I know, innumerable sorts of ideas or sensations, as different from one another, and from all that I have perceived, as colors are from sounds. But, how ready soever I may be to acknowledge the scantiness of my comprehension with regard to the endless variety of spirits and ideas that may possibly exist, yet for anyone to pretend to a notion of entity or existence, *abstracted* from *spirit* and *idea*, from perceived and being perceived, is, I suspect, a downright repugnancy and trifling with words.

It remains that we consider the objections which may possibly be made on the part of religion.

82. Some there are who think that, though the arguments for the real existence of bodies which are drawn from reason be allowed not to amount to demonstration, yet the Holy Scriptures are so clear in the point as will sufficiently convince every good Christian that bodies do really exist, and are something more than mere ideas; there being in Holy Writ innumerable facts related which evidently suppose the reality of timber and stone, mountains and rivers, and cities, and human bodies. To which I answer that no sort of writings whatever, sacred or profane, which use those and the like words in the vulgar acceptation, or so as to have a meaning in them, are in danger of having their truth called in question by our doctrine. That all those things do really exist, that there are

bodies, even corporeal substances, when taken in the vulgar sense, has been shewn to be agreeable to our principles: and the difference betwixt *things* and *ideas*, *realities* and *chimeras*, has been distinctly explained. (See Secs. 29, 30, 33, 36, etc.) And I do not think that either what philosophers call *matter*, or the existence of objects without the mind, is anywhere mentioned in Scripture.

83. Again, whether there can be or be not external things, it is agreed on all hands that the proper use of words is the marking our conceptions, or things only as they are known and perceived by us; whence it plainly follows that in the tenets we have laid down there is nothing inconsistent with the right use and significancy of language, and that discourse, of what kind soever, so far as it is intelligible, remains undisturbed. But all this seems so manifest, from what has been largely set forth in the premises, that it is needless to insist any farther on it.

84. But, it will be urged that miracles do, at least, lose much of their stress and import by our principles. What must we think of Moses' rod: was it not *really* turned into a serpent; or was there only a change of *ideas* in the minds of the spectators? And, can it be supposed that our Saviour did no more at the marriage-feast in Cana than impose on the sight, and smell, and taste of the guests, so as to create in them the appearance or idea only of wine? The same may be said of all other miracles; which, in consequence of the foregoing principles, must be looked upon only as so many cheats, or illusions of fancy. To this I reply, that the rod was changed into a real serpent, and the water into real wine. That this does not in the least contradict what I have elsewhere said will be evident from Secs. 34 and 35. But this business of *real* and *imaginary* hath been already so plainly and fully explained, and so often referred to, and the difficulties about it are so easily answered from what hath gone before, that it were an affront to the reader's understanding to resume the explication of it in its place. I shall only observe that if at table all who were present should see, and smell, and taste, and drink wine, and find the effects of it, with me there could be no doubts of its reality; so that at bottom the scruple concerning real miracles has no place at all on ours, but only on the received principles, and consequently makes rather for than against what hath been said.

85. Having done with the objections, which I endeavored

to propose in the clearest light, and gave them all the force and weight I could, we proceed in the next place to take a view of our tenets in their *consequences*. Some of these appear at first sight: as that several difficult and obscure questions, on which abundance of speculation has been thrown away, are entirely banished from philosophy. "Whether corporeal substance can think," "whether matter be infinitely divisible," and "how it operates on spirit"—these and like inquiries have given infinite amusement to philosophers in all ages; but, depending on the existence of matter, they have no longer any place on our principles. Many other advantages there are, as well with regard to religion as the sciences, which it is easy for anyone to deduce from what has been premised; but this will appear more plainly in the sequel.

86. From the principles we have laid down it follows human knowledge may naturally be reduced to two heads: that of *ideas* and that of *spirits*. Of each of these I shall treat in order.

And *first* as to ideas or unthinking things. Our knowledge of these hath been very much obscured and confounded, and we have been led into very dangerous errors, by supposing a twofold existence of the objects of sense—the one *intelligible* or in the mind, the other *real* and without the mind; whereby unthinking things are thought to have a natural subsistence of their own distinct from being perceived by spirits. This, which, if I mistake not, hath been shewn to be a most groundless and absurd notion, is the very root of scepticism; for, so long as men thought that real things subsisted without the mind, and that their knowledge was not so far forth *real* as it was conformable to *real things*, it follows they could not be certain they had any real knowledge at all. For how can it be known that the things which are perceived are conformable to those which are not perceived, or exist without the mind?

87. Color, figure, motion, extension, and the like, considered only as so many *sensations* in the mind, are perfectly known, there being nothing in them which is not perceived. But, if they are looked on as notes or images, referred to *things* or *archetypes* existing without the mind, then are we involved all in scepticism. We see only the appearances, and not the real qualities of things. What may be the extension, figure, or motion of anything really and absolutely, or in itself, it is impossible for us to know, but only the proportion or relation they bear to our senses. Things remaining the same, our ideas

vary, and which of them, or even whether any of them at all, represent the true quality really existing in the thing, it is out of our reach to determine. So that, for aught we know, all we see, hear, and feel may be only phantom and vain chimera, and not at all agree with the real things existing in our *rerum natura.* All this scepticism follows from our supposing a difference between *things* and *ideas,* and that the former have a subsistence without the mind or unperceived. It were easy to dilate on this subject, and show how the arguments urged by sceptics in all ages depend on the supposition of external objects.

88. So long as we attribute a real existence to unthinking things, distinct from their being perceived, it is not only impossible for us to know with evidence the nature of any real unthinking being, but even that it exists. Hence it is that we see philosophers distrust their senses, and doubt of the existence of heaven and earth, of everything they see or feel, even of their own bodies. And, after all their labor and struggle of thought, they are forced to own we cannot attain to any self-evident or demonstrative knowledge of the existence of sensible things. But, all this doubtfulness, which so bewilders and confounds the mind and makes philosophy ridiculous in the eyes of the world, vanishes if we annex a meaning to our words, and not amuse ourselves with the terms 'absolute,' 'external,' 'exist,' and such like, signifying we know not what. I can as well doubt of my own being as of the being of those things which I actually perceive by sense; it being a manifest contradiction that any sensible object should be immediately perceived by sight or touch, and at the same time have no existence in nature, since the very *existence* of an unthinking being consists in *being perceived.*

89. Nothing seems of more importance towards erecting a firm system of sound and real knowledge, which may be proof against the assaults of scepticism, than to lay the beginning in a distinct explication of what is meant by *thing, reality, existence*; for in vain shall we dispute concerning the real existence of things, or pretend to any knowledge thereof, so long as we have not fixed the meaning of those words. *Thing* or *Being* is the most general name of all; it comprehends under it two kinds entirely distinct and heterogeneous, and which have nothing common but the name, to wit, *spirits* and *ideas.* The former are active, indivisible substances: the latter are inert, fleeting, dependent beings, which subsist not by them-

selves, but are supported by, or exist in minds or spiritual substances. We comprehend our own existence by inward feeling or reflection, and that of other spirits by reason. We may be said to have some knowledge or notion of our own minds, of spirits and active beings, whereof in a strict sense we have not ideas. In like manner we know and have a notion of relations between things or ideas—which relations are distinct from the ideas or things related, inasmuch as the latter may be perceived by us without our perceiving the former. To me it seems that *ideas, spirits*, and *relations* are all in their respective kinds the object of human knowledge and subject of discourse; and that the term 'idea' would be improperly extended to signify everything we know or have any notion of.

90. Ideas imprinted on the senses are real things, or do really exist; this we do not deny, but we deny they can subsist without the minds which perceive them, or that they are resemblances of any archetypes existing without the mind; since the very being of a sensation or idea consists in being perceived, and an idea can be like nothing but an idea. Again, the things perceived by sense may be termed *external*, with regard to their origin: in that they are not generated from within by the mind itself, but imprinted by a Spirit distinct from that which perceives them. Sensible objects may likewise be said to be 'without the mind' in another sense, namely when they exist in some other mind; thus, when I shut my eyes, the things I saw may still exist, but it must be in another mind.

91. It were a mistake to think that what is here said derogates in the least from the reality of things. It is acknowledged, on the received principles, that extension, motion, and in a word all sensible qualities have need of a support, as not being able to subsist by themselves. But the objects perceived by sense are allowed to be nothing but combinations of those qualities, and consequently cannot subsist by themselves. Thus far it is agreed on all hands. So that in denying the things perceived by sense an existence independent of a substance of support wherein they may exist, we detract nothing from the received opinion of their *reality*, and are guilty of no innovation in that respect. All the difference is that, according to us, the unthinking beings perceived by sense have no existence distinct from being perceived, and cannot therefore exist in any other substance than those unextended indivisible substances or *spirits* which act and think and perceive them;

whereas philosophers vulgarly hold that the sensible qualities do exist in an inert, extended, unperceiving substance which they call *matter*, to which they attribute a natural subsistence, exterior to all thinking beings, or distinct from being perceived by any mind whatsoever, even the eternal mind of the Creator, wherein they suppose only ideas of the corporeal substances created by Him; if indeed they allow them to be at all created.

92. For, as we have shewn the doctrine of matter or corporeal substance to have been the main pillar and support of scepticism, so likewise upon the same foundation have been raised all the impious schemes of atheism and irreligion. Nay, so great a difficulty hath it been thought to conceive matter produced out of nothing, that the most celebrated among the ancient philosophers, even of those who maintained the being of God, have thought matter to be uncreated and coeternal with Him. How great a friend *material substance* hath been to atheists in all ages were needless to relate. All their monstrous systems have so visible and necessary a dependence on it that, when this cornerstone is once removed, the whole fabric cannot choose but fall to the ground, insomuch that it is no longer worth while to bestow a particular consideration on the absurdities of every wretched sect of atheists.

93. That impious and profane persons should readily fall in with those systems which favor their inclinations, by deriding immaterial substance, and supposing the soul to be divisible and subject to corruption as the body; which exclude all freedom, intelligence, and design from the formation of things, and instead thereof make a self-existent, stupid, unthinking substance the root and origin of all beings; that they should hearken to those who deny a Providence, or inspection of a Superior Mind over the affairs of the world, attributing the whole series of events either to blind chance or fatal necessity arising from the impulse of one body or another—all this is very natural. And, on the other hand, when men of better principles observe the enemies of religion lay so great a stress on *unthinking matter*, and all of them use so much industry and artifice to reduce everything to it, methinks they should rejoice to see them deprived of their grand support, and driven from that only fortress, without which your Epicureans, Hobbists, and the like, have not even the shadow of a pretense, but become the most cheap and easy triumph in the world.

94. The existence of matter, or bodies unperceived, has not only been the main support of atheists and fatalists, but on

the same principle doth idolatry likewise in all its various forms depend. Did men but consider that the sun, moon, and stars, and every other object of the senses are not so many sensations in their minds, which have no other existence but barely being perceived, doubtless they would never fall down and worship their own *ideas*, but rather address their homage to that Eternal Invisible Mind which produces and sustains all things.

95. The same absurd principle, by mingling itself with the articles of our faith, has occasioned no small difficulties to Christians. For example, about the Resurrection, how many scruples and objections have been raised by Socinians and others? But do not the most plausible of them depend on the supposition that a body is denominated the *same*, with regard not to the form or that which is perceived by sense, but the material substance, which remains the same under several forms? Take away this *material substance*, about the identity whereof all the dispute is, and mean by *body* what every plain ordinary person means by that word, to wit, that which is immediately seen and felt, which is only a combination of sensible qualities or ideas, and then their most unanswerable objections come to nothing.

96. Matter being once expelled out of nature drags with it so many sceptical and impious notions, such an incredible number of disputes and puzzling questions, which have been thorns in the sides of divines as well as philosophers, and made so much fruitless work for mankind, that if the arguments we have produced against it are not found equal to demonstration (as to me they evidently seem), yet I am sure all friends to knowledge, peace, and religion have reason to wish they were.

97. Beside the external existence of the objects of perception, another great source of errors and difficulties with regard to ideal knowledge is the doctrine of *abstract ideas*, such as it hath been set forth in the Introduction. The plainest things in the world, those we are most intimately acquainted with and perfectly know, when they are considered in an abstract way, appear strangely difficult and incomprehensible. Time, place, and motion, taken in particular or concrete, are what everybody knows, but, having passed through the hands of a metaphysician, they become too abstract and fine to be apprehended by men of ordinary sense. Bid your servant meet you at such a *time* in such a *place*, and he shall never stay to

deliberate on the meaning of those words; in conceiving that particular time and place, or the motion by which he is not to get thither, he finds not the least difficulty. But if *time* be taken exclusive of all those particular actions and ideas that diversify the day, merely for the continuation of existence or duration in abstract, then it will perhaps gravel even a philosopher to comprehend it.

98. For my own part, whenever I attempt to frame a simple idea of *time*, abstracted from the succession of ideas in my mind, which flows uniformly and is participated by all beings, I am lost and embrangled in inextricable difficulties. I have no notion of it at all, only I hear others say it is infinitely divisible, and speak of it in such a manner as leads me to entertain odd thoughts of my existence; since that doctrine lays one under an absolute necessity of thinking, either that he passes away innumerable ages without a thought, or else that he is annihilated every moment of his life, both which seem equally absurd. Time therefore being nothing, abstracted from the succession of ideas in our minds, it follows that the duration of any finite spirit must be estimated by the number of ideas or actions succeeding each other in that same spirit or mind. Hence, it is a plain consequence that the soul always thinks; and in truth whoever shall go about to divide in his thoughts, or abstract the *existence* of a spirit from its *cogitation*, will, I believe, find it no easy task.

99. So likewise when we attempt to abstract extension and motion from all other qualities, and consider them by themselves, we presently lose sight of them, and run into great extravagances. All which depend on a twofold abstraction; first, it is supposed that extension, for example, may be abstracted from all other sensible qualities; and secondly, that the entity of extension may be abstracted from its being perceived. But, whoever shall reflect, and take care to understand what he says, will, if I mistake not, acknowledge that all sensible qualities are alike *sensations* and alike *real*; that where the extension is, there is the color, too, to wit, in his mind, and that their archetypes can exist only in some other *mind*; and that the objects of sense are nothing but those sensations combined, blended, or (if one may so speak) concreted together; none of all which can be supposed to exist unperceived.

100. What it is for a man to be happy, or an object good, everyone may think he knows. But to frame an abstract idea of happiness, prescinded from all particular pleasure, or of

goodness from everything that is good, this is what few can pretend to. So likewise a man may be just and virtuous without having precise ideas of justice and virtue. The opinion that those and the like words stand for general notions, abstracted from all particular persons and actions, seems to have rendered morality very difficult, and the study thereof of small use to mankind. And in effect the doctrine of *abstraction* has not a little contributed towards spoiling the most useful parts of knowledge.

101. The two great provinces of speculative science conversant about ideas received from sense, are *natural philosophy* and *mathematics*; with regard to each of these I shall make some observations. And first I shall say somewhat of natural philosophy. On this subject it is that the sceptics triumph. All that stock of arguments they produce to depreciate our faculties and make mankind appear ignorant and low, are drawn principally from this head, namely, that we are under an invincible blindness as to the *true* and *real* nature of things. This they exaggerate, and love to enlarge on. We are miserably bantered, say they, by our senses, and amused only with the outside and show of things. The real essence, the internal qualities and constitution of every the meanest object, is hid from our view; something there is in every drop of water, every grain of sand, which it is beyond the power of human understanding to fathom or comprehend. But it is evident from what has been shewn that all this complaint is groundless, and that we are influenced by false principles to that degree as to mistrust our senses, and think we know nothing of those things which we perfectly comprehend.

102. One great inducement to our pronouncing ourselves ignorant of the nature of things is the current opinion that everything includes within itself the cause of its properties; or that there is in each object an inward essence which is the source whence its discernible qualities flow, and whereon they depend. Some have pretended to account for appearances by occult qualities, but of late they are mostly resolved into mechanical causes, to wit, the figure, motion, weight, and suchlike qualities, of insensible particles; whereas, in truth, there is no other agent or efficient cause than *spirit*, it being evident that motion, as well as all other *ideas*, is perfectly inert. (See Sec. 25.) Hence, to endeavor to explain the production of colors or sounds, by figure, motion, magnitude, and the like, must needs be labor in vain. And accordingly

we see the attempts of that kind are not at all satisfactory. Which may be said in general of those instances wherein one idea or quality is assigned for the cause of another. I need not say how many hypotheses and speculations are left out, and how much the study of nature is abridged by this doctrine.

103. The great mechanical principle now in vogue is *attraction*. That a stone falls to the earth, or the sea swells towards the moon, may to some appear sufficiently explained thereby. But how are we enlightened by being told this is done by attraction? Is it that that word signifies the manner of the tendency, and that it is by the mutual drawing of bodies instead of their being impelled or protruded towards each other? But nothing is determined of the manner or action, and it may as truly (for aught we know) be termed 'impulse,' or 'protrusion,' as 'attraction.' Again, the parts of steel we see cohere firmly together, and this also is accounted for by attraction; but, in this as in the other instances, I do not perceive that anything is signified besides the effect itself; for as to the manner of the action whereby it is produced, or the cause which produces it, these are not so much as aimed at.

104. Indeed, if we take a view of the several phenomena, and compare them together, we may observe some likeness and conformity between them. For example, in the falling of a stone to the ground, in the rising of the sea towards the moon, in cohesion, crystallization, etc., there is something alike, namely, an union or mutual approach of bodies. So that any one of these or the like phenomena may not seem strange or surprising to a man who has nicely observed and compared the effects of nature. For that only is thought so which is uncommon, or a thing by itself, and out of the ordinary course of our observation. That bodies should tend towards the center of the earth is not thought strange, because it is what we perceive every moment of our lives. But that they should have a like gravitation towards the center of the moon may seem odd and unaccountable to most men, because it is discerned only in the tides. But a philosopher, whose thoughts take in a larger compass of nature, having observed a certain similitude of appearances, as well in the heavens as the earth, that argue innumerable bodies to have a mutual tendency towards each other, which he denotes by the general name 'attraction,' whatever can be reduced to that he thinks justly accounted for. Thus he explains the tides by the attraction of the terraqueous globe towards the moon, which to him

doth not appear odd or anomalous, but only a particular example of a general rule or law of nature.

105. If therefore we consider the difference there is betwixt natural philosophers and other men, with regard to their knowledge of the phenomena, we shall find it consists not in an exacter knowledge of the efficient cause that produces them, for that can be no other than the *will of a spirit;* but only in a greater largeness of comprehension, whereby analogies, harmonies, and agreements are discovered in the works of nature, and the particular effect explained, that is, reduced to general rules (see Sec. 62), which rules, grounded on the analogy and uniformness observed in the production of natural effects, are most agreeable and sought after by the mind; for that they extend our prospect beyond what is present and near to us, and enable us to make very probable conjectures touching things that may have happened at very great distances of time and place, as well as to predict things to come; which sort of endeavor towards omniscience is much affected by the mind.

106. But we should proceed warily in such things, for we are apt to lay too great stress on analogies, and, to the prejudice of truth, humor that eagerness of the mind whereby it is carried to extend its knowledge into general theorems. For example, in the business of gravitation or mutual attraction, because it appears in many instances, some are straightway for pronouncing it *universal;* and that to attract and be attracted by every other body is an essential quality inherent in all bodies whatsoever. Whereas it is evident the fixed stars have no such tendency towards each other; and, so far is that gravitation from being *essential* to bodies that in some instances a quite contrary principle seems to shew itself; as in the perpendicular growth of plants, and the elasticity of the air. There is nothing necessary or essential in the case, but it depends entirely on the will of the Governing Spirit, who causes certain bodies to cleave together or tend towards each other according to various laws, whilst He keeps others at a fixed distance; and to some He gives a quite contrary tendency to fly asunder just as He sees convenient.

107. After what has been premised, I think we may lay down the following conclusions. First, it is plain philosophers amuse themselves in vain, when they inquire for any natural efficient cause, distinct from a *mind* or *spirit.* Secondly, considering the whole creation is the workmanship of a *wise and*

good Agent, it should seem to become philosophers to employ their thoughts (contrary to what some hold) about the final causes of things; and I confess I see no reason why pointing out the various ends to which natural things are adapted, and for which they were originally with unspeakable wisdom contrived, should not be thought one good way of accounting for them, and altogether worthy a philosopher. Thirdly, from what hath been premised no reason can be drawn why the history of nature should not still be studied, and observations and experiments made, which, that they are of use to mankind, and enable us to draw any general conclusions, is not the result of any immutable habitudes or relations between things themselves, but only of God's goodness and kindness to men in the administration of the world. (See Secs. 30 and 31.) Fourthly, by a diligent observation of the phenomena within our view, we may discover the general laws of nature, and from them deduce the other phenomena; I do not say *demonstrate*, for all deductions of that kind depend on a supposition that the Author of Nature always operates uniformly, and in a constant observance of those rules we take for principles: which we cannot evidently know.

108. Those men who frame general rules from the phenomena and afterwards derive the phenomena from those rules, seem to consider signs rather than causes. A man may well understand natural signs without knowing their analogy, or being able to say by what rule a thing is so or so. And, as it is very possible to write improperly, through too strict an observance of general grammar rules; so, in arguing from general laws of nature, it is not impossible we may extend the analogy too far, and by that means run into mistakes.

109. As in reading other books a wise man will choose to fix his thoughts on the sense and apply it to use, rather than lay them out in grammatical remarks on the language; so, in perusing the volume of nature, it seems beneath the dignity of the mind to affect an exactness in reducing each particular phenomenon to general rules, or shewing how it follows from them. We should propose to ourselves nobler views, namely, to recreate and exalt the mind with a prospect of the beauty, order, extent, and variety of natural things: hence, by proper inferences, to enlarge our notions of the grandeur, wisdom, and beneficence of the Creator; and lastly, to make the several parts of the creation, so far as in us lies, subservient to the

ends they were designed for, God's glory, and the sustenation and comfort of ourselves and fellow-creatures.

110. The best key for the aforesaid analogy or natural science will be easily acknowledged to be a certain celebrated treatise of *mechanics*. In the entrance of which justly admired treatise, time, space, and motion are distinguished into *absolute* and *relative, true* and *apparent, mathematical* and *vulgar;* which distinction, as it is at large explained by the author, does suppose these quantities to have an existence without the mind; and that they are ordinarily conceived with relation to sensible things, to which nevertheless in their own nature they bear no relation at all.

111. As for *time,* as it is there taken in an absolute or abstracted sense, for the duration or perseverance of the existence of things, I have nothing more to add concerning it after what has been already said on that subject. (Secs. 97 and 98.) For the rest, this celebrated author holds there is an *absolute space,* which, being unperceivable to sense, remains in itself similar and immovable; and relative space to be the measure thereof, which, being movable and defined by its situation in respect of sensible bodies, is vulgarly taken for immovable space. *Place* he defines to be that part of space which is occupied by any body; and according as the space is absolute or relative so also is the place. *Absolute motion* is said to be the translation of a body from absolute place to absolute place, as relative motion is from one relative place to another. And, because the parts of absolute space do not fall under our senses, instead of them we are obliged to use their sensible measures, and so define both place and motion with respect to bodies which we regard as immovable. But, it is said in philosophical matters we must abstract from our senses, since it may be that none of those bodies which seem to be quiescent are truly so, and the same thing which is moved relatively may be really at rest; as likewise one and the same body may be in relative rest and motion, or even moved with contrary relative motions at the same time, according as its place is variously defined. All which ambiguity is to be found in the apparent motions, but not at all in the true or absolute, which should therefore be alone regarded in philosophy. And the true as we are told are distinguished from apparent or relative motions by the following properties. First, in true or absolute motion all parts which preserve the same position with respect of the whole, partake of the motions of the whole. Secondly,

the place being moved, that which is placed therein is also moved; so that a body moving in a place which is in motion doth participate the motion of its place. Thirdly, true motion is never generated or changed otherwise than by force impressed on the body itself. Fourthly, true motion is always changed by force impressed on the body moved. Fifthly, in circular motion barely relative there is no centrifugal force, which, nevertheless, in that which is true or absolute, is proportional to the quantity of motion.

112. But, notwithstanding what hath been said, I must confess it doth not appear to me that there can be any motion other than *relative*; so that to conceive motion there must be at least conceived two bodies, whereof the distance or position in regard to each other is varied. Hence, if there was one only body in being it could not possibly be moved. This seems evident, in that the idea I have of motion doth necessarily include relation.

113. But, though in every motion it be necessary to conceive more bodies than one, yet it may be that one only is moved, namely, that on which the force causing the change in the distance or situation of the bodies, is impressed. For, however some may define relative motion, so as to term that body *moved* which changes its distance from some other body, whether the force or action causing that change were impressed on it or no, yet as relative motion is that which is perceived by sense, and regarded in the ordinary affairs of life, it should seem that every man of common sense knows what it is as well as the best philosopher. Now, I ask anyone whether, in his sense of motion as he walks along the streets, the stones he passes over may be said to *move*, because they change distance with his feet? To me it appears that though motion includes a relation of one thing to another, yet it is not necessary that each term of the relation be denominated from it. As a man may think of somewhat which does not think, so a body may be moved to or from another body which is not therefore itself in motion.

114. As the place happens to be variously defined, the motion which is related to it varies. A man in a ship may be said to be quiescent with relation to the sides of the vessel, and yet move with relation to the land. Or he may move eastward in respect of the one, and westward in respect of the other. In the common affairs of life men never go beyond the earth to define the place of any body; and what is quiescent

in respect of that is accounted *absolutely* to be so. But philosophers, who have a greater extent of thought, and juster notions of the system of things, discover even the earth itself to be moved. In order therefore to fix their notions they seem to conceive the corporeal world as finite, and the utmost unmoved walls or shell thereof to be the place whereby they estimate true motions. If we sound our own conceptions, I believe we may find all the absolute motion we can frame an idea of to be at bottom no other than relative motion thus defined. For, as hath been already observed, absolute motion, exclusive of all external relation, is incomprehensible; and to this kind of relative motion all the above-mentioned properties, causes, and effects ascribed to absolute motion will, if I mistake not, be found to agree. As to what is said of the centrifugal force, that it doth not at all belong to circular relative motion, I do not see how this follows from the experiment which is brought to prove it. (See *Philosophiae Naturalis Principia Mathematica, in Schol. Def.* *VIII.*) For the water in the vessel at that time wherein it is said to have the greatest relative circular motion, hath, I think, no motion at all; as is plain from the foregoing section.

115. For to denominate a body *moved* it is requisite, first, that it change its distance or situation with regard to some other body; and secondly, that the force occasioning that change be applied to it. If either of these be wanting, I do not think that, agreeably to the sense of mankind, or the propriety of language, a body can be said to be in motion. I grant indeed that it is possible for us to think a body which we see change its distance from some other to be moved, though it have no force applied to it (in which sense there may be apparent motion), but then it is because the force causing the change of distance is imagined by us to be applied or impressed on that body thought to move; which indeed shews we are capable of mistaking a thing to be in motion which is not, and that is all.

116. From what hath been said it follows that the philosophic consideration of motion doth not imply the being of an *absolute space*, distinct from that which is perceived of sense and related bodies; which that it cannot exist without the mind is clear upon the same principles that demonstrate the like of all other objects of sense. And perhaps, if we inquire narrowly, we shall find we cannot even frame an idea of *pure space* exclusive of all body. This I must confess seems

impossible, as being a most abstract idea. When I excite a motion in some part of my body, if it be free or without resistance, I say there is *space*; but if I find a resistance, then I say there is *body*; and in proportion as the resistance to motion is lesser or greater, I say the space is more or less *pure*. So that when I speak of pure or empty space, it is not to be supposed that the word 'space' stands for an idea distinct from or conceivable without body and motion. Though indeed we are apt to think every noun substantive stands for a distinct idea that may be separated from all others; which has occasioned infinite mistakes. When, therefore, supposing all the world to be annihilated besides my own body, I say there still remains *pure space*, thereby nothing else is meant but only that I conceive it possible for the limbs of my body to be moved on all sides without the least resistance, but if that, too, were annihilated then there could be no motion, and consequently no space. Some, perhaps, may think the sense of seeing doth furnish them with the idea of pure space; but it is plain from what we have elsewhere shewn, that the ideas of space and distance are not obtained by that sense. (See the Essay concerning Vision.)

117. What is here laid down seems to put an end to all those disputes and difficulties that have sprung up amongst the learned concerning the nature of *pure space*. But the chief advantage arising from it is that we are freed from that dangerous dilemma, to which several who have employed their thoughts on that subject imagine themselves reduced, to wit, of thinking either that real space is God, or else that there is something beside God which is eternal, uncreated, infinite, indivisible, immutable. Both which may justly be thought pernicious and absurd notions. It is certain that not a few divines, as well as philosophers of great note, have, from the difficulty they found in conceiving either limits or annihilation of space, concluded it must be divine. And some of late have set themselves particularly to shew the incommunicable attributes of God agree to it. Which doctrine, how unworthy soever it may seem of the Divine Nature, yet I do not see how we can get clear of it, so long as we adhere to the received opinions.

118. Hitherto of natural philosophy: we come now to make some inquiry concerning that other great branch of speculative knowledge, to wit, mathematics. These, how celebrated soever they may be for their clearness and certainty of demonstration,

which is hardly anyhere else to be found, cannot nevertheless be supposed altogether free from mistakes, if in their principles there lurks some secret error which is common to the professors of those sciences with the rest of mankind. Mathematicians, though they deduce their theorems from a great height of evidence, yet their first principles are limited by the consideration of quantity; and they do not ascend into any inquiry concerning those transcendental maxims which influence all the particular sciences, each part whereof, mathematics not excepted, does consequently participate of the errors involved in them. That the principles laid down by mathematicians are true, and their way of deduction from those principles clear and incontestible, we do not deny; but we hold there may be certain erroneous maxims of greater extent than the object of mathematics, and for that reason not expressly mentioned, though tacitly supposed throughout the whole progress of that science; and that the ill effects of those secret unexamined errors are diffused through all the branches thereof. To be plain, we suspect the mathematicians are as well as other men concerned in the errors arising from the doctrine of abstract general ideas, and the existence of objects without the mind.

119. Arithmetic has been thought to have for its object abstract ideas of *number*; of which to understand the properties and mutual habitudes, is supposed no mean part of speculative knowledge. The opinion of the pure and intellectual nature of numbers in abstract hath made them in esteem with those philosophers who seem to have affected an uncommon fineness and elevation of thought. It hath set a price on the most trifling numerical speculations which in practice are of no use, but serve only for amusement; and hath therefore so far infected the minds of some, that they have dreamed of mighty mysteries involved in numbers, and attempted the explication of natural things by them. But, if we inquire into our own thoughts, and consider what hath been premised, we may perhaps entertain a low opinion of those high flights and abstractions, and look on all inquiries, about numbers only as so many *difficiles nugae*, so far as they are not subservient to practice, and promote the benefit of life.

120. Unity in abstract we have before considered in Sec. 13, from which and what hath been said in the Introduction, it plainly follows there is not any such idea. But, number being defined a 'collection of units,' we may conclude that, if there

be no such thing as unity or unit in abstract, there are no ideas of number in abstract denoted by the numeral names and figures. The theories therefore in arithmetic, if they are abstracted from the names and figures, as likewise from all use and practice, as well as from the particular things numbered, can be supposed to have nothing at all for their object; hence we may see how entirely the science of numbers is subordinate to practice, and how jejune and trifling it becomes when considered as a matter of mere speculation.

121. However, since there may be some who, deluded by the specious show of discovering abstracted verities, waste their time in arithmetical theorems and problems which have not any use, it will not be amiss if we more fully consider and expose the vanity of that pretense; and this will plainly appear by taking a view of arithmetic in its infancy, and observing what it was that originally put men on the study of that science, and to what scope they directed it. It is natural to think that at first, men, for ease of memory and help of computation, made use of counters, or in writing of single strokes, points, or the like, each whereof was made to signify an unit, i.e., some one thing of whatever kind they had occasion to reckon. Afterwards they found out the more compendious ways of making one character stand in place of several strokes or points. And, lastly, the notation of the Arabians or Indians came into use, wherein, by the repetition of a few characters or figures, and varying the significance of each figure according to the place it obtains, all numbers may be most aptly expressed; which seems to have been done in imitation of language, so that an exact analogy is observed betwixt the notation by figures and names, the nine simple figures answering the nine first numeral names and places in the former, corresponding to denominations in the latter. And agreeably to those conditions of the simple and local value of figures, were contrived methods of finding, from the given figures or marks of the parts, what figures and how placed are proper to denote the whole, or *vice versa*. And having found the sought figures, the same rule or analogy being observed throughout, it is easy to read them into words; and so the number becomes perfectly known. For then the number of any particular things is said to be known, when we know the name or figures (with their due arrangement) that according to the standing analogy belong to them. For, these signs being known, we can by the operations of arithmetic

know the signs of any part of the particular sums signified by them; and, thus computing in signs (because of the connection established betwixt them and the distinct multitudes of things whereof one is taken for an unit), we may be able rightly to sum up, divide, and proportion the things themselves that we intend to number.

122. In arithmetic, therefore, we regard not the *things*, but the *signs*, which nevertheless are not regarded for their own sake, but because they direct us how to act with relation to things, and dispose rightly of them. Now, agreeably to what we have before observed of words in general (Sec. 19, Introd.) it happens here likewise that abstract ideas are thought to be signified by numeral names or characters, while they do not suggest ideas of particular things to our minds. I shall not at present enter into a more particular dissertation on this subject, but only observe that it is evident from what hath been said, those things which pass for abstract truths and theorems concerning numbers, are in reality conversant about no object distinct from particular numeral things, except only names and characters, which originally came to be considered on no other account but their being signs, or capable to represent aptly whatever particular things men had need to compute. Whence it follows that to study them for their own sake would be just as wise, and to as good purpose as if a man, neglecting the true use or original intention and subserviency of language, should spend his time in impertinent criticisms upon words, or reasonings and controversies purely verbal.

123. From numbers we proceed to speak of *extension*, which, considered as relative, is the object of geometry. The *infinite* divisibility of *finite* extension, though it is not expressly laid down either as an axiom or theorem in the elements of that science, yet is throughout the same everywhere supposed and thought to have so inseparable and essential a connection with the principles and demonstrations in geometry, that mathematicians never admit it into doubt, or make the least question of it. And, as this notion is the source from whence do spring all those amusing geometrical paradoxes which have such a direct repugnancy to the plain common sense of mankind, and are admitted with so much reluctance into a mind not yet debauched by learning; so it is the principal occasion of all that nice and extreme subtilty which renders the study of mathematics so difficult and tedious. Hence, if we can make it appear that no finite extension con-

tains innumerable parts, or is infinitely divisible, it follows that we shall at once clear the science of geometry from a great number of difficulties and contradictions which have ever been esteemed a reproach to human reason, and withal make the attainment thereof a business of much less time and pains than it hitherto hath been.

124. Every particular finite extension which may possibly be the object of our thought is an *idea* existing only in the mind, and consequently each part thereof must be perceived. If, therefore, I cannot perceive innumerable parts in any finite extension that I consider, it is certain they are not contained in it; but it is evident that I cannot distinguish innumerable parts in any particular line, surface, or solid, which I either perceive by sense, or figure to myself in my mind: wherefore I conclude they are not contained in it. Nothing can be plainer to me than that the extensions I have in view are no other than my own ideas; and it is no less plain that I cannot resolve any one of my ideas into an infinite number of other ideas, that is, that they are not infinitely divisible. If by finite extension be meant something distinct from a finite idea, I declare I do not know what that is, and so cannot affirm or deny anything of it. But if the terms 'extension,' 'parts,' etc., are taken in any sense conceivable, that is, for ideas, then to say a finite quantity or extension consists of parts infinite in number is so manifest a contradiction, that everyone at first sight acknowledges it to be so; and it is impossible it should ever gain the assent of any reasonable creature who is not brought to it by gentle and slow degrees, as a converted Gentile to the belief of transubstantiation. Ancient and rooted prejudices do often pass into principles; and those propositions which once obtain the force and credit of a *principle*, are not only themselves, but likewise whatever is deducible from them, thought privileged from all examination. And there is no absurdity so gross, which, by this means, the mind of man may not be prepared to swallow.

125. He whose understanding is possessed with the doctrine of abstract general ideas may be persuaded that (whatever be thought of the ideas of sense) extension in *abstract* is infinitely divisible. And one who thinks the objects of sense exist without the mind will perhaps in virtue thereof be brought to admit that a line but an inch long may contain innumerable parts—really existing, though too small to be discerned. These errors are grafted as well in the minds of geometricians as of

other men, and have a like influence on their reasonings; and it were no difficult thing to shew how the arguments from geometry made use of to support the infinite divisibility of extension are bottomed on them. At present we shall only observe in general whence it is the mathematicians are all so fond and tenacious of that doctrine.

126. It hath been observed in another place that the theorems and demonstrations in geometry are conversant about universal ideas (Sec. 15, Introd.); where it is explained in what sense this ought to be understood, to wit, the particular lines and figures included in the diagram are supposed to stand for innumerable others of different sizes; or, in other words, the geometer considers them abstracting from their magnitude—which does not imply that he forms an abstract idea, but only that he cares not what the particular magnitude is, whether great or small, but looks on that as a thing different to the demonstration. Hence it follows that a line in the scheme but an inch long must be spoken of as though it contained ten thousand parts, since it is regarded not in itself, but as it is universal; and it is universal only in its signification, whereby it represents innumerable lines greater than itself, in which may be distinguished ten thousand parts or more, though there may not be above an inch in it. After this manner, the properties of the lines signified are (by a very usual figure) transferred to the sign, and thence, through mistake, thought to appertain to it considered in its own nature.

127. Because there is no number of parts so great but it is possible there may be a line containing more, the inch-line is said to contain parts more than any assignable number; which is true, not of the inch taken absolutely, but only for the things signified by it. But men, not retaining that distinction in their thoughts, slide into a belief that the small particular line described on paper contains in itself parts innumerable. There is no such thing as the ten-thousandth part of an inch; but there is of a mile or diameter of the earth, which may be signified by that inch. When therefore I delineate a triangle on paper, and take one side not above an inch, for example, in lengths to be the radius, this I consider as divided into ten thousand or an hundred thousand parts or more; for, though the ten-thousandth part of that line considered in itself is nothing at all, and consequently may be neglected without an error or inconveniency, yet these described lines, being only marks standing for greater quantities, whereof it may be the

ten-thousandth part is very considerable, it follows that, to prevent notable errors in practice, the radius must be taken of ten thousand parts or more.

128. From what hath been said the reason is plain why, to the end any theorem become universal in its use, it is necessary we speak of the lines described on paper as though they contained parts which really they do not. In doing of which, if we examine the matter thoroughly, we shall perhaps discover that we cannot conceive an inch itself as consisting of, or being divisible into, a thousand parts, but only some other line which is far greater than an inch, and represented by it; and that when we say a line is infinitely divisible, we must mean a line which is infinitely great. What we have here observed seems to be the chief cause why, to suppose the infinite divisibility of finite extension hath been thought necessary in geometry.

129. The several absurdities and contradictions which flowed from this false principle might, one would think, have been esteemed so many demonstrations against it. But, by I know not what logic, it is held that proofs *a posteriori* are not to be admitted against propositions relating to infinity, as though it were not impossible even for an infinite mind to reconcile contradictions; or as if anything absurd and repugnant could have a necessary connection with truth or flow from it. But whoever considers the weakness of this pretense will think it was contrived on purpose to humor the laziness of the mind which had rather acquiesce in an indolent scepticism than be at the pains to go through with a severe examination of those principles it hath ever embraced for true.

130. Of late the speculations about infinites have run so high, and grown to such strange notions, as have occasioned no scruples and disputes among the geometers of the present age. Some there are of great note who, not content with holding that finite lines may be divided into an infinite number of parts, do yet farther maintain that each of those infinitesimals is itself subdivisible into an infinity of other parts or infinitesimals of a second order, and so on *ad infinitum*. These, I say, assert there are infinitesimals of infinitesimals of infinitesimals, etc., without ever coming to an end! so that according to them an inch does not barely contain an infinite number of parts, but an infinity of an infinity of an infinity *ad infinitum* of parts. Others there be who hold all orders of infinitesimals below the first to be nothing at all; thinking it

with good reason absurd to imagine there is any positive quantity or part of extension which, though multiplied infinitely, can never equal the smallest given extension. And yet on the other hand it seems no less absurd to think the square, cube or other power of a positive real root, should itself be nothing at all; which they who hold infinitesimals of the first order, denying all of the subsequent orders, are obliged to maintain.

131. Have we not therefore reason to conclude they are *both* in the wrong, and that there is in effect no such thing as parts infinitely small, or an infinite number of parts contained in any finite quantity? But you will say that if this doctrine obtains it will follow the very foundations of geometry are destroyed, and those great men who have raised that science to so astonishing a height, have been all the while building a castle in the air. To this it may be replied that whatever is useful in geometry, and promotes the benefit of human life, does still remain firm and unshaken on our principles; that science considered as practical will rather receive advantage than any prejudice from what has been said. But to set this in a due light may be the proper business of another place. For the rest, though it should follow that some of the more intricate and subtle parts of speculative mathematics may be pared off without any prejudice to truth, yet I do not see what damage will be thence derived to mankind. On the contrary, I think it were highly to be wished that men of great abilities and obstinate application would draw off their thoughts from those amusements, and employ them in the study of such things as lie nearer the concerns of life, or have a more direct influence on the manners.

132. If it be said that several theorems undoubtedly true are discovered by methods in which infinitesimals are made use of, which could never have been if their existence included a contradiction in it; I answer that upon a thorough examination it will not be found that in any instance it is necessary to make use of or conceive infinitesimal parts of finite lines, or even quantities less than the *minimum sensible*; nay, it will be evident this is never done, it being impossible.

133. By what we have premised, it is plain that very numerous and important errors have taken their rise from those false principles which were impugned in the foregoing parts of this treatise; and the opposites of those erroneous tenets at the same time appear to be most fruitful principles, from whence do flow innumerable consequences highly advanta-

geous to true philosophy, as well as to religion. Particularly *matter*, or *the absolute existence of corporeal objects*, hath been shewn to be that wherein the most avowed and pernicious enemies of all knowledge, whether human or divine, have ever placed their chief strength and confidence. And surely, if by distinguishing the real existence of unthinking things from their being perceived, and allowing them a subsistence of their own out of the minds of spirits, no one thing is explained in nature, but on the contrary a great many inexplicable difficulties arise; if the supposition of matter is barely precarious, as not being grounded on so much as one single reason; if its consequences cannot endure the light of examination and free inquiry, but screen themselves under the dark and general pretense of 'infinites being incomprehensible'; if withal the removal of this *matter* be not attended with the least evil consequence; if it be not even missed in the world, but everything as well, nay much easier conceived without it; if, lastly, both sceptics and atheists are forever silenced upon supposing only spirits and ideas, and this scheme of things is perfectly agreeable both to reason and religion: methinks we may expect it should be admitted and firmly embraced, though it were proposed only as an *hypothesis*, and the existence of matter had been allowed possible, which yet I think we have evidently demonstrated that it is not.

134. True it is that, in consequence of the foregoing principles, several disputes and speculations which are esteemed no mean parts of learning, are rejected as useless. But, how great a prejudice soever against our notions this may give to those who have already been deeply engaged, and made large advances in studies of that nature, yet by others we hope it will not be thought any just ground of dislike to the principles and tenets herein laid down, that they abridge the labor of study, and make human sciences far more clear, compendious and attainable than they were before.

135. Having despatched what we intended to say concerning the knowledge of *ideas*, the method we proposed leads us in the next place to treat of *spirits*—with regard to which, perhaps, human knowledge is not so deficient as is vulgarly imagined. The great reason that is assigned for our being thought ignorant of the nature of spirits is our not having an *idea* of it. But surely it ought not to be looked on as a defect in a human understanding that it does not perceive the idea of spirit, if it is manifestly impossible there should be any

such idea. And this if I mistake not has been demonstrated in Section 27; to which I shall here add that a spirit has been shewn to be the only substance or support wherein unthinking beings or ideas can exist; but that this *substance* which supports or perceives ideas should itself be an idea or like an idea is evidently absurd.

136. It will perhaps be said that we want a sense (as some have imagined) proper to know substances withal, which, if we had, we might know our own soul as we do a triangle. To this I answer, that, in case we had a new sense bestowed upon us, we could only receive thereby some new sensations or ideas of sense. But I believe nobody will say that what he means by the terms *soul* and *substance* is only some particular sort of idea or sensation. We may therefore infer that, all things duly considered, it is not more reasonable to think our faculties defective, in that they do not furnish us with an idea of spirit or active thinking substance, than it would be if we should blame them for not being able to comprehend a *round square*.

137. From the opinion that spirits are to be known after the manner of an idea or sensation have risen many absurd and heterodox tenets, and much scepticism about the nature of the soul. It is even probable that this opinion may have produced a doubt in some whether they had any soul at all distinct from their body, since upon inquiry they could not find they had an idea of it. That an *idea*, which is inactive and the existence whereof consists in being perceived, should be the image or likeness of an agent subsisting by itself, seems to need no other refutation than barely attending to what is meant by those words. But perhaps you will say that though an idea cannot resemble a spirit in its thinking, acting, or subsisting by itself, yet it may in some other respects; and it is not necessary that an idea or image be in all respects like the original.

138. I answer, if it does not in those mentioned, it is impossible it should represent it in any other thing. Do but leave out the power of willing, thinking, and perceiving ideas, and there remains nothing else wherein the idea can be like a spirit. For by the word 'spirit' we mean only that which thinks, wills, and perceives; this, and this alone, constitutes the signification of that term. If therefore it is impossible that any degree of those powers should be represented in an idea, it is evident there can be no idea of a spirit.

139. But it will be objected that, if there is no idea signified by the terms 'soul,' 'spirit,' and 'substance,' they are wholly insignificant, or have no meaning in them. I answer, those words do mean or signify a real thing, which is neither an idea nor like an idea, but that which perceives ideas, and wills, and reasons about them. What I am myself, that which I denote by the term 'I,' is the same with what is meant by 'soul' or 'spiritual substances.' If it be said that this is only quarreling at a word, and that, since the immediate significations of other names are by common consent called 'ideas' no reason can be assigned why that which is signified by the name 'spirit' or 'soul' may not partake in the same appellation: I answer, all the unthinking objects of the mind agree in that they are entirely passive, and their existence consists only in being perceived: whereas a soul or spirit is an active being, whose existence consists, not in being perceived, but in perceiving ideas and thinking. It is therefore necessary, in order to prevent equivocation and confounding natures perfectly disagreeing and unlike, that we distinguish between *spirit* and *idea*. (See Sec. 27.)

140. In a large sense, indeed, we may be said to have an idea or rather a notion of *spirit*, that is, we understand the meaning of the word, otherwise we could not affirm or deny anything of it. Moreover, as we conceive the ideas that are in the minds of other spirits by means of our own, which we suppose to be resemblances of them; so we know other spirits by means of our own soul; which in that sense is the image or idea of them; it having a like respect to other spirits that blueness or heat by me perceived has to those ideas perceived by another.

141. It must not be supposed that they who assert the natural immortality of the soul are of opinion that it is absolutely incapable of annihilation even by the infinite power of the Creator who first gave it being, but only that it is not liable to be broken or dissolved by the ordinary laws of nature or motion. They indeed who hold the soul of man to be only a thin vital flame, or system of animal spirits, make it perishing and corruptible as the body; since there is nothing more easily dissipated than such a being, which it is naturally impossible should survive the ruin of the tabernacle wherein it is enclosed. And this notion hath been greedily embraced and cherished by the worst part of mankind, as the most effectual antidote against all impressions of virtue and religion. But it

hath been made evident that bodies of what frame or texture soever, are barely passive ideas in the mind, which is more distant and heterogeneous from them than light is from darkness. We have shewn that the soul is indivisible, incorporeal, unextended, and it is consequently incorruptible. Nothing can be plainer than that the motions, changes, decays, and dissolutions which we hourly see befall natural bodies (and which is what we mean by the *course of nature*) cannot possibly affect an active, simple, uncompounded substance; such a being therefore is indissoluble by the force of nature; that is to say, *the soul of man is naturally immortal.*

142. After what hath been said, it is, I suppose, plain that our souls are not to be known in the same manner as senseless, inactive objects, or by way of *idea. Spirits* and *ideas* are things so wholly different, that when we say 'they exist,' 'they are known,' or the like, these words must not be thought to signify anything common to both natures. There is nothing alike or common in them: and to expect that by any multiplication or enlargement of our faculties we may be enabled to know a spirit as we do a triangle, seems as absurd as if we should hope to see a sound. This is inculcated because I imagine it may be of moment towards clearing several important questions, and preventing some very dangerous errors concerning the nature of the soul. We may not, I think, strictly be said to have an *idea* of an active being, or of an action, although we may be said to have a *notion* of them. I have some knowledge or notion of my mind, and its acts about ideas, inasmuch as I know or understand what is meant by these words. What I know, that I have some notion of. I will not say that the terms 'idea' and 'notion' may not be used convertibly, if the world will have it so; but yet it conduceth to clearness and propriety that we distinguish things very different by different names. It is also to be remarked that, all relations including an act of the mind, we cannot so properly be said to have an idea, but rather a notion of the relations and habitudes between things. But if, in the modern way, the word 'idea' is extended to spirits, and relations, and acts, this is, after all, an affair of verbal concern.

143. It will not be amiss to add, that the doctrine of *abstract ideas* hath had no small share in rendering those sciences intricate and obscure which are particularly conversant about spiritual things. Men have imagined they could frame abstract notions of the powers and acts of the mind, and con-

sider them prescinded as well from the mind or spirit itself, as from their respective objects and effects. Hence a great number of dark and ambiguous terms, presumed to stand for abstract notions, have been introduced into metaphysics and morality, and from these have grown infinite distractions and disputes amongst the learned.

144. But nothing seems more to have contributed towards engaging men in controversies and mistakes with regard to the nature and operations of the mind, than the being used to speak of those things in terms borrowed from sensible ideas. For example, the will is termed the *motion* of the soul: this infuses a belief that the mind of man is as a ball in motion, impelled and determined by the objects of sense, as necessarily as that is by the stroke of a racket. Hence arise endless scruples and errors of dangerous consequence in morality. All which, I doubt not, may be cleared, and truth appear plain, uniform, and consistent, could but philosophers be prevailed on to retire into themselves, and attentively consider their own meaning.

145. From what hath been said, it is plain that we cannot know the existence of other spirits otherwise than by their operations, or the ideas by them excited in us. I perceive several motions, changes, and combinations of ideas, that inform me there are certain particular agents, like myself, which accompany them and concur in their production. Hence, the knowledge I have of other spirits is not immediate, as is the knowledge of my ideas; but depending on the intervention of ideas, by me referred to agents or spirits distinct from myself, as effects or concomitant signs.

146. But though there be some things which convince us human agents are concerned in producing them; yet it is evident to everyone that those things which are called the works of nature, that is, the far greater part of the ideas or sensations perceived by us, are not produced by, or dependent on, the wills of men. There is therefore some other Spirit that causes them; since it is repugnant that they should subsist by themselves. (See Sec. 29.) But if we attentively consider the constant regularity, order, and concatenation of natural things, the surprising magnificence, beauty, and perfection of the larger, and the exquisite contrivance of the smaller parts of creation, together with the exact harmony and correspondence of the whole, but above all the never enough admired laws of pain and pleasure, and the instincts or natural inclinations,

appetites, and passions of animals; I say if we consider all these things, and at the same time attend to the meaning and import of the attributes One, Eternal, Infinitely Wise, Good, and Perfect, we shall clearly perceive that they belong to the aforesaid Spirit, "who works all in all," and "by whom all things consist."

147. Hence, it is evident that God is known as certainly and immediately as any other mind or spirit whatsoever distinct from ourselves. We may even assert that the existence of God is far more evidently perceived than the existence of men; because the effects of nature are infinitely more numerous and considerable than those ascribed to human agents. There is not any one mark that denotes a man, or effect produced by him, which does not more strongly evince the being of that Spirit who is the Author of Nature. For it is evident that in affecting other persons the will of man hath no other object than barely the motion of the limbs of his body; but that such a motion should be attended by, or excite any idea in the mind of another, depends wholly on the will of the Creator. He alone it is who, "upholding all things by the word of His power," maintains that intercourse between spirits whereby they are able to perceive the existence of each other. And yet this pure and clear light which enlightens everyone is itself invisible.

148. It seems to be a general pretense of the unthinking herd that they cannot *see* God. Could we but see Him, say they, as we see a man, we should believe that He is, and believing obey His commands. But alas, we need only open our eyes to see the Sovereign Lord of all things, with a more full and clear view than we do any one of our fellow-creatures. Not that I imagine we see God (as some will have it) by a direct and immediate view; or see corporeal things, not by themselves, but by seeing that which represents them in the essence of God, which doctrine is, I must confess, to me incomprehensible. But I shall explain my meaning. A human spirit or person is not perceived by sense, as not being an idea; when therefore we see the color, size, figure, and motions of a man, we perceive only certain sensations or ideas excited in our own minds; and these being exhibited to our view in sundry distinct collections, serve to mark out unto us the existence of finite and created spirits like ourselves. Hence it is plain we do not see a man—if by *man* is meant that which lives, moves, perceives, and thinks as we do—but only such a certain col-

lection of ideas as directs us to think there is a distinct principle of thought and motion, like to ourselves, accompanying and represented by it. And after the same manner we see God; all the difference is that, whereas some one finite and narrow assemblage of ideas denotes a particular human mind, whithersoever we direct our view, we do at all times and in all places perceive manifest tokens of the Divinity: everything we see, hear, feel, or anywise perceive by sense being a sign or effect of the power of God; as is our perception of those very motions which are produced by men.

149. It is therefore plain that nothing can be more evident to anyone that is capable of the least reflection that the existence of God, or a Spirit who is intimately present to our minds, producing in them all that variety of ideas or sensations which continually affect us, on whom we have an absolute and entire dependence, in short "in whom we live, and move, and have our being." That the discovery of this great truth, which lies so near and obvious to the mind, should be attained to by the reason of so very few, is a sad instance of the stupidity and inattention of men, who, though they are surrounded with such clear manifestations of the Deity, are yet so little affected by them that they seem, as it were, blinded with excess of light.

150. But you will say, Hath Nature no share in the production of natural things, and must they be all ascribed to the immediate and sole operation of God? I answer, if by 'Nature' is meant only the visible *series* of effects or sensations imprinted on our minds, according to certain fixed and general laws, then it is plain that Nature, taken in this sense, cannot produce anything at all. But, if by 'Nature' is meant some being distinct from God, as well as from the laws of nature, and things perceived by sense, I must confess that word is to me an empty sound without any intelligible meaning annexed to it. Nature, in this acceptation, is a vain chimera, introduced by those heathens who had not just notions of the omnipresence and infinite perfection of God. But it is more unaccountable that it should be received among Christians, professing belief in the Holy Scriptures, which constantly ascribe those effects to the immediate hand of God that heathen philosophers are wont to impute to Nature. "The Lord He causeth the vapors to ascend; He maketh lightnings with rain; He bringeth forth the wind out of his treasures." (Jerem. x. 13.) "He turneth the shadow of death into the

morning, and maketh the day dark with night." (Amos. v. 8.) "He visiteth the earth, and maketh it soft with showers: He blesseth the springing thereof, and crowneth the year with His goodness; so that the pastures are clothed with flocks, and the valleys are covered over with corn." (See Psalm lxv.) But notwithstanding that this is the constant language of Scripture, yet we have I know not what aversion from believing that God concerns Himself so nearly in our affairs. Fain would we suppose Him at a great distance off, and substitute some blind unthinking deputy in His stead, though (if we may believe Saint Paul) "He be not far from every one of us."

151. It will, I doubt not, be objected that the slow and gradual methods observed in the production of natural things do not seem to have for their cause the immediate hand of an Almighty Agent. Besides, monsters, untimely births, fruits blasted in the blossom, rains falling in desert places, miseries incident to human life, and the like, are so many arguments that the whole frame of nature is not immediately actuated and superintended by a Spirit of infinite wisdom and goodness. But the answer to this objection is in a good measure plain from Section 62; it being visible that the aforesaid methods of nature are absolutely necessary, in order to working by the most simple and general rules, and after a steady and consistent manner; which argues both the wisdom and goodness of God. Such is the artificial contrivance of this mighty machine of nature that, whilst its motions and various phenomena strike on our senses, the hand which actuates the whole is itself unperceivable to men of flesh and blood. "Verily," saith the prophet, "thou art a God that hidest thyself." (Isaiah xlv. 15.) But though the Lord conceal Himself from the eyes of the sensual and lazy, who will not be at the least expense of thought, yet to an unbiased and attentive mind nothing can be more plainly legible than the intimate presence of an all-wise Spirit, who fashions, regulates, and sustains the whole system of beings. It is clear, from what we have elsewhere observed, that the operating according to general and stated laws is so necessary for our guidance in the affairs of life, and letting us into the secret of nature, that without it all reach and compass of thought, all human sagacity and design, could serve to no manner of purpose; it were even impossible there should be any such faculties or powers in the mind. (See Sec. 31.) Which one consideration abundantly outbalances whatever particular inconveniences may thence arise.

152. We should further consider that the very blemishes and defects of nature are not without their use, in that they make an agreeable sort of variety, and augment the beauty of the rest of the creation, as shades in a picture serve to set off the brighter and more enlightened parts. We would likewise do well to examine whether our taxing the waste of seeds and embryos, and accidental destruction of plants and animals, before they come to full maturity, as an imprudence in the Author of nature, be not the effect of prejudice contracted by our familiarity with impotent and saving mortals. In man indeed a thrifty management of those things which he cannot procure without much pains and industry may be esteemed wisdom. But we must not imagine that the inexplicably fine machine of an animal or vegetable costs the great Creator any more pains or trouble in its production than a pebble does; nothing being more evident than that an Omnipotent Spirit can indifferently produce everything by a mere *fiat* or act of His will. Hence, it is plain that the splendid profusion of natural things should not be interpreted weakness or prodigality in the Agent who produces them, but rather be looked on as an argument of the riches of His power.

153. As for the mixture of pain or uneasiness which is in the world, pursuant to the general laws of nature, and the actions of finite, imperfect spirits, this, in the state we are in at present, is indispensably necessary to our well-being. But our prospects are too narrow. We take, for instance, the idea of some one particular pain into our thoughts and account it *evil*; whereas, if we enlarge our view, so as to comprehend the various ends, connections, and dependencies of things, on what occasions and in what proportions we are affected with pain and pleasure, the nature of human freedom, and the design with which we are put into the world; we shall be forced to acknowledge that those particular things which, considered in themselves, appear to be evil, have the nature of good, when considered as linked with the whole system of beings.

154. From what hath been said, it will be manifest to any considering person, that it is merely for want of attention and comprehensiveness of mind that there are any favorers of atheism or the Manichean heresy to be found. Little and unreflecting souls may indeed burlesque the works of Providence, the beauty and order whereof they have not capacity, or will not be at the pains, to comprehend; but those who are masters

of any justness and extent of thought, and are withal used to reflect, can never sufficiently admire the divine traces of wisdom and goodness that shine throughout the economy of nature. But what truth is there which shineth so strongly on the mind that by an aversion of thought, a willful shutting of the eyes, we may not escape seeing it? Is it therefore to be wondered at, if the generality of men, who are ever intent on business or pleasure, and little used to fix or open the eye of their mind, should not have all that conviction and evidence of the Being of God which might be expected in reasonable creatures?

155. We should rather wonder that men can be found so stupid as to neglect, than that neglecting they should be unconvinced of such an evident and momentous truth. And yet it is to be feared that too many of parts and leisure, who live in Christian countries, are, merely through a supine and dreadful negligence, sunk into atheism; since it is downright impossible that a soul pierced and enlightened with a thorough sense of the omnipresence, holiness, and justice of that Almighty Spirit should persist in a remorseless violation of His laws. We ought, therefore, earnestly to meditate and dwell on those important points; that so we may attain conviction without all scruple "that the eyes of the Lord are in every place beholding the evil and the good; that He is with us and keepeth us in all places whither we go, and giveth us bread to eat and raiment to put on;" that He is present and conscious to our innermost thoughts; and that we have a most absolute and immediate dependence on Him. A clear view of which great truths cannot choose but fill our hearts with an awful circumspection and holy fear, which is the strongest incentive to *virtue*, and the best guard against *vice*.

156. For, after all, what deserves the first place in our studies is the consideration of God and our *duty*; which to promote, as it was the main drift and design of my labors, so shall I esteem them altogether useless and ineffectual if, by what I have said, I cannot inspire my readers with a pious sense of the Presence of God; and, having shewn the falseness or vanity of those barren speculations which make the chief employment of learned men, the better dispose them to reverence and embrace the salutary truths of the Gospel, which to know and to practice is the highest perfection of human nature.

George Berkeley

THREE DIALOGUES

BETWEEN HYLAS AND PHILONOUS, IN OPPOSITION TO SCEPTICS AND ATHEISTS

THE FIRST DIALOGUE

Philonous. Good morrow, Hylas: I did not expect to find you abroad so early.

Hylas. It is indeed something unusual: but my thoughts were so taken up with a subject I was discoursing of last night, that finding I could not sleep, I resolved to rise and take a turn in the garden.

Phil. It happened well, to let you see what innocent and agreeable pleasures you lose every morning. Can there be a pleasanter time of the day, or a more delightful season of the year? That purple sky, those wild but sweet notes of birds, the fragrant bloom upon the trees and flowers, the gentle influence of the rising sun, these and a thousand nameless beauties of nature inspire the soul with secret transports; its faculties too being at this time fresh and lively, are fit for these meditations, which the solitude of a garden and tranquillity of the morning naturally dispose us to. But I am afraid I interrupt your thoughts; for you seemed very intent on something.

Hyl. It is true, I was, and shall be obliged to you if you will permit me to go on in the same vein; not that I would by any means deprive myself of your company, for my thoughts always flow more easily in conversation with a friend, than when I am alone: but my request is, that you would suffer me to impart my reflections to you.

Phil. With all my heart, it is what I should have requested myself, if you had not prevented me.

Hyl. I was considering the odd fate of those men who have in all ages, through an affectation of being distinguished from the vulgar, or some unaccountable turn of thought, pretended either to believe nothing at all, or to believe the most extravagant things in the world. This however might be borne, if their paradoxes and scepticism did not draw after them some consequences of general disadvantage to mankind. But the mischief lieth here; that when men of less leisure see them who are supposed to have spent their whole time in the pursuits of knowledge, professing an entire ignorance of all things, or advancing such notions as are repugnant to plain and commonly received principles, they will be tempted to entertain suspicions concerning the most important truths, which they had hitherto held sacred and unquestionable.

Phil. I entirely agree with you, as to the ill tendency of the affected doubts of some philosophers, and fantastical conceits of others. I am even so far gone of late in this way of thinking, that I have quitted several of the sublime notions I had got in their schools for vulgar opinions. And I give it you on my word, since this revolt from metaphysical notions to the plain dictates of nature and common sense, I find my understanding strangely enlightened, so that I can now easily comprehend a great many things which before were all mystery and riddle.

Hyl. I am glad to find there was nothing in the accounts I heard of you.

Phil. Pray, what were those?

Hyl. You were represented in last night's conversation, as one who maintained the most extravagant opinion that ever entered into the mind of man, to wit, that there is no such thing as *material substance* in the world.

Phil. That there is no such thing as what philosophers call *material substance,* I am seriously persuaded: but if I were made to see any thing absurd or sceptical in this, I should then have the same reason to renounce this, that I imagine I have now to reject the contrary opinion.

Hyl. What! can any thing be more fantastical, more repugnant to common sense, or a more manifest piece of scepticism, than to believe there is no such thing as *matter*?

Phil. Softly, good Hylas. What if it should prove, that you who hold there is, are by virtue of that opinion a greater sceptic, and maintain more paradoxes and repugnancies to common sense, than I who believe no such thing?

Hyl. You may as soon persuade me, the part is greater than the whole, as that, in order to avoid absurdity and scepticism, I should ever be obliged to give up my opinion in this point.

Phil. Well then, are you content to admit that opinion for true, which upon examination shall appear most agreeable to common sense, and remote from scepticism?

Hyl. With all my heart. Since you are for raising disputes about the plainest things in nature, I am content for once to hear what you have to say.

Phil. Pray, Hylas, what do you mean by a *sceptic?*

Hyl. I mean what all men mean, one that doubts of every thing.

Phil. He then who entertains no doubt concerning some particular point, with regard to that point cannot be thought a *sceptic.*

Hyl. I agree with you.

Phil. Whether doth doubting consist in embracing the affirmative or negative side of a question?

Hyl. In neither; for whoever understands English, cannot but know that *doubting* signifies a suspense between both.

Phil. He then that denieth any point, can no more be said to doubt of it than he who affirmeth it with the same degree of assurance.

Hyl. True.

Phil. And consequently, for such his denial is no more to be esteemed a *sceptic* than the other.

Hyl. I acknowledge it.

Phil. How cometh it to pass then, Hylas, that you pronounce me a *sceptic,* because I deny what you affirm, to wit, the existence of matter? Since, for ought you can tell, I am as peremptory in my denial, as you in your affirmation.

Hyl. Hold, Philonous, I have been a little out in my definition; but every false step a man makes in discourse is not to be insisted on. I said, indeed, that a *sceptic* was one who doubted of every thing; but I should have added, or who denies the reality and truth of things.

Phil. What things? Do you mean the principles and theorems of sciences? but these you know are universal intellectual notions, and consequently independent of matter; the denial therefore of this doth not imply the denying them.

Hyl. I grant it. But are there no other things? What think you of distrusting the senses, of denying the real existence of sensible things, or pretending to know nothing of them? Is not this sufficient to denominate a man a *sceptic?*

Phil. Shall we therefore examine which of us it is that denies the reality of sensible things, or professes the greatest ignorance of them; since, if I take you rightly, he is to be esteemed the greatest *sceptic?*

Hyl. That is what I desire.

Phil. What mean you by sensible things?

Hyl. Those things which are perceived by the senses. Can you imagine that I mean any thing else?

Phil. Pardon me, Hylas, if I am desirous clearly to apprehend your notions, since this may much shorten our inquiry. Suffer me then to ask you this further question. Are those things only perceived by the senses which are perceived immediately? or may those things properly be said to be *sensible,* which are perceived mediately, or not without the intervention of others?

Hyl. I do not sufficiently understand you.

Phil. In reading a book, what I immediately perceive are the letters, but mediately, or by means of these, are suggested to my mind the notions of God, virtue, truth, &c. Now that the letters are truly sensible things, or perceived by sense, there is no doubt: but I would know whether you take the things suggested by them to be so too.

Hyl. No, certainly, it were absurd to think *God* or *virtue* sensible things, though they may be signified and suggested to the mind by sensible marks, with which they have an arbitrary connexion.

Phil. It seems then, that by *sensible things* you mean those only which can be perceived immediately by sense.

Hyl. Right.

Phil. Doth it not follow from this, that though I see one part of the sky red, and another blue, and that my reason doth thence evidently conclude there must be some cause of that diversity of colours, yet that cause cannot be said to be a sensible thing, or perceived by the sense of seeing?

Hyl. It doth.

Phil. In like manner, though I hear variety of sounds, yet I cannot be said to hear the causes of those sounds.

Hyl. You cannot.

Phil. And when by my touch I perceive a thing to be hot and heavy, I cannot say with any truth or propriety, that I feel the cause of its heat or weight.

Hyl. To prevent any more questions of this kind, I tell you once for all, that by *sensible things* I mean those only which are perceived by sense, and that in truth the senses perceive nothing which they do not perceive immediately: for they make no inferences. The deducing therefore of causes or occasions from effects and appearances, which alone are perceived by sense, entirely relates to reason.

Phil. This point then is agreed between us, that *sensible things are those only which are immediately perceived by sense.* You will further inform me, whether we immediately perceive by sight any thing beside light, and colours, and figures: or by hearing any thing but sounds: by the palate, any thing besides tastes: by the smell, besides odours: or by the touch, more than tangible qualities.

Hyl. We do not.

Phil. It seems therefore, that if you take away all sensible qualities, there remains nothing sensible.

Hyl. I grant it.

Phil. Sensible things therefore are nothing else but so many sensible qualities, or combinations of sensible qualities.

Hyl. Nothing else.

Phil. Heat then is a sensible thing.

Hyl. Certainly.

Phil. Doth the reality of sensible things consist in being perceived? or, is it something distinct from their being perceived, and that bears no relation to the mind?

Hyl. To *exist* is one thing, and to be *perceived* is another.

Phil. I speak with regard to sensible things only; and of these I ask, whether by their real existence you mean a subsistence exterior to the mind, and distinct from their being perceived?

Hyl. I mean a real absolute being, distinct from, and without any relation to their being perceived.

Phil. Heat, therefore, if it be allowed a real being, must exist without the mind.

Hyl. It must.

Phil. Tell me, Hylas, is this real existence equally compatible to all degrees of heat, which we perceive: or is there any reason why we should attribute it to some, and deny it others? and if there be, pray let me know that reason.

Hyl. Whatever degree of heat we perceive by sense, we may be sure the same exists in the object that occasions it.

Phil. What, the greatest as well as the least?

Hyl. I tell you, the reason is plainly the same in respect of both: they are both perceived by sense; nay, the greater degree of heat is more sensibly perceived; and consequently, if there is any difference, we are more certain of its real existence than we can be of the reality of a lesser degree.

Phil. But is not the most vehement and intense degree of heat a very great pain?

Hyl. No one can deny it.

Phil. And is any unperceiving thing capable of pain or pleasure?

Hyl. No, certainly.

Phil. Is your material substance a senseless being, or a being endowed with sense and perception?

Hyl. It is senseless without doubt.

Phil. It cannot therefore be the subject of pain.

Hyl. By no means.

Phil. Nor consequently of the greatest heat perceived by sense, since you acknowledge this to be no small pain.

Hyl. I grant it.

Phil. What shall we say then of your external object; is it a material substance, or no?

Hyl. It is a material substance with the sensible qualities inhering in it.

Phil. How then can a great heat exist in it, since you own it cannot in a material substance? I desire you would clear this point.

Hyl. Hold, Philonous; I fear I was out in yielding intense heat to be a pain. It should seem rather, that pain is something distinct from heat, and the consequence or effect of it.

Phil. Upon putting your hand near the fire, do you perceive one simple uniform sensation, or two distinct sensations?

Hyl. But one simple sensation.

Phil. Is not the heat immediately perceived?

Hyl. It is.

Phil. And the pain?

Hyl. True.

Phil. Seeing therefore they are both immediately perceived at the same time, and the fire affects you only with one simple, or uncompounded idea, it follows that this same simple idea is both the intense heat immediately perceived, and the pain; and consequently, that the intense heat immediately perceived, is nothing distinct from a particular sort of pain.

Hyl. It seems so.

Phil. Again, try in your thoughts, Hylas, if you can conceive a vehement sensation to be without pain, or pleasure.

Hyl. I cannot.

Phil. Or can you frame to yourself an idea of sensible pain or pleasure in general, abstracted from every particular idea of heat, cold, tastes, smells, &c.?

Hyl. I do not find that I can.

Phil. Doth it not therefore follow, that sensible pain is nothing distinct from those sensations or ideas, in an intense degree?

Hyl. It is undeniable; and to speak the truth, I begin to suspect a very great heat cannot exist but in a mind perceiving it.

Phil. What! are you then in that *sceptical* state of suspense, between affirming and denying?

Hyl. I think I may be positive in the point. A very violent and painful heat cannot exist without the mind.

Phil. It hath not therefore, according to you, any real being.

Hyl. I own it.

Phil. Is it therefore certain, that there is no body in nature really hot?

Hyl. I have not denied there is any real heat in bodies. I only say, there is no such thing as an intense real heat.

Phil. But did you not say before, that all degrees of heat were equally real: or if there was any difference, that the greater were more undoubtedly real than the lesser?

Hyl. True: but it was, because I did not then consider the ground there is for distinguishing between them, which I now plainly see. And it is this: because intense heat is nothing else but a particular kind of painful sensation; and pain cannot exist but in a perceiving being; it follows that no intense heat can really exist in an unperceiving corporeal substance. But this is no reason why we should deny heat in an inferior degree to exist in such a substance.

Phil. But how shall we be able to discern those degrees of heat which exist only in the mind, from those which exist without it?

Hyl. That is no difficult matter. You know, the least pain cannot exist unperceived; whatever therefore degree of heat is a pain, exists only in the mind. But as for all other degrees of heat, nothing obliges us to think the same of them.

Phil. I think you granted before, that no unperceiving being was capable of pleasure, any more than of pain.

Hyl. I did.

Phil. And is not warmth, or a more gentle degree of heat than what causes uneasiness, a pleasure?

Hyl. What then?

Phil. Consequently it cannot exist without the mind in any unperceiving substance, or body.

Hyl. So it seems.

Phil. Since therefore, as well those degrees of heat that are not painful, as those that are, can exist only in a thinking substance; may we not conclude that external bodies are absolutely incapable of any degree of heat whatsoever?

Hyl. On second thoughts, I do not think it so evident that warmth is a pleasure, as that a great degree of heat is a pain.

Phil. I do not pretend that warmth is as great a pleasure as heat is a pain. But if you grant it to be even a small pleasure, it serves to make good my conclusion.

Hyl. I could rather call it an *indolence.* It seems to be nothing more than a privation of both pain and pleasure. And that such a quality or state as this may agree to an unthinking substance, I hope you will not deny.

Phil. If you are resolved to maintain that warmth, or a gentle degree of heat, is no pleasure, I know not how to convince you otherwise, than by appealing to your own sense. But what think you of cold?

Hyl. The same that I do of heat. An intense degree of cold is a pain; for to feel a very great cold, is to perceive a great uneasiness: it cannot therefore exist without the mind; but a lesser degree of cold may, as well as a lesser degree of heat.

Phil. Those bodies therefore, upon whose application to our own we perceive a moderate degree of heat, must be concluded to have a moderate degree of heat or warmth in them; and those, upon whose application we feel a like degree of cold, must be thought to have cold in them.

Hyl. They must.

Phil. Can any doctrine be true that necessarily leads a man into an absurdity?

Hyl. Without doubt it cannot.

Phil. Is it not an absurdity to think that the same thing should be at the same time both cold and warm?

Hyl. It is.

Phil. Suppose now one of your hands hot, and the other cold, and that they are both at once put into the same vessel of water, in an intermediate state; will not the water seem cold to one hand, and warm to the other?

Hyl. It will.

Phil. Ought we not therefore by your principles to conclude, it is really both cold and warm at the same time, that is, according to your own concession, to believe an absurdity?

Hyl. I confess it seems so.

Phil. Consequently, the principles themselves are false, since you have granted that no true principle leads to an absurdity.

Hyl. But after all, can any thing be more absurd than to say, *there is no heat in the fire?*

Phil. To make the point still clearer; tell me, whether in two cases exactly alike, we ought not to make the same judgment?

Hyl. We ought.

Phil. When a pin pricks your finger, doth it not rend and divide the fibres of your flesh?

Hyl. It doth.

Phil. And when a coal burns your finger, doth it any more?

Hyl. It doth not.

Phil. Since therefore you neither judge the sensation itself occasioned by the pin, nor any thing like it to be in the pin; you should not, conformably to what you have now granted, judge the sensation occasioned by the fire, or any thing like it, to be in the fire.

Hyl. Well, since it must be so, I am content to yield this point, and acknowledge, that heat and cold are only sensations existing in our minds: but there still remain qualities enough to secure the reality of external things.

Phil. But what will you say, Hylas, if it shall appear that the case is the same with regard to all other sensible qualities, and that they can no more be supposed to exist without the mind, than heat and cold?

Hyl. Then indeed you will have done something to the purpose; but that is what I despair of seeing proved.

Phil. Let us examine them in order. What think you of tastes, do they exist without the mind, or no?

Hyl. Can any man in his senses doubt whether sugar is sweet, or wormwood bitter?

Phil. Inform me, Hylas. Is a sweet taste a particular kind of pleasure or pleasant sensation, or is it not?

Hyl. It is.

Phil. And is not bitterness some kind of uneasiness or pain?

Hyl. I grant it.

Phil. If therefore sugar and wormwood are unthinking corporeal substances existing without the mind, how can sweetness and bitterness, that is, pleasure and pain, agree to them?

Hyl. Hold, Philonous; I now see what it was deluded me all this time. You asked whether heat and cold, sweetness and bitterness, were not particular sorts of pleasure and pain; to which I answered simply, that they were. Whereas I should have thus distinguished: those qualities, as perceived by us, are pleasures or pains, but not as existing in the external objects. We must not therefore conclude absolutely, that there is no heat in the fire, or sweetness in the sugar, but only that heat or sweetness, as perceived by us, are not in the fire or sugar. What say you to this?

Phil. I say it is nothing to the purpose. Our discourse proceeded altogether concerning sensible things, which you defined to be the things we *immediately perceive by our senses.* Whatever other qualities therefore you speak of, as distinct from these, I know nothing of them, neither do they at all belong to the point in dispute. You may indeed pretend to have discovered certain qualities which you do not perceive, and assert those insensible qualities exist in fire and sugar. But what use can be made of this to your present purpose, I am at a loss to conceive. Tell me then once more, do you acknowledge that heat and cold, sweetness and bitterness (meaning those qualities which are perceived by the senses), do not exist without the mind?

Hyl. I see it is to no purpose to hold out, so I give up the cause as to those mentioned qualities. Though I profess it sounds oddly, to say that sugar is not sweet.

Phil. But for your further satisfaction, take this along with you: that which at other times seems sweet, shall to a distempered palate appear bitter. And nothing can be plainer, than that divers persons perceive different tastes in the same food, since that which one man delights in, another abhors. And how could this be, if the taste was something really inherent in the food?

Hyl. I acknowledge I know not how.

Phil. In the next place, odours are to be considered. And with regard to these, I would fain know, whether what hath been said of tastes doth not exactly agree to them? Are they not so many pleasing or displeasing sensations?

Hyl. They are.

Phil. Can you then conceive it possible that they should exist in an unperceiving thing?

Hyl. I cannot.

Phil. Or can you imagine, that filth and ordure affect those brute animals that feed on them out of choice, with the same smells which we perceive in them?

Hyl. By no means.

Phil. May we not therefore conclude of smells, as of the other forementioned qualities, that they cannot exist in any but a perceiving substance or mind?

Hyl. I think so.

Phil. Then as to sounds, what must we think of them: are they accidents really inherent in external bodies, or not?

Hyl. That they inhere not in the sonorous bodies, is plain from hence; because a bell struck in the exhausted receiver of an air-pump, sends forth no sound. The air therefore must be thought the subject of sound.

Phil. What reason is there for that, Hylas?

Hyl. Because when any motion is raised in the air, we perceive a sound greater or lesser, in proportion to the air's motion; but without some motion in the air, we never hear any sound at all.

Phil. And granting that we never hear a sound but when some motion is produced in the air, yet I do not see how you can infer from thence, that the sound itself is in the air.

Hyl. It is this very motion in the external air, that produces in the mind the sensation of *sound.* For striking on the drum of the ear, it causeth a vibration, which by the auditory nerves being communicated to the brain, the soul is thereupon affected with the sensation called *sound.*

Phil. What! is sound then a sensation?

Hyl. I tell you, as perceived by us, it is a particular sensation in the mind.

Phil. And can any sensation exist without the mind?

Hyl. No, certainly.

Phil. How then can sound, being a sensation, exist in the air, if by the *air* you mean a senseless substance existing without the mind.

Hyl. You must distinguish, Philonous, between sound, as it is perceived by us, and as it is in itself; or, (which is the same thing) between the sound we immediately perceive, and that which exists without us. The former indeed is a particular kind of sensation, but the latter is merely a vibrative or undulatory motion in the air.

Phil. I thought I had already obviated that distinction by the answer I gave when you were applying it in a like case before. But to say no more of that: are you sure then that sound is really nothing but motion?

Hyl. I am.

Phil. Whatever therefore agrees to real sound, may with truth be attributed to motion.

Hyl. It may.

Phil. It is then good sense to speak of *motion*, as of a thing that is *loud, sweet, acute*, or *grave*.

Hyl. I see you are resolved not to understand me. Is it not evident, those accidents or modes belong only to sensible sound, or *sound* in the common acceptation of the word, but not to *sound* in the real and philosophic sense, which, as I just now told you, is nothing but a certain motion of the air?

Phil. It seems then there are two sorts of sound, the one vulgar, or that which is heard, the other philosophical and real.

Hyl. Even so.

Phil. And the latter consists in motion.

Hyl. I told you so before.

Phil. Tell me, Hylas, to which of the senses, think you, the idea of motion belongs: to the hearing?

Hyl. No, certainly, but to the sight and touch.

Phil. It should follow then, that according to you, real sounds may possibly be *seen* or *felt*, but never *heard*.

Hyl. Look you, Philonous, you may if you please make a jest of my opinion, but that will not alter the truth of things. I own, indeed, the inferences you draw me into sound something oddly: but common language, you know, is framed by, and for the use of the vulgar: we must not therefore wonder, if expressions adapted to exact philosophic notions, seem uncouth and out of the way.

Phil. Is it come to that? I assure you, I imagine myself to have gained no small point, since you make so light of departing from common phrases and opinions; it being a main part of our inquiry, to examine whose notions are widest of the common road, and most repugnant to the general sense of the world. But can you think it no more than a philosophical paradox, to say that *real sounds are never heard*, and that the idea of them is obtained by some other sense. And is there nothing in this contrary to nature and the truth of things?

Hyl. To deal ingenuously, I do not like it. And after the concessions already made, I had as well grant that sounds too have no real being without the mind.

Phil. And I hope you will make no difficulty to acknowledge the same of colours.

Hyl. Pardon me; the case of colours is very different. Can any thing be plainer, than that we see them on the objects?

Phil. The objects you speak of are, I suppose, corporeal substances existing without the mind.

Hyl. They are.

Phil. And have true and real colours inhering in them?

Hyl. Each visible object hath that colour which we see in it.

Phil. How! is there any thing visible but what we perceive by sight.

Hyl. There is not.

Phil. And do we perceive any thing by sense, which we do not perceive immediately?

Hyl. How often must I be obliged to repeat the same thing? I tell you, we do not.

Phil. Have patience, good Hylas; and tell me once more whether there is any thing immediately perceived by the senses, except sensible qualities. I know you asserted there was not: but I would now be informed, whether you still persist in the same opinion.

Hyl. I do.

Phil. Pray, is your corporeal substance either a sensible quality or made up of sensible qualities?

Hyl. What a question that is! who ever thought it was?

Phil. My reason for asking was, because in saying, *each visible object hath that colour which we see in it*, you make visible objects to be corporeal substances; which implies either that corporeal substances are sensible qualities, or else that there is something beside sensible qualities perceived by sight: but as this point was formerly agreed between us, and is still maintained by you, it is a clear consequence, that your corporeal substance is nothing distinct from sensible qualities.

Hyl. You may draw as many absurd consequences as you please, and endeavour to perplex the plainest things; but you shall never persuade me out of my senses. I clearly understand my own meaning.

Phil. I wish you would make me understand it too. But since you are unwilling to have your notion of corporeal substance examined, I shall urge that point no further. Only be pleased to let me know, whether the same colours which we see, exist in external bodies, or some other.

Hyl. The very same.

Phil. What! are then the beautiful red and purple we see on yonder clouds, really in them? Or do you imagine they have in themselves any other form than that of a dark mist or vapour?

Hyl. I must own, Philonous, those colours are not really in the clouds as they seem to be at this distance. They are only apparent colours.

Phil. *Apparent* call you them? how shall we distinguish these apparent colours from real?

Hyl. Very easily. Those are to be thought apparent, which, appearing only at a distance, vanish upon a nearer approach.

Phil. And those I suppose are to be thought real, which are discovered by the most near and exact survey.

Hyl. Right.

Phil. Is the nearest and exactest survey made by the help of a microscope, or by the naked eye?

Hyl. By a microscope, doubtless.

Phil. But a microscope often discovers colours in an object different from those perceived by the unassisted sight. And in case we had microscopes magnifying to any assigned degree; it is certain, that no object whatsoever viewed through them, would appear in the same colour which it exhibits to the naked eye.

Hyl. And what will you conclude from all this? You cannot argue that there are really and naturally no colours on objects; because by artificial managements they may be altered, or made to vanish.

Phil. I think it may evidently be concluded from your own concessions, that all the colours we see with our naked eyes, are only apparent as those on the clouds, since they vanish upon a more close and accurate inspection, which is afforded us by a microscope. Then as to what you say by way of prevention; I ask you, whether the real and natural state of an object is better discovered by a very sharp and piercing sight, or by one which is less sharp.

Hyl. By the former without doubt.

Phil. Is it not plain from *dioptrics*, that microscopes make the sight more penetrating, and represent objects as they would appear to the eye, in case it were naturally endowed with a most exquisite sharpness?

Hyl. It is.

Phil. Consequently the microscopical representation is to be thought that which best sets forth the real nature of the thing, or what it is in itself. The colours therefore by it perceived, are more genuine and real, than those perceived otherwise.

Hyl. I confess there is something in what you say.

Phil. Besides, it is not only possible but manifest, that there actually are animals, whose eyes are by nature framed to perceive those things, which by reason of their minuteness escape our sight. What think you of those inconceivably small animals perceived by glasses? must we suppose they are all stark blind? Or, in case they see, can it be imagined their sight hath not the same use in preserving their bodies from injuries, which appears in that of all other animals? And if it hath, is it not evident, they must see particles less than their own bodies, which will present them with a far different view in each object, from that which strikes our senses? Even our own eyes do not always represent objects to us after the same manner. In the *jaundice*, every one knows that all things seem yellow. Is it not therefore highly probable, those animals in whose eyes we discern a very different texture from that of ours, and whose bodies abound with different humours, do not see the same colours in every object that we do? From all of which, should it not seem to follow that all colours are equally apparent, and that none of those which we perceive are really inherent in any outward object?

Hyl. It should.

Phil. The point will be past all doubt, if you consider, that in case colours were real properties or affections inherent in external bodies, they could admit of no alteration, without some change wrought in the very bodies themselves; but is it not evident from what hath been said, that upon the use of microscopes, upon a change happening in the humours of the eye, or a variation of distance, without any manner of real alteration in the thing itself, the colours of any object are either changed, or totally disappear? Nay, all other circumstances remaining the same, change but the situation of some objects, and they shall present different colours to the eye. The same thing happens upon viewing an object in various degrees of light. And what is more known, than that the same bodies appear differently coloured by candle-light from what they do in the open day? Add to these the experiment of a prism, which, separating the heterogeneous rays of light, alters the colour of any object; and will cause the whitest to appear of a deep blue or red to the naked eye. And now tell me, whether you are still of opinion, that every body hath its true, real colour inhering in it; and if you think it hath, I would fain know further from you, what certain distance and position of the object, what peculiar texture and formation of the eye, what degree or kind of light is necessary for ascertaining that true colour, and distinguishing it from apparent ones.

Hyl. I own myself entirely satisfied, that they are all equally apparent; and that there is no such thing as colour really inhering in external bodies, but that it is altogether in the light. And what confirms me in this opinion, is, that in proportion to the light, colours are still more or less vivid; and if there be no light, then are there no colours perceived. Besides, allowing there are colours on external objects, yet how is it possible for us to perceive them? For no external body affects the mind, unless it act first on our organs of sense. But the only action of bodies is motion; and motion cannot be communicated otherwise than by impulse. A distant object therefore cannot act on the eye, nor consequently make itself or its properties perceivable to the soul. Whence it plainly follows, that it is immediately some contiguous substance, which operating on the eye occasions a perception of colours: and such is light.

Phil. How! is light then a substance?

Hyl. I tell you, Philonous, external light is nothing but a thin fluid substance, whose minute particles being agitated with a brisk motion, and in various manners reflected from the different surfaces of outward objects to the eyes, communicate different motions to the optic nerves; which being propagated to the brain, cause therein various impressions: and these are attended with the sensations of red, blue, yellow, &c.

Phil. It seems, then, the light doth no more than shake the optic nerves.

Hyl. Nothing else.

Phil. And consequent to each particular motion of the nerves the mind is affected with a sensation, which is some particular colour.

Hyl. Right.

Phil. And these sensations have no existence without the mind.

Hyl. They have not.

Phil. How then do you affirm that colours are in the light, since by *light* you understand a corporeal substance external to the mind?

Hyl. Light and colours, as immediately perceived by us, I grant cannot exist without the mind. But in themselves they are only the motions and configurations of certain insensible particles of matter.

Phil. Colours then, in the vulgar sense, or taken for the immediate objects of sight, cannot agree to any but a perceiving substance.

Hyl. That is what I say.

Phil. Well then, since you give up the point as to those sensible qualities, which are alone thought colours by all mankind beside, you may hold what you please with regard to those invisible ones of the philosophers. It is not my business to dispute about them; only I would advise you to bethink yourself, whether, considering the inquiry we are upon, it be prudent for you to affirm *the red and blue which we see are not real colours, but certain unknown motions and figures which no man ever did or can see, are truly so.* Are not these shocking notions, and are not they subject to as many ridiculous inferences, as those you were obliged to renounce before in the case of sounds?

Hyl. I frankly own, Philonous, that it is in vain to stand out any longer. Colours, sounds, tastes, in a word, all those termed *secondary qualities,* have certainly no existence without the mind. But by this acknowledgment I must not be supposed to derogate any thing from the reality of matter or external objects, seeing it is no more than several philosophers maintain, who nevertheless are the furthest imaginable from denying matter. For the clearer understanding of this, you must know sensible qualities are by philosophers divided into *primary* and *secondary.* The former are extension, figure, solidity, gravity, motion, and rest. And these they hold exist really in bodies. The latter are those above enumerated; or briefly, all sensible qualities beside the primary, which they assert are only so many sensations or ideas existing no where but in the mind. But all this, I doubt not, you are already apprised of. For my part, I have been a long time sensible there was such an opinion current among philosophers, but was never thoroughly convinced of its truth till now.

Phil. You are still then of opinion, that extension and figures are inherent in external unthinking substances.

Hyl. I am.

Phil. But what if the same arguments which are brought against secondary qualities, will hold proof against these also?

Hyl. Why then I shall be obliged to think, they too exist only in the mind.

Phil. Is it your opinion, the very figure and extension which you perceive by sense, exist in the outward object or material substance?

Hyl. It is.

Phil. Have all other animals as good grounds to think the same of the figure and extension which they see and feel?

Hyl. Without doubt, if they have any thought at all.

Phil. Answer me, Hylas. Think you the senses were bestowed upon all animals for their preservation and well-being in life? or were they given to men alone for this end?

Hyl. I make no question but they have the same use in all other animals.

Phil. If so, is it not necessary they should be enabled by them to perceive their own limbs, and those bodies which are capable of harming them?

Hyl. Certainly.

Phil. A mite therefore must be supposed to see his own foot, and things equal or even less than it, as bodies of some considerable dimension; though at the same time they appear to you scarce discernible, or at best as so many visible points.

Hyl. I cannot deny it.

Phil. And to creatures less than the mite they will seem yet larger.

Hyl. They will.

Phil. Insomuch that what you can hardly discern, will to another extremely minute animal appear as some huge mountain.

Hyl. All this I grant.

Phil. Can one and the same thing be at the same time in itself of different dimensions?

Hyl. That were absurd to imagine.

Phil. But from what you have laid down it follows, that both the extension by you perceived, and that perceived by the mite itself, as likewise all those perceived by lesser animals, are each of them the true extension of the mite's foot, that is to say, by your own principles you are led into an absurdity.

Hyl. There seems to be some difficulty in the point.

Phil. Again, have you not acknowledged that no real inherent property of any object can be changed, without some change in the thing itself?

Hyl. I have.

Phil. But as we approach to or recede from an object, the visible extension varies, being at one distance ten or a hundred times greater than at another. Doth it not therefore follow from hence likewise, that it is not really inherent in the object?

Hyl. I own I am at a loss what to think.

Phil. Your judgment will soon be determined, if you will venture to think as freely concerning this quality, as you have done concerning the rest. Was it not admitted as a good argument, that neither heat nor cold was in the water, because it seemed warm to one hand, and cold to the other?

Hyl. It was.

Phil. Is it not the very same reasoning to conclude, there is no extension or figure in an object, because to one eye it shall seem little, smooth, and round, when at the same time it appears to the other, great, uneven, and angular?

Hyl. The very same. But doth this latter fact ever happen?

Phil. You may at any time make the experiment, by looking with one eye bare, and with the other through a microscope.

Hyl. I know not how to maintain it, and yet I am loath to give up *extension*, I see so many odd consequences following upon such a concession.

Phil. Odd, say you? After the concessions already made, I hope you will stick at nothing for its oddness. But on the other hand should it not seem very odd, if the general reasoning which includes all other sensible qualities did not also include extension? If it be allowed that no idea nor any thing like an idea can exist in an unperceiving substance, then surely it follows, that no figure or mode of extension, which we can either perceive or imagine, or have any idea of, can be really inherent in matter; not to mention the peculiar difficulty there must be, in conceiving a material substance, prior to and distinct from extension, to be the *substratum* of extension. Be the sensible quality what it will, figure, or sound, or colour; it seems alike impossible it should subsist in that which doth not perceive it.

Hyl. I give up the point for the present, reserving still a right to retract my opinion, in case I shall hereafter discover any false step in my progress to it.

Phil. That is a right you cannot be denied. Figures and extension being despatched, we proceed next to *motion.* Can a real motion in any external body be at the same time both very swift and very slow?

Hyl. It cannot.

Phil. Is not the motion of a body swift in a reciprocal proportion to the time it takes up in describing any given space? Thus a body that describes a mile in an hour, moves three times faster than it would in case it described only a mile in three hours.

Hyl. I agree with you.

Phil. And is not time measured by the succession of ideas in our minds?

Hyl. It is.

Phil. And is it not possible ideas should succeed one another twice as fast in your mind, as they do in mine, or in that of some spirit of another kind.

Hyl. I own it.

Phil. Consequently the same body may to another seem to perform its motion over any space in half the time that it doth to you. And the same reasoning will hold as to any other proportion: that is to say, according to your principles (since the motions perceived are both really in the object) it is possible one and the same body shall be really moved the same way at once, both very swift and very slow. How is this consistent either with common sense, or with what you just now granted?

Hyl. I have nothing to say to it.

Phil. Then as for *solidity*: either you do not mean any sensible quality by that word, and so it is beside our inquiry: or if you do, it must be either hardness or resistance. But both the one and the other are plainly relative to our senses: it being evident, that what seems hard to one animal, may appear soft to another, who hath greater force and firmness of limbs. Nor is it less plain, that the resistance I feel is not in the body.

Hyl. I own the very sensation of resistance, which is all you immediately perceive, is not in the *body*, but the cause of that sensation is.

Phil. But the causes of our sensations are not things immediately perceived, and therefore not sensible. This point I thought had been already determined.

Hyl. I own it was; but you will pardon me if I seem a little embarrassed: I know not how to quit my old notions.

Phil. To help you out, do but consider, that if extension be once acknowledged to have no existence without the mind, the same must necessarily be granted of motion, solidity, and gravity, since they all evidently suppose extension. It is therefore superfluous to inquire particularly concerning each of them. In denying extension, you have denied them all to have any real existence.

Hyl. I wonder, Philonous, if what you say be true, why those philosophers who deny the secondary qualities any real existence, should yet attribute it to the primary. If there is no difference between them, how can this be accounted for?

Phil. It is not my business to account for every opinion of the philosophers. But among other reasons which may be assigned for this, it seems probable, that pleasure and pain being rather annexed to the former than the latter, may be one. Heat and cold, tastes and smells, have something more vividly pleasing or disagreeable than the ideas of extension, figure, and motion, affect us with. And it being too visibly absurd to hold, that pain or pleasure can be in an unperceiving substance, men are more easily weaned from believing the external existence of the secondary, than the primary qualities. You will be satisfied there is something in this, if you recollect the difference you made between an intense and more moderate degree of heat, allowing the one a real existence, while you denied it to the other. But after all, there is no rational ground for that distinction; for surely an indifferent sensation is as truly *a sensation,* as one more pleasing or painful; and consequently should not any more than they be supposed to exist in an unthinking subject.

Hyl. It is just come into my head, Philonous, that I have somewhere heard of a distinction between absolute and sensible extension. Now though it be acknowledged that *great* and *small,* consisting merely in the relation which other extended beings have to the parts of our own bodies, do not really inhere in the substances themselves; yet nothing obliges us to hold the same with regard to *absolute extension,* which is something abstracted from *great and small,* from this or that particular magnitude or figure. So likewise as to motion, *swift* and *slow* are altogether relative to the succession of ideas in our own minds. But it doth not follow, because those modifications of motion exist not without the mind, that therefore absolute motion abstracted from them doth not.

Phil. Pray what is it that distinguishes one motion, or one part of extension from another? Is it not something sensible, as some degree of swiftness or slowness, some certain magnitude or figure peculiar to each?

Hyl. I think so.

Phil. These qualities therefore, stripped of all sensible properties, are without all specific and numerical differences, as the schools call them.

Hyl. They are.

Phil. That is to say, they are extension in general, and motion in general.

Hyl. Let it be so.

Phil. But it is a universally received maxim, that *everything which exists is particular*. How then can motion in general, or extension in general, exist in any corporeal substance?

Hyl. I will take time to solve your difficulty.

Phil. But I think the point may be speedily decided. Without doubt you can tell, whether you are able to frame this or that idea. Now I am content to put our dispute on this issue. If you can frame in your thoughts a distinct abstract idea of motion or extension, divested of all those sensible modes, as swift and slow, great and small, round and square, and the like, which are acknowledged to exist only in the mind, I will then yield the point you contend for. But if you cannot, it will be unreasonable on your side to insist any longer upon what you have no notion of.

Hyl. To confess ingenuously, I cannot.

Phil. Can you even separate the ideas of extension and motion, from the ideas of all those qualities which they who make the distinction term *secondary*?

Hyl. What! is it not an easy matter, to consider extension and motion by themselves, abstracted from all other sensible qualities? Pray how do the mathematicians treat of them?

Phil. I acknowledge, Hylas, it is not difficult to form general propositions and reasonings about those qualities, without mentioning any other; and in this sense to consider or treat of them abstractedly. But how doth it follow that because I can pronounce the word *motion* by itself, I can form the idea of it in my mind exclusive of body? Or because theorems may be made of extension and figures, without any mention of *great* or *small*, or any other sensible mode or quality; that therefore it is possible such an abstract idea of extension, without any particular size or figure, or sensible quality, should be distinctly formed, and apprehended by the mind? Mathematicians treat of quantity, without regarding what other sensible qualities it is attended with, as being altogether indifferent to their demonstrations. But when laying aside the words, they contemplate the bare ideas, I believe you will find, they are not the pure abstracted ideas of extension.

Hyl. But what say you to *pure intellect?* May not abstracted ideas be framed by that faculty?

Phil. Since I cannot frame abstract ideas at all, it is plain, I cannot frame them by the help of *pure intellect*, whatsoever faculty you understand by those words. Besides—not to inquire into the nature of pure intellect and its spiritual objects, as *virtue—reason, God*, or the like, thus much seems manifest, that sensible things are only to be perceived by sense, or represented by the imagination. Figures therefore and extension, being originally perceived by sense, do not belong to pure intellect. But for your further satisfaction, try if you can frame the idea of any figure, abstracted from all particularities of size, or even from other sensible qualities.

Hyl. Let me think a little——I do not find that I can.

Phil. And can you think it possible, that should really exist in nature, which implies a repugnancy in its conception?

Hyl. By no means.

Phil. Since therefore it is impossible even for the mind to disunite the ideas of extension and motion from all other sensible qualities, doth it not follow, that where the one exist, there necessarily the other exist likewise?

Hyl. It should seem so.

Phil. Consequently the very same arguments which you admitted, as conclusive against the secondary qualities, are without any further application of force against the primary too. Besides, if you will trust your senses, is it not plain all sensible qualities co-exist, or to them appear as being in the same place? Do they ever represent a motion, or figure, as being divested of all other visible and tangible qualities?

Hyl. You need say no more on this head. I am free to own, if there be no secret error or oversight in our proceedings hitherto, that all sensible qualities are alike to be denied existence without the mind. But my fear is, that I have been too liberal in my former concessions, or overlooked some fallacy or other. In short, I did not take time to think.

Phil. For that matter, Hylas, you may take what time you please in reviewing the progress of our inquiry. You are at liberty to recover any slips you might have made, or offer whatever you have omitted, which makes for your first opinion.

Hyl. One great oversight I take to be this: that I did not sufficiently distinguish the *object* from the *sensation.* Now though this latter may not exist without the mind, yet it will not thence follow that the former cannot.

Phil. What object do you mean? The object of the senses?

Hyl. The same.

Phil. It is then immediately perceived?

Hyl. Right.

Phil. Make me to understand the difference between what is immediately perceived, and a sensation.

Hyl. The sensation I take to be an act of the mind perceiving; beside which, there is something perceived; and this I call the *object.* For example, there is red and yellow on that tulip. But then the act of perceiving those colours is in me only, and not in the tulip.

Phil. What tulip do you speak of? is it that which you see?

Hyl. The same.

Phil. And what do you see beside colour, figure, and extension?

Hyl. Nothing.

Phil. What you would say then is, that the red and yellow are co-existent with the extension; is it not?

Hyl. That is not all: I would say, they have a real existence without the mind, in some unthinking substance.

Phil. That the colours are really in the tulip which I see, is manifest. Neither can it be denied, that this tulip may exist independent of your mind or mine; but that any immediate object of the senses, that is, any idea, or combination of ideas, should exist in an unthinking substance, or exterior to all minds, is in itself an evident contradiction. Nor can I imagine how this follows from what you said just now, to wit that the red and yellow were on the tulip *you saw,* since you do not pretend to *see* that unthinking substance.

Hyl. You have an artful way, Philonous, of diverting our inquiry from the subject.

Phil. I see you have no mind to be pressed that way. To return then to your distinction between *sensation* and *object;*

if I take you right, you distinguish in every perception two things, the one an action of the mind, the other not.

Hyl. True.

Phil. And this action cannot exist in, or belong to any unthinking thing; but whatever beside is implied in a perception, may.

Hyl. That is my meaning.

Phil. So that if there was a perception without any act of the mind, it were possible such a perception should exist in an unthinking substance.

Hyl. I grant it. But it is impossible there should be such a perception.

Phil. When is the mind said to be active?

Hyl. When it produces, puts an end to, or changes any thing.

Phil. Can the mind produce, discontinue, or change any thing but by an act of the will?

Hyl. It cannot.

Phil. The mind therefore is to be accounted active in its perceptions, so far forth as volition is included in them.

Hyl. It is.

Phil. In plucking this flower, I am active, because I do it by the motion of my hand, which was consequent upon my volition; so likewise in applying it to my nose. But is either of these smelling?

Hyl. No.

Phil. I act too in drawing the air through my nose; because my breathing so rather than otherwise, is the effect of my volition. But neither can this be called *smelling*: for if it were, I should smell every time I breathed in that manner.

Hyl. True.

Phil. Smelling then is somewhat consequent to all this.

Hyl. It is.

Phil. But I do not find my will concerned any further. Whatever more there is, as that I perceive such a particular smell or any smell at all, this is independent of my will, and therein I am altogether passive. Do you find it otherwise with you, Hylas?

Hyl. No, the very same.

Phil. Then as to seeing, is it not in your power to open your eyes, or keep them shut; to turn them this or that way?

Hyl. Without doubt.

Phil. But doth it in like manner depend on your will, that in looking on this flower, you perceive *white* rather than any other colour? Or directing your open eyes towards yonder part of the heaven, can you avoid seeing the sun? Or is light or darkness the effect of your volition?

Hyl. No, certainly.

Phil. You are then in these respects altogether passive.

Hyl. I am.

Phil. Tell me now, whether *seeing* consists in perceiving light and colours, or in opening and turning the eyes?

Hyl. Without doubt, in the former.

Phil. Since, therefore you are in the very perception of light and colours altogether passive, what is become of that action you were speaking of, as an ingredient in every sensation? And doth it not follow from your own concessions, that the perception of light and colours, including no action in it, may exist in an unperceiving substance? And is not this a plain contradiction?

Hyl. I know not what to think of it.

Phil. Besides, since you distinguish the *active* and *passive* in every perception, you must do it in that of pain. But how is it possible that pain, be it as little active as you please, should exist in an unperceiving substance? In short, do but consider the point, and then confess ingenuously, whether light and colours, tastes, sounds, &c., are not all equally passions or sensations in the soul. You may indeed call them *external objects*, and give them in words what subsistence you please. But examine your own thoughts, and then tell me whether it be not as I say?

Hyl. I acknowledge, Philonous, that upon a fair observation of what passes in my mind, I can discover nothing else, but that I am a thinking being, affected with variety of sensations; neither is it possible to conceive how a sensation should exist in an unperceiving substance. But then on the other hand, when I look on sensible things in a different view, considering them as so many modes and qualities, I find it necessary to suppose a material *substratum*, without which they cannot be conceived to exist.

Phil. Material substratum call you it? Pray, by which of your senses came you acquainted with that being?

Hyl. It is not itself sensible; its modes and qualities only being perceived by the senses.

Phil. I presume then, it was by reflection and reason you obtained the idea of it.

Hyl. I do not pretend to any proper positive idea of it. However I conclude it exists, because qualities cannot be conceived to exist without a support.

Phil. It seems then you have only a relative notion of it, or that you conceive it not otherwise than by conceiving the relation it bears to sensible qualities.

Hyl. Right.

Phil. Be pleased therefore to let me know wherein that relation consists.

Hyl. Is it not sufficiently expressed in the term *substratum*, or *substance?*

Phil. If so, the word *substratum* should import, that it is spread under the sensible qualities or accidents.

Hyl. True.

Phil. And consequently under extension.

Hyl. I own it.

Phil. It is therefore somewhat in its own nature entirely distinct from extension.

Hyl. I tell you, extension is only a mode, and matter is something that supports modes. And is it not evident the thing supported is different from the thing supporting?

Phil. So that something distinct from, and exclusive of extension, is supposed to be the *substratum* of extension?

Hyl. Just so.

Phil. Answer me, Hylas. Can a thing be spread without extension? or is not the idea of extension necessarily included in *spreading?*

Hyl. It is.

Phil. Whatsoever therefore you suppose spread under any thing, must have in itself an extension distinct from the extension of that thing under which it is spread.

Hyl. It must.

Phil. Consequently every corporeal substance being the *substratum* of extension, must have in itself another extension by which it is qualified to be a *substratum:* and so on to infinity. And I ask whether this be not absurd in itself, and repugnant to what you granted just now, to wit, that the *substratum* was something distinct from, and exclusive of extension.

Hyl. Aye but Philonous, you take me wrong. I do not mean that matter is *spread* in a gross literal sense under extension. The word *substratum* is used only to express in general the same thing with *substance.*

Phil. Well then, let us examine the relation implied in the term *substance.* Is it not that it stands under accidents?

Hyl. The very same.

Phil. But that one thing may stand under or support another, must it not be extended?

Hyl. It must.

Phil. Is not therefore this supposition liable to the same absurdity with the former?

Hyl. You still take things in a strict literal sense: that is not fair, Philonous.

Phil. I am not for imposing any sense on your words: you are at liberty to explain them as you please. Only I beseech you, make me understand something by them. You tell me, matter supports or stands under accidents. How! is it as your legs support your body?

Hyl. No; that is the literal sense.

Phil. Pray let me know any sense, literal or not literal, that you understand it in.——How long must I wait for an answer, Hylas?

Hyl. I declare I know not what to say. I once thought I understood well enough what was meant by matter's supporting accidents. But now the more I think on it, the less can I comprehend it; in short, I find that I know nothing of it.

Phil. It seems then you have no idea at all, neither relative nor positive, of matter; you know neither what it is in itself, nor what relation it bears to accidents.

Hyl. I acknowledge it.

Phil. And yet you asserted, that you could not conceive how qualities or accidents should really exist, without conceiving at the same time a material support of them.

Hyl. I did.

Phil. That is to say, when you conceive the real existence of qualities, you do withal conceive something which you cannot conceive.

Hyl. It was wrong, I own. But still I fear there is some fallacy or other. Pray what think you of this? It is just come into my head, that the ground of all our mistake lies in your treating of each quality by itself. Now, I grant that each quality cannot singly subsist without the mind. Colour cannot without extension, neither can figure without some other sensible quality. But as the several qualities united or blended together form entire sensible things, nothing hinders why such things may not be supposed to exist without the mind.

Phil. Either, Hylas, you are jesting, or have a very bad memory. Though indeed we went through all the qualities by name one after another; yet my arguments, or rather your concessions no where tended to prove, that the secondary qualities did not subsist each alone by itself: but that they were not *at all* without the mind. Indeed in treating of figure and motion, we concluded they could not exist without the mind, because it was impossible even in thought to separate them from all secondary qualities, so as to conceive them existing by themselves. But then this was not the only argument made use of upon that occasion. But (to pass by all that hath been hitherto said, and reckon it for nothing, if you will have it so) I am content to put the whole upon this issue. If you can conceive it possible for any mixture or combination of qualities, or any sensible object whatever, to exist without the mind, then I will grant it actually to be so.

Hyl. If it comes to that, the point will soon be decided. What more easy than to conceive a tree or house existing by itself, independent of, and unperceived by any mind whatsoever? I do at this present time conceive them existing after that manner.

Phil. How say you, Hylas, can you see a thing which is at the same time unseen?

Hyl. No, that were a contradiction.

Phil. Is it not as great a contradiction to talk of *conceiving* a thing which is *unconceived?*

Hyl. It is.

Phil. The tree or house therefore which you think of, is conceived by you.

Hyl. How should it be otherwise?

Phil. And what is conceived is surely in the mind.

Hyl. Without question, that which is conceived is in the mind.

Phil. How then came you to say, you conceived a house or tree existing independent and out of all minds whatsoever?

Hyl. That was, I own, an oversight; but stay, let me consider what led me into it.—It is a pleasant mistake enough. As I was thinking of a tree in a solitary place, where no one was present to see it, methought that was to conceive a tree as existing unperceived or unthought of, not considering that I myself conceived it all the while. But now I plainly see, that all I can do is to frame ideas in my own mind. I may indeed conceive in my own thoughts the idea of a tree, or a house, or a mountain, but that is all. And this is far from proving, that I can conceive them *existing out of the minds of all spirits*.

Phil. You acknowledge then that you cannot possibly conceive how any one corporeal sensible thing should exist otherwise than in a mind.

Hyl. I do.

Phil. And yet you will earnestly contend for the truth of that which you cannot so much as conceive.

Hyl. I profess I know not what to think, but still there are some scruples remain with me. Is it not certain I see things at a distance? Do we not perceive the stars and moon, for example, to be a great way off? Is not this, I say, manifest to the senses?

Phil. Do you not in a dream too perceive those or the like objects?

Hyl. I do.

Phil. And have they not then the same appearance of being distant?

Hyl. They have.

Phil. But you do not thence conclude the apparitions in a dream to be without the mind?

Hyl. By no means.

Phil. You ought not therefore to conclude that sensible objects are without the mind, from their appearance or manner wherein they are perceived.

Hyl. I acknowledge it. But doth not my sense deceive me in those cases?

Phil. By no means. The idea or thing which you immediately perceive, neither sense nor reason inform you that it actually exists without the mind. By sense you only know that you are affected with such certain sensations of light and colours, &c. And these you will not say are without the mind.

Hyl. True: but beside all that, do you not think the sight suggests something of *outness* or *distance?*

Phil. Upon approaching a distant object, do the visible size and figure change perpetually, or do they appear the same at all distances?

Hyl. They are in a continual change.

Phil. Sight therefore doth not suggest or in any way inform you, that the visible object you immediately perceive, exists at a distance, or will be perceived when you advance further onward, there being a continued series of visible objects succeeding each other, during the whole time of your approach.

Hyl. It doth not; but still I know, upon seeing an object, what object I shall perceive after having passed over a certain distance: no matter whether it be exactly the same or no: there is still something of distance suggested in the case.

Phil. Good Hylas, do but reflect a little on the point, and then tell me whether there be any more in it than this. From the ideas you actually perceive by sight, you have by experience learned to collect what other ideas you will (according to the standing order of nature) be affected with, after such a certain succession of time and motion.

Hyl. Upon the whole, I take it to be nothing else.

Phil. Now is it not plain, that if we suppose a man born blind was on a sudden made to see, he could at first have no experience of what may be suggested by sight.

Hyl. It is.

Phil. He would not then, according to you, have any notion of distance annexed to the things he saw; but would take them for a new set of sensations existing only in his mind.

Hyl. It is undeniable.

Phil. But to make it still more plain: is not *distance* a line turned endwise to the eye?

Hyl. It is.

Phil. And can a line so situated be perceived by sight?

Hyl. It cannot.

Phil. Doth it not therefore follow that distance is not properly and immediately perceived by sight?

Hyl. It should seem so.

Phil. Again, is it your opinion that colours are at a distance?

Hyl. It must be acknowledged, they are only in the mind.

Phil. But do not colours appear to the eye as co-existing in the same place with extension and figures?

Hyl. They do.

Phil. How can you then conclude from sight, that figures exist without, when you acknowledge colours do not; the sensible appearance being the very same with regard to both?

Hyl. I know not what to answer.

Phil. But allowing that distance was truly and immediately perceived by the mind, yet it would not thence follow it existed out of the mind. For whatever is immediately perceived is an idea: and can any *idea* exist out of the mind?

Hyl. To suppose that were absurd: but inform me, Philonous, can we perceive or know nothing beside our ideas?

Phil. As for the rational deducing of causes from effects, that is beside our inquiry. And by the senses you can best tell, whether you perceive any thing which is not immediately perceived. And I ask you, whether the things immediately perceived, are other than your own sensations or ideas? You have indeed more than once, in the course of this conversation, declared yourself on those points; but you seem, by this last question, to have departed from what you then thought.

Hyl. To speak the truth, Philonous, I think there are two kinds of objects, the one perceived immediately, which are likewise called *ideas*; the other are real things or external objects perceived by the mediation of ideas, which are their images and representations. Now I own, ideas do not exist without the mind; but the latter sort of objects do. I am sorry I did not think of this distinction sooner; it would probably have cut short your discourse.

Phil. Are those external objects perceived by sense, or by some other faculty?

Hyl. They are perceived by sense.

Phil. How! is there any thing perceived by sense, which is not immediately perceived?

Hyl. Yes, Philonous, in some sort there is. For example, when I look on a picture or statue of Julius Cæsar, I may be said, after a manner, to perceive him (though not immediately) by my senses.

Phil. It seems, then, you will have our ideas, which alone are immediately perceived, to be pictures of external things: and that these also are perceived by sense, inasmuch as they have a conformity or resemblance to our ideas.

Hyl. That is my meaning.

Phil. And in the same way that Julius Cæsar, in himself invisible, is nevertheless perceived by sight; real things, in themselves imperceptible, are perceived by sense.

Hyl. In the very same.

Phil. Tell me, Hylas, when you behold the picture of Julius Cæsar, do you see with your eyes any more than some colours and figures, with a certain symmetry and composition of the whole?

Hyl. Nothing else.

Phil. And would not a man, who had never known any thing of Julius Cæsar, see as much?

Hyl. He would.

Phil. Consequently he hath his sight, and the use of it, in as perfect a degree as you.

Hyl. I agree with you.

Phil. Whence comes it then that your thoughts are directed to the Roman emperor and his are not? This cannot proceed from the sensations or ideas of sense by you then perceived; since you acknowledge you have no advantage over him in that respect. It should seem therefore to proceed from reason and memory: should it not?

Hyl. It should.

Phil. Consequently it will not follow from that instance, that any thing is perceived by sense which is not immediately perceived. Though I grant we may in one acceptation be said to perceive sensible things mediately by sense: that is, when from a frequently perceived connexion, the immediate perception of ideas by one sense suggests to the mind others perhaps belonging to another sense, which are wont to be connected with them, For instance, when I hear a coach drive along the streets, immediately I perceive only the sound; but from the experience I have had that such a sound is connected with a coach, I am said to hear the coach. It is nevertheless evident, that in truth and strictness, nothing can be *heard* but *sound:* and the coach is not then properly perceived by sense, but suggested from experience. So likewise when we are said to see a red-hot bar of iron; the solidity and heat of the iron are not the objects of sight, but suggested to the imagination by the colour and figure, which are properly perceived by that sense. In short, those things alone are actually and strictly perceived by any sense, which would have been perceived, in case that same sense had then been first conferred on us. As for other things, it is plain they are only suggested to the mind by experience grounded on former perceptions. But to return to your comparison of Cæsar's picture, it is plain, if you keep to that, you must hold the real things or archetypes of our ideas are not perceived by sense, but by some internal faculty of the soul, as reason or memory. I would therefore fain know, what arguments you can draw from reason for the existence of what you call *real things* or *material objects*; or whether you remember to have seen them formerly as they are in themselves; or if you have heard or read of any one that did.

Hyl. I see, Philonous, you are disposed to raillery; but that will never convince me.

Phil. My aim is only to learn from you the way to come at the knowledge of *material beings.* Whatever we perceive, is perceived either immediately or mediately: by sense, or by reason and reflection. But as you have excluded sense, pray show me what reason you have to believe their existence; or what *medium* you can possibly make use of to prove it, either to mine or your own understanding.

Hyl. To deal ingenuously, Philonous, now I consider the point, I do not find I can give you any good reason for it. But thus much seems pretty plain, that it is at least possible such things may really exist; and as long as there is no absurdity in supposing them, I am resolved to believe as I did, till you bring good reasons to the contrary.

Phil. What! is it come to this, that you only believe the existence of material objects, and that your belief is founded barely on the possibility of its being true? Then you will have me bring reasons against it: though another would think it reasonable, the proof should lie on him who holds the affirmative. And after all, this very point which you are now resolved to maintain without any reason, is, in effect, what you have more than once, during this discourse, seen good reason to give up. But to pass over all this; if I understand you rightly, you say our ideas do not exist without the mind; but that they are copies, images, or representations of certain originals that do.

Hyl. You take me right.

Phil. They are then like external things.

Hyl. They are.

Phil. Have those things a stable and permanent nature independent of our senses; or are they in a perpetual change, upon our producing any motions in our bodies, suspending, exerting, or altering our faculties or organs of sense.

Hyl. Real things, it is plain, have a fixed and real nature, which remains the same, notwithstanding any change in our senses, or in the posture and motion of our bodies; which, indeed, may affect the ideas in our minds, but it were absurd to think they had the same effect on things existing without the mind.

Phil. How then is it possible, that things perpetually fleeting and variable as our ideas, should be copies or images of any thing fixed and constant? or in other words, since all sensible qualities, as size, figure, colour, &c., that is, our ideas, are continually changing upon every alteration in the distance, medium, or instruments of sensation; how can any determinate material objects be properly represented or painted forth by several distinct things, each of which is so different from and unlike the rest? Or if you say it resembles some one only of our ideas, how shall we be able to distinguish the true copy from all the false ones?

Hyl. I profess, Philonous, I am at a loss. I know not what to say to this.

Phil. But neither is this all. Which are material objects in themselves, perceptible or imperceptible?

Hyl. Properly and immediately nothing can be perceived but ideas. All material things therefore are in themselves insensible, and to be perceived only by their ideas.

Phil. Ideas then are sensible, and their archetypes or originals insensible.

Hyl. Right.

Phil. But how can that which is sensible be like that which is insensible? Can a real thing in itself *invisible* be like a *colour;* or a real thing which is not *audible,* be like a *sound?* In a word, can any thing be like a sensation or idea, but another sensation or idea?

Hyl. I must own, I think not.

Phil. Is it possible there should be any doubt in the point? Do you not perfectly know your own ideas?

Hyl. I know them perfectly; since what I do not perceive or know, can be no part of my idea.

Phil. Consider therefore, and examine them, and then tell me if there be any thing in them which can exist without the mind: or if you can conceive any thing like them existing without the mind.

Hyl. Upon inquiry, I find it is impossible for me to conceive or understand how any thing but an idea can be like an idea. And it is most evident, that *no idea can exist without the mind.*

Phil. You are therefore by your principles forced to deny the reality of sensible things, since you made it to consist in an absolute existence exterior to the mind. That is to say, you are a downright sceptic. So I have gained my point, which was to show your principles led to scepticism.

Hyl. For the present I am, if not entirely convinced, at least silenced.

Phil. I would fain know what more you would require in order to a perfect conviction. Have you not had the liberty of explaining yourself all manner of ways? Were any little slips in discourse laid hold and insisted on? Or were you not allowed to retract or reinforce any thing you had offered, as best served your purpose? Hath not every thing you could say been heard and examined with all the fairness imaginable? In a word, have you not in every point been convinced out of your own mouth? And if you can at present discover any flaw in any of your former concessions, or think of any remaining subterfuge, any new distinction, colour, or comment whatsoever, why do you not produce it?

Hyl. A little patience, Philonous. I am at present so amazed to see myself ensnared, and as it were imprisoned in the labyrinths you have drawn me into, that on the sudden it cannot be expected I should find my way out. You must give me time to look about me, and recollect myself.

Phil. Hark; is not this the college-bell?

Hyl. It rings for prayers.

Phil. We will go in then if you please, and meet here again to-morrow morning. In the mean time you may employ your thoughts on this morning's discourse, and try if you can find any fallacy in it, or invent any new means to extricate yourself.

Hyl. Agreed.

THE SECOND DIALOGUE

Hylas. I beg your pardon, Philonous, for not meeting you sooner. All this morning my head was so filled with our late conversation, that I had not leisure to think of the time of the day, or indeed of any thing else.

Philonous. I am glad you were so intent upon it, in hopes if there were any mistakes in your concessions, or fallacies in my reasonings from them, you will now discover them to me.

Hyl. I assure you, I have done nothing ever since I saw you, but search after mistakes and fallacies, and with that view have minutely examined the whole series of yesterday's discourse: but all in vain, for the notions it led me into, upon review appear still more clear and evident; and the more I consider them, the more irresistibly do they force my assent.

Phil. And is not this, think you, a sign that they are genuine, that they proceed from nature, and are conformable to right reason? Truth and beauty are in this alike, that the strictest survey sets them both off to advantage. While the false lustre of error and disguise cannot endure being reviewed, or too nearly inspected.

Hyl. I own there is a great deal in what you say. Nor can any one be more entirely satisfied of the truth of those odd consequences, so long as I have in view the reasonings that lead to them. But when these are out of my thoughts, there seems on the other hand something so satisfactory, so natural and intelligible in the modern way of explaining things, that I profess I know not how to reject it.

Phil. I know not what way you mean.

Hyl. I mean the way of accounting for our sensations or ideas.

Phil. How is that?

Hyl. It is supposed the soul makes her residence in some part of the brain, from which the nerves take their rise, and are thence extended to all parts of the body: and that outward objects, by the different impressions they make on the organs of sense, communicate certain vibrative motions to the nerves; and these being filled with spirits, propagate them to the brain or seat of the soul, which according to the various impressions or traces thereby made in the brain, is variously affected with ideas.

Phil. And call you this an explication of the manner whereby we are affected with ideas?

Hyl. Why not, Philonous? have you any thing to object against it?

Phil. I would first know whether I rightly understand your hypothesis. You make certain traces in the brain to be the causes or occasions of our ideas. Pray tell me, whether by the *brain* you mean any sensible thing?

Hyl. What else think you I could mean?

Phil. Sensible things are all immediately perceivable; and those things which are immediately perceivable, are ideas; and these exist only in the mind. Thus much you have, if I mistake not, long since agreed to.

Hyl. I do not deny it.

Phil. The brain therefore you speak of, being a sensible thing, exists only in the mind. Now, I would fain know whether you think it reasonable to suppose, that one idea or thing existing in the mind, occasions all other ideas. And if you think so, pray how do you account for the origin of that primary idea or brain itself?

Hyl. I do not explain the origin of our ideas by that brain which is perceivable to sense, this being itself only a combination of sensible ideas, but by another which I imagine.

Phil. But are not things imagined as truly in the mind as things perceived?

Hyl. I must confess they are.

Phil. It comes therefore to the same thing; and you have been all this while accounting for ideas, by certain motions or impressions in the brain, that is, by some alterations in an idea, whether sensible or imaginable, it matters not.

Hyl. I begin to suspect my hypothesis.

Phil. Beside spirits, all that we know or conceive are our own ideas. When therefore you say, all ideas are occasioned by impressions in the brain, do you conceive this brain or no? If you do, then you talk of ideas imprinted in an idea, causing that same idea, which is absurd. If you do not conceive it, you talk unintelligibly, instead of forming a reasonable hypothesis.

Hyl. I now clearly see it was a mere dream. There is nothing in it.

Phil. You need not be much concerned at it; for after all, this way of explaining things, as you called it, could never have satisfied any reasonable man. What connexion is there between a motion in the nerves, and the sensations of sound or colour in the mind? Or how is it possible these should be the effect of that?

Hyl. But I could never think it had so little in it, as now it seems to have.

Phil. Well then, are you at length satisfied that no sensible things have a real existence; and that you are in truth an arrant *sceptic*?

Hyl. It is too plain to be denied.

Phil. Look! are not the fields covered with a delightful verdure? Is there not something in the woods and groves, in the rivers and clear springs, that soothes, that delights, that transports the soul? At the prospect of the wide and deep ocean, or some huge mountain whose top is lost in the clouds, or of an old gloomy forest, are not our minds filled with a pleasing horror? Even in rocks and deserts, is there not an agreeable wildness? How sincere a pleasure is it to behold the natural beauties of the earth! to preserve and renew our relish for them, is not the veil of night alternately drawn over her face, and doth she not change her dress with the seasons? How aptly are the elements disposed! What variety and use in the meanest production of nature! What delicacy, what beauty, what contrivance in animal and vegetable bodies? How exquisitely are all things suited as well to their particular ends, as to constitute opposite parts of the whole! and while they mutually aid and support, do they not also set off and illustrate each other! Raise now your thoughts from this ball of earth, to all those glorious luminaries that adorn the high arch of heaven. The motion and situation of the planets, are they not admirable for use and order. Were those (miscalled *erratic*) globes ever known to stray, in their repeated journeys through the pathless void? Do they not measure areas round the sun ever proportioned to the times? So fixed, so immutable are the laws by which the unseen Author of nature actuates the universe. How vivid and radiant is the lustre of the fixed stars! how magnificent and rich that negligent profusion, with which they appear to be scattered throughout the whole azure vault! yet if you take the telescope, it brings into your sight a new host of stars that escape the naked eye. Here they seem contiguous and minute, but to a nearer view immense orbs of light at various distances, far sunk in the abyss of space. Now you must call imagination to your aid. The feeble narrow sense cannot descry innumerable worlds revolving round the central fires; and in those worlds the energy of an all-perfect mind displayed in endless forms. But neither sense nor imagination are big enough to comprehend the boundless extent with all its glittering furniture. Though the labouring mind exert and strain each power to its utmost reach, there still stands out ungrasped a surplusage immeasurable. Yet all the vast bodies that compose this mighty frame, how distant and remote soever, are by some secret mechanism, some divine art and force, linked in a mutual dependence and intercourse with each other, even with this earth, which was almost slipped from my thoughts, and lost in the crowd of worlds. Is not the whole system immense, beautiful, glorious beyond expression and beyond thought? What treatment then do those philosophers deserve, who would deprive these noble and delightful scenes of all reality? How should those principles be entertained, that lead us to think all the visible beauty of the creation a false imaginary glare? To be plain, can you expect this scepticism of yours will not be thought extravagantly absurd by all men of sense?

Hyl. Other men may think as they please: but for your part you have nothing to reproach me with. My comfort is, you are as much a *sceptic* as I am.

Phil. There, Hylas, I must beg leave to differ from you.

Hyl. What! have you all along agreed to the premises, and do you now deny the conclusion, and leave me to maintain those paradoxes by myself which you led me into? This surely is not fair.

Phil. I deny that I agreed with you in those notions that led to scepticism. You indeed said, the reality of sensible things consisted in an *absolute existence* out of the minds of spirits, or distinct from their being perceived. And pursuant to this notion of reality, you are obliged to deny sensible things any real existence: that is, according to your own definition, you profess yourself a *sceptic*. But I neither said nor thought the reality of sensible things was to be defined after that manner. To me it is evident, for the reasons you allow of, that sensible things cannot exist otherwise than in a mind or spirit. Whence I conclude, not that they have no real existence, but that seeing they depend not on my thought, and have an existence distinct from being perceived by me, *there must be some other mind wherein they exist*. As sure therefore as the sensible world really exists, so sure is there an infinite, omnipresent Spirit who contains and supports it.

Hyl. What! this is no more than I and all Christians hold; nay, and all others too who believe there is a God, and that he knows and comprehends all things.

Phil. Ay, but here lies the difference. Men commonly believe that all things are known or perceived by God, because they believe the being of a God, whereas I, on the other side, immediately and necessarily conclude the being of a God, because all sensible things must be perceived by him.

Hyl. But so long as we all believe the same thing, what matter is it how we come by that belief?

Phil. But neither do we agree in the same opinion. For philosophers, though they acknowledge all corporeal beings to be perceived by God, yet they attribute to them an absolute subsistence distinct from their being perceived by any mind whatever, which I do not. Besides, is there no difference between saying, *there is a God, therefore he perceives all things*: and saying, *sensible things do really exist: and if they really exist, they are necessarily perceived by an infinite mind: therefore there is an infinite mind,* or *God.* This furnishes you with a direct and immediate demonstration, from a most evident principle, of the *being of a God.* Divines and philosophers had proved beyond all controversy, from the beauty and usefulness of the several parts of the creation, that it was the workmanship of God. But that setting aside all help of astronomy and natural philosophy, all contemplation of the contrivance, order, and adjustment of things, an infinite mind should be necessarily inferred from the bare existence of the sensible world, is an advantage peculiar to them only who have made this easy reflection: that the sensible world is that which we perceive by our several senses; and that nothing is perceived by the senses beside ideas; and that no idea or archetype of an idea can exist otherwise than in a mind. You may now, without any laborious search into the sciences, without any subtilty of reason, or tedious length of discourse, oppose and baffle the most strenuous advocate for atheism. Those miserable refuges, whether in an eternal succession of unthinking causes and effects, or in a fortuitous concourse of atoms; those wild imaginations of Vanini, Hobbes, and Spinoza; in a word, the whole system of atheism, is it not entirely overthrown by this single reflection on the repugnancy included in supposing the whole, or any part, even the most rude and shapeless of the visible world, to exist without a mind? Let any one of those abettors of impiety but look into his own thoughts, and there try if he can conceive how so much as a rock, a desert, a chaos, or confused jumble of atoms; how any thing at all, either sensible or imaginable, can exist independent of a mind, and he need go no further to be convinced of his folly. Can any thing be fairer than to put a dispute on such an issue, and leave it to a man himself to see if he can conceive, even in thought, what he holds to be true in fact, and from a notional to allow it a real existence?

Hyl. It cannot be denied, there is something highly serviceable to religion in what you advance. But do you not think it looks very like a notion entertained by some eminent moderns, of *seeing all things in God?*

Phil. I would gladly know that opinion; pray explain it to me.

Hyl. They conceive that the soul being immaterial, is incapable of being united with material things, so as to perceive them in themselves, but that she perceives them by her union with the substance of God, which being spiritual is therefore purely intelligible, or capable of being the immediate object of a spirit's thought. Besides, the divine essence contains in it perfections correspondent to each created being; and which are, for that reason, proper to exhibit or represent them to the mind.

Phil. I do not understand how our ideas, which are things altogether passive and inert, can be the essence, or any part (or like any part) of the essence or substance of God, who is an impassive, indivisible, purely active being. Many more difficulties and objections there are, which occur at first view against this hypothesis; but I shall only add, that it is liable to all the absurdities of the common hypotheses, in making a created world exist otherwise than in the mind of a spirit. Beside all which it hath this peculiar to itself, that it makes that material world serve to no purpose. And if it pass for a good argument against other hypotheses in the sciences, that they suppose nature or the Divine Wisdom to make something in vain, or do that by tedious roundabout methods, which might have been performed in a much more easy and compendious way, what shall we think of that hypothesis which supposes the whole world made in vain?

Hyl. But what say you, are not you too of opinion that we see all things in God? If I mistake not, what you advance comes near it.

Phil. Few men think, yet all will have opinions. Hence men's opinions are superficial and confused. It is nothing strange that tenets, which in themselves are ever so different, should nevertheless be confounded with each other by those who do not consider them attentively. I shall not therefore be surprised, if some men imagine that I run into the enthusiasm of Malebranche, though in truth I am very remote from it. He builds on the most abstract general ideas, which I entirely disclaim. He asserts an absolute external world, which I deny. He maintains that we are deceived by our senses, and know not the real natures, or the true forms and figures of extended beings; of all which I hold the direct contrary. So that, upon the whole, there are no principles more fundamentally opposite than his and mine. It must be owned I entirely agree with what the holy scripture saith, that "in God we live, and move, and have our being." But that we see things in his essence, after the manner above set forth, I am far from believing. Take here in brief my meaning. It is evident, that the things I perceive are my own ideas, and that no idea can exist unless it be in a mind. Nor is it less plain that these ideas, or things by me perceived, either themselves or their archetypes, exist independently of my mind, since I know myself not to be their author, it being out of my power to determine at pleasure, what particular ideas I shall be affected with upon opening my eyes or ears. They must therefore exist in some other mind, whose will it is they should be exhibited to me. The things, I say, immediately perceived, are ideas or sensations, call them which you will. But how can any idea or sensation exist in, or be produced by, any thing but a mind or spirit? This indeed is inconceivable; and to assert that which is inconceivable, is to talk nonsense: is it not?

Hyl. Without doubt.

Phil. But on the other hand, it is very conceivable that they should exist in, and be produced by, a spirit: since this is no more than I daily experience in myself, inasmuch as I perceive numberless ideas: and by an act of my will can form a great variety of them, and raise them up in my imagination: though it must be confessed, these creatures of the fancy are not altogether so distinct, so strong, vivid, and permanent, as those perceived by my senses, which latter are called *real things*. From all which I conclude, *there is a mind which affects me every moment with all the sensible impressions I perceive*. And from the variety, order, and manner of these, I conclude the author of them to be *wise, powerful, and good, beyond comprehension*. Mark it well: I do not say, I see things by perceiving that which represents them in the intelligible substance of God. This I do not understand; but I say, the things by me perceived are known by the understanding, and produced by the will, of an infinite Spirit. And is not all this most plain and evident? Is there any more in it, than what a little observation of our own minds, and that which passes in them, not only enableth us to conceive, but also obligeth us to acknowledge?

Hyl. I think I understand you very clearly; and own the proof you give of a Deity seems no less evident, than it is surprising. But allowing that God is the supreme and universal cause of all things, yet may not there be still a third nature besides spirits and ideas? May we not admit a subordinate and limited cause of our ideas? In a word, may there not for all that be *matter*?

Phil. How often must I inculcate the same thing? You allow the things immediately perceived by sense to exist no where without the mind; but there is nothing perceived by sense, which is not perceived immediately: therefore there is nothing sensible that exists without the mind. The matter therefore which you still insist on, is something intelligible, I suppose; something that may be discovered by reason, and not by sense.

Hyl. You are in the right.

Phil. Pray let me know what reasoning your belief of matter is grounded on; and what this matter is in your present sense of it.

Hyl. I find myself affected with various ideas, whereof I know I am not the cause; neither are they the cause of themselves or of one another, or capable of subsisting by themselves, as being altogether inactive, fleeting, dependent beings. They have therefore some cause distinct from me and them: of which I pretend to know no more, than that it is *the cause of my ideas*. And this thing, whatever it be, I call matter.

Phil. Tell me, Hylas, hath every one a liberty to change the current proper signification annexed to a common name in any language? For example, suppose a traveller should tell you, that in a certain country men might pass unhurt through the fire; and, upon explaining himself, you found he meant by the word *fire* that which others call *water*: or if he should assert there are trees which walk upon two legs, meaning men by the term *trees*. Would you think this reasonable?

Hyl. No; I should think it very absurd. Common custom is the standard of propriety in language. And for any man to affect speaking improperly, is to pervert the use of speech, and can never serve to a better purpose, than to protract and multiply disputes where there is no difference in opinion.

Phil. And doth not *matter*, in the common current acceptation of the word, signify an extended, solid, moveable, unthinking, inactive substance?

Hyl. It doth.

Phil. And hath it not been made evident, that no such substance can possibly exist? And though it should be allowed to exist, yet how can that which is *inactive* be a *cause*; or that which is *unthinking* be a *cause of thought?* You may indeed, if you please, annex to the word *matter* a contrary meaning to what is vulgarly received; and tell me you understand by it an unextended, thinking, active being, which is the cause of our ideas. But what else is this, than to play with words, and run into that very fault you just now condemned with so much reason? I do by no means find fault with your reasoning, in that you collect a cause from the phenomena: but I deny that the cause deducible by reason can properly be termed *matter*.

Hyl. There is indeed something in what you say. But I am afraid you do not thoroughly comprehend my meaning. I would by no means be thought to deny that God, or an infinite spirit, is the supreme cause of all things. All I contend for, is that subordinate to the supreme agent there is a cause of a limited and inferior nature, which concurs in the production of our ideas, not by any act of will or spiritual efficiency, but by that kind of action which belongs to matter, viz. *motion*.

Phil. I find, you are at every turn relapsing into your old exploded conceit, of a moveable and consequently an extended substance existing without the mind. What! have you already forgot you were convinced, or are you willing I should repeat what has been said on that head? In truth this is not fair dealing in you, still to suppose the being of that which you have so often acknowledged to have no being. But not to insist further on what has been so largely handled, I ask whether all your ideas are not perfectly passive and inert, including nothing of action in them?

Hyl. They are.

Phil. And are sensible qualities any thing else but ideas?

Hyl. How often have I acknowledged that they are not?

Phil. But is not motion a sensible quality?

Hyl. It is.

Phil. Consequently it is no action.

Hyl. I agree with you. And indeed it is very plain, that when I stir my finger, it remains passive; but my will which produced the motion, is active.

Phil. Now I desire to know in the first place, whether motion being allowed to be no action, you can conceive any action besides volition: and in the second place, whether to say something and conceive nothing be not to talk nonsense: and lastly, whether having considered the premises, you do not perceive that to suppose any efficient or active cause of our ideas, other than *spirit*, is highly absurd and unreasonable?

Hyl. I give up the point entirely. But though matter may

not be a cause, yet what hinders it being an *instrument* subservient to the supreme agent in the production of our ideas?

Phil. An instrument, say you; pray what may be the figure, springs, wheels, and motions of that instrument?

Hyl. Those I pretend to determine nothing of, both the substance and its qualities being entirely unknown to me.

Phil. What? You are then of opinion, it is made up of unknown parts, that it hath unknown motions, and an unknown shape.

Hyl. I do not believe it hath any figure or motion at all, being already convinced, that no sensible qualities can exist in an unperceiving substance.

Phil. But what notion is it possible to frame of an instrument void of all sensible qualities, even extension itself?

Hyl. I do not pretend to have any notion of it.

Phil. And what reason have you to think, this unknown, this inconceivable somewhat doth exist? Is it that you imagine God cannot act as well without it, or that you find by experience the use of some such thing, when you form ideas in your own mind?

Hyl. You are always teasing me for reasons of my belief. Pray what reasons have you not to believe it?

Phil. It is to me a sufficient reason not to believe the existence of any thing, if I see no reason for believing it. But not to insist on reasons for believing, you will not so much as let me know what it is you would have me believe, since you say you have no manner of notion of it. After all, let me entreat you to consider whether it be like a philosopher, or even like a man of common sense, to pretend to believe you know not what and you know not why.

Hyl. Hold, Philonous. When I tell you matter is an *instrument*, I do not mean altogether nothing. It is true, I know not the particular kind of instrument: but however I have some notion of *instrument in general*, which I apply to it.

Phil. But what if it should prove that there is something, even in the most general notion of *instrument*, as taken in a distinct sense from *cause*, which makes the use of it inconsistent with the divine attributes?

Hyl. Make that appear, and I shall give up the point.

Phil. What mean you by the general nature or notion of *instrument?*

Hyl. That which is common to all particular instruments, composeth the general notion.

Phil. Is it not common to all instruments, that they are applied to the doing those things only, which cannot be performed by the mere act of our wills? Thus for instance, I never use an instrument to move my finger, because it is done by a volition. But I should use one, if I were to remove part of a rock, or tear up a tree by the roots. Are you of the same mind? Or can you show any example where an instrument is made use of in producing an effect immediately depending on the will of the agent?

Hyl. I own, I cannot.

Phil. How therefore can you suppose, that an all-perfect Spirit, on whose will all things have an absolute and immediate dependence, should need an instrument in his operations, or not needing it make use of it? Thus it seems to me that you are obliged to own the use of a lifeless inactive instrument, to be incompatible with the infinite perfection of God; that is, by your own confession to give up the point.

Hyl. It doth not readily occur what I can answer you.

Phil. But methinks you should be ready to own the truth, when it hath been fairly proved to you. We indeed, who are beings of finite powers, are forced to make use of instruments. And the use of an instrument showeth the agent to be limited by rules of another's prescription, and that he cannot obtain his end, but in such a way and by such conditions. Whence it seems a clear consequence, that the supreme unlimited agent useth no tool or instrument at all. The will of an omnipotent Spirit is no sooner exerted than executed, without the application of means, which, if they are employed by inferior agents, it is not upon account of any real efficacy that is in them, or necessary aptitude to produce any effect, but merely in compliance with the laws of nature, or those conditions prescribed to them by the first cause, who is himself above all limitation or prescription whatsoever.

Hyl. I will no longer maintain that matter is an instrument. However, I would not be understood to give up its existence neither; since, notwithstanding what hath been said, it may still be an *occasion*.

Phil. How many shapes is your matter to take? Or how often must it be proved not to exist, before you are content to part with it? But to say no more of this (though by all the laws of disputation I may justly blame you for so frequently changing the signification of the principal term) I would fain know what you mean by affirming that matter is an occasion, having already denied it to be a cause. And when you have shown in what sense you understand *occasion*, pray in the next place be pleased to show me what reason induceth you to believe there is such an occasion of our ideas.

Hyl. As to the first point: by *occasion* I mean an inactive, unthinking being, at the presence whereof God excites ideas in our minds.

Phil. And what may be the nature of that inactive, unthinking being?

Hyl. I know nothing of its nature.

Phil. Proceed then to the second point, and assign some reason why we should allow an existence to this inactive, unthinking, unknown thing.

Hyl. When we see ideas produced in our minds after an orderly and constant manner, it is natural to think they have some fixed and regular occasions, at the presence of which they are excited.

Phil. You acknowledge then God alone to be the cause of our ideas, and that he causes them at the presence of those occasions.

Hyl. That is my opinion.

Phil. Those things which you say are present to God, without doubt he perceives.

Hyl. Certainly; otherwise they could not be to him an occasion of acting.

Phil. Not to insist now on your making sense of this hypothesis, or answering all the puzzling questions and difficulties it is liable to: I only ask whether the order and regularity observable in the series of our ideas, or the course of nature, be not sufficiently accounted for by the wisdom and power of God; and whether it doth not derogate from those attributes, to suppose he is influenced, directed, or put in mind, when and what he is to act, by any unthinking substance. And lastly, whether in case I granted all you contend for, it would make any thing to your purpose, it not being easy to conceive how the external or absolute existence of an unthinking substance, distinct from its being perceived, can be inferred from my allowing that there are certain things perceived by the mind of God, which are to him the occasion of producing ideas in us.

Hyl. I am perfectly at a loss what to think, this notion of *occasion* seeming now altogether as groundless as the rest.

Phil. Do you not at length perceive, that in all these different acceptations of *matter*, you have been only supposing you know not what, for no manner of reason, and to no kind of use?

Hyl. I freely own myself less fond of my notions, since they have been so accurately examined. But still, methinks I have some confused perception that there is such a thing as *matter*.

Phil. Either you perceive the being of matter immediately, or mediately. If immediately, pray inform me by which of the senses you perceive it. If mediately, let me know by what reasoning it is inferred from those things which you perceive immediately. So much for the perception. Then for the matter itself, I ask whether it is object, substratum, cause, instrument, or occasion? You have already pleaded for each of these, shifting your notions, and making matter to appear sometimes in one shape, then in another. And what you have offered hath been disapproved and rejected by yourself. If you have any thing new to advance, I would gladly hear it.

Hyl. I think I have already offered all I had to say on those heads. I am at a loss what more to urge.

Phil. And yet you are loath to part with your old prejudice. But to make you quit it more easily, I desire that, besides what has been hitherto suggested, you will further consider whether, upon supposition that matter exists, you can possibly conceive how you should be affected by it? Or supposing it did not exist, whether it be not evident you might for all that be affected with the same ideas you now are, and consequently have the very same reasons to believe its existence that you now can have?

Hyl. I acknowledge it is possible we might perceive all things just as we do now, though there was no matter in the world; neither can I conceive, if there be matter, how it should produce any idea in our minds. And I do further grant, you have entirely satisfied me, that it is impossible there should be such a thing as matter in any of the foregoing acceptations. But still I cannot help supposing that there is *matter* in some sense or other. What that is I do not indeed pretend to determine.

Phil. I do not expect you should define exactly the nature of that unknown being. Only be pleased to tell me, whether it is a substance: and if so, whether you can suppose a substance without accidents: or in case you suppose it to have accidents or qualities, I desire you will let me know what those qualities are, at least what is meant by matter's supporting them.

Hyl. We have already argued on those points. I have no more to say to them. But to prevent any further questions, let me tell you, I at present understand by *matter* neither substance nor accident, thinking nor extended being, neither cause, instrument, nor occasion, but something entirely unknown, distinct from all these.

Phil. It seems then you include in your present notion of matter, nothing but the general abstract of idea of *entity*.

Hyl. Nothing else, save only that I superadd to this general idea the negation of all those particular things, qualities, or ideas that I perceive, imagine, or in any wise apprehend.

Phil. Pray where do you suppose this unknown matter to exist?

Hyl. Oh Philonous! now you think you have entangled me; for if I say it exists in place, then you will infer that it exists in the mind, since it is agreed, that place or extension exists only in the mind: but I am not ashamed to own my ignorance. I know not where it exists; only I am sure it exists not in place. There is a negative answer for you: and you must expect no other to all the questions you put for the future about matter.

Phil. Since you will not tell me where it exists, be pleased to inform me after what manner you suppose it to exist, or what you mean by its *existence*.

Hyl. It neither thinks nor acts, neither perceives, nor is perceived.

Phil. But what is there positive in your abstracted notion of its existence?

Hyl. Upon a nice observation, I do not find I have any positive notion or meaning at all. I tell you again I am not ashamed to own my ignorance. I know not what is meant by its *existence*, or how it exists.

Phil. Continue, good Hylas, to act the same ingenuous part, and tell me sincerely whether you can frame a distinct idea of entity in general, prescinded from and exclusive of all thinking and corporeal beings, all particular things whatsoever.

Hyl. Hold, let me think a little——I profess, Philonous, I do not find that I can. At first glance methought I had some dilute and airy notion of pure entity in abstract; but upon closer attention it hath quite vanished out of sight. The more I think on it, the more am I confirmed in my prudent resolution of giving none but negative answers, and not pretending to the least degree of any positive knowledge or conception of matter, its *where*, its *how*, its *entity*, or any thing belonging to it.

Phil. When therefore you speak of the existence of matter, you have not any notion in your mind.

Hyl. None at all.

Phil. Pray tell me if the case stands not thus: at first, from a belief of material substance you would have it that the immediate objects existed without the mind; then that their archetypes; then causes; next instruments: then occasions: lastly, *something in general*, which being interpreted proves *nothing*. So matter comes to nothing. What think you, Hylas? is not this a fair summary of your whole proceeding?

Hyl. Be that as it will, yet I still insist upon it, that our not being able to conceive a thing, is no argument against its existence.

Phil. That from a cause, effect, operation, sign, or other circumstance, there may reasonably be inferred the existence of a thing not immediately perceived, and that it were absurd for any man to argue against the existence of that thing, from his having no direct and positive notion of it, I freely own. But where there is nothing of all this; where neither reason nor revelation induces us to believe the existence of a thing; where we have not even a relative notion of it; where an abstraction is made from perceiving and being perceived, from spirit and idea: lastly, where there is not so much as the most inadequate or faint idea pretended to: I will not indeed thence conclude against the reality of any notion or existence of any thing: but my inference shall be, that you mean nothing at all: that you imply words to no manner of purpose, without any design or signification whatsoever. And I leave it to you to consider how mere jargon should be treated.

Hyl. To deal frankly with you, Philonous, your arguments seem in themselves unanswerable, but they have not so great an effect on me as to produce that entire conviction, that hearty acquiescence which attends demonstration. I find myself still relapsing into an obscure surmise of I know not what, *matter*.

Phil. But are you not sensible, Hylas, that two things must concur to take away all scruple, and work a plenary assent in the mind? Let a visible object be set in never so clear a light, yet if there is any imperfection in the sight, or if the eye is not directed towards it, it will not be distinctly seen. And though a demonstration be never so well grounded and fairly proposed, yet if there is withal a stain of prejudice, or a wrong bias on the understanding, can it be expected on a sudden to perceive clearly and adhere firmly to the truth? No, there is need of time and pains; the attention must be awakened and detained by a frequent repetition of the same thing placed oft in the same, oft in different lights. I have said it already, and I find I must still repeat and inculcate, that it is an unaccountable license you take in pretending to maintain you know not what, for you know not what reason, to you know not what purpose. Can this be paralleled in any art or science, any sect or profession of men? Or is there any thing so barefacedly groundless and unreasonable to be met with even in the lowest of common conversation? But perhaps you will still say, matter may exist, though at the same time you neither know what is meant by *matter*, nor by its *existence*. This indeed is surprising, and the more so because it is altogether voluntary, you not being led to it by any one reason; for I challenge you to show me that thing in nature which needs matter to explain or account for it.

Hyl. The reality of things cannot be maintained without supposing the existence of matter. And is not this, think you, a good reason why I should be earnest in its defence?

Phil. The reality of things! What things, sensible or intelligible?

Hyl. Sensible things.

Phil. My glove, for example?

Hyl. That or any other thing perceived by the senses.

Phil. But to fix on some particular thing; is it not a sufficient evidence to me of the existence of this *glove*, that I see it, and feel it, and wear it? Or if this will not do, how is it possible I should be assured of the reality of this thing, which I actually see in this place, by supposing that some unknown thing, which I never did or can see, exists after an unknown manner, in an unknown place, or in no place at all? How can the supposed reality of that which is intangible, be a proof that any thing tangible really exists? Or of that which is invisible, that any visible thing, or in general of any thing which is imperceptible, that a perceptible exists? Do but explain this, and I shall think nothing too hard for you.

Hyl. Upon the whole, I am content to own the existence

of matter is highly improbable; but the direct and absolute impossibility of it does not appear to me.

Phil. But granting matter to be possible, yet upon that account merely it can have no more claim to existence, than a golden mountain or a centaur.

Hyl. I acknowledge it; but still you do not deny it is possible; and that which is possible, for aught you know, may actually exist.

Phil. I deny it to be possible; and have, if I mistake not, evidently proved from your own concessions that it is not. In the common sense of the word *matter*, is there any more implied than an extended, solid, figured, moveable substance, existing without the mind? And have not you acknowledged over and over, that you have seen evident reason for denying the possibility of such a substance.

Hyl. True, but that is only one sense of the term *matter*.

Phil. But is it not the only proper genuine received sense? and if matter in such a sense be proved impossible, may it not be thought with good grounds absolutely impossible? Else how could any thing be proved impossible? Or indeed how could there be any proof at all one way or other, to a man who takes the liberty to unsettle and change the common signification of words?

Hyl. I thought philosophers might be allowed to speak more accurately than the vulgar, and were not always confined to the common acceptation of a term.

Phil. But this now mentioned is the common received sense among philosophers themselves. But not to insist on that, have you not been allowed to take matter in what sense you pleased? And have you not used this privilege in the utmost extent, sometimes entirely changing, at others leaving out or putting into the definition of it whatever for the present best served your design, contrary to all the known rules of reason and logic? And hath not this shifting, unfair method of yours spun out our dispute to an unnecessary length; matter having been particularly examined, and by your own confession refuted in each of those senses? And can any more be required to prove the absolute impossibility of a thing, than the proving it impossible in every particular sense, that either you or any one else understands it in?

Hyl. But I am not so thoroughly satisfied that you have proved the impossibility of matter in the last most obscure, abstracted and indefinite sense.

Phil. When is a thing shown to be impossible?

Hyl. When a repugnancy is demonstrated between the ideas comprehended in its definition.

Phil. But where there are no ideas, there no repugnancy can be demonstrated between ideas.

Hyl. I agree with you.

Phil. Now in that which you call the obscure, indefinite sense of the word *matter*, it is plain, by your own confession, there was included no idea at all, no sense except an unknown sense, which is the same thing as none. You are not therefore to expect I should prove a repugnancy between ideas where there are no ideas, or the impossibility of matter taken in an *unknown* sense, that is no sense at all. My business was only to show, you meant *nothing*: and this you were brought to own. So that in all your various senses, you have been shown either to mean nothing at all, or if any thing, an absurdity. And if this be not sufficient to prove the impossibility of a thing, I desire you will let me know what is.

Hyl. I acknowledge you have proved that matter is impossible; nor do I see what more can be said in defence of it. But at the same time that I give up this, I suspect all my other notions. For surely none could be more seemingly evident than this once was: and yet it now seems as false and absurd as ever it did true before. But I think we have discussed the point sufficiently for the present. The remaining part of the day I would willingly spend, in running over in my thoughts the several heads of this morning's conversation, and to-morrow shall be glad to meet you here again about the same time.

Phil. I will not fail to attend you.

THE THIRD DIALOGUE

Philonous. Tell me, Hylas, what are the fruits of yesterday's meditation? Hath it confirmed you in the same mind you were in at parting? or have you since seen cause to change your opinion?

Hylas. Truly my opinion is, that all our opinions are alike vain and uncertain. What we approve to-day, we condemn tomorrow. We keep a stir about knowledge, and spend our lives in the pursuit of it, when, alas! we know nothing all the while: nor do I think it possible for us ever to know any thing in this life. Our faculties are too narrow and too few. Nature certainly never intended us for speculation.

Phil. What! say you we can know nothing, Hylas?

Hyl. There is not that single thing in the world, whereof we can know the real nature, or what it is in itself.

Phil. Will you tell me I do not really know what fire or water is?

Hyl. You may indeed know that fire appears hot, and water fluid: but this is no more than knowing what sensations are produced in your own mind, upon the application of fire and water to your organs of sense. Their internal constitution, their true and real nature, you are utterly in the dark as to that.

Phil. Do I not know this to be a real stone that I stand on, and that which I see before my eyes to be a real tree?

Hyl. Know? No, it is impossible you or any man alive should know it. All you know is, that you have such a certain idea or appearance in your own mind. But what is this to the real tree or stone? I tell you, that colour, figure, and hardness, which you perceive, are not the real natures of those things, or in the least like them. The same may be said of all other real things or corporeal substances which compose the world. They have none of them any thing in themselves, like those sensible qualities by us perceived. We should not therefore pretend to affirm or know any thing of them, as they are in their own nature.

Phil. But surely, Hylas, I can distinguish gold, for example, from iron: and how could this be, if I knew not what either truly was?

Hyl. Believe me, Philonous, you can only distinguish between your own ideas. That yellowness, that weight, and other sensible qualities, think you they are really in the gold? They are only relative to the senses, and have no absolute existence in nature. And in pretending to distinguish the species of real things, by the appearances in your mind, you may perhaps act as wisely as he that should conclude two men were of a different species, because their clothes were not of the same colour.

Phil. It seems then we are altogether put off with the appearances of things, and those false ones too. The very meat

I eat, and the cloth I wear, have nothing in them like what I see and feel.

Hyl. Even so.

Phil. But is it not strange the whole world should be thus imposed on and so foolish as to believe their senses? And yet I know not how it is, but men eat, and drink, and sleep, and perform all the offices of life as comfortably and conveniently, as if they really knew the things they are conversant about.

Hyl. They do so: but you know ordinary practice does not require a nicety of speculative knowledge. Hence the vulgar retain their mistakes, and for all that, make a shift to bustle through the affairs of life. But philosophers know better things.

Phil. You mean, they know that they *know nothing.*

Hyl. That is the very top and perfection of human knowledge.

Phil. But are you all this while in earnest, Hylas; and are you seriously persuaded that you know nothing real in the world? Suppose you are going to write, would you not call for pen, ink, and paper, like another man; and do you not know what it is you call for?

Hyl. How often must I tell you, that I know not the real nature of any one thing in the universe? I may, indeed, upon occasion, make use of pen, ink, and paper. But what any one of them is in its own true nature, I declare positively I know not. And the same is true with regard to every other corporeal thing. And, what is more, we are not only ignorant of the true and real nature of things, but even of their existence. It cannot be denied that we perceive such certain appearances or ideas; but it cannot be concluded from thence that bodies really exist. Nay, now I think on it, I must, agreeably to my former concessions, further declare, that it is impossible any real corporeal thing should exist in nature.

Phil. You amaze me. Was ever any thing more wild and extravagant than the notions you now maintain: and is it not evident you are led into all these extravagancies by the belief of *material substance?* This makes you dream of those unknown natures in every thing. It is this occasions your distinguishing between the reality and sensible appearances of things. It is to this you are indebted for being ignorant of what every body else knows perfectly well. Nor is this all: you are not only ignorant of the true nature of every thing, but you know not whether any thing really exists, or whether there are any true natures at all; forasmuch as you attribute to your material beings an absolute or external existence, wherein you suppose their reality consists. And as you are forced in the end to acknowledge such an existence means either a direct repugnancy, or nothing at all, it follows that you are obliged to pull down your own hypothesis of material substance, and positively to deny the real existence of any part of the universe. And so you are plunged into the deepest and most deplorable *scepticism* that ever man was. Tell me, Hylas, is it not as I say?

Hyl. I agree with you. *Material substance* was no more than an hypothesis, and a false and groundless one too. I will no longer spend my breath in defence of it. But whatever hypothesis you advance, or whatsoever scheme of things you introduce in its stead, I doubt not it will appear every whit as false: let me but be allowed to question you upon it. That is, suffer me to serve you in your own kind, and I warrant it shall conduct you through as many perplexities and contradictions, to the very same state of scepticism that I myself am in at present.

Phil. I assure you, Hylas, I do not pretend to frame any hypothesis at all. I am of a vulgar cast, simple enough to believe my senses, and leave things as I find them. To be plain, it is my opinion, that the real things are those very things I see and feel, and perceive by my senses. These I know, and finding they answer all the necessities and purposes of life, have no reason to be solicitous about any other unknown beings. A piece of sensible bread, for instance, would stay my stomach better than ten thousand times as much of that insensible, unintelligible, real bread you speak of. It is likewise my opinion, that colours and other sensible qualities are on the objects. I cannot for my life help thinking that snow is white, and fire hot. You indeed, who by *snow* and *fire* mean certain external, unperceived, unperceiving substances, are in the right to deny whiteness or heat to be affections inherent in them. But I, who understand by those words the things I see and feel, am obliged to think like other folks. And as I am no sceptic with regard to the nature of things, so neither am I as to their existence. That a thing should be really perceived by my senses, and at the same time not really exist, is to me a plain contradiction; since I cannot prescind or abstract, even in thought, the existence of a sensible thing from its being perceived. Wood, stones, fire, water, flesh, iron, and the like things, which I name and discourse of, are things that I know. And I should not have known them, but that I perceived them by my senses; and things perceived by the senses are immediately perceived; and things immediately perceived are ideas; and ideas cannot exist without the mind; their existence therefore consists in being perceived; when therefore they are actually perceived, there can be no doubt of their existence. Away then with all that scepticism, all those ridiculous philosophical doubts. What a jest is it for a philosopher to question the existence of sensible things, till he hath it proved to him from the veracity of God: or to pretend our knowledge in this point falls short of intuition or demonstration! I might as well doubt of my own being, as of the being of those things I actually see and feel.

Hyl. Not so fast, Philonous: you say you cannot conceive how sensible things should exist without the mind. Do you not?

Phil. I do.

Hyl. Supposing you were annihilated, cannot you conceive it possible that things perceivable by sense may still exist?

Phil. I can; but then it must be in another mind. When I deny sensible things an existence out of the mind, I do not mean my mind in particular, but all minds. Now it is plain they have an existence exterior to my mind, since I find them by experience to be independent of it. There is therefore some other mind wherein they exist, during the intervals between the times of my perceiving them: as likewise they did before my birth, and would do after my supposed annihilation. And as the same is true with regard to all other finite created spirits, it necessarily follows, there is an *omnipresent, eternal Mind*, which knows and comprehends all things, and exhibits them to our view in such a manner, and according to such rules as he himself hath ordained, and are by us termed the *laws of nature*.

Hyl. Answer me, Philonous. Are all our ideas perfectly inert beings? Or have they any agency included in them?

Phil. They are altogether passive and inert.

Hyl. And is not God an agent, a being purely active?

Phil. I acknowledge it.

Hyl. No idea therefore can be like unto, or represent the nature of God.

Phil. It cannot.

Hyl. Since therefore you have no idea of the mind of God,

how can you conceive it possible, that things should exist in his mind? Or, if you can conceive the mind of God without having an idea of it, why may not I be allowed to conceive the existence of matter, notwithstanding that I have no idea of it?

Phil. As to your first question: I own I have properly no idea, either of God or any other spirit; for these being active, cannot be represented by things perfectly inert, as our ideas are. I do nevertheless know, that I, who am a spirit or thinking substance, exist as certainly, as I know my ideas exist. Further, I know what I mean by the terms *I* and *myself*; and I know this immediately, or intuitively, though I do not perceive it as I perceive a triangle, a colour, or a sound. The mind, spirit, or soul, is that indivisible, unextended thing, which thinks, acts, and perceives. I say *indivisible*, because unextended; and *unextended*, because extended, figured, moveable things, are ideas; and that which perceives ideas, which thinks and wills, is plainly itself no idea, nor like an idea. Ideas are things inactive, and perceived: and spirits a sort of beings altogether different from them. I do not therefore say my soul is an idea, or like an idea. However, taking the word *idea* in a large sense, my soul may be said to furnish me with an idea, that is, an image, or likeness of God, though indeed extremely inadequate. For all the notion I have of God, is obtained by reflecting on my own soul, heightening its powers, and removing its imperfections. I have therefore, though not an inactive idea, yet in myself some sort of an active thinking image of the Deity. And though I perceive him not by sense, yet I have a notion of him, or know him by reflection and reasoning. My own mind and my own ideas I have an immediate knowledge of; and by the help of these, do mediately apprehend the possibility of the existence of other spirits and ideas. Further, from my own being, and from the dependency I find in myself and my ideas, I do by an act of reason necessarily infer the existence of a God, and of all created things in the mind of God. So much for your first question. For the second: I suppose by this time you can answer it yourself. For you neither perceive matter objectively, as you do an inactive being or idea, nor know it, as you do yourself, by a reflex act: neither do you mediately apprehend it by similitude of the one or the other: nor yet collect it by reasoning from that which you know immediately. All which makes the case of *matter* widely different from that of the *Deity*.

Hyl. You say your own soul supplies you with some sort of

an idea or image of God. But at the same time you acknowledge you have, properly speaking, no idea of your own soul. You even affirm that spirits are a sort of beings altogether different from ideas. Consequently that no idea can be like a spirit. We have therefore no idea of any spirit. You admit nevertheless that there is spiritual substance, although you have no idea of it; while you deny there can be such a thing as material substance, because you have no notion or idea of it. Is this fair dealing? To act consistently, you must either admit matter or reject spirit. What say you to this?

Phil. I say in the first place, that I do not deny the existence of material substance merely because I have no notion of it, but because the notion of it is inconsistent, or in other words, because it is repugnant that there should be a notion of it. Many things, for aught I know, may exist, whereof neither I nor any other man hath or can have any idea or notion whatsoever. But then those things must be possible, that is, nothing inconsistent must be included in their definition. I say secondly, that although we believe things to exist which we do not perceive; yet we may not believe that any particular thing exists, without some reason for such belief: but I have no reason for believing the existence of matter. I have no immediate intuition thereof: neither can I mediately from my sensations, ideas, notions, actions, or passions, infer an unthinking, unperceiving, inactive substance, either by probable deduction, or necessary consequence. Whereas the being of myself, that is, my own soul, mind, or thinking principle, I evidently know by reflection. You will forgive me if I repeat the same things in answer to the same objections. In the very notion or definition of material substance, there is included a manifest repugnance and inconsistency. But this cannot be said of the notion of spirit. That ideas should exist in what doth not perceive, or be produced by what doth not act, is repugnant. But it is no repugnancy to say, that a perceiving thing should be the subject of ideas, or an active thing the cause of them. It is granted we have neither an immediate evidence nor a demonstrative knowledge of the existence of other finite spirits; but it will not thence follow that such spirits are on a foot with material substances: if to suppose the one be inconsistent, and it be not inconsistent to suppose the other; if the one can be inferred by no argument, and there is a probability for the other; if we see signs and effects indicating distinct finite agents like ourselves, and see no sign or symptom whatever that leads to a rational belief of matter. I say lastly, that I have a notion of spirit, though I have not, strictly speaking, an idea of it. I do not perceive it as an idea or by means of an idea, but know it by reflection.

Hyl. Notwithstanding all you have said, to me it seems, that according to your own way of thinking, and in consequence of your own principles, it should follow that you are only a system of floating ideas, without any substance to support them. Words are not to be used without a meaning. And as there is no more meaning in spiritual substance than in material substance, the one is to be exploded as well as the other.

Phil. How often must I repeat, that I know or am conscious of my own being; and that I myself am not my ideas, but somewhat else, a thinking, active principle that perceives, knows, wills, and operates about ideas? I know that I, one and the same self, perceive both colours and sounds: that a colour cannot perceive a sound, nor a sound a colour: that I am therefore one individual principle, distinct from colour and sound; and, for the same reason, from all other sensible things and inert ideas. But I am not in like manner conscious either of the existence or essence of matter. On the contrary, I know that nothing inconsistent can exist, and that the existence of matter implies an inconsistency. Further, I know what I mean, when I affirm that there is a spiritual substance or support of ideas, that is, that a spirit knows and perceives ideas. But I do not know what is meant, when it is said, that an unperceiving substance hath inherent in it and supports either ideas or the archetypes of ideas. There is therefore upon the whole no parity of case between spirit and matter.

Hyl. I own myself satisfied in this point. But do you in earnest think, the real existence of sensible things consists in their being actually perceived? If so, how comes it that all mankind distinguish between them? Ask the first man you meet, and he shall tell you, *to be perceived* is one thing, and *to exist* is another.

Phil. I am content, Hylas, to appeal to the common sense of the world for the truth of my notion. Ask the gardener, why he thinks yonder cherry-tree exists in the garden, and he shall tell you, because he sees and feels it; in a word, because he perceives it by his senses. Ask him, why he thinks an orange-tree not to be there, and he shall tell you, because he does not perceive it. What he perceives by sense, that he terms a real being, and saith it *is*, or *exists*; but that which is not perceivable, the same, he saith, hath no being.

Hyl. Yes, Philonous, I grant the existence of a sensible thing consists in being perceivable, but not in being actually perceived.

Phil. And what is perceivable but an idea? And can an idea exist without being actually perceived? These are points long since agreed between us.

Hyl. But be your opinion never so true, yet surely you will not deny it is shocking, and contrary to the common sense of men. Ask the fellow, whether yonder tree hath an existence out of his mind: what answer, think you, he would make?

Phil. The same that I should myself, to wit, that it doth exist out of his mind. But then to a Christian it cannot surely be shocking to say, the real tree existing without his mind is truly known and comprehended by (that is, *exists in*) the infinite mind of God. Probably he may not at first glance be aware of the direct and immediate proof there is of this, inasmuch as the very being of a tree, or any other sensible thing, implies a mind wherein it is. But the point itself he cannot deny. The question between the materialists and me is not, whether things have a real existence out of the mind of this or that person, but whether they have an absolute existence, distinct from being perceived by God, and exterior to all minds. This indeed some heathens and philosophers have affirmed, but whoever entertains notions of the Deity suitable to the holy scriptures, will be of another opinion.

Hyl. But according to your notions, what difference is there between real things, and chimeras formed by the imagination, or the visions of a dream, since they are all equally in the mind?

Phil. The ideas formed by the imagination are faint and indistinct; they have besides an entire dependence on the will. But the ideas perceived by sense, that is, real things, are more vivid and clear, and being imprinted on the mind by a spirit distinct from us, have not a like dependence on our will. There is therefore no danger of confounding these with the foregoing: and there is as little of confounding them with the visions of a dream, which are dim, irregular, and confused. And though they should happen to be never so lively and natural, yet by their not being connected, and of a piece with the preceding and subsequent transactions of our lives, they might easily be distinguished from realities. In short, by whatever method you distinguish *things* from *chimeras* on your own scheme, the same, it is evident, will hold also upon mine. For it must be, I presume, by some perceived difference, and I am not for depriving you of any one thing that you perceive.

Hyl. But still, Philonous, you hold, there is nothing in the world but spirits and ideas. And this, you must needs acknowledge, sounds very oddly.

Phil. I own the word *idea*, not being commonly used for *thing*, sounds something out of the way. My reason for using it was, because a necessary relation to the mind is understood to be implied by that term; and it is now commonly used by philosophers, to denote the immediate objects of the understanding. But however oddly the proposition may sound in words, yet it includes nothing so very strange or shocking in its sense, which in effect amounts to no more than this, to wit, that there are only things perceiving, and things perceived; or that every unthinking being is necessarily, and from the very nature of its existence, perceived by some mind; if not by any finite created mind, yet certainly by the infinite mind of God, in whom "we live, and move, and have our being." Is this as strange as to say, the sensible qualities are not on the objects: or, that we cannot be sure of the existence of things, or know any thing of their real natures, though we both see and feel them, and perceive them by all our senses?

Hyl. And in consequence of this, must we not think there are no such things as physical or corporeal causes; but that a spirit is the immediate cause of all the phenomena in nature? Can there be any thing more extravagant than this?

Phil. Yes, it is infinitely more extravagant to say, a thing which is inert, operates on the mind, and which is unperceiving, is the cause of our perceptions. Besides, that which to you, I know not for what reason, seems so extravagant, is no more than the holy scriptures assert in a hundred places. In them God is represented as the sole and immediate author of all those effects, which some heathens and philosophers are wont to ascribe to nature, matter, fate, or the like unthinking principle. This is so much the constant language of scripture, that it were needless to confirm it by citations.

Hyl. You are not aware, Philonous, that in making God the immediate author of all the motions in nature, you make him the author of murder, sacrilege, adultery, and the like heinous sins.

Phil. In answer to that, I observe first, that the imputation of guilt is the same, whether a person commits an action with or without an instrument. In case therefore you suppose God to act by the mediation of an instrument, or occasion, called *matter*, you as truly make him the author of sin as I, who think him the immediate agent in all those operations vulgarly ascribed to nature. I further observe, that sin or moral turpitude doth not consist in the outward physical action or motion, but in the internal deviation of the will from the laws of reason and religion. This is plain, in that the killing an enemy in a battle, or putting a criminal legally to death, is not thought sinful, though the outward act be the very same with that in the case of murder. Since therefore sin doth not consist in the physical action, the making God an immediate cause of all such actions, is not making him the author of sin. Lastly, I have no where said that God is the only agent who produces all the motions in bodies. It is true, I have denied there are any other agents beside spirits: but this is very consistent with allowing to thinking, rational beings, in the production of motions, the use of limited powers, ultimately indeed derived from God, but immediately under the direction of their own wills, which is sufficient to entitle them to all the guilt of their actions.

Hyl. But the denying matter, Philonous, or corporeal substance; there is the point. You can never persuade me that this is not repugnant to the universal sense of mankind. Were our dispute to be determined by most voices, I am confident you would give up the point, without gathering the votes.

Phil. I wish both our opinions were fairly stated and submitted to the judgment of men who had plain common sense, without the prejudices of a learned education. Let me be represented as one who trusts his senses, who thinks he knows the things he sees and feels, and entertains no doubts of their existence; and you fairly set forth with all your doubts, your paradoxes, and your scepticism about you, and I shall willingly acquiesce in the determination of any indifferent person. That there is no substance wherein ideas can exist beside spirit, is to me evident. And that the objects immediately perceived are ideas, is on all hands agreed. And that sensible qualities are objects immediately perceived, no one can deny. It is therefore evident there can be no *substratum* of those qualities but spirit, in which they exist, not by way of mode or property, but as a thing perceived in that which perceives it. I deny therefore that there is any unthinking *substratum* of the objects of sense, and in that acceptation that there is any material substance. But if by *material substance* is meant only sensible body, that which is seen and felt (and the unphilosophical part of the world, I dare say, mean no more), then I am more certain of matter's existence than you, or any other philosopher, pretend to be. If there be any thing which makes the generality of mankind averse from the notions I espouse, it is a misapprehension that I deny the reality of sensible things: but as it is you who are guilty of that and not I, it follows that in truth their aversion is against your notions, and not mine. I do therefore assert that I am as certain as of my own being, that there are bodies or corporeal substances (meaning the things I perceive by my senses); and that granting this, the bulk of mankind will take no thought about, nor think themselves at all concerned in the fate of those unknown natures, and philosophical quiddities, which some men are so fond of.

Hyl. What say you to this? Since, according to you, men judge of the reality of things by their senses, how can a man be mistaken in thinking the moon a plain lucid surface, about a foot in diameter; or a square tower, seen at a distance, round; or an oar, with one end in the water, crooked?

Phil. He is not mistaken with regard to the ideas he actually perceives; but in the inferences he makes from his present perceptions. Thus in the case of the oar, what he immediately perceives by sight is certainly crooked; and so far he is in the right. But if he thence conclude, that upon taking the oar out of the water he shall perceive the same crookedness, or that it would affect his touch as crooked things are wont to do, in that he is mistaken. In like manner, if he should conclude from what he perceives in one station, that in case he advances toward the moon or tower, he should still be affected with the like ideas, he is mistaken. But his mistake lies not in what he perceives immediately and at present (it being a manifest contradiction to suppose he should err in respect of that), but in the wrong judgment he makes concerning the ideas he apprehends to be connected with those immediately perceived: or concerning the ideas that, from what he perceives at present, he imagines would be perceived in other circumstances. The case is the same with regard to the Copernican system. We do not here perceive any motion of the earth: but it were erroneous thence to conclude, that in case we were placed at as great a distance from that, as we are now from the other planets, we should not then perceive its motion.

Hyl. I understand you; and must needs own you say things plausible enough: but give me leave to put you in mind of one thing. Pray, Philonous, were you not formerly as positive that matter existed, as you are now that it does not?

Phil. I was. But here lies the difference. Before, my positiveness was founded without examination, upon prejudice; but now, after inquiry, upon evidence.

Hyl. After all, it seems our dispute is rather about words than things. We agree in the thing, but differ in the name. That we are affected with ideas from without is evident; and it is no less evident, that there must be (I will not say archetypes, but) powers without the mind, corresponding to those ideas. And as these powers cannot subsist by themselves, there is some subject of them necessarily to be admitted, which I call *matter*, and you call *spirit*. This is all the difference.

Phil. Pray, Hylas, is that powerful being, or subject of powers, extended?

Hyl. It hath not extension; but it hath the power to raise in you the idea of extension.

Phil. It is therefore itself unextended.

Hyl. I grant it.

Phil. Is it not also active?

Hyl. Without doubt: otherwise, how could we attribute powers to it?

Phil. Now let me ask you two questions: first, whether it be agreeable to the usage either of philosophers or others, to give the name *matter* to an unextended active being? And secondly, whether it be not ridiculously absurd to misapply names contrary to the common use of language?

Hyl. Well then, let it not be called matter, since you will have it so, but some *third nature* distinct from matter and spirit. For, what reason is there why you should call it spirit? Does not the notion of spirit imply, that it is thinking as well as active and unextended?

Phil. My reason is this: because I have a mind to have some notion or meaning in what I say; but I have no notion of any action distinct from volition, neither can I conceive volition to be any where but in a spirit: therefore when I speak of an active being, I am obliged to mean a spirit. Beside, what can be plainer than that a thing which hath no ideas in itself, cannot impart them to me; and if it hath ideas, surely it must be a spirit. To make you comprehend the point still more clearly, if it be possible: I assert as well as you, that since we are affected from without, we must allow powers to be without in a being distinct from ourselves. So far we are agreed. But then we differ as to the kind of this powerful being. I will have it to be spirit, you matter, or I know not what (I may add too, you know not what) third nature. Thus I prove it to be spirit. From the effects I see produced, I conclude there are actions; and because actions, volitions; and because there are volitions, there must be a will. Again, the things I perceive must have an existence, they or their archetypes, out of my mind: but being ideas, neither they nor their archetypes can exist otherwise than in an understanding: there is therefore an understanding. But will and understanding constitute in the strictest sense a mind or spirit. The powerful cause therefore of my ideas, is in strict propriety of speech a *spirit*.

Hyl. And now I warrant you think you have made the point very clear, little suspecting that what you advance leads directly to a contradiction. Is it not an absurdity to imagine any imperfection in God?

Phil. Without doubt.

Hyl. To suffer pain is an imperfection.

Phil. It is.

Hyl. Are we not sometimes affected with pain and uneasiness by some other being?

Phil. We are.

Hyl. And have you not said that being is a spirit, and is not that spirit God?

Phil. I grant it.

Hyl. But you have asserted, that whatever ideas we perceive from without, are in the mind which affects us. The ideas therefore of pain and uneasiness are in God; or in other words, God suffers pain: that is to say, there is an imperfection in the divine nature, which you acknowledged was absurd. So you are caught in a plain contradiction.

Phil. That God knows or understands all things, and that he knows among other things what pain is, even every sort of painful sensation, and what it is for his creatures to suffer pain, I make no question. But that God, though he knows and sometimes causes painful sensations in us, can himself suffer pain, I positively deny. We who are limited and dependent spirits, are liable to impressions of sense, the effects of an external agent, which being produced against our wills, are sometimes painful and uneasy. But God, whom no external being can affect, who perceives nothing by sense as we do, whose will is absolute and independent, causing all things, and liable to be thwarted or resisted by nothing; it is evident, such a being as this can suffer nothing, nor be affected with any painful sensation, or indeed any sensation at all. We are chained to a body, that is to say, our perceptions are connected with corporeal motions. By the law of our nature we are affected upon every alteration in the nervous parts of our sensible body: which sensible body rightly considered, is nothing but a complexion of such qualities or ideas, as have no existence distinct from being perceived by a mind; so that this connexion of sensations with corporeal motions, means no more than a correspondence in the order of nature between two sets of ideas, or things immediately perceivable. But God is a pure spirit, disengaged from all such sympathy or natural ties. No corporeal motions are attended with the sensations of pain or pleasure in his mind. To know every thing knowable is certainly a perfection; but to endure, or suffer, or feel any thing by sense, is an imperfection. The former, I say, agrees to God, but not the latter. God knows or hath ideas: but his ideas are not conveyed to him by sense, as ours are. Your not distinguishing where there is so manifest a difference, makes you fancy you see an absurdity where there is none.

Hyl. But all this while you have not considered, that the quantity of matter hath been demonstrated to be proportioned to the gravity of bodies. And what can withstand demonstration?

Phil. Let me see how you demonstrate that point?

Hyl. I lay it down for a principle, that the moments or quantities of motion in bodies, are in a direct compounded reason of the velocities and quantities of matter contained in them. Hence, where the velocities are equal, it follows, the moments are directly as the quantity of matter in each. But it is found by experience, that all bodies (bating the small inequalities arising from the resistance of the air) descend with an equal velocity; the motion therefore of descending bodies, and consequently their gravity, which is the cause or principle of that motion, is proportional to the quantity of matter: which was to be demonstrated.

Phil. You lay it down as a self-evident principle, that the quantity of motion in any body is proportional to the velocity and *matter* taken together: and this is made use of to prove a proposition, from whence the existence of *matter* is inferred. Pray is not this arguing in a circle?

Hyl. In the premise I only mean, that the motion is proportional to the velocity, jointly with the extension and solidity.

Phil. But allowing this to be true, yet it will not thence follow, that gravity is proportional to *matter*, in your philosophic sense of the word; except you take it for granted, that unknown *substratum*, or whatever else you call it, is proportional to those sensible qualities; which to suppose is plainly begging the question. That there is magnitude, and solidity, or resistance, perceived by sense, I readily grant; as likewise that gravity may be proportional to those qualities, I will not dispute. But that either these qualities as perceived by us, or the powers producing them, do exist in a *material substratum;* this is what I deny, and you indeed affirm, but notwithstanding your demonstration, have not yet proved.

Hyl. I shall insist no longer on that point. Do you think, however, you shall persuade me that natural philosophers have been dreaming all this while? pray what becomes of all their hypotheses and explications of the phenomena, which suppose the existence of matter?

Phil. What mean you, Hylas, by the phenomena?

Hyl. I mean the appearances which I perceive by my senses.

Phil. And the appearances perceived by sense, are they not ideas?

Hyl. I have told you so a hundred times.

Phil. Therefore, to explain the phenomena, is to show how we come to be affected with ideas, in that manner and order wherein they are imprinted on our senses. Is it not?

Hyl. It is.

Phil. Now if you can prove, that any philosopher hath explained the production of any one idea in our minds by the help of *matter*, I shall for ever acquiesce, and look on all that hath been said against it as nothing: but if you cannot, it is in vain to urge the explication of phenomena. That a being endowed with knowledge and will, should produce or exhibit ideas, is easily understood. But that a being which is utterly destitute of these faculties should be able to produce ideas, or in any sort to affect an intelligence, this I can never understand. This I say, though we had some positive conception of matter, though we knew its qualities, and could comprehend its existence, would yet be so far from explaining things, that it is itself the most inexplicable thing in the world. And yet for all this, it will not follow, that philosophers have been doing nothing; for by observing and reasoning upon the connexion of ideas, they discover the laws and methods of nature, which is a part of knowledge both useful and entertaining.

Hyl. After all, can it be supposed God would deceive all mankind? Do you imagine, he would have induced the whole world to believe the being of matter, if there was no such thing?

Phil. That every epidemical opinion arising from prejudice, or passion, or thoughtlessness, may be imputed to God, as the author of it, I believe you will not affirm. Whatsoever opinion we father on him, it must be either because he has discovered it to us by supernatural revelation, or because it is so evident to our natural faculties, which were framed and given us by God, that it is impossible we should withhold our assent from it. But where is the revelation, or where is the evidence that extorts the belief of matter? Nay, how does it appear that matter, taken for something distinct from what we perceive by our senses, is thought to exist by all mankind, or indeed by any except a few philosophers, who do not know what they would be at? Your question supposes these points are clear; and when you have cleared them, I shall think myself obliged to give you another answer. In the mean time let it suffice that I tell you, I do not suppose God has deceived mankind at all.

Hyl. But the novelty, Philonous, the novelty! There lies the danger. New notions should always be discountenanced; they unsettle men's minds, and nobody knows where they will end.

Phil. Why the rejecting a notion that hath no foundation either in sense, or in reason, or in divine authority, should be thought to unsettle the belief of such opinions as are grounded on all or any of these, I cannot imagine. That innovations in government and religion are dangerous, and ought to be discountenanced, I freely own. But is there the like reason why they should be discouraged in philosophy? The making any thing known which was unknown before, is an innovation in knowledge: and if all such innovations had been forbidden, men would have made a notable progress in the arts and sciences. But it is none of my business to plead for novelties and paradoxes. That the qualities we perceive are not on the objects: that we must not believe our senses: that we know nothing of the real nature of things, and can never be assured even of their existence: that real colours and sounds are nothing but certain unknown figures and motions: that motions are in themselves neither swift nor slow: that there are in bodies absolute extensions, without any particular magnitude or figure: that a thing stupid, thoughtless, and inactive, operates on a spirit: that the least particle of a body contains innumerable extended parts. These are the novelties, these are the strange notions which shock the genuine uncorrupted judgment of all mankind; and being once admitted, embarrass the mind with endless doubts and difficulties. And it is against these and the like innovations, I endeavour to vindicate common sense. It is true, in doing this, I may perhaps be obliged to use some *ambages*, and ways of speech not common. But if my notions are once thoroughly understood, that which is most singular in them will in effect be found to amount to no more than this: that it is absolutely impossible, and a plain contradiction to suppose, any unthinking being should exist without being perceived by a mind. And if this notion be singular, it is a shame it should be so at this time of day, and in a Christian country.

Hyl. As for the difficulties other opinions may be liable to, those are out of the question. It is your business to defend your own opinion. Can any thing be plainer, than that you are for changing all things into ideas? You, I say, who are not ashamed to charge me with *scepticism*. This is so plain, there is no denying it.

Phil. You mistake me. I am not for changing things into ideas, but rather ideas into things; since those immediate objects of perception, which, according to you, are only appearances of things, I take to be the real things themselves.

Hyl. Things! you may pretend what you please; but it is certain, you leave us nothing but the empty forms of things, the outside only which strikes the senses.

Phil. What you call the empty forms and outside of things, seems to me the very things themselves. Nor are they empty or incomplete otherwise, than upon your supposition, that matter is an essential part of all corporeal things. We both therefore agree in this, that we perceive only sensible forms: but herein we differ, you will have them to be empty appearances, I real beings. In short you do not trust your senses, I do.

Hyl. You say you believe your senses; and seem to applaud yourself that in this you agree with the vulgar. According to you therefore, the true nature of a thing is discovered by the senses. If so, whence comes that disagreement? Why is not the same figure, and other sensible qualities, perceived all manner of ways? and why should we use a microscope, the better to discover the true nature of a body, if it were discoverable to the naked eye?

Phil. Strictly speaking, Hylas, we do not see the same object that we feel; neither is the same object perceived by the microscope, which was by the naked eye. But in case every variation was thought sufficient to constitute a new kind or individual, the endless number or confusion of names would render language impracticable. Therefore to avoid this as well as other inconveniences which are obvious upon a little thought, men combine together several ideas, apprehended by divers senses, or by the same sense at different times, or in different circumstances, but observed however to have some connexion in nature, either with respect to co-existence or succession; all which they refer to one name, and consider as one thing. Hence it follows that when I examine by my other senses a thing I have seen, it is not in order to understand better the same object which I had perceived by sight, the object of one sense not being perceived by the other senses. And when I look through a microscope, it is not that I may perceive more clearly what I perceived already with my bare eyes, the object perceived by the glass being quite different from the former. But in both cases my aim is only to know what ideas are connected together; and the more a man knows of the connexion of ideas, the more he is said to know of the nature of things. What therefore if our ideas are variable? What if our senses are not in all circumstances affected with the same appearances? It will not thence follow, they are not to be trusted, or that they are inconsistent either with themselves or any thing else, except it be with your preconceived notion of (I know not what) one single, unchanged, unperceivable, real nature, marked by each name: which prejudice seems to have taken its rise from not rightly understanding the common language of men speaking of several distinct ideas, as united into one thing by the mind. And indeed there is cause to suspect several erroneous conceits of the philosophers are owing to the same original: while they began to build their schemes, not so much on notions as words, which were framed by the vulgar, merely for conveniency and despatch in the common actions of life, without any regard to speculation.

Hyl. Methinks I apprehend your meaning.

Phil. It is your opinion, the ideas we perceive by our senses are not real things, but images, or copies of them. Our knowledge therefore is no further real, than as our ideas are the true representations of those originals. But as these supposed originals are in themselves unknown, it is impossible to know how far our ideas resemble them; or whether they resemble them at all. We cannot therefore be sure we have any real knowledge. Further, as our ideas are perpetually varied, without any change in the supposed real things, it necessarily follows they cannot all be true copies of them; or if some are, and others are not, it is impossible to distinguish the former from the latter. And this plunges us yet deeper in uncertainty. Again, when we consider the point, we cannot conceive how any idea, or any thing like an idea, should have an absolute existence out of a mind; nor consequently, according to you, how there should be any real thing in nature. The result of all which is, that we are thrown into the most hopeless and abandoned *scepticism*. Now give me leave to ask you, first, whether your referring ideas to certain absolutely existing unperceived substances, as their originals, be not the source of all this *scepticism?* Secondly, whether you are informed, either by sense or reason, of the existence of those unknown originals? And in case you are not, whether it be not absurd to suppose them? Thirdly, whether upon inquiry, you find there is any thing distinctly conceived or meant by the *absolute or external existence of unperceiving substances?* Lastly, whether, the premises considered, it be not the wisest way to follow nature, trust your senses, and laying aside all anxious thought about unknown natures or substances, admit with the vulgar those for real things, which are perceived by the senses?

Hyl. For the present, I have no inclination to the answering part. I would much rather see how you can get over what follows. Pray are not the objects perceived by the senses of one, likewise perceivable to others present? If there were a hundred more here, they would all see the garden, the trees, and flowers as I see them. But they are not in the same manner affected with the ideas I frame in my imagination. Does not this make a difference between the former sort of objects and the latter?

Phil. I grant it does. Nor have I ever denied a difference between the objects of sense and those of imagination. But what would you infer from thence? You cannot say that sensible objects exist unperceived, because they are perceived by many.

Hyl. I own, I can make nothing of that objection, but it hath led me into another. Is it not your opinion that by our senses we perceive only the ideas existing in our minds?

Phil. It is.

Hyl. But the same idea which is in my mind, cannot be in yours, or in any other mind. Doth it not therefore follow from your principles, that no two can see the same thing? And is not this highly absurd?

Phil. If the term *same* be taken in the vulgar acceptation, it is certain (and not at all repugnant to the principles I maintain) that different persons may perceive the same thing; or the same thing or idea exist in different minds. Words are of arbitrary imposition; and since men are used to apply the word *same* where no distinction or variety is perceived, and I do not pretend to alter their perceptions, it follows, that as men have said before, *several saw the same thing,* so they may upon like occasions still continue to use the same phrase, without any deviation either from propriety of language, or the truth of things. But if the term *same* be used in the acceptation of philosophers, who pretend to an abstracted notion of identity, then, according to their sundry definitions of this notion (for it is not yet agreed wherein that philosophic identity consists), it may or may not be possible for divers persons to perceive the same thing. But whether philosophers shall think fit to call a thing the *same* or no, is, I conceive, of small importance. Let us suppose several men together, all endued with the same faculties, and consequently affected in like sort by their senses, and who had yet never known the use of language; they would without question agree in their perceptions. Though perhaps, when they came to the use of speech, some regarding the uniformness of what was perceived, might call it the *same* thing: others especially regarding the diversity of persons who perceived, might choose the denomination of different things. But who sees not that all the dispute is about a word; to wit, whether what is perceived by different persons, may yet have the term *same* applied to it? Or suppose a house, whose walls or outward shell remaining unaltered, the chambers are all pulled down, and new ones built in their place; and that you should call this the *same*, and I should say it was not the *same* house: would we not for all this perfectly agree in our thoughts of the house, considered in itself? And would not all the difference consist in a sound? If you should say, we differ in our notions; for that you superadded to your idea of the house the simple abstracted idea of identity, whereas I did not; I would tell you I know not what you mean by that *abstracted idea of identity*; and should desire you to look into your own thoughts, and be sure you understood yourself.——Why so silent, Hylas? Are you not yet satisfied, men may dispute about identity and diversity, without any real difference in their thoughts and opinions, abstracted from names? Take this further reflection with you: that whether matter be allowed to exist or no, the case is exactly the same as to the point in hand. For the materialists themselves acknowledge what we immediately perceive by our senses to be our own ideas. Your difficulty therefore, that no two see the same thing, makes equally against the materialists and me.

Hyl. But they suppose an external archetype, to which referring their several ideas, they may truly be said to perceive the same thing.

Phil. And (not to mention your having discovered those archetypes) so may you suppose an external archetype on my principles: *external*, I mean, to your own mind; though indeed it must be supposed to exist in that mind which comprehends all things; but then this serves all the ends of identity, as well as if it existed out of a mind. And I am sure you yourself will not say, it is less intelligible.

Hyl. You have indeed clearly satisfied me, either that there is no difficulty at bottom in this point; or if there be, that it makes equally against both opinions.

Phil. But that which makes equally against two contradictory opinions, can be a proof against neither.

Hyl. I acknowledge it. But after all, Philonous, when I consider the substance of what you advance against scepticism, it amounts to no more than this. We are sure that we really see, hear, feel; in a word, that we are affected with sensible impressions.

Phil. And how are we concerned any further? I see this *cherry*, I feel it, I taste it: and I am sure *nothing* cannot be seen, or felt, or tasted: it is therefore *real*. Take away the sensations of softness, moisture, redness, tartness, and you take away the *cherry*. Since it is not a being distinct from sensations; a *cherry*, I say, is nothing but a congeries of sensible impressions, or ideas perceived by various senses; which ideas are united into one thing (or have one name given them) by the mind; because they are observed to attend each other. Thus when the palate is affected with such a particular taste, the sight is affected with a red colour, the touch with roundness, softness, &c. Hence, when I see, and feel, and taste, in sundry certain manners, I am sure the *cherry* exists, or is real; its reality being in my opinion nothing abstracted from those sensations. But if by the word *cherry* you mean an unknown nature distinct from all those sensible qualities, and by its existence something distinct from its being perceived; then indeed I own, neither you, nor I, nor any one else can be sure it exists.

Hyl. But what would you say, Philonous, if I should bring the very same reasons against the existence of sensible things in a mind, which you have offered against their existing in a material *substratum?*

Phil. When I see your reasons, you shall hear what I have to say to them.

Hyl. Is the mind extended or unextended?

Phil. Unextended, without doubt.

Hyl. Do you say the things you perceive are in your mind?

Phil. They are.

Hyl. Again, have I not heard you speak of sensible impressions?

Phil. I believe you may.

Hyl. Explain to me now, O Philonous! how it is possible there should be room for all those trees and houses to exist in your mind. Can extended things be contained in that which is unextended? or are we to imagine impressions made on a thing void of all solidity? You cannot say objects are in your mind, as books in your study: or that things are imprinted on it, as the figure of a seal upon wax. In what sense therefore are we to understand those expressions? Explain me this if you can: and I shall then be able to answer all those queries you formerly put to me about my substratum.

Phil. Look you, Hylas, when I speak of objects as existing in the mind or imprinted on the senses, I would not be understood in the gross literal sense, as when bodies are said to exist in a place, or a seal to make an impression upon wax. My meaning is only that the mind comprehends or perceives them; and that it is affected from without, or by some being distinct from itself. This is my explication of your difficulty; and how it can serve to make your tenet of an unperceiving material substratum intelligible, I would fain know.

Hyl. Nay, if that be all, I confess I do not see what use can be made of it. But are you not guilty of some abuse of language in this?

Phil. None at all: it is no more than common custom, which you know is the rule of language, hath authorized: nothing being more usual, than for philosophers to speak of the immediate objects of the understanding as things existing in the mind. Nor is there any thing in this, but what is conformable to the general analogy of language; most part of the mental operations being signified by words borrowed from sensible things; as is plain in the terms *comprehend, reflect, discourse,* &c., which being applied to the mind, must not be taken in their gross original sense.

Hyl. You have, I own, satisfied me in this point; but there still remains one great difficulty, which I know not how you will get over. And, indeed, it is of such importance, that if you could solve all others, without being able to find a solution for this, you must never expect to make me a proselyte to your principles.

Phil. Let me know this mighty difficulty.

Hyl. The scripture account of the creation is what appears to me utterly irreconcilable with your notions. Moses tells us of a creation: a creation of what? of ideas? No, certainly, but of things, of real things, solid corporeal substances. Bring your principles to agree with this, and I shall perhaps agree with you.

Phil. Moses mentions the sun, moon, and stars, earth and sea, plants and animals: that all these do really exist, and were in the beginning created by God, I make no question. If by *ideas* you mean fictions and fancies of the mind, then these are no ideas. If by *ideas* you mean immediate objects of the understanding, or sensible things which cannot exist unperceived, or out of a mind, then these things are ideas. But whether you do or do not call them *ideas,* it matters little. The difference is only about a name. And whether that name be retained or rejected, the sense, the truth, and reality of things continues the same. In common talk, the objects of our senses are not termed *ideas,* but *things.* Call them so still; provided you do not attribute to them any absolute external existence, and I shall never quarrel with you for a word. The creation, therefore, I allow to have been a creation of things, of *real* things. Neither is this in the least inconsistent with my principles, as is evident from what I have now said; and would have been evident to you without this, if you had not forgotten what had been so often said before. But as for solid corporeal substances, I desire you to show where Moses makes any mention of them; and if they should be mentioned by him, or any other inspired writer, it would still be incumbent on you to show those words were not taken in the vulgar acceptation, for things falling under our senses, but in the philosophic acceptation, for matter, or an unknown quiddity, with an absolute existence. When you have proved these points, then (and not till then) may you bring the authority of Moses into our dispute.

Hyl. It is in vain to dispute about a point so clear. I am content to refer it to your own conscience. Are you not satisfied there is some peculiar repugnancy between the Mosaic account of the creation and your notions?

Phil. If all possible sense, which can be put on the first chapter of Genesis, may be conceived as consistently with my principles as any other, then it has no peculiar repugnancy with them. But there is no sense you may not as well conceive, believing as I do. Since, beside spirits, all you conceive are ideas, and the existence of these I do not deny. Neither do you pretend they exist without the mind.

Hyl. Pray let me see any sense you can understand it in.

Phil. Why I imagine that if I had been present at the creation, I should have seen things produced into being; that is, become perceptible, in the order described by the sacred historian. I ever before believed the Mosaic account of the creation, and now find no alteration in my manner of believing it. When things are said to begin or end their existence, we do not mean this with regard to God, but his creatures. All objects are eternally known by God, or, which is the same thing, have an eternal existence in his mind: but when things before imperceptible to creatures, are by a decree of God, made perceptible to them; then are they said to begin a relative existence with respect to created minds. Upon reading therefore the Mosaic account of the creation, I understand that the several parts of the world became gradually perceivable to finite spirits, endowed with proper faculties; so that, whoever such were present, they were in truth perceived by them. This is the literal, obvious sense suggested to me by the words of the holy scripture: in which is included no mention or no thought, either of substratum, instrument, occasion, or absolute existence. And upon inquiry, I doubt not it will be found, that most plain, honest men, who believe the creation, never think of those things any more than I. What metaphysical sense you may understand it in, you only can tell.

Hyl. But, Philonous, you do not seem to be aware, that you allow created things in the beginning only a relative, and, consequently, hypothetical being; that is to say, upon supposition there were men to perceive them, without which they have no actuality of absolute existence, wherein creation might terminate. Is it not, therefore, according to you plainly impossible, the creation of any inanimate creatures should precede that of man? And is not this directly contrary to the Mosaic account?

Phil. In answer to that I say, first, created beings might begin to exist in the mind of other created intelligences, beside men. You will not therefore be able to prove any contradiction between Moses and my notions, unless you first show, there was no other order of finite created spirits in being before man. I say further, in case we conceive the creation, as we should at this time a parcel of plants or vegetables of all sorts, produced by an invisible power, in a desert where nobody was present: that this way of explaining or conceiving it, is consistent with my principles, since they deprive you of nothing, either sensible or imaginable: that it exactly suits with the common, natural, undebauched notions of mankind: that it manifests the dependence of all things on God; and consequently hath all the good effect or influence, which it is possible that important article of our faith should have in making men humble, thankful, and resigned to their Creator. I say moreover, that in this naked conception of things, divested of words, there will not be found any notion of what you call the *actuality of absolute existence*. You may indeed raise a dust with those terms, and so lengthen our dispute to no purpose. But I entreat you calmly to look into your own thoughts, and then tell me if they are not a useless and unintelligible jargon.

Hyl. I own I have no very clear notion annexed to them. But what say you to this? Do you not make the existence of sensible things consist in their being in a mind? and were not all things eternally in the mind of God? Did they not therefore exist from all eternity, according to you? And how could that which was eternal be created in time? Can any thing be clearer or better connected than this?

Phil. And are not you too of opinion, that God knew all things from eternity?

Hyl. I am.

Phil. Consequently they always had a being in the divine intellect.

Hyl. This I acknowledge.

Phil. By your own confession therefore, nothing is new, or begins to be, in respect of the mind of God. So we are agreed in that point.

Hyl. What shall we make then of the creation?

Phil. May we not understand it to have been entirely in respect of finite spirits; so that things, with regard to us, may properly be said to begin their existence, or be created, when God decreed they should become perceptible to intelligent creatures, in that order and manner which he then established, and we now call the laws of nature? You may call this a *relative*, or *hypothetical existence* if you please. But so long as it supplies us with the most natural, obvious, and literal sense of the Mosaic history of the creation; so long as it answers all the religious ends of that great article; in a word, so long as you can assign no other sense or meaning in its stead; why should we reject this? Is it to comply with a ridiculous sceptical humour of making every thing nonsense and unintelligible? I am sure you cannot say it is for the glory of God. For allowing it to be a thing possible and conceivable, that the corporeal world should have an absolute subsistence extrinsical to the mind of God, as well as to the minds of all created spirits: yet how could this set forth either the immensity or omniscience of the Deity, or the necessary and immediate dependence of all things on him? Nay, would it not rather seem to derogate from those attributes?

Hyl. Well, but as to this decree of God's, for making things perceptible: what say you, Philonous, is it not plain, God did either execute that decree from all eternity, or at some certain time began to will what he had not actually willed before, but only designed to will? If the former, then there could be no creation or beginning of existence in finite things. If the latter, then we must acknowledge something new to befall the

Deity; which implies a sort of change; and all change argues imperfection.

Phil. Pray consider what you are doing. Is it not evident, this objection concludes equally against a creation in any sense; nay, against every other act of the Deity, discoverable by the light of nature? None of which can we conceive, otherwise than as performed in time, and having a beginning. God is a being of transcendent and unlimited perfections: his nature therefore is incomprehensible to finite spirits. It is not therefore to be expected, that any man, whether *materialist* or *immaterialist*, should have exactly just notions of the Deity, his attributes, and ways of operation. If then you would infer any thing against me, your difficulty must not be drawn from the inadequateness of our conceptions of the divine nature, which is unavoidable on any scheme: but from the denial of matter, of which there is not one word, directly or indirectly, in what you have now objected.

Hyl. I must acknowledge the difficulties you are concerned to clear, are such only as arise from the non-existence of matter, and are peculiar to that notion. So far you are in the right. But I cannot by any means bring myself to think there is no such peculiar repugnancy between the creation and your opinion; though indeed where to fix it, I do not distinctly know.

Phil. What would you have? Do I not acknowledge a twofold state of things, the one ectypal or natural, the other archetypal and eternal? The former was created in time; the latter existed from everlasting in the mind of God. Is not this agreeable to the common notions of divines? or is any more than this necessary in order to conceive the creation? But you suspect some peculiar repugnancy, though you know not where it lies. To take away all possibility of scruple in the case, do but consider this one point. Either you are not able to conceive the creation on any hypothesis whatsoever; and if so, there is no ground for dislike or complaint against my particular opinion on that score: or you are able to conceive it; and if so, why not on my principles, since thereby nothing conceivable is taken away? You have all along been allowed the full scope of sense, imagination, and reason. Whatever therefore you could before apprehend, either immediately or mediately by your senses, or by ratiocination from your senses; whatever you could perceive, imagine, or understand, remains still with you. If therefore the notion you have of the creation by other principles be intelligible, you have it still upon mine; if it be not intelligible, I conceive it to be no notion at all; and so there is no loss of it. And indeed it seems to me very plain, that the supposition of matter, that is, a thing perfectly unknown and inconceivable, cannot serve to make us conceive any thing. And I hope, it need not be proved to you, that if the existence of matter doth not make the creation conceivable, the creation's being without it inconceivable, can be no objection against its non-existence.

Hyl. I confess, Philonous, you have almost satisfied me in this point of the creation.

Phil. I would fain know why you are not quite satisfied. You tell me indeed of a repugnancy between the Mosaic history and immaterialism: but you know not where it lies. Is this reasonable, Hylas? Can you expect I should solve a difficulty without knowing what it is? But to pass by all that, would not a man think you were assured there is no repugnancy between the received notions of materialists and the inspired writings?

Hyl. And so I am.

Phil. Ought the historical part of scripture to be understood in a plain, obvious sense, or in a sense which is metaphysical and out of the way?

Hyl. In the plain sense, doubtless.

Phil. When Moses speaks of herbs, earth, water, &c., as having been created by God; think you not the sensible things, commonly signified by those words, are suggested to every unphilosophical reader?

Hyl. I cannot help thinking so.

Phil. And are not all ideas, or things perceived by sense, to be denied a real existence by the doctrine of the materialists?

Hyl. This I have already acknowledged.

Phil. The creation therefore, according to them, was not the creation of things sensible, which have only a relative being, but of certain unknown natures, which have an absolute being, wherein creation might terminate.

Hyl. True.

Phil. Is it not therefore evident, the asserters of matter destroy the plain obvious sense of Moses, with which their notions are utterly inconsistent; and instead of it obtrude on us I know not what, something equally unintelligible to themselves and me.

Hyl. I cannot contradict you.

Phil. Moses tells us of a creation. A creation of what? of unknown quiddities, of occasions, or substratums? No, certainly; but of things obvious to the senses. You must first reconcile this with your notions, if you expect I should be reconciled to them.

Hyl. I see you can assault me with my own weapons.

Phil. Then as to *absolute existence;* was there ever known a more jejune notion than that? Something it is, so abstracted and unintelligible, that you have frankly owned you could not conceive it, much less explain any thing by it. But allowing matter to exist, and the notion of absolute existence to be as clear as light, yet was this ever known to make the creation more credible? Nay, hath it not furnished the atheists and infidels of all ages with the most plausible argument against a creation? That a corporeal substance, which hath an absolute existence without the minds of spirits, should be produced out of nothing by the mere will of a spirit, hath been looked upon as a thing so contrary to all reason, so impossible and absurd, that not only the most celebrated among the ancients, but even divers modern and Christian philosophers, have thought matter co-eternal with the Deity. Lay these things together, and then judge you whether materialism disposes men to believe the creation of things.

Hyl. I own, Philonous, I think it does not. This of the *creation* is the last objection I can think of; and I must needs own it hath been sufficiently answered as well as the rest. Nothing now remains to be overcome, but a sort of unaccountable backwardness that I find in myself toward your notions.

Phil. When a man is swayed, he knows not why, to one side of a question, can this, think you, be any thing else but the effect of prejudice, which never fails to attend old and rooted notions? And indeed in this respect I cannot deny the belief of matter to have very much the advantage over the contrary opinion, with men of a learned education.

Hyl. I confess it seems to be as you say.

Phil. As a balance therefore to this weight of prejudice, let us throw into the scale the great advantages that arise from the belief of immaterialism, both in regard to religion and human learning. The being of a God, and incorruptibility of the soul, those great articles of religion, are they not proved with the clearest and most immediate evidence? When I say the being of a *God,* I do not mean an obscure, general cause of things, whereof we have no conception, but *God,* in the strict and proper sense of the word. A being whose spirituality, omnipresence, providence, omniscience, infinite power, and goodness, are as conspicuous as the existence of sensible things, of which (notwithstanding the fallacious pretences and affected scruples of sceptics) there is no more reason to doubt than of our own being. Then with relation to human sciences; in natural philosophy, what intricacies, what obscurities, what contradictions, hath the belief of matter led men into! To say nothing of the numberless disputes about its extent, continuity, homogeneity, gravity, divisibility, &c., do they not pretend to explain all things by bodies operating on bodies, according to the laws of motion? and yet, are they able to comprehend how any one body should move another? Nay, admitting there was no difficulty in reconciling the notion of an inert being with a cause; or in conceiving how an accident might pass from one body to another; yet by all their strained thoughts and extravagant suppositions, have they been able to reach the mechanical production of any one animal or vegetable body? Can they account by the laws of motion, for sounds, tastes, smells, or colours, or for the regular course of things? Have they accounted by physical principles for the aptitude and contrivance, even of the most inconsiderable parts of the universe? But laying aside matter and corporeal causes, and admitting only the efficiency of an all-perfect mind, are not all the effects of nature easy and intelligible? If the phenomena are nothing else but *ideas*; God is a *spirit*, but matter an unintelligent, unperceiving being. If they demonstrate an unlimited power in their cause; God is active and omnipotent, but matter an inert mass. If the order, regularity, and usefulness of them can never be sufficiently admired; God is infinitely wise and provident, but matter destitute of all contrivance and design. These surely are great advantages in *physics*. Not to mention that the apprehension of a distant Deity naturally disposes men to a negligence in their *moral* actions, which they would be more cautious of in case they thought him immediately present, and acting on their minds without the interposition of matter, or unthinking second causes. Then in *metaphysics*; what difficulties concerning entity in abstract, substantial forms, hylarchic principles, plastic natures, substance and accident, principle of individuation, possibility of matter's thinking, origin of ideas, the manner how two independent substances, so widely different as *spirit* and *matter*, should mutually operate on each other!

what difficulties, I say, and endless disquisitions concerning these and innumerable other the like points, do we escape by supposing only spirits and ideas? Even the *mathematics* themselves, if we take away the absolute existence of extended things, become much more clear and easy; the most shocking paradoxes and intricate speculations in those sciences, depending on the infinite divisibility of finite extension, which depends on that supposition. But what need is there to insist on the particular sciences? Is not that opposition to all science whatsoever, that frenzy of the ancient and modern sceptics, built on the same foundation? Or can you produce so much as one argument against the reality of corporeal things, or in behalf of that avowed utter ignorance of their natures, which doth not suppose their reality to consist in an external absolute existence. Upon this supposition indeed, the objections from the change of colours in a pigeon's neck, or the appearances of a broken oar in the water, must be allowed to have weight. But those and the like objections vanish, if we do not maintain the being of absolute external originals, but place the reality of things in ideas, fleeting indeed, and changeable; however not changed at random, but according to the fixed order of nature. For herein consists that constancy and truth of things, which secures all the concerns of life, and distinguishes that which is *real* from the irregular visions of the fancy.

Hyl. I agree to all you have now said, and must own that nothing can incline me to embrace your opinion, more than the advantages I see it is attended with. I am by nature lazy, and this would be a mighty abridgment in knowledge. What doubts, what hypotheses, what labyrinths of amusement, what fields of disputation, what an ocean of false learning, may be avoided by that single notion of *immaterialism!*

Phil. After all, is there any thing further remaining to be done? You may remember you promised to embrace that opinion which upon examination should appear most agreeable to common sense, and remote from scepticism. This, by your own confession, is that which denies matter, or the absolute existence of corporeal things. Nor is this all; the same notion has been proved several ways, viewed in different lights, pursued in its consequences, and all objections against it cleared. Can there be a greater evidence of its truth? or is it possible it should have all the marks of a true opinion, and yet be false?

Hyl. I own myself entirely satisfied for the present in all respects. But what security can I have that I shall still continue the same full assent to your opinion, and that no unthought-of objection or difficulty will occur hereafter?

Phil. Pray, Hylas, do you in other cases, when a point is once evidently proved, withhold your assent on account of objections or difficulties it may be liable to? Are the difficulties that attend the doctrine of incommensurable quantities, of the angle of contact, of the asymptotes to curves, or the like, sufficient to make you hold out against mathematical demonstration? Or will you disbelieve the providence of God, because there may be some particular things which you know not how to reconcile with it? If there are difficulties attending immaterialism, there are at the same time direct and evident proofs for it. But for the existence of matter there is not one proof, and far more numerous and insurmountable objections lie against it. But where are those mighty difficulties you insist on? Alas! you know not where or what they are; something which may possibly occur hereafter. If this be a sufficient pretence for withholding your full assent, you should never yield it to any proposition, how free soever from exceptions, how clearly and solidly soever demonstrated.

Hyl. You have satisfied me, Philonous.

Phil. But to arm you against all future objections, do but consider, that which bears equally hard on two contradictory opinions, can be a proof against neither. Whenever therefore any difficulty occurs, try if you can find a solution for it on the hypothesis of the *materialists*. Be not deceived by words; but sound your own thoughts. And in case you cannot conceive it easier by the help of *materialism*, it is plain it can be no objection against *immaterialism*. Had you proceeded all along by this rule, you would probably have spared yourself abundance of trouble in objecting; since of all your difficulties I challenge you to show one that is explained by matter; nay, which is not more unintelligible with, than without that supposition, and consequently makes rather *against* than *for* it. You should consider in each particular, whether the difficulty arises from the *non-existence of matter*. If it doth not, you might as well argue from the infinite divisibility of extension against the divine prescience, as from such a difficulty against *immaterialism*. And yet upon recollection I believe you will find this to have been often, if not always the case. You should likewise take heed not to argue on a *petitio prin-*

cipii. One is apt to say, the unknown substances ought to be esteemed real things, rather than the ideas in our minds: and who can tell but the unthinking external substance may concur as a cause or instrument in the production of our ideas? But is not this proceeding on a supposition that there are such external substances? And to suppose this, is it not begging the question? But above all things you should beware of imposing on yourself by that vulgar sophism, which is called *ignoratio elenchi*. You talked often as if you thought I maintained the non-existence of sensible things: whereas in truth no one can be more thoroughly assured of their existence than I am, and it is you who doubt; I should have said, positively deny it. Every thing that is seen, felt, heard, or any way perceived by the senses, is, on the principles I embrace, a real being, but not on yours. Remember the matter you contend for is an unknown somewhat (if indeed it may be termed *somewhat*), which is quite stripped of all sensible qualities, and can neither be perceived by sense, nor apprehended by the mind. Remember, I say, that it is not any object which is hard or soft, hot or cold, blue or white, round or square, &c. For all these things I affirm do exist. Though indeed I deny they have any existence distinct from being perceived; or that they exist out of all minds whatsoever. Think on these points; let them be attentively considered and still kept in view. Otherwise you will not comprehend the state of the question; without which your objections will always be wide of the mark, and instead of mine, may possibly be directed (as more than once they have been) against your own notions.

Hyl. I must needs own, Philonous, nothing seems to have kept me from agreeing with you more than this same *mistaking the question*. In denying matter, at first glimpse I am tempted to imagine you deny the things we see and feel; but upon reflection find there is no ground for it. What think you therefore of retaining the name *matter*, and applying it to sensible things? This may be done without any change in your sentiments: and believe me it would be a means of reconciling them to some persons, who may be more shocked at an innovation in words than in opinion.

Phil. With all my heart: retain the word *matter*, and apply it to the objects of sense, if you please, provided you do not attribute to them any subsistence distinct from their being perceived. I shall never quarrel with you for an expression. *Matter*, or *material substance*, are terms introduced by philosophers; and as used by them, imply a sort of independency, or a subsistence distinct from being perceived by a mind: but are never used by common people; or if ever, it is to signify the immediate objects of sense. One would think therefore, so long as the names of all particular things, with the terms *sensible*, *substance*, *body*, *stuff*, and the like, are retained, the word *matter* should be never missed in common talk. And in philosophical discourses it seems the best way to leave it quite out; since there is not perhaps any one thing that hath more favoured and strengthened the depraved bent of the mind toward *atheism*, than the use of that general confused term.

Hyl. Well but, Philonous, since I am content to give up the notion of an unthinking substance exterior to the mind, I think you ought not to deny me the privilege of using the word *matter* as I please, and annexing it to a collection of sensible qualities subsisting only in the mind. I freely own there is no other substance in a strict sense, than *spirit*. But I have been so long accustomed to the term *matter*, that I know not how to part with it. To say, there is no *matter* in the world, is still shocking to me. Whereas to say, there is no *matter*, if by that term be meant an unthinking substance existing without the mind; but if by matter is meant some sensible thing, whose existence consists in being perceived, then there is *matter*: this distinction gives it quite another turn: and men will come into your notions with small difficulty, when they are proposed in that manner. For after all, the controversy about matter, in the strict acceptation of it, lies altogether between you and the philosophers, whose principles, I acknowledge, are not near so natural, or so agreeable to the common sense of mankind, and holy scripture, as yours. There is nothing we either desire or shun, but as it makes, or is apprehended to make some part of our happiness or misery. But what hath happiness or misery, joy or grief, pleasure or pain, to do with absolute existence, or with unknown entities, abstracted from all relation to us? It is evident, things regard us only as they are pleasing or displeasing: and they can please or displease only so far forth as they are perceived. Further therefore we are not concerned; and thus far you leave things as you found them. Yet still there is something new in this doctrine. It is plain, I do not now think with the philosophers, nor yet altogether with the vulgar. I would know how the case stands in that respect: precisely, what you have added to, or altered in my former notions.

Phil. I do not pretend to be a setter-up of *new notions.* My endeavours tend only to unite and place in a clearer light that truth, which was before shared between the vulgar and the philosophers: the former being of opinion, that *those things they immediately perceive are the real things*: and the latter, that *the things immediately perceived are ideas which exist only in the mind.* Which two notions put together, do in effect constitute the substance of what I advance.

Hyl. I have been a long time distrusting my senses; methought I saw things by a dim light, and through false glasses. Now the glasses are removed, and a new light breaks in upon my understanding. I am clearly convinced that I see things in their native forms; and am no longer in pain about their unknown natures or absolute existence. This is the state I find myself in at present: though indeed the course that brought me to it I do not yet thoroughly comprehend. You set out upon the same principles that Academics, Cartesians, and the like sects, usually do; and for a long time it looked as if you were advancing their philosophical scepticism; but in the end your conclusions are directly opposite to theirs.

Phil. You see, Hylas, the water of yonder fountain, how it is forced upwards, in a round column, to a certain height; at which it breaks and falls back into the basin from whence it rose: its ascent, as well as descent, proceeding from the same uniform law or principle of *gravitation.* Just so, the same principles which at first view lead to scepticism, pursued to a certain point, bring men back to common sense.

David Hume

AN ENQUIRY CONCERNING HUMAN UNDERSTANDING

SECTION I

OF THE DIFFERENT SPECIES OF PHILOSOPHY

Moral philosophy, or the science of human nature, may be treated after two different manners; each of which has its peculiar merit, and may contribute to the entertainment, instruction, and reformation of mankind. The one considers man chiefly as born for action; and as influenced in his measures by taste and sentiment; pursuing one object, and avoiding another, according to the value which these objects seem to possess, and according to the light in which they present themselves. As virtue, of all objects, is allowed to be the most valuable, this species of philosophers paint her in the most amiable colors; borrowing all helps from poetry and eloquence, and treating their subject in an easy and obvious manner, and such as is best fitted to please the imagination, and engage the affections. They select the most striking observations and instances from common life; place opposite characters in a proper contrast; and alluring us into the paths of virtue by the views of glory and happiness, direct our steps in these paths by the soundest precepts and most illustrious examples. They make us *feel* the difference between vice and virtue; they excite and regulate our sentiments; and so they can but bend our hearts to the love of probity and true honor, they think, that they have fully attained the end of all their labors.

The other species of philosophers consider man in the light of a reasonable rather than an active being, and endeavor to form his understanding more than cultivate his manners. They regard human nature as a subject of speculation; and with a narrow scrutiny examine it, in order to find those principles, which regulate our understanding, excite our sentiments, and make us to approve or blame any particular object, action, or behavior. They think it a reproach to all literature, that philosophy should not yet have fixed, beyond controversy, the foundation of morals, reasoning, and criticism; and should for ever talk of truth and falsehood, vice and virtue, beauty and deformity, without being able to determine the source of these distinctions. While they attempt this arduous task, they are deterred by no difficulties; but proceeding from particular instances to general principles, they still push on their inquiries to principles more general, and rest not satisfied till they arrive at those original principles, by which, in every science, all human curiosity must be bounded. Though their speculations seem abstract, and even unintelligible to common readers, they aim at the approbation of the learned and the wise; and think themselves sufficiently compensated for the labor of their whole lives, if they can discover some hidden truths, which may contribute to the instruction of posterity.

It is certain that the easy and obvious philosophy will always, with the generality of mankind, have the preference above the accurate and abstruse; and by many will be recommended, not only as more agreeable, but more useful than the other. It enters more into common life; molds the heart and affections; and, by touching those principles which actuate men, reforms their conduct, and brings them nearer to that model of perfection which it describes. On the contrary, the abstruse philosophy, being founded on a turn of mind, which cannot enter into business and action, vanishes when the philosopher leaves the shade, and comes into open day; nor can its principles easily retain any influence over our conduct and behavior. The feelings of our heart, the agitation of our passions, the vehemence of our affections, dissipate all its conclusions, and reduce the profound philosopher to a mere plebeian.

This also must be confessed, that the most durable, as well as justest fame, has been acquired by the easy philosophy, and that abstract reasoners seem hitherto to have enjoyed only a momentary reputation, from the caprice or ignorance of their own age, but have not been able to support their renown with more equitable posterity. It is easy for a profound philosopher to commit a mistake in his subtle reasonings; and one mistake is the necessary parent of another, while he pushes on his consequences, and is not deterred from embracing any conclusion, by its unusual appearance, or its contradiction to popular opinion. But a philosopher, who purposes only to represent the common sense of mankind in more beautiful and more engaging colors, if by accident he falls into error, goes no farther; but renewing his appeal to common sense, and the natural sentiments of the mind, returns into the right path, and secures himself from any dangerous illusions. The fame of Cicero flourishes at present; but that of Aristotle is utterly decayed. La Bruyère passes the seas, and still maintains his reputation: But the glory of Malebranche is confined to his own nation, and to his own age. And Addison, perhaps, will be read with pleasure, when Locke shall be entirely forgotten.

The mere philosopher is a character, which is commonly but little acceptable in the world, as being supposed to contribute nothing either to the advantage or pleasure of society; while he lives remote from communication with mankind, and is wrapped up in principles and notions equally remote from their comprehension. On the other hand, the mere ignorant is still more despised; nor is anything deemed a surer sign of an illiberal genius in an age and nation where the sciences flourish, than to be entirely destitute of all relish for those noble entertainments. The most perfect character is supposed to lie between those extremes; retaining an equal ability and taste for books, company, and business; preserving in conversation that discernment and delicacy which arise from polite letters; and in business, that probity and accuracy which are the natural result of a just philosophy. In order to diffuse and cultivate so accomplished a character, nothing can be more useful than compositions of the easy style and manner, which draw not too much from life, require no deep application or retreat to be comprehended, and send back the student among mankind full of noble sentiments and wise precepts, applicable to every exigence of human life. By means of such compositions, virtue becomes amiable, science agreeable, company instructive, and retirement entertaining.

Man is a reasonable being; and as such, receives from science his proper food and nourishment: But so narrow are the bounds of human understanding, that little satisfaction can be hoped for in this particular, either from the extent or security of his acquisitions. Man is a sociable, no less than a reasonable being: But neither can he always enjoy company agreeable and amusing, or preserve the proper relish for them.

Man is also an active being; and from that disposition, as well as from the various necessities of human life, must submit to business and occupation: But the mind requires some relaxation, and cannot always support its bent to care and industry. It seems, then, that nature has pointed out a mixed kind of life as most suitable to the human race, and secretly admonished them to allow none of these biases to *draw* too much, so as to incapacitate them for other occupations and entertainments. Indulge your passion for science, says she, but let your science be human, and such as may have a direct reference to action and society. Abstruse thought and profound researches I prohibit, and will severely punish, by the pensive melancholy which they introduce, by the endless uncertainty in which they involve you, and by the cold reception which your pretended discoveries shall meet with, when communicated. Be a philosopher; but, amidst all your philosophy, be still a man.

Were the generality of mankind contented to prefer the easy philosophy to the abstract and profound, without throwing any blame or contempt on the latter, it might not be improper, perhaps, to comply with this general opinion, and allow every man to enjoy, without opposition, his own taste and sentiment. But as the matter is often carried farther, even to the absolute rejecting of all profound reasonings, or what is commonly called *metaphysics*, we shall now proceed to consider what can reasonably be pleaded in their behalf.

We may begin with observing, that one considerable advantage, which results from the accurate and abstract philosophy, is, its subserviency to the easy and humane, which, without the former, can never attain a sufficient degree of exactness in its sentiments, precepts, or reasonings. All polite letters are nothing but pictures of human life in various attitudes and situations; and inspire us with different sentiments, of praise or blame, admiration or ridicule, according to the qualities of the object, which they set before us. An artist must be better qualified to succeed in this undertaking, who, besides a delicate taste and a quick apprehension, possesses an accurate knowledge of the internal fabric, the operations of the understanding, the workings of the passions, and the various species of sentiment which discriminate vice and virtue. How painful soever this inward search or inquiry may appear, it becomes, in some measure, requisite to those, who would describe with success the obvious and outward appearances of life and manners. The anatomist presents to the eye the most hideous and disagreeable objects; but his science is useful to the painter in delineating even a Venus or an Helen. While the latter employs all the richest colors of his art, and gives his figures the most graceful and engaging airs; he must still carry his attention to the inward structure of the human body, the position of the muscles, the fabric of the bones, and the use and figure of every part or organ. Accuracy is, in every case, advantageous to beauty, and just reasoning to delicate sentiment. In vain would we exalt the one by depreciating the other.

Besides, we may observe, in every art or profession, even those which most concern life or action, that a spirit of accuracy, however acquired, carries all of them nearer their perfection, and renders them more subservient to the interests of society. And though a philosopher may live remote from business, the genius of philosophy, if carefully cultivated by several, must gradually diffuse itself throughout the whole society, and bestow a similar correctness on every art and calling. The politician will acquire greater foresight and subtlety, in the subdividing and balancing of power; the lawyer more method and finer principles in his reasonings; and the general more regularity in his discipline, and more caution in his plans and operations. The stability of modern governments above the ancient, and the accuracy of modern philosophy, have improved, and probably will still improve, by similar gradations.

Were there no advantage to be reaped from these studies, beyond the gratification of an innocent curiosity, yet ought not even this to be despised; as being one accession to those few safe and harmless pleasures, which are bestowed on the human race. The sweetest and most inoffensive path of life leads through the avenues of science and learning; and whoever can either remove any obstructions in this way, or open up any new prospect, ought so far to be esteemed a benefactor to mankind. And though these researches may appear painful and fatiguing, it is with some minds as with some bodies, which being endowed with vigorous and florid health, require severe exercise, and reap a pleasure from what, to the generality of mankind, may seem burdensome and laborious. Obscurity, indeed, is painful to the mind as well as to the eye; but to bring light from obscurity, by whatever labor, must needs be delightful and rejoicing.

But this obscurity in the profound and abstract philosophy, is objected to, not only as painful and fatiguing, but as the inevitable source of uncertainty and error. Here indeed lies the justest and most plausible objection against a considerable part of metaphysics, that they are not properly a science; but arise either from the fruitless efforts of human vanity, which would penetrate into subjects utterly inaccessible to the understanding, or from the craft of popular superstitions, which, being unable to defend themselves on fair ground, raise these entangling brambles to cover and protect their weakness. Chased from the open country, these robbers fly into the forest, and lie in wait to break in upon every unguarded avenue of the mind, and overwhelm it with religious fears and prejudices. The stoutest antagonist, if he remit his watch a moment, is oppressed. And many, through cowardice and folly, open the gates to the enemies, and willingly receive them with reverence and submission, as their legal sovereigns.

But is this a sufficient reason, why philosophers should desist from such researches, and leave superstition still in possession of her retreat? Is it not proper to draw an opposite conclusion, and perceive the necessity of carrying the war into the most secret recesses of the enemy? In vain do we hope, that men, from frequent disappointment, will at last abandon such airy sciences, and discover the proper province of human reason. For, besides, that many persons find too sensible an interest in perpetually recalling such topics; besides this, I say, the motive of blind despair can never reasonably have place in the sciences; since, however unusccessful former attempts may have proved, there is still room to hope, that the industry, good fortune, or improved sagacity of succeeding generations may reach discoveries unknown to former ages. Each adventurous genius will leap at the arduous prize, and find himself stimulated, rather than discouraged, by the failures of his predecessors; while he hopes that the glory of achieving so hard an adventure is reserved for him alone. The only method of freeing learning, at once, from these abstruse questions, is to inquire seriously into the nature of human understanding, and show, from an exact analysis of its powers and capacity, that it is by no means fitted for such remote and abstruse subjects. We must submit to this fatigue, in order to live at ease ever after: And must cultivate true metaphysics with some care, in order to destroy the false and adulterate. Indolence, which, to some persons, affords a safeguard against this deceitful philosophy, is, with others, over-balanced by curiosity; and despair, which, at some moments, prevails, may give place afterwards to sanguine hopes and expectations. Accurate and just reasoning is the only catholic remedy, fitted for all persons and all dispositions; and is alone able to subvert that abstruse philosophy and metaphysical jargon, which, being mixed up with popular superstition, renders it in a manner impenetrable to careless reasoners, and gives it the air of science and wisdom.

Besides this advantage of rejecting, after deliberate inquiry, the most uncertain and disagreeable part of learning, there are many positive advantages, which result from an accurate scrutiny into the powers and faculties of human nature. It is remarkable concerning the operations of the mind, that, though most intimately present to us, yet, whenever they become the object of reflection, they seem involved in obscurity; nor can the eye readily find those lines and boundaries, which discriminate and distinguish them. The objects are too fine to remain long in the same aspect or situation; and must be apprehended in an instant, by a superior penetration, derived from nature, and improved by habit and reflection. It becomes, therefore, no inconsiderable part of science barely to know the different operations of the mind, to separate them from each other, to class them under their proper heads, and to correct all that seeming disorder, in which they lie involved, when made the object of reflection and inquiry. This talk of ordering and distinguishing, which has no merit, when performed with regard to external bodies, the objects of our senses, rises in its value, when directed towards the operations of the mind, in proportion to the difficulty and labor, which we meet with in performing it. And if we can go no farther than this mental geography, or delineation of the distinct parts and powers of the mind, it is at least a satisfaction to go so far; and the more obvious this science may appear (and it is by no means obvious) the more contemptible still must the ignorance of it be esteemed, in all pretenders to learning and philosophy.

Nor can there remain any suspicion, that this science is uncertain and chimerical; unless we should entertain such a scepticism as is entirely subversive of all speculation, and even action. It cannot be doubted, that the mind is endowed with several powers and faculties, that these powers are distinct from each other, that what is really distinct to the immediate perception may be distinguished by reflection; and consequently, that there is a truth and falsehood in all propositions on this subject, and a truth and falsehood, which lie not beyond the compass of human understanding. There are many obvious distinctions of this kind, such as those between the will and understanding, the imagination and passions, which fall within the comprehension of every human creature; and the finer and more philosophical distinctions are no less real and certain, though more difficult to be comprehended. Some instances, especially late ones, of success in these inquiries, may give us a juster notion of the certainty and solidity of this branch of learning. And shall we esteem it worthy the labor of a philosopher to give us a true system of the planets, and adjust the position and order of those remote bodies; while we affect to overlook those, who, with so much success, delineate the parts of the mind, in which we are so intimately concerned?

But may we not hope, that philosophy, if cultivated with care, and encouraged by the attention of the public, may carry its researches still farther, and discover, at least in some degree, the secret springs and principles, by which the human mind is actuated in its operations? Astronomers had long contented themselves with proving, from the phenomena, the true motions, order, and magnitude of the heavenly bodies: Till a philosopher, at last, arose, who seems, from the happiest reasoning, to have also determined the laws and forces, by which the revolutions of the planets are governed and directed. The like has been performed with regard to other parts of nature. And there is no reason to despair of equal success in our inquiries concerning the mental powers and economy, if prosecuted with equal capacity and caution. It is probable, that one operation and principle of the mind depends on another; which, again, may be resolved into one more general and universal: And how far these researches may possibly be carried, it will be difficult for us, before, or even after, a careful trial, exactly to determine. This is certain, that attempts of this kind are every day made even by those who philosophize the most negligently: And nothing can be more requisite than to enter upon the enterprise with thorough care and attention; that, if it lie within the compass of human understanding, it may at last be happily achieved; if not, it may, however, be rejected with some confidence and security. This last conclusion, surely, is not desirable; nor ought it to be embraced too rashly. For how much must we diminish from the beauty and value of this species of philosophy, upon such a supposition?

Moralists have hitherto been accustomed, when they considered the vast multitude and diversity of those actions that excite our approbation or dislike, to search for some common principle, on which this variety of sentiments might depend. And though they have sometimes carried the matter too far, by their passion for some one general principle; it must, however, be confessed, that they are excusable in expecting to find some general principles, into which all the vices and virtues were justly to be resolved. The like has been the endeavor of critics, logicians, and even politicians: Nor have their attempts been wholly unsuccessful; though perhaps longer time, greater accuracy, and more ardent application may bring these sciences still nearer their perfection. To throw up at once all pretensions of this kind may justly be deemed more rash, precipitate, and dogmatical, than even the boldest and most affirmative philosophy, that has ever attempted to impose its crude dictates and principles on mankind.

What though these reasonings concerning human nature seem abstract, and of difficult comprehension? This affords no presumption of their falsehood. On the contrary, it seems impossible, that what has hitherto escaped so many wise and profound philosophers can be very obvious and easy. And whatever pains these researches may cost us, we may think ourselves sufficiently rewarded, not only in point of profit but of pleasure, if, by that means, we can make any addition to our stock of knowledge, in subjects of such unspeakable importance.

But as, after all, the abstractedness of these speculations is no recommendation, but rather a disadvantage to them, and as this difficulty may perhaps be surmounted by care and art, and the avoiding of all unnecessary detail, we have, in the following inquiry, attempted to throw some light upon subjects, from which uncertainty has hitherto deterred the wise, and obscurity the ignorant. Happy, if we can unite the boundaries of the different species of philosophy, by reconciling profound inquiry with clearness, and truth with novelty! And still more happy, if reasoning in this easy manner, we can undermine the foundations of an abstruse philosophy, which seems to have hitherto served only as a shelter to superstition, and a cover to absurdity and error!

SECTION II

OF THE ORIGIN OF IDEAS

Everyone will readily allow that there is a considerable difference between the perceptions of the mind, when a man feels the pain of excessive heat, or the pleasure of moderate warmth, and when he afterwards recalls to his memory this sensation, or anticipates it by his imagination. These faculties may mimic or copy the perceptions of the senses; but they never can entirely reach the force and vivacity of the original sentiment. The utmost we say of them, even when they operate with greatest vigor, is, that they represent their object in so lively a manner, that we could *almost* say we feel or see it: But, except the mind be disordered by disease or madness, they never can arrive at such a pitch of vivacity, as to render these perceptions altogether undistinguishable. All the colors of poetry, however splendid, can never paint natural objects in such a manner as to make the description be taken for a real landscape. The most lively thought is still inferior to the dullest sensation.

We may observe a like distinction to run through all the other perceptions of the mind. A man in a fit of anger, is actuated in a very different manner from one who only thinks of that emotion. If you tell me, that any person is in love, I easily understand your meaning, and form a just conception of his situation; but never can mistake that conception for the real disorders and agitations of the passion. When we reflect on our past sentiments and affections, our thought is a faithful mirror, and copies its objects truly; but the colors which it employs are faint and dull, in comparison of those in which our original perceptions were clothed. It requires no nice discernment or metaphysical head to mark the distinction between them.

Here therefore we may divide all the perceptions of the mind into two classes or species, which are distinguished by their different degrees of force and vivacity. The less forcible and lively are commonly denominated *thoughts* or *ideas*. The other species want a name in our language, and in most others;

I suppose, because it was not requisite for any, but philosophical purposes, to rank them under a general term or appellation. Let us, therefore, use a little freedom, and call them *impressions;* employing that word in a sense somewhat different from the usual. By the term *impression,* then, I mean all our more lively perceptions, when we hear, or see, or feel, or love, or hate, or desire, or will. And impressions are distinguished from ideas, which are the less lively perceptions, of which we are conscious, when we reflect on any of those sensations or movements above mentioned.

Nothing, at first view, may seem more unbounded than the thought of man, which not only escapes all human power and authority, but is not even restrained within the limits of nature and reality. To form monsters, and join incongruous shapes and appearances, costs the imagination no more trouble than to conceive the most natural and familiar objects. And while the body is confined to one planet, along which it creeps with pain and difficulty; the thought can in an instant transport us into the most distant regions of the universe; or even beyond the universe, into the unbounded chaos, where nature is supposed to lie in total confusion. What never was seen, or heard of, may yet be conceived; nor is anything beyond the power of thought, except what implies an absolute contradiction.

But though our thought seems to possess this unbounded liberty, we shall find, upon a nearer examination, that it is really confined within very narrow limits, and that all this creative power of the mind amounts to no more than the faculty of compounding, transposing, augmenting, or diminishing the materials afforded us by the senses and experience. When we think of a golden mountain, we only join two consistent ideas, *gold,* and *mountain,* with which we were formerly acquainted. A virtuous horse we can conceive; because, from our own feeling, we can conceive virtue; and this we may unite to the figure and shape of a horse, which is an animal familiar to us. In short, all the materials of thinking are derived either from our outward or inward sentiment: the mixture and composition of these belongs alone to the mind and will. Or, to express myself in philosophical language, all our ideas or more feeble perceptions are copies of our impressions or more lively ones.

To prove this, the two following arguments will, I hope, be sufficient. First, when we analyze our thoughts or ideas, however compounded or sublime, we always find that they resolve themselves into such simple ideas as were copied from a precedent feeling or sentiment. Even those ideas, which, at first view, seem the most wide of this origin, are found, upon a nearer scrutiny, to be derived from it. The idea of God, as meaning an infinitely intelligent, wise, and good Being, arises from reflecting on the operations of our own mind, and augmenting, without limit, those qualities of goodness and wisdom. We may prosecute this inquiry to what length we please; where we shall always find, that every idea which we examine is copied from a similar impression. Those who would assert that this position is not universally true nor without exception, have only one, and that an easy method of refuting it; by producing that idea, which, in their opinion, is not derived from this source. It will then be incumbent on us, if we would maintain our doctrine, to produce the impression, or lively perception, which corresponds to it.

Secondly. If it happen, from a defect of the organ, that a man is not susceptible of any species of sensation, we always find that he is as little susceptible of the correspondent ideas. A blind man can form no notion of colors; a deaf man of sounds. Restore either of them that sense in which he is deficient; by opening this new inlet for his sensations, you also open an inlet for the ideas; and he finds no difficulty in conceiving these objects. The case is the same, if the object, proper for exciting any sensation, has never been applied to the organ. A Laplander or Negro has no notion of the relish of wine. And though there are few or no instances of a like deficiency in the mind, where a person has never felt or is wholly incapable of a sentiment or passion that belongs to his species; yet we find the same observation to take place in a less degree. A man of mild manners can form no idea of inveterate revenge or cruelty; nor can a selfish heart easily conceive the heights of friendship and generosity. It is readily allowed, that other beings may possess many senses of which we can have no conception; because the ideas of them have never been introduced to us in the only manner by which an idea can have access to the mind, to wit, by the actual feeling and sensation.

There is, however, one contradictory phenomenon, which may prove that it is not absolutely impossible for ideas to arise, independent of their correspondent impressions. I believe it will readily be allowed, that the several distinct ideas of color, which enter by the eye, or those of sound, which are conveyed by the ear, are really different from each other; though, at the same time, resembling. Now if this be true of different colors, it must be no less so of the different shades of the same color; and each shade produces a distinct idea, independent of the rest. For if this should be denied, it is possible, by the continual gradation of shades, to run a color insensibly into what is most remote from it; and if you will not allow any of the means to be different, you cannot, without absurdity, deny the extremes to be the same. Suppose, therefore, a person to have enjoyed his sight for thirty years, and to have become perfectly acquainted with colors of all kinds except one particular shade of blue, for instance, which it never has been his fortune to meet with. Let all the different shades of that color, except that single one, be placed before him, descending gradually from the deepest to the lightest; it is plain that he will perceive a blank, where that shade is wanting, and will be sensible that there is a greater distance in that place between the contiguous colors than in any other. Now I ask, whether it be possible for him, from his own imagination, to supply this deficiency, and raise up to himself the idea of that particular shade, though it had never been conveyed to him by his senses? I believe there are few but will be of opinion that he can: and this may serve as a proof that the simple ideas are not always, in every instance, derived from the correspondent impressions; though this instance is so singular, that it is scarcely worth our observing, and does not merit that for it alone we should alter our general maxim.

Here, therefore, is a proposition, which not only seems, in itself, simple and intelligible; but, if a proper use were made of it, might render every dispute equally intelligible, and banish all that jargon, which has so long taken possession of metaphysical reasonings, and drawn disgrace upon them. All ideas, especially abstract ones, are naturally faint and obscure: the mind has but a slender hold of them: they are apt to be confounded with other resembling ideas; and when we have often employed any term, though without a distinct meaning, we are apt to imagine it has a determinate idea annexed to it. On the contrary, all impressions, that is, all sensations, either outward or inward, are strong and vivid: the limits between them are more exactly determined: nor is it easy to fall into any error or mistake with regard to them. When we entertain, therefore, any suspicion that a philosophical term is employed without any meaning or idea (as is but too frequent), we need but inquire, *from what impression is that supposed idea derived?* And if it be impossible to assign any, this will serve to confirm our suspicion.[1] By bringing ideas into so clear a light we may reasonably hope to remove all dispute, which may arise, concerning their nature and reality.

words must have ideas behind them or they have no meaning

SECTION III

OF THE ASSOCIATION OF IDEAS

It is evident that there is a principle of connection between the different thoughts or ideas of the mind, and that, in their appearance to the memory or imagination, they introduce each other with a certain degree of method and regularity. In

[1] It is probable that no more was meant by those, who denied innate ideas, than that all ideas were copies of our impressions; though it must be confessed, that the terms, which they employed, were not chosen with such caution, nor so exactly defined, as to prevent all mistakes about their doctrine. For what is meant by *innate?* If innate be equivalent to natural, then all the perceptions and ideas of the mind must be allowed to be innate or natural, in whatever sense we take the latter word, whether in opposition to what is uncommon, artificial, or miraculous. If by innate be meant, contemporary to our birth, the dispute seems to be frivolous; nor is it worth while to inquire at what time thinking begins, whether before, at, or after our birth. Again, the word *idea,* seems to be commonly taken in a very loose sense, by Locke and others; as standing for any of our perceptions, our sensations and passions, as well as thoughts. Now in this sense, I should desire to know, what can be meant by asserting, that self-love, or resentment of injuries, or the passion between the sexes is not innate?

But admitting these terms, *impressions* and *ideas,* in the sense above explained, and understanding by *innate,* what is original or copied from no precedent perception, then may we assert that all our impressions are innate and our ideas not innate.

To be ingenuous, I must own it to be my opinion, that Locke was betrayed into this question by the schoolmen, who, making use of undefined terms, draw out their disputes to a tedious length, without ever touching the point in question. A like ambiguity and circumlocution seem to run through that philosopher's reasonings on this as well as most other subjects.

our more serious thinking or discourse this is so observable that any particular thought, which breaks in upon the regular tract or chain of ideas, is immediately remarked and rejected. And even in our wildest and most wandering reveries, nay in our very dreams, we shall find, if we reflect, that the imagination ran not altogether at adventures, but that there was still a connection upheld among the different ideas, which succeeded each other. Were the loosest and freest conversation to be transcribed, there would immediately be observed something which connected it in all its transitions. Or where this is wanting, the person who broke the thread of discourse might still inform you, that there had secretly revolved in his mind a succession of thought, which had gradually led him from the subject of conversation. Among different languages, even where we cannot suspect the least connection or communication, it is found, that the words, expressive of ideas, the most compounded, do yet nearly correspond to each other: a certain proof that the simple ideas, comprehended in the compound ones, were bound together by some universal principle, which had an equal influence on all mankind.

Though it be too obvious to escape observation, that different ideas are connected together; I do not find that any philosopher has attempted to enumerate or class all the principles of association; a subject, however, that seems worthy of curiosity. To me, there appear to be only three principles of connection among ideas, namely, *resemblance*, *contiguity* in time or place, and *cause* or *effect*.

That these principles serve to connect ideas will not, I believe, be much doubted. A picture naturally leads our thoughts to the original:[2] the mention of one apartment in a building naturally introduces an inquiry or discourse concerning the others:[3] and if we think of a wound, we can scarcely forbear reflecting on the pain which follows it.[4] But that this enumeration is complete, and that there are no other principles of association except these, may be difficult to prove to the satisfaction of the reader, or even to a man's own satisfaction. All we can do, in such cases, is to run over several instances, and examine carefully the principle which binds the different thoughts to each other, never stopping till we render the prin-

[2] Resemblance.
[3] Contiguity.
[4] Cause and effect.

ciple as general as possible.[5] The more instances we examine, and the more care we employ, the more assurance shall we acquire, that the enumeration, which we form from the whole, is complete and entire.

SECTION IV

SCEPTICAL DOUBTS CONCERNING THE OPERATIONS OF THE UNDERSTANDING

Part I

All the objects of human reason or inquiry may naturally be divided into two kinds, to wit, *relations of ideas*, and *matters of fact.* Of the first kind are the sciences of geometry, algebra, and arithmetic; and in short, every affirmation which is either intuitively or demonstratively certain. *That the square of the hypothenuse is equal to the squares of the two sides*, is a proposition which expresses a relation between these figures. *That three times five is equal to the half of thirty*, expresses a relation between these numbers. Propositions of this kind are discoverable by the mere operation of thought, without dependence on what is anywhere existent in the universe. Though there never was a circle or triangle in nature, the truths demonstrated by Euclid would for ever retain their certainty and evidence.

Matters of fact, which are the second objects of human reason, are not ascertained in the same manner; nor is our evidence of their truth, however great, of a like nature with the foregoing. The contrary of every matter of fact is still possible; because it can never imply a contradiction, and is conceived by the mind with the same facility and distinctness, as if ever so comformable to reality. *That the sun will not rise tomorrow* is no less intelligible a proposition, and implies

[5] For instance, *contrast* or *contrariety* is also a connection among ideas but it may, perhaps, be considered as a mixture of *causation* and *resemblance*. Where two objects are contrary, the one destroys the other; that is, the cause of its annihilation and the idea of the annihilation of an object implies the idea of its former existence.

no more contradiction than the affirmation, *that it will rise.* We should in vain, therefore, attempt to demonstrate its falsehood. Were it demonstratively false, it would imply a contradiction, and could never be distinctly conceived by the mind.

It may, therefore, be a subject worthy of curiosity, to inquire what is the nature of that evidence which assures us of any real existence and matter of fact, beyond the present testimony of our senses, or the records of our memory. This part of philosophy, it is observable, has been little cultivated, either by the ancients or moderns; and therefore our doubts and errors, in the prosecution of so important an inquiry, may be the more excusable; while we march through such difficult paths without any guide or direction. They may even prove useful, by exciting curiosity, and destroying that implicit faith and security, which is the bane of all reasoning and free inquiry. The discovery of defects in the common philosophy, if any such there be, will not, I presume, be a discouragement, but rather an incitment, as is usual, to attempt something more full and satisfactory than has yet been proposed to the public.

All reasonings concerning matter of fact seem to be founded on the relation of *cause and effect*. By means of that relation alone we can go beyond the evidence of our memory and senses. If you were to ask a man, why he believes any matter of fact, which is absent; for instance, that his friend is in the country, or in France; he would give you a reason; and this reason would be some other fact; as a letter received from him, or the knowledge of his former resolutions and promises. A man finding a watch or any other machine in a desert island, would conclude that there had once been men in that island. All our reasonings concerning fact are of the same nature. And here it is constantly supposed that there is a connection between the present fact and that which is inferred from it. Were there nothing to bind them together, the inference would be entirely precarious. The hearing of an articulate voice and rational discourse in the dark assures us of the presence of some person: Why? because these are the effects of the human make and fabric, and closely connected with it. If we anatomize all the other reasonings of this nature, we shall find that they are founded on the relation of cause and effect, and that this relation is either near or remote, direct or collateral. Heat and light are collateral effects of fire, and the one effect may justly be inferred from the other.

If we would satisfy ourselves, therefore, concerning the nature of that evidence, which assures us of matters of fact, we must inquire how we arrive at the knowledge of cause and effect.

I shall venture to affirm, as a general proposition, which admits of no exception, that the knowledge of this relation is not, in any instance, attained by reasonings *a priori*; but arises entirely from experience, when we find that any particular objects are constantly conjoined with each other. Let an object be presented to a man of ever so strong natural reason and abilities; if that object be entirely new to him, he will not be able, by the most accurate examination of its sensible qualities, to discover any of its causes or effects. Adam, though his rational faculties be supposed, at the very first, entirely perfect, could not have inferred from the fluidity and transparency of water that it would suffocate him, or from the light and warmth of fire that it would consume him. No object ever discovers, by the qualities which appear to the senses, either the causes which produced it, or the effects which will arise from it; nor can our reason, unassisted by experience, ever draw any inference concerning real existence and matter of fact.

This proposition, *that causes and effects are discoverable, not by reason but by experience*, will readily be admitted with regard to such objects, as we remember to have once been altogether unknown to us; since we must be conscious of the utter inability, which we then lay under, of foretelling what would arise from them. Present two smooth pieces of marble to a man who has no tincture of natural philosophy; he will never discover that they will adhere together in such a manner as to require great force to separate them in a direct line, while they make so small a resistance to a lateral pressure. Such events, as bear little analogy to the common course of nature, are also readily confessed to be known only by experience; nor does any man imagine that the explosion of gunpowder, or the attraction of a loadstone, could ever be discovered by arguments *a priori*. In like manner, when an effect is supposed to depend upon an intricate machinery or secret structure of parts, we make no difficulty in attributing all our knowledge of it to experience. Who will assert that he can give the ultimate reason, why milk or bread is proper nourishment for a man, not for a lion or a tiger?

But the same truth may not appear, at first sight, to have the same evidence with regard to events, which have become familiar to us from our first appearance in the world, which bear a close analogy to the whole course of nature, and which are supposed to depend on the simple qualities of objects, without any secret structure of parts. We are apt to imagine that we could discover these effects by the mere operation of our reason, without experience. We fancy, that were we brought on a sudden into this world, we could at first have inferred that one billiard ball would communicate motion to another upon impulse; and that we needed not to have waited for the event, in order to pronounce with certainty concerning it. Such is the influence of custom, that, where it is strongest, it not only covers our natural ignorance, but even conceals itself, and seems not to take place, merely because it is found in the highest degree.

But to convince us that all the laws of nature, and all the operations of bodies without exception, are known only by experience, the following reflections may, perhaps, suffice. Were any object presented to us, and were we required to pronounce concerning the effect, which will result from it, without consulting past observation; after what manner, I beseech you, must the mind proceed in this operation? It must invent or imagine some event, which it ascribes to the object as its effect; and it is plain that this invention must be entirely arbitrary. The mind can never possibly find the effect in the supposed cause, by the most accurate scrutiny and examination. For the effect is totally different from the cause, and consequently can never be discovered in it. Motion in the second billiard ball is a quite distinct event from motion in the first: nor is there anything in the one to suggest the smallest hint of the other. A stone or piece of metal raised into the air, and left without any support, immediately falls: but to consider the matter *a priori*, is there anything we discover in this situation which can beget the idea of a downward, rather than an upward, or any other motion, in the stone or metal?

And as the first imagination or invention of a particular effect, in all natural operations, is arbitrary, where we consult not experience; so must we also esteem the supposed tie or connection between the cause and effect, which binds them together, and renders it impossible that any other effect could result from the operation of that cause. When I see, for instance, a billiard ball moving in a straight line towards another; even suppose motion in the second ball should by accident be suggested to me, as the result of their contact or impulse; may I not conceive, that a hundred different events might as well follow from that cause? May not both these balls remain at absolute rest? May not the first ball return in a straight line, or leap off from the second in any line or direction? All these suppositions are consistent and conceivable. Why then should we give the preference to one, which is no more consistent or conceivable than the rest? All our reasonings *a priori* will never be able to show us any foundation for this preference.

In a word, then, every effect is a distinct event from its cause. It could not, therefore, be discovered in the cause, and the first invention or conception of it, *a priori*, must be entirely arbitrary. And even after it is suggested, the conjunction of it with the cause must appear equally arbitrary; since there are always many other effects, which, to reason, must seem fully as consistent and natural. In vain, therefore, should we pretend to determine any single event, or infer any cause or effect, without the assistance of observation and experience.

Hence we may discover the reason why no philosopher, who is rational and modest, has ever pretended to assign the ultimate cause of any natural operation, or to show distinctly the action of that power, which produces any single effect in the universe. It is confessed, that the utmost effort of human reason is to reduce the principles, productive of natural phenomena, to a greater simplicity, and to resolve the many particular effects into a few general causes, by means of reasonings from analogy, experience, and observation. But as to the causes of these general causes, we should in vain attempt their discovery; nor shall we ever be able to satisfy ourselves, by any particular explication of them. These ultimate springs and principles are totally shut up from human curiosity and inquiry. Elasticity, gravity, cohesion of parts, communication of motion by impulse; these are probably the ultimate causes and principles which we ever discover in nature; and we may esteem ourselves sufficiently happy, if, by accurate inquiry and reasoning, we can trace up the particular phenomena to, or near to, these general principles. The most perfect philosophy of the natural kind only staves off our ignorance a little longer:

as perhaps the most perfect philosophy of the moral or metaphysical kind serves only to discover larger portions of it. Thus the observation of human blindness and weakness is the result of all philosophy, and meets us at every turn, in spite of our endeavors to elude or avoid it.

Nor is geometry, when taken into the assistance of natural philosophy, ever able to remedy this defect, or lead us into the knowledge of ultimate causes, by all that accuracy of reasoning for which it is so justly celebrated. Every part of mixed mathematics proceeds upon the supposition that certain laws are established by nature in her operations; and abstract reasonings are employed, either to assist experience in the discovery of these laws, or to determine their influence in particular instances, where it depends upon any precise degree of distance and quantity. Thus, it is a law of motion, discovered by experience, that the moment or force of any body in motion is in the compound ratio or proportion of its solid contents and its velocity; and consequently, that a small force may remove the greatest obstacle or raise the greatest weight, if, by any contrivance or machinery, we can increase the velocity of that force, so as to make it an overmatch for its antagonist. Geometry assists us in the application of this law, by giving us the just dimensions of all the parts and figures which can enter into any species of machine; but still the discovery of the law itself is owing merely to experience, and all the abstract reasonings in the world could never lead us one step towards the knowledge of it. When we reason *a priori*, and consider merely any object or cause, as it appears to the mind, independent of all observation, it never could suggest to us the notion of any distinct object, such as its effect; much less, show us the inseparable and inviolable connection between them. A man must be very sagacious who could discover by reasoning that crystal is the effect of heat, and ice of cold, without being previously acquainted with the operation of these qualities.

Part II

But we have not yet attained any tolerable satisfaction with regard to the question first proposed. Each solution still gives rise to a new question as difficult as the foregoing, and leads us on to farther inquiries. When it is asked, *What is the nature of all our reasonings concerning matter of fact?* the proper answer seems to be, that they are founded on the relation of cause and effect. When again it is asked, *What is the foundation of all our reasonings and conclusions concerning that relation?* it may be replied in one word, *experience.* But if we still carry on our sifting humor, and ask, *What is the foundation of all conclusions from experience?* this implies a new question, which may be of more difficult solution and explication. Philosophers, that give themselves airs of superior wisdom and sufficiency, have a hard task when they encounter persons of inquisitive dispositions, who push them from every corner to which they retreat, and who are sure at last to bring them to some dangerous dilemma. The best expedient to prevent this confusion, is to be modest in our pretensions; and even to discover the difficulty ourselves before it is objected to us. By this means, we may make a kind of merit of our very ignorance.

I shall content myself, in this section, with an easy task, and shall pretend only to give a negative answer to the question here proposed. I say then, that, even after we have experience of the operations of cause and effect, our conclusions from that experience are *not* founded on reasoning, or any process of the understanding. This answer we must endeavor both to explain and to defend.

It must certainly be allowed, that nature has kept us at a great distance from all her secrets, and has afforded us only the knowledge of a few superficial qualities of objects; while she conceals from us those powers and principles on which the influence of those objects entirely depends. Our senses inform us of the color, weight, and consistence of bread; but neither sense nor reason can ever inform us of those qualities which fit it for the nourishment and support of a human body. Sight or feeling conveys an idea of the actual motion of bodies; but as to that wonderful force or power, which would carry on a moving body for ever in a continued change of place, and which bodies never lose but by communicating it to others; of this we cannot form the most distant conception. But notwithstanding this ignorance of natural powers[6] and principles, we always presume, when we see like sensible quali-

[6] The word, *power,* is here used in a loose and popular sense. The more accurate explication of it would give additional evidence to this argument. See Sect. 7.

ties, that they have like secret powers, and expect that effects, similar to those which we have experienced, will follow from them. If a body of like color and consistence with that bread, which we have formerly eat, be presented to us, we make no scruple of repeating the experiment, and foresee, with certainty, like nourishment and support. Now this is a process of the mind or thought, of which I would willingly know the foundation. It is allowed on all hands that there is no known connection between the sensible qualities and the secret powers; and consequently, that the mind is not led to form such a conclusion concerning their constant and regular conjunction, by anything which it knows of their nature. As to past *experience*, it can be allowed to give *direct* and *certain* information of those precise objects only, and that precise period of time, which fell under its cognizance: but why this experience should be extended to future times, and to other objects, which, for aught we know, may be only in appearance similar; this is the main question on which I would insist. The bread, which I formerly eat, nourished me; that is, a body of such sensible qualities was, at that time, endued with such secret powers: but does it follow, that other bread must also nourish me at another time, and that like sensible qualities must always be attended with like secret powers? The consequence seems no wise necessary. At least, it must be acknowledged that there is here a consequence drawn by the mind; that there is a certain step taken; a process of thought, and an inference, which wants to be explained. These two propositions are far from being the same, *I have found that such an object has always been attended with such an effect*, and *I foresee, that other objects, which are, in appearance, similar, will be attended with similar effects*. I shall allow, if you please, that the one proposition may justly be inferred from the other; I know, in fact, that it always is inferred. But if you insist that the inference is made by a chain of reasoning, I desire you to produce that reasoning. The connection between these propositions is not intuitive. There is required a medium, which may enable the mind to draw such an inference, if indeed it be drawn by reasoning and argument. What that medium is, I must confess, passes my comprehension; and it is incumbent on those to produce it, who assert that it really exists, and is the origin of all our conclusions concerning matter of fact.

This negative argument must certainly, in process of time,

become altogether convincing, if many penetrating and able philosophers shall turn their inquiries this way and no one be ever able to discover any connecting proposition or intermediate step, which supports the understanding in this conclusion. But as the question is yet new, every reader may not trust so far to his own penetration, as to conclude, because an argument escapes his inquiry, that therefore it does not really exist. For this reason it may be requisite to venture upon a more difficult task; and enumerating all the branches of human knowledge, endeavor to show that none of them can afford such an argument.

All reasonings may be divided into two kinds, namely demonstrative reasoning, or that concerning relations of ideas, and moral reasoning, or that concerning matter of fact and existence. That there are no demonstrative arguments in the case seems evident; since it implies no contradiction that the course of nature may change, and that an object, seemingly like those which we have experienced, may be attended with different or contrary effects. May I not clearly and distinctly conceive that a body, falling from the clouds, and which, in all other respects, resembles snow, has yet the taste of salt or feeling of fire? Is there any more intelligible proposition than to affirm, that all the trees will flourish in December and January, and decay in May and June? Now whatever is intelligible, and can be distinctly conceived, implies no contradiction, and can never be proved false by any demonstrative argument or abstract reasoning *a priori.*

If we be, therefore, engaged by arguments to put trust in past experience, and make it the standard of our future judgment, these arguments must be probable only, or such as regard matter of fact and real existence, according to the division above mentioned. But that there is no argument of this kind, must appear, if our explication of that species of reasoning be admitted as solid and satisfactory. We have said that all arguments concerning existence are founded on the relation of cause and effect; that our knowledge of that relation is derived entirely from experience; and that all our experimental conclusions proceed upon the supposition that the future will be conformable to the past. To endeavor, therefore, the proof of this last supposition by probable arguments, or arguments regarding existence, must be evidently going in a circle, and taking that for granted, which is the very point in question.

In reality, all arguments from experience are founded on

the similarity which we discover among natural objects, and by which we are induced to expect effects similar to those which we have found to follow from such objects. And though none but a fool or madman will ever pretend to dispute the authority of experience, or to reject that great guide of human life, it may surely be allowed a philosopher to have so much curiosity at least as to examine the principle of human nature, which gives this mighty authority to experience, and makes us draw advantage from that similarity which nature has placed among different objects. From causes which appear *similar* we expect similar effects. This is the sum of all our experimental conclusions. Now it seems evident that, if this conclusion were formed by reason, it would be as perfect at first, and upon one instance, as after ever so long a course of experience. But the case is far otherwise. Nothing so like as eggs; yet no one, on account of this appearing similarity, expects the same taste and relish in all of them. It is only after a long course of uniform experiments in any kind, that we attain a firm reliance and security with regard to a particular event. Now where is that process of reasoning which, from one instance, draws a conclusion, so different from that which it infers from a hundred instances that are nowise different from that single one? This question I propose as much for the sake of information, as with an intention of raising difficulties. I cannot find, I cannot imagine any such reasoning. But I keep my mind still open to instruction, if anyone will vouchsafe to bestow it on me.

Should it be said that, from a number of uniform experiments, we *infer* a connection between the sensible qualities and the secret powers; this, I must confess, seems the same difficulty, couched in different terms. The question still recurs, on what process of argument this *inference* is founded? Where is the medium, the interposing ideas, which join propositions so very wide of each other? It is confessed that the color, consistence, and other sensible qualities of bread appear not, of themselves, to have any connection with the secret powers of nourishment and support. For otherwise we could infer these secret powers from the first appearance of these sensible qualities, without the aid of experience; contrary to the sentiment of all philosophers, and contrary to plain matter of fact. Here, then, is our natural state of ignorance with regard to the powers and influence of all objects. How is this remedied by experience? It only shows us a number of uniform effects, resulting from certain objects, and teaches us that those particular objects, at that particular time, were endowed with such powers and forces. When a new object, endowed with similar sensible qualities, is produced, we expect similar powers and forces, and look for a like effect. From a body of like color and consistence with bread we expect like nourishment and support. But this surely is a step or progress of the mind, which wants to be explained. When a man says, *I have found, in all past instances, such sensible qualities conjoined with such secret powers*: And when he says, *Similar sensible qualities will always be conjoined with similar secret powers*, he is not guilty of a tautology, nor are these propositions in any respect the same. You say that the one proposition is an inference from the other. But you must confess that the inference is not intuitive; neither is it demonstrative: Of what nature is it, then? To say it is experimental, is begging the question. For all inferences from experience suppose, as their foundation, that the future will resemble the past, and that similar powers will be conjoined with similar sensible qualities. If there be any suspicion that the course of nature may change, and that the past may be no rule for the future, all experience becomes useless, and can give rise to no inference or conclusion. It is impossible, therefore, that any arguments from experience can prove this resemblance of the past to the future; since all these arguments are founded on the supposition of that resemblance. Let the course of things be allowed hitherto ever so regular; that alone, without some new argument or inference, proves not that, for the future, it will continue so. In vain do you pretend to have learned the nature of bodies from your past experience. Their secret nature, and consequently all their effects and influence, may change, without any change in their sensible qualities. This happens sometimes, and with regard to some objects: Why may it not happen always, and with regard to all objects? What logic, what process of argument secures you against this supposition? My practice, you say, refutes my doubts. But you mistake the purport of my question. As an agent, I am quite satisfied in the point; but as a philosopher, who has some share of curiosity, I will not say scepticism, I want to learn the foundation of this inference. No reading, no inquiry has yet been able to remove my difficulty, or give me satisfaction in a matter of such importance. Can I do better than propose the difficulty to the public, even though, perhaps, I have small hopes of obtaining a solution? We shall, at least, by this means, be sensible of our ignorance, if we do not augment our knowledge.

I must confess that a man is guilty of unpardonable arrogance who concludes, because an argument has escaped his own investigation, that therefore it does not really exist. I must also confess that, though all the learned, for several ages, should have employed themselves in fruitless search upon any subject, it may still, perhaps, be rash to conclude positively that the subject must, therefore, pass all human comprehension. Even though we examine all the sources of our knowledge, and conclude them unfit for such a subject, there may still remain a suspicion, that the enumeration is not complete, or the examination not accurate. But with regard to the present subject, there are some considerations which seem to remove all this accusation of arrogance or suspicion of mistake.

It is certain that the most ignorant and stupid peasants—nay infants, nay even brute beasts—improve by experience, and learn the qualities of natural objects, by observing the effects which result from them. When a child has felt the sensation of pain from touching the flame of a candle, he will be careful not to put his hand near any candle; but will expect a similar effect from a cause which is similar in its sensible qualities and appearance. If you assert, therefore, that the understanding of the child is led into this conclusion by any process of argument or ratiocination, I may justly require you to produce that argument; nor have you any pretense to refuse so equitable a demand. You cannot say that the argument is abstruse, and may possibly escape your inquiry; since you confess that it is obvious to the capacity of a mere infant. If you hesitate, therefore, a moment, or if, after reflection, you produce any intricate or profound argument, you, in a manner, give up the question, and confess that it is not reasoning which engages us to suppose the past resembling the future, and to expect similar effects from causes which are, to appearance, similar. This is the proposition which I intended to enforce in the present section. If I be right, I pretend not to have made any mighty discovery. And if I be wrong, I must acknowledge myself to be indeed a very backward scholar; since I cannot now discover an argument which, it seems, was perfectly familiar to me long before I was out of my cradle.

SECTION V

SCEPTICAL SOLUTION OF THESE DOUBTS

Part I

The passion for philosophy, like that for religion, seems liable to this inconvenience, that, though it aims at the correction of our manners, and extirpation of our vices, it may only serve, by imprudent management, to foster a predominant inclination, and push the mind, with more determined resolution, towards that side which already *draws* too much, by the bias and propensity of the natural temper. It is certain that, while we aspire to the magnanimous firmness of the philosophic sage, and endeavor to confine our pleasures altogether within our own minds, we may, at last, render our philosophy like that of Epictetus, and other *stoics*, only a more refined system of selfishness, and reason ourselves out of all virtue as well as social enjoyment. While we study with attention the vanity of human life, and turn all our thoughts towards the empty and transitory nature of riches and honors, we are, perhaps, all the while flattering our natural indolence, which, hating the bustle of the world, and drudgery of business, seeks a pretense of reason to give itself a full and uncontrolled indulgence. There is, however, one species of philosophy which seems little liable to this inconvenience, and that because it strikes in with no disorderly passion of the human mind, nor can mingle itself with any natural affection or propensity; and that is the *academic* or *sceptical* philosophy. The academics always talk of doubt and suspense of judgment, of danger in hasty determinations, of confining to very narrow bounds the inquiries of the understanding, and of renouncing all speculations which lie not within the limits of common life and practice. Nothing, therefore, can be more contrary than such a philosophy to the supine indolence of the mind, its rash arrogance, its lofty pretensions, and its superstitious credulity. Every passion is mortified by it, except the love of truth; and that passion never is, nor can be, carried to too high a degree. It is surprising, therefore, that this philosophy, which, in almost every instance, must be harmless and innocent, should be the subject of so much groundless reproach and obloquy. But, perhaps, the very circumstance which renders it so innocent is what chiefly exposes it to the public hatred and resentment. By flattering no irregular passion, it gains few partisans: By opposing so many vices and follies, it raises to itself abundance of enemies, who stigmatize it as libertine, profane, and irreligious.

Nor need we fear that this philosophy, while it endeavors to limit our inquiries to common life, should ever undermine the reasonings of common life, and carry its doubts so far as to destroy all action, as well as speculation. Nature will always maintain her rights, and prevail in the end over any abstract reasoning whatsoever. Though we should conclude, for instance, as in the foregoing section, that, in all reasonings from experience, there is a step taken by the mind which is not supported by any argument or process of the understanding; there is no danger that these reasonings, on which almost all knowledge depends, will ever be affected by such a discovery. If the mind be not engaged by argument to make this step, it must be induced by some other principle of equal weight and authority; and that principle will preserve its influence as long as human nature remains the same. What that principle is may well be worth the pains of inquiry.

Suppose a person, though endowed with the strongest faculties of reason and reflection, to be brought on a sudden into this world; he would, indeed, immediately observe a continual succession of objects, and one event following another; but he would not be able to discover anything farther. He would not, at first, by any reasoning, be able to reach the idea of cause and effect; since the particular powers, by which all natural operations are performed, never appear to the senses; nor is it reasonable to conclude, merely because one event, in one instance, precedes another, that therefore the one is the cause, the other the effect. Their conjunction may be arbitrary and casual. There may be no reason to infer the existence of one from the appearance of the other. And in a word, such a person, without more experience, could never employ his conjecture or reasoning concerning any matter of fact, or be assured of anything beyond what was immediately present to his memory and senses.

Suppose, again, that he has acquired more experience, and has lived so long in the world as to have observed familiar objects or events to be constantly conjoined together; what is the consequence of this experience? He immediately infers the existence of one object from the appearance of the other. Yet he has not, by all his experience, acquired any idea or knowledge of the secret power by which the one object produces the other; nor is it, by any process of reasoning, he is engaged to draw this inference. But still he finds himself determined to draw it: And though he should be convinced that his understanding has no part in the operation, he would nevertheless continue in the same course of thinking. There is some other principle which determines him to form such a conclusion.

This principle is *custom* or *habit*. For wherever the repetition of any particular act or operation produces a propensity to renew the same act or operation, without being impelled by any reasoning or process of the understanding, we always say, that this propensity is the effect of *custom*. By employing that word, we pretend not to have given the ultimate reason of such a propensity. We only point out a principle of human nature, which is universally acknowledged, and which is well known by its effects. Perhaps we can push our inquiries no farther, or pretend to give the cause of this cause; but must rest contented with it as the ultimate principle, which we can assign, of all our conclusions from experience. It is sufficient satisfaction, that we can go so far, without repining at the narrowness of our faculties because they will carry us no farther. And it is certain we here advance a very intelligible proposition at least, if not a true one, when we assert that, after the constant conjunction of two objects—heat and flame, for instance, weight and solidity—we are determined by custom alone to expect the one from the appearance of the other. This hypothesis seems even the only one which explains the difficulty, why we draw, from a thousand instances, an inference which we are not able to draw from one instance, that is, in no respect, different from them. Reason is incapable of any such variation. The conclusions which it draws from considering one circle are the same which it would form upon surveying all the circles in the universe. But no man, having seen only one body move after being impelled by another, could infer that every other body will move after a like impulse. All inferences from experience, therefore, are effects of custom, not of reasoning.[7]

[7] Nothing is more useful than for writers, even, on *moral*, *political*, or *physical* subjects, to distinguish between *reason* and *experience*,

Custom, then, is the great guide of human life. It is that principle alone which renders our experience useful to us, and makes us expect, for the future, a similar train of events with those which have appeared in the past. Without the influence of custom, we should be entirely ignorant of every matter

---

and to suppose, that these species of argumentation are entirely different from each other. The former are taken for the mere result of our intellectual faculties, which, by considering *a priori* the nature of things, and examining the effects, that must follow from their operation, establish particular principles of science and philosophy. The latter are supposed to be derived entirely from sense and observation, by which we learn what has actually resulted from the operation of particular objects, and are thence able to infer, what will, for the future, result from them. Thus, for instance, the limitations and restraints of civil government, and a legal constitution, may be defended, either from *reason*, which reflecting on the great frailty and corruption of human nature, teaches, that no man can safely be trusted with unlimited authority; or from *experience* and history, which inform us of the enormous abuses, that ambition, in every age and country, has been found to make of so imprudent a confidence.

The same distinction between reason and experience is maintained in all our deliberations concerning the conduct of life; while the experienced statesman, general, physician, or merchant is trusted and followed; and the unpracticed novice, with whatever natural talents endowed, neglected and despised. Though it be allowed, that reason may form very plausible conjectures with regard to the consequences of such a particular conduct in such particular circumstances; it is still supposed imperfect, without the assistance of experience, which is alone able to give stability and certainly to the maxims, derived from study and reflection.

But notwithstanding that this distinction be thus universally received, both in the active and speculative scenes of life, I shall not scruple to pronounce, that it is, at bottom, erroneous, at least, superficial.

If we examine those arguments, which, in any of the sciences above mentioned, are supposed to be the mere effects of reasoning and reflection, they will be found to terminate, at last, in some general principle or conclusion, for which we can assign no reason but observation and experience. The only difference between them and those maxims, which are vulgarly esteemed the result of pure experience, is, that the former cannot be established without some process of thought, and some reflection on what we have observed, in order to distinguish its circumstances, and trace its consequences: Whereas in the latter, the experienced event is exactly and fully familiar to that which we infer as the result of any particular situa-

of fact beyond what is immediately present to the memory and senses. We should never know how to adjust means to ends, or to employ our natural powers in the production of any effect. There would be an end at once of all action, as well as of the chief part of speculation.

But here it may be proper to remark, that though our conclusions from experience carry us beyond our memory and senses, and assure us of matters of fact which happened in the most distant places and most remote ages, yet some fact must always be present to the senses or memory, from which we may first proceed in drawing these conclusions. A man, who should find in a desert country the remains of pompous buildings, would conclude that the country had, in ancient times, been cultivated by civilized inhabitants; but did nothing of this nature occur to him, he could never form such an inference. We learn the events of former ages from history; but then we must peruse the volumes in which this instruction is contained, and thence carry up our inferences from one

---

tion. The history of a Tiberius or a Nero makes us dread a like tyranny, were our monarchs freed from the restraints of laws and senates. But the observation of any fraud or cruelty in private life is sufficient, with the aid of a little thought, to give us the same apprehension; while it serves as an instance of the general corruption of human nature, and shows us the danger which we must incur by reposing an entire confidence in mankind. In both cases, it is experience which is ultimately the foundation of our inference and conclusion.

There is no man so young and unexperienced, as not to have formed, from observation, many general and just maxims concerning human affairs and the conduct of life; but it must be confessed, that, when a man comes to put these in practice, he will be extremely liable to error, till time and farther experience both enlarge these maxims, and teach him their proper use and application. In every situation or incident, there are many particular and seemingly minute circumstances, which the man of greatest talent is, at first, apt to overlook, though on them the justness of his conclusions, and consequently the prudence of his conduct, entirely depend. Not to mention, that, to a young beginner, the general observations and maxims occur not always on the proper occasions, nor can be immediately applied with due calmness and distinction. The truth is, an unexperienced reasoner could be no reasoner at all, were he absolutely unexperienced; and when we assign that character to anyone, we mean it only in a comparative sense, and suppose him possessed of experience, in a smaller and more imperfect degree.

testimony to another, till we arrive at the eyewitnesses and spectators of these distant events. In a word, if we proceed not upon some fact, present to the memory or senses, our reasonings would be merely hypothetical; and however the particular links might be connected with each other, the whole chain of inferences would have nothing to support it, nor could we ever, by its means, arrive at the knowledge of any real existence. If I ask why you believe any particular matter of fact, which you relate, you must tell me some reason; and this reason will be some other fact, connected with it. But as you cannot proceed after this manner, *in infinitum*, you must at last terminate in some fact, which is present to your memory or senses; or must allow that your belief is entirely without foundation.

What, then, is the conclusion of the whole matter? A simple one; though, it must be confessed, pretty remote from the common theories of philosophy. All belief of matter of fact or real existence is derived merely from some object, present to the memory or senses, and a customary conjunction between that and some other object. Or in other words; having found, in many instances, that any two kinds of objects—flame and heat, snow and cold—have always been conjoined together; if flame or snow be presented anew to the senses, the mind is carried by custom to expect heat or cold, and to *believe* that such a quality does exist, and will discover itself upon a nearer approach. This belief is the necessary result of placing the mind in such circumstances. It is an operation of the soul, when we are so situated, as unavoidable as to feel the passion of love, when we receive benefits; or hatred, when we meet with injuries. All these operations are a species of natural instincts, which no reasoning or process of the thought and understanding is able either to produce or to prevent.

At this point, it would be very allowable for us to stop our philosophical researches. In most questions we can never make a single step farther; and in all questions we must terminate here at last, after our most restless and curious inquiries. But still our curiosity will be pardonable, perhaps commendable, if it carry us on to still farther researches, and make us examine more accurately the nature of this *belief*, and of the *customary conjunction*, whence it is derived. By this means we may meet with some explications and analogies that will give satisfaction; at least to such as love the abstract sciences, and can be entertained with speculations, which, however accurate, may still retain a degree of doubt and uncertainty. As to readers of a different taste; the remaining part of this section is not calculated for them, and the following inquiries may well be understood, though it be neglected.

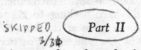

Part II

Nothing is more free than the imagination of man; and though it cannot exceed that original stock of ideas furnished by the internal and external senses, it has unlimited power of mixing, compounding, separating, and dividing these ideas, in all the varieties of fiction and vision. It can feign a train of events, with all the appearance of reality, ascribe to them a particular time and place, conceive them as existent, and paint them out to itself with every circumstance, that belongs to any historical fact, which it believes with the greatest certainty. Wherein, therefore, consists the difference between such a fiction and belief? It lies not merely in any peculiar idea, which is annexed to such a conception as commands our assent, and which is wanting to every known fiction. For as the mind has authority over all its ideas, it could voluntarily annex this particular idea to any fiction, and consequently be able to believe whatever it pleases; contrary to what we find by daily experience. We can, in our conception, join the head of a man to the body of a horse; but it is not in our power to believe that such an animal has ever really existed.

It follows, therefore, that the difference between *fiction* and *belief* lies in some sentiment or feeling, which is annexed to the latter, not to the former, and which depends not on the will, nor can be commanded at pleasure. It must be excited by nature, like all other sentiments; and must arise from the particular situation, in which the mind is placed at any particular juncture. Whenever any object is presented to the memory or senses, it immediately, by the force of custom, carries the imagination to conceive that object, which is usually conjoined to it; and this conception is attended with a feeling or sentiment, different from the loose reveries of the fancy. In this consists the whole nature of belief. For as there is no matter of fact which we believe so firmly that we cannot conceive the contrary, there would be no difference between the conception assented to and that which is rejected, were it not for some sentiment which distinguishes the one from the other. If I see a billiard ball moving towards another, on a smooth table, I can easily conceive it to stop upon contact. This conception implies no contradiction; but still it feels very differently from that conception by which I represent to myself the impulse and the communication of motion from one ball to another.

Were we to attempt a *definition* of this sentiment, we should, perhaps, find it a very difficult, if not an impossible task; in the same manner as if we should endeavor to define the feeling of cold or passion of anger, to a creature who never had any experience of these sentiments. Belief is the true and proper name of this feeling; and no one is ever at a loss to know the meaning of that term; because every man is every moment conscious of the sentiment represented by it. It may not, however, be improper to attempt a *description* of this sentiment; in hopes we may, by that means, arrive at some analogies, which may afford a more perfect explication of it. I say, then, that belief is nothing but a more vivid, lively, forcible, firm, steady conception of an object, than what the imagination alone is ever able to attain. This variety of terms, which may seem so unphilosophical, is intended only to express that act of the mind, which renders realities, or what is taken for such, more present to us than fictions, causes them to weigh more in the thought, and gives them a superior influence on the passions and imagination. Provided we agree about the thing, it is needless to dispute about the terms. The imagination has the command over all its ideas, and can join and mix and vary them, in all the ways possible. It may conceive fictitious objects with all the circumstances of place and time. It may set them, in a manner, before our eyes, in their true colors, just as they might have existed. But as it is impossible that this faculty of imagination can ever, of itself, reach belief, it is evident that belief consists not in the peculiar nature or order of ideas, but in the *manner* of their conception, and in their *feeling* to the mind. I confess, that it is impossible perfectly to explain this feeling or manner of conception. We may make use of words which express something near it. But its true and proper name, as we observed before, is *belief*; which is a term that every one sufficiently understands in common life. And in philosophy, we can go no farther than assert, that *belief* is something felt by the mind, which distinguishes the ideas of the judgment from the fictions of the imagination. It gives them more weight and influence; makes them appear of greater importance; enforces them in the mind; and renders them the governing principle of our actions. I hear at present, for instance, a person's voice, with whom I am acquainted; and the sound comes as from the next room. This impression of my senses immediately conveys my thought to the person, together with all the surrounding objects. I paint them out to myself as existing at present, with the same qualities and relations, of which I formerly knew them possessed. These ideas take faster hold of my mind than ideas of an enchanted castle. They are very different to the feeling, and have a much greater influence of every kind, either to give pleasure or pain, joy or sorrow.

Let us, then, take in the whole compass of this doctrine, and allow, that the sentiment of belief is nothing but a conception more intense and steady than what attends the mere fictions of the imagination, and that this *manner* of conception arises from a customary conjunction of the object with something present to the memory or senses: I believe that it will not be difficult, upon these suppositions, to find other operations of the mind analogous to it, and to trace up these phenomena to principles still more general.

We have already observed that nature has established connections among particular ideas, and that no sooner one idea occurs to our thoughts than it introduces its correlative, and carries our attention towards it, by a gentle and insensible movement. These principles of connection or association we have reduced to three, namely *resemblance*, *contiguity* and *causation*; which are the only bonds that unite our thoughts together, and beget that regular train of reflection or discourse, which, in a greater or less degree, takes place among mankind. Now here arises a question, on which the solution of the present difficulty will depend. Does it happen, in all these relations, that, when one of the objects is presented to the senses or memory, the mind is not only carried to the conception of the correlative, but reaches a steadier and stronger conception of it than what otherwise it would have been able to attain? This seems to be the case with that belief which arises from the relation of cause and effect. And if the case be the same with the other relations or principles of association, this may be established as a general law, which takes place in all the operations of the mind.

We may, therefore, observe, as the first experiment to our present purpose, that, upon the appearance of the picture of an absent friend, our idea of him is evidently enlivened by the *resemblance*, and that every passion, which that idea occasions, whether of joy or sorrow, acquires new force and vigor. In producing this effect, there concur both a relation and a present impression. Where the picture bears him no resemblance, at least was not intended for him, it never so much as conveys our thought to him: And where it is absent, as well as the person, though the mind may pass from the thought of the one to that of the other, it feels its idea to be rather weakened than enlivened by that transition. We take a pleasure in viewing the picture of a friend, when it is set before us; but when it is removed, rather choose to consider him directly than by reflection in an image, which is equally distant and obscure.

The ceremonies of the Roman Catholic religion may be considered as instances of the same nature. The devotees of that superstition usually plead in excuse for the mummeries, with which they were upbraided, that they feel the good effect of those external motions, and postures, and actions, in enlivening their devotion and quickening their fervor which otherwise would decay, if directed entirely to distant and immaterial objects. We shadow out the objects of our faith, say they, in sensible types and images, and render them more present to us by the immediate presence of these types, than it is possible for us to do merely by an intellectual view and contemplation. Sensible objects have always a greater influence on the fancy than any other; and this influence they readily convey to those ideas to which they are related, and which they resemble. I shall only infer from these practices, and this reasoning, that the effect of resemblance in enlivening the ideas is very common; and as in every case a resemblance and a present impression must concur, we are abundantly supplied with experiments to prove the reality of the foregoing principle.

We may add force to these experiments by others of a different kind, in considering the effects of *contiguity* as well as of *resemblance*. It is certain that distance diminishes the force of every idea, and that upon our approach to any object; though it does not discover itself to our senses; it operates upon the mind with an influence, which imitates an immediate impression. The thinking on any object readily transports the mind to what is contiguous; but it is only the actual presence of an object, that transports it with a superior vivacity. When I am a few miles from home, whatever relates to it touches me more nearly than when I am two hundred leagues distant; though even at that distance the reflecting on anything in the neighborhood of my friends or family naturally produces an idea of them. But as in this latter case, both the objects of the mind are ideas; notwithstanding there is an easy transition between them; that transition alone is not able to give a superior vivacity to any of the ideas, for want of some immediate impression.

No one can doubt but causation has the same influence as the other two relations of resemblance and contiguity. Superstitious people are fond of the relics of saints and holy men, for the same reason, that they seek after types or images, in order to enliven their devotion, and give them a more intimate and strong conception of those exemplary lives, which they desire to imitate. Now it is evident, that one of the best relics, which a devotee could procure, would be the handiwork of a saint; and if his clothes and furniture are ever to be considered in this light, it is because they were once at his disposal, and were moved and affected by him; in which respect they are to be considered as imperfect effects, and as connected with him by a shorter chain of consequences than any of those, by which we learn the reality of his existence.

Suppose, that the son of a friend, who had been long dead or absent, were presented to us; it is evident, that this object would instantly revive its correlative idea, and recall to our thoughts all past intimacies and familiarities, in more lively colors than they would otherwise have appeared to us. This is another phenomenon, which seems to prove the principle above mentioned.

We may observe, that, in these phenomena, the belief of the correlative object is always presupposed: without which the relation could have no effect. The influence of the picture supposes, that we *believe* our friend to have once existed. Contiguity to home can never excite our ideas of home, unless we *believe* that it really exists. Now I assert, that this belief, where it reaches beyond the memory or senses, is of a similar nature, and arises from similar causes, with the transition of thought and vivacity of conception here explained. When I throw a piece of dry wood into a fire, my mind is immediately carried to conceive, that it augments, not extinguishes the flame. This transition of thought from the cause to the effect proceeds not from reason. It derives its origin altogether from custom and experience. And as it first begins from an object, present to the senses, it renders the idea or conception of flame more strong and lively than any loose, floating reverie of the imagination. That idea arises immediately. The thought moves instantly towards it, and conveys to it all that force of conception, which is derived from the impression present to the senses. When a sword is leveled at my breast, does not the idea of wound and pain strike me more strongly, than when a glass of wine is presented to me, even though by accident this idea should occur after the appearance of the latter object? But what is there in this whole matter to cause such a strong conception, except only a present object and a customary transition to the idea of another object, which we have been accustomed to conjoin with the former? This is the whole operation of the mind, in all our conclusions concerning matter of fact and existence; and it is a satisfaction to find some analogies, by which it may be explained. The transition from a present object does in all cases give strength and solidity to the related idea.

Here, then, is a kind of pre-established harmony between the course of nature and the succession of our ideas; and though the powers and forces, by which the former is governed, be wholly unknown to us; yet our thoughts and conceptions have still, we find, gone on in the same train with the other works of nature. Custom is that principle, by which this correspondence has been effected; so necessary to the subsistence of our species, and the regulation of our conduct, in every circumstance and occurrence of human life. Had not the presence of an object, instantly excited the idea of those objects, commonly conjoined with it, all our knowledge must have been limited to the narrow sphere of our memory and senses; and we should never have been able to adjust means to ends, or employ our natural powers, either to the producing of good, or avoiding of evil. Those, who delight in the discovery and contemplation of *final causes,* have here ample subject to employ their wonder and admiration.

I shall add, for a further confirmation of the foregoing theory, that, as this operation of the mind, by which we infer like effects from like causes, and *vice versa,* is so essential to the subsistence of all human creatures, it is not probable, that it could be trusted to the fallacious deductions of our reason, which is slow in its operations; appears not, in any degree, during the first years of infancy; and at best is, in every age and period of human life, extremely liable to error and mistake. It is more conformable to the ordinary wisdom of nature to secure so necessary an act of the mind, by some instinct or mechanical tendency, which may be infallible in its operations, may discover itself at the first appearance of life and thought, and may be independent of all the labored deductions of the understanding. As nature has taught us the use of our limbs, without giving us the knowledge of the muscles and nerves, by which they are actuated; so has she implanted in us an instinct, which carries forward the thought in a correspondent course to that which she has established among external objects; though we are ignorant of those powers and forces, on which this regular course and succession of objects totally depends.

SECTION VI

OF PROBABILITY[8]

Though there be no such thing as *chance* in the world; our ignorance of the real cause of any event has the same influence on the understanding, and begets a like species of belief or opinion.

There is certainly a probability, which arises from a superiority of chances on any side; and according as this superiority increases, and surpasses the opposite chances, the probability receives a proportionable increase, and begets still a higher degree of belief or assent to that side, in which we discover the superiority. If a die were marked with one figure or number of spots on four sides, and with another figure or number of spots on the two remaining sides, it would be more probable, that the former would turn up than the latter; though, if it had a thousand sides marked in the same manner, and only one side different, the probability would be much higher,

[8] Mr. Locke divides all arguments into demonstrative and probable. In this view, we must say, that it is only probable all men must die, or that the sun will rise tomorrow. But to conform our language more to common use, we ought to divide arguments into *demonstrations*, *proofs*, and *probabilities*. By proofs meaning such arguments from experience as leave no room for doubt or opposition.

and our belief or expectation of the event more steady and secure. This process of the thought or reasoning may seem trivial and obvious; but to those who consider it more narrowly, it may, perhaps, afford matter for curious speculation.

It seems evident, that, when the mind looks forward to discover the event, which may result from the throw of such a die, it considers the turning up of each particular side as alike probable; and this is the very nature of chance, to render all the particular events, comprehended in it, entirely equal. But finding a greater number of sides concur in the one event than in the other, the mind is carried more frequently to that event, and meets it oftener, in revolving the various possibilities or chances, on which the ultimate result depends. This concurrence of several views in one particular event begets immediately, by an inexplicable contrivance of nature, the sentiment of belief, and gives that event the advantage over its antagonist, which is supported by a smaller number of views, and recurs less frequently to the mind. If we allow, that belief is nothing but a firmer and stronger conception of an object than what attends the mere fictions of the imagination, this operation may, perhaps, in some measure, be accounted for. The concurrence of these several views or glimpses imprints the idea more strongly on the imagination; gives it superior force and vigor; renders its influence on the passions and affections more sensible; and in a word, begets that reliance or security, which constitutes the nature of belief and opinion.

The case is the same with the probability of causes, as with that of chance. There are some causes, which are entirely uniform and constant in producing a particular effect; and no instance has ever yet been found of any failure or irregularity in their operation. Fire has always burned, and water suffocated every human creature: the production of motion by impulse and gravity is an universal law, which has hitherto admitted of no exception. But there are other causes which have been found more irregular and uncertain; nor has rhubarb always proved a purge, or opium a soporific to everyone, who has taken these medicines. It is true, when any cause fails of producing its usual effect, philosophers ascribe not this to any irregularity in nature; but suppose, that some secret causes, in the particular structure of parts, have prevented the operation. Our reasonings, however, and conclusions concerning the event are the same as if this principle had no place. Being determined by custom to transfer the past to the future, in all our inferences; where the past has been entirely regular and uniform, we expect the event with the greatest assurance, and leave no room for any contrary supposition. But where different effects have been found to follow from causes, which are to *appearance* exactly similar, all these various effects must occur to the mind in transferring the past to the future, and enter into our consideration, when we determine the probability of the event. Though we give the preference to that which has been found most usual, and believe that this effect will exist, we must not overlook the other effects, but must assign to each of them a particular weight and authority, in proportion as we have found it to be more or less frequent. It is more probable, in almost every country of Europe, that there will be frost sometime in January, than that the weather will continue open throughout the whole month; though this probability varies according to the different climates, and approaches to a certainty in the more northern kingdoms. Here then it seems evident, that, when we transfer the past to the future, in order to determine the effect, which will result from any cause, we transfer all the different events, in the same proportion as they have appeared in the past, and conceive one to have existed a hundred times, for instance, another ten times, and another once. As a great number of views do here concur in one event, they fortify and confirm it to the imagination, beget that sentiment which we call *belief*, and give its object the preference above the contrary event, which is not supported by an equal number of experiments, and recurs not so frequently to the thought in transferring the past to the future. Let anyone try to account for this operation of the mind upon any of the received systems of philosophy, and he will be sensible of the difficulty. For my part, I shall think it sufficient, if the present hints excite the curiosity of philosophers, and make them sensible how defective all common theories are in treating of such curious and such sublime subjects.

SECTION VII

OF THE IDEA OF NECESSARY CONNECTION

Part I

The great advantage of the mathematical sciences above the moral consists in this, that the ideas of the former, being sensible, are always clear and determinate, the smallest distinction between them is immediately perceptible, and the same terms are still expressive of the same ideas, without ambiguity or variation. An oval is never mistaken for a circle, nor an hyperbola for an ellipsis. The isosceles and scalenum are distinguished by boundaries more exact than vice and virtue, right and wrong. If any term be defined in geometry, the mind readily, of itself, substitutes, on all occasions, the definition for the term defined: or even when no definition is employed, the object itself may be presented to the senses, and by that means be steadily and clearly apprehended. But the finer sentiments of the mind, the operations of the understanding, the various agitations of the passions, though really in themselves distinct, easily escape us, when surveyed by reflection; nor is it in our power to recall the original object, as often as we have occasion to contemplate it. Ambiguity, by this means, is gradually introduced into our reasonings: similar objects are readily taken to be the same: and the conclusion becomes at last very wide of the premises.

One may safely, however, affirm, that, if we consider these sciences in a proper light, their advantages and disadvantages nearly compensate each other, and reduce both of them to a state of equality. If the mind, with greater facility, retains the ideas of geometry clear and determinate, it must carry on a much longer and more intricate chain of reasoning, and compare ideas much wider of each other, in order to reach the abstruser truths of that science. And if moral ideas are apt, without extreme care, to fall into obscurity and confusion, the inferences are always much shorter in these disquisitions, and the intermediate steps, which lead to the conclusion, much fewer than in the sciences which treat of quantity and number. In reality, there is scarcely a proposition in Euclid so simple, as not to consist of more parts, than are to be found in any moral reasoning which runs not into chimera and conceit. Where we trace the principles of the human mind through a few steps, we may be very well satisfied with our progress; considering how soon nature throws a bar to all our inquiries concerning causes, and reduces us to an acknowledgment of our ignorance. The chief obstacle, therefore, to our improvement in the moral or metaphysical sciences is the obscurity of the ideas, and ambiguity of the terms. The principal difficulty in the mathematics is the length of inferences and compass of thought, requisite to the forming of any conclusion. And, perhaps, our progress in natural philosophy is chiefly retarded by the want of proper experiments and phenomena, which are often discovered by chance, and cannot always be found, when requisite, even by the most diligent and prudent inquiry. As moral philosophy seems hitherto to have received less improvement than either geometry or physics, we may conclude, that, if there be any difference in this respect among these sciences, the difficulties, which obstruct the progress of the former, require superior care and capacity to be surmounted.

There are no ideas, which occur in metaphysics more obscure and uncertain, than those of *power*, *force*, *energy* or *necessary connection*, of which it is every moment necessary for us to treat in all our disquisitions. We shall, therefore, endeavor, in this section, to fix, if possible, the precise meaning of these terms, and thereby remove some part of that obscurity, which is so much complained of in this species of philosophy.

It seems a proposition, which will not admit of much dispute, that all our ideas are nothing but copies of our impressions, or, in other words, that it is impossible for us to *think* of anything, which we have not antecedently *felt*, either by our external or internal senses. I have endeavored[9] to explain and prove this proposition, and have expressed my hopes, that, by a proper application of it, men may reach a greater clearness and precision in philosophical reasonings, than what they have hitherto been able to attain. Complex ideas may, perhaps, be well known by definition, which is nothing but an enumeration of those parts or simple ideas, that compose them. But when we have pushed up definitions to the most

[9] Section II.

simple ideas, and find still some ambiguity and obscurity; what resource are we then possessed of? By what invention can we throw light upon these ideas, and render them altogether precise and determinate to our intellectual view! Produce the impressions or original sentiments, from which the ideas are copied. These impressions are all strong and sensible. They admit not of ambiguity. They are not only placed in a full light themselves, but may throw light on their correspondent ideas, which lie in obscurity. And by this means, we may, perhaps, attain a new microscope or species of optics, by which, in the moral sciences, the most minute, and most simple ideas may be so enlarged as to fall readily under our apprehension, and be equally known with the grossest and most sensible ideas, that can be the object of our inquiry.

To be fully acquainted, therefore, with the idea of power or necessary connection, let us examine its impression; and in order to find the impression with greater certainty, let us search for it in all the sources, from which it may possibly be derived.

When we look about us towards external objects, and consider the operation of causes, we are never able, in a single instance, to discover any power or necessary connection; any quality, which binds the effect to the cause, and renders the one an infallible consequence of the other. We only find, that the one does actually, in fact, follow the other. The impulse of one billiard ball is attended with motion in the second. This is the whole that appears to the *outward* senses. The mind feels no sentiment or *inward* impression from this succession of objects: consequently there is not, in any single, particular instance of cause and effect, anything which can suggest the idea of power or necessary connection.

From the first appearance of an object, we never can conjecture what effect will result from it. But were the power or energy of any cause discoverable by the mind, we could foresee the effect, even without experience; and might, at first, pronounce with certainty concerning it, by mere dint of thought and reasoning.

In reality, there is no part of matter, that does ever, by its sensible qualities, discover any power or energy, or give us ground to imagine, that it could produce anything, or be followed by any other object, which we could denominate its effect. Solidity, extension, motion; these qualities are all complete in themselves, and never point out any other event which may result from them. The scenes of the universe are continually shifting, and one object follows another in an uninterrupted succession; but the power of force, which actuates the whole machine, is entirely concealed from us, and never discovers itself in any of the sensible qualities of body. We know, that, in fact, heat is a constant attendant of flame; but what is the connection between them, we have no room so much as to conjecture or imagine. It is impossible, therefore, that the idea of power can be derived from the contemplation of bodies, in single instances of their operation; because no bodies ever discover any power, which can be the original of this idea.[10]

Since, therefore, external objects as they appear to the senses, give us no idea of power or necessary connection, by their operation in particular instances, let us see, whether this idea be derived from reflection on the operations of our own minds, and be copied from any internal impression. It may be said, that we are every moment conscious of internal power; while we feel, that, by the simple command of our will, we can move the organs of our body, or direct the faculties of our mind. An act of volition produces motion in our limbs, or raises a new idea in our imagination. This influence of the will we know by consciousness. Hence we acquire the idea of power or energy; and are certain, that we ourselves and all other intelligent beings are possessed of power. This idea, then, is an idea of reflection, since it arises from reflecting on the operations of our own mind, and on the command which is exercised by will, both over the organs of the body and faculties of the soul.

We shall proceed to examine this pretension; and first with regard to the influence of volition over the organs of the body. This influence, we may observe, is a fact, which, like all other natural events, can be known only by experience, and can never be foreseen from any apparent energy or power in the cause, which connects it with the effect, and renders the one an infallible consequence of the other. The motion of our

[10] Mr. Locke, in his chapter on power, says, that, finding from experience, that there are several new productions in matter, and concluding that there must somewhere be a power capable of producing them, we arrive at last by this reasoning at the idea of power. But no reasoning can ever give us a new original, simple idea; as this philosopher himself confesses. This, therefore, can never be the origin of that idea.

body follows upon the command of our will. Of this we are every moment conscious. But the means, by which this is effected; the energy, by which the will performs so extraordinary an operation; of this we are so far from being immediately conscious, that it must for ever escape our most diligent inquiry.

For *first*, Is there any principle in all nature more mysterious than the union of soul with body; by which a supposed spiritual substance acquires such an influence over a material one, that the most refined thought is able to actuate the grossest matter? Were we empowered, by a secret wish, to remove mountains, or control the planets in their orbit; this extensive authority would not be more extraordinary, nor more beyond our comprehension. But if by consciousness we perceived any power or energy in the will, we must know this power; we must know its connection with the effect; we must know the secret union of soul and body, and the nature of both these substances; by which the one is able to operate, in so many instances, upon the other.

Secondly, We are not able to move all the organs of the body with a like authority; though we cannot assign any reason besides experience, for so remarkable a difference between one and the other. Why has the will an influence over the tongue and fingers, not over the heart and liver? This question would never embarrass us, were we conscious of a power in the former case, not in the latter. We should then perceive, independent of experience, why the authority of will over the organs of the body is circumscribed within such particular limits. Being in that case fully acquainted with the power or force, by which it operates, we should also know, why its influence reaches precisely to such boundaries, and no farther.

A man, suddenly struck with palsy in the leg or arm, or who had newly lost those members, frequently endeavors, at first to move them, and employ them in their usual offices. Here he is as much conscious of power to command such limbs, as a man in perfect health is conscious of power to actuate any member which remains in its natural state and condition. But consciousness never deceives. Consequently, neither in the one case nor in the other, are we ever conscious of any power. We learn the influence of our will from experience alone. And experience only teaches us, how one event constantly follows another; without instructing us in the secret connection, which binds them together, and renders them inseparable.

Thirdly, We learn from anatomy, that the immediate object of power in voluntary motion, is not the member itself which is moved, but certain muscles, and nerves, and animal spirits, and, perhaps, something still more minute and more unknown, through which the motion is successfully propagated, ere it reach the member itself whose motion is the immediate object of volition. Can there be a more certain proof that the power, by which this whole operation is performed, so far from being directly and fully known by an inward sentiment or consciousness, is, to the last degree, mysterious and unintelligible? Here the mind wills a certain event: immediately another event, unknown to ourselves, and totally different from the one intended, is produced: this event produces another, equally unknown: till at last, through a long succession, the desired event is produced. But if the original power were felt, it must be known: were it known, its effect also must be known; since all power is relative to its effect. And *vice versa*, if the effect be not known, the power cannot be known nor felt. How indeed can we be conscious of a power to move our limbs, when we have no such power; but only that to move certain animal spirits, which, though they produce at last the motion of our limbs, yet operate in such a manner as is wholly beyond our comprehension?

We may, therefore, conclude from the whole, I hope, without any temerity, though with assurance; that our idea of power is not copied from any sentiment or consciousness of power within ourselves, when we give rise to animal motion, or apply our limbs, to their proper use and office. That their motion follows the command of the will is a matter of common experience, like other natural events: but the power or energy by which this is effected, like that in other natural events, is unknown and inconceivable.[11]

[11] It may be pretended, that the resistance which we meet with in bodies, obliging us frequently to exert our force, and call up all our power, this gives us the idea of force and power. It is this *nisus*, or strong endeavor, of which we are conscious, that is the original impression from which this idea is copied. But, *first*, We attribute power to a vast number of objects, where we never can suppose this resistance or exertion of force to take place; to the Supreme Being, who never meets with any resistance; to the mind in its command over its ideas and limbs, in common thinking and motion, where

Shall we then assert, that we are conscious of a power or energy in our own minds, when, by an act or command of our will, we raise up a new idea, fix the mind to the contemplation of it, turn it on all sides, and at last dismiss it for some other idea, when we think that we have surveyed it with sufficient accuracy? I believe the same arguments will prove, that even this command of the will gives us no real idea of force or energy.

First, It must be allowed, that, when we know a power, we know that very circumstance in the cause, by which it is enabled to produce the effect: for these are supposed to be synonymous. We must, therefore, know both the cause and effect, and the relation between them. But do we pretend to be acquainted with the nature of the human soul and the nature of an idea, or the aptitude of the one to produce the other? This is a real creation; a production of something out of nothing: which implies a power so great, that it may seem, at first sight, beyond the reach of any being, less than infinite. At least it must be owned, that such a power is not felt, nor known, nor even conceivable by the mind. We only feel the event, namely, the existence of an idea, consequent to a command of the will: but the manner, in which this operation is performed, the power by which it is produced, is entirely beyond our comprehension.

Secondly, The command of the mind over itself is limited, as well as its command over the body; and these limits are not known by reason, or any acquaintance with the nature of cause and effect, but only by experience and observation, as in all other natural events and in the operation of external objects. Our authority over our sentiments and passions is much weaker than that over our ideas; and even the latter authority is circumscribed within very narrow boundaries. Will anyone pretend to assign the ultimate reason of these boundaries, or show why the power is deficient in one case, not in another?

---

the effect follows immediately upon the will, without any exertion or summoning up of force; to inanimate matter, which is not capable of this sentiment. *Secondly*, This sentiment of an endeavor to overcome resistance has no known connection with any event: what follows it, we know by experience; but could not know it *a priori*. It must, however, be confessed, that the animal *nisus*, which we experience, though it can afford no accurate precise idea of power, enters very much into that vulgar, inaccurate idea, which is formed of it.

Thirdly, This self-command is very different at different times. A man in health possesses more of it than one languishing with sickness. We are more master of our thoughts in the morning than in the evening; fasting, than after a full meal. Can we give any reason for these variations, except experience? Where then is the power, of which we pretend to be conscious? Is there not here, either in a spiritual or material substance, or both, some secret mechanism or structure of parts, upon which the effect depends, and which, being entirely unknown to us, renders the power of energy of the will equally unknown and incomprehensible?

Volition is surely an act of the mind, with which we are sufficiently acquainted. Reflect upon it. Consider it on all sides. Do you find anything in it like this creative power, by which it raises from nothing a new idea, and with a kind of *fiat,* imitates the omnipotence of its Maker, if I may be allowed so to speak, who called forth into existence all the various scenes of nature? So far from being conscious of this energy in the will, it requires as certain experience as that of which we are possessed, to convince us that such extraordinary effects do ever result from a simple act of volition.

The generality of mankind never find any difficulty in accounting for the more common and familiar operations of nature—such as the descent of heavy bodies, the growth of plants, the generation of animals, or the nourishment of bodies by food; but suppose that, in all these cases, they perceive the very force or energy of the cause, by which it is connected with its effect, and is forever infallible in its operation. They acquire, by long habit, such a turn of mind, that, upon the appearance of the cause, they immediately expect with assurance its usual attendant, and hardly conceive it possible that any other event could result from it. It is only on the discovery of extraordinary phenomena, such as earthquakes, pestilence, and prodigies of any kind, that they find themselves at a loss to assign a proper cause, and to explain the manner in which the effect is produced by it. It is usual for men, in such difficulties, to have recourse to some invisible intelligent principle as the immediate cause of that event which surprises them, and which, they think, cannot be accounted for from the common powers of nature. But philosophers, who carry their scrutiny a little farther, immediately perceive that, even in the most familiar events, the energy of the cause is as unintelligible as in the most unusual, and that we only learn by experience the frequent *conjunction* of objects, without being ever able to comprehend anything like *connection* between them. Here, then, many philosophers think themselves obliged by reason to have recourse, on all occasions, to the same principle, which the vulgar never appeal to but in cases that appear miraculous and supernatural. They acknowledge mind and intelligence to be, not only the ultimate and original cause of all things, but the immediate and sole cause of every event which appears in nature. They pretend that those objects which are commonly denominated *causes*, are in reality nothing but *occasions*; and that the true and direct principle of every effect is not any power or force in nature, but a volition of the Supreme Being, who wills that such particular objects should forever be conjoined with each other. Instead of saying that one billiard ball moves another by a force which it has derived from the author of nature, it is the Deity himself, they say, who, by a particular volition, moves the second ball, being determined to this operation by the impulse of the first ball, in consequence of those general laws which he has laid down to himself in the government of the universe. But philosophers advancing still in their inquiries, discover that, as we are totally ignorant of the power on which depends the mutual operation of bodies, we are no less ignorant of that power on which depends the operation of mind on body, or of body on mind; nor are we able, either from our senses or consciousness, to assign the ultimate principle in one case more than in the other. The same ignorance, therefore, reduces them to the same conclusion. They assert that the Deity is the immediate cause of the union between soul and body; and that they are not the organs of sense, which, being agitated by external objects, produce sensations in the mind; but that it is a particular volition of our omnipotent Maker, which excites such a sensation, in consequence of such a motion in the organ. In like manner, it is not any energy in the will that produces local motion in our members; it is God himself, who is pleased to second our will, in itself impotent, and to command that motion which we erroneously attribute to our own power and efficacy. Nor do philosophers stop at this conclusion. They sometimes extend the same inference to the mind itself, in its internal operations. Our mental vision or conception of ideas is nothing but a revelation made to us by our Maker. When we voluntarily turn our thoughts to any object, and raise up its image in the fancy, it is not the will which creates that idea; it is the universal Creator, who discovers it to the mind, and renders it present to us.

Thus, according to these philosophers, everything is full of God. Not content with the principle, that nothing exists but by his will, that nothing possesses any power but by his concession; they rob nature, and all created beings, of every power, in order to render their dependence on the Deity still more sensible and immediate. They consider not that, by this theory, they diminish, instead of magnifying, the grandeur of those attributes, which they affect so much to celebrate. It argues surely more power in the Deity to delegate a certain degree of power to inferior creatures, than to produce everything by his own immediate volition. It argues more wisdom to contrive at first the fabric of the world with such perfect foresight that, of itself, and by its proper operation, it may serve all the purposes of providence, than if the great Creator were obliged every moment to adjust its parts, and animate by his breath all the wheels of that stupendous machine.

But if we would have a more philosophical confutation of this theory, perhaps the two following reflections may suffice.

First, It seems to me that this theory of the universal energy and operation of the Supreme Being is too bold ever to carry conviction with it to a man, sufficiently apprised of the weakness of human reason, and the narrow limits to which it is confined in all its operations. Though the chain of arguments which conduct to it were ever so logical, there must arise a strong suspicion, if not an absolute assurance, that it has carried us quite beyond the reach of our faculties, when it leads to conclusions so extraordinary, and so remote from common life and experience. We are got into fairy land, long ere we have reached the last steps of our theory; and *there* we have no reason to trust our common methods of argument, or to think that our usual analogies and probabilities have any authority. Our line is too short to fathom such immense abysses. And however we may flatter ourselves that we are guided, in every step which we take, by a kind of verisimilitude and experience, we may be assured that this fancied experience has no authority when we thus apply it to subjects that lie entirely out of the sphere of experience. But on this we shall have occasion to touch afterwards.[12]

Secondly, I cannot perceive any force in the arguments on

[12] Section XII.

which this theory is founded. We are ignorant, it is true, of the manner in which bodies operate on each other: their force or energy is entirely incomprehensible: but are we not equally ignorant of the manner or force by which a mind, even the supreme mind, operates either on itself or on body? Whence, I beseech you, do we acquire any idea of it? We have no sentiment or consciousness of this power in ourselves. We have no idea of the Supreme Being but what we learn from reflection on our own faculties. Were our ignorance, therefore, a good reason for rejecting anything, we should be led into that principle of denying all energy in the Supreme Being as much as in the grossest matter. We surely comprehend as little the operations of one as of the other. Is it more difficult to conceive that motion may arise from impulse than that it may arise from volition? All we know is our profound ignorance in both cases.[13]

Part II

But to hasten to a conclusion of this argument, which is already drawn out to too great a length: we have sought in

[13] I need not examine at length the *vis inertiae* which is so much talked of in the new philosophy, and which is ascribed to matter. We find by experience, that a body at rest or in motion continues forever in its present state, till put from it by some new cause; and that a body impelled takes as much motion from the impelling body as it acquires itself. These are facts. When we call this a *vis inertiae*, we only mark these facts, without pretending to have any idea of the inert power; in the same manner as, when we talk of gravity, we mean certain effects, without comprehending that active power. It was never the meaning of Sir Isaac Newton to rob second causes of all force or energy; though some of his followers have endeavored to establish that theory upon his authority. On the contrary, that great philosopher had recourse to an etherial active fluid to explain his universal attraction; though he was so cautious and modest as to allow, that it was a mere hypothesis, not to be insisted on, without more experiments. I must confess, that there is something in the fate of opinions a little extraordinary. Descartes insinuated that doctrine of the universal and sole efficiency of the Deity, without insisting on it. Malebranche and other Cartesians made it the foundation of all their philosophy. It had, however, no authority in England. Locke, Clarke, and Cudworth, never so much as take notice of it, but suppose all along, that matter has a real, though subordinate and derived power. By what means has it become so prevalent among our modern metaphysicians?

vain for an idea of power or necessary connection in all the sources from which we could suppose it to be derived. It appears that, in single instances of the operation of bodies, we never can, by our utmost scrutiny, discover anything but one event following another, without being able to comprehend any force or power by which the cause operates, or any connection between it and its supposed effect. The same difficulty occurs in contemplating the operations of mind on body—where we observe the motion of the latter to follow upon the volition of the former, but are not able to observe or conceive the tie which binds together the motion and volition, or the energy by which the mind produces this effect. The authority of the will over its own faculties and ideas is not a whit more comprehensible: so that, upon the whole, there appears not, throughout all nature, any one instance of connection which is conceivable by us. All events seem entirely loose and separate. One event follows another; but we never can observe any tie between them. They seem *conjoined*, but never *connected*. And as we can have no idea of anything which never appeared to our outward sense or inward sentiment, the necessary conclusion *seems* to be that we have no idea of connection or power at all, and that these words are absolutely without any meaning, when employed either in philosophical reasonings or common life.

But there still remains one method of avoiding this conclusion, and one source which we have not yet examined. When any natural object or event is presented, it is impossible for us, by any sagacity or penetration, to discover, or even conjecture, without experience, what event will result from it, or to carry our foresight beyond that object which is immediately present to the memory and senses. Even after one instance or experiment where we have observed a particular event to follow upon another, we are not entitled to form a general rule, or foretell what will happen in like cases; it being justly esteemed an unpardonable temerity to judge of the whole course of nature from one single experiment, however accurate or certain. But when one particular species of event has always, in all instances, been conjoined with another, we make no longer any scruple of foretelling one upon the appearance of the other, and of employing that reasoning which can alone assure us of any matter of fact or existence. We then call the one object, *cause*; the other, *effect*. We suppose that there is some connection between them; some power in the one, by which it infallibly produces the other, and operates with the greatest certainty and strongest necessity.

It appears, then, that this idea of a necessary connection among events arises from a number of similar instances which occur of the constant conjunction of these events; nor can that idea ever be suggested by any one of these instances, surveyed in all possible lights and positions. But there is nothing in a number of instances, different from every single instance, which is supposed to be exactly similar; except only, that after a repetition of similar instances, the mind is carried by habit, upon the appearance of one event, to expect its usual attendant, and to believe that it will exist. This connection, therefore, which we *feel* in the mind, this customary transition of the imagination from one object to its usual attendant, is the sentiment or impression from which we form the idea of power or necessary connection. Nothing farther is in the case. Contemplate the subject on all sides; you will never find any other origin of that idea. This is the sole difference between one instance, from which we can never receive the idea of connection, and a number of similar instances, by which it is suggested. The first time a man saw the communication of motion by impulse, as by the shock of two billiard balls, he could not pronounce that the one event was *connected*; but only that it was *conjoined* with the other. After he has observed several instances of this nature, he then pronounces them to be *connected*. What alteration has happened to give rise to this new idea of *connection*? Nothing but that he now *feels* these events to be *connected* in his imagination, and can readily foretell the existence of one from the appearance of the other. When we say, therefore, that one object is connected with another, we mean only that they have acquired a connection in our thought, and give rise to this inference, by which they become proofs of each other's existence: a conclusion which is somewhat extraordinary, but which seems founded on sufficient evidence. Nor will its evidence be weakened by any general diffidence of the understanding, or sceptical suspicion concerning every conclusion which is new and extraordinary. No conclusions can be more agreeable to scepticism than such as make discoveries concerning the weakness and narrow limits of human reason and capacity.

And what stronger instance can be produced of the surprising ignorance and weakness of the understanding than the present? For surely, if there be any relation among objects which it imports to us to know perfectly, it is that of cause and effect. On this are founded all our reasonings concerning matter of fact or existence. By means of it alone we attain any assurance concerning objects which are removed from the present testimony of our memory and senses. The only immediate utility of all sciences, is to teach us, how to control and regulate future events by their causes. Our thoughts and inquiries are, therefore, every moment, employed about this relation: yet so imperfect are the ideas which we form concerning it, that it is impossible to give any just definition of cause, except what is drawn from something extraneous and foreign to it. Similar objects are always conjoined with similar. Of this we have experience. Suitably to this experience, therefore, we may define a cause to be *an object, followed by another, and where all the objects similar to the first are followed by objects similar to the second.* Or in other words *where, if the first object had not been, the second never had existed.* The appearance of a cause always conveys the mind, by a customary transition, to the idea of the effect. Of this also we have experience. We may, therefore, suitably to this experience, form another definition of cause, and call it, *an object followed by another, and whose appearance always conveys the thought to that other.* But though both these definitions be drawn from circumstances foreign to the cause, we cannot remedy this inconvenience, or attain any more perfect definition, which may point out that circumstances in the cause, which gives it a connection with its effect. We have no idea of this connection, nor even any distinct notion what it is we desire to know, when we endeavor at a conception of it. We say, for instance, that the vibration of this string is the cause of this particular sound. But what do we mean by that affirmation? We either mean *that this vibration is followed by this sound, and that all similar vibrations have been followed by similar sounds*: Or, *that this vibration is followed by this sound, and that upon the appearance of one the mind anticipates the senses, and forms immediately an idea of the other.* We may consider the relation of cause and effect in either of these two lights; but beyond these, we have no idea of it.[14]

[14] According to these explications and definitions, the idea of *power* is relative as much as that of *cause*; and both have a reference to an effect, or some other event constantly conjoined with the former. When we consider the *unknown* circumstance of an object,

To recapitulate, therefore, the reasonings of this section: every idea is copied from some preceding impression or sentiment; and where we cannot find any impression, we may be certain that there is no idea. In all single instances of the operation of bodies or minds, there is nothing that produces any impression, nor consequently can suggest any idea of power or necessary connection. But when many uniform instances appear, and the same object is always followed by the same event; we then begin to entertain the notion of cause and connection. We then feel a new sentiment or impression, to wit, a customary connection in the thought or imagination between one object and its usual attendant; and this sentiment is the original of that idea which we seek for. For as this idea arises from a number of similar instances, and not from any single instance, it must arise from that circumstance, in which the number of instances differ from every individual instance. But this customary connection or transition of the imagination is the only circumstance in which they differ. In

---

by which the degree or quantity of its effect is fixed and determined, we call that its power: And accordingly, it is allowed by all philosophers, that the effect is the measure of the power. But if they had any idea of power, as it is in itself, why could not they measure it in itself? The dispute whether the force of a body in motion be as its velocity, or the square of its velocity; this dispute, I say, needed not be decided by comparing its effects in equal or unequal times; but by a direct mensuration and comparison.

As to the frequent use of the words, *force*, *power*, *energy*, etc., which everywhere occur in common conversation, as well as in philosophy; that is no proof, that we are acquainted, in any instance, with the connecting principle between cause and effect, or can account ultimately for the production of one thing to another. These words, as commonly used, have very loose meanings annexed to them; and their ideas are very uncertain and confused. No animal can put external bodies in motion without the sentiment of a *nisus* or endeavor; and every animal has a sentiment or feeling from the stroke or blow of an external object, that is in motion. These sensations, which are merely animal, and from which we can *a priori* draw no inference, we are apt to transfer to inanimate objects, and to suppose, that they have some such feelings, whenever they transfer or receive motion. With regard to energies, which are exerted, without our annexing to them any idea of communicated motion, we consider only the constant experienced conjunction of the events; and as we *feel* a customary connection between the ideas, we transfer that feeling to the objects; as nothing is more usual than to apply to external bodies every internal sensation which they occasion.

every other particular they are alike. The first instance which we saw of motion communicated by the shock of two billiard balls (to return to this obvious illustration) is exactly similar to any instance that may, at present, occur to us; except only, that we could not, at first, *infer* one event from the other; which we are enabled to do at present, after so long a course of uniform experience. I know not whether the reader will readily apprehend this reasoning. I am afraid that, should I multiply words about it, or throw it into a greater variety of lights, it would only become more obscure and intricate. In all abstract reasonings there is one point of view which, if we can happily hit, we shall go farther towards illustrating the subject than by all the eloquence in the world. This point of view we should endeavor to reach, and reserve the flowers of rhetoric for subjects which are more adapted to them.

SECTION VIII

OF LIBERTY AND NECESSITY

Part I

It might reasonably be expected in questions which have been convassed and disputed with great eagerness, since the first origin of science and philosophy, that the meaning of all the terms, at least, should have been agreed upon among the disputants; and our inquiries, in the course of two thousand years, been able to pass from words to the true and real subject of the controversy. For how easy may it seem to give exact definitions of the terms employed in reasoning, and make these definitions, not the mere sound of words, the object of future scrutiny and examination? But if we consider the matter more narrowly, we shall be apt to draw a quite opposite conclusion. From this circumstance alone, that a controversy has been long kept on foot, and remains still undecided, we may presume that there is some ambiguity in the expression, and that the disputants affix different ideas to the terms employed in the controversy. For as the faculties of the mind are supposed to be naturally alike in every individual; otherwise nothing could be more fruitless than to reason or dispute together; it were impossible, if men affix the same ideas to their terms, that they could so long form different opinions of the same subject; especially when they communicate their views, and each party turn themselves on all sides, in search of arguments which may give them the victory over their antagonists. It is true, if men attempt the discussion of questions which lie entirely beyond the reach of human capacity, such as those concerning the origin of worlds, or the economy of the intellectual system or region of spirits, they may long beat the air in their fruitless contests, and never arrive at any determinate conclusion. But if the question regard any subject of common life and experience, nothing, one would think, could preserve the dispute so long undecided but some ambiguous expressions, which keep the antagonists still at a distance, and hinder them from grappling with each other.

This has been the case in the long disputed question concerning liberty and necessity; and to so remarkable a degree that, if I be not much mistaken, we shall find, that all mankind, both learned and ignorant, have always been of the same opinion with regard to this subject, and that a few intelligible definitions would immediately have put an end to the whole controversy. I own that this dispute has been so much canvassed on all hands, and has led philosophers into such a labyrinth of obscure sophistry, that it is no wonder, if a sensible reader indulge his ease so far as to turn a deaf ear to the proposal of such a question, from which he can expect neither instruction nor entertainment. But the state of the argument here proposed may, perhaps, serve to renew his attention; as it has more novelty, promises at least some decision of the controversy, and will not much disturb his ease by any intricate or obscure reasoning.

I hope, therefore, to make it appear that all men have ever agreed in the doctrine both of necessity and of liberty, according to any reasonable sense, which can be put on these terms; and that the whole controversy has hitherto turned merely upon words. We shall begin with examining the doctrine of necessity.

It is universally allowed that matter, in all its operations, is actuated by a necessary force, and that every natural effect is so precisely determined by the energy of its cause that no other effect, in such particular circumstances, could possibly have resulted from it. The degree and direction of every motion is, by the laws of nature, prescribed with such exactness that a living creature may as soon arise from the shock of two bodies as motion in any other degree or direction than what is actually produced by it. Would we, therefore, form a just and precise idea of *necessity*, we must consider whence that idea arises when we apply it to the operation of bodies.

It seems evident that, if all the scenes of nature were continually shifted in such a manner that no two events bore any resemblance to each other, but every object was entirely new, without any similitude to whatever had been seen before, we should never, in that case, have attained the least idea of necessity, or of a connection among these objects. We might say, upon such a supposition, that one object or event has followed another; not that one was produced by the other. The relation of cause and effect must be utterly unknown to mankind. Inference and reasoning concerning the operations of nature would, from that moment, be at an end; and the memory and senses remain the only canals, by which the knowledge of any real existence could possibly have access to the mind. Our idea, therefore, of necessity and causation arises entirely from the uniformity observable in the operations of nature, where similar objects are constantly conjoined together, and the mind is determined by custom to infer the one from the appearance of the other. These two circumstances form the whole of that necessity, which we ascribe to matter. Beyond the constant *conjunction* of similar objects, and the consequent *inference* from one to the other, we have no notion of any necessity or connection.

If it appear, therefore, that all mankind have ever allowed, without any doubt or hesitation, that these two circumstances take place in the voluntary actions of men, and in the operations of mind; it must follow, that all mankind have ever agreed in the doctrine of necessity, and that they have hitherto disputed, merely for not understanding each other.

As to the first circumstance, the constant and regular conjunction of similar events, we may possibly satisfy ourselves by the following considerations. It is universally acknowledged that there is a great uniformity among the actions of men, in all nations and ages, and that human nature remains still the same, in its principles and operations. The same motives always produce the same actions; the same events follow from the same causes. Ambition, avarice, self-love, vanity, friendship, generosity, public spirit: these passions, mixed in various degrees, and distributed through society, have been, from the beginning of the world, and still are, the source of all the actions and enterprises, which have ever been observed among mankind. Would you know the sentiments, inclinations, and course of life of the Greeks and Romans? Study well the temper and actions of the French and English: you cannot be much mistaken in transferring to the former *most* of the observations which you have made with regard to the latter. Mankind are so much the same, in all times and places, that history informs us of nothing new or strange in this particular. Its chief use is only to discover the constant and universal principles of human nature, by showing men in all varieties of circumstances and situations, and furnishing us with materials from which we may form our observations and become acquainted with the regular springs of human action and behavior. These records of wars, intrigues, factions, and revolutions, are so many collections of experiments, by which the politician or moral philosopher fixes the principles of his science, in the same manner as the physician or natural philosopher becomes acquainted with the nature of plants, minerals, and other external objects, by the experiments which he forms concerning them. Nor are the earth, water, and other elements, examined by Aristotle, and Hippocrates, more like to those which at present lie under our observation than the men described by Polybius and Tacitus are to those who now govern the world.

Should a traveler, returning from a far country, bring us an account of men, wholly different from any with whom we were ever acquainted; men, who were entirely divested of avarice, ambition, or revenge; who knew no pleasure but friendship, generosity, and public spirit; we should immediately, from these circumstances, detect the falsehood, and prove him a liar, with the same certainty as if he had stuffed his narration with stories of centaurs and dragons, miracles and prodigies. And if we would explode any forgery in history, we cannot make us of a more convincing argument, than to prove, that the actions ascribed to any person are directly contrary to the course of nature, and that no human motives, in such circumstances, could ever induce him to such a conduct. The veracity of Quintus Curtius is as much to be suspected, when he describes the supernatural courage of Alexander, by which he was hurried on singly to attack multitudes, as when he describes his supernatural force and activity, by which he was able to resist them. So readily and universally do we acknowledge a uniformity in human motives and actions as well as in the operations of body.

Hence likewise the benefit of that experience, acquired by long life and a variety of business and company, in order to instruct us in the principles of human nature, and regulate our future conduct, as well as speculation. By means of this guide, we mount up to the knowledge of men's inclinations and motives, from their actions, expressions, and even gestures; and again descend to the interpretation of their actions from our knowledge of their motives and inclinations. The general observations treasured up by a course of experience, give us the clue of human nature, and teach us to unravel all its intricacies. Pretexts and appearances no longer deceive us. Public declarations pass for the specious coloring of a cause. And though virtue and honor be allowed their proper weight and authority, that perfect disinterestedness, so often pretended to, is never expected in multitudes and parties; seldom in their leaders; and scarcely even in individuals of any rank or station. But were there no uniformity in human actions, and were every experiment which we could form of this kind irregular and anomalous, it were impossible to collect any general observations concerning mankind; and no experience, however accurately digested by reflection, would ever serve to any purpose. Why is the aged husbandman more skillful in his calling than the young beginner but because there is a certain uniformity in the operation of the sun, rain, and earth towards the production of vegetables; and experience teaches the old practitioner the rules by which this operation is governed and directed.

We must not, however, expect that this uniformity of human actions should be carried to such a length as that all men, in the same circumstances, will always act precisely in the same manner, without making any allowance for the diversity of characters, prejudices, and opinions. Such a uniformity in every particular, is found in no part of nature. On the contrary, from observing the variety of conduct in different men, we are enabled to form a greater variety of maxims, which still suppose a degree of uniformity and regularity.

Are the manners of men different in different ages and countries? We learn thence the great force of custom and education, which mold the human mind from its infancy and form it into a fixed and established character. Is the behavior and conduct of the one sex very unlike that of the other? Is it thence we become acquainted with the different characters which nature has impressed upon the sexes, and which she preserves with constancy and regularity? Are the actions of the same person much diversified in the different periods of his life, from infancy to old age? This affords room for many general observations concerning the gradual change of our sentiments and inclinations, and the different maxims which prevail in the different ages of human creatures. Even the characters, which are peculiar to each individual, have a uniformity in their influence; otherwise our acquaintance with the persons and our observation of their conduct could never teach us their dispositions, or serve to direct our behavior with regard to them.

I grant it possible to find some actions, which seem to have no regular connection with any known motives, and are exceptions to all the measures of conduct which have ever been established for the government of men. But if we would willingly know what judgment should be formed of such irregular and extraordinary actions, we may consider the sentiments commonly entertained with regard to those irregular events which appear in the course of nature, and the operations of external objects. All causes are not conjoined to their usual effects with like uniformity. An artificer, who handles only dead matter, may be disappointed of his aim, as well as the politician, who directs the conduct of sensible and intelligent agents.

The vulgar, who take things according to their first appearance, attribute the uncertainty of events to such an uncertainty in the causes as makes the latter often fail of their usual influence; though they meet with no impediment in their operation. But philosophers, observing that, almost in every part of nature, there is contained a vast variety of springs and principles, which are hid, by reason of their minuteness or remoteness, find, that it is at least possible the contrariety of events may not proceed from any contingency in the cause, but from the secret operation of contrary causes. This possibility is converted into certainty by farther observation, when they remark that, upon an exact scrutiny, a contrariety of effects always betrays a contrariety of causes, and proceeds from their mutual opposition. A peasant can give no better reason for the stopping of any clock or watch than to say that it does not commonly go right: but an artist easily perceives that the same force in the spring or pendulum has always the same influence on the wheels; but fails of its usual effect, perhaps by reason of a grain of dust, which puts a stop to the whole movement. From the observation of several parallel instances, philosophers form a maxim that the connection between all causes and effects is equally necessary, and that its seeming uncertainty in some instances proceeds from the secret opposition of contrary causes.

Thus, for instance, in the human body, when the usual symptoms of health or sickness disappoint our expectation; when medicines operate not with their wonted powers; when irregular events follow from any particular cause; the philosopher and physician are not surprised at the matter, nor are ever tempted to deny, in general, the necessity and uniformity of those principles by which the animal economy is conducted. They know that a human body is a mighty complicated machine; that many secret powers lurk in it, which are altogether beyond our comprehension; that to us it must often appear very uncertain in its operations; and that therefore the irregular events, which outwardly discover themselves, can be no proof that the laws of nature are not observed with the greatest regularity in its internal operations and government.

The philosopher, if he be consistent, must apply the same reasoning to the actions and volitions of intelligent agents. The most irregular and unexpected resolutions of men may frequently be accounted for by those who know every particular circumstance of their character and situation. A person of an obliging disposition gives a peevish answer; but he has the toothache, or has not dined. A stupid fellow discovers an uncommon alacrity in his carriage; but he has met with a sudden piece of good fortune. Or even when an action, as something happens, cannot be particularly accounted for, either by the person himself or by others; we know, in general, that the characters of men are, to a certain degree, inconstant and irregular. This is, in a manner, the constant character of human nature; though it be applicable, in a more particular manner, to some persons who have no fixed rule for their conduct, but proceed in a continued course of caprice and inconstancy. The internal principles and motives may operate in a uniform manner, notwithstanding these seeming irregularities; in the same manner as the winds, rain, clouds, and other variations of the weather are supposed to be governed by steady principles; though not easily discoverable by human sagacity and inquiry.

Thus it appear, not only that the conjunction between motives and voluntary actions is as regular and uniform as that between the cause and effect in any part of nature; but also that this regular conjunction has been universally acknowledged among mankind, and has never been the subject of dispute, either in philosophy or common life. Now, as it is from past experience that we draw all inferences concerning the future, and as we conclude that objects will always be conjoined together which we find to have always been conjoined; it may seem superfluous to prove that this experienced uniformity in human actions is a source whence we draw *inferences* concerning them. But in order to throw the argument into a greater variety of lights we shall also insist, though briefly, on this latter topic.

The mutual dependence of men is so great in all societies that scarce any human action is entirely complete in itself, or is performed without some reference to the actions of others, which are requisite to make it answer fully the intention of the agent. The poorest artificer, who labors alone, expects at least the protection of the magistrate, to ensure him the enjoyment of the fruits of his labor. He also expects that, when he carries his goods to market, and offers them at a reasonable price, he shall find purchasers, and shall be able, by the money he acquires, to engage others to supply him with those commodities which are requisite for his subsistence. In proportion as men extend their dealings, and render their intercourse with others more complicated, they always comprehend, in their schemes of life, a greater variety of voluntary actions, which they expect, from the proper motives, to cooperate with their own. In all these conclusions they take their measures from past experience, in the same manner as in their reasonings concerning external objects; and firmly believe that men, as well as all the elements, are to continue, in their operations, the same that they have ever found them. A manufacturer reckons upon the labor of his servants for the execution of any work as much as upon the tools which he employs, and would be equally surprised were his expectations disappointed. In short, this experimental inference and reasoning concerning the actions of others enters so much into human life, that no man, while awake, is ever a moment without employing it. Have we not reason, therefore, to affirm that all mankind have always agreed in the doctrine of necessity according to the foregoing definition and explication of it?

Nor have philosophers ever entertained a different opinion from the people in this particular. For, not to mention that almost every action of their life supposes that opinion, there are even few of the speculative parts of learning to which it is not essential. What would become of *history*, had we not a dependence on the veracity of the historian according to the experience which we have had of mankind? How could *politics* be a science, if laws and forms of government had not a uniform influence upon society? Where would be the foundation of *morals*, if particular characters had no certain or determinate power to produce particular sentiments, and if these sentiments had no constant operation on actions? And with what pretense could we employ our *criticism* upon any poet or polite author, if we could not pronounce the conduct and sentiments of his actors either natural or unnatural to such characters, and in such circumstances? It seems almost impossible, therefore, to engage either in science or action of any kind without acknowledging the doctrine of necessity, and this *inference* from motive to voluntary actions, from characters to conduct.

And indeed, when we consider how aptly *natural* and *moral* evidence link together, and form only one chain of argument, we shall make no scruple to allow that they are of the same nature, and derived from the same principles. A prisoner who has neither money nor interest, discovers the impossibility of his escape, as well when he considers the obstinacy of the goaler, as the walls and bars with which he is surrounded; and, in all attempts for his freedom, chooses rather to work upon the stone and iron of the one, than upon the inflexible nature of the other. The same prisoner, when conducted to the scaffold, foresees his death as certainly from the constancy and fidelity of his guards, as from the operation of the axe or wheel. His mind runs along a certain train of ideas: the refusal of the soldiers to consent to his escape; the action of the executioner; the separation of the head and body; bleeding, convulsive motions, and death. Here is a connected chain of natural causes and voluntary actions; but the mind feels no difference between them in passing from one link to another. Nor is less certain of the future event than if it were connected with the objects present to the memory or senses, by a train of causes, cemented together by what we are pleased to call a *physical* necessity. The same experienced union has the same effect on the mind, whether the united objects be motives, volition, and actions; or figure and motion. We may change the name of things; but their nature and their operation on the understanding never change.

Were a man, whom I know to be honest and opulent, and with whom I live in intimate friendship, to come into my house, where I am surrounded with my servants, I rest assured that he is not to stab me before he leaves it in order to rob me of my silver standish; and I no more suspect this event than the falling of the house itself, which is new, and solidly built and founded.—*But he may have been seized with a sudden and unknown frenzy.*—So may a sudden earthquake arise, and shake and tumble my house about my ears. I shall therefore change the suppositions. I shall say that I know with certainty that he is not to put his hand into the fire and hold it there till it be consumed: and this event, I think I can foretell with the same assurance, as that, if he throw himself out at the window, and meet with no obstruction, he will not remain a moment suspended in the air. No suspicion of an unknown frenzy can give the least possibility to the former event, which is so contrary to all the known principles of human nature. A man who at noon leaves his purse full of gold on the pavement at Charing Cross, may as well expect that it will fly away like a feather, as that he will find it untouched an hour after. Above one half of human reasonings contain inferences of a similar nature, attended with more or less degrees of certainty proportioned to our experience of the usual conduct of mankind in such particular situations.

I have frequently considered, what could possibly be the reason why all mankind, though they have ever, without hesitation, acknowledged the doctrine of necessity in their whole practice and reasoning, have yet discovered such a reluctance to acknowledge it in words, and have rather shown a propensity, in all ages, to profess the contrary opinion. The matter, I think, may be accounted for after the following manner. If we examine the operations of body, and the production of effects from their causes, we shall find that all our faculties can never carry us farther in our knowledge of this relation than barely to observe that particular objects are *constantly conjoined* together, and that the mind is carried, by a *customary transition*, from the appearance of one to the belief of the other. But though this conclusion concerning human ignorance be the result of the strictest scrutiny of this subject, men still entertain a strong propensity to believe that they penetrate farther into the powers of nature, and perceive something like a necessary connection between the cause and the effect. When again they turn their reflections towards the operations of their own minds, and *feel* no such connection of the motive and the action; they are thence apt to suppose, that there is a difference between the effects which result from material force, and those which arise from thought and intelligence. But being once convinced that we know nothing farther of causation of any kind than merely the *constant conjunction* of objects, and the consequent *inference* of the mind from one to another, and finding that these two circumstances are universally allowed to have place in voluntary actions; we may be more easily led to own the same necessity common to all causes. And though this reasoning may contradict the systems of many philosophers, in ascribing necessity to the determinations of the will, we shall find, upon reflection, that they dissent from it in words only, not in their real sentiment. Necessity, according to the sense in which it is here taken, has never yet been rejected, nor can ever, I think, be rejected by any philosopher. It may only, perhaps, be pretended that the mind can perceive, in the operations of matter, some farther connection between the cause and effect; and connection that has not place in voluntary actions of intelligent beings. Now whether it be so or not, can only appear upon examination; and it is incumbent on these philosophers to make good their assertion, by defining or describing that necessity, and pointing it out to us in the operations of material causes.

It would seem, indeed, that men begin at the wrong end of this question concerning liberty and necessity, when they enter upon it by examining the faculties of the soul, the influence of the understanding, and the operations of the will. Let them first discuss a more simple question, namely, the operations of body and of brute unintelligent matter; and try whether they can there form any idea of causation and necessity, except that of a constant conjunction of objects, and subsequent inference of the mind from one to another. If these circumstances form, in reality, the whole of that necessity, which we conceive in matter, and if these circumstances be also universally acknowledged to take place in the operations of the mind, the dispute is at an end; at least, must be owned to be thenceforth merely verbal. But as long as we will rashly suppose, that we have some farther idea of necessity and causation in the operations of external objects; at the same time, that we can find nothing farther in the voluntary actions of the mind; there is no possibility of bringing the question to any determinate issue, while we proceed upon so erroneous a supposition. The only method of undeceiving us is to mount up higher; to examine the narrow extent of science when applied to material causes; and to convince ourselves that all we know of them is the constant conjunction and inference above mentioned. We may, perhaps, find that it is with difficulty we are induced to fix such narrow limits to human understanding: but we can afterwards find no difficulty when we come to apply this doctrine to the actions of the will. For as it is evident that these have a regular conjunction with motives and circumstances and characters, and as we always draw inferences from one to the other, we must be obliged to acknowledge in words that necessity, which we have already avowed, in every deliberation of our lives, and in every step of our conduct and behavior.[15]

[15] The prevalence of the doctrine of liberty may be accounted for, from another cause, viz., a false sensation or seeming experience which we have, or may have, of liberty or indifference, in many of our actions. The necessity of any action, whether of matter or of mind, is not, properly speaking, a quality in the agent, but in any thinking or intelligent being, who may consider the action; and it consists chiefly in the determination of his thoughts to infer the existence of that action from some preceeding objects; as liberty, when opposed to necessity, is nothing but the want of that determination, and a certain looseness or indifference, which we feel, in passing, or not passing, from the idea of one object to that of any succeeding one. Now we may observe, that, though, in *reflecting* on human actions, we seldom feel such a looseness, or indifference, but are commonly able to infer them with considerable certainty from their motives, and from the dispositions of the agent; yet it frequently happens, that, in *performing* the actions themselves, we are sensible of something like it. And as all assembling objects are readily taken for each other, this has been employed as a demonstrative and even intuitive proof of human liberty. We feel, that our actions are subject to our will, on most occasions; and imagine we feel, that the will itself is subject to nothing, because, when by a denial of it we are provoked to try, we feel, that it moves easily every way, and produces an image of itself (or a *velleïty*, as it is called in the schools) even on that side, on which it did not settle. This image, or faint motion, we persuade ourselves, could, at that time, have been completed into the thing itself; because, should that be denied, we find, upon a second trial, that, at present, it can. We consider not, that the fantastical desire of shewing liberty, is here the motive of our

But to proceed in this reconciling project with regard to the question of liberty and necessity; the most contentious question of metaphysics, the most contentious science; it will not require many words to prove, that all mankind have ever agreed in the doctrine of liberty as well as in that of necessity, and that the whole dispute, in this respect also, has been hitherto merely verbal. For what is meant by liberty, when applied to voluntary actions? We cannot surely mean that actions have so little connection with motives, inclinations, and circumstances, that one does not follow with a certain degree of uniformity from the other, and that one affords no inference by which we can conclude the existence of the other. For these are plain and acknowledged matters of fact. By liberty, then, we can only mean *a power of acting or not acting, according to the determinations of the will*; that is, if we choose to remain at rest, we may; if we choose to move, we also may. Now this hypothetical liberty is universally allowed to belong to everyone who is not a prisoner and in chains. Here, then, is no subject of dispute.

Whatever definition we may give of liberty, we should be careful to observe two requisite circumstances; *first*, that it be consistent with plain matter of fact; *secondly*, that it be consistent with itself. If we observe these circumstances, and render our definition intelligible, I am persuaded that all mankind will be found of one opinion with regard to it.

It is universally allowed that nothing exists without a cause of its existence, and that chance, when strictly examined, is a mere negative word, and means not any real power which has anywhere a being in nature. But it is pretended that some causes are necessary, some not necessary. Here then is the advantage of definitions. Let anyone *define* a cause, without comprehending, as a part of the definition, a *necessary connection* with its effect; and let him show distinctly the origin of the idea, expressed by the definition; and I shall readily give up the whole controversy. But if the foregoing explication of the matter be received, this must be absolutely impracticable.

---

actions. And it seems certain, that, however we may imagine we feel a liberty within ourselves, a spectator can commonly infer our action from our motives and character; and even where he cannot, he concludes in general, that he might, were he perfectly acquainted with every circumstance of our situation and temper, and the most secret springs of our complexion and disposition. Now this is the very essence of necessity, according to the foregoing doctrine.

Had not objects a regular conjunction with each other, we should never have entertained any notion of cause and effect; and this regular conjunction produces that inference of the understanding, which is the only connection, that we can have any comprehension of. Whoever attempts a definition of cause, exclusive of these circumstances, will be obliged either to employ unintelligible terms or such as we are synonymous to the term which he endeavors to define.[16] And if the definition above mentioned be admitted; liberty, when opposed to necessity, not to constraint, is the same thing with chance; which is universally allowed to have no existence.

Part II

There is no method of reasoning more common, and yet none more blamable, than, in philosophical disputes, to endeavor the refutation of any hypothesis, by a pretense of its dangerous consequences to religion and morality. When any opinion leads to absurdities, it is certainly false; but it is not certain that an opinion is false, because it is of dangerous consequence. Such topics, therefore, ought entirely to be forborne; as serving nothing to the discovery of truth, but only to make the person of an antagonist odious. This I observe in general, without pretending to draw any advantage from it. I frankly submit to an examination of this kind, and shall venture to affirm that the doctrines, both of necessity and of liberty, as above explained, are not only consistent with morality, but are absolutely essential to its support.

Necessity may be defined two ways, conformably to the two definitions of *cause*, of which it makes an essential part. It consists either in the constant conjunction of like objects, or in the inference of the understanding from one object to another. Now necessity, in both these senses (which, indeed, are at bottom the same), has universally, though tacitly, in the

[16] Thus, if a cause be defined, *that which produces any thing*; it is easy to observe, that *producing* is synonymous to *causing*. In like manner, if a cause be defined, *that by which any thing exists*; this is liable to the same objection. For what is meant by these words, *by which?* Had it been said, that a cause is *that* after which *any thing constantly exists* we should have understood the terms. For this is, indeed, all we know of the matter. And this constancy forms the very essence of necessity, nor have we any other idea of it.

schools, in the pulpit, and in common life, been allowed to belong to the will of man; and no one has ever pretended to deny that we can draw inferences concerning human actions, and that those inferences are founded on the experienced union of like actions, with like motives, inclinations, and circumstances. The only particular in which anyone can differ, is, that either, perhaps, he will refuse to give the name of necessity to this property of human actions: but as long as the meaning is understood, I hope the word can do no harm; or that he will maintain it possible to discover something farther in the operations of matter. But this, it must be acknowledged, can be of no consequence to morality or religion, whatever it may be to natural philosophy or metaphysics. We may here be mistaken in asserting that there is no idea of any other necessity or connection in the actions of body; but surely we ascribe nothing to the actions of the mind, but what everyone does, and must readily allow of. We change no circumstance in the received orthodox system with regard to the will, but only in that with regard to material objects and causes. Nothing, therefore, can be more innocent, at least, than this doctrine.

All laws being founded on rewards and punishments, it is supposed as a fundamental principle, that these motives have a regular and uniform influence on the mind, and both produce the good and prevent the evil actions. We may give to this influence what name we please; but, as it is usually conjoined with the action, it must be esteemed a *cause*, and be looked upon as an instance of that necessity, which we would here establish.

The only proper object of hatred or vengeance is a person or creature, endowed with thought and consciousness; and when any criminal or injurious actions excite that passion, it is only by their relation to the person, or connection with him. Actions are, by their very nature, temporary and perishing; and where they proceed not from some *cause* in the character and disposition of the person who performed them, they can neither redound to his honor, if good; nor infamy, if evil. The actions themselves may be blamable; they may be contrary to all the rules of morality and religion. But the person is not answerable for them; and as they proceeded from nothing in him that is durable and constant, and leave nothing of that nature behind them, it is impossible he can, upon their account, become the object of punishment or vengeance. According to the principle therefore, which denies necessity, and consequently causes, a man is as pure and untainted, after having committed the most horrid crime, as at the first moment of his birth, nor is his character anywise concerned in his actions, since they are not derived from it, and the wickedness of the one can never be used as a proof of the depravity of the other.

Men are not blamed for such actions as they perform ignorantly and casually, whatever may be the consequences. Why? but because the principles of these actions are only momentary, and terminate in them alone. Men are less blamed for such actions as they perform hastily and unpremeditately than for such as proceed from deliberation. For what reason? but because a hasty temper, though a constant cause or principle in the mind, operates only by intervals, and infects not the whole character. Again, repentance wipes off every crime, if attended with a reformation of life and manners. How is this to be accounted for? but by asserting that actions render a person criminal merely as they are proofs of criminal principles in the mind; and when, by an alteration of these principles, they cease to be just proofs, they likewise cease to be criminal. But, except upon the doctrine of necessity, they never were just proofs, and consequently never were criminal.

It will be equally easy to prove, and from the same arguments, that *liberty*, according to that definition above mentioned, in which all men agree, is also essential to morality, and that no human actions, where it is wanting, are susceptible of any moral qualities, or can be the objects either of approbation or dislike. For as actions are objects of our moral sentiment, so far only as they are indications of the internal character, passions, and affections; it is impossible that they can give rise either to praise or blame, where they proceed not from these principles, but are derived altogether from external violence.

I pretend not to have obviated or removed all objections to this theory, with regard to necessity and liberty. I can foresee other objections, derived from topics which have not here been treated of. It may be said, for instance, that, if voluntary actions be subjected to the same laws of necessity with the operations of matter, there is a continued chain of necessary causes, pre-ordained and pre-determined, reaching from the original cause of all to every single volition of every human creature. No contingency anywhere in the universe; no indifference; no liberty. While we act, we are, at the same time, acted upon. The ultimate Author of all our volitions is the Creator of the world, who first bestowed motion on this immense machine, and placed all beings in that particular position, whence every subsequent event, by an inevitable necessity, must result. Human actions, therefore, either can have no moral turpitude at all, as proceeding from so good a cause; or if they have any turpitude, they must involve our Creator in the same guilt, while he is acknowledged to be their ultimate cause and author. For as a man, who fired a mine, is answerable for all the consequences whether the train he employed be long or short; so wherever a continued chain of necessary causes is fixed, that Being, either finite or infinite, who produces the first, is likewise the author of all the rest, and must both bear the blame and acquire the praise which belong to them. Our clear and unalterable ideas of morality establish this rule, upon unquestionable reasons, when we examine the consequences of any human action; and these reasons must still have greater force when applied to the volitions and intentions of a Being infinitely wise and powerful. Ignorance or impotence may be pleaded for so limited a creature as man; but these imperfections have no place in our Creator. He foresaw, he ordained, he intended all those actions of men, which we so rashly pronounce criminal. And we must therefore conclude, either that they are not criminal, or that the Deity, not man, is accountable for them. But as either of these positions is absurd and impious, it follows, that the doctrine from which they are deduced cannot possibly be true, as being liable to all the same objections. An absurd consequence, if necessary, proves the original doctrine to be absurd in the same manner as criminal actions render criminal the original cause, if the connection between them be necessary and inevitable.

This objection consists of two parts, which we shall examine separately. *First*, that, if human actions can be traced up, by a necessary chain, to the Deity, they can never be criminal; on account of the infinite perfection of that Being from whom they are derived, and who can intend nothing but what is altogether good and laudable. Or, *Secondly*, if they be criminal, we must retract the attribute of perfection, which we ascribe to the Deity, and must acknowledge him to be the ultimate author of guilt and moral turpitude in all his creatures.

The answer to the first objection seems obvious and convincing. There are many philosophers who, after an exact scrutiny of all the phenomena of nature, conclude, that the *whole*, considered as one system, is, in every period of its existence, ordered with perfect benevolence; and that the utmost possible happiness will, in the end, result to all created beings, without any mixture of positive or absolute ill or misery. Every physical ill, say they, makes an essential part of this benevolent system, and could not possibly be removed, even by the Deity himself, considered as a wise agent, without giving entrance to greater ill, or excluding greater good, which will result from it. From this theory, some philosophers, and the ancient Stoics among the rest, derived a topic of consolation under all afflictions, while they taught their pupils that those ills under which they labored were, in reality, goods to the universe; and that to an enlarged view, which could comprehend the whole system of nature, every event became an object of joy and exultation. But though this topic be specious and sublime, it was soon found in practice weak and ineffectual. You would surely more irritate than appease a man lying under the racking pains of the gout by preaching up to him the rectitude of those general laws, which produced the malignant humors in his body, and led them through the proper canals, to the sinews and nerves, where they now excite such acute torments. These enlarged views may, for a moment, please the imagination of a speculative man, who is placed in ease and security; but neither can they dwell with constancy on his mind, even though undisturbed by the emotions of pain or passion; much less can they maintain their ground when attacked by such powerful antagonists. The affections take a narrower and more natural survey of their object; and by an economy, more suitable to the infirmity of human minds, regard alone the beings around us, and are actuated by such events as appear good or ill to the private system.

The case is the same with *moral* as with *physical* ill. It cannot reasonably be supposed, that those remote considerations, which are found of so little efficacy with regard to one, will have a more powerful influence with regard to the other. The mind of man is so formed by nature that, upon the appearance of certain characters, dispositions, and actions, it immediately feels the sentiment of approbation or blame; nor are there any emotions more essential to its frame and constitution. The characters which engage our approbation are chiefly such as contribute to the peace and security of human society; as the characters which excite blame are chiefly such as tend to public detriment and disturbance: whence it may reasonably be presumed, that the moral sentiments arise, either mediately or immediately, from a reflection of these opposite interests. What though philosophical meditations establish a different opinion or conjecture; that everything is right with regard to the *whole*, and that the qualities, which disturb society, are, in the main, as beneficial, and are as suitable to the primary intention of nature as those which more directly promote its happiness and welfare? Are such remote and uncertain speculations able to counterbalance the sentiments which arise from the natural and immediate view of the objects? A man who is robbed of a considerable sum; does he find his vexation for the loss anywise diminished by these sublime reflections? Why then should his moral resentment against the crime be supposed incompatible with them? Or why should not the acknowledgment of a real distinction between vice and virtue be reconcilable to all speculative systems of philosophy, as well as that of a real distinction between personal beauty and deformity? Both these distinctions are founded in the natural sentiments of the human mind; and these sentiments are not to be controlled or altered by any philosophical theory or speculation whatsoever.

The *second* objection admits not so easy and satisfactory an answer; nor is it possible to explain distinctly, how the Deity can be the mediate cause of all the actions of men, without being the author of sin and moral turpitude. These are mysteries, which mere natural and unassisted reason is very unfit to handle; and whatever system she embraces, she must find herself involved in inextricable difficulties, and even contradictions, at every step which she takes with regard to such subjects. To reconcile the indifference and contingency of human actions with prescience; or to defend absolute decrees, and yet free the Deity from being the author of sin, has been found hitherto to exceed all the power of philosophy. Happy, if she be thence sensible of her temerity, when she pries into these sublime mysteries; and leaving a scene so full of obscurities and perplexities, return, with suitable modesty, to her true and proper province, the examination of common life; where she will find difficulties enough to employ her inquiries, without launching into so boundless an ocean of doubt, uncertainty, and contradiction!

SECTION IX

OF THE REASON OF ANIMALS

All our reasonings concerning matter of fact are founded on a species of *analogy*, which leads us to expect from any cause the same events, which we have observed to result from similar causes. Where the causes are entirely similar, the analogy is perfect, and the inference, drawn from it, is regarded as certain and conclusive: nor does any man ever entertain a doubt, when he sees a piece of iron, that it will have weight and cohesion of parts; as in all other instances, which have ever fallen under his observation. But where the objects have not so exact a similarity, the analogy is less perfect, and the inference is less conclusive; though still it has some force, in proportion to the degree of similarity and resemblance. The anatomical observations, formed upon one animal, are, by this species of reasoning, extended to all animals; and it is certain, that when the circulation of the blood, for instance, is clearly proved to have place in one creature, as a frog, or fish, it forms a strong presumption, that the same principle has place in all. These analogical observations may be carried farther, even to this science, of which we are now treating; and any theory, by which we explain the operations of the understanding, or the origin and connection of the passions in man, will acquire additional authority, if we find, that the same theory is requisite to explain the same phenomena in all other animals. We shall make trial of this, with regard to the hypothesis, by which we have, in the foregoing discourse, endeavored to account for all experimental reasonings; and it is hoped, that this new point of view will serve to confirm all our former observations.

First, It seems evident, that animals as well as men learn many things from experience, and infer, that the same events will always follow from the same causes. By this principle they become acquainted with the more obvious properties of external objects, and gradually, from their birth, treasure up a knowledge of the nature of fire, water, earth, stones, heights, depths, etc., and of the effects which result from their operation. The ignorance and inexperience of the young are here plainly distinguishable from the cunning and sagacity of the old, who have learned, by long observation, to avoid what hurt them, and to pursue what gave ease or pleasure. A horse, that has been accustomed to the field, becomes acquainted with the proper height which he can leap, and will never attempt what exceeds his force and ability. An old greyhound will trust the more fatiguing part of the chase to the younger, and will place himself so as to meet the hare in her doubles; nor are the conjectures, which he forms on this occasion, founded in anything but his observation and experience.

This is still more evident from the effects of discipline and education on animals, who, by the proper application of rewards and punishments, may be taught any course of action, and most contrary to their natural instincts and propensities. Is it not experience, which renders a dog apprehensive of pain, when you menace him, or lift up the whip to beat him? Is it not even experience, which makes him answer to his name, and infer, from such an arbitrary sound, that you mean him rather than any of his fellows, and intend to call him, when you pronounce it in a certain manner, and with a certain tone and accent?

In all these cases, we may observe, that the animal infers some fact beyond what immediately strikes his senses; and that this inference is altogether founded on past experience, while the creature expects from the present object the same consequences, which it has always found in its observation to result from similar objects.

Secondly, It is impossible, that this inference of the animal can be founded on any process of argument or reasoning, by which he concludes, that like events must follow like objects, and that the course of nature will always be regular in its operations. For if there be in reality any arguments of this nature, they surely lie too abstruse for the observation of such imperfect understandings; since it may well employ the utmost care and attention of a philosophic genius to discover and observe them. Animals, therefore, are not guided in these inferences by reasoning; neither are children; neither are the generality of mankind, in their ordinary actions and conclusions; neither are philosophers themselves, who, in all the active parts of life, are, in the main, the same with the vulgar, and are governed by the same maxims. Nature must have provided some other principle, of more ready, and more general use and application; nor can an operation of such immense consequence in life, as that of inferring effects from causes, be trusted to the uncertain process of reasoning and argumentation. Were this doubtful with regard to men, it seems to admit of no question with regard to the brute creation; and the conclusion being once firmly established in the one, we have a strong presumption, from all the rules of analogy, that it ought to be universally admitted, without any exception or reserve. It is custom alone, which engages animals, from every object, that strikes their senses, to infer its usual attendant, and carries their imagination, from the appearance of the one, to conceive the other, in that particular manner, which we denominate *belief*. No other explication can be given of this operation, in all the higher, as well as lower classes of sensitive beings, which fall under our notice and observation.[17]

[17] Since all reasoning concerning facts or causes is derived merely from custom, it may be asked how it happens, that men so much surpass animals in reasoning, and one man so much surpasses another? Has not the same custom the same influence on all?

We shall here endeavor briefly to explain the great difference in human understandings; after which the reason of the difference between men and animals will easily be comprehended.

1. When we have lived any time, and have been accustomed to the uniformity of nature, we acquire a general habit, by which we always transfer the known to the unknown, and conceive the latter to resemble the former. By means of this general habitual principle, we regard even one experiment as the foundation of reasoning and expect a similar event with some degree of certainty, where the experiment has been made accurately, and free from all foreign circumstances. It is therefore considered as a matter of great importance to observe the consequences of things; and as one man may very much surpass another in attention and memory and observation, this will make a very great difference in their reasoning.

2. Where there is a complication of causes to produce any effect, one mind may be much larger than another, and better able to comprehend the whole system of objects, and to infer justly their consequences.

3. One man is able to carry on a chain of consequences to a greater length than another.

4. Few men can think long without running into a confusion of

But though animals learn many parts of their knowledge from observation, there are also many parts of it, which they derive from the original hand of nature; which much exceed the share of capacity they possess on ordinary occasions; and in which they improve, little or nothing, by the longest practice and experience. These we denominate *instincts*, and are so apt to admire as something very extraordinary, and inexplicable by all the disquisitions of human understanding. But our wonder will, perhaps, cease or diminish, when we consider, that the experimental reasoning itself, which we possess in common with beasts, and on which the whole conduct of life depends, is nothing but a species of instinct or mechanical power, that acts in us unknown to ourselves; and in its chief operations, is not directed by any such relations or comparisons of ideas, as are the proper objects of our intellectual faculties. Though the instinct be different, yet still it is an instinct, which teaches a man to avoid the fire; as much as that, which teaches a bird, with such exactness, the art of incubation, and the whole economy and order of its nursery.

---

ideas, and mistaking one for another; and there are various degrees of this infirmity.

5. The circumstance, on which the effect depends, is frequently involved in other circumstances, which are foreign and extrinsic. The separation of it often requires great attention, accuracy, and subtlety.

6. The forming of general maxims from particular observation is a very nice operation; and nothing is more usual, from haste or narrowness of mind which sees not on all sides, than to commit mistakes in this particular.

7. When we reason from analogies, the man, who has the greater experience or the greater promptitude of suggesting analogies, will be the better reasoner.

8. Biases from prejudice, education, passion, party, etc., hang more upon one mind than another.

9. After we have acquired a confidence in human testimony, books and conversation enlarge much more the sphere of one man's experience and thought than those of another.

It would be easy to discover many other circumstances that make a difference in the understandings of men.

SECTION X

OF MIRACLES

Part I

There is, in Dr. Tillotson's writings, an argument against the *real presence*, which is as concise, and elegant, and strong as any argument can possibly be supposed against a doctrine, so little worthy of a serious refutation. It is acknowledged on all hands, says that learned prelate, that the authority, either of the scripture or of tradition, is founded merely in the testimony of the apostles, who were eye-witnesses to those miracles of our Saviour, by which he proved his divine mission. Our evidence, then, for the truth of the *Christian* religion is less than the evidence for the truth of our senses; because, even in the first authors of our religion, it was no greater; and it is evident it must diminish in passing from them to their disciples; nor can anyone rest such confidence in their testimony, as in the immediate object of his senses. But a weaker evidence can never destroy a stronger; and therefore, were the doctrine of the real presence ever so clearly revealed in scripture, it were directly contrary to the rules of just reasoning to give our assent to it. It contradicts sense, though both the scripture and tradition, on which it is supposed to be built, carry not such evidence with them as sense; when they are considered merely as external evidences, and are not brought home to everyone's breast, by the immediate operation of the Holy Spirit.

Nothing is so convenient as a decisive argument of this kind, which must at least *silence* the most arrogant bigotry and superstition, and free us from their impertinent solicitations. I flatter myself, that I have discovered an argument of a like nature, which, if just, will, with the wise and learned, be an everlasting check to all kinds of superstitious delusion, and consequently, will be useful as long as the world endures. For so long, I presume, will the accounts of miracles and prodigies be found in all history, sacred and profane.

Though experience be our only guide in reasoning concerning matters of fact; it must be acknowledged, that this guide is not altogether infallible, but in some cases is apt to lead us into errors. One, who in our climate, should expect better weather in any week of June than in one of December, would reason justly, and comformably to experience; but it is certain, that he may happen, in the event, to find himself mistaken. However, we may observe, that, in such a case, he would have no cause to complain of experience; because it commonly informs us beforehand of the uncertainty, by that contrariety of events, which we may learn from a diligent observation. All effects follow not with like certainty from their supposed causes. Some events are found, in all countries and all ages, to have been constantly conjoined together. Others are found to have been more variable, and sometimes to disappoint our expectations; so that, in our reasonings concerning matter of fact, there are all imaginable degrees of assurance, from the highest certainty to the lowest species of moral evidence.

A wise man, therefore, proportions his belief to the evidence. In such conclusions as are founded on an infallible experience, he expects the event with the last degree of assurance, and regards his past experience as a full *proof* of the future existence of that event. In other cases, he proceeds with more caution; he weighs the opposite experiments; he considers which side is supported by the greater number of experiments; to that side he inclines, with doubt and hesitation; and when at last he fixes his judgment, the evidence exceeds not what we properly call *probability*. All probability, then, supposes an opposition of experiments and observations, where the one side is found to overbalance the other, and to produce a degree of evidence, proportioned to the superiority. A hundred instances or experiments on one side, and fifty on another, afford a double expectation of any event; though a hundred uniform experiments, with only one that is contradictory, reasonably begets a pretty strong degree of assurance. In all cases, we must balance the opposite experiments, where they are opposite, and deduct the smaller number from the greater, in order to know the exact force of the superior evidence.

To apply these principles to a particular instance; we may observe, that there is no species of reasoning more common, more useful, and even necessary to human life, than that which is derived from the testimony of men, and the reports of eye-witnesses and spectators. This species of reasoning, perhaps, one may deny to be founded on the relation of cause and effect. I shall not dispute about a word. It will be sufficient to observe that our assurance in any argument of this kind is derived from no other principle than our observation of the veracity of human testimony, and of the usual conformity of facts to the reports of witnesses. It being a general maxim, that no objects have any discoverable connection together, and that all the inferences, which we can draw from one to another, are founded merely on our experience of their constant and regular conjunction; it is evident, that we ought not to make an exception to this maxim in favor of human testimony, whose connection with any event seems, in itself, as little necessary as any other. Were not the memory tenacious to a certain degree; had not men commonly an inclination to truth and a principle of probity, were they not sensible to shame, when detected in a falsehood: were not these, I say, discovered by *experience* to be qualities, inherent in human nature, we should never repose the least confidence in human testimony. A man delirious, or noted for falsehood and villainy, has no manner of authority with us.

And as the evidence, derived from witnesses and human testimony, is founded on past experience, so it varies with the experience, and is regarded either as *proof* or a *probability*, according as the conjunction between any particular kind of report and any kind of object has been found to be constant or variable. There are a number of circumstances to be taken into consideration in all judgments of this kind; and the ultimate standard, by which we determine all disputes, that may arise concerning them, is always derived from experience and observation. Where this experience is not entirely uniform on any side, it is attended with an unavoidable contrariety in our judgments, and with the same opposition and mutual destruction of argument as in every other kind of evidence. We frequently hesitate concerning the reports of others. We balance the opposite circumstances, which cause any doubt or uncertainty; and when we discover a superiority on one side, we incline to it; but still with a diminution of assurance, in proportion to the force of its antagonist.

This contrariety of evidence, in the present case, may be derived from several different causes; from the opposition of contrary testimony; from the character or number of the witnesses; from the manner of their delivering their testimony; or from the union of all these circumstances. We entertain a suspicion concerning any matter of fact, when the witnesses contradict each other; when they are but few, or of a doubtful character; when they have an interest in what they affirm; when they deliver their testimony with hesitation, or on the contrary, with too violent asseverations. There are many other particulars of the same kind, which may diminish or destroy the force of any argument, derived from human testimony.

Suppose, for instance, that the fact, which the testimony endeavors to establish, partakes of the extraordinary and marvellous; in that case, the evidence, resulting from the testimony, admits of a diminution, greater or less, in proportion as the fact is more or less unusual. The reason why we place any credit in witnesses and historians, is not derived from any *connection*, which we perceive *a priori*, between testimony and reality, but because we are accustomed to find a conformity between them. But when the fact attested is such a one as has seldom fallen under our observation, here is a contest of two opposite experiences; of which the one destroys the other, as far as its force goes, and the superior can only operate on the mind by the force, which remains. The very same principle of experience, which gives us a certain degree of assurance in the testimony of witnesses, gives us also, in this case, another degree of assurance against the fact, which they endeavor to establish; from which contradiction there necessarily arises a counterpoise, and mutual destruction of belief and authority.

I should not believe such a story were it told me by Cato, was a proverbial saying in Rome, even during the lifetime of that philosophical patriot.[18] The incredibility of a fact, it was allowed, might invalidate so great an authority.

The Indian prince, who refused to believe the first relations concerning the effects of frost, reasoned justly; and it naturally required very strong testimony to engage his assent to fact, that arose from a state of nature, with which he was unacquainted, and which bore so little analogy to those events, of which he had had constant and uniform experience. Though

[18] Plutarch, in *Vita Catonis*.

they were not contrary to his experience, they were not conformable to it.[19]

But in order to increase the probability against the testimony of witnesses, let us suppose, that the fact, which they affirm, instead of being only marvellous, is really miraculous; and suppose also, that the testimony considered apart and in itself, amounts to an entire proof; in that case, there is proof against proof, of which the strongest must prevail, but still with a diminution of its force, in proportion to that of its antagonist.

A miracle is a violation of the laws of nature; and as a firm and unalterable experience has established these laws, the proof against a miracle, from the very nature of the fact, is as entire as any argument from experience can possibly be imagined. Why is it more than probable, that all men must die; that lead cannot, of itself, remain suspended in the air; that fire consumes wood, and is extinguished by water; unless it be, that these events are found agreeable to the laws of nature, and there is required a violation of these laws, or in other words, a miracle to prevent them? Nothing is esteemed a miracle, if it ever happen in the common course of nature. It is no miracle that a man, seemingly in good health, should die on a sudden: because such a kind of death, though more

[19] No Indian, it is evident, could have experience that water did not freeze in cold climates. This is placing nature in a situation quite unknown to him; and it is impossible for him to tell *a priori* what will result from it. It is making a new experiment, the consequence of which is always uncertain. One may sometimes conjecture from analogy what will follow; but still this is but conjecture. And it must be confessed, that, in the present case of freezing, the event follows contrary to the rules of analogy, and is such as a rational Indian would not look for. The operations of cold upon water are not gradual, according to the degrees of cold; but whenever it comes to the freezing point, the water passes in a moment, from the utmost liquidity to perfect hardness. Such an event, therefore, may be denominated *extraordinary*, and requires a pretty strong testimony, to render it credible to people in a warm climate: But still it is not *miraculous*, nor contrary to uniform experience of the course of nature in cases where all the circumstances are the same. The inhabitants of Sumatra have always seen water fluid in their own climate, and the freezing of their rivers ought to be deemed a prodigy; but they never saw water in Muscovy during the winter; and therefore they cannot reasonably be positive what would there be the consequence.

unusual than any other, has yet been frequently observed to happen. But it is a miracle that a dead man should come to life; because that has never been observed in any age or country. There must, therefore, be a uniform experience against every miraculous event, otherwise the event would not merit that appellation. And as a uniform experience amounts to a proof, there is here a direct and full *proof*, from the nature of the fact, against the existence of any miracle; nor can such a proof be destroyed, or the miracle rendered credible, but by an opposite proof, which is superior.[20]

The plain consequence is (and it is a general maxim worthy of our attention), 'That no testimony is sufficient to establish a miracle, unless the testimony be of such a kind, that its falsehood would be more miraculous, than the fact, which it endeavors to establish: and even in that case there is a mutual destruction of arguments, and the superior only gives us an assurance suitable to that degree of force, which remains, after deducting the inferior.' When anyone tells me, that he saw a dead man restored to life, I immediately consider with myself, whether it be more probable, that this person should either deceive or be deceived, or that the fact, which he relates, should really have happened. I weigh the one miracle against

[20] Sometimes an event may not, *in itself, seem* to be contrary to the laws of nature, and yet, if it were real, it might, by reason of some circumstances, be denominated a miracle; because, *in fact*, it is contrary to these laws. Thus if a person, claiming a divine authority, should command a sick person to be well, a healthful man to fall down dead, the clouds to pour rain, the winds to blow, in short, should order many natural events, which immediately follow upon his command; these might justly be esteemed miracles, because they are really, in this case, contrary to the laws of nature. For if any suspicion remain, that the event and command concurred by accident, there is no miracle and no transgression of the laws of nature. If this suspicion be removed, there is evidently a miracle, and a transgression of these laws; because nothing can be more contrary to nature than that the voice or command of a man should have such an influence. A miracle may be accurately defined, *a transgression of a law of nature by a particular volition of the Deity, or by the interposition of some invisible agent.* A miracle may either be discoverable by men or not. This alters not its nature and essence. The raising of a house or ship into the air is a visible miracle. The raising of a feather, when the wind wants ever so little of a force requisite for that purpose, is as real a miracle, though not so sensible with regard to us.

the other; and according to the superiority, which I discover, I pronounce my decision, and always reject the greater miracle. If the falsehood of his testimony would be more miraculous, than the event which he relates; then, and not till then, can he pretend to command my belief or opinion.

Part II

In the foregoing reasoning we have supposed, that the testimony, upon which a miracle is founded, may possibly amount to an entire proof, and that the falsehood of that testimony would be a real prodigy. But it is easy to show, that we have been a great deal too liberal in our concession, and that there never was a miraculous event established on so full an evidence.

For *first*, there is not to be found, in all history, any miracle attested by a sufficient number of men, of such unquestioned good sense, education, and learning, as to secure us against all delusion in themselves; of such undoubted integrity, as to place them beyond all suspicion of any design to deceive others; of such credit and reputation in the eyes of mankind, as to have a great deal to lose in case of their being detected in any falsehood; and at the same time, attesting facts performed in such a public manner and in so celebrated a part of the world, as to render the detection unavoidable: all which circumstances are requisite to give us a full assurance in the testimony of men.

Secondly. We may observe in human nature a principle which, if strictly examined, will be found to diminish extremely the assurance, which we might, from human testimony, have, in any kind of prodigy. The maxim, by which we commonly conduct ourselves in our reasonings, is, that the objects, of which we have no experience, resemble those, of which we have; that what we have found to be most usual is always most probable; and that where there is an opposition of arguments, we ought to give the preference to such as are founded on the greatest number of past observations. But though, in proceeding by this rule, we readily reject any fact which is unusual and incredible in an ordinary degree; yet in advancing farther, the mind observes not always the same rule; but when anything is affirmed utterly absurd and miraculous, it rather the more readily admits of such a fact, upon account of that very circumstance, which ought to destroy all its authority. The passion of *surprise* and *wonder*, arising from miracles, being an agreeable emotion, gives a sensible tendency towards the belief of those events, from which it is derived. And this goes so far, that even those who cannot enjoy this pleasure immediately, nor can believe those miraculous events, of which they are informed, yet love to partake of the satisfaction at second hand or by rebound, and place a pride and delight in exciting the admiration of others.

With what greediness are the miraculous accounts of travelers received; their descriptions of sea and land monsters, their relations of wonderful adventures, strange men, and uncouth manners? But if the spirit of religion join itself to the love of wonder, there is an end of common sense; and human testimony, in these circumstances, loses all pretensions to authority. A religionist may be an enthusiast, and imagine he sees what has no reality: he may know his narrative to be false, and yet persevere in it, with the best intentions in the world, for the sake of promoting so holy a cause: or even where this delusion has not place, vanity, excited by so strong a temptation, operates on him more powerfully than on the rest of mankind in any other circumstances; and self-interest with equal force. His auditors may not have, and commonly have not, sufficient judgment to canvass his evidence: what judgment they have, they renounce by principle, in these sublime and mysterious subjects: or if they were ever so willing to employ it, passion and a heated imagination disturb the regularity of its operations. Their credulity increases his impudence: and his impudence overpowers their credulity.

Eloquence, when at its highest pitch, leaves little room for reason or reflection; but addressing itself entirely to the fancy or the affections, captivates the willing hearers, and subdues their understanding. Happily, this pitch it seldom attains. But what a Tully or a Demosthenes could scarcely effect over a Roman or Athenian audience, every *Capuchin*, every itinerant or stationary teacher can perform over the generality of mankind, and in a higher degree, by touching such gross and vulgar passions.

The many instances of forged miracles, and prophecies, and supernatural events, which, in all ages, have either been detected by contrary evidence, or which detect themselves by their absurdity, prove sufficiently the strong propensity of mankind to the extraordinary and the marvellous, and ought reasonably to beget a suspicion against all relations of this kind. This is our natural way of thinking, even with regard to the most common and most credible events. For instance: there is no kind of report which rises so easily, and spreads so quickly, especially in country places and provincial towns, as those concerning marriages; insomuch that two young persons of equal condition never see each other twice, but the whole neighborhood immediately join them together. The pleasure of telling a piece of news so interesting, of propagating it, and of being the first reporters of it, spreads the intelligence. And this is so well known, that no man of sense gives attention to these reports, till he find them confirmed by some greater evidence. Do not the same passions, and others still stronger, incline the generality of mankind to believe and report, with the greatest vehemence and assurance, all religious miracles?

Thirdly. It forms a strong presumption against all supernatural and miraculous relations, that they are observed chiefly to abound among ignorant and barbarous nations; or if a civilized people has ever given admission to any of them, that people will be found to have received them from ignorant and barbarous ancestors, who transmitted them with that inviolable sanction and authority, which always attend received opinions. When we peruse the first histories of all nations, we are apt to imagine ourselves transported into some new world; where the whole frame of nature is disjointed, and every element performs its operations in a different manner, from what it does at present. Battles, revolutions, pestilence, famine and death, are never the effect of those natural causes, which we experience. Prodigies, omens, oracles, judgments, quite obscure the few natural events, that are intermingled with them. But as the former grow thinner every page, in proportion as we advance nearer the enlightened ages, we soon learn, that there is nothing mysterious or supernatural in the case, but that all proceeds from the usual propensity of mankind towards the marvellous, and that, though this inclination may at intervals receive a check from sense and learning, it can never be thoroughly extirpated from human nature.

It is strange, a judicious reader is apt to say, upon the perusal of these wonderful historians, *that such prodigious events never happen in our days.* But it is nothing strange, I hope, that men should lie in all ages. You must surely have seen instances enough of that frailty. You have yourself heard many such marvellous relations started, which, being treated with scorn by all the wise and judicious, have at last been abandoned even by the vulgar. Be assured, that those renowned lies, which have spread and flourished to such a monstrous height, arose from like beginnings; but being sown in a more proper soil, shot up at last into prodigies almost equal to those which they relate.

It was a wise policy in that false prophet, Alexander, who though now forgotten, was once so famous, to lay the first scene of his impostures in Paphlagonia, where, as Lucian tells us, the people were extremely ignorant and stupid, and ready to swallow even the grossest delusion. People at a distance, who are weak enough to think the matter at all worth inquiry, have no opportunity of receiving better information. The stories come magnified to them by a hundred circumstances. Fools are industrious in propagating the imposture; while the wise and learned are contented, in general, to deride its absurdity, without informing themselves of the particular facts, by which it may be distinctly refuted. And thus the impostor above mentioned was enabled to proceed, from his ignorant Paphlagonians, to the enlisting of votaries, even among the Grecian philosophers, and men of the most eminent rank and distinction in Rome: nay, could engage the attention of that sage emperor Marcus Aurelius, so far as to make him trust the success of a military expedition to his delusive prophecies.

The advantages are so great, of starting an imposture among an ignorant people, that, even though the delusion should be too gross to impose on the generality of them (*which, though seldom, is sometimes the case*) it has a much better chance for succeeding in remote countries, than if the first scene had been laid in a city renowned for arts and knowledge. The most ignorant and barbarous of these barbarians carry the report abroad. None of their countrymen have a large correspondence, or sufficient credit and authority to contradict and beat down the delusion. Men's inclination to the marvellous has full opportunity to display itself. And thus a story, which is universally exploded in the place where it was first started, shall pass for certain at a thousand miles distance. But had Alexander fixed his residence at Athens, the philosophers of that renowned mart of learning had immediately spread, throughout the whole Roman empire, their sense of the matter; which, being supported by so great authority, and displayed by all the force of reason and eloquence, had entirely opened the eyes of mankind. It is true; Lucian, passing by chance through Paphlagonia, had an opportunity of performing this good office. But, though much to be wished, it does not always happen that every Alexander meets with a Lucian, ready to expose and detect his impostures.

I may add as a *fourth* reason, which diminishes the authority of prodigies, that there is no testimony for any, even those which have not been expressly detected, that is not opposed by an infinite number of witnesses; so that not only the miracle destroys the credit of testimony, but the testimony destroys itself. To make this the better understood, let us consider, that, in matters of religion, whatever is different is contrary; and that it is impossible the religions of ancient Rome, of Turkey, of Siam, and of China should, all of them, be established on any solid foundation. Every miracle, therefore, pretended to have been wrought in any of these religions (and all of them abound in miracles), as its direct scope is to establish the particular system to which it is attributed; so has it the same force, though more indirectly, to overthrow every other system. In destroying a rival system, it likewise destroys the credit of those miracles, on which that system was established; so that all the prodigies of different religions are to be regarded as contrary facts, and the evidences of these prodigies, whether weak or strong, as opposite to each other. According to this method of reasoning, when we believe any miracle of Mahomet or his successors, we have for our warrant the testimony of a few barbarous Arabians. And on the other hand, we are to regard the authority of Titus Livius, Plutarch, Tacitus, and, in short, of all the authors and witnesses, Grecian, Chinese, and Roman Catholic, who have related any miracle in their particular religion; I say, we are to regard their testimony in the same light as if they had mentioned that Mohammedan miracle, and had in express terms contradicted it, with the same certainty as they have for the miracle they relate. This argument may appear oversubtle and refined; but is not in reality different from the reasoning of a judge, who supposes, that the credit of two witnesses, maintaining a crime against anyone, is destroyed by the testimony of two others, who affirm him to have been two hundred leagues distant, at the same instant when the crime is said to have been committed.

One of the best attested miracles in all profane history, is that which Tacitus reports of Vespasian, who cured a blind man in Alexandria, by means of his spittle, and a lame man by the mere touch of his foot; in obedience to a vision of the god Serapis, who had enjoined them to have recourse to the Emperor, for these miraculous cures. The story may be seen in that fine historian:[21] where every circumstance seems to add weight to the testimony, and might be displayed at large with all the force of argument and eloquence, if anyone were now concerned to enforce the evidence of that exploded and idolatrous superstition. The gravity, solidity, age, and probity of so great an emperor, who, through the whole course of his life, conversed in a familiar manner with his friends and courtiers, and never affected those extraordinary airs of divinity assumed by Alexander and Demetrius. The historian, a contemporary writer, noted for candor and veracity, and withal, the greatest and most penetrating genius, perhaps, of all antiquity; and so free from any tendency to credulity, that he even lies under the contrary imputation, of atheism and profaneness; the persons, from whose authority he related the miracle, of established character for judgment and veracity, as we may well presume; eye-witnesses of the fact, and confirming their testimony, after the Flavian family was despoiled of the empire, and could no longer give any reward, as the price of a lie. *Utrumque, qui interfuere, nunc quoque memorant, postquam nullum mendacio pretium.* To which if we add the public nature of the facts, as related, it will appear, that no evidence can well be supposed stronger for so gross and so palpable a falsehood.

There is also a memorable story related by Cardinal de Retz, which may well deserve our consideration. When that intriguing politician fled into Spain, to avoid the persecution of his enemies, he passed through Saragossa, the capital of Aragon, where he was shown, in the cathedral, a man, who had served seven years as a doorkeeper, and was well known to everybody in town, that had ever paid his devotions at that church. He had been seen, for so long a time, wanting a leg; but recovered that limb by the rubbing of holy oil upon the stump; and the cardinal assures us that he saw him with two legs. This miracle was vouched by all the canons of the church; and the whole company in town were appealed to for a confirmation of the fact; whom the cardinal found, by their zealous devotion, to be thorough believers of the miracle.

21 Hist, lib. v. cap. 8. Suetonius gives nearly the same account *in vita* Vesp.

Here the relater was also contemporary to the supposed prodigy, of an incredulous and libertine character, as well as of great genius; the miracle of so *singular* a nature as could scarcely admit of a counterfeit, and the witnesses very numerous, and all of them, in a manner, spectators of the fact, to which they gave their testimony. And what adds mightily to the force of the evidence, and may double our surprise on this occasion, is, that the cardinal himself, who relates the story, seems not to give any credit to it, and consequently cannot be suspected of any concurrence in the holy fraud. He considered justly, that it was not requisite, in order to reject a fact of this nature, to be able accurately to disprove the testimony, and to trace its falsehood, through all the circumstances of knavery and credulity which produced it. He knew, that, as this was commonly altogether impossible at any small distance of time and place; so was it extremely difficult, even where one was immediately present, by reason of the bigotry, ignorance, cunning, and roguery of a great part of mankind. He therefore concluded, like a just reasoner, that such an evidence carried falsehood upon the very face of it, and that a miracle, supported by any human testimony, was more properly a subject of derision than of argument.

There surely never was a greater number of miracles ascribed to one person, than those, which were lately said to have been wrought in France upon the tomb of Abbé Paris, the famous Jansenist, with whose sanctity the people were so long deluded. The curing of the sick, giving hearing to the deaf, and sight to the blind, were everywhere talked of as the usual effects of that holy sepulchre. But what is more extraordinary; many of the miracles were immediately proved upon the spot, before judges of unquestioned integrity, attested by witnesses of credit and distinction, in a learned age, and on the most eminent theater that is now in the world. Nor is this all: a relation of them was published and dispersed everywhere; nor were the *Jesuits*, though a learned body, supported by the civil magistrate, and determined enemies to those opinions, in whose favor the miracles were said to have been wrought, ever able distinctly to refute or detect them. Where shall we find such a number of circumstances, agreeing to the corroboration of one fact? And what have we to oppose to such a cloud of witnesses, but the absolute impossibility or miraculous nature of the events, which they relate? And this surely, in the eyes of all reasonable people, will alone be regarded as a sufficient refutation.

Is the consequence just, because some human testimony has the utmost force and authority in some cases, when it relates the battle of Philippi or Pharsalia for instance; that therefore all kinds of testimony must, in all cases, have equal force and authority? Suppose that the Caesarean and Pompeian factions had, each of them, claimed the victory in these battles, and that the historians of each party had uniformly ascribed the advantage to their own side; how could mankind, at this distance, have been able to determine between them? The contrariety is equally strong between the miracles related by Herodotus or Plutarch, and those delivered by Mariana, Bede, or any monkish historian.

The wise lend a very academic faith to every report which favors the passion of the reporter; whether it magnifies his country, his family, or himself, or in any other way strikes in with his natural inclinations and propensities. But what greater temptation than to appear a missionary, a prophet, an ambassador from heaven? Who would not encounter many dangers and difficulties, in order to attain so sublime a character? Or if, by the help of vanity and a heated imagination, a man has first made a convert of himself, and entered seriously into the delusion; whoever scruples to make use of pious frauds, in support of so holy and meritorious a cause?

The smallest spark may here kindle into the greatest flame; because the materials are always prepared for it. The *avidum genus auricularum*, the gazing populace, receive greedily, without examination, whatever soothes superstition, and promotes wonder.

How many stories of this nature have, in all ages, been detected and exploded in their infancy? How many more have been celebrated for a time, and have afterwards sunk into neglect and oblivion? Where such reports, therefore, fly about, the solution of the phenomenon is obvious; and we judge in conformity to regular experience and observation, when we account for it by the known and natural principles of credulity and delusion. And shall we, rather than have a recourse to so natural a solution, allow of a miraculous violation of the most established laws of nature?

I need not mention the difficulty of detecting a falsehood in any private or even public history, at the place, where it is said to happen; much more when the scene is removed to ever so small a distance. Even a court of judicature, with all the authority, accuracy, and judgment, which they can employ, find themselves often at a loss to distinguish between truth and falsehood in the most recent actions. But the matter never comes to any issue, if trusted to the common method of altercations and debate and flying rumors; especially when men's passions have taken part on either side.

In the infancy of new religions, the wise and learned commonly esteem the matter too inconsiderable to deserve their attention or regard. And when afterwards they would willingly detect the cheat, in order to undeceive the deluded multitude, the season is now past, and the records and witnesses, which might clear up the matter, have perished beyond recovery. No means of detection remain, but those which must be drawn from the very testimony itself of the reporters: and these, though always sufficient with the judicious and knowing, are commonly too fine to fall under the comprehension of the vulgar.

Upon the whole, then, it appears, that no testimony for any kind of miracle has ever amounted to a probability, much less to a proof; and that, even supposing it amounted to a proof, it would be opposed by another proof; derived from the very nature of the fact, which it would endeavor to establish. It is experience only, which gives authority to human testimony; and it is the same experience, which assures us of the laws of nature. When, therefore, these two kinds of experience are contrary, we have nothing to do but substract the one from the other, and embrace an opinion, either on one side or the other, with that assurance which arises from the remainder. But according to the principle here explained, this substraction, with regard to all popular religions, amounts to an entire annihilation; and therefore we may establish it as a maxim, that no human testimony can have such force as to prove a miracle, and make it a just foundation for any such system of religion.

I beg the limitations here made may be remarked, when I say, that a miracle can never be proved, so as to be the foundation of a system of religion. For I own, that otherwise, there may possibly be miracles, or violations of the usual course of nature, of such a kind as to admit of proof from human testimony; though, perhaps, it will be impossible to find any such in all the records of history. Thus, suppose, all authors, in all languages, agree, that, from the first of January

1600, there was a total darkness over the whole earth for eight days: suppose that the tradition of this extraordinary event is still strong and lively among the people: that all travelers, who return from foreign countries, bring us accounts of the same tradition, without the least variation or contradiction: it is evident, that our present philosophers, instead of doubting the fact, ought to receive it as certain, and ought to search for the causes whence it might be derived. The decay, corruption, and dissolution of nature, is an event rendered probable by so many analogies, that any phenomenon, which seems to have a tendency towards that catastrophe, comes within the reach of human testimony, if that testimony be very extensive and uniform.

But suppose, that all the historians who treat of England, should agree, that, on the first of January 1600, Queen Elizabeth died; that both before and after her death she was seen by her physicians and the whole court, as is usual with persons of her rank; that her successor was acknowledged and proclaimed by the parliament; and that, after being interred a month, she again appeared, resumed the throne, and governed England for three years. I must confess that I should be surprised at the concurrence of so many odd circumstances, but should not have the least inclination to believe so miraculous an event. I should not doubt of her pretended death, and of those other public circumstances that followed it; I should only assert it to have been pretended, and that it neither was, nor possibly could be real. You would in vain object to me the difficulty, and almost impossibility of deceiving the world in an affair of such consequence; the wisdom and solid judgment of that renowned queen; with the little or no advantage which she could reap from so poor an artifice. All this might astonish me; but I would still reply, that the knavery and folly of men are such common phenomena, that I should rather believe the most extraordinary events to arise from their concurrence, than admit of so signal a violation of the laws of nature.

But should this miracle be ascribed to any new system of religion; men, in all ages, have been so much imposed on by ridiculous stories of that kind, that this very circumstance would be a full proof of a cheat, and sufficient, with all men of sense, not only to make them reject the fact, but even reject it without farther examination. Though the Being to whom the miracle is ascribed, be, in this case, Almighty, it does not, upon that account, become a whit more probable; since it is impossible for us to know the attributes or actions of such a Being, otherwise than from the experience which we have of his productions, in the usual course of nature. This still reduces us to past observation, and obliges us to compare the instances of the violation of truth in the testimony of men, with those of the violation of the laws of nature by miracles, in order to judge which of them is most likely and probable. As the violations of truth are more common in the testimony concerning religious miracles, than in that concerning any other matter of fact; this must diminish very much the authority of the former testimony, and make us form a general resolution, never to lend any attention to it, with whatever specious pretense it may be covered.

Lord Bacon seems to have embraced the same principles of reasoning. "We ought," says he, "to make a collection or particular history of all monsters and prodigious births or productions, and in a word of everything new, rare, and extraordinary in nature. But this must be done with the most severe scrutiny, lest we depart from truth. Above all, every relation must be considered as suspicious, which depends in any degree upon religion, as the prodigies of Livy. And no less so, everything that is to be found in the writers of natural magic or alchemy, or such authors, who seem, all of them, to have an unconquerable appetite for falsehood and fable."[22]

I am the better pleased with the method of reasoning here delivered, as I think it may serve to confound those dangerous friends or disguised enemies to the *Christian Religion*, who have undertaken to defend it by the principles of human reason. Our most holy religion is founded on *faith*, not on reason; and it is a sure method of exposing it to put it to such a trial as it is, by no means, fitted to endure. To make this more evident, let us examine those miracles, related in scripture; and not to lose ourselves in too wide a field, let us confine ourselves to such as we find in the *Pentateuch*, which we shall examine, according to the principles of these pretended Christians, not as the word or testimony of God himself, but as the production of a mere human writer and historian. Here then we are first to consider a book, presented to us by a barbarous and ignorant people, written in an age when they were still more barbarous, and in all probability long after the facts which it relates, corroborated by no concurring testimony, and

[22] Nov. Org. lib. ii. aph. 29.

resembling those fabulous accounts, which every nation gives of its origin. Upon reading this book, we find it full of prodigies and miracles. It gives an account of a state of the world and of human nature entirely different from the present: of our fall from that state; of the age of man, extended to near a thousand years; of the destruction of the world by a deluge; of the arbitrary choice of one people, as the favorites of heaven; and that people the countrymen of the author; of their deliverance from bondage by prodigies the most astonishing imaginable. I desire anyone to lay his hand upon his heart, and after a serious consideration declare, whether he thinks that the falsehood of such a book, supported by such a testimony, would be more extraordinary and miraculous than all the miracles it relates; which is, however, necessary to make it be received, according to the measures of probability above established.

What we have said of miracles may be applied, without any variation, to prophecies; and indeed, all prophecies are real miracles, and as such only, can be admitted as proofs of any revelation. If it did not exceed the capacity of human nature to foretell future events, it would be absurd to employ any prophecy as an argument for a divine mission or authority from heaven. So that, upon the whole, we may conclude, that the *Christian Religion* not only was at first attended with miracles, but even at this day cannot be believed by any reasonable person without one. Mere reason is insufficient to convince us of its veracity: and whoever is moved by *faith* to assent to it, is conscious of a continued miracle in his own person, which subverts all the principles of his understanding, and gives him a determination to believe what is most contrary to custom and experience.

SECTION XI

OF A PARTICULAR PROVIDENCE AND OF A FUTURE STATE

I was lately engaged in conversation with a friend who loves sceptical paradoxes; where, though he advanced many principles, of which I can by no means approve, yet as they seem to be curious, and to bear some relation to the chain of reasoning carried on throughout this inquiry, I shall here copy them from my memory as accurately as I can, in order to submit them to the judgment of the reader.

Our conversation began with my admiring the singular good fortune of philosophy, which, as it requires entire liberty above all other privileges, and chiefly flourishes from the free opposition of sentiments and argumentation, received its first birth in an age and country of freedom and toleration, and was never cramped, even in its most extravagant principles, by any creeds, concessions, or penal statutes. For, except the banishment of Protagoras, and the death of Socrates, which last event proceeded partly from other motives, there are scarcely any instances to be met with, in ancient history, of this bigoted jealousy, with which the present age is so much infested. Epicurus lived at Athens to an advanced age, in peace and tranquillity; Epicureans were even admitted to receive the sacerdotal character, and to officiate at the altar, in the most sacred rites of the established religion. And the public encouragement of pensions and salaries was afforded equally, by the wisest of all the Roman emperors, to the professors of every sect of philosophy. How requisite such kind of treatment was to philosophy, in her early youth, will easily be conceived, if we reflect, that, even at present, when she may be supposed more hardy and robust, she bears with much difficulty the inclemency of the seasons, and those harsh winds of calumny and persecution, which blow upon her.

You admire, says my friend, as the singular good fortune of philosophy, what seems to result from the natural course of things, and to be unavoidable in every age and nation. This pertinacious bigotry, of which you complain, as so fatal to philosophy, is really her offspring, who, after allying with superstition, separates himself entirely from the interest of his parent, and becomes her most inveterate enemy and persecutor. Speculative dogmas of religion, the present occasions of such furious dispute, could not possibly be conceived or admitted in the early ages of the world; when mankind, being wholly illiterate, formed an idea of religion more suitable to their weak apprehension, and composed there sacred tenets of such tales chiefly as were the objects of traditional belief, more than of argument or disputation. After the first alarm, therefore, was over, which arose from the new paradoxes and principles of the philosophers; these teachers seem ever after, during the ages of antiquity, to have lived in great harmony with the established superstition, and to have made a fair partition of mankind between them; the former claiming all the learned and wise, the latter possessing all the vulgar and illiterate.

It seems then, say I, that you leave politics entirely out of the question, and never suppose, that a wise magistrate can justly be jealous of certain tenets of philosophy, such as those of Epicurus, which, denying a divine existence, and consequently a providence and a future state, seem to loosen, in a great measure, the ties of morality, and may be supposed, for that reason, pernicious to the peace of civil society.

I know, replied he, that in fact these persecutions never, in any age, proceeded from calm reason, or from experience of the pernicious consequences of philosophy; but arose entirely from passion and prejudice. But what if I should advance farther, and assert, that if Epicurus had been accused before the people, by any of the *sycophants* or informers of those days, he could easily have defended his cause, and proved his principles of philosophy to be as salutary as those of his adversaries, who endeavored, with such zeal, to expose him to the public hatred and jealousy?

I wish, said I, you would try your eloquence upon so extraordinary a topic, and make a speech for Epicurus, which might satisfy, not the mob of Athens, if you will allow that ancient and polite city to have contained any mob, but the more philosophical part of his audience, such as might be supposed capable of comprehending his arguments.

The matter would not be difficult, upon such conditions, replied he. And if you please, I shall suppose myself Epicurus for a moment, and make you stand for the Athenian people, and shall deliver you such an harangue as will fill all the urn with white beans, and leave not a black one to gratify the malice of my adversaries.

Very well: pray proceed upon these suppositions.

I come hither, O ye Athenians, to justify in your assembly what I maintained in my school, and I find myself impeached by furious antagonists, instead of reasoning with calm and dispassionate inquirers. Your deliberations, which of right should be directed to questions of public good, and the interest of the commonwealth, are diverted to the disquisitions of speculative philosophy; and these magnificent, but perhaps fruitless inquiries, take place of your more familiar but more useful occupations. But so far as in me lies, I will prevent this abuse. We shall not here dispute concerning the origin and government of worlds. We shall only inquire how far such questions concern the public interest. And if I can persuade you, that they are entirely indifferent to the peace of society and security of government, I hope that you will presently send us back to our schools, there to examine, at leisure, the question the most sublime, but at the same time, the most speculative of all philosophy.

The religious philosophers, not satisfied with the tradition of your forefathers, and doctrine of your priests (in which I willingly acquiesce), indulge a rash curiosity, in trying how far they can establish religion upon the principles of reason; and they thereby excite, instead of satisfying, the doubts, which naturally arise from a diligent and scrutinous inquiry. They paint, in the most magnificent colors, the order, beauty, and wise arrangement of the universe; and then ask, if such a glorious display of intelligence could proceed from the fortuitous concourse of atoms, or if chance could produce what the greatest genius can never sufficiently admire. I shall not examine the justness of this argument. I shall allow it to be as solid as my antagonists and accusers can desire. It is sufficient, if I can prove, from this very reasoning, that the question is entirely speculative, and that, when, in my philosophical disquisitions, I deny a providence and a future state, I undermine not the foundations of society, but advance principles, which they themselves, upon their own topics, if they argue consistently, must allow to be solid and satisfactory.

You then, who are my accusers, have acknowledged, that the chief or sole argument for a divine existence (which I never questioned) is derived from the order of nature; where there appear such marks of intelligence and design, that you think it extravagant to assign for its cause, either chance, or the blind and unguided force of matter. You allow, that this is an argument drawn from effects to causes. From the order of the work, you infer, that there must have been project and forethought in the workman. If you cannot make out this point, you allow, that your conclusion fails; and you pretend not to establish the conclusion in a greater latitude than the phenomena of nature will justify. These are your concessions. I desire you to mark the consequences.

When we infer any particular cause from an effect, we must proportion the one to the other, and can never be allowed to ascribe to the cause any qualities, but what are exactly sufficient to produce the effect. A body of ten ounces raised in any scale may serve as a proof, that the counterbalancing weight exceeds ten ounces; but can never afford a reason that it exceeds a hundred. If the cause, assigned for any effect, be not sufficient to produce it, we must either reject that cause, or add to it such qualities as will give it a just proportion to the effect. But if we ascribe to it further qualities, or affirm it capable of producing other effects, we can only indulge the license of conjecture, and arbitrarily suppose the existence of qualities and energies, without reason or authority.

The same rule holds, whether the cause assigned be brute unconscious matter, or a rational intelligent being. If the cause be known only by the effect, we never ought to ascribe to it any qualities, beyond what are precisely requisite to produce the effect; nor can we, by any rules of just reasoning, return back from the cause, and infer other effects from it, beyond those by which alone it is known to us. No one, merely from the sight of one of Zeuxis's pictures, could know, that he was also a statuary or architect, and was an artist no less skillful in stone and marble than in colors. The talents and taste, displayed in the particular work before us; these we may safely conclude the workman to be possessed of. The cause must be proportioned to the effect; and if we exactly and precisely proportion it, we shall never find in it any qualities, that point farther, or afford an inference concerning any other design or performance. Such qualities must be somewhat beyond what is merely requisite for producing the effect, which we examine.

Allowing, therefore, the gods to be the authors of the existence or order of the universe; it follows, that they possess that precise degree of power, intelligence, and benevolence, which appears in their workmanship; but nothing farther can ever be proved, except we call in the assistance of exaggeration and flattery to supply the defects of argument and reasoning. So far as the traces of any attributes, at present, appear, so far may we conclude these attributes to exist. The supposition of farther attributes is mere hypothesis; much more the supposition, that, in distant regions of space or periods of time, there has been, or will be, a more magnificent display of these attributes, and a scheme of administration more suitable to such imaginary virtues. We can never be allowed to mount up from the universe, the effect, to Jupiter, the cause; and then descend downwards, to infer any new effect from that cause;

as if the present effects alone were not entirely worthy of the glorious attributes, which we ascribe to that deity. The knowledge of the cause being derived solely from the effect, they must be exactly adjusted to each other; and the one can never refer to anything farther, or be the foundation of any new inference and conclusion.

You find certain phenomena in nature. You seek a cause or author. You imagine that you have found him. You afterwards become so enamored of this offspring of your brain, that you imagine it impossible, but he must produce something greater and more perfect than the present scene of things, which is so full of ill and disorder. You forget, that this superlative intelligence and benevolence are entirely imaginary, or, at least, without any foundation in reason; and that you have no ground to ascribe to him any qualities, but what you see he has actually exerted and displayed in his productions. Let your gods, therefore, O philosophers, be suited to the present appearances of nature: and presume not to alter these appearances by arbitrary suppositions, in order to suit them to the attributes, which you so fondly ascribe to your deities.

When priests and poets, supported by your authority, O Athenians, talk of a golden or silver age, which preceded the present state of vice and misery, I hear them with attention and with reverence. But when philosophers, who pretend to neglect authority, and to cultivate reason, hold the same discourse, I pay them not, I own, the same obsequious submission and pious deference. I ask, who carried them into the celestial regions, who admitted them into the councils of the gods, who opened to them the book of fate, that they thus rashly affirm, that their deities have executed, or will execute, any purpose beyond what has actually appeared? If they tell me, that they have mounted on the steps or by the gradual ascent of reason, and by drawing inferences from effects to causes, I still insist, that they have aided the ascent of reason by the wings of imagination; otherwise they could not thus change their manner of inference, and argue from causes to effects; presuming, that a more perfect production than the present world would be more suitable to such perfect beings as the gods, and forgetting that they have no reason to ascribe to these celestial beings any perfection or any attribute, but what can be found in the present world.

Hence all the fruitless industry to account for the ill appearances of nature, and save the honor of the gods; while we must acknowledge the reality of that evil and disorder, with which the world so much abounds. The obstinate and intractable qualities of matter, we are told, or the observance of general laws, or some such reason, is the sole cause, which controlled the power and benevolence of Jupiter, and obliged him to create mankind and every sensible creature so imperfect and so unhappy. These attributes then, are, it seems, beforehand, taken for granted, in their greatest latitude. And upon that supposition, I own that such conjectures may, perhaps, be admitted as plausible solutions of the ill phenomena. But still I ask, Why take these attributes for granted, or why ascribe to the cause any qualities but what actually appear in the effect? Why torture your brain to justify the course of nature upon suppositions, which, for aught you know, may be entirely imaginary, and of which there are to be found no traces in the course of nature?

The religious hypothesis, therefore, must be considered only as a particular method of accounting for the visible phenomena of the universe: but no just reasoner will ever presume to infer from it any single fact, and alter or add to the phenomena, in any single particular. If you think, that the appearances of things prove such causes, it is allowable for you to draw an inference concerning the existence of these causes. In such complicated and sublime subjects, everyone should be indulged in the liberty of conjecture and argument. But here you ought to rest. If you come backward, and arguing from your inferred causes, conclude, that any other fact has existed, or will exist, in the course of nature, which may serve as a fuller display of particular attributes; I must admonish you, that you have departed from the method of reasoning, attached to the present subject, and have certainly added something to the attributes of the cause, beyond what appears in the effect; otherwise you could never, with tolerable sense or propriety, add anything to the effect, in order to render it more worthy of the cause.

Where, then, is the odiousness of that doctrine, which I teach in my school, or rather, which I examine in my gardens? Or what do you find in this whole question, wherein the security of good morals, or the peace and order of society, is in the least concerned?

I deny a providence, you say, and supreme governor of the world, who guides the course of events, and punishes the vicious with infamy and disappointment, and rewards the virtuous with honor and success, in all their undertakings. But surely, I deny not the course itself of events, which lies open to everyone's inquiry and examination. I acknowledge, that, in the present order of things, virtue is attended with more peace of mind than vice, and meets with a more favorable reception from the world. I am sensible, that, according to the past experience of mankind, friendship is the chief joy of human life, and moderation the only source of tranquillity and happiness. I never balance between the virtuous and the vicious course of life; but am sensible, that, to a well-disposed mind, every advantage is on the side of the former. And what can you say more, allowing all your suppositions and reasonings? You tell me, indeed, that this disposition of things proceeds from intelligence and design. But whatever it proceeds from, the disposition itself, on which depends our happiness or misery, and consequently our conduct and deportment in life, is still the same. It is still open for me, as well as you, to regulate my behavior, by my experience of past events. And if you affirm, that, while a divine providence is allowed, and a supreme distributive justice in the universe, I ought to expect some more particular reward of the good, and punishment of the bad, beyond the ordinary course of events; I here find the same fallacy, which I have before endeavored to detect. You persist in imagining, that, if we grant that divine existence, for which you so earnestly contend, you may safely infer consequences from it, and add something to the experienced order of nature, by arguing from the attributes which you ascribe to your gods. You seem not to remember, that all your reasonings on this subject can only be drawn from effects to causes; and that every argument, deducted from causes to effects, must of necessity be a gross sophism; since it is impossible for you to know anything of the cause, but what you have antecedently, not inferred, but discovered to the full, in the effect.

But what must a philosopher think of those vain reasoners, who, instead of regarding the present scene of things as the sole object of their contemplation, so far reverse the whole course of nature, as to render this life merely a passage to something farther; a porch, which leads to a greater, and vastly different building; a prologue, which serves only to introduce the piece, and give it more grace and propriety? Whence, do you think, can such philosophers derive their idea of the gods?

From their own conceit and imagination surely. For if they derived it from the present phenomena, it would never point to anything farther, but must be exactly adjusted to them. That the divinity may *possibly* be endowed with attributes, which we have never seen exerted; may be governed by principles of action, which we cannot discover to be satisfied: all this will freely be allowed. But still this is mere *possibility* and hypothesis. We never can have reason to *infer* any attributes, or any principles of action in him, but so far as we know them to have been exerted and satisfied.

Are there any marks of a distributive justice in the world? If you answer in the affirmative, I conclude, that, since justice here exerts itself, it is satisfied. If you reply in the negative, I conclude, that you have then no reason to ascribe justice, in our sense of it, to the gods. If you hold a medium between affirmation and negation, by saying, that the justice of the gods, at present, exerts itself in part, but not in its full extent; I answer, that you have no reason to give it any particular extent, but only so far as you see it, *at present*, exert itself.

Thus I bring the dispute, O Athenians, to a short issue with my antagonists. The course of nature lies open to my contemplation as well as to theirs. The experienced train of events is the great standard, by which we all regulate our conduct. Nothing else can be appealed to in the field, or in the senate. Nothing else ought ever to be heard of in the school, or in the closet. In vain would our limited understanding break through those boundaries, which are too narrow for our fond imagination. While we argue from the course of nature, and infer a particular intelligent cause, which first bestowed, and still preserves order in the universe, we embrace a principle, which is both uncertain and useless. It is uncertain; because the subject lies entirely beyond the reach of human experience. It is useless; because our knowledge of this cause being derived entirely from the course of nature, we can never, according to the rules of just reasoning, return back from the cause with any new inference, or making additions to the common and experienced course of nature, establish any new principles of conduct and behavior.

I observe (said I, finding he had finished his harangue) that you neglect not the artifice of the demagogues of old; and as you were pleased to make me stand for the people, you insinuate yourself into my favor by embracing those principles, to which, you know, I have always expressed a particular attachment. But allowing you to make experience (as indeed I think you ought) the only standard of our judgment concerning this, and all other questions of fact; I doubt not but, from the very same experience, to which you appeal, it may be possible to refute this reasoning, which you have put into the mouth of Epicurus. If you saw, for instance, a half-finished building, surrounded with heaps of brick and stone and mortar, and all the instruments of masonry; could you not *infer* from the effect, that it was a work of design and contrivance? And could you not return again, from this inferred cause, to infer new additions to the effect, and conclude, that the building would soon be finished, and receive all the further improvements, which art could bestow upon it? If you saw upon the seashore the print of one human foot, you would conclude, that a man had passed that way, and that he had also left the traces of the other foot, though effaced by the rolling of the sands or inundation of the waters. Why then do you refuse to admit the same method of reasoning with regard to the order of nature? Consider the world and the present life only as an imperfect building, from which you can infer a superior intelligence; and arguing from that superior intelligence, which can leave nothing imperfect; why may you not infer a more finished scheme or plan, which will receive its completion in some distant point of space or time? Are not these methods of reasoning exactly similar? And under what pretense can you embrace the one, while you reject the other?

The infinite difference of the subjects, replied he, is a sufficient foundation for this difference in my conclusions. In works of *human* art and contrivance, it is allowable to advance from the effect to the cause, and returning back from the cause, to form new inferences concerning the effect, and examine the alterations, which it has probably undergone, or may still undergo. But what is the foundation of this method of reasoning? Plainly this: that man is a being, whom we know by experience, whose motives and designs we are acquainted with, and whose projects and inclinations have a certain connection and coherence, according to the laws which nature has established for the government of such a creature. When, therefore, we find, that any work has proceeded from the skill and industry of man; as we are otherwise acquainted with the nature of the animal, we can draw a hundred inferences concerning what may be expected from him; and these inferences will all be founded in experience and observation. But did we know man only from the single work or production which we examine, it were impossible for us to argue in this manner; because our knowledge of all the qualities, which we ascribe to him, being in that case derived from the production, it is impossible they could point to anything further, or be the foundation of any new inference. The print of a foot in the sand can only prove, when considered alone, that there was some figure adapted to it, by which it was produced: but the print of a human foot proves likewise, from our other experience, that there was probably another foot, which also left its impression, though effaced by time or other accidents. Here we mount from the effect to the cause; and descending again from the cause, infer alterations in the effect; but this is not a continuation of the same simple chain of reasoning. We comprehend in this case a hundred other experiences and observations, concerning the *usual* figure and members of that species of animal, without which this method of argument must be considered as fallacious and sophistical.

The case is not the same with our reasonings from the works of nature. The Deity is known to us only by his productions, and is a single being in the universe, not comprehended under any species or genus, from whose experienced attributes or qualities, we can, by analogy, infer any attribute or quality in him. As the universe shows wisdom and goodness, we infer wisdom and goodness. As it shows a particular degree of these perfections, we infer a particular degree of them, precisely adapted to the effect which we examine. But further attributes or further degrees of the same attributes, we can never be authorized to infer or suppose, by any rules of just reasoning. Now, without some such license of supposition, it is impossible for us to argue from the cause, or infer any alteration in the effect, beyond what has immediately fallen under our observation. Greater good produced by this Being must still prove a greater degree of goodness; a more impartial distribution of rewards and punishments must proceed from a greater regard to justice and equity. Every supposed addition to the works of nature makes an addition to the attributes of the Author of nature; and consequently, being entirely unsupported by any reason or argument, can never be admitted but as mere conjecture and hypothesis.[23]

[23] In general, it may, I think, be established as a maxim, that where any cause is known only by its particular effects, it must be impossible to infer any new effects from that cause; since the quali-

The great source of our mistake in this subject, and of the unbounded license of conjecture, which we indulge, is, that we tacitly consider ourselves, as in the place of the Supreme Being, and conclude, that he will, on every occasion, observe the same conduct, which we ourselves, in his situation, would have embraced as reasonable and eligible. But, besides that the ordinary course of nature may convince us, that almost everything is regulated by principles and maxims very different from ours; besides this, I say, it must evidently appear contrary to all rules of analogy to reason, from the intentions and project of men, to those of a Being so different, and so much superior. In human nature, there is a certain experienced coherence of designs and inclinations; so that when, from any fact, we have discovered one intention of any man, it may often be reasonable, from experience, to infer another, and draw a long chain of conclusions concerning his past or future conduct. But this method of reasoning can never have place with regard to a Being, so remote and incomprehensible, who bears much less analogy to any other being in the universe than the sun to a waxen taper, and who discovers himself only by some faint traces or outlines, beyond which we have no authority to ascribe to him any attribute or perfection. What we imagine to be a superior perfection, may really be a defect. Or were it ever so much a perfection, the ascribing of it to the Supreme Being, where it appears not to have been really exerted, to the full, in his works, savors more

---

ties, which are requisite to produce these new effects along with the former, must either be different, or superior, or of more extensive operation, than those which simply produced the effect, whence alone the cause is supposed to be known to us. We can never, therefore, have any reason to suppose the existence of these qualities. To say, that the new effects proceed only from a continuation of the same energy, which is already known from the first effects, will not remove the difficulty. For even granting this to be the case (which can seldom be supposed), the very continuation and exertion of a like energy (for it is impossible it can be absolutely the same), I say, this exertion of a like energy, in a different period of space and time, is a very arbitary supposition, and what there cannot possibly be any traces of in the effects, from which all our knowledge of the cause is originally derived. Let the *inferred* cause be exactly proportioned (as it should be) to the known effect; and it is impossible that it can possess any qualities, from which new or different effects can be *inferred*.

of flattery and panegyric, than of just reasoning and sound philosophy. All the philosophy, therefore, in the world, and all the religion, which is nothing but a species of philosophy, will never be able to carry us beyond the usual course of experience, or give us measures of conduct and behavior different from those which are furnished by reflections on common life. No new fact can ever be inferred from the religious hypothesis; no event foreseen or foretold; no reward or punishment expected or dreaded, beyond what is already known by practice and observation. So that my apology for Epicurus will still appear solid and satisfactory; nor have the political interests of society any connection with the philosophical disputes concerning metaphysics and religion.

There is still one circumstance, replied I, which you seem to have overlooked. Though I should allow your premises, I must deny your conclusion. You conclude, that religious doctrines and reasonings *can* have no influence on life, because they *ought* to have no influence; never considering, that men reason not in the same manner you do, but draw many consequences from the belief of a divine existence, and suppose that the Deity will inflict punishments on vice, and bestow rewards on virtue, beyond what appear in the ordinary course of nature. Whether this reasoning of theirs be just or not, is no matter. Its influence on their life and conduct must still be the same. And, those, who attempt to disabuse them of such prejudices, may, for aught I know, be good reasoners, but I cannot allow them to be good citizens and politicians; since they free men from one restraint upon their passions, and make the infringement of the laws of society, in one respect, more easy and secure.

After all, I may, perhaps, agree to your general conclusion in favor of liberty, though upon different premises from those, on which you endeavor to found it. I think, that the state ought to tolerate every principle of philosophy; nor is there an instance, that any government has suffered in its political interests by such indulgence. There is no enthusiasm among philosophers; their doctrines are not very alluring to the people; and no restraint can be put upon their reasonings, but what must be of dangerous consequence to the sciences, and even to the state, by paving the way for persecution and oppression in points, where the generality of mankind are more deeply interested and concerned.

But there occurs to me (continued I) with regard to your

main topic, a difficulty, which I shall just propose to you without insisting on it; lest it lead into reasonings of too nice and delicate a nature. In a word, I much doubt whether it be possible for a cause to be known only by its effect (as you have all along supposed) or to be of so singular and particular a nature as to have no parallel and no similiarity with any other cause or object, that has ever fallen under our observation. It is only when two *species* of objects are found to be constantly conjoined, that we can infer the one from the other; and were an effect presented, which was entirely singular, and could not be comprehended under any known *species*, I do not see, that we could form any conjecture or inference at all concerning its cause. If experience and observation and analogy be, indeed, the only guides which we can reasonably follow in inferences of this nature; both the effect and cause must bear a similarity and resemblance to other effects and causes, which we know, and which we have found, in many instances, to be conjoined with each other. I leave it to your own reflection to pursue the consequences of this principle. I shall just observe, that, as the antagonists of Epicurus always suppose the universe, an effect quite singular and unparalleled, to be the proof of a Deity, a cause no less singular and unparalleled; your reasonings, upon that supposition, seem, at least, to merit our attention. There is, I own, some difficulty, how we can ever return from the cause to the effect, and, reasoning from our ideas of the former, infer any alteration on the latter, or any addition to it.

SECTION XII

OF THE ACADEMICAL OR SCEPTICAL PHILOSOPHY

Part I

There is not a greater number of philosophical reasonings, displayed upon any subject, than those, which prove the existence of a Deity, and refute the fallacies of *atheists*; and yet the most religious philosophers still dispute whether any man can be so blinded as to be a speculative atheist. How shall we reconcile these contradictions? The knights-errant, who wandered about to clear the world of dragons and giants, never entertained the least doubt with regard to the existence of these monsters.

The *sceptic* is another enemy of religion, who naturally provokes the indignation of all divines and graver philosophers; though it is certain, that no man ever met with any such absurd creature, or conversed with a man, who had no opinion or principle concerning any subject, either of action or speculation. This begets a very natural question; What is meant by a sceptic? And how far is it possible to push these philosophical principles of doubt and uncertainty?

There is a species of scepticism, *antecedent* to all study and philosophy, which is much inculcated by Descartes and others, as a sovereign preservative against error and precipitate judgment. It recommends an universal doubt, not only of all our former opinions and principles, but also of our very faculties; of whose veracity, say they, we must assure ourselves, by a chain of reasoning, deduced from some original principle, which cannot possibly be fallacious or deceitful. But neither is there any such original principle, which has a prerogative above others, that are self-evident and convincing: or if there were, could we advance a step beyond it, but by the use of those very faculties, of which we are supposed to be already diffident. The Cartesian doubt, therefore, were it ever possible to be attained by any human creature (as it plainly is not) would be entirely incurable; and no reasoning could ever bring us to a state of assurance and conviction upon any subject.

It must, however, be confessed, that this species of scepticism, when more moderate, may be understood in a very reasonable sense, and is a necessary preparative to the study of philosophy, by preserving a proper impartiality in our judgments, and weaning our mind from all those prejudices, which we may have imbibed from education or rash opinion. To begin with clear and self-evident principles, to advance by timorous and sure steps, to review frequently our conclusions, and examine accurately all their consequences; though by these means we shall make both a slow and a short progress in our systems; are the only methods, by which we can ever hope to reach truth, and attain a proper stability and certainty in our determinations.

There is another species of scepticism, *consequent* to science and inquiry, when men are supposed to have discovered either the absolute fallaciousness of their mental faculties, or their unfitness to reach any fixed determination in all those curious subjects of speculation, about which they are commonly employed. Even our very senses are brought into dispute, by a certain species of philosophers; and the maxims of common life are subjected to the same doubt as the most profound principles or conclusions of metaphysics and theology. As these paradoxical tenets (if they may be called tenets) are to be met with in some philosophers, and the refutation of them in several, they naturally excite our curiosity, and make us inquire into the arguments, on which they may be founded.

I need not insist upon the more trite topics, employed by the sceptics in all ages, against the evidence of *sense*; such as those which are derived from the imperfection and fallaciousness of our organs, on numberless occasions; the crooked appearance of an oar in water; the various aspects of objects, according to their different distances; the double images which arise from the pressing one eye; with many other appearances of a like nature. These sceptical topics, indeed, are only sufficient to prove, that the senses alone are not implicitly to be depended on; but that we must correct their evidence by reason, and by considerations, derived from the nature of the medium, the distance of the object, and the disposition of the organ, in order to render them, within their sphere, the proper *criteria* of truth and falsehood. There are other more profound arguments against the senses, which admit not of so easy a solution.

It seems evident, that men are carried, by a natural instinct or pre-possession, to repose faith in their senses; and that, without any reasoning, or even almost before the use of reason, we always suppose an external universe, which depends not on our perception, but would exist, though we and every sensible creature were absent or annihilated. Even the animal creation are governed by a like opinion, and preserve this belief of external objects, in all their thoughts, designs, and actions.

It seems also evident, that, when men follow this blind and powerful instinct of nature, they always suppose the very images, presented by the senses, to be the external objects, and never entertain any suspicion, that the one are nothing but representations of the other. This very table, which we see white, and which we feel hard, is believed to exist, independent of our perception, and to be something external to our mind, which perceives it. Our presence bestows not being on it; our absence does not annihilate it. It preserves its existence uniform and entire, independent of the situation of intelligent beings, who perceive or contemplate it.

But this universal and primary opinion of all men is soon destroyed by the slightest philosophy, which teaches us, that nothing can ever be present to the mind but an image or perception, and that the senses are only the inlets, through which these images are conveyed, without being able to produce any immediate intercourse between the mind and the object. The table, which we see, seems to diminish, as we remove farther from it; but the real table, which exists independent of us, suffers no alteration: it was, therefore, nothing but its image, which was present to the mind. These are the obvious dictates of reason; and no man, who reflects, ever doubted, that the existences, which we consider, when we say, *this house* and *that tree*, are nothing but perceptions in the mind, and fleeting copies or representations of other existences, which remain uniform and independent.

So far, then, are we necessitated by reasoning to contradict or depart from the primary instincts of nature, and to embrace a new system with regard to the evidence of our senses. But here philosophy finds herself extremely embarrassed, when she would justify this new system, and obviate the cavils and objections of the sceptics. She can no longer plead the infallible and irresistible instinct of nature: for that led us to a quite different system, which is acknowledged fallible and even erroneous. And to justify this pretended philosophical system, by a chain of clear and convincing argument, or even any appearance of argument, exceeds the power of all human capacity.

By what argument can it be proved, that the perceptions of the mind must be caused by external objects, entirely different from them, though resembling them (if that be possible) and could not arise either from the energy of the mind itself, or from the suggestion of some invisible and unknown spirit, or from some other cause still more unknown to us? It is acknowledged, that, in fact, many of these perceptions arise not from anything external, as in dreams, madness, and other diseases. And nothing can be more inexplicable than the manner, in which body should so operate upon mind as ever to convey an image of itself to a substance, supposed of so different, and even contrary a nature.

It is a question of fact, whether the perceptions of the senses be produced by external objects, resembling them: how shall this question be determined? By experience surely; as all other questions of a like nature. But here experience is, and must be entirely silent. The mind has never anything present to it but the perceptions, and cannot possibly reach any experience of their connection with objects. The supposition of such a connection is, therefore, without any foundation in reasoning.

To have recourse to the veracity of the supreme Being, in order to prove the veracity of our senses, is surely making a very unexpected circuit. If this veracity were at all concerned in this matter, our senses would be entirely infallible; because it is not possible that he can ever deceive. Not to mention, that, if the external world be once called in question, we shall be at a loss to find arguments, by which we may prove the existence of that Being or any of his attributes.

This is a topic, therefore, in which the profounder and more philosophical sceptics will always triumph, when they endeavor to introduce an universal doubt into all subjects of human knowledge and inquiry. Do you follow the instincts and propensities of nature, may they say, in assenting to the veracity of sense? But these lead you to believe that the very perception or sensible image is the external object. Do you disclaim this principle, in order to embrace a more rational opinion, that the perceptions are only representations of something external? You here depart from your natural propensities and more obvious sentiments; and yet are not able to satisfy your reason, which can never find any convincing argument from experience to prove, that the perceptions are connected with any external objects.

There is another sceptical topic of a like nature, derived from the most profound philosophy; which might merit our attention, were it requisite to dive so deep, in order to discover arguments and reasonings, which can so little serve to any serious purpose. It is universally allowed by modern inquirers, that all the sensible qualities of objects, such as hard, soft, hot, cold, white, black, etc. are merely secondary, and exist not in the objects themselves, but are perceptions of the mind, without any external archetype or model, which they represent. If this be allowed, with regard to secondary qualities, it must also follow, with regard to the supposed primary qualities of extension and solidity; nor can the latter be any more entitled to that denomination than the former. The idea of extension is entirely acquired from the senses of sight and feeling; and if all the qualities, perceived by the senses, be in the mind, not in the object, the same conclusion must reach the idea of extension, which is wholly dependent on the sensible ideas or the ideas of secondary qualities. Nothing can save us from this conclusion, but the asserting, that the ideas of those primary qualities are attained by *abstraction*, an opinion, which, if we examine it accurately, we shall find to be unintelligible, and even absurd. An extension, that is neither tangible nor visible, cannot possibly be conceived; and a tangible or visible extension, which is neither hard nor soft, black or white, is equally beyond the reach of human conception. Let any man try to conceive a triangle in general, which is neither *isosceles* nor *scalenum*, nor has any particular length or proportion of sides; and he will soon perceive the absurdity of all the scholastic notions with regard to abstraction and general ideas.[24]

Thus the first philosophical objection to the evidence of sense or to the opinion of external existence consists in this, that such an opinion, if rested on natural instinct, is contrary to reason, and if referred to reason, is contrary to natural instinct, and at the same time carries no rational evidence with it, to convince an impartial inquirer. The second objection goes farther, and represents this opinion as contrary to reason, at least, if it be a principle of reason, that all sensible qualities are in the mind, not in the object. Bereave matter of all its intelligible qualities, both primary and secondary, you in a manner annihilate it, and leave only a certain unknown, inexplicable *something*, as the cause of our perceptions; a notion so imperfect, that no sceptic will think it worth while to contend against it.

24 This argument is drawn from Dr. Berkeley; and indeed most of the writings of that very ingenious author form the best lessons of scepticism, which are to be found either among the ancient or modern philosophers, Bayle not excepted. He professes, however, in his title-page (and undoubtedly with great truth) to have composed his book against the sceptics as well as against the atheists and free-thinkers. But that all his arguments, though otherwise intended, are, in reality, merely sceptical, appears from this, *that they admit of no answer and produce no conviction*. Their only effect is to cause that momentary amazement and irresolution and confusion, which is the result of scepticism.

Part II

It may seem a very extravagant attempt of the sceptics to destroy *reason* by argument and ratiocination; yet is this the grand scope of all their inquiries and disputes. They endeavor to find objections, both to our abstract reasonings, and to those which regard matter of fact and existence.

The chief objection against all *abstract* reasonings is derived from the ideas of space and time; ideas, which, in common life and to a careless view, are very clear and intelligible, but when they pass through the scrutiny of the profound sciences (and they are the chief object of these sciences) afford principles, which seem full of absurdity and contradiction. No priestly *dogmas*, invented on purpose to tame and subdue the rebellious reason of mankind, ever shocked common sense more than the doctrine of the infinite divisibility of extension, with its consequences; as they are pompously displayed by all geometricians and metaphysicians, with a kind of triumph and exultation. A real quantity, infinitely less than any finite quantity, containing quantities infinitely less than itself, and so on *in infinitum*; this is an edifice so bold and prodigious, that it is too weighty for any pretended demonstration to support, because it shocks the clearest and most natural principles of human reason.[25] But what renders the matter more extraordinary, is, that these seemingly absurd opinions are supported by a chain of reasoning, the clearest and most natural; nor is it possible for us to allow the premises without admitting the consequences. Nothing can be more convincing and satisfactory than all the conclusions concerning the properties of circles and triangles; and yet, when these are once received, how can we deny, that the angle of contact between a circle

[25] Whatever disputes there may be about mathematical points, we must allow that there are physical points; that is, parts of extension, which cannot be divided or lessened, either by the eye or imagination. These images, then, which are present to the fancy or senses, are absolutely indivisible, and consequently must be allowed by mathematicians to be infinitely less than any real part of extension; and yet nothing appears more certain to reason, than that an infinite number of them composes an infinite extension. How much more an infinite number of those infinitely small parts of extension, which are still supposed infinitely divisible.

and its tangent is infinitely less than any rectilineal angle, that as you may increase the diameter of the circle *in infinitum*, this angle of contact becomes still less, even *in infinitum*, and that the angle of contact between other curves and their tangents may be infinitely less than those between any circle and its tangent, and so on, *in infinitum*? The demonstration of these principles seems as unexceptionable as that which proves the three angles of a triangle to be equal to two right ones, though the latter opinion be natural and easy, and the former big with contradiction and absurdity. Reason here seems to be thrown into a kind of amazement and suspense, which, without the suggestions of any sceptic, gives her a diffidence of herself, and of the ground on which she treads. She sees a full light, which illuminates certain places; but that light borders upon the most profound darkness. And between these she is so dazzled and confounded, that she scarcely can pronounce with certainty and assurance concerning any one object.

The absurdity of these bold determinations of the abstract sciences seems to become, if possible, still more palpable with regard to time than extension. An infinite number of real parts of time, passing in succession, and exhausted one after another, appears so evident a contradiction, that no man, one should think, whose judgment is not corrupted, instead of being improved, by the sciences, would ever be able to admit of it.

Yet still reason must remain restless, and unquiet, even with regard to that scepticism, to which she is driven by these seeming absurdities and contradictions. How any clear, distinct idea can contain circumstances, contradictory to itself, or to any other clear, distinct idea, is absolutely incomprehensible; and is, perhaps, as absurd as any proposition, which can be formed. So that nothing can be more sceptical, or more full of doubt and hesitation, than this scepticism itself, which arises from some of the paradoxical conclusions of geometry or the science of quantity.[26]

[26] It seems to me not impossible to avoid these absurdities and contradictions, if it be admitted, that there is no such thing as abstract or general ideas, properly speaking; but that all general ideas are, in reality, particular ones, attached to a general term, which recalls, upon occasion, other particular ones, that resemble, in certain circumstances, the idea, present to the mind. Thus when the term *horse* is pronounced, we immediately figure to ourselves the idea of

The sceptical objections to *moral* evidence, or to the reasonings concerning matter of fact, are either *popular* or *philosophical.* The popular objections are derived from the natural weakness of human understanding; the contradictory opinions, which have been entertained in different ages and nations; the variations of our judgment in sickness and health, youth and old age, prosperity and adversity; the perpetual contradiction of each particular man's opinions and sentiments; with many other topics of that kind. It is needless to insist farther on this head. These objections are but weak. For as, in common life, we reason every moment concerning fact and existence, and cannot possibly subsist, without continually employing this species of argument, any popular objections, derived from thence, must be insufficient to destroy that evidence. The great subverter of *Pyrrhonism* or the excessive principles of scepticism is action, and employment, and the occupations of common life. These principles may flourish and triumph in the schools; where it is, indeed, difficult, if not impossible, to refute them. But as soon as they leave the shade, and by the presence of the real objects, which actuate our passions and sentiments, are put in opposition to the more powerful principles of our nature, they vanish like smoke, and leave the most determined sceptic in the same condition as other mortals.

The sceptic, therefore, had better keep within his proper sphere, and display those *philosophical* objections, which arise from more profound researches. Here he seems to have ample matter of triumph; while he justly insists, that all our evidence for any matter of fact, which lies beyond the testimony of sense or memory, is derived entirely from the relation of cause

---

a black or a white animal, of a particular size or figure: but as that term is also usually applied to animals of others colors, figures and sizes, these ideas, though not actually present to the imagination, are easily recalled; and our reasoning and conclusion proceed in the same way, as if they were actually present. If this be admitted (as seems reasonable) it follows that all the ideas of quantity, upon which mathematicians reason, are nothing but particular, and such as are suggested by the senses and imagination, and consequently, cannot be infinitely divisible. It is sufficient to have dropped this hint at present, without prosecuting it any farther. It certainly concerns all lovers of science not to expose themselves to the ridicule and contempt of the ignorant by their conclusions; and this seems the readiest solution of these difficulties.

and effect; that we have no other idea of this relation than that of two objects, which have been frequently *conjoined* together; that we have no argument to convince us, that objects, which have, in our experience, been frequently conjoined, will likewise, in other instances, be conjoined in the same manner; and that nothing leads us to this inference but custom or a certain instinct of our nature; which it is indeed difficult to resist, but which, like other instincts, may be fallacious and deceitful. While the sceptic insists upon these topics, he shows his force, or rather, indeed, his own and our weakness; and seems, for the time at least, to destroy all assurance and conviction. These arguments might be displayed at greater length, if any durable good or benefit to society could ever be expected to result from them.

For here is the chief and most confounding objection to *excessive* scepticism, that no durable good can ever result from it; while it remains in its full force and vigor. We need only ask such a sceptic, *What his meaning is? And what he proposes by all these curious researches?* He is immediately at a loss, and knows not what to answer. A Copernican of Ptolemaic, who supports each his different system of astronomy, may hope to produce a conviction, which will remain constant and durable, with his audience. A Stoic or Epicurean displays principles, which may not be durable, but which have an effect on conduct and behavior. But a Pyrrhonian cannot expect, that his philosophy will have any constant influence on the mind: or if it had, that its influence would be beneficial to society. On the contrary, he must acknowledge, if he will acknowledge anything, that all human life must perish, were his principles universally and steadily to prevail. All discourse, all action would immediately cease; and men remain in a total lethargy, till the necessities of nature, unsatisfied, put an end to their miserable existence. It is true; so fatal an event is very little to be dreaded. Nature is always too strong for principle. And though a Pyrrhonian may throw himself or others into a momentary amazement and confusion by his profound reasonings; the first and most trival event in life will put to flight all his doubts and scruples, and leave him the same, in every point of action and speculation, with the philosophers of every other sect, or with those who never concerned themselves in any philosophical researches. When he awakes from his dream, he will be the first to join in the laugh against himself, and to confess, that all his objections are mere amusement, and can have no other tendency than to show the whimsical condition of mankind, who must act and reason and believe; though they are not able, by their most diligent inquiry, to satisfy themselves concerning the foundation of these operations, or to remove the objections, which may be raised against them.

Part III

There is, indeed, a more *mitigated* scepticism or *academical* philosophy, which may be both durable and useful, and which may, in part, be the result of this Pyrrhonism, or *excessive* scepticism, when its undistinguished doubts are, in some measure, corrected by common sense and reflection. The greater part of mankind are naturally apt to be affirmative and dogmatical in their opinions; and while they see objects only on one side, and have no idea of any counterpoising argument, they throw themselves precipitately into the principles, to which they are inclined; nor have they any indulgence for those who entertain opposite sentiments. To hesitate or balance perplexes their understanding, checks their passion, and suspends their action. They are, therefore, impatient till they escape from a state, which to them is so uneasy: and they think, that they could never remove themselves far enough from it, by the violence of their affirmations and obstinacy of their belief. But could such dogmatical reasoners become sensible of the strange infirmities of human understanding, even in its most perfect state, and when most accurate and cautious in its determinations; such a reflection would naturally inspire them with more modesty and reserve, and diminish their fond opinion of themselves, and their prejudice against antagonists. The illiterate may reflect on the disposition of the learned, who, amidst all the advantages of study and reflection, are commonly still diffident in their determinations: and if any of the learned be inclined, from their natural temper, to haughtiness and obstinacy, a small tincture of Pyrrhonism might abate their pride, by showing them, that the few advantages, which they may have attained over their fellows, are but inconsiderable, if compared with the universal perplexity and confusion, which is inherent in human nature. In general, there is a degree of doubt, and caution, and modesty, which, in all kinds of scrutiny and decision, ought forever to accompany a just reasoner.

Another species of *mitigated* scepticism which may be of advantage to mankind, and which may be the natural result of the Pyrrhonian doubts and scruples, is the limitation of our inquiries to such subjects as are best adapted to the narrow capacity of human understanding. The *imagination* of man is naturally sublime, delighted with whatever is remote and extraordinary, and running, without control, into the most distant parts of space and time in order to avoid the objects, which custom has rendered too familiar to it. A correct *judgment* observes a contrary method, and avoiding all distant and high inquiries, confines itself to common life, and to such subjects as fall under daily practice and experience; leaving the more sublime topics to the embellishment of poets and orators, or to the arts of priests and politicians. To bring us to so salutary a determination, nothing can be more serviceable, than to be once thoroughly convinced of the force of the Pyrrhonian doubt, and of the impossibility, that anything, but the strong power of natural instinct, could free us from it. Those who have a propensity to philosophy, will still continue their researches; because they reflect, that, besides the immediate pleasure, attending such an occupation, philosophical decisions are nothing but the reflections of common life, methodized and corrected. But they will never be tempted to go beyond common life, so long as they consider the imperfection of those faculties which they employ, their narrow reach, and their inaccurate operations. While we cannot give a satisfactory reason, why we believe, after a thousand experiments, that a stone will fall, or fire burn; can we ever satisfy ourselves concerning any determination, which we may form, with regard to the origin of worlds, and the situation of nature, from, and to eternity?

This narrow limitation, indeed, of our inquiries, is, in every respect, so reasonable, that it suffices to make the slightest examination into the natural powers of the human mind and to compare them with their objects, in order to recommend it to us. We shall then find what are the proper subjects of science and inquiry.

It seems to me, that the only objects of the abstract science or of demonstration are quantity and number, and that all attempts to extend this more perfect species of knowledge beyond these bounds are mere sophistry and illusion. As the component parts of quantity and number are entirely similar, their relations become intricate and involved; and nothing can be more curious, as well as useful, than to trace, by a variety of mediums, their equality or inequality, through their different appearances. But as all other ideas are clearly distinct and different from each other, we can never advance farther, by our utmost scrutiny, than to observe this diversity, and, by an obvious reflection, pronounce one thing not to be another. Or if there be any difficulty in these decisions, it proceeds entirely from the undeterminate meaning of words, which is corrected by juster definitions. That *the square of the hypothenuse is equal to the squares of the other two sides*, cannot be known, let the terms be ever so exactly defined, without a train of reasoning and inquiry. But to convince us of this proposition, *that where there is no property, there can be no injustice*, it is only necessary to define the terms, and explain injustice to be a violation of property. This proposition is, indeed, nothing but a more imperfect definition. It is the same case with all those pretended syllogistical reasonings, which may be found in every other branch of learning, except the sciences of quantity and number; and these may safely, I think, be pronounced the only proper objects of knowledge and demonstration.

All other inquiries of men regard only matter of fact and existence; and these are evidently incapable of demonstration. Whatever *is* may *not be*. No negation of a fact can involve a contradiction. The non-existence of any being, without exception, is as clear and distinct an idea as its existence. The proposition, which affirms it not to be, however false, is no less conceivable and intelligible, than that which affirms it to be. The case is different with the sciences, properly so called. Every proposition, which is not true, is there confused and unintelligible. That the cube root of 64 is equal to the half of 10, is a false proposition, and can never be distinctly conceived. But that Caesar, or the angel Gabriel, or any being never existed, may be a false proposition, but still is perfectly conceivable, and implies no contradiction.

The existence, therefore, of any being can only be proved by arguments from its cause or its effect; and these arguments are founded entirely on experience. If we reason *a priori*, anything may appear able to produce anything. The falling of a pebble may, for aught we know, extinguish the sun; or the wish of a man control the planets in their orbits. It is only experience, which teaches us the nature and bounds of cause and effect, and enables us to infer the existence of one object from that of another.[27] Such is the foundation of moral reasoning, which forms the greater part of human knowledge, and is the source of all human action and behavior.

Moral reasonings are either concerning particular or general facts. All deliberations in life regard the former; as also all disquisitions in history, chronology, geography, and astronomy.

The sciences, which treat of general facts, are politics, natural philosophy, physics, chemistry, etc., where the qualities, causes and effects of a whole species of objects are inquired into.

Divinity or Theology, as it proves the existence of a Deity, and the immortality of souls, is composed partly of reasonings concerning particular, partly concerning general facts. It has a foundation in *reason*, so far as it is supported by experience. But its best and most solid foundation is *faith* and divine revelation.

Morals and criticism are not so properly objects of the understanding as of taste and sentiment. Beauty, whether moral or natural, is felt, more properly than perceived. Or if we reason concerning it, and endeavor to fix its standard, we regard a new fact, to wit, the general tastes of mankind, or some such fact, which may be the object of reasoning and inquiry.

When we run over libraries, persuaded of these principles, what havoc must we make? If we take in our hand any volume; of divinity or school metaphysics, for instance; let us ask, *Does it contain any abstract reasoning concerning quantity or number?* No. *Does it contain any experimental reasoning concerning matter of fact and existence?* No. Commit it then to the flames: for it can contain nothing but sophistry and illusion.

27 That impious maxim of the ancient philosophy, *Ex nihilo, nihil fit*, by which the creation of matter was excluded, ceases to be a maxim, according to this philosophy. Not only the will of the supreme Being may create matter; but, for aught we know *a priori*, the will of any other being might create it, or any other cause, that the most whimsical imagination can assign.

David Hume

DIALOGUES CONCERNING NATURAL RELIGION

PAMPHILUS TO HERMIPPUS

It has been remarked, my Hermippus, that, though the ancient philosophers conveyed most of their instruction in the form of dialogue, this method of composition has been little practiced in later ages, and has seldom succeeded in the hands of those, who have attempted it. Accurate and regular argument, indeed, such as is now expected of philosophical inquirers, naturally throws a man into the methodical and didactic manner; where he can immediately, without preparation, explain the point, at which he aims; and thence proceed, without interruption, to deduce the proofs, on which it is established. To deliver a system in conversation scarcely appears natural; and while the dialogue-writer desires, by departing from the direct style of composition, to give a freer air to his performance, and avoid the appearance of *Author* and *Reader*, he is apt to run into a worse inconvenience, and convey the image of *Pedagogue* and *Pupil*. Or if he carries on the dispute in the natural spirit of good company, by throwing in a variety of topics, and preserving a proper balance among the speakers; he often loses so much time in preparations and transitions, that the reader will scarcely think himself compensated, by all the graces of dialogue, for the order, brevity, and precision, which are sacrificed to them.

There are some subjects, however, to which dialogue-writing is peculiarly adapted, and where it is still preferable to the direct and simple method of composition.

Any point of doctrine, which is so *obvious*, that it scarcely admits of dispute, but at the same time so *important*, that it cannot be too often inculcated, seems to require some such method of handling it; where the novelty of the manner may compensate the triteness of the subject, where the vivacity of conversation may enforce the precept, and where the variety of lights, presented by various personages and characters, may appear neither tedious nor redundant.

Any question of philosophy, on the other hand, which is so *obscure* and *uncertain*, that human reason can reach no fixed determination with regard to it; if it should be treated at all; seems to lead us naturally into the style of dialogue and conversation. Reasonable men may be allowed to differ, where no one can reasonably be positive: Opposite sentiments, even without any decision, afford an agreeable amusement: and if the subject be curious and interesting, the book carries us, in a manner, into company; and unites the two greatest and purest pleasures of human life, study and society.

Happily, these circumstances are all to be found in the subject of *Natural Religion*. What truth so obvious, so certain, as the *being* of a God, which the most ignorant ages have acknowledged, for which the most refined geniuses have ambitiously striven to produce new proofs and arguments? What truth so important as this, which is the ground of all our hopes, the surest foundation of morality, the firmest support of society, and the only principle, which ought never to be a moment absent from our thoughts and meditations? But in treating of this obvious and important truth; what obscure questions occur, concerning the *nature* of that divine being; his attributes, his decrees, his plan of providence? These have been always subjected to the disputations of men: Concerning these, human reason has not reached any certain determination: But these are topics so interesting, that we cannot restrain our restless inquiry with regard to them; though nothing but doubt, uncertainty and contradiction, have, as yet, been the result of our most accurate researches.

This I had lately occasion to observe, while I passed, as usual, part of the summer season with Cleanthes, and was present at those conversations of his with Philo and Demea, of which I gave you lately some imperfect account. Your curiosity, you then told me, was so excited, that I must of necessity enter into a more exact detail of their reasonings, and display those various systems, which they advanced with regard to so delicate a subject as that of Natural Religion. The remarkable contrast in their characters still farther raised your expectations; while you opposed the accurate philosophical turn of Cleanthes to the careless scepticism of Philo, or compared either of their dispositions with the rigid inflexible orthodoxy of Demea. My youth rendered me a mere auditor of their disputes; and that curiosity, natural to the early season of life, has so deeply imprinted in my memory the whole chain and connection of their arguments, that, I hope, I shall not omit or confound any considerable part of them in the recital.

Part I

After I joined the company, whom I found sitting in Cleanthes's library, Demea paid Cleanthes some compliments, on the great care which he took of my education, and on his unwearied perseverance and constancy in all his friendships. The father of Pamphilus, said he, was your intimate friend: The son is your pupil, and may indeed be regarded as your adopted son; were we to judge by the pains which you bestow in conveying to him every useful branch of literature and science. You are no more wanting, I am persuaded, in prudence than in industry. I shall, therefore, communicate to you a maxim, which I have observed with regard to my own children, that I may learn how far it agrees with your practice. The method I follow in their education is founded on the saying of an ancient, 'That students of philosophy ought first to learn Logic, then Ethics, next Physics, last of all, of the nature of the Gods.' This science of Natural Theology, according to him, being the most profound and abstruse of any, required the maturest judgment in its students; and none but a mind, enriched with all the other sciences, can safely be entrusted with it.

Are you so late, says Philo, in teaching your children the principles of religion? Is there no danger of their neglecting or rejecting altogether those opinions, of which they have heard so little, during the whole course of their education? It is only as a science, replied Demea, subjected to human reasoning and disputation, that I postpone the study of Natural Theology. To season their minds with early piety is my chief care; and by continual precept and instruction, and I hope too, by example, I imprint deeply on their tender minds an habitual reverence for all the principles of religion. While they pass through every other science, I still remark the uncertainty of each part, the eternal disputations of men, the obscurity of all philosophy, and the strange, ridiculous conclusions, which some of the greatest geniuses have derived from the principles of mere human reason. Having thus tamed their mind to a proper submission and self-diffidence, I have no longer any scruple of opening to them the greatest mysteries of religion, nor apprehend any danger from that assuming arrogance of philosophy, which may lead them to reject the most established doctrines and opinions.

Your precaution, says Philo, of seasoning your children's minds with early piety, is certainly very reasonable; and no more than is requisite, in this profane and irreligious age. But what I chiefly admire in your plan of education, is your method of drawing advantage from the very principles of philosophy and learning, which, by inspiring pride and self-sufficiency, have commonly, in all ages, been found so destructive to the principles of religion. The vulgar, indeed, we may remark, who are unacquainted with science and profound inquiry, observing the endless disputes of the learned, have commonly a thorough contempt for philosophy; and rivet themselves the faster, by that means, in the great points of theology, which have been taught them. Those, who enter a little into study and inquiry, finding many appearances of evidence in doctrines the newest and most extraordinary, think nothing too difficult for human reason; and presumptuously breaking through all fences, profane the inmost sanctuaries of the temple. But Cleanthes will, I hope, agree with me, that after we have abandoned ignorance, the surest remedy, there is still one expedient left to prevent this profane liberty. Let Demea's principles be improved and cultivated: Let us become thoroughly sensible of the weakness, blindness, and narrow limits of human reason: Let us duly consider its uncertainty and endless contrarieties, even in subjects of common life and practice: Let the errors and deceits of our very senses be set before us; the insuperable difficulties, which attend first principles in all systems; the contradictions, which adhere to the very ideas of matter, cause and effect, extension, space, time, motion; and in a word, quantity of all kinds, the object of the only science, that can fairly pretend to any certainty or evidence. When these topics are displayed in their full light, as they are by some philosophers and almost all divines; who can retain such confidence in this frail faculty of reason as to pay any regard to its determinations in points so sublime, so abstruse, so remote from common life and experience? When the coherence of the parts of a stone, or even that composition of parts, which renders it extended; when these familiar objects, I say, are so inexplicable, and contain circumstances so repugnant and contradictory; with what assurance can we decide concerning the origin of worlds, or trace their history from eternity to eternity?

While Philo pronounced these words, I could observe a smile in the countenances both of Demea and Cleanthes. That of Demea seemed to imply an unreserved satisfaction in the doctrines delivered: But in Cleanthes's features, I could distinguish an air of finesse, as if he perceived some raillery or artificial malice in the reasonings of Philo.

You propose then, Philo, said Cleanthes, to erect religious faith on philosophical scepticism; and you think, that if certainty or evidence be expelled from every other subject of inquiry, it will all retire to these theological doctrines, and there acquire a superior force and authority. Whether your scepticism be as absolute and sincere as you pretend, we shall learn by and by, when the company breaks up: We shall then see, whether you go out at the door or the window; and whether you really doubt, if your body has gravity, or can be injured by its fall; according to popular opinion, derived from our fallacious senses and more fallacious experience. And this consideration, Demea, may, I think, fairly serve to abate our ill-will to this humorous sect of the sceptics. If they be thoroughly in earnest, they will not long trouble the world with their doubts, cavils, and disputes: If they be only in jest, they are, perhaps, bad ralliers, but can never be very dangerous, either to the state, to philosophy, or to religion.

In reality, Philo, continued he, it seems certain, that though a man, in a flush of humor, after intense reflection on the many contradictions and imperfections of human reason, may entirely renounce all belief and opinion; it is impossible for him to persevere in this total scepticism, or make it appear in his conduct for a few hours. External objects press in upon him: passions solicit him: His philosophical melancholy dissipates; and even the utmost violence upon his own temper will not be able, during any time, to preserve the poor appearance of scepticism. And for what reason impose on himself such a violence? This is a point, in which it will be impossible for him ever to satisfy himself, consistent with his sceptical principles: So that upon the whole nothing could be more ridiculous than the principles of the ancient Pyrrhonians; if in reality they endeavored, as is pretended, to extend throughout, the same scepticism, which they had learned from the declamations of their schools, and which they ought to have confined to them.

In this view, there appears a great resemblance between the sects of the Stoics and Pyrrhonians, though perpetual antagonists: and both of them seem founded on this erroneous maxim: That what a man can perform sometimes, and in some dispositions, he can perform always, and in every disposition. When the mind, by Stoical reflections, is elevated into a sublime enthusiasm of virtue, and strongly smit with any species of honor or public good, the utmost bodily pain and sufferance will not prevail over such a high sense of duty; and 'tis possible, perhaps, by its means, even to smile and exult in the midst of tortures. If this sometimes may be the case in fact and reality, much more may a philosopher, in his school, or even in his closet, work himself up to such an enthusiasm, and support in imagination the acutest pain or most calamitous event, which he can possibly conceive. But how shall he support this enthusiasm itself? The bent of his mind relaxes, and cannot be recalled at pleasure: avocations lead him astray: misfortunes attack him unawares: and the *philosopher* sinks by degrees into the *plebeian*.

I allow of your comparison between the Stoics and Sceptics, replied Philo. But you may observe, at the same time, that though the mind cannot, in Stoicism, support the highest flights of philosophy, yet even when it sinks lower, it still retains somewhat of its former disposition; and the effects of the Stoic's reasoning will appear in his conduct in common life, and through the whole tenor of his actions. The ancient schools, particularly that of Zeno, produced examples of virtue and constancy which seem astonishing to present times.

> Vain Wisdom all and false Philosophy.
> Yet with a pleasing sorcery could charm
> Pain, for a while, or anguish, and excite
> Fallacious Hope, or arm the obdurate breast
> With stubborn Patience, as with triple steel.[1]

In like manner, if a man has accustomed himself to sceptical considerations on the uncertainty and narrow limits of reason,

[1] Paradise Lost, II.

he will not entirely forget them when he turns his reflection on other subjects; but in all his philosophical principles and reasoning, I dare not say, in his common conduct, he will be found different from those, who either never formed any opinions in the case, or have entertained sentiments more favorable to human reason.

To whatever length anyone may push his speculative principles of scepticism, he must act, I own, and live, and converse like other men; and for this conduct he is not obliged to give any other reason than the absolute necessity he lies under of so doing. If he ever carries his speculations farther than this necessity constrains him, and philosophises, either on natural or moral subjects, he is allured by a certain pleasure and satisfaction, which he finds in employing himself after that manner. He considers besides, that everyone, even in common life, is constrained to have more or less of this philosophy; that from our earliest infancy we make continual advances in forming more general principles of conduct and reasoning; that the larger experience we acquire, and the stronger reason we are endued with, we always render our principles the more general and comprehensive; and that what we call *philosophy* is nothing but a more regular and methodical operation of the same kind. To philosophize on such subjects is nothing essentially different from reasoning on common life; and we may only expect greater stability, if not greater truth, from our philosophy, on account of its exacter and more scrupulous method of proceeding.

But when we look beyond human affairs and the properties of the surrounding bodies: when we carry our speculations into the two eternities, before and after the present state of things; into the creation and formation of the universe; the existence and properties of spirits; the powers and operations of one universal spirit, existing without beginning and without end; omnipotent, omniscient, immutable, infinite, and incomprehensible: we must be far removed from the smallest tendency to scepticism not to be apprehensive, that we have here got quite beyond the reach of our faculties. So long as we confine our speculations to trade, or morals, or politics, or criticism, we make appeals, every moment, to common sense and experience, which strengthen our philosophical conclusions, and remove (at least, in part) the suspicion, which we so justly entertain with regard to every reasoning, that is very subtile and refined. But in theological reasonings, we have not this advantage; while at the same time we are employed upon objects, which, we must be sensible, are too large for our grasp, and of all others, require most to be familiarized to our apprehension. We are like foreigners in a strange country, to whom everything must seem suspicious, and who are in danger every moment of transgressing against the laws and customs of the people, with whom they live and converse. We know not how far we ought to trust our vulgar methods of reasoning in such a subject; since, even in common life and in that province, which is peculiarly appropriated to them, we cannot account for them, and are entirely guided by a kind of instinct or necessity in employing them.

All sceptics pretend, that, if reason be considered in an abstract view, it furnishes invincible arguments against itself, and that we could never retain any conviction or assurance, on any subject, were not the sceptical reasonings so refined and subtile, that they are not able to counterpoise the more solid and more natural arguments, derived from the senses and experience. But it is evident, whenever our arguments lose this advantage, and run wide of common life, that the most refined scepticism comes to be upon a footing with them, and is able to oppose and counterbalance them. The one has no more weight than the other. The mind must remain in suspense between them; and it is that very suspense or balance, which is the triumph of scepticism.

But I observe, says Cleanthes, with regard to you, Philo, and all speculative sceptics, that your doctrine and practice are as much at variance in the most abstruse points of theory as in the conduct of common life. Wherever evidence discovers itself, you adhere to it, notwithstanding your pretended scepticism; and I can observe, too, some of your sect to be as decisive as those, who make greater professions of certainty and assurance. In reality, would not a man be ridiculous, who pretended to reject Newton's explication of the wonderful phenomenon of the rainbow, because that explication gives a minute anatomy of the rays of light; a subject, forsooth, too refined for human comprehension? And what would you say to one, who having nothing particular to object to the arguments of Copernicus and Galileo for the motion of the earth, should withhold his assent, on that general principle, that these subjects were too magnificent and remote to be explained by the narrow and fallacious reason of mankind?

There is indeed a kind of brutish and ignorant scepticism,

as you well observed, which gives the vulgar a general prejudice against what they do not easily understand, and makes them reject every principle, which requires elaborate reasoning to prove and establish it. This species of scepticism is fatal to knowledge, not to religion; since we find, that those who make greatest profession of it, give often their assent, not only to the great truths of theism, and natural theology, but even to the most absurd tenets, which a traditional superstition has recommended to them. They firmly believe in witches; though they will not believe nor attend to the most simple proposition of Euclid. But the refined and philosophical sceptics fall into an inconsistence of an opposite nature. They push their researches into the most abstruse corners of science; and their assent attends them in every step, proportioned to the evidence which they meet with. They are even obliged to acknowledge, that the most abstruse and remote objects are those, which are best explained by philosophy. Light is in reality anatomized: the true system of the heavenly bodies is discovered and ascertained. But the nourishment of bodies by food is still an inexplicable mystery: the cohesion of the parts of matter is still incomprehensible. These sceptics, therefore, are obliged, in every question, to consider each particular evidence apart, and proportion their assent to the precise degree of evidence, which occurs. This is their practice in all natural, mathematical, moral, and political science. And why not the same, I ask, in the theological and religious? Why must conclusions of this nature be alone rejected on the general presumption of the insufficiency of human reason, without any particular discussion of the evidence? Is not such an unequal conduct a plain proof of prejudice and passion?

Our senses, you say, are fallacious, our understanding erroneous, our ideas even of the most familiar objects, extension, duration, motion, full of absurdities and contradictions. You defy me to solve the difficulties, or reconcile the repugnances, which you discover in them. I have not capacity for so great an undertaking: I have not leisure for it: I perceive it to be superfluous. Your own conduct, in every circumstance, refutes your principles; and shows the firmest reliance on all the received maxims of science, morals, prudence, and behavior.

I shall never assent to so harsh an opinion as that of a celebrated writer,[2] who says, that the sceptics are not a sect of

[2] L'art de penser.

philosophers: they are only a sect of liars. I may, however, affirm (I hope without offense), that they are a sect of jesters or ralliers. But for my part, whenever I find myself disposed to mirth and amusement, I shall certainly choose my entertainment of a less perplexing and abstruse nature. A comedy, a novel, or at most a history, seems a more natural recreation than such metaphysical subtilties and abstractions.

In vain would the sceptic make a distinction between science and common life, or between one science and another. The arguments, employed in all, if just, are of a similar nature, and contain the same force and evidence. Or if there be any difference among them, the advantage lies entirely on the side of theology and natural religion. Many principles of mechanics are founded on very abstruse reasoning; yet no man, who has any pretensions to science, even no speculative sceptic, pretends to entertain the least doubt with regard to them. The Copernican system contains the most surprising paradox, and the most contrary to our natural conceptions, to appearances, and to our very senses: yet even monks and inquisitors are now constrained to withdraw their opposition to it. And shall Philo, a man of so liberal a genius, and extensive knowledge, entertain any general undistinguished scruples with regard to the religious hypothesis, which is founded on the simplest and most obvious arguments, and, unless it meet with artificial obstacles, has such easy access and admission into the mind of man?

And here we may observe, continued he, turning himself towards Demea, a pretty curious circumstance in the history of the sciences. After the union of philosophy with the popular religion, upon the first establishment of Christianity, nothing was more usual, among all religious teachers, than declamations against reason, against the senses, against every principle, derived merely from human research and inquiry. All the topics of the ancient Academics were adopted by the fathers; and thence propagated for several ages in every school and pulpit throughout Christendom. The reformers embraced the same principles of reasoning, or rather declamation; and all panegyrics on the excellency of faith were sure to be interlarded with some severe strokes of satire against natural reason. A celebrated prelate too,[3] of the Romish communion, a man of the most extensive learning, who wrote a demonstra-

[3] Mons. Huet.

tion of Christianity, has also composed a treatise, which contains all the cavils of the boldest and most determined Pyrrhonism. Locke seems to have been the first Christian, who ventured openly to assert, that *faith* was nothing but a species of *reason*, that religion was only a branch of philosophy, and that a chain of arguments, similar to that which established any truth in morals, politics, or physics, was always employed in discovering all the principles of theology, natural and revealed. The ill use, which Bayle and other libertines made of the philosophical scepticism of the fathers and first reformers, still farther propagated the judicious sentiment of Mr. Locke: and it is now, in a manner, avowed, by all pretenders to reasoning and philosophy, that atheist and sceptic are almost synonymous. And as it is certain, that no man is in earnest, when he professes the latter principle; I would fain hope that there are as few, who seriously maintain the former.

Don't you remember, said Philo, the excellent saying of Lord Bacon on this head? That a little philosophy, replied Cleanthes, makes a man an atheist: a great deal converts him to religion. That is a very judicious remark too, said Philo. But what I have in my eye is another passage, where, having mentioned David's fool, who said in his heart there is no God, this great philosopher observes, that the atheists nowadays have a double share of folly: for they are not contented to say in their hearts there is no God, but they also utter that impiety with their lips, and are thereby guilty of multiplied indiscretion and imprudence. Such people, though they were ever so much in earnest, cannot, methinks, be very formidable.

But though you should rank me in this class of fools, I cannot forbear communicating a remark, that occurs to me, from the history of the religious and irreligious scepticism, with which you have entertained us. It appears to me, that there are strong symptoms of priestcraft in the whole progress of this affair. During ignorant ages, such as those which followed the dissolution of the ancient schools, the priests perceived, that atheism, deism, or heresy of any kind, could only proceed from the presumptuous questioning of received opinions, and from a belief, that human reason was equal to everything. Education had then a mighty influence over the minds of men, and was almost equal in force to those suggestions of the senses and common understanding, by which the most determined sceptic must allow himself to be governed. But at present, when the influence of education is much diminished, and men, from a more open commerce of the world, have learned to compare the popular principles of different nations and ages, our sagacious divines have changed their whole system of philosophy, and talk the language of Stoics, Platonists, and Peripatetics, not that of Pyrrhonians and Academics. If we distrust human reason, we have now no other principle to lead us into religion. Thus sceptics, in one age, dogmatists in another; whichever system best suits the purpose of these reverend gentlemen, in giving them an ascendant over mankind, they are sure to make it their favorite principle, and established tenet.

It is very natural, said Cleanthes, for men to embrace those principles, by which they find they can best defend their doctrines; nor need we have any recourse to priestcraft to account for so reasonable an expedient. And surely nothing can afford a stronger presumption, that any set of principles are true, and ought to be embraced, than to observe, that they tend to the confirmation of true religion, and serve to confound the cavils of atheists, libertines, and freethinkers of all denominations.

Part II

I must own, Cleanthes, said Demea, that nothing can more surprise me, than the light, in which you have, all along, put this argument. By the whole tenor of your discourse, one would imagine that you were maintaining the being of a God, against the cavils of atheists and infidels; and were necessitated to become a champion for that fundamental principle of all religion. But this, I hope, is not by any means a question among us. No man; no man, at least, of common sense, I am persuaded, ever entertained a serious doubt with regard to a truth, so certain and self-evident. The question is not concerning the *being*, but the *nature* of God. This, I affirm, from the infirmities of human understanding, to be altogether incomprehensible and unknown to us. The essence of that supreme mind, his attributes, the manner of his existence, the very nature of his duration; these and every particular, which regards so divine a being, are mysterious to men. Finite, weak, and blind creatures, we ought to humble ourselves in his august presence, and, conscious of our frailties, adore in silence his infinite perfections, which eye hath not seen, ear hath not heard, neither hath it entered into the heart of man to conceive them. They are covered in a deep cloud from human curiosity: it is profaneness to attempt penetrating through these sacred obscurities: and next to the impiety of denying his existence, is the temerity of prying into his nature and essence, decrees and attributes.

But lest you should think, that my *piety* has here got the better of my *philosophy*, I shall support my opinion, if it needs any support, by a very great authority. I might cite all the divines almost, from the foundation of Christianity, who have ever treated of this or any other theological subject: but I shall confine myself, at present, to one equally celebrated for piety and philosophy. It is Father Malebranche, who, I remember, thus expresses himself.[4] 'One ought not so much (says he) to call God a spirit, in order to express positively what he is, as in order to signify that he is not matter. He is a Being infinitely perfect: of this we cannot doubt. But in the same manner as we ought not to imagine, even supposing him corporeal, that he is clothed with a human body, as the Anthropomorphites asserted, under color that that figure was the most perfect of any; so neither ought we to imagine, that the spirit of God has human ideas, or bears *any* resemblance to our spirit; under color that we know nothing more perfect than a human mind. We ought rather to believe, that as he comprehends the perfections of matter without being material . . . . he comprehends also the perfections of created spirits, without being spirit, in the manner we conceive spirit: that his true name is, *He that is*, or, in other words, Being without restriction, All Being, the Being infinite and universal.' INCOMPREHENSIBLE

After so great an authority, Demea, replied Philo, as that which you have produced, and a thousand more, which you might produce, it would appear ridiculous in me to add my sentiment, or express my approbation of your doctrine. But surely, where reasonable men treat these subjects, the question can never be concerning the being, but only the nature of the Deity. The former truth, as you well observe, is unquestionable and self-evident. Nothing exists without a cause; and the original cause of this universe (whatever it be) we call God; and piously ascribe to him every species of perfection. Whoever scruples this fundamental truth, deserves every pun-

[4] Recherche de la Vérité, liv. 3, chap. 9.

ishment, which can be inflicted among philosophers, to wit, the greatest ridicule, contempt and disapprobation. But as all perfection is entirely relative, we ought never to imagine, that we comprehend the attributes of this divine Being, or to suppose, that his perfections have any analogy or likeness to the perfections of a human creature. Wisdom, thought, design, knowledge; these we justly ascribe to him; because these words are honorable among men, and we have no other language or other conceptions, by which we can express our adoration of him. But let us beware, lest we think, that our ideas any wise correspond to his perfections, or that his attributes have any resemblance to these qualities among men. He is infinitely superior to our limited view and comprehension; and is more the object of worship in the temple, than of disputation in the schools.

In reality, Cleanthes, continued he, there is no need of having recourse to that affected scepticism, so displeasing to you, in order to come at this determination. Our ideas reach no farther than our experience: we have no experience of divine attributes and operations: I need not conclude my syllogism: you can draw the inference yourself. And it is a pleasure to me (and I hope to you too) that just reasoning and sound piety here concur in the same conclusion, and both of them establish the adorably mysterious and incomprehensible nature of the Supreme Being.

Not to lose any time in circumlocutions, said Cleanthes, addressing himself to Demea, much less in replying to the pious declamations of Philo; I shall briefly explain how I conceive this matter. Look round the world: contemplate the whole and every part of it: you will find it to be nothing but one great machine, subdivided into an infinite number of lesser machines, which again admit of subdivisions, to a degree beyond what human senses and faculties can trace and explain. All these various machines, and even their most minute parts, are adjusted to each other with an accuracy, which ravishes into admiration all men, who have ever contemplated them. The curious adapting of means to ends, throughout all nature, resembles exactly, though it much exceeds, the productions of human contrivance; of human design, thought, wisdom, and intelligence. Since therefore the effects resemble each other, we are led to infer, by all the rules of analogy, that the causes also resemble; and that the Author of Nature is somewhat similar to the mind of men;

though possessed of much larger faculties, proportioned to the grandeur of the work, which he has executed. By this argument *a posteriori*, and by this argument alone, do we prove at once the existence of a Deity, and his similarity to human mind and intelligence.

I shall be so free, Cleanthes, said Demea, as to tell you, that from the beginning, I could not approve of your conclusion concerning the similarity of the Deity to men; still less can I approve of the mediums, by which you endeavor to establish it. What! No demonstration of the being of a God! No abstract arguments! No proofs *a priori!* Are these, which have hitherto been so much insisted on by philosophers, all fallacy, all sophism? Can we reach no farther in this subject than experience and probability? I will not say, that this is betraying the cause of a deity: but surely, by this affected candor, you give advantage to atheists, which they never could obtain, by the mere dint of argument and reasoning.

What I chiefly scruple in this subject, said Philo, is not so much, that all religious arguments are by Cleanthes reduced to experience, as that they appear not to be even the most certain and irrefragable of that inferior kind. That a stone will fall, that fire will burn, that the earth has solidity, we have observed a thousand and a thousand times; and when any new instance of this nature is presented, we draw without hesitation the accustomed inference. The exact similarity of the cases gives us a perfect assurance of a similar event; and a stronger evidence is never desired nor sought after. But wherever you depart, in the least, from the similarity of the cases, you diminish proportionably the evidence; and may at last bring it to a very weak *analogy*, which is confessedly liable to error and uncertainty. After having experienced the circulation of the blood in human creatures, we make no doubt that it takes place in Titius and Maevius: but from its circulation in frogs and fishes, it is only a presumption, though a strong one, from analogy, that it takes place in men and other animals. The analogical reasoning is much weaker, when we infer the circulation of the sap in vegetables from our experience, that the blood circulates in animals; and those, who hastily followed that imperfect analogy, are found, by more accurate experiments, to have been mistaken.

If we see a house, Cleanthes, we conclude, with the greatest certainty, that it had an architect or builder; because this is precisely that species of effect, which we have experienced to proceed from that species of cause. But surely you will not affirm, that the universe bears such a resemblance to a house, that we can with the same certainty infer a similar cause, or that the analogy is here entire and perfect. The dissimilitude is so striking, that the utmost you can here pretend to is a guess, a conjecture, a presumption concerning a similar cause; and how that pretension will be received in the world, I leave you to consider.

It would surely be very ill received, replied Cleanthes; and I should be deservedly blamed and detested, did I allow, that the proofs of a Deity amounted to no more than a guess or conjecture. But is the whole adjustment of means to ends in a house and in the universe so slight a resemblance? The economy of final causes? The order, proportion, and arrangement of every part? Steps of a stair are plainly contrived, that human legs may use them in mounting; and this inference is certain and infallible. Human legs are also contrived for walking and mounting; and this inference, I allow, is not altogether so certain, because of the dissimilarity which you remark; but does it, therefore, deserve the name only of presumption or conjecture?

Good God! cried Demea, interrupting him, where are we? Zealous defenders of religion allow, that the proofs of a Deity fall short of perfect evidence! And you, Philo, on whose assistance I depended, in proving the adorable mysteriousness of the Divine Nature, do you assent to all these extravagant opinions of Cleanthes? For what other name can I give them? Or why spare my censure, when such principles are advanced, supported by such an authority, before so young a man as Pamphilus?

You seem not to apprehend, replied Philo, that I argue with Cleanthes in his own way; and by showing him the dangerous consequences of his tenets, hope at last to reduce him to our opinion. But what sticks most with you, I observe, is the representation which Cleanthes has made of the argument *a posteriori*; and finding, that that argument is likely to escape your hold and vanish into air, you think it so disguised, that you can scarcely believe it to be set in its true light. Now, however much I may dissent, in other respects, from the dangerous principles of Cleanthes, I must allow, that he has fairly represented that argument; and I shall endeavor so to state the matter to you, that you will entertain no farther scruples with regard to it.

Were a man to abstract from everything which he knows or has seen, he would be altogether incapable, merely from his own ideas, to determine what kind of scene the universe must be, or to give the preference to one state or situation of things above another. For as nothing which he clearly conceives, could be esteemed impossible or implying a contradiction, every chimera of his fancy would be upon an equal footing; nor could he assign any just reason, why he adheres to one idea or system, and rejects the others, which are equally possible.

Again; after he opens his eyes, and contemplates the world, as it really is, it would be impossible for him, at first, to assign the cause of any one event; much less, of the whole of things or of the universe. He might set his fancy a rambling; and she might bring him in an infinite variety of reports and representations. These would all be possible; but being all equally possible, he would never, of himself, give a satisfactory account for his preferring one of them to the rest. Experience alone can point out to him the true cause of any phenomenon.

Now, according to this method of reasoning, Demea, it follows (and is, indeed, tacitly allowed by Cleanthes himself) that order, arrangement, or the adjustment of final causes is not, of itself, any proof of design; but only so far as it has been experienced to proceed from that principle. For aught we can know *a priori*, matter may contain the source or spring of order originally, within itself, as well as mind does; and there is no more difficulty in conceiving, that the several elements, from an internal unknown cause, may fall into the most exquisite arrangement, than to conceive that their ideas, in the great, universal mind, from a like internal, unknown cause, fall into that arrangement. The equal possibility of both these suppositions is allowed. But by experience we find (according to Cleanthes), that there is a difference between them. Throw several pieces of steel together, without shape or form; they will never arrange themselves so as to compose a watch: stone, and mortar, and wood, without an architect, never erect a house. But the ideas in a human mind, we see, by an unknown, inexplicable economy, arrange themselves so as to form the plan of a watch or house. Experience, therefore, proves, that there is an original principle of order in mind, not in matter. From similar effects we infer similar causes. The adjustment of means to ends is alike in the universe, as in a machine of human contrivance. The causes, therefore, must be resembling.

I was from the beginning scandalized, I must own, with this resemblance, which is asserted, between the Deity and human creatures; and must conceive it to imply such a degradation of the Supreme Being as no sound theist could endure. With your assistance, therefore, Demea, I shall endeavor to defend what you justly called the adorable mysteriousness of the Divine Nature, and shall refute this reasoning of Cleanthes, provided he allows, that I have made a fair representation of it.

When Cleanthes had assented, Philo, after a short pause, proceeded in the following manner.

That all inferences, Cleanthes, concerning fact, are founded on experience, and that all experimental reasonings are founded on the supposition, that similar causes prove similar effects, and similar effects similar causes; I shall not, at present, much dispute with you. But observe, I entreat you, with what extreme caution all just reasoners proceed in the transferring of experiments to similar cases. Unless the cases be exactly similar, they repose no perfect confidence in applying their past observation to any particular phenomenon. Every alteration of circumstances occasions a doubt concerning the event; and it requires new experiments to prove certainly, that the new circumstances are of no moment or importance. A change in bulk, situation, arrangement, age, disposition of the air, or surrounding bodies; any of these particulars may be attended with the most unexpected consequences: and unless the objects be quite familiar to us, it is the highest temerity to expect with assurance, after any of these changes, an event similar to that which before fell under our observation. The slow and deliberate steps of philosophers, here, if anywhere, are distinguished from the precipitate march of the vulgar, who, hurried on by the smallest similitudes, are incapable of all discernment or consideration.

But can you think, Cleanthes, that your usual phlegm and philosophy have been preserved in so wide a step as you have taken, when you compared to the universe, houses, ships, furniture, machines; and from their similarity in some circumstances inferred a similarity in their causes? Thought, design, intelligence, such as we discover in men and other animals, is no more than one of the springs and principles of the universe, as well as heat or cold, attraction or repulsion, and a hundred others, which fall under daily observation. It is an active cause, by which some particular parts of nature, we find, produce alterations on other parts. But can a conclusion, with any propriety, be transferred from parts to the whole? Does not the great disproportion bar all comparison and inference? From observing the growth of a hair, can we learn anything concerning the generation of a man? Would the manner of a leaf's blowing, even though perfectly known, afford us any instruction concerning the vegetation of a tree?

But allowing that we were to take the *operations* of one part of nature upon another for the foundation of our judgment concerning the *origin* of the whole (which never can be admitted), yet why select so minute, so weak, so bounded a principle as the reason and design of animals is found to be upon this planet? What peculiar privilege has this little agitation of the brain which we call *thought*, that we must thus make it the model of the whole universe? Our partiality in our own favor does indeed present it on all occasions; but sound philosophy ought carefully to guard against so natural an illusion.

So far from admitting, continued Philo, that the operations of a part can afford us any just conclusion concerning the origin of the whole, I will not allow any one part to form a rule for another part, if the latter be very remote from the former. Is there any reasonable ground to conclude, that the inhabitants of other planets possess thought, intelligence, reason, or anything similar to these faculties in men? When Nature has so extremely diversified her manner of operation in this small globe; can we imagine, that she incessantly copies herself throughout so immense a universe? And if thought, as we may well suppose, be confined merely to this narrow corner, and has even there so limited a sphere of action; with what propriety can we assign it for the original cause of all things? The narrow views of a peasant, who makes his domestic economy the rule for the government of kingdoms, is in comparison a pardonable sophism.

But were we ever so much assured, that a thought and reason, resembling the human, were to be found throughout the whole universe, and were its activity elsewhere vastly greater and more commanding than it appears in this globe; yet I cannot see, why the operations of a world, constituted, arranged, adjusted, can with any propriety be extended to a world, which is in its embryo state, and is advancing towards that constitution and arrangement. By observation, we know somewhat of the economy, action, and nourishment of a finished animal; but we must transfer with great caution that observation to the growth of a fetus in the womb, and still more, to the formation of an animalcule in the loins of its male parent. Nature, we find, even from our limited experience, possesses an infinite number of springs and principles, which incessantly discover themselves on every change of her position and situation. And what new and unknown principles would actuate her in so new and unknown a situation as that of the formation of a universe, we cannot, without the utmost temerity, pretend to determine.

A very small part of this great system, during a very short time, is very imperfectly discovered to us: and do we thence pronounce decisively concerning the origin of the whole?

Admirable conclusion! Stone, wood, brick, iron, brass, have not, at this time, in this minute globe of earth, an order or arrangement without human art and contrivance: therefore the universe could not originally attain its order and arrangement, without something similar to human art. But is a part of nature a rule for another part very wide of the former? Is it a rule for the whole? Is a very small part a rule for the universe? Is nature in one situation, a certain rule for nature in another situation, vastly different from the former?

And can you blame me, Cleanthes, if I here imitate the prudent reserve of Simonides, who, according to the noted story, being asked by Hiero, *What God was?* desired a day to think of it, and then two days more; and after that manner continually prolonged the term, without ever bringing in his definition or description? Could you even blame me, if I had answered at first *that I did not know*, and was sensible that this subject lay vastly beyond the reach of my faculties? You might cry out sceptic and rallier as much as you pleased: but having found, in so many other subjects, much more familiar, the imperfections and even contradictions of human reason, I never should expect any success from its feeble conjectures, in a subject, so sublime, and so remote from the sphere of our observation. When two species of objects have always been observed to be conjoined together, I can infer, by custom, the existence of one wherever I see the existence of the other: and this I call an argument from experience. But how this argument can have place, where the objects, as in the present case, are single, individual, without parallel, or specific resemblance, may be difficult to explain. And will any man tell me with a serious countenance, that an orderly universe must arise from some thought and art, like the human; because we have experience of it? To ascertain this reasoning, it were requisite, that we had experience of the origin of worlds; and it is not sufficient surely, that we have seen ships and cities arise from human art and contrivance . . . .

Philo was proceeding in this vehement manner, somewhat between jest and earnest, as it appeared to me; when he observed some signs of impatience in Cleanthes, and then immediately stopped short. What I had to suggest, said Cleanthes, is only that you would not abuse terms, or make use of popular expressions to subvert philosophical reasonings. You know, that the vulgar often distinguish reason from experience, even where the question relates only to matter of fact and existence; though it is found, where that reason is properly analyzed, that it is nothing but a species of experience. To prove by experience the origin of the universe from mind is not more contrary to common speech than to prove the motion of the earth from the same principle. And a caviler might raise all the same objections to the Copernican system, which you have urged against my reasonings. Have you other earths, might he say, which you have seen to move? Have . . . .

Yes! cried Philo, interrupting him, we have other earths. Is not the moon another earth, which we see to turn round its center? Is not Venus another earth, where we observe the same phenomenon? Are not the revolutions of the sun also a confirmation, from analogy, of the same theory? All the planets, are they not earths, which revolve about the sun? Are not the satellites moons, which move round Jupiter and Saturn, and along with these primary planets, round the sun? These analogies and resemblances, with others, which I have not mentioned, are the sole proofs of the Copernican system: and to you it belongs to consider, whether you have any analogies of the same kind to support your theory.

In reality, Cleanthes, continued he, the modern system of astronomy is now so much received by all inquirers, and has become so essential a part even of our earliest education, that we are not commonly very scrupulous in examining the reasons upon which it is founded. It is now become a matter of mere curiosity to study the first writers on that subject, who had the full force of prejudice to encounter, and were obliged to turn their arguments on every side, in order to render them popular and convincing. But if we peruse Galileo's famous Dialogues concerning the system of the world, we shall find, that that great genius, one of the sublimest that ever existed, first bent all his endeavors to prove, that there was no foundation for the distinction commonly made between elementary and celestial substances. The schools, proceeding from the illusions of sense, had carried this distinction very far; and had established the latter substances to be ingenerable, incorruptible, unalterable, impassable; and had assigned all the opposite qualities to the former. But Galileo, beginning with the moon, proved its similarity in every particular to the earth; its convex figure, its natural darkness when not illuminated, its density, its distinction into solid and liquid, the variations of its phases, the mutual illuminations of the earth and moon, their mutual eclipses, the inequalities of the lunar surface, etc. After many instances of this kind, with regard to all the planets, men plainly saw, that these bodies became proper objects of experience; and that the similarity of their nature enabled us to extend the same arguments and phenomena from one to the other.

In this cautious proceeding of the astronomers, you may read your own condemnation, Cleanthes; or rather may see, that the subject in which you are engaged exceeds all human reason and inquiry. Can you pretend to show any such similarity between the fabric of a house, and the generation of a universe? Have you ever seen nature in any such situation as resembles the first arrangement of the elements? Have worlds ever been formed under your eye? and have you had leisure to observe the whole progress of the phenomenon, from the first appearance of order to its final consummation? If you have, then cite your experience, and deliver your theory.

Part III

How the most absurd argument, replied Cleanthes, in the hands of a man of ingenuity and invention, may acquire an air of probability! Are you not aware, Philo, that it became necessary for Copernicus and his first disciples to prove the similarity of the terrestrial and celestial matter; because several philosophers, blinded by old systems, and supported by some sensible appearances, had denied this similarity? But that it is by no means necessary, that theists should prove the similarity of the works of nature to those of art; because this similarity is self-evident and undeniable? The same matter, a like form: what more is requisite to show an analogy between their causes, and to ascertain the origin of all things from a divine purpose and intention? Your objections, I must freely tell you, are no better than the abstruse cavils of those philosophers who denied motion; and ought to be refuted in the same manner, by illustrations, examples, and instances, rather than by serious argument and philosophy.

Suppose, therefore, that an articulate voice were heard in the clouds, much louder and more melodious than any which human art could ever reach: suppose, that this voice were extended in the same instant over all nations, and spoke to each nation in its own language and dialect: suppose, that the words delivered not only contain a just sense and meaning, but convey some instruction altogether worthy of a benevolent being, superior to mankind: could you possibly hesitate a moment concerning the cause of this voice? and must you not instantly ascribe it to some design or purpose? Yet I cannot see but all the same objections (if they merit that appellation) which lie against the system of theism, may also be produced against this inference.

Might you not say, that all conclusions concerning fact were founded on experience: that when we hear an articulate voice in the dark, and thence infer a man, it is only the resemblance of the effects, which leads us to conclude that there is a like resemblance in the cause: but that this extraordinary voice, by its loudness, extent, and flexibility to all languages, bears so little analogy to any human voice, that we have no reason to suppose any analogy in their causes: and consequently, that a rational, wise, coherent speech proceeded, you knew not whence, from some accidental whistling of the winds, not from any divine reason or intelligence? You see clearly your own objections in these cavils; and I hope too, you see clearly, that they cannot possibly have more force in the one case than in the other.

But to bring the case still nearer the present one of the universe, I shall make two suppositions, which imply not any absurdity or impossibility. Suppose, that there is a natural, universal, invariable language, common to every individual of human race, and that books are natural productions, which perpetuate themselves in the same manner with animals and vegetables, by descent and propagation. Several expressions of our passions contain a universal language: all brute animals have a natural speech, which, however limited, is very intelligible to their own species. And as there are infinitely fewer parts and less contrivance in the finest composition of eloquence, than in the coarsest organized body, the propagation of an *Iliad* or *Aeneid* is an easier supposition than that of any plant or animal.

Suppose, therefore, that you enter into your library, thus peopled by natural volumes, containing the most refined reason and most exquisite beauty: could you possibly open one of them, and doubt, that its original cause bore the strongest analogy to mind and intelligence? When it reasons and discourses; when it expostulates, argues, and enforces its views and topics; when it applies sometimes to the pure intellect, sometimes to the affections; when it collects, disposes, and adorns every consideration suited to the subject: could you persist in asserting, that all this, at the bottom, had really no meaning, and that the first formation of this volume in the loins of its original parent proceeded not from thought and design? Your obstinacy, I know, reaches not that degree of firmness: even your sceptical play and wantonness would be abashed at so glaring an absurdity.

But if there be any difference, Philo, between this supposed case and the real one of the universe, it is all to the advantage of the latter. The anatomy of an animal affords many stronger instances of design than the perusal of Livy or Tacitus: and any objection which you start in the former case, by carrying me back to so unusual and extraordinary a scene as the first formation of worlds, the same objection has place on the supposition of our vegetating library. Choose, then, your party, Philo, without ambiguity or evasion; assert either that a rational volume is no proof of a rational cause, or admit of a similar cause to all the works of nature.

Let me here observe too, continued Cleanthes, that this religious argument, instead of being weakened by that scepticism, so much affected by you, rather acquires force from it, and becomes more firm and undisputed. To exclude all argument or reasoning of every kind is either affectation or madness. The declared profession of every reasonable sceptic is only to reject abstruse, remote and refined arguments; to adhere to common sense and the plain instincts of nature; and to assent, wherever any reasons strike him with so full a force, that he cannot, without the greatest violence, prevent it. Now the arguments for Natural Religion are plainly of this kind; and nothing but the most perverse, obstinate metaphysics can reject them. Consider, anatomize the eye; survey its structure and contrivance; and tell me, from your own feeling, if the idea of a contriver does not immediately flow in upon you with a force like that of sensation. The most obvious conclusion surely is in favor of design; and it requires time, reflection and study, to summon up those frivolous, though abstruse objections, which can support infidelity. Who can behold the male and female of each species, the correspondence of their parts and instincts, their passions and whole course of life before and after generation, but must be sensible, that the propagation of the species is intended by Nature? Millions and millions of such instances present themselves through every part of the universe; and no language can convey a more intelligible, irresistible meaning, than the curious adjustment of final causes. To what degree, therefore, of blind dogmatism must one have attained, to reject such natural and such convincing arguments?

Some beauties in writing we may meet with, which seem contrary to rules, and which gain the affections, and animate the imagination, in opposition to all the precepts of criticism, and to the authority of the established masters of art. And if the argument for theism be, as you pretend, contradictory to the principles of logic; its universal, its irresistible influence proves clearly, that there may be arguments of a like irregular nature. Whatever cavils may be urged; an orderly world, as well as a coherent, articulate speech, will still be received as an incontestable proof of design and intention.

It sometimes happens, I own, that the religious arguments have not their due influence on an ignorant savage and barbarian; not because they are obscure and difficult, but because he never asks himself any question with regard to them. Whence arises the curious structure of an animal? From the copulation of its parents. And these whence? From *their* parents. A few removes set the objects at such a distance, that to him they are lost in darkness and confusion; nor is he actuated by any curiosity to trace them farther. But this is neither dogmatism nor scepticism, but stupidity; a state of mind very different from your sifting, inquisitive disposition, my ingenious friend. You can trace causes from effects: you can compare the most distant and remote objects: and your greatest errors proceed not from barrenness of thought and invention, but from too luxuriant a fertility, which suppresses your natural good sense, by a profusion of unnecessary scruples and objections.

Here I could observe, Hermippus, that Philo was a little embarrassed and confounded: but while he hesitated in delivering an answer, luckily for him, Demea broke in upon the discourse, and saved his countenance.

Your instance, Cleanthes, said he, drawn from books and languages, being familiar, has, I confess, so much more force on that account; but is there not some danger too in this very circumstance; and may it not render us presumptuous, by making us imagine we comprehend the Deity, and have some adequate idea of his nature and attributes? When I read a volume, I enter into the mind and intention of the author: I become him, in a manner, for the instant; and have an immediate feeling and conception of those ideas which revolved in his imagination while employed in that composition. But so near an approach we never surely can make to the Deity. His ways are not our ways. His attributes are perfect, but incomprehensible. And this volume of Nature contains a great and inexplicable riddle, more than any intelligible discourse or reasoning.

The ancient Platonists, you know, were the most religious and devout of all the pagan philosophers: yet many of them, particularly Plotinus, expressly declare, that intellect or understanding is not to be ascribed to the Deity, and that our most perfect worship of him consists, not in acts of veneration, reverence, gratitude or love; but in a certain mysterious self-annihilation or total extinction of all our faculties. These ideas are, perhaps, too far stretched; but still it must be acknowledged, that, by representing the Deity as so intelligible, and comprehensible, and so similar to a human mind, we are guilty of the grossest and most narrow partiality, and make ourselves the model of the whole universe.

All the *sentiments* of the human mind, gratitude, resentment, love, friendship, approbation, blame, pity, emulation, envy, have a plain reference to the state and situation of man, and are calculated for preserving the existence, and promoting the activity of such a being in such circumstances. It seems therefore unreasonable to transfer such sentiments to a supreme existence, or to suppose him actuated by them; and the phenomena, besides, of the universe will not support us in such a theory. All our *ideas*, derived from the senses, are confusedly false and illusive; and cannot, therefore, be supposed to have place in a supreme intelligence: and as the ideas of internal sentiment, added to those of the external senses, compose the whole furniture of human understanding, we may conclude, that none of the *materials* of thought are in any respect similar in the human and in the divine intelligence. Now, as to the *manner* of thinking; how can we make any comparison between them, or suppose them anywise resembling? Our thought is fluctuating, uncertain, fleeting, successive, and compounded; and were we to remove these circumstances, we absolutely annihilate its essence, and it would, in such a case, be an abuse of terms to apply to it the name of thought or reason. At least, if it appear more pious and respectful (as it really is) still to retain these terms, when we mention the Supreme Being, we ought to acknowledge, that their meaning, in that case, is totally incomprehensible; and that the infirmities of our nature do not permit us to reach any ideas, which in the least correspond to the ineffable sublimity of the divine attributes.

Part IV

It seems strange to me, said Cleanthes, that you, Demea, who are so sincere in the cause of religion, should still maintain the mysterious, incomprehensible nature of the Deity, and should insist so strenuously, that he has no manner of likeness or resemblance to human creatures. The Deity, I can readily allow, possesses many powers and attributes, of which we can have no comprehension: but if our ideas, so far as they go, be not just and adequate, and correspondent to his real nature, I know not what there is in this subject worth insisting on. Is the name, without any meaning, of such mighty importance? Or how do you mystics, who maintain the absolute incomprehensibility of the Deity, differ from sceptics or atheists, who assert, that the first cause of all is unknown and unintelligible? Their temerity must be very great, if, after rejecting the production by a mind; I mean, a mind resembling the human (for I know of no other), they pretend to assign, with certainty, any other specific, intelligible cause: and their conscience must be very scrupulous indeed, if they refuse to call the universal, unknown cause a God or Deity;

and to bestow on him as many sublime eulogies and unmeaning epithets, as you shall please to require of them.

Who could imagine, replied Demea, that Cleanthes, the calm, philosophical Cleanthes, would attempt to refute his antagonists, by affixing a nickname to them; and like the common bigots and inquisitors of the age, have recourse to invective and declamation, instead of reasoning? Or does he not perceive, that these topics are easily retorted, and that *anthropomorphite* is an appellation as invidious, and implies as dangerous consequences, as the epithet of *mystic*, with which he has honored us? In reality, Cleanthes, consider what it is you assert, when you represent the Deity as similar to a human mind and understanding. What is the soul of man? A composition of various faculties, passions, sentiments, ideas; united, indeed, into one self or person, but still distinct from each other. When it reasons, the ideas, which are the parts of its discourse, arrange themselves in a certain form or order; which is not preserved entire for a moment, but immediately gives place to another arrangement. New opinions, new passions, new affections, new feelings arise, which continually diversify the mental scene, and produce in it the greatest variety, and most rapid succession imaginable. How is this compatible with that perfect immutability and simplicity which all true theists ascribe to the Deity? By the same act, say they, he sees past, present, and future: his love and his hatred, his mercy and his justice, are one individual operation: he is entire in every point of space; and complete in every instant of duration. No succession, no change, no acquisition, no diminution. What he is implies not in it any shadow of distinction or diversity. And what he is, this moment, he ever has been, and ever will be, without any new judgment, sentiment, or operation. He stands fixed in one simple, perfect state; nor can you ever say, with any propriety, that this act of his is different from that other, or that this judgment or idea has been lately formed, and will give place, by succession, to any different judgment or idea.

I can readily allow, said Cleanthes, that those who maintain the perfect simplicity of the Supreme Being, to the extent in which you have explained it, are complete mystics, and chargeable with all the consequences which I have drawn from their opinion. They are, in a word, atheists, without knowing it. For though it be allowed, that the Deity possesses attributes, of which we have no comprehension; yet ought we never to ascribe to him any attributes, which are absolutely incompatible with that intelligent nature, essential to him. A mind, whose acts and sentiments and ideas are not distinct and successive; one, that is wholly simple, and totally immutable; is a mind which has no thought, no reason, no will, no sentiment, no love, no hatred; or in a word, is no mind at all. It is an abuse of terms to give it that appellation; and we may as well speak of limited extension without figure, or of number without composition.

Pray consider, said Philo, whom you are at present inveighing against. You are honoring with the appellation of atheist all the sound, orthodox divines almost, who have treated of this subject; and you will, at last, be, yourself, found, according to your reckoning, the only sound theist in the world. But if idolaters be atheists, as, I think, may justly be asserted, and Christian theologians the same; what becomes of the argument, so much celebrated, derived from the universal consent of mankind?

But because I know you are not much swayed by names and authorities, I shall endeavor to show you, a little more distinctly, the inconveniences of that anthropomorphism which you have embraced; and I shall prove, that there is no ground to suppose a plan of the world to be formed in the divine mind, consisting of distinct ideas, differently arranged; in the same manner as an architect forms in his head the plan of a house which he intends to execute.

It is not easy, I own, to see, what is gained by this supposition, whether we judge of the matter by *reason* or by *experience*. We are still obliged to mount higher, in order to find the cause of this cause, which you had assigned as satisfactory and conclusive.

If *reason* (I mean abstract reason, derived from inquiries *a priori*) be not alike mute with regard to all questions concerning cause and effect; this sentence at least it will venture to pronounce, that a mental world, or universe of ideas, requires a cause as much, as does a material world, or universe of objects; and if similar in its arrangement must require a similar cause. For what is there in this subject, which should occasion a different conclusion or inference? In an abstract view, they are entirely alike; and no difficulty attends the one supposition, which is not common to both of them.

Again, when we will needs force *experience* to pronounce some sentence, even on these subjects, which lie beyond her sphere; neither can she perceive any material difference in this particular, between these two kinds of worlds, but finds them to be governed by similar principles, and to depend upon an equal variety of causes in their operations. We have specimens in miniature of both of them. Our own mind resembles the one: a vegetable or animal body the other. Let experience, therefore, judge from these samples. Nothing seems more delicate with regard to its causes than thought; and as these causes never operate in two persons after the same manner, so we never find two persons, who think exactly alike. Nor indeed does the same person think exactly alike at any two different periods of time. A difference of age, of the disposition of his body, of weather, of food, of company, of books, of passions; any of these particulars, or others more minute, are sufficient to alter the curious machinery of thought, and communicate to it very different movements and operations. As far as we can judge, vegetables and animal bodies are not more delicate in their motions, nor depend upon a greater variety or more curious adjustment of springs and principles.

How therefore shall we satisfy ourselves concerning the cause of that Being, whom you suppose the Author of Nature, or, according to your system of anthropomorphism, the ideal world, into which you trace the material? Have we not the same reason to trace that ideal world into another ideal world, or new intelligent principle? But if we stop, and go no farther; why go so far? Why not stop at the material world? How can we satisfy ourselves without going on *in infinitum?* And after all, what satisfaction is there in that infinite progression? Let us remember the story of the Indian philosopher and his elephant. It was never more applicable than to the present subject. If the material world rests upon a similar ideal world, this ideal world must rest upon some other; and so on, without end. It were better, therefore, never to look beyond the present material world. By supposing it to contain the principle of its order within itself, we really assert it to be God; and the sooner we arrive at that Divine Being, so much the better. When you go one step beyond the mundane system, you only excite an inquisitive humor, which it is impossible ever to satisfy.

To say, that the different ideas, which compose the reason of the Supreme Being, fall into order, of themselves, and by their own nature, is really to talk without any precise meaning. If it has a meaning, I would fain know, why it is not as good sense to say, that the parts of the material world fall into order, of themselves, and by their own nature. Can the one opinion be intelligible, while the other is not so?

We have, indeed, experience of ideas, which fall into order, of themselves, and without any *known* cause; but, I am sure, we have a much larger experience of matter, which does the same; as, in all instances of generation and vegetation, where the accurate analysis of the cause exceeds all human comprehension. We have also experience of particular systems of thought and of matter, which have no order; of the first, in madness; of the second, in corruption. Why then should we think, that order is more essential to one than the other? And if it requires a cause in both, what do we gain by your system, in tracing the universe of objects into a similar universe of ideas? The first step, which we make, leads us on forever. It were, therefore, wise in us, to limit all our inquiries to the present world, without looking farther. No satisfaction can ever be attained by these speculations, which so far exceed the narrow bounds of human understanding.

It was usual with the Peripatetics, you know, Cleanthes, when the cause of any phenomenon was demanded, to have recourse to their *faculties* or *occult qualities*, and to say, for instance, that bread nourished by its nutritive faculty, and senna purged by its purgative: but it has been discovered, that this subterfuge was nothing but the disguise of ignorance; and that these philosophers, though less ingenuous, really said the same thing with the sceptics or the vulgar, who fairly confessed, that they knew not the cause of these phenomena. In like manner, when it is asked, what cause produces order in the ideas of the Supreme Being, can any other reason be assigned to you, Anthropomorphites, than that it is a *rational* faculty, and that such is the nature of the Deity? But why a similar answer will not be equally satisfactory in accounting for the order of the world, without having recourse to any such intelligent creator, as you insist on, may be difficult to determine. It is only to say, that such is the nature of material objects, and that they are all originally possessed of a *faculty* of order and proportion. These are only more learned and elaborate ways of confessing our ignorance; nor has the one hypothesis any real advantage above the other, except in its greater conformity to vulgar prejudices.

You have displayed this argument with great emphasis, replied Cleanthes: you seem not sensible, how easy it is to answer it. Even in common life, if I assign a cause for any event; is it any objection, Philo, that I cannot assign the cause of that cause, and answer every new question, which may incessantly be started? And what philosophers could possibly submit to so rigid a rule? Philosophers, who confess ultimate causes to be totally unknown, and are sensible, that the most refined principles, into which they trace the phenomena, are still to them as inexplicable as these phenomena themselves are to the vulgar. The order and arrangement of nature, the curious adjustment of final causes, the plain use and intention of every part and organ; all these bespeak in the clearest language an intelligent cause or author. The heavens and the earth join in the same testimony: the whole chorus of Nature raises one hymn to the praises of its creator: you alone, or almost alone, disturb this general harmony. You start abstruse doubts, cavils, and objections: you ask me, what is the cause of this cause? I know not; I care not; that concerns not me. I have found a Deity; and here I stop my inquiry. Let those go farther, who are wiser or more enterprising.

I pretend to be neither, replied Philo: and for that very reason, I should never perhaps have attempted to go so far; especially when I am sensible, that I must at last be contented to sit down with the same answer, which, without farther trouble, might have satisfied me from the beginning. If I am still to remain in utter ignorance of causes, and can absolutely give an explication of nothing, I shall never esteem it any advantage to shove off for a moment a difficulty, which, you acknowledge, must immediately, in its full force, recur upon me. Naturalists indeed very justly explain particular effects by more general causes, though these general causes themselves should remain in the end totally inexplicable: but they never surely thought it satisfactory to explain a particular effect by a particular cause, which was no more to be accounted for than the effect itself. An ideal system, arranged of itself, without a precedent design, is not a whit more explicable than a material one, which attains its order in a like manner; nor is there any more difficulty in the latter supposition than in the former.

Part V

But to show you still more inconveniences, continued Philo, in your anthropomorphism; please to take a new survey of your principles. *Like effects prove like causes.* This is the experimental argument; and this, you say too, is the sole theological argument. Now it is certain, that the liker the effects are, which are seen, and the liker the causes, which are inferred, the stronger is the argument. Every departure on either side diminishes the probability, and renders the experiment less conclusive. You cannot doubt of the principle: neither ought you to reject its consequences.

All the new discoveries in astronomy, which prove the immense grandeur and magnificence of the works of nature, are so many additional arguments for a Deity, according to the true system of theism: but according to your hypothesis of experimental theism, they become so many objections, by removing the effect still farther from all resemblance to the effects of human art and contrivance. For if Lucretius,[5] even following the old system of the world, could exclaim,

> Quis regere immensi summan, quis habere profundi
> Indu manu validas potis est moderanter habenas?
> Quis pariter coelos omnes convertere? et omnes
> Ignibus aetheriis terras suffire feraces?
> Omnibus inque locis esse omni tempore praesto?

If Tully[6] esteemed this reasoning so natural as to put it into the mouth of his Epicurean. *Quibus enim oculis animi intueri potuit vester Plato fabricam illam tanti operis, qua construi a Deo atque aedificari mundum facit? quae molitio? quae ferramenta? qui vectes? quae machinae? qui ministri tanti muneris fuerunt? quemadmodum autem obedire et parere voluntati architecti aer, ignis, aqua, terra potuerunt?* If this argument, I say, has any force in former ages: how much greater must it have at present; when the bonds of nature are so infinitely enlarged, and such a magnificent scene is opened to us? It is still more unreasonable to form our idea of so unlimited a cause from our experience of the narrow productions of human design and invention.

The discoveries by microscopes, as they open a new universe in miniature, are still objections, according to you; arguments, according to me. The farther we push our researches of this kind, we are still led to infer the universal causes of all to be vastly different from mankind, or from any object of human experience and observation.

[5] Lib. xi. 1094.
[6] De Nat. Deor., lib. i.

And what say you to the discoveries in anatomy, chemistry, botany? . . . . These surely are no objections, replied Cleanthes: they only discover new instances of art and contrivance. It is still the image of mind reflected on us from innumerable objects. Add, a mind *like the human*, said Philo. I know of no other, replied Cleanthes. And the liker the better, insisted Philo. To be sure, said Cleanthes.

Now, Cleanthes, said Philo, with an air of alacrity and triumph, mark the consequences. *First*, By this method of reasoning, you renounce all claim to infinity in any of the attributes of the Deity. For as the cause ought only to be proportioned to the effect, and the effect, so far as it falls under our cognizance, is not infinite; what pretensions have we, upon your suppositions, to ascribe that attribute to the Divine Being? You will still insist, that, by removing him so much from all similarity to human creatures, we give in to the most arbitrary hypothesis, and at the same time weaken all proofs of his existence.

Secondly, You have no reason, on your theory, for ascribing perfection to the Deity, even in his finite capacity; or for supposing him free from every error, mistake, or incoherence in his undertakings. There are many inexplicable difficulties in the works of nature, which, if we allow a perfect author to be proved *a priori*, are easily solved, and become only seeming difficulties, from the narrow capacity of man, who cannot trace infinite relations. But according to your method of reasoning, these difficulties become all real; and perhaps will be insisted on, as new instances of likeness to human art and contrivance. At least, you must acknowledge, that it is impossible for us to tell, from our limited views, whether this system contains any great faults, or deserves any considerable praise, if compared to other possible, and even real systems. Could a peasant, if the *Aeneid* were read to him, pronounce that poem to be absolutely faultless, or even assign to it its proper rank among the productions of human wit; he, who had never seen any other production?

But were this world ever so perfect a production, it must still remain uncertain, whether all the excellences of the work can justly be ascribed to the workman. If we survey a ship, what an exalted idea must we form of the ingenuity of the carpenter, who framed so complicated, useful, and beautiful a machine? And what surprise must we feel, when we find him a stupid mechanic, who imitated others, and copied an art, which, through a long succession of ages, after multiplied trials, mistakes, corrections, deliberations, and controversies, had been gradually improving? Many worlds might have been botched and bungled, throughout an eternity, ere this system was struck out: much labor lost: many fruitless trials made: and a slow, but continued improvement carried on during infinite ages in the art of world-making. In such subjects, who can determine, where the truth; nay, who can conjecture where the probability lies; amidst a great number of hypotheses which may be proposed, and a still greater number which may be imagined?

And what shadow of an argument, continued Philo, can you produce, from your hypothesis, to prove the unity of the Deity? A great number of men join in building a house or ship, in rearing a city, in framing a commonwealth: why may not several deities combine in contriving and framing a world? This is only so much greater similarity to human affairs? By sharing the work among several, we may so much further limit the attributes of each, and get rid of that extensive power and knowledge, which must be supposed in one deity, and which, according to you, can only serve to weaken the proof of his existence. And if such foolish, such vicious creatures as man can yet often unite in framing and executing one plan; how much more those deities or demons, whom we may suppose several degrees more perfect?

To multiply causes, without necessity, is indeed contrary to true philosophy: but this principle applies not to the present case. Were one deity antecedently proved by your theory, who were possessed of every attribute, requisite to the production of the universe; it would be needless, I own (though not absurd) to suppose any other deity existent. But while it is still a question, whether all these attributes are united in one subject, or dispersed among several independent beings: by what phenomena in nature can we pretend to decide the controversy? Where we see a body raised in a scale, we are sure that there is in the opposite scale, however concealed from sight, some counterpoising weight equal to it: but it is still allowed to doubt, whether that weight be an aggregate of several distinct bodies, or one uniform united mass. And if the weight requisite very much exceeds anything which we have ever seen conjoined in any single body, the former supposition becomes still more probable and natural. An intelligent being of such vast power and capacity, as is necessary to produce the universe, or, to speak in the language of ancient philosophy, so prodigious an animal, exceeds all analogy, and even comprehension.

But farther, Cleanthes; men are mortal, and renew their species by generation; and this is common to all living creatures. The two great sexes of male and female, says Milton, animate the world. Why must this circumstance, so universal, so essential, be excluded from those numerous and limited deities? Behold then the theogony of ancient times brought back upon us.

And why not become a perfect anthropomorphite? Why not assert the deity or deities to be corporeal, and to have eyes, a nose, mouth, ears, etc? Epicurus maintained, that no man had ever seen reason but in a human figure; therefore the gods must have a human figure. And this argument, which is deservedly so much ridiculed by Cicero, becomes, according to you, solid and philosophical.

In a word, Cleanthes, a man, who follows your hypothesis, is able, perhaps, to assert, or conjecture, that the universe, sometime, arose from something like design: but beyond that position he cannot ascertain one single circumstance, and is left afterwards to fix every point of his theology, by the utmost license of fancy and hypothesis. This world, for aught he knows, is very faulty and imperfect compared to a superior standard; and was only the first rude essay of some infant deity, who afterwards abandoned it, ashamed of his lame performance; it is the work only of some dependent, inferior deity; and is the object of derision to his superiors: it is the production of old age and dotage in some superannuated deity; and ever since his death, has run on at adventures, from the first impulse and active force, which it received from him. You justly give signs of horror, Demea, at these strange suppositions: but these, and a thousand more of the same kind, are Cleanthes's suppositions, not mine. From the moment the attributes of the Deity are supposed finite, all these have place. And I cannot, for my part, think, that so wild and unsettled a system of theology is, in any respect, preferable to none at all.

These suppositions I absolutely disown, cried Cleanthes: they strike me, however, with no horror; especially, when proposed in that rambling way in which they drop from you. On the contrary, they give me pleasure, when I see, that, by the utmost indulgence of your imagination, you never get rid of the hypothesis of design in the universe; but are obliged, at every turn, to have recourse to it. To this concession I adhere steadily; and this I regard as a sufficient foundation for religion.

Part VI

It must be a slight fabric, indeed, said Demea, which can be erected on so tottering a foundation. While we are uncertain, whether there is one deity or many; whether the deity or deities, to whom we owe our existence, be perfect or imperfect, subordinate or supreme, dead or alive; what trust or confidence can we repose in them? What devotion or worship address to them? What veneration or obedience pay them? To all the purposes of life, the theory of religion becomes altogether useless: and even with regard to speculative consequences, its uncertainty, according to you, must render it totally precarious and unsatisfactory.

To render it still more unsatisfactory, said Philo, there occurs to me another hypothesis, which must acquire an air of probability from the method of reasoning so much insisted on by Cleanthes. That like effects arise from like causes: this principle he supposes the foundation of all religion. But there is another principle of the same kind, no less certain, and derived from the same source of experience: that where several known circumstances are *observed* to be similar, the unknown will also be *found* similar. Thus, if we see the limbs of a human body, we conclude, that it is also attended with a human head, though hid from us. Thus, if we see, through a chink in a wall, a small part of the sun, we conclude that, were the wall removed, we should see the whole body. In short, this method of reasoning is so obvious and familiar, that no scruple can ever be made with regard to its solidity.

Now if we survey the universe, so far as it falls under our knowledge, it bears a great resemblance to an animal or organized body, and seems actuated with a like principle of life and motion. A continual circulation of matter in it produces no disorder: a continual waste in every part is incessantly repaired; the closest sympathy is perceived throughout the entire system: and each part or member, in performing its proper offices, operates both to its own preservation and to that of the whole. The world, therefore, I infer, is an animal, and the Deity is the *soul* of the world, actuating it, and actuated by it.

You have too much learning, Cleanthes, to be at all surprised at this opinion, which, you know, was maintained by almost all the theists of antiquity, and chiefly prevails in their discourses and reasonings. For though sometimes the ancient philosophers reason from final causes, as if they thought the world the workmanship of God; yet it appears rather their favorite notion to consider it as his body, whose organization renders it subservient to him. And it must be confessed, that as the universe resembles more a human body than it does the works of human art and contrivance; if our limited analogy could ever, with any propriety, be extended to the whole of nature, the inference seems juster in favor of the ancient than the modern theory.

There are many other advantages too, in the former theory, which recommend it to the ancient theologians. Nothing more repugnant to all their notions, because nothing more repugnant to common experience than mind without body; a mere spiritual substance, which fell not under their senses nor comprehension, and of which they had not observed one single instance throughout all nature. Mind and body they knew, because they felt both: an order, arrangement, organization, or internal machinery in both they likewise knew, after the same manner; and it could not but seem reasonable to transfer this experience to the universe, and to suppose the divine mind and body to be also coeval, and to have, both of them, order and arrangement naturally inherent in them, and inseparable from them.

Here therefore is a new species of anthropomorphism, Cleanthes, on which you may deliberate; and a theory which seems not liable to any considerable difficulties. You are too much superior surely to systematical prejudices, to find any more difficulty in supposing an animal body to be, originally, of itself, or from unknown causes, possessed of order and organization, than in supposing a similar order to belong to mind. But the vulgar prejudice, that body and mind ought always to accompany each other, ought not, one should think, to be entirely neglected; since it is founded on vulgar experience, the only guide which you profess to follow in all these theological inquiries. And if you assert, that our limited experience is an unequal standard, by which to judge of the unlimited extent of nature; you entirely abandon your own hypothesis, and must thenceforward adopt our mysticism, as you call it, and admit of the absolute incomprehensibility of the Divine Nature.

This theory, I own, replied Cleanthes, has never before occurred to me, though a pretty natural one; and I cannot readily, upon so short an examination and reflection, deliver any opinion with regard to it. You are very scrupulous, indeed, said Philo; were I to examine any system of yours, I should not have acted with half that caution and reserve, in stating objections and difficulties to it. However, if anything occur to you, you will oblige us by proposing it.

Why then, replied Cleanthes, it seems to me that, though the world does, in many circumstances, resemble an animal body; yet is the analogy also defective in many circumstances, the most material: no organs of sense; no seat of thought or reason; no one precise origin of motion and action. In short, it seems to bear a stronger resemblance to a vegetable than to an animal, and your inference would be so far inconclusive in favor of the soul of the world.

But, in the next place, your theory seems to imply the eternity of the world; and that is a principle which, I think, can be refuted by the strongest reasons and probabilities. I shall suggest an argument to this purpose, which, I believe, has not been insisted on by any writer. Those, who reason from the late origin of arts and sciences, though their inference wants not force, may perhaps be refuted by considerations, derived from the nature of human society, which is in continual revolution between ignorance and knowledge, liberty and slavery, riches and poverty; so that it is impossible for us, from our limited experience, to foretell with assurance what events may or may not be expected. Ancient learning and history seem to have been in great danger of entirely perishing after the inundation of the barbarous nations; and had these convulsions continued a little longer, or been a little more violent, we should not probably have now known what passed in the world a few centuries before us. Nay, were it not for the superstition of the popes, who preserved a little jargon of Latin, in order to support the appearance of an ancient and universal church, that tongue must have been utterly lost: in which case, the Western world, being totally barbarous, would not have been in a fit disposition for receiving the Greek language and learning, which was conveyed to them after the sacking of Constantinople. When learning and books had been extinguished, even the mechanical arts would have fallen considerably to decay; and it is easily imagined, that fable or tradition might ascribe to them a much later origin than the true one. This vulgar argument, therefore, against the eternity of the world, seems a little precarious.

But here appears to be the foundation of a better argument. Lucullus was the first that brought cherry-trees from Asia to Europe; though that tree thrives so well in many European climates, that it grows in the woods without any culture. Is it possible, that, throughout a whole eternity, no European had ever passed into Asia, and thought of transplanting so delicious a fruit into his own country? Or if the tree was once transplanted and propagated, how could it ever afterwards perish? Empires may rise and fall; liberty and slavery succeed alternately; ignorance and knowledge give place to each other; but the cherry-tree will still remain in the woods of Greece, Spain and Italy, and will never be affected by the revolutions of human society.

It is not two thousand years since vines were transplanted into France; though there is no climate in the world more favorable to them. It is not three centuries since horses, cows, sheep, swine, dogs, corn, were known in America. Is it possible, that, during the revolutions of a whole eternity, there never arose a Columbus, who might open the communication between Europe and that continent? We may as well imagine, that all men would wear stockings for ten thousand years, and never have the sense to think of garters to tie them. All these seem convincing proofs of the youth, or rather infancy, of the world; as being founded on the operation of principles more constant and steady, than those by which human society is governed and directed. Nothing less than a total convulsion of the elements will ever destroy all the European animals and vegetables, which are now to be found in the Western world.

And what argument have you against such convulsions? replied Philo. Strong and almost incontestable proofs may be traced over the whole earth, that every part of this globe has continued for many ages entirely covered with water. And though order were supposed inseparable from matter, and inherent in it; yet may matter be susceptible of many and great revolutions, through the endless periods of eternal duration. The incessant changes, to which every part of it is subject, seem to intimate some such general transformations; though at the same time, it is observable, that all the changes and corruptions, of which we have ever had experience, are but passages from one state of order to another; nor can matter ever rest in total deformity and confusion. What we see in the parts, we may infer in the whole; at least, that is the method of reasoning on which you rest your whole theory. And were I obliged to defend any particular system of this nature (which I never willingly should do), I esteem none more plausible than that which ascribes an eternal, inherent principle of order to the world; though attended with great and continual revolutions and alterations. This at once solves all difficulties; and if the solution, by being so general, is not entirely complete and satisfactory, it is, at least, a theory, that we must, sooner or later, have recourse to, whatever system we embrace. How could things have been as they are, were there not an original, inherent principle of order somewhere, in thought or in matter? And it is very indifferent to which of these we give the preference. Chance has no place, on any hypothesis, sceptical or religious. Everything is surely governed by steady, inviolable laws. And were the inmost essence of things laid open to us, we should then discover a scene, of which, at present, we can have no idea. Instead of admiring the order of natural beings, we should clearly see that it was absolutely impossible for them, in the smallest article, ever to admit of any other disposition.

Were anyone inclined to revive the ancient pagan theology, which maintained, as we learn from Hesiod, that this globe was governed by 30,000 deities, who arose from the unknown powers of nature: you would naturally object, Cleanthes, that nothing is gained by this hypothesis; and that it is as easy to suppose all men animals, beings more numerous, but less perfect, to have sprung immediately from a like origin. Push the same inference a step farther; and you will find a numerous society of deities as explicable as one universal deity, who possesses, within himself, the powers and perfections of the whole society. All these systems, then, of scepticism, polytheism, and theism, you must allow, on your principles, to be on a like footing, and that no one of them has any advantages over the others. You may thence learn the fallacy of your principles.

Part VII

But here, continued Philo, in examining the ancient system of the soul of the world, there strikes me, all on a sudden, a new idea, which, if just, must go near to subvert all your reasoning, and destroy even your first inferences, on which you repose such confidence. If the universe bears a greater likeness to animal bodies and to vegetables, than to the works of human art, it is more probable that its cause resembles the cause of the former than that of the latter, and its origin ought rather to be ascribed to generation or vegetation than to reason or design. Your conclusion, even according to your own principles, is therefore lame and defective.

Pray open up this argument a little farther, said Demea. For I do not rightly apprehend it, in that concise manner, in which you have expressed it.

Our friend, Cleanthes, replied Philo, as you have heard, asserts, that since no question of fact can be proved otherwise than by experience, the existence of a Deity admits not of proof from any other medium. The world, says he, resembles the works of human contrivance: therefore its cause must also resemble that of the other. Here we may remark, that the operation of one very small part of nature, to wit man, upon another very small part, to wit that inanimate matter lying within his reach, is the rule, by which Cleanthes judges of the origin of the whole; and he measures objects, so widely disproportioned, by the same individual standard. But to waive all objections drawn from this topic; I affirm, that there are other parts of the universe (besides the machines of human invention) which bear still a greater resemblance to the fabric of the world, and which therefore afford a better conjecture concerning the universal origin of this system. These parts are animals and vegetables. The world plainly resembles more an animal or a vegetable, than it does a watch or a knitting-loom. Its cause, therefore, it is more probable, resembles the cause of the former. The cause of the former is generation or vegetation. The cause, therefore, of the world, we may infer to be some thing similar or analogous to generation or vegetation.

But how is it conceivable, said Demea, that the world can arise from anything similar to vegetation or generation?

Very easily, replied Philo. In like manner as a tree sheds its seed into the neighboring fields, and produces other trees; so the great vegetable the world, or this planetary system, produces within itself certain seeds, which, being scattered into the surrounding chaos, vegetate into new worlds. A comet, for instance, is the seed of a world; and after it has been fully ripened, by passing from sun to sun, and star to star, it is at last tossed into the unformed elements, which everywhere surround this universe, and immediately sprouts up into a new system.

Or if, for the sake of variety (for I see no other advantage), we should suppose this world to be an animal; a comet is the egg of this animal; and in like manner as an ostrich lays its egg in the sand, which, without any farther care, hatches the egg, and produces a new animal; so . . . . I understand you, says Demea: but what wild, arbitrary suppositions are these? What *data* have you for such extraordinary conclusions? And is the slight, imaginary resemblance of the world to a vegetable or an animal sufficient to establish the same inference with regard to both? Objects, which are in general so widely different; ought they to be a standard for each other?

Right, cries Philo: this is the topic on which I have all along insisted. I have still asserted, that we have no *data* to establish any system of cosmogony. Our experience, so imperfect in itself, and so limited both in extent and duration, can afford us no probable conjecture concerning the whole of things. But if we must needs fix on some hypothesis; by what rule, pray ought we to determine our choice? Is there any other rule than the greater similarity of the objects compared? And does not a plant or an animal, which springs from vegetation or generation, bear a stronger resemblance to the world, than does any artificial machine, which arises from reason and design?

But what is this vegetation and generation of which you talk? said Demea. Can you explain their operations, and anatomize that fine internal structure, on which they depend?

As much, at least, replied Philo, as Cleanthes can explain the operations of reason, or anatomize that internal structure, on which *it* depends. But without any such elaborate disquisitions, when I see an animal, I infer, that it sprang from generation; and that with as great certainty as you conclude a house to have been reared by design. These words, *generation, reason,* mark only certain powers and energies in nature, whose effects are known, but whose essence is incomprehensible; and one of these principles, more than the other, has no privilege for being made a standard to the whole of nature.

In reality, Demea, it may reasonably be expected, that the larger the views are which we take of things, the better will they conduct us in our conclusions concerning such extraordinary and such magnificent subjects. In this little corner of the world alone, there are four principles, *reason*, *instinct*, *generation*, *vegetation*, which are similar to each other, and are the causes of similar effects. What a number of other principles may we naturally suppose in the immense extent and variety of the universe, could we travel from planet to planet and from system to system, in order to examine each part of this mighty fabric? Any one of these four principles above mentioned (and a hundred others which lie open to our conjecture) may afford us a theory, by which to judge of the origin of the world; and it is a palpable and egregious partiality, to confine our view entirely to that principle, by which our own minds operate. Were this principle more intelligent on that account, such a partiality might be somewhat excusable. But reason, in its internal fabric and structure, is really as little known to us as instinct or vegetation; and perhaps even that vague, undeterminate word, *Nature*, to which the vulgar refer everything, is not at the bottom more inexplicable. The effects of these principles are all known to us from experience: but the principles themselves, and their manner of operation, are totally unknown: nor is it less intelligible, or less conformable to experience to say, that the world arose by vegetation from a seed shed by another world, than to say that it arose from a divine reason or contrivance, according to the sense in which Cleanthes understands it.

But methinks, said Demea, if the world had a vegetative quality, and could sow the seeds of new worlds into the infinite chaos, this power would be still an additional argument for design in its author. For whence could arise so wonderful a faculty but from design? Or how can order spring from anything, which perceives not that order which it bestows?

You need only look around you, replied Philo, to satisfy yourself with regard to this question. A tree bestows order and organization on that tree, which springs from it, without knowing the order: an animal, in the same manner, on its offspring: a bird, on its nest: and instances of this kind are even more frequent in the world, than those of order, which arise from reason and contrivance. To say, that all this order in animals and vegetables proceeds ultimately from design, is begging the question; nor can that great point be ascertained otherwise than by proving *a priori*, both that order is, from its nature, inseparably attached to thought, and that it can never, of itself, or from original unknown principles, belong to matter.

But farther, Demea; this objection, which you urge, can never be made use of by Cleanthes, without renouncing a defense, which he has already made against one of my objections. When I inquired concerning the cause of that supreme reason and intelligence, into which he resolves everything; he told me, that the impossibility of satisfying such inquiries could never be admitted as an objection in any species of philosophy. *We must stop somewhere*, says he; *nor is it ever within the reach of human capacity to explain ultimate causes, or show the last connections of any objects. It is sufficient, if our steps, so far as we go, are supported by experience and observation.* Now, that vegetation and generation, as well as reason, are experienced to be principles of order in nature, is undeniable. If I rest my system of cosmogony on the former, preferably to the latter, 'tis at my choice. The matter seems entirely arbitrary. And when Cleanthes asks me what is the cause of my great vegetative or generative faculty, I am equally entitled to ask him the cause of his great reasoning principle. These questions we have agreed to forebear on both sides; and it is chiefly his interest on the present occasion to stick to this agreement. Judging by our limited and imperfect experience, generation has some privileges above reason: for we see every day the latter arise from the former, never the former from the latter.

Compare, I beseech you, the consequences on both sides. The world, say I, resembles an animal, therefore it is an animal, therefore it arose from generations. The steps, I confess, are wide; yet there is some small appearance of analogy in each step. The world, says Cleanthes, resembles a machine, therefore it is a machine, therefore it arose from design. The steps are here equally wide, and the analogy less striking. And if he pretends to carry on *my* hypothesis a step farther, and to infer design or reason from the great principle of generation, on which I insist; I may, with better authority, use the same freedom to push farther *his* hypothesis, and infer a divine generation or theogony from his principle of reason. I have at least some faint shadow of experience, which is the utmost that can ever be attained in the present subject. Reason, in innumerable instances, is observed to arise from the principle of generation, and never to arise from any other principle.

Hesiod, and all the ancient mythologists, were so struck with this analogy, that they universally explained the origin of nature from an animal birth, and copulation. Plato too, so far as he is intelligible, seems to have adopted some such notion in his *Timaeus*.

The Brahmins assert, that the world arose from an infinite spider, who spun this whole complicated mass from his bowels, and annihilates afterwards the whole or any part of it, by absorbing it again, and resolving it into his own essence. Here is a species of cosmogony, which appears to us ridiculous; because a spider is a little contemptible animal, whose operations we are never likely to take for a model of the whole universe. But still here is a new species of analogy, even in our globe. And were there a planet wholly inhabited by spiders (which is very possible), this inference would there appear as natural and irrefragable as that which in our planet ascribes the origin of all things to design and intelligence, as explained by Cleanthes. Why an orderly system may not be spun from the belly as well as from the brain, it will be difficult for him to give a satisfactory reason.

I must confess, Philo, replied Cleanthes, that of all men living, the task which you have undertaken, of raising doubts and objections, suits you best, and seems, in a manner, natural and unavoidable to you. So great is your fertility of invention, that I am not ashamed to acknowledge myself unable, on a sudden, to solve regularly such out-of-the-way difficulties as you incessantly start upon me: though I clearly see, in general, their fallacy and error. And I question not, but you are yourself, at present, in the same case, and have not the solution so ready as the objection; while you must be sensible, that common sense and reason are entirely against you, and that such whimsies as you have delivered, may puzzle, but never can convince us.

Part VIII

What you ascribe to the fertility of my invention, replied Philo, is entirely owing to the nature of the subject. In subjects, adapted to the narrow compass of human reason, there is commonly but one determination, which carries probability or conviction with it; and to a man of sound judgment, all other suppositions, but that one, appear entirely absurd and chimerical. But in such questions, as the present, a hundred contradictory views may preserve a kind of imperfect analogy; and invention has here full scope to exert itself. Without any great effort of thought, I believe that I could, in an instant, propose other systems of cosmogony, which would have some faint appearance of truth; though it is a thousand, a million to one, if either yours or any one of mine be the true system.

For instance; what if I should revive the old Epicurean hypothesis? This is commonly, and I believe, justly, esteemed the most absurd system, that has yet been proposed; yet, I know not, whether, with a few alterations, it might not be brought to bear a faint appearance of probability. Instead of supposing matter infinite, as Epicurus did; let us suppose it finite. A finite number of particles is only susceptible of finite transpositions: and it must happen, in an eternal duration, that every possible order or position must be tried an infinite number of times. This world, therefore, with all its events, even the most minute, has before been produced and destroyed, and will again be produced and destroyed, without any bounds and limitations. No one, who has a conception of the powers of infinite, in comparison of finite, will ever scruple this determination.

But this supposes, said Demea, that matter can acquire motion, without any voluntary agent or first mover.

And where is the difficulty, replied Philo, of that supposition? Every event, before experience, is equally difficult and incomprehensible; and every event, after experience, is equally easy and intelligible. Motion, in many instances, from gravity, from elasticity, from electricity, begins in matter, without any known voluntary agent; and to suppose always, in these cases, an unknown voluntary agent, is mere hypothesis; and hypothesis attended with no advantages. The beginning of motion in matter itself is as conceivable *a priori* as its communication from mind and intelligence.

Besides; why may not motion have been propagated by impulse through all eternity, and the same stock of it, or nearly the same, be still upheld in the universe? As much as is lost by the composition of motion, as much is gained by its resolution. And whatever the causes are, the fact is certain, that matter is, and always has been in continual agitation, as far as human experience or tradition reaches. There is not probably, at present, in the whole universe, one particle of matter at absolute rest.

And this very consideration too, continued Philo, which we have stumbled on in the course of argument, suggests a new hypothesis of cosmogony, that is not absolutely absurd and improbable. Is there a system, an order, an economy of things, by which matter can preserve that perpetual agitation, which seems essential to it, and yet maintain a constancy in the forms, which it produces? There certainly is such an economy: for this is actually the case with the present world. The continual motion of matter, therefore, in less than infinite transpositions, must produce this economy or order; and by its very nature, that order, when once established, supports itself, for many ages, if not to eternity. But wherever matter is so poised, arranged, and adjusted as to continue in perpetual motion, and yet preserve a constancy in the forms, its situation must, of necessity, have all the same appearance of art and contrivance, which we observe at present. All the parts of each form must have a relation to each other, and to the whole: and the whole itself must have a relation to the other parts of the universe; to the element, in which the form subsists; to the materials, with which it repairs its waste and decay; and to every other form, which is hostile or friendly. A defect in any of these particulars destroys the form; and the matter, of which it is composed, is again set loose, and is thrown into irregular motions and fermentations, till it unite itself to some other regular form. If no such form be prepared to receive it, and if there be a great quantity of this corrupted matter in the universe, the universe itself is entirely disordered; whether it be the feeble embryo of a world in its first beginnings, that is thus destroyed, or the rotten carcass of one, languishing in old age and infirmity. In either case, a chaos ensues; till finite, though innumerable revolutions produce at last some forms, whose parts and organs are so adjusted as to support the forms amidst a continued succession of matter.

Suppose (for we shall endeavor to vary the expression), that matter were thrown into any position, by a blind, unguided force; it is evident that this first position must in all probability be the most confused and most disorderly imaginable, without any resemblance to those works of human contrivance, which, along with a symmetry of parts, discover an adjustment of means to ends and a tendency to self-preservation. If the actuating force cease after this operation, matter must remain forever in disorder, and continue an immense chaos, without any proportion or activity. But suppose, that the actuating force, whatever it be, still continues in matter, this first position will immediately give place to a second, which will likewise in all probability be as disorderly as the first, and so on, through many successions of changes and revolutions. No particular order or position ever continues a moment unaltered. The original force, still remaining in activity, gives a perpetual restlessness to matter. Every possible situation is produced, and instantly destroyed. If a glimpse or dawn of order appears for a moment, it is instantly hurried away, and confounded, by that never-ceasing force, which actuates every part of matter.

Thus the universe goes on for many ages in a continued succession of chaos and disorder. But is it not possible that it may settle at last, so as not to lose its motion and active force (for that we have supposed inherent in it) yet so as to preserve an uniformity of appearance, amidst the continual motion and fluctuation of its parts? This we find to be the case with the universe at present. Every individual is perpetually changing, and every part of every individual, and yet the whole remains, in appearance, the same. May we not hope for such a position, or rather be assured of it, from the eternal revolutions of unguided matter, and may not this account for all the appearing wisdom and contrivance, which is in the universe? Let us contemplate the subject a little, and we shall find, that this adjustment, if attained by matter, of a seeming stability in the forms, with a real and perpetual revolution or motion of parts, affords a plausible, if not a true solution of the difficulty.

It is in vain, therefore, to insist upon the uses of the parts in animals or vegetables and their curious adjustment to each other. I would fain know how an animal could subsist, unless its parts were so adjusted? Do we not find, that it immediately perishes whenever this adjustment ceases, and that its matter corrupting tries some new form. It happens, indeed, that the parts of the world are so well adjusted, that some regular form immediately lays claim to this corrupted matter: and if it were not so, could the world subsist? Must it not dissolve as well as the animal, and pass through new positions and situations; till in a great, but finite succession, it fall at last into the present or some such order?

It is well, replied Cleanthes, you told us, that this hypothesis was suggested on a sudden, in the course of the argument. Had you had leisure to examine it, you would soon have perceived the insuperable objections, to which it is exposed. No form, you say, can subsist, unless it possess those powers and organs, requisite for its subsistence: some new order or economy must be tried, and so on, without intermission; till at last some order, which can support and maintain itself, is fallen upon. But according to this hypothesis, whence arise the many conveniences and advantages which men and all animals possess? Two eyes, two ears, are not absolutely necessary for the subsistence of the species. Human race might have been propagated and preserved, without horses, dogs, cows, sheep and those innumerable fruits and products which serve to our satisfaction and enjoyment. If no camels had been created for the use of man in the sandy deserts of Africa and Arabia, would the world have been dissolved? If no loadstone had been framed to give that wonderful and useful direction to the needle, would human society and the human kind have been immediately extinguished? Though the maxims of Nature be in general very frugal, yet instances of this kind are far from being rare; and any one of them is a sufficient proof of design, and of a benevolent design, which gave rise to the order and arrangement of the universe.

At least, you may safely infer, said Philo, that the foregoing hypothesis is so far incomplete and imperfect; which I shall not scruple to allow. But can we ever reasonably expect greater success in any attempts of this nature? Or can we ever hope to erect a system of cosmogony, that will be liable to no exceptions, and will contain no circumstance repugnant to our limited and imperfect experience of the analogy of nature? Your theory itself cannot surely pretend to any such advantage; even though you have run into anthropomorphism, the better to preserve a conformity to common experience. Let us once more put it to trial. In all instances which we have ever seen, ideas are copied from real objects, and are ectypal, not archetypal, to express myself in learned terms: you reverse this order, and give thought the precedence. In all instances which we have ever seen, thought has no influence upon matter, except where that matter is so conjoined with it, as to have an equal reciprocal influence upon it. No animal can move immediately anything but the members of its own body; and indeed, the equality of action and reaction seems to be an universal law of nature: but your theory implies a contradiction to this experience. These instances, with many more, which it were easy to collect (particularly the supposition of a mind or system of thought that is eternal, or in other words, an animal ingenerable and immortal), these instances, I say, may teach, all of us, sobriety in condemning each other; and let us see, that as no system of this kind ought ever to be received from a slight analogy, so neither ought any to be rejected on account of a small incongruity. For that is an inconvenience, from which we can justly pronounce no one to be exempted.

All religious systems, it is confessed, are subject to great and insuperable difficulties. Each disputant triumphs in his turn; while he carries on an offensive war, and exposes the absurdities, barbarities, and pernicious tenets of his antagonist. But all of them, on the whole, prepare a complete triumph for the sceptic; who tells them, that no system ought ever to be embraced with regard to such subjects: for this plain reason, that no absurdity ought ever to be assented to with regard to any subject. A total suspense of judgment is here our only reasonable resource. And if every attack, as is commonly observed, and no defense, among theologians, is successful; how complete must be *his* victory, who remains always, with all mankind, on the offensive, and has himself no fixed station or abiding city, which he is ever, on any occasion, obliged to defend?

Part IX

But if so many difficulties attend the argument *a posteriori*, said Demea; had we not better adhere to that simple and sublime argument *a priori*, which, by offering to us infallible demonstration, cuts off at once all doubt and difficulty? By this argument, too, we may prove the *infinity* of the divine attributes, which, I am afraid, can never be ascertained with certainty from any other topic. For how can an effect, which either is finite, or, for aught we know, may be so; how can such an effect, I say, prove an infinite cause? The unity too of the Divine Nature, it is very difficult, if not absolutely impossible, to deduce merely from contemplating the works of nature; nor will the uniformity alone of the plan, even were it allowed, give us any assurance of that attribute. Whereas the argument *a priori* . . . .

You seem to reason, Demea, interposed Cleanthes, as if those advantages and conveniences in the abstract argument were full proofs of its solidity. But it is first proper, in my opinion, to determine what argument of this nature you choose to insist on; and we shall afterwards, from itself, better than from its useful consequences, endeavor to determine what value we ought to put upon it.

The argument, replied Demea, which I would insist on is the common one. Whatever exists must have a cause or reason of its existence; it being absolutely impossible for anything to produce itself, or be the cause of its own existence. In mounting up; therefore, from effects to causes, we must either go on in tracing an infinite succession, without any ultimate cause at all; or must at last have recourse to some ultimate cause, that is *necessarily* existent. Now that the first supposition is absurd may be thus proved. In the infinite chain or succession of causes and effects, each single effect is determined to exist by the power and efficacy of that cause, which immediately preceded; but the whole eternal chain or succession, taken together, is not determined or caused by anything: and yet it is evident that it requires a cause or reason, as much as any particular object, which begins to exist in time. The question is still reasonable, why this particular succession of causes existed from eternity, and not any other succession, or no succession at all. If there be no necessarily existent being, any supposition, which can be formed, is equally possible; nor is there any more absurdity in *nothing's* having existed from eternity, than there is in that succession of causes, which constitutes the universe. What was it then, which determined something to exist rather than nothing, and bestowed being on a particular possibility, exclusive of the rest? *External causes*, there are supposed to be none. *Chance* is a word without a meaning. Was it *nothing*? But that can never produce anything. We must, therefore, have recourse to a necessarily existent Being, who carries the reason of his existence in himself; and who cannot be supposed not to exist without an express contradiction. There is consequently such a Being, that is, there is a Deity.

I shall not leave it to Philo, said Cleanthes (though I know that the starting objections is his chief delight), to point out the weakness of this metaphysical reasoning. It seems to me so obviously ill-grounded, and at the same time of so little consequence to the cause of true piety and religion, that I shall myself venture to show the fallacy of it.

I shall begin with observing, that there is an evident absurdity in pretending to demonstrate a matter of fact, or to prove it by any arguments *a priori*. Nothing is demonstrable, unless the contrary implies a contradiction. Nothing, that is distinctly conceivable, implies a contradiction. Whatever we conceive as existent, we can also conceive as non-existent. There is no being, therefore, whose non-existence implies a contradiction. Consequently there is no being, whose existence is demonstrable. I propose this argument as entirely decisive, and am willing to rest the whole controversy upon it.

It is pretended that the Deity is a necessarily existent being; and this necessity of his existence is attempted to be explained by asserting, that, if we knew his whole essence or nature, we should perceive it to be as impossible for him not to exist as for twice two not to be four. But it is evident, that this can never happen, while our faculties remain the same as at present. It will still be possible for us, at any time, to conceive the non-existence of what we formerly conceived to exist; nor can the mind ever lie under a necessity of supposing any object to remain always in being; in the same manner as we lie under a necessity of always conceiving twice two to be four. The words, therefore, *necessary existence*, have no meaning; or, which is the same thing, none that is consistent.

But farther; why may not the material universe be the necessarily existent Being, according to this pretended explication of necessity? We dare not affirm that we know all the qualities of matter; and for aught we can determine, it may contain some qualities, which, were they known, would make its non-existence appear as great a contradiction as that twice two is five. I find only one argument employed to prove, that the material world is not the necessarily existent Being; and this argument is derived from the contingency both of the matter and the form of the world. 'Any particle of matter,' 'tis said,[7] 'may be *conceived* to be annihilated; and any form may be *conceived* to be altered. Such an annihilation or alteration, therefore, is not impossible.' But it seems a great partiality not to perceive, that the same argument extends equally to the Deity, so far as we have any conception of him; and that the mind can at least imagine him to be non-existent, or his attributes to be altered. It must be some unknown, inconceivable qualities, which can make his non-existence appear impossible, or his attributes inalterable. And no reason can be assigned, why these qualities may not belong to matter. As they are altogether unknown and inconceivable, they can never be proved incompatible with it.

[7] Dr. Clarke.

Add to this, that in tracing an eternal succession of objects, it seems absurd to inquire for a general cause or first author. How can anything, that exists from eternity, have a cause, since that relation implies a priority in time and a beginning of existence?

In such a chain too, or succession of objects, each part is caused by that which preceded it, and causes that which succeeds it. Where then is the difficulty? But the *whole*, you say, wants a cause. I answer, that the uniting of these parts into a whole, like the uniting of several distinct counties into one kingdom, or several distinct members into one body, is performed merely by an arbitrary act of the mind, and has no influence on the nature of things. Did I show you the particular causes of each individual in a collection of twenty particles of matter, I should think it very unreasonable, should you afterwards ask me, what was the cause of the whole twenty. This is sufficiently explained in explaining the cause of the parts.

Though the reasonings, which you have urged, Cleanthes, may well excuse me, said Philo, from starting any farther difficulties; yet I cannot forbear insisting still upon another topic. 'Tis observed by arithmeticians, that the products of 9 compose always either 9 or some lesser product of 9; if you add together all the characters, of which any of the former products is composed. Thus, of 18, 27, 36, which are products of 9, you make 9 by adding 1 to 8, 2 to 7, 3 to 6. Thus, 369 is a product also of 9; and if you add 3, 6, and 9, you make 18, a lesser product of 9.[8] To a superficial observer, so wonderful a regularity may be admired as the effect either of chance or design: but a skillful algebraist immediately concludes it to be the work of necessity, and demonstrates, that it must forever result from the nature of these numbers. Is it not probable, I ask, that the whole economy of the universe is conducted by a like necessity, though no human algebra can furnish a key, which solves the difficulty? And instead of admiring the order of natural beings, may it not happen, that, could we penetrate into the intimate nature of bodies, we should clearly see why it was absolutely impossible, they could ever admit of any other disposition? So dangerous is it to introduce this idea of necessity into the present question! And so naturally does it

[8] République des Lettres, Août 1685.

afford an inference directly opposite to the religious hypothesis!

But dropping all these abstractions, continued Philo; and confining ourselves to more familiar topics; I shall venture to add an observation, that the argument *a priori* has seldom been found very convincing, except to people of a metaphysical head, who have accustomed themselves to abstract reasoning, and who finding from mathematics, that the understanding frequently leads to truth, through obscurity, and contrary to first appearances, have transferred the same habit of thinking to subjects, where it would not seem to have place. Other people, even of good sense and the best inclined to religion, feel always some deficiency in such arguments, though they are not perhaps able to explain distinctly where it lies. A certain proof, that men ever did, and ever will derive their religion from other sources than from this species of reasoning.

Part X

It is my opinion, I own, replied Demea, that each man feels, in a manner, the truth of religion within his own breast; and from a consciousness of his imbecility and misery, rather than from any reasoning, is led to seek protection from that Being, on whom he and all nature is dependent. So anxious or so tedious are even the best scenes of life, that futurity is still the object of all our hopes and fears. We incessantly look forward, and endeavor, by prayers, adoration, and sacrifice, to appease those unknown powers, whom we find, by experience, so able to afflict and oppress us. Wretched creatures that we are! what resource for us amidst the innumerable ills of life, did not religion suggest some methods of atonement, and appease those terrors, with which we are incessantly agitated and tormented?

I am indeed persuaded, said Philo, that the best and indeed the only method of bringing everyone to a due sense of religion, is by just representations of the misery and wickedness of men. And for that purpose a talent of eloquence and strong imagery is more requisite than that of reasoning and argument. For is it necessary to prove, what everyone feels within himself? 'Tis only necessary to make us feel it, if possible, more intimately and sensibly.

The people, indeed, replied Demea, are sufficiently convinced of this great and melancholy truth. The miseries of life, the unhappiness of men, the general corruptions of our nature, the unsatisfactory enjoyment of pleasures, riches, honors; these phrases have become almost proverbial in all languages. And who can doubt of what all men declare from their own immediate feeling and experience?

In this point, said Philo, the learned are perfectly agreed with the vulgar; and in all letters, sacred and profane, the topic of human misery has been insisted on with the most pathetic eloquence that sorrow and melancholy could inspire. The poets, who speak from sentiment, without a system, and whose testimony has therefore the more authority, abound in images of this nature. From Homer down to Dr. Young, the whole inspired tribe have ever been sensible, that no other representation of things would suit the feeling and observation of each individual.

As to authorities, replied Demea, you need not seek them. Look round this library of Cleanthes. I shall venture to affirm, that, except authors of particular sciences, such as chemistry or botany, who have no occasion to treat of human life, there scarce is one of those innumerable writers, from whom the sense of human misery has not, in some passage or other, extorted a complaint and confession of it. At least, the chance is entirely on that side; and no one author has ever, so far as I can recollect, been so extravagant as to deny it.

There you must excuse me, said Philo: Leibnitz has denied it; and is perhaps the first,[9] who ventured upon so bold and paradoxical an opinion; at least, the first, who made it essential to his philosophical system.

And by being the first, replied Demea, might he not have been sensible of his error? For is this a subject, in which philosophers can propose to make discoveries, especially in so late an age? And can any man hope by a simple denial (for the subject scarcely admits of reasoning) to bear down the united testimony of mankind, founded on sense and consciousness?

And why should man, added he, pretend to an exemption from the lot of all other animals? The whole earth, believe me, Philo, is cursed and polluted. A perpetual war is kindled amongst all living creatures. Necessity, hunger, want, stimu-

[9] That sentiment had been maintained by Dr. King and some few others, before Leibnitz, though by none of so great fame as that German philosopher.

late the strong and courageous: fear, anxiety, terror, agitate the weak and infirm. The first entrance into life gives anguish to the new-born infant and to its wretched parent: weakness, impotence, distress, attend each stage of that life: and 'tis at last finished in agony and horror.

Observe too, says Philo, the curious artifices of nature, in order to embitter the life of every living being. The stronger prey upon the weaker, and keep them in perpetual terror and anxiety. The weaker too, in their turn, often prey upon the stronger, and vex and molest them without relaxation. Consider that innumerable race of insects, which either are bred on the body of each animal, or flying about infix their stings in him. These insects have others still less than themselves, which torment them. And thus on each hand, before and behind, above and below, every animal is surrounded with enemies, which incessantly seek his misery and destruction.

Man alone, said Demea, seems to be, in part, an exception to this rule. For by combination in society, he can easily master lions, tigers, and bears, whose greater strength and agility naturally enable them to prey upon him.

On the contrary, it is here chiefly, cried Philo, that the uniform and equal maxims of nature are most apparent. Man, it is true, can, by combination, surmount all his *real* enemies, and become master of the whole animal creation: but does he not immediately raise up to himself *imaginary* enemies, the demons of his fancy, who haunt him with superstitious terrors, and blast every enjoyment of life? His pleasure, as he imagines, becomes, in their eyes, a crime: his food and repose give them umbrage and offense: his very sleep and dreams furnish new materials to anxious fear: and even death, his refuge from every other ill, presents only the dread of endless and innumerable woes. Nor does the wolf molest more the timid flock, than superstition does the anxious breast of wretched mortals.

Besides, consider, Demea; this very society, by which we surmount those wild beasts, our natural enemies; what new enemies does it not raise to us? What woe and misery does it not occasion? Man is the greatest enemy of man. Oppression, injustice, contempt, contumely, violence, sedition, war, calumny, treachery, fraud; by these they mutually torment each other: and they would soon dissolve that society which they had formed, were it not for the dread of still greater ills, which must attend their separation.

But though these external insults, said Demea, from animals, from men, from all the elements, which assault us, form a frightful catalogue of woes, they are nothing in comparison of those, which arise within ourselves, from the distempered condition of our mind and body. How many lie under the lingering torment of diseases? Hear the pathetic enumeration of the great poet.

> Intestine stone and ulcer, colic-pangs,
> Demoniac frenzy, moping melancholy,
> And moon-struck madness, pining atrophy,
> Marasmus and wide-wasting pestilence.
> Dire was the tossing, deep the groans: Despair
> Tended the sick, busiest from couch to couch.
> And over them triumphant Death his dart
> Shook, but delay'd to strike, tho' oft invok'd
> With vows, as their chief good and final hope.[10]

The disorders of the mind, continued Demea, though more secret, are not perhaps less dismal and vexatious. Remorse, shame, anguish, rage, disappointment, anxiety, fear, dejection, despair; who has ever passed through life without cruel inroads from these tormentors? How many have scarcely ever felt any better sensations? Labor and poverty, so abhorred by everyone, are the certain lot of the far greater number; and those few privileged persons, who enjoy ease and opulence, never reach contentment or true felicity. All the goods of life united would not make a very happy man: but all the ills united would make a wretch indeed; and anyone of them almost (and who can be free from everyone), nay often the absence of one good (and who can possess all), is sufficient to render life ineligible.

Were a stranger to drop, on a sudden, into this world, I would show him, as a specimen of its ills, an hospital full of diseases, a prison crowded with malefactors and debtors, a field of battle strewed with carcasses, a fleet floundering in the ocean, a nation languishing under tyranny, famine, or pestilence. To turn the gay side of life to him, and give him a notion of its pleasures; whither should I conduct him? to a ball, to an opera, to court? He might justly think, that I was only showing him a diversity of distress and sorrow.

There is no evading such striking instances, said Philo, but by apologies, which still farther aggravate the charge. Why

[10] Milton: Paradise Lost, XI.

have all men, I ask, in all ages, complained incessantly of the miseries of life? . . . . They have no just reason, says one: these complaints proceed only from their discontented, repining, anxious disposition. . . . And can there possibly, I reply, be a more certain foundation of misery, than such a wretched temper?

But if they were really as unhappy as they pretend, says my antagonist, why do they remain in life? . . . .

Not satisfied with life, afraid of death.

This is the secret chain, say I, that holds us. We are terrified, not bribed to the continuance of our existence.

It is only a false delicacy, he may insist, which a few refined spirits indulge, and which has spread these complaints among the whole race of mankind. . . . And what is this delicacy, I ask, which you blame? Is it anything but a greater sensibility to all the pleasures and pains of life? and if the man of a delicate, refined temper, by being so much more alive than the rest of the world, is only so much more unhappy; what judgment must we form in general of human life?

Let men remain at rest, says our adversary; and they will be easy. They are willing artificers of their own misery. . . . No! reply I; an anxious languor follows their repose: disappointment, vexation, trouble, their activity and ambition.

I can observe something like what you mention in some others, replied Cleanthes: but I confess, I feel little or nothing of it in myself, and hope that it is not so common as you represent it.

If you feel not human misery yourself, cried Demea, I congratulate you on so happy a singularity. Others, seemingly the most prosperous, have not been ashamed to vent their complaints in the most melancholy strains. Let us attend to the great, the fortunate Emperor, Charles V, when, tired with human grandeur, he resigned all his extensive dominions into the hands of his son. In the last harangue, which he made on that memorable occasion, he publicly avowed, *that the greatest prosperities which he had ever enjoyed, had been mixed with so many adversities, that he might truly say he had never enjoyed any satisfation or contentment*. But did the retired life, in which he sought for shelter, afford him any greater happiness? If we may credit his son's account, his repentance commenced the very day of his resignation.

Cicero's fortune, from small beginnings, rose to the greatest luster and renown; yet what pathetic complaints of the ills of life do his familiar letters, as well as philosophical discourses, contain? And suitably to his own experience, he introduces Cato, the great, the fortunate Cato, protesting in his old age, that, had he a new life in his offer, he would reject the present.

Ask yourself, ask any of your acquaintance, whether they would live over again the last ten or twenty years of their lives. No! but the next twenty, they say, will be better:

> And from the dregs of life, hope to receive
> What the first sprightly running could not give.[11]

Thus at last they find (such is the greatest of human misery; it reconciles even contradictions) that they complain, at once, of the shortness of life, and of its vanity and sorrow.

And is it possible, Cleanthes, said Philo, that after all these reflections, and infinitely more, which might be suggested, you can still persevere in your anthropomorphism, and assert the moral attributes of the Deity, his justice, benevolence, mercy, and rectitude, to be of the same nature with these virtues in human creatures? His power we allow infinite: whatever he wills is executed: but neither man nor any other animal is happy: therefore he does not will their happiness. His wisdom is infinite: he is never mistaken in choosing the means to any end: but the course of nature tends not to human or animal felicity: therefore it is not established for that purpose. Through the whole compass of human knowledge, there are no inferences more certain and infallible than these. In what respect, then, do his benevolence and mercy resemble the benevolence and mercy of men?

Epicurus's old questions are yet unanswered.

Is he willing to prevent evil, but not able? then is he impotent. Is he able, but not willing? then is he malevolent. Is he both able and willing? whence then is evil?

You ascribe, Cleanthes, (and I believe justly) a purpose and intention to nature. But what, I beseech you, is the object of that curious artifice and machinery, which she has displayed in all animals? The preservation alone of individuals and propagation of the species. It seems enough for her purpose, if such a rank be barely upheld in the universe, without any care or concern for the happiness of the members that compose it. No resource for this purpose: no machinery, in order

[11] Dryden: Aurungzebe, Act IV., sc. i.

merely to give pleasure or ease: no fund of pure joy and contentment: no indulgence without some want or necessity accompanying it. At least, the few phenomena of this nature are overbalanced by opposite phenomena of still greater importance.

Our sense of music, harmony, and indeed beauty of all kinds, gives satisfaction, without being absolutely necessary to the preservation and propagation of the species. But what racking pains, on the other hand, arise from gouts, gravels, megrims, toothaches, rheumatisms; where the injury to the animal-machinery is either small or incurable? Mirth, laughter, play, frolic, seem gratuitous satisfactions, which have no farther tendency: spleen, melancholy, discontent, superstition, are pains of the same nature. How then does the divine benevolence display itself, in the sense of you anthropomorphites? None but we mystics, as you were pleased to call us, can account for this strange mixture of phenomena, by deriving it from attributes, infinitely perfect, but incomprehensible.

And have you at last, said Cleanthes smiling, betrayed your intentions, Philo? Your long agreement with Demea did indeed a little surprise me; but I find you were all the while erecting a concealed battery against me. And I must confess, that you have now fallen upon a subject, worthy of your noble spirit of opposition and controversy. If you can make out the present point, and prove mankind to be unhappy or corrupted, there is an end at once of all religion. For to what purpose establish the natural attributes of the Deity, while the moral are still doubtful and uncertain?

You take umbrage very easily, replied Demea, at opinions the most innocent, and the most generally received even amongst the religious and devout themselves: and nothing can be more surprising than to find a topic like this, concerning the wickedness and misery of man, charged with no less than atheism and profaneness. Have not all pious divines and preachers, who have indulged their rhetoric on so fertile a subject: have they not easily, I say, given a solution of any difficulties, which may attend it? This world is but a point in comparison of the universe; this life but a moment in comparison of eternity. The present evil phenomena, therefore, are rectified in other regions, and in some future period of existence. And the eyes of men, being then opened to larger views of things, see the whole connection of general laws; and trace, with adoration, the benevolence and rectitude of the

Deity, through all the mazes and intricacies of his providence.

No! replied Cleanthes, No! These arbitrary suppositions can never be admitted, contrary to matter of fact, visible and uncontroverted. Whence can any cause be known but from its known effects? Whence can any hypothesis be proved but from the apparent phenomena? To establish one hypothesis upon another, is building entirely in the air; and the utmost we ever attain, by these conjectures and fictions, is to ascertain the bare possibility of our opinion; but never can we, upon such terms, establish its reality.

The only method of supporting divine benevolence (and it is what I willingly embrace) is to deny absolutely the misery and wickedness of man. Your representations are exaggerated: your melancholy views mostly fictitious: your inferences contrary to fact and experience. Health is more common than sickness: pleasure than pain: happiness than misery. And for one vexation, which we meet with, we attain, upon computation, a hundred enjoyments.

Admitting your position, replied Philo, which yet is extremely doubtful, you must, at the same time, allow, that, if pain be less frequent than pleasure, it is infinitely more violent and durable. One hour of it is often able to outweigh a day, a week, a month of our common insipid enjoyments. And how many days, weeks, and months are passed by several in the most acute torments? Pleasure, scarcely in one instance, is ever able to reach ecstasy and rapture: and in no one instance can it continue for any time at its highest pitch and altitude. The spirits evaporate; the nerves relax; the fabric is disordered; and the enjoyment quickly degenerates into fatigue and uneasiness. But pain often, good God, how often! rises to torture and agony; and the longer it continues, it becomes still more genuine agony and torture. Patience is exhausted; courage languishes; melancholy seizes us; and nothing terminates our misery but the removal of its cause, or another event, which is the sole cure of all evil, but which, from our natural folly, we regard with still greater horror and consternation.

But not to insist upon these topics, continued Philo, though most obvious, certain, and important; I must use the freedom to admonish you, Cleanthes, that you have put this controversy upon a most dangerous issue, and are unawares introducing a total scepticism, into the most essential articles of natural and revealed theology. What! no method of fixing a just foundation for religion, unless we allow the happiness of human life, and maintain a continued existence even in this world, with all our present pains, infirmities, vexations, and follies, to be eligible and desirable! But this is contrary to everyone's feeling and experience: it is contrary to an authority so established as nothing can subvert: no decisive proofs can ever be produced against this authority; nor is it possible for you to compute, estimate, and compare all the pains and all the pleasures in the lives of all men and of all animals: and thus by your resting the whole system of religion on a point, which, from its very nature, must forever be uncertain, you tacitly confess, that that system is equally uncertain.

But allowing you, what never will be believed; at least, what you never possibly can prove, that animal, or at least, human happiness, in this life, exceeds its misery; you have yet done nothing: for this is not, by any means, what we expect from infinite power, infinite wisdom, and infinite goodness. Why is there any misery at all in the world? Not by chance surely. From some cause then. Is it from the intention of the Deity? But he is perfectly benevolent. Is it contrary to his intention? But he is almighty. Nothing can shake the solidity of this reasoning, so short, so clear, so decisive; except we assert, that these subjects exceed all human capacity, and that our common measures of truth and falsehood are not applicable to them; a topic, which I have all along insisted on, but which you have, from the beginning, rejected with scorn and indignation.

But I will be contented to retire still from this intrenchment: for I deny that you can ever force me in it: I will allow, that pain or misery in man is *compatible* with infinite power and goodness in the Deity, even in your sense of these attributes: what are you advanced by all these concessions? A mere possible compatibility is not sufficient. You must *prove* these pure, unmixed, and uncontrollable attributes from the present mixed and confused phenomena, and from these alone. A hopeful undertaking! Were the phenomena ever so pure and unmixed, yet being finite, they would be insufficient for that purpose. How much more, where they are also so jarring and discordant!

Here, Cleanthes, I find myself at ease in my argument. Here I triumph. Formerly, when we argued concerning the natural attributes of intelligence and design, I needed all my sceptical and metaphysical subtilty to elude your grasp. In many views of the universe, and of its parts, particularly the latter, the beauty and fitness of final causes strikes us with such irresistible force, that all objections appear (what I believe they really are) mere cavils and sophisms; nor can we then imagine how it was ever possible for us to repose any weight on them. But there is no view of human life or of the condition of mankind, from which, without the greatest violence, we can infer the moral attributes, or learn that infinite benevolence, conjoined with infinite power and infinite wisdom, which we must discover by the eyes of faith alone. It is your turn now to tug the laboring oar, and to support your philosophical subtilties against the dictates of plain reason and experience.

Part XI

I scruple not to allow, said Cleanthes, that I have been apt to suspect the frequent repetition of the word, *infinite*, which we meet with in all theological writers, to savor more of panegyric than of philosophy, and that any purposes of reasoning, and even of religion, would be better served, were we to rest contented with more accurate and more moderate expressions. The terms, *admirable*, *excellent*, *superlatively great*, *wise*, and *holy*; these sufficiently fill the imaginations of men; and anything beyond, besides that it leads into absurdities, has no influence on your affections or sentiments. Thus, in the present subject, if we abandon all human analogy, as seems your intention, Demea, I am afraid we abandon all religion, and retain no conception of the great object of our adoration. If we preserve human analogy, we must forever find it impossible to reconcile any mixture of evil in the universe with infinite attributes; much less can we ever prove the latter from the former. But supposing the Author of Nature to be finitely perfect, though far exceeding mankind; a satisfactory account may then be given of natural and moral evil, and every untoward phenomenon be explained and adjusted. A less evil may then be chosen, in order to avoid a greater; inconveniences be submitted to, in order to reach a desirable end: and in a word, benevolence, regulated by wisdom, and limited by necessity, may produce just such a world as the present. You, Philo, who are so prompt at starting views, and reflections, and analogies, I would gladly hear, at length, without interruption, your opinion of this new theory; and if it deserve our attention, we may afterwards, at more leisure, reduce it into form.

My sentiments, replied Philo, are not worth being made a mystery of; and therefore, without any ceremony, I shall deliver what occurs to me with regard to the present subject. It must, I think, be allowed, that, if a very limited intelligence, whom we shall suppose utterly unacquainted with the universe, were assured, that it were the production of a very good, wise, and powerful being, however infinite, he would, from his conjectures, form *beforehand* a different notion of it from what we find it to be by *experience*; nor would he ever imagine, merely from these attributes of the cause, of which he is informed, that the effect could be so full of vice and misery and disorder, as it appears in his life. Supposing now, that this person were brought into the world, still assured, that it was the workmanship of such a sublime and benevolent Being; he might, perhaps, be surprised at the disappointment; but would never retract his former belief, if founded on any very solid argument; since such a limited intelligence must be sensible of his own blindness and ignorance, and must allow, that there may be many solutions of those phenomena, which will forever escape his comprehension. But supposing, which is the real case with regard to man, that this creature is not antecedently convinced of a supreme intelligence, benevolent, and powerful, but is left to gather such a belief from the appearance of things; this entirely alters the case, nor will he ever find any reason for such a conclusion. He may be fully convinced of the narrow limits of his understanding; but this will not help him in forming an inference concerning the goodness of superior powers, since he must form that inference from what he knows, not from what he is ignorant of. The more you exaggerate his weakness and ignorance, the more diffident you render him, and give him the greater suspicion, that such subjects are beyond the reach of his faculties. You are obliged, therefore, to reason with him merely from the known phenomena, and to drop every arbitrary supposition or conjecture.

Did I show you a house or palace, where there was not one apartment convenient or agreeable; where the windows, doors, fires, passages, stairs, and the whole economy of the building were the source of noise, confusion, fatigue, darkness, and extremes of heat and cold; you would certainly blame the contrivance, without any farther examination. The architect would in vain display his subtilty, and prove to you, that if this door or that window were altered, greater ills would ensue. What he says, may be strictly true: the alteration of one particular, while the other parts of the building remain, may only augment the inconveniences. But still you would assert in general, that, if the architect had had skill and good intentions, he might have formed such a plan of the whole, and might have adjusted the parts in such a manner, as would have remedied all or most of these inconveniences. His ignorance, or even your own ignorance of such a plan, will never convince you of the impossibility of it. If you find many inconveniences and deformities in the building, you will always, without entering into any detail, condemn the architect.

In short, I repeat the question: is the world considered in general, and as it appears to us in this life, different from what a man or such a limited being would, beforehand, expect from a very powerful, wise, and benevolent Deity? It must be strange prejudice to assert the contrary. And from thence I conclude, that, however consistent the world may be, allowing certain suppositions and conjectures, with the idea of such a Deity, it can never afford us an inference concerning his existence. The consistency is not absolutely denied, only the inference. Conjectures, especially where infinity is excluded from the Divine attributes, may perhaps be sufficient to prove a consistency; but can never be foundations for any inference.

There seem to be four circumstances, on which depend all, or the greatest parts of the ills, that molest sensible creatures; and it is not impossible but all these circumstances may be necessary and unavoidable. We know so little beyond common life, or even of common life, that, with regard to the economy of a universe, there is no conjecture, however wild, which may not be just; nor any one, however plausible, which may not be erroneous. All that belongs to human understanding, in this deep ignorance and obscurity, is to be sceptical, or at least cautious; and not to admit of any hypothesis, whatever; much less, of any which is supported by no appearance of probability. Now this I assert to be the case with regard to all the causes of evil, and the circumstances, on which it depends. None of them appear to human reason, in the least degree, necessary or unavoidable; nor can we suppose them such, without the utmost license of imagination.

The *first* circumstance which introduces evil, is that contrivance or economy of the animal creation, by which pains, as well as pleasures, are employed to excite all creatures to action, and make them vigilant in the great work of self-preservation. Now pleasure alone, in its various degrees, seems to human understanding sufficient for this purpose. All animals might be constantly in a state of enjoyment; but when urged by any of the necessities of nature, such as thirst, hunger, weariness; instead of pain, they might feel a diminution of pleasure, by which they might be prompted to seek that object, which is necessary to their subsistence. Men pursue pleasure as eagerly as they avoid pain; at least, might have been so constituted. It seems, therefore, plainly possible to carry on the business of life without any pain. Why then is any animal ever rendered susceptible of such a sensation? If animals can be free from it an hour, they might enjoy a perpetual exemption from it; and it required as particular a contrivance of their organs to produce that feeling, as to endow them with sight, hearing, or any of the senses. Shall we conjecture, that such a contrivance was necessary, without any appearance of reason? and shall we build on that conjecture as on the most certain truth?

But a capacity of pain would not alone produce pain, were it not for the *second* circumstance, viz., the conducting of the world by general laws; and this seems nowise necessary to a very perfect being. It is true; if everything were conducted by particular volitions, the course of nature would be perpetually broken, and no man could employ his reason in the conduct of life. But might not other particular volitions remedy this inconvenience? In short, might not the Deity exterminate all ill, wherever it were to be found; and produce all good, without any preparation or long progress of causes and effects?

Besides, we must consider, that, according to the present economy of the world, the course of nature, though supposed exactly regular, yet to us appears not so, and many events are uncertain, and many disappoint our expectations. Health and sickness, calm and tempest, with an infinite number of other accidents, whose causes are unknown and variable, have a great influence both on the fortunes of particular persons and on the prosperity of public societies: and indeed all human life, in a manner, depends on such accidents. A being, therefore, who knows the secret springs of the universe, might easily, by particular volitions, turn all these accidents to the good of mankind, and render the whole world happy, without discovering himself in any operation. A fleet, whose purposes were salutary to society, might always meet with a fair wind: good princes enjoy sound health and long life: persons, born to power and authority, be framed with good tempers and virtuous dispositions. A few such events as these, regularly and wisely conducted, would change the face of the world; and yet would no more seem to disturb the course of nature or confound human conduct, than the present economy of things, where the causes are secret, and variable, and compounded. Some small touches, given to Caligula's brain in his infancy, might have converted him into a Trajan: one wave, a little higher than the rest, by burying Caesar and his fortune in the bottom of the ocean, might have restored liberty to a considerable part of mankind. There may, for aught we know, be good reasons, why Providence interposes not in this manner; but they are unknown to us: and though the mere supposition, that such reasons exist, may be sufficient to *save* the conclusion concerning the divine attributes, yet surely it can never be sufficient to *establish* that conclusion.

If everything in the universe be conducted by general laws, and if animals be rendered susceptible of pain, it scarcely seems possible but some ill must arise in the various shocks of matter, and the various concurrence and opposition of general laws. But this ill would be very rare, were it not for the *third* circumstance, which I proposed to mention, viz., the great frugality with which all powers and faculties are distributed to every particular being. So well adjusted are the organs and capacities of all animals, and so well fitted to their preservation, that, as far as history or tradition reaches, there appears not to be any single species, which has yet been extinguished in the universe. Every animal has the requisite endowments; but these endowments are bestowed with so scrupulous an economy, that any considerable diminution must entirely destroy the creature. Wherever one power is increased, there is a proportional abatement in the others. Animals, which excel in swiftness, are commonly defective in force. Those, which possess both, are either imperfect in some of their senses, or are oppressed with the most craving wants. The human species, whose chief excellency is reason and sagacity, is of all others the most necessitous, and the most deficient in bodily advantages; without clothes, without arms, without food, without lodging, without any convenience of life, except what they owe to their own skill and industry. In short, nature seems to have formed an exact calculation of the necessities of her creatures; and like a *rigid master*, has afforded them little more powers or endowments, than what are strictly sufficient to supply those necessities. An *indulgent parent* would have bestowed a large stock, in order to guard against accidents, and secure the happiness and welfare of the creature, in the most unfortunate concurrence of circumstances. Every course of life would not have been so surrounded with precipices, that the least departure from the true path, by mistake or necessity, must involve us in misery and ruin. Some reserve, some fund would have been provided to ensure happiness; nor would the powers and the necessities have been adjusted with so rigid an economy. The Author of Nature is inconceivably powerful: his force is supposed great, if not altogether inexhaustible: nor is there any reason, as far as we can judge, to make him observe this strict frugality in his dealings with his creatures. It would have been better, were his power extremely limited, to have created fewer animals, and to have endowed these with more faculties for their happiness and preservation. A builder is never esteemed prudent, who undertakes a plan, beyond what his stock will enable him to finish.

In order to cure most of the ills of human life, I require not that man should have the wings of the eagle, the swiftness of the stag, the force of the ox, the arms of the lion, the scales of the crocodile or rhinoceros; much less do I demand the sagacity of an angel or cherub. I am contented to take an increase in one single power or faculty of his soul. Let him be endowed with a greater propensity to industry and labor; a more vigorous spring and activity of mind; a more constant bent to business and application. Let the whole species possess naturally an equal diligence with that which many individuals are able to attain by habit and reflection; and the most beneficial consequences, without any alloy of ill, is the immediate and necessary result of this endowment. Almost all the moral, as well as natural evils of human life arise from idleness; and were our species, by the original constitution of their frame, exempt from this vice or infirmity, the perfect cultivation of land, the improvement of arts and manufactures, the exact execution of every office and duty, immediately follow; and men at once may fully reach that state of society, which is so imperfectly attained by the best-regulated government. But as industry is a power, and the most valuable of any, nature seems determined, suitably to her usual maxims, to bestow it on men with a very sparing hand; and rather to punish him severely for his deficiency in it, than to reward him for his attainments. She has so contrived his frame, that nothing but the most violent necessity can oblige him to labor; and she employs all his other wants to overcome, at least in part, the want of diligence, and to endow him with some share of a faculty, of which she has thought fit naturally to bereave him. Here our demands may be allowed very humble, and therefore the more reasonable. If we required the endowments of superior penetration and judgment, of a more delicate taste of beauty, of a nicer sensibility to benevolence and friendship; we might be told, that we impiously pretend to break the order of nature, that we want to exalt ourselves into a higher rank of being, that the presents which we require, not being suitable to our state and condition, would only be pernicious to us. But it is hard; I dare to repeat it, it is hard, that being placed in a world so full of wants and necessities; where almost every being and element is either our foe or refuses us their assistance, we should also have our own temper to struggle with, and should be deprived of that faculty, which can alone fence against these multiplied evils.

The *fourth* circumstance, whence arises the misery and ill of the universe, is the inaccurate workmanship of all the springs and principles of the great machine of nature. It must be acknowledged, that there are few parts of the universe, which seem not to serve some purpose, and whose removal would not produce a visible defect and disorder in the whole. The parts hang all together; nor can one be touched without affecting the rest in a greater or less degree. But at the same time, it must be observed, that none of these parts or principles, however useful, are so accurately adjusted, as to keep precisely within those bounds, in which their utility consists; but they are, all of them, apt, on every occasion, to run into the one extreme or the other. One would imagine, that this grand production had not received the last hand of the maker; so little finished in every part, and so coarse are the strokes, with which it is executed. Thus, the winds are requisite to convey the vapors along the surface of the globe, and to assist men in navigation: but how oft, rising up to tempests and hurricanes, do they become pernicious? Rains are necessary to nourish all the plants and animals of the earth: but how often are they defective? how often excessive? Heat is requisite to all life and vegetation; but is not always found in the due proportion. On the mixture and secretion of the humors and juices of the body depend the health and prosperity of the animal: but the parts perform not regularly their proper function. What more useful than all the passions of the mind, ambition, vanity, love, anger? But how oft do they break their bounds, and cause the greatest convulsions in society? There is nothing so advantageous in the universe, but what frequently becomes pernicious, by its excess or defect; nor has nature guarded, with the requisite accuracy, against all disorder or confusion. The irregularity is never, perhaps, so great as to destroy any species; but is often sufficient to involve the individuals in ruin and misery.

On the concurrence, then, of these four circumstances does all, or the greatest part of natural evil depend. Were all living creatures incapable of pain, or were the world administered by particular volitions, evil never could have found access into the universe: and were animals endowed with a large stock of powers and faculties, beyond what strict necessity requires; or were the several springs and principles of the universe so accurately framed as to preserve always the just temperament and medium; there must have been very little ill in comparison of what we feel at present. What then shall we pronounce on this occasion? Shall we say, that these circumstances are not necessary, and that they might easily have been altered in the contrivance of the universe? This decision seems too presumptuous for creatures, so blind and ignorant. Let us be more modest in our conclusions. Let us allow, that, if the goodness of the Deity (I mean a goodness like the human) could be established on any tolerable reasons *a priori*, these phenomena, however untoward, would not be sufficient to subvert that principle; but might easily, in some unknown manner, be reconcilable to it. But let us still assert, that as this goodness is not antecedently established, but must be inferred from the phenomena, there can be no grounds for such an inference, while there are so many ills in the universe, and while these ills might so easily have been remedied, as far as human understanding can be allowed to judge on such a subject. I am sceptic enough to allow, that the bad appearances, notwithstanding all my reasonings, may be compatible with such attributes as you suppose: but surely they can never prove these attributes. Such a conclusion cannot result from scepticism; but must arise from the phenomena, and from our confidence in the reasonings, which we deduce from these phenomena.

Look round this universe. What an immense profusion of beings, animated and organized, sensible and active! You admire this prodigious variety and fecundity. But inspect a little more narrowly these living existences, the only beings worth regarding. How hostile and destructive to each other! How insufficient all of them for their own happiness! How contemptible or odious to the spectator! The whole presents nothing but the idea of a blind nature, impregnated by a great vivifying principle, and pouring forth from her lap, without discernment or parental care, her maimed and abortive children!

Here the Manichaean system occurs as a proper hypothesis to solve the difficulty: and no doubt, in some respects, it is very specious, and has more probability than the common hypothesis, by giving a plausible account of the strange mixture of good and ill, which appears in life. But if we consider, on the other hand, the perfect uniformity and agreement of the parts of the universe, we shall not discover in it any marks of the combat of a malevolent with a benevolent being. There is indeed an opposition of pains and pleasures in the feelings of sensible creatures: but are not all the operations of nature carried on by an opposition of principles, of hot and cold, moist and dry, light and heavy? The true conclusion is, that the original source of all things is entirely indifferent to all these principles, and has no more regard to good above ill than to heat above cold, or to drought above moisture, or to light above heavy.

There may four hypotheses be framed concerning the first causes of the universe: that they are endowed with perfect goodness, that they have perfect malice, that they are opposite and have both goodness and malice, that they have neither goodness nor malice. Mixed phenomena can never prove the two former unmixed principles. And the uniformity and steadiness of general laws seem to oppose the third. The fourth, therefore, seems by far the most probable.

What I have said concerning natural evil will apply to moral, with little or no variation; and we have no more reason to infer, that the rectitude of the Supreme Being resembles human rectitude than that his benevolence resembles the human. Nay, it will be thought, that we have still greater cause to exclude from him moral sentiments, such as we feel them; since moral evil, in the opinion of many, is much more predominant above moral good than natural evil above natural good.

But even though this should not be allowed, and though the virtue, which is in mankind, should be acknowledged much superior to the vice; yet so long as there is any vice at all in the universe, it will very much puzzle you anthropomorphites, how to account for it. You must assign a cause for it, without having recourse to the first cause. But as every effect must have a cause, and that cause another; you must either carry on the progression *in infinitum*, or rest on that original principle, who is the ultimate cause of all things . . .

Hold! hold! cried Demea: Whither does your imagination hurry you? I joined in alliance with you, in order to prove the incomprehensible nature of the Divine Being, and refute the principles of Cleanthes, who would measure everything by a human rule and standard. But I now find you running into all the topics of the greatest libertines and infidels; and betraying that holy cause, which you seemingly espoused. Are you secretly, then, a more dangerous enemy than Cleanthes himself?

And are you so late in perceiving it? replied Cleanthes. Believe me, Demea; your friend Philo, from the beginning, has been amusing himself at both our expense; and it must be confessed, that the injudicious reasoning of our vulgar theology has given him but too just a handle of ridicule. The total infirmity of human reason, the absolute incomprehensibility of the Divine Nature, the great and universal misery and still greater wickedness of men; these are strange topics surely to be so fondly cherished by orthodox divines and doctors. In ages of stupidity and ignorance, indeed, these principles may safely be espoused; and perhaps, no views of things are more proper to promote superstition, than such as encourage the blind amazement, the diffidence, and melancholy of mankind. But at present . . .

Blame not so much, interposed Philo, the ignorance of these reverend gentlemen. They know how to change their style with the times. Formerly it was a most popular theological topic to maintain, that human life was vanity and misery, and to exaggerate all the ills and pains, which are incident to men. But of late years, divines, we find, begin to retract this position, and maintain, though still with some hesitation, that there are more goods than evils, more pleasures than pains, even in this life. When religion stood entirely upon temper and education, it was thought proper to encourage melancholy; as indeed, mankind never have recourse to superior powers so readily as in that disposition. But as men have now learned to form principles, and to draw consequences, it is necessary to change the batteries, and to make use of such arguments as will endure, at least some scrutiny and examination. This variation is the same (and from the same causes) with that which I formerly remarked with regard to scepticism.

Thus Philo continued to the last his spirit of opposition, and his censure of established opinions. But I could observe, that Demea did not at all relish the latter part of the discourse; and he took occasion soon after on some pretense or other, to leave the company.

Part XII

After Demea's departure, Cleanthes and Philo continued the conversation in the following manner. Our friend, I am afraid, said Cleanthes, will have little inclination to revive this topic of discourse, while you are in company; and to tell truth, Philo, I should rather wish to reason with either of you apart on a subject so sublime and interesting. Your spirit of controversy, joined to your abhorrence of vulgar superstition, carries you strange lengths, when engaged in an argument; and there is nothing so sacred and venerable, even in your own eyes, which you spare on that occasion.

I must confess, replied Philo, that I am less cautious on the subject of Natural Religion than on any other; both because I know that I can never, on that head, corrupt the principles of any man of common sense, and because no one, I am confident, in whose eyes I appear a man of common sense, will ever mistake my intentions. You, in particular, Cleanthes, with whom I live in unreserved intimacy; you are sensible, that, notwithstanding the freedom of my conversation, and my love of singular arguments, no one has a deeper sense of religion impressed on his mind, or pays more profound adoration to the Divine Being, as he discovers himself to reason, in the inexplicable contrivance and artifice of nature. A purpose, an intention, a design strikes everywhere the most careless, the most stupid thinker; and no man can be so hardened in absurd systems, as at all times to reject it. *That Nature does nothing in vain*, is a maxim established in all the schools, merely from the contemplation of the works of nature, without any religious purpose; and, from a firm conviction of its truth, an anatomist, who had observed a new organ or canal, would never be satisfied, till he had also discovered its use and intention. One great foundation of the Copernican system is the maxim, *That Nature acts by the simplest methods, and chooses the most proper means to any end*; and astronomers often, without thinking of it, lay this strong foundation of piety and religion. The same thing is observable in other parts of philosophy: and thus all the sciences almost lead us insensibly to acknowledge a first intelligent Author; and their authority is often so much the greater, as they do not directly profess that intention.

It is with pleasure I hear Galen reason concerning the structure of the human body. The anatomy of a man, says he,[12] discovers above 600 different muscles; and whoever duly considers these, will find, that in each of them Nature must have adjusted at least ten different circumstances, in order to attain the end which she proposed; proper figure, just magnitude, right disposition of the several ends, upper and lower position of the whole, the due insertion of the several nerves, veins, and arteries: so that in the muscles alone, above 6000 several views and intentions must have been formed and executed. The bones he calculates to be 284: the distinct purposes, aimed at in the structure of each, above forty. What a prodigious display of artifice, even in these simple and homogeneous parts! But if we consider the skin, ligaments, vessels, glandules, humors, the several limbs and members of the body; how must our astonishment rise upon us, in proportion to the number and intricacy of the parts so artificially adjusted! The farther we advance in these researches, we discover new scenes of art and wisdom: but descry still, at a distance, farther scenes beyond our reach; in the fine internal structure of the parts, in the economy of the brain, in the fabric of the seminal vessels. All these artifices are repeated in every different species of animal, with wonderful variety, and with exact propriety, suited to the different intentions of Nature, in framing each species. And if the infidelity of Galen, even when these natural sciences were still imperfect, could not withstand such striking appearances; to what pitch

[12] De formatione foetus.

of pertinacious obstinacy must a philosopher in this age have attained, who can now doubt of a Supreme Intelligence?

Could I meet with one of this species (who, I thank God, are very rare) I would ask him: Supposing there were a God, who did not discover himself immediately to our senses; were it possible for him to give stronger proofs of his existence, than what appear on the whole face of nature? What indeed could such a divine Being do, but copy the present economy of things; render many of his artifices so plain, that no stupidity could mistake them; afford glimpses of still greater artifices, which demonstrate his prodigious superiority above our narrow apprehensions; and conceal altogether a great many from such imperfect creatures? Now according to all rules of just reasoning, every fact must pass for undisputed, when it is supported by all the arguments, which its nature admits of; even though these arguments be not, in themselves, very numerous or forcible: How much more, in the present case, where no human imagination can compute their number, and no understanding estimate their cogency!

I shall farther add, said Cleanthes, to what you have so well urged, that one great advantage of the principle of theism, is, that it is the only system of cosmogony, which can be rendered intelligible and complete, and yet can throughout preserve a strong analogy to what we every day see and experience in the world. The comparison of the universe to a machine of human contrivance is so obvious and natural, and is justified by so many instances of order and design in nature, that it must immediately strike all unprejudiced apprehensions, and procure universal approbation. Whoever attempts to weaken this theory, cannot pretend to succeed by establishing in its place any other, that is precise and determinate: it is sufficient for him, if he start doubts and difficulties; and by remote and abstract views of things, reach that suspense of judgment, which is here the utmost boundary of his wishes. But besides, that this state of mind is in itself unsatisfactory, it can never be steadily maintained against such striking appearances, as continually engage us into the religious hypothesis. A false, absurd system, human nature, from the force of prejudice, is capable of adhering to, with obstinacy and perseverance: But no system at all, in opposition to a theory, supported by strong and obvious reason, by natural propensity, and by early education, I think it absolutely impossible to maintain or defend.

So little, replied Philo, do I esteem this suspense of judgment in the present case to be possible, that I am apt to suspect there enters somewhat of a dispute of words into this controversy, more than is usually imagined. That the works of nature bear a great analogy to the productions of art is evident: and according to all the rules of good reasoning, we ought to infer, if we argue at all concerning them, that their causes have a proportional analogy. But as there are also considerable differences, we have reason to suppose a proportional difference in the causes; and in particular ought to attribute a much higher degree of power and energy to the supreme cause than any we have ever observed in mankind. Here then the existence of a Deity is plainly ascertained by reason; and if we make it a question, whether, on account of these analogies, we can properly call him a *mind* or *intelligence*, notwithstanding the vast difference, which may reasonably be supposed between him and human minds; what is this but a mere verbal controversy? No man can deny the analogies between the effects: to restrain ourselves from inquiring concerning the causes is scarcely possible: from this inquiry, the legitimate conclusion is, that the causes have also an analogy: And if we are not contented with calling the first and supreme cause a God or Deity, but desire to vary the expression; what can we call him but Mind or Thought, to which he is justly supposed to bear a considerable resemblance?

All men of sound reason are disgusted with verbal disputes, which abound so much in philosophical and theological inquiries; and it is found, that the only remedy for this abuse must arise from clear definitions, from the precision of those ideas which enter into any argument, and from the strict and uniform use of those terms which are employed. But there is a species of controversy, which, from the very nature of language and of human ideas, is involved in perpetual ambiguity, and can never, by any precaution or any definitions, be able to reach a reasonable certainty or precision. These are the controversies concerning the degrees of any quality or circumstance. Men may argue to all eternity, whether Hannibal be a great, or a very great, or a superlatively great man, what degree of beauty Cleopatra possessed, what epithet of praise Livy or Thucydides is entitled to, without bringing the controversy to any determination. The disputants may here agree in their sense, and differ in the terms, or *vice versa*; yet never be able to define their terms, so as to enter into each other's meaning: because the degrees of these qualities are not, like quantity or number, susceptible of any exact mensuration, which may be the standard in the controversy. That the dispute concerning theism is of this nature, and consequently is merely verbal, or perhaps, if possible, still more incurably ambiguous, will appear upon the slightest inquiry. I ask the theist, if he does not allow, that there is a great and immeasurable, because incomprehensible, difference between the *human* and the *divine* mind. The more pious he is, the more readily will he assent to the affirmative, and the more will he be disposed to magnify the difference: he will even assert, that the difference is of a nature which cannot be too much magnified. I next turn to the atheist, who, I assert, is only nominally so, and can never possibly be in earnest; and I ask him, whether, from the coherence and apparent sympathy in all the parts of this world, there be not a certain degree of analogy among all the operations of nature, in every situation and in every age; whether the rotting of a turnip, the generation of an animal, and the structure of human thought be not energies that probably bear some remote analogy to each other. It is impossible he can deny it: he will readily acknowledge it. Having obtained this concession, I push him still farther in his retreat; and I ask him, if it be not probable, that the principle which first arranged, and still maintains order in this universe, bears not also some remote inconceivable analogy to the other operations of nature, and among the rest to the economy of human mind and thought. However reluctant, he must give his assent. Where then, cry I to both these antagonists, is the subject of your dispute? The theist allows, that the original intelligence is very different from human reason: The atheist allows, that the original principle of order bears some remote analogy to it. Will you quarrel, gentlemen, about the degrees, and enter into a controversy, which admits not of any precise meaning, nor consequently of any determination? If you should be so obstinate, I should not be surprised to find you insensibly change sides; while the theist on the one hand exaggerates the dissimilarity between the Supreme Being, and frail, imperfect, variable, fleeting, and mortal creatures; and the atheist on the other magnifies the analogy among all the operations of nature, in every period, every situation, and every position. Consider then, where the real point of controversy lies, and if you cannot lay aside your disputes, endeavor, at least, to cure yourselves of your animosity.

And here I must also acknowledge, Cleanthes, that, as the

works of nature have a much greater analogy to the effects of *our* art and contrivance, than to those of *our* benevolence and justice; we have reason to infer that the natural attributes of the Deity have a greater resemblance to those of man, than his moral have to human virtues. But what is the consequence? Nothing but this, that the moral qualities of man are more defective in their kind than his natural abilities. For, as the Supreme Being is allowed to be absolutely and entirely perfect, whatever differs most from him departs the farthest from the supreme standard of rectitude and perfection.[13]

These, Cleanthes, are my unfeigned sentiments on this subject; and these sentiments, you know, I have ever cherished and maintained. But in proportion to my veneration for true religion, is my abhorrence of vulgar superstitions; and I indulge a peculiar pleasure, I confess, in pushing such principles, sometimes into absurdity, sometimes into impiety. And you are sensible, that all bigots, notwithstanding their great aversion to the latter above the former, are commonly equally guilty of both.

My inclination, replied Cleanthes, lies, I own, a contrary way. Religion, however corrupted, is still better than no religion at all. The doctrine of a future state is so strong and necessary a security to morals, that we never ought to abandon or neglect it. For if finite and temporary rewards and punishments have so great an effect, as we daily find; how much greater must be expected from such as are infinite and eternal?

How happens it then, said Philo, if vulgar superstition be so salutary to society, that all history abounds so much with accounts of its pernicious consequences on public affairs? Factions, civil wars, persecutions, subversions of government,

[13] It seems evident, that the dispute between the sceptics and dogmatists is entirely verbal, or at least regards only the degrees of doubt and assurance, which we ought to indulge with regard to all reasoning: and such disputes are commonly, at the bottom, verbal, and admit not of any precise determination. No philosophical dogmatist denies, that there are difficulties both with regard to the senses and to all science; and that these difficulties are in a regular, logical method, absolutely insolvable. No sceptic denies, that we lie under an absolute necessity, notwithstanding these difficulties, of thinking, and believing, and reasoning with regard to all kind of subjects, and even of frequently assenting with confidence and security. The only difference, then, between these sects, if they merit that name, is that the sceptic, from habit, caprice, or inclination, insists most on the difficulties; the dogmatist, for like reasons, on the necessity.

oppression, slavery; these are the dismal consequences which always attend its prevalency over the minds of men. If the religious spirit be ever mentioned in any historical narration, we are sure to meet afterwards with a detail of the miseries, which attend it. And no period of time can be happier or more prosperous, than those in which it is never regarded, or heard of.

The reason of this observation, replied Cleanthes, is obvious. The proper office of religion is to regulate the heart of men, humanize their conduct, infuse the spirit of temperance, order, and obedience; and as its operation is silent, and only enforces the motives of morality and justice, it is in danger of being overlooked, and confounded with these other motives. When it distinguishes itself, and acts as a separate principle over men, it has departed from its proper sphere, and has become only a cover to faction and ambition.

And so will all religion, said Philo, except the philosophical and rational kind. Your reasonings are more easily eluded than my facts. The inference is not just, because finite and temporary rewards and punishments have so great influence, that therefore such as are infinite and eternal must have so much greater. Consider, I beseech you, the attachment, which we have to present things, and the little concern which we discover for objects, so remote and uncertain. When divines are declaiming against the common behavior and conduct of the world, they always represent this principle as the strongest imaginable (which indeed it is) and describe almost all human kind as lying under the influence of it, and sunk into the deepest lethargy and unconcern about their religious interests. Yet these same divines, when they refute their speculative antagonists, suppose the motives of religion to be so powerful, that, without them, it were impossible for civil society to subsist; nor are they ashamed of so palpable a contradiction. It is certain, from experience, that the smallest grain of natural honesty and benevolence has more effect on men's conduct, than the most pompous views suggested by theological theories and systems. A man's natural inclination works incessantly upon him; it is forever present to the mind, and mingles itself with every view and consideration: whereas religious motives, where they act at all, operate only by starts and bounds; and it is scarcely possible for them to become altogether habitual to the mind. The force of the greatest gravity, say the philosophers, is infinitely small, in comparison of that of the least impulse; yet it is certain, that the smallest gravity will, in the end, prevail above a great impulse; because no strokes or blows can be repeated with such constancy as attraction and gravitation.

Another advantage of inclination: it engages on its side all the wit and ingenuity of the mind; and when set in opposition to religious principles, seeks every method and art of eluding them: in which it is almost always successful. Who can explain the heart of man, or account for those strange salvos and excuses, with which people satisfy themselves, when they follow their inclinations in opposition to their religious duty! This is well understood in the world; and none but fools ever repose less trust in a man, because they hear, that, from study and philosophy, he has entertained some speculative doubts with regard to theological subjects. And when we have to do with a man, who makes a great profession of religion and devotion; has this any other effect upon several, who pass for prudent, than to put them on their guard, lest they be cheated and deceived by him?

We must farther consider, that philosophers, who cultivate reason and reflection, stand less in need of such motives to keep them under the restraint of morals; and that the vulgar, who alone may need them, are utterly incapable of so pure a religion, as represents the Deity to be pleased with nothing but virtue in human behavior. The recommendations to the Divinity are generally supposed to be either frivolous observances, or rapturous ecstasies, or a bigoted credulity. We need not run back into antiquity, or wander into remote regions, to find instances of this degeneracy. Amongst ourselves, some have been guilty of that atrociousness, unknown to the Egyptian and Grecian superstitions, of declaiming, in express terms, against morality, and representing it as a sure forfeiture of the Divine favor, if the least trust or reliance be laid upon it.

But even though superstition or enthusiasm should not put itself in direct opposition to morality; the very diverting of the attention, the raising up a new and frivolous species of merit, the preposterous distribution, which it makes of praise and blame; must have the most pernicious consequences, and weaken extremely men's attachment to the natural motives of justice and humanity.

Such a principle of action likewise, not being any of the familiar motives of human conduct, acts only by intervals on the temper, and must be roused by continual efforts, in order to render the pious zealot satisfied with his own conduct, and make him fulfil his devotional task. Many religious exercises are entered into with seeming fervor, where the heart, at the time, feels cold and languid: a habit of dissimulation is by degrees contracted: and fraud and falsehood become the predominant principle. Hence the reason of that vulgar observation, that the highest zeal in religion and the deepest hypocrisy, so far from being inconsistent, are often or commonly united in the same individual character.

The bad effects of such habits, even in common life, are easily imagined: but where the interests of religion are concerned, no morality can be forcible enough to bind the enthusiastic zealot. The sacredness of the cause sanctifies every measure, which can be made use of to promote it.

The steady attention alone to so important an interest as that of eternal salvation is apt to extinguish the benevolent affections, and beget a narrow, contracted selfishness. And when such a temper is encouraged, it easily eludes all the general precepts of charity and benevolence.

Thus the motives of vulgar superstition have no great influence on general conduct; nor is their operation very favorable to morality, in the instances where they predominate.

Is there any maxim in politics more certain and infallible, than that both the number and authority of priests should be confined within very narrow limits, and that the civil magistrate ought, for ever, to keep his *fasces* and *axes* from such dangerous hands? But if the spirit of popular religion were so salutary to society, a contrary maxim ought to prevail. The greater number of priests, and their greater authority and riches, will always augment the religious spirit. And though the priests have the guidance of this spirit, why may we not expect a superior sanctity of life, and greater benevolence and moderation, from persons who are set apart for religion, who are continually inculcating it upon others, and who must themselves imbibe a greater share of it? Whence comes it then, that in fact, the utmost a wise magistrate can propose with regard to popular religions, is, as far as possible, to make a saving game of it, and to prevent their pernicious consequences with regard to society? Every expedient which he tries for so humble a purpose is surrounded with inconveniences. If he admits only one religion among his subjects, he must sacrifice, to an uncertain prospect of tranquillity, every consideration of public liberty, science, reason, industry, and even his own independency. If he gives indulgence to several sects, which is the wiser maxim, he must preserve a very philosophical indifference to all of them, and carefully restrain the pretensions of the prevailing sect; otherwise he can expect nothing but endless disputes, quarrels, factions, persecutions, and civil commotions.

True religion, I allow, has no such pernicious consequences: but we must treat of religion, as it has commonly been found in the world; nor have I anything to do with that speculative tenet of theism, which, as it is a species of philosophy, must partake of the beneficial influence of that principle, and at the same time must lie under a like inconvenience of being always confined to very few persons.

Oaths are requisite in all courts of judicature; but it is a question whether their authority arises from any popular religion. 'Tis the solemnity and importance of the occasion, the regard to reputation, and the reflecting on the general interests of society, which are the chief restraints upon mankind. Custom-house oaths and political oaths are but little regarded even by some who pretend to principles of honesty and religion: and a Quaker's asseveration is with us justly put upon the same footing with the oath of any other person. I know, that Polybius[14] ascribes the infamy of Greek faith to the prevalency of the Epicurean philosophy; but I know also, that Punic faith had as bad a reputation in ancient times, as Irish evidence has in modern; though we cannot account for these vulgar observations by the same reason. Not to mention, that Greek faith was infamous before the rise of the Epicurean philosophy; and Euripides,[15] in a passage which I shall point out to you, has glanced a remarkable stroke of satire against his nation, with regard to this circumstance.

Take care, Philo, replied Cleanthes, take care; push not matters too far: allow not your zeal against false religion to undermine your veneration for the true. Forfeit not this principle, the chief, the only great comfort in life; and our principal support amidst all the attacks of adverse fortune. The most agreeable reflection, which it is possible for human imagination to suggest, is that of genuine theism, which represents us as the workmanship of a Being perfectly good, wise, and powerful; who created us for happiness, and who, having implanted in us

[14] Lib. 6, cap. 54.
[15] Iphigenia in Tauride.

immeasurable desires for good, will prolong our existence to all eternity, and will transfer us into an infinite variety of scenes, in order to satisfy those desires, and render our felicity complete and durable. Next to such a Being himself (if the comparison be allowed) the happiest lot which we can imagine, is that of being under his guardianship and protection.

These appearances, said Philo, are most engaging and alluring; and with regard to the true philosopher, they are more than appearances. But it happens here, as in the former case, that, with regard to the greater part of mankind, the appearances are deceitful, and that the terrors of religion commonly prevail above its comforts.

It is allowed, that men never have recourse to devotion so readily as when dejected with grief or depressed with sickness. Is not this a proof, that the religious spirit is not so nearly allied to joy as to sorrow?

But men, when afflicted, find consolation in religion, replied Cleanthes. Sometimes, said Philo: but it is natural to imagine, that they will form a notion of those unknown beings, suitably to the present gloom and melancholy of their temper, when they betake themselves to the contemplation of them. Accordingly, we find the tremendous images to predominate in all religions; and we ourselves, after having employed the most exalted expressions in our descriptions of the Deity, fall into the flattest contradiction, in affirming, that the damned are infinitely superior in number to the elect.

I shall venture to affirm, that there never was a popular religion, which represented the state of departed souls in such a light, as would render it eligible for human kind, that there should be such a state. These fine models of religion are the mere product of philosophy. For as death lies between the eye and the prospect of futurity, that event is so shocking to nature, that it must throw a gloom on all the regions which lie beyond it; and suggest to the generality of mankind the idea of Cerberus and Furies; devils, and torrents of fire and brimstone.

It is true; both fear and hope enter into religion; because both these passions, at different times, agitate the human mind, and each of them forms a species of divinity, suitable to itself. But when a man is in a cheerful disposition, he is fit for business or company or entertainment of any kind; and he naturally applies himself to these, and thinks not of religion. When melancholy, and dejected, he has nothing to do but brood upon the terrors of the invisible world, and to plunge himself still deeper in affliction. It may, indeed, happen, that after he has, in this manner, engraved the religious opinions deep into his thought and imagination, there may arrive a change of health or circumstances, which may restore his good humor, and raising cheerful prospects of futurity, make him run into the other extreme of joy and triumph. But still it must be acknowledged, that, as terror is the primary principle of religion, it is the passion, which always predominates in it, and admits but of short intervals of pleasure.

Not to mention, that these fits of excessive, enthusiastic joy, by exhausting the spirits, always prepare the way for equal fits of superstitious terror and dejection; nor is there any state of mind so happy as the calm and equable. But this state it is impossible to support, where a man thinks that he lies in such profound darkness and uncertainty, between an eternity of happiness and an eternity of misery. No wonder, that such an opinion disjoints the ordinary frame of the mind, and throws it into the utmost confusion. And though that opinion is seldom so steady in its operation as to influence all the actions; yet it is apt to make a considerable breach in the temper, and to produce that gloom and melancholy, so remarkable in all devout people.

It is contrary to common sense to entertain apprehensions or terrors, upon account of any opinion whatsoever, or to imagine that we run any risk hereafter, by the freest use of our reason. Such a sentiment implies both an *absurdity* and an *inconsistency*. It is an absurdity to believe that the Deity has human passions, and one of the lowest of human passions, a restless appetite for applause. It is an inconsistency to believe, that, since the Deity has this human passion, he has not others also; and, in particular, a disregard to the opinions of creatures so much inferior.

To know God, says Seneca, *is to worship him*. All other worship is indeed absurd, superstitious, and even impious. It degrades him to the low condition of mankind, who are delighted with entreaty, solicitation, presents, and flattery. Yet is this impiety the smallest of which superstition is guilty. Commonly, it depresses the Deity far below the condition of mankind; and represents him as a capricious demon, who exercises his power without reason and without humanity! And were that Divine Being disposed to be offended at the vices and follies of silly mortals, who are his own workmanship; ill would it surely fare with the votaries of most popular superstitions. Nor would any of human race merit his *favor*, but a very few, the philosophical theists, who entertain, or rather indeed endeavor to entertain, suitable notions of his divine perfections: as the only persons entitled to his *compassion* and *indulgence* would be the philosophical sceptics, a sect almost equally rare, who, from a natural diffidence of their own capacity, suspend, or endeavor to suspend all judgment with regard to such sublime and such extraordinary subjects.

If the whole of Natural Theology, as some people seem to maintain, revolves itself into one simple, though somewhat ambiguous, at least undefined proposition, *That the cause or causes of order in the universe probably bear some remote analogy to human intelligence*: if this proposition be not capable of extension, variation, or more particular explication: if it afford no inference that affects human life, or can be the source of any action or forbearance: and if the analogy, imperfect as it is, can be carried no farther than to the human intelligence; and cannot be transferred, with any appearance of probability, to the other qualities of the mind: if this really be the case, what can the most inquisitive, contemplative, and religious man do more than give a plain, philosophical assent to the proposition, as often as it occurs; and believe that the arguments, on which it is established, exceed the objections, which lie against it? Some astonishment indeed will naturally arise from the greatness of the object: some melancholy from its obscurity: some contempt of human reason, that it can give no solution more satisfactory with regard to so extraordinary and magnificent a question. But believe me, Cleanthes, the most natural sentiment, which a well-disposed mind will feel on this occasion, is a longing desire and expectation, that heaven would be pleased to dissipate, at least alleviate, this profound ignorance, by affording some more particular revelation to mankind, and making discoveries of the nature, attributes, and operations of the divine object of our faith. A person, seasoned with a just sense of the imperfections of natural reason, will fly to revealed truth with the greatest avidity: while the haughty dogmatist, persuaded that he can erect a complete system of theology by the mere help of philosophy, disdains any farther aid, and rejects this adventitious instructor. To be a philosophical sceptic is, in a man of letters, the first and most essential step towards being a sound, believing Christian; a proposition which I would willingly recommend to the attention of Pamphilus: And I hope Cleanthes will forgive me for interposing so far in the education and instruction of his pupil.

Cleanthes and Philo pursued not this conversation much farther; and as nothing ever made greater impression on me, than all the reasonings of that day; so I confess, that, upon a serious review of the whole, I cannot but think that Philo's principles are more probable than Demea's; but that those of Cleanthes approach still nearer to the truth.